Law of Evidence
IN SOUTH AFRICA

PROCEDURAL LAW

Law of Evidence
IN SOUTH AFRICA

PROCEDURAL LAW

ADRIAN BELLENGÈRE (Editor)
CONSTANTINE THEOPHILOPOULOS (Editor)
ROBIN PALMER (Editor)
ZAKHELE HLOPHE | THEA ILLSLEY
NEVILLE JOHN MELVILLE | LESALA MOFOKENG
BOBBY NAUDÉ | MATHOBELA SHADRACK NKUTHA
ELIZABETH PICARRA | SHANTA REDDY
LEE SWALES | LES ROBERTS
ANNETTE VAN DER MERWE | BENITA WHITCHER

Oxford University Press is a department of the University of Oxford.
It furthers the University's objective of excellence in research, scholarship,
and education by publishing worldwide. Oxford is a registered trade mark of
Oxford University Press in the UK and in certain other countries

Published in South Africa by
Oxford University Press Southern Africa (Pty) Limited

Vasco Boulevard, Goodwood, N1 City, Cape Town, South Africa, 7460
P O Box 12119, N1 City, Cape Town, South Africa, 7463

The moral rights of the author have been asserted

First published 2013
Second Edition published in 2019

All rights reserved. No part of this publication may be reproduced, stored in
a retrieval system, or transmitted, in any form or by any means, without the
prior permission in writing of Oxford University Press Southern Africa (Pty) Ltd,
or as expressly permitted by law, by licence, or under terms agreed
with the appropriate reprographic rights organisation, DALRO, The Dramatic, Artistic
and Literary Rights Organisation atdalro@dalro.co.za. Enquiries concerning
reproduction outside the scope of the above should be sent to the Rights Department,
Oxford University Press Southern Africa (Pty) Ltd, at the above address.

You must not circulate this work in any other form
and you must impose this same condition on any acquirer.

The Law of Evidence in South Africa

978 0 19 073346 9

Second edition 2019
Sixth impression 2024

Typeset in UtopiaStd 9.5pt on 12pt
Printed on 70gsm woodfree paper

Acknowledgements
Publisher: Penny Lane
Development Editor: Edward Ndiloseh
Project manager: Lindsay-Jane Lücks
Copy-editor: Angela Voges
Proofreader: Language Mechanics
Indexer: Language Mechanics
Typesetter: Aptara
Cover reproduction by: Judith Cross
Printed and bound by Creda Communications

The authors and publisher gratefully acknowledge permission to reproduce copyright material in this book.
Every effort has been made to trace copyright holders, but if any copyright infringements have been made,
the publisher would be grateful for information that would enable any omissions or errors to be corrected in
subsequent impressions.

Links to third party websites are provided by Oxford in good faith and for information only.
Oxford disclaims any responsibility for the materials contained in any third party website referenced in this
work.

To my son, Arasen Hugh

Adrian Bellengère

For Pamela Victoria Palmer
Intemperans adulescentia effetum corpus tradit senectuti

Robin Palmer

Contents in brief

PART ONE	**GENERAL INTRODUCTION**	**1**
CHAPTER 1	DEFINING EVIDENCE	2
CHAPTER 2	BRIEF HISTORY AND SOURCES OF THE SOUTH AFRICAN LAW OF EVIDENCE	4
CHAPTER 3	SYSTEMS OF LEGAL FACT-FINDING	10
CHAPTER 4	TRUTH VERIFICATION, FACT FINDING AND RULES OF EVIDENCE IN AFRICAN ORAL TRADITIONAL LAW	18
CHAPTER 5	IMPACT OF THE CONSTITUTION ON THE LAW OF EVIDENCE	44
PART TWO	**BASIC CONCEPTS**	**51**
CHAPTER 6	ADMISSIBILITY AND WEIGHT OF EVIDENCE	52
CHAPTER 7	EVIDENCE AND PROOF	61
CHAPTER 8	*PRIMA FACIE*, CONCLUSIVE AND SUFFICIENT PROOF	69
CHAPTER 9	EVIDENCE: SUBSTANTIVE OR PROCEDURAL LAW?	74
PART THREE	**KINDS OF EVIDENCE**	**79**
CHAPTER 10	ORAL EVIDENCE	80
CHAPTER 11	DOCUMENTARY EVIDENCE	99
CHAPTER 12	REAL EVIDENCE	110
CHAPTER 13	FORMS OF ANALOGUE EVIDENCE	116
CHAPTER 14	ELECTRONIC AND CYBER EVIDENCE	119
PART FOUR	**RULES FOR EXCLUDING EVIDENCE**	**157**
CHAPTER 15	THE GENERAL TEST FOR RELEVANCE	158
CHAPTER 16	UNCONSTITUTIONALLY OBTAINED EVIDENCE IN CRIMINAL CASES: SECTION 35(5) OF THE CONSTITUTION	174
CHAPTER 17	SIMILAR FACT EVIDENCE	197
CHAPTER 18	OPINION AND EXPERT EVIDENCE	207

viii

CHAPTER 19 CHARACTER EVIDENCE ... 222

CHAPTER 20 EVIDENCE IN SEXUAL OFFENCES CASES ... 235

CHAPTER 21 SELF-CORROBORATION ... 244

CHAPTER 22 COLLATERAL EVIDENCE ... 246

CHAPTER 23 *RES GESTAE* ... 250

CHAPTER 24 PREVIOUS CONSISTENT STATEMENTS ... 256

CHAPTER 25 HEARSAY EVIDENCE ... 264

CHAPTER 26 PRIVILEGE ... 280

PART FIVE **THE RULES OF TRIAL** ... **307**

CHAPTER 27 WITNESSES: COMPETENCE AND COMPELLABILITY ... 308

CHAPTER 28 OPENING STATEMENTS ... 319

CHAPTER 29 EVIDENCE-IN-CHIEF ... 325

CHAPTER 30 CROSS-EXAMINATION ... 335

CHAPTER 31 RE-EXAMINATION ... 346

CHAPTER 32 CLOSING ADDRESS ... 350

CHAPTER 33 OBJECTIONS ... 357

CHAPTER 34 REFRESHING MEMORY ... 360

CHAPTER 35 PREVIOUS INCONSISTENT STATEMENTS ... 365

CHAPTER 36 HOSTILE WITNESSES ... 368

PART SIX **EVALUATION OF EVIDENCE** ... **373**

CHAPTER 37 EVALUATION OF EVIDENCE ... 374

CHAPTER 38 CREDITWORTHINESS: CREDIBILITY AND RELIABILITY ... 382

CHAPTER 39 INHERENT PROBABILITIES ... 388

CHAPTER 40 CONTRADICTIONS AND DISCREPANCIES ... 391

CHAPTER 41 THE CAUTIONARY RULE ... 394

CHAPTER 42	CORROBORATION	404
CHAPTER 43	IDENTIFICATION: VISUAL AND VOICE	408
CHAPTER 44	CIRCUMSTANTIAL EVIDENCE	412
CHAPTER 45	DEMEANOUR	416
CHAPTER 46	ASSESSMENT OF MENDACITY	419
CHAPTER 47	FAILURE TO TESTIFY	422
CHAPTER 48	JUDICIAL NOTICE	426
CHAPTER 49	PRESUMPTIONS	433
CHAPTER 50	ADMISSIONS, POINTINGS OUT AND CONFESSIONS	440

PART SEVEN SCIENTIFIC FORENSIC EVIDENCE **463**

CHAPTER 51	FINGERPRINTS AND BODY-PRINTS	464
CHAPTER 52	BLOOD TYPING AND DNA TESTING	468
CHAPTER 53	POLYGRAPHS AND VOICE-STRESS ANALYSERS	474
CHAPTER 54	NEUROTECHNOLOGY AND NEUROLOGICAL EVIDENCE	480

PART EIGHT SPECIAL EVIDENTIARY PROCEDURES **489**

CHAPTER 55	THE TRIAL-WITHIN-A-TRIAL	490
CHAPTER 56	ESTOPPEL	498
CHAPTER 57	THE PAROL EVIDENCE RULE	504
CHAPTER 58	CHILDREN'S EVIDENCE	508
CHAPTER 59	EVIDENCE IN LABOUR MATTERS	514
CHAPTER 60	EVIDENCE OBTAINED BY MEANS OF ENTRAPMENT	533
CHAPTER 61	EVIDENTIARY PROBLEMS WITH THE PREVENTION OF ORGANISED CRIME ACT, 1998 (POCA)	538

BIBLIOGRAPHY	545
TABLE OF CASES	549
TABLE OF LEGISLATION	573
GLOSSARY	581
INDEX	591

Contents

PART ONE   GENERAL INTRODUCTION ... 1

CHAPTER 1   DEFINING EVIDENCE ... 2

CHAPTER 2   BRIEF HISTORY AND SOURCES OF THE SOUTH AFRICAN LAW OF EVIDENCE ... 4
2.1   Background: the reception of the English law of evidence in South Africa ... 4
2.2   The 30 May 1961 rule: the residuary sections ... 5
2.3   The impact of the interim (1993) and final Constitution, 1996 ... 7
2.4   Overview of the main evidence statutes ... 7
2.5   The South African Law Reform Commission (SALRC) Project 126
        Review of the Law of Evidence ... 8

CHAPTER 3   SYSTEMS OF LEGAL FACT-FINDING ... 10
3.1   Introduction ... 10
3.2   Different systems in use in Africa ... 11
3.3   Evidentiary differences between the adversarial and inquisitorial justice models in Africa ... 11
        3.3.1   The adversarial system is jury-centred and an inquisitorial
                  system is judge-centred ... 11
        3.3.2   A strict system versus a free natural system of evidence ... 11
        3.3.3   The difference in approach to evidence is particularly striking in criminal matters ... 12
        3.3.4   Other major differences between these two models ... 12
3.4   The South African adversarial system ... 13
3.5   The basic jurisprudential principles of an adversarial trial ... 13
3.6   The basic rules of the South African adversarial trial system ... 14
3.7   The role of evidence in the South African adversarial system ... 15
        3.7.1   The place of the law of evidence ... 15
        3.7.2   The scope of the law of evidence ... 15

**CHAPTER 4   TRUTH VERIFICATION, FACT FINDING AND RULES OF
                EVIDENCE IN AFRICAN ORAL TRADITIONAL LAW** ... 18
4.1   Introduction ... 18
4.2   Verification of existence, and ascertainment of content, of customary law ... 20
4.3   Proof of existence, content and applicability of customary law by the litigant ... 21
        4.3.1   No evidence required ... 21
        4.3.2   Evidence of existence ... 22
        4.3.3   Evidence of content ... 23
        4.3.4   Proof of affiliation to, or membership of, a traditional community ... 23
4.4   The notion of a 'living version of customary law' and its relevance in evidence ... 25
        4.4.1   Presiding officer's own knowledge: is it proof of 'living' customary law? ... 27
        4.4.2   Court assessors' opinions ... 31
4.5   Rules of evidence in the courts of traditional leaders ... 31
4.6   Truth verification ... 33
        4.6.1   Narrative methods of evidence presentation ... 33
        4.6.2   Rituals and customs as evidence of a juristic act ... 36
        4.6.3   Presumptions concerning hearsay ... 38
        4.6.4   Presumptions in sex and marriage matters ... 40

CHAPTER 5 IMPACT OF THE CONSTITUTION ON THE LAW OF EVIDENCE   **44**

5.1 Introduction   44
5.2 The impact of the Constitution on the law of evidence in criminal matters   45
　　5.2.1 General fundamental rights and specific legal protections   45
　　5.2.2 Reverse onus clauses   46
　　5.2.3 Docket privilege   47
　　5.2.4 The admissibility of unconstitutionally obtained evidence   48
5.3 The impact of the Constitution on the law of evidence in civil matters in general   48

PART TWO BASIC CONCEPTS   **51**

CHAPTER 6 ADMISSIBILITY AND WEIGHT OF EVIDENCE   **52**

6.1 Introduction   52
6.2 Admissibility   54
　　6.2.1 Relevance   54
　　6.2.2 Determination of admissibility   55
　　　　6.2.2.1 The issues to be proved   55
　　　　6.2.2.2 Collateral issues   55
　　　　6.2.2.3 Potential weight   56
　　　　6.2.2.4 Unreliable evidence   56
　　　　6.2.2.5 Prejudice versus probative value   56
　　　　6.2.2.6 Precedent   56
　　　　6.2.2.7 Completeness   56
　　6.2.3 Procedure to determine admissibility   57
6.3 Weight   57
　　6.3.1 Fundamental principles   57
　　　　6.3.1.1 Evidence weighed as a whole   57
　　　　6.3.1.2 Inferences versus speculation   57
　　6.3.2 Factors   57
　　　　6.3.2.1 Corroboration   58
　　　　6.3.2.2 Credibility   58
　　　　6.3.2.3 Direct or circumstantial evidence   59

CHAPTER 7 EVIDENCE AND PROOF   **61**

7.1 Introduction   61
7.2 The pursuit of truth   62
7.3 Evidence and proof   63
7.4 Burden of proof   63
　　7.4.1 General principles applicable to criminal and civil cases   64
　　7.4.2 Criminal cases   64
　　7.4.3 Civil cases   65
7.5 Evidentiary burden   65
　　7.5.1 Criminal cases   66
　　7.5.2 Civil cases   67
7.6 Duty to begin   67
　　7.6.1 High Court Rule 39 and Magistrates' Courts Rule 29   67

CHAPTER 8 *PRIMA FACIE*, CONCLUSIVE AND SUFFICIENT PROOF **69**

8.1 Introduction 69
8.2 *Prima facie* proof 69
    8.2.1 *Prima facie*: the term 69
    8.2.2 A *prima facie* case 70
    8.2.3 *Prima facie* proof 71
    8.2.4 Frequently occurring examples of *prima facie* evidence 71
8.3 Conclusive proof 72
8.4 Sufficient proof 72

CHAPTER 9 EVIDENCE: SUBSTANTIVE OR PROCEDURAL LAW? **74**

9.1 Introduction 74
9.2 The importance of distinguishing between substantive and procedural law 74
9.3 Problem areas 75
    9.3.1 Burden of proof 75
    9.3.2 Irrebuttable presumptions 76
    9.3.3 Estoppel 76
    9.3.4 Parol evidence rule 77

PART THREE KINDS OF EVIDENCE **79**

CHAPTER 10 ORAL EVIDENCE **80**

10.1 Introduction 80
10.2 Testimony must be given on oath or affirmation 81
10.3 Exceptions 82
    10.3.1 Unsworn evidence 82
    10.3.2 The intermediary 82
        10.3.2.1 The role of intermediaries when examining and
                cross-examining child witnesses 82
        10.3.2.2 Principles to consider when appointing an intermediary 84
    10.3.3 Closed-circuit television and other electronic media 85
    10.3.4 Evidence on commission 85
    10.3.5 Interrogatories 86
    10.3.6 Testimony by way of affidavit 86
        10.3.6.1 Types of affidavits 87
        10.3.6.2 The use of affidavits in civil application proceedings 88
        10.3.6.3 The form and content of civil affidavits 88
        10.3.6.4 Inadmissible evidence in affidavits 90
            10.3.6.4.1 Hearsay 90
            10.3.6.4.2 Privileged communications 90
            10.3.6.4.3 Scandalous, vexatious or irrelevant matter 90
            10.3.6.4.4 Inadmissible new matter 90
            10.3.6.4.5 Matter excluded by the use of inherent jurisdiction 91
        10.3.6.5 The court's powers in application proceedings 91
            10.3.6.5.1 If no real dispute of fact has arisen on the papers 91
            10.3.6.5.2 If a real dispute of fact has arisen on the papers 92
            10.3.6.5.2 (i) The court may decide the matter on the affidavits
                      alone 92

10.3.6.5.2	(ii) The court may refer the matter to oral evidence	92
10.3.6.5.2	(iii) The court may refer the matter to trial	93
10.3.6.5.2	(iv) The court may dismiss the matter with costs	93
10.3.6.5.2	(v) In certain cases, the court may decide to make no order	93

10.3.6.6 Perjury: the consequences of being untruthful in affidavits 93
10.4 When is oral evidence used? 93
    10.4.1 Criminal trials 94
    10.4.2 Civil matters 94
10.5 Method and procedure of presenting oral evidence 95
    10.5.1 Criminal trials 95
    10.5.2 Civil matters 96
    10.5.3 Precognition versus putting words in the witness's mouth 96
    10.5.4 Use of interpreters 96
    10.5.5 Perjury 96

CHAPTER 11 DOCUMENTARY EVIDENCE — 99

11.1 Introduction 99
11.2 Categories of documents 100
11.3 Admissibility 101
    11.3.1 Inspection and discovery 102
    11.3.2 The production of the original document 102
        11.3.2.1 The best evidence versus secondary evidence 102
        11.3.2.2 Admissibility of secondary evidence 103
    11.3.3 Proof of authenticity 105
    11.3.4 Current applicability of the Stamp Duties Act, 1968 107
11.4 The procedural steps in admitting a document in civil proceedings 108

CHAPTER 12 REAL EVIDENCE — 110

12.1 Introduction 110
12.2 Immediate versus reported real evidence 111
12.3 Appearance of persons 111
12.4 Tape recordings 112
12.5 Fingerprints 112
12.6 Handwriting 113
12.7 Blood tests, tissue typing and DNA 113
12.8 Inspections *in loco* 114

CHAPTER 13 FORMS OF ANALOGUE EVIDENCE — 116

13.1 Introduction 116
13.2 Cinematographic films and photographs 116
13.3 Video and audio tape recordings 117

CHAPTER 14 ELECTRONIC AND CYBER EVIDENCE — 119

14.1 Introduction 120
14.2 History of electronic evidence in South Africa 121
    14.2.1 Background and context 121
    14.2.2 History of electronic evidence in South Africa 121

| | | 14.2.2.1 | Position prior to the Electronic Communications and Transactions Act 25 of 2002 | 121 |

14.2.2.1 Position prior to the Electronic Communications and Transactions Act 25 of 2002 ... 121

14.2.2.2 Background to the Electronic Communications and Transactions Act 25 of 2002 ... 122

14.2.2.3 Functional equivalence ... 123

14.3 Electronic Communications and Transactions Act, 2002 ... 123

14.3.1 Overview ... 123

14.3.2 Data messages ... 124

14.3.3 Legal recognition of data messages ... 124

14.3.4 Writing ... 124

14.3.5 Original ... 125

14.3.6 Electronic signature ... 126

14.3.7 Production of document or information ... 126

14.4 Admissibility and evidential weight of electronic evidence ... 127

14.4.1 Overview of Section 15 of the Electronic Communications and Transactions Act ... 127

14.4.2 Section 15(1) of the Electronic Communications and Transactions Act ... 127

14.4.3 Best evidence rule ... 128

14.4.4 Hearsay electronic evidence ... 128

14.4.4.1 Business records exceptions – section 15(4) of the Electronic Communications and Transactions Act ... 128

14.4.4.2 Can electronic evidence (a data message) constitute hearsay within the meaning of section 3 of the Law of Evidence Amendment Act? ... 130

14.4.4.3 The interaction between the statutory exceptions to hearsay contained in the Electronic Communications and Transactions Act, the Law of Evidence Amendment Act, the Civil Proceedings Evidence Act and the Criminal Procedure Act in the context of hearsay electronic evidence ... 131

14.4.4.3.1 The Civil Proceedings Evidence Act ... 131

14.4.4.3.2 The Criminal Procedure Act ... 131

14.4.4.3.3 The Law of Evidence Amendment Act ... 132

14.4.4.3.4 Electronic Communications and Transactions Act and the interaction between the various exceptions ... 132

14.4.4.4 Data messages as real evidence ... 133

14.4.4.5 Requirements for a data message to be admissible ... 136

14.4.5 Evidential weight of data messages ... 136

14.5 Distinctions between civil and criminal proceedings ... 137

14.5.1 Criminal Procedure Act ... 138

14.5.2 Cybercrimes and Cybersecurity Bill ... 138

14.6 Presumption of reliability ... 139

14.6.1 Background ... 139

14.6.2 A presumption of reliability or regularity? ... 140

14.7 Overview of search and seizure of electronic evidence ... 141

14.7.1 Search and seizure in criminal cases (South Africa) ... 141

14.7.2 Search and seizure in criminal cases (foreign) ... 142

14.7.3 Search and seizure in civil cases ... 143

14.8 Overview of forensic science ... 144

14.9 Overview of the South African Law Reform Commission's review of electronic evidence ... 145

14.10 Overview of foreign law in respect of electronic evidence ... 148

14.10.1 England and Wales		148
14.10.2 Canada		149
14.10.3 The United States of America		151
14.11 Conclusion		153

PART FOUR   RULES FOR EXCLUDING EVIDENCE   157

CHAPTER 15   THE GENERAL TEST FOR RELEVANCE   158

15.1	The relationship between relevance and admissibility	158
15.2	The practical meaning of relevance	159
	15.2.1 The general test of relevance	160
15.3	The inquiry into logical relevance	162
	15.3.1 The facts in issue	162
	15.3.1.1 Identify the facts in issue	162
	15.3.1.2 Establish the relationship between the evidentiary fact and the issue	162
	15.3.2 The closeness or remoteness of the logical connection	163
15.4	The inquiry into admissibility	164
	15.4.1 Admissibility and the degree of probative value: a cost–benefit analysis	164
	15.4.2 The use of the term 'legal relevance'	166
	15.4.3 The meaning of procedural prejudice	167
15.5	Exclusion or inclusion of relevant evidence for policy or constitutional reasons	168
	15.5.1 Exclusion of relevant evidence	168
	15.5.2 Exclusion in terms of the Constitution	168
	15.5.3 Inclusion of immaterial evidence	168
	15.5.4 Inclusion of evidence not connected to a material fact in issue	168
	15.5.5 Precedent	169
15.6	The practical application of relevance	169
	15.6.1 Basic functional elements	169
	15.6.1.1 Relevance is a relational question of fact	169
	15.6.1.2 Multiple relevance and admissibility	169
	15.6.1.3 Provisional or conditional relevance	170
	15.6.2 The practical test of relevance	170
15.7	The court's general discretion to exclude relevant evidence	171
	15.7.1 The discretion to exclude evidence in criminal cases	171
	15.7.2 The discretion to exclude evidence in civil cases	172

**CHAPTER 16   UNCONSTITUTIONALLY OBTAINED EVIDENCE IN CRIMINAL CASES:
SECTION 35(5) OF THE CONSTITUTION   174**

16.1	Introduction	174
16.2	Theoretical basis for excluding unconstitutionally obtained evidence	175
	16.2.1 Rationales for excluding unconstitutionally obtained evidence	176
	16.2.1.1 The condonation rationale	176
	16.2.1.2 The deterrence rationale	177
	16.2.1.3 The corrective justice rationale	177
	16.2.2 Some critiques of the rationales for excluding unconstitutionally obtained evidence	178
	16.2.3 Rationales used by the courts to exclude unconstitutionally obtained evidence	179

	16.2.4 Implications of excluding unconstitutionally obtained evidence	179
16.3	Overview of section 35 of the Constitution	180
16.4	The section 35(5) test for excluding unconstitutionally obtained evidence	181
	16.4.1 First leg of the test: whether admission would render a trial unfair	182
	16.4.2 Second leg of the test: whether admission would be detrimental to the administration of justice	186
16.5	Procedural issues	189
	16.5.1 Section 35(5): onus of proof	190
	16.5.2 Section 35(5): *locus standi*	191
	16.5.3 Section 35(5): trial-within-a-trial	193
16.6	A section 35(5) case study of *S v Van Deventer and Another*	193
	16.6.1 Background	193
	16.6.2 Facts of the case	193
	16.6.3 The admissibility test to be applied in terms of section 35(5) of the Constitution	194
	16.6.4 Applying this test in terms of section 35(5) to the facts of this case	194

CHAPTER 17   SIMILAR FACT EVIDENCE   197

17.1	Meaning of similar fact evidence	197
17.2	Purpose of similar fact evidence	197
17.3	Admissibility and evidentiary aspects of similar fact evidence	198
17.4	Evolution of the similar fact rule	199
	17.4.1 The *Makin* formulation	199
	17.4.2 Criticism of the *Makin* formulation	200
	17.4.3 Explaining the similarity away as mere coincidence	201
	17.4.4 Further categories of similar fact evidence	202
17.5	Similar fact evidence: the present-day rule	203
	17.5.1 The test in *DPP v Boardman*	203
	17.5.2 Extension of the *Boardman test*	203
17.6	Other supporting evidence	204
17.7	Additional examples	204
17.8	An example of the non-admittance of similar fact evidence	205

CHAPTER 18   OPINION AND EXPERT EVIDENCE   207

18.1	Introduction	207
18.2	Basis of the opinion rule	208
18.3	Admissibility of opinion evidence	209
	18.3.1 Admissibility of a layperson's opinion	209
	18.3.2 Admissibility of an expert's opinion	210
	18.3.2.1 Introduction	210
	18.3.2.2 The expert witness	211
	18.3.2.3 Procedure for leading expert evidence	217
18.4	The opinion of a court and the *Hollington* rule	218

CHAPTER 19   CHARACTER EVIDENCE   222

19.1	Introduction: what is character evidence?	222
19.2	Admissibility of character evidence in the common law	223
19.3	Character evidence: admissibility in criminal cases	224

xviii

19.3.1	The accused	224
	19.3.1.1 The State's power to present evidence of an accused's bad character: the common law	224
	19.3.1.2 Admissibility of previous convictions: section 211 of the Criminal Procedure Act, 1977	225
	19.3.1.3 The express provision in section 241 of the Criminal Procedure Act, 1977: evidence of previous conviction on charge of receiving stolen property	227
	19.3.1.4 Lifting the shield: proving previous convictions, previous charges or bad character in terms of section 197 of the Criminal Procedure Act, 1977	228
	19.3.1.5 Proving previous convictions for purposes of sentencing	231
19.3.2	The character of the complainant in criminal cases	231
19.4	The character of the plaintiff and defendant in civil cases	231
19.5	Character of witnesses: credibility	232

CHAPTER 20   EVIDENCE IN SEXUAL OFFENCES CASES — **235**

20.1	Introduction	235
20.2	Previous consistent statement	235
	20.2.1 Common law position	236
	20.2.1.1 The victim should make the complaint voluntarily	236
	20.2.1.2 The victim should make the complaint at the first reasonable opportunity	236
	20.2.1.3 The complainant must testify	237
	20.2.2 Statutory position	237
20.3	Evidence regarding previous sexual history	238
	20.3.1 Common law position	238
	20.3.2 Statutory position	239
	20.3.2.1 1989 amendments	239
	20.3.2.2 2007 amendments	240
20.4	Cautionary rule	241
	20.4.1 Common law	241
	20.4.2 Judicial abolition of the cautionary rule	241
	20.4.3 Statutory abolition of the cautionary rule	242

CHAPTER 21   SELF-CORROBORATION — **244**

21.1	Introduction	244
21.2	Basis of the rule against self-corroboration	244
21.3	Purpose of the rule against self-corroboration	244
21.4	Scope and ambit of the rule against self-corroboration	245

CHAPTER 22   COLLATERAL EVIDENCE — **246**

22.1	Introduction	246
22.2	Legal rules applicable to collateral evidence	247
	22.2.1 Questions as to credit	247
	22.2.1.1 Previous convictions	248
	22.2.1.2 Bias	249

CHAPTER 23   *RES GESTAE* **250**

23.1   Definition of *res gestae* 250
23.2   Kinds of evidence forming part of the *res gestae* 251
      23.2.1   Statements that accompany and explain a relevant act 251
      23.2.2   Spontaneous statements 252
      23.2.3   Statements that prove state of mind 253
      23.2.4   Statements of physical sensations 254

CHAPTER 24   PREVIOUS CONSISTENT STATEMENTS **256**

24.1   Introduction 256
24.2   The rule against previous consistent statements 256
24.3   Admissibility of previous consistent statements 257
      24.3.1   To rebut a suggestion of recent fabrication 257
      24.3.2   Complaints in sexual cases where there is a victim 258
            24.3.2.1   A voluntary complaint 258
            24.3.2.2   The victim must testify 259
            24.3.2.3   The first reasonable opportunity 259
            24.3.2.4   A victim of a sexual offence 260
      24.3.3   Prior identification 261
      24.3.4   Other circumstances in which previous consistent statements are admissible 262
            24.3.4.1   Sections 34(2) of the Civil Proceedings Evidence Act, 1965 and
                       222 of the Criminal Procedure Act, 1977 262
            24.3.4.2   *Res gestae* 262
            24.3.4.3   Section 213 of the Criminal Procedure Act, 1977 262
            24.3.4.4   Refreshing memory 263
            24.3.4.5   Statements made on arrest 263

CHAPTER 25   HEARSAY EVIDENCE **264**

25.1   Introduction 265
25.2   The general rule 265
      25.2.1   On oath 265
      25.2.2   Cross-examination 265
      25.2.3   Demeanour and credibility 266
25.3   Statutory definition of hearsay 266
      25.3.1   Section 3 of the Law of Evidence Amendment Act, 1988 267
      25.3.2   Constitutionality of section 3 268
25.4   Admissibility of hearsay 268
      25.4.1   By agreement: section 3(1)(*a*) 269
      25.4.2   Where the person testifies: sections 3(1)(*b*) and 3(3) 270
      25.4.3   In the interests of justice: section 3(1)(*c*) 270
            25.4.3.1   The nature of the proceedings 270
            25.4.3.2   The nature of evidence 270
            25.4.3.3   The purpose for which the evidence is tendered 271
            25.4.3.4   The probative value of the evidence 271
            25.4.3.5   The reason why the evidence is not given by the person on whose
                       credibility the probative value depends 272
            25.4.3.6   Prejudice to opponents 272

	25.4.3.7 Any other factor which in the opinion of the court should be taken into account	273
25.5	Other statutory exceptions	273
	25.5.1 The Criminal Procedure Act, 1977	273
	25.5.1.1 Affidavits	274
	25.5.1.2 Written statements	274
	25.5.1.3 Preparatory examinations	274
	25.5.1.4 Former trials	274
	25.5.1.5 Business records	274
	25.5.1.6 Judicial proceedings	275
	25.5.1.7 Bankers' books	275
	25.5.2 The Civil Proceedings Evidence Act, 1965	275
	25.5.2.1 Affidavits	275
	25.5.2.2 Sunrise and sunset	275
	25.5.2.3 Bankers' books	275
	25.5.2.4 Documentary evidence	275
	25.5.3 Other examples	275
	25.5.3.1 Electronic evidence	275
	25.5.3.2 Companies' books	276
	25.5.3.3 Age	276
	25.5.3.4 Public documents	276
25.6	The South African Law Reform Commission (SALRC) Project 126 *Review of the Law of Evidence* Discussion Paper 113 *Hearsay and Relevance*	276

CHAPTER 26 PRIVILEGE **280**

26.1	Definition of privilege	280
26.2	Private privilege	281
	26.2.1 Legal professional privilege	281
	26.2.1.1 The legal professional must act in a professional capacity	282
	26.2.1.2 The client must intend that the communication be made to a legal professional in confidence	282
	26.2.1.3 For the purpose of obtaining legal advice	283
	26.2.1.4 In respect of a pending or contemplated litigation	283
	26.2.1.5 The client must claim the privilege	283
	26.2.1.6 Legal professional privilege as a limited fundamental right	284
	26.2.1.7 Litigation privilege as opposed to legal professional privilege	285
	26.2.2 Witness's privilege against self-incrimination	285
	26.2.2.1 Legal basis of a witness's privilege against self-incrimination	285
	26.2.2.2 Rationales for a witness's privilege against self-incrimination	286
	26.2.2.3 Application of a witness's privilege against self-incrimination	286
	26.2.3 Accused's right to silence	288
	26.2.3.1 Common law right to silence	289
	26.2.3.2 Constitutional right to silence	290
	26.2.4 Other private privileges	293
	26.2.4.1 Professional privileges	293
	26.2.4.2 Marital privilege	294
	26.2.4.3 Statements made without prejudice	294
26.3	State privilege	294

26.3.1	The common law development of state privilege	295
26.3.2	Post-constitutional state privilege	296
26.3.3	The Promotion of Access to Information Act, 2000 (PAIA)	298
26.3.4	Police docket privilege	299
	26.3.4.1 Police docket	299
	26.3.4.2 Consultations with state witnesses	301
26.3.5	Crime detection privileges	301
26.3.6	Other state privileges	303
	26.3.6.1 Judicial proceedings	304
	26.3.6.2 Statutory privileges	304

PART FIVE   THE RULES OF TRIAL 307

CHAPTER 27   WITNESSES: COMPETENCE AND COMPELLABILITY 308

27.1	Introduction	309
27.2	Competence	309
27.3	Compellability	309
27.4	Legal rules applicable	309
	27.4.1 Civil law	309
	27.4.2 Criminal law	309
	27.4.3 General rules	310
27.5	Exclusions	310
	27.5.1 Mentally incompetent and intoxicated witnesses	310
	27.5.2 Evidence of the accused	311
	27.5.3 Evidence of the co-accused	311
	27.5.4 Husband and wife	312
	27.5.4.1 Communications between husband and wife	312
	27.5.4.2 Questions that a spouse may refuse to answer	312
	27.5.4.3 Accused's spouse as a witness for the defence	312
	27.5.4.4 Accused's spouse as a witness for the prosecution	313
	27.5.4.5 Spouses as co-accused	313
	27.5.5 Child witnesses	314
	27.5.6 Hearing and speech impaired persons as witnesses	314
	27.5.7 Foreign language speakers as witnesses	314
	27.5.8 Judicial officers as witnesses	314
	27.5.9 Officers of the court as witnesses	315
	27.5.10 Members of Parliament as witnesses	315
	27.5.11 Foreign heads of state and diplomats as witnesses	315
	27.5.12 The President as a witness	315
27.6	Procedural aspects of competence and compellability	315
	27.6.1 Objections	315
	27.6.2 Recalcitrant witnesses	315
	27.6.3 Section 205: means of compelling witnesses to testify	316
	27.6.4 Deciding on competence and compellability of witnesses	317

CHAPTER 28   OPENING STATEMENTS 319

28.1	Introduction: the sequence of the trial	319
28.2	Legal basis for the opening statement	319

xxii

28.3 Content of the opening statement 320
28.4 Procedure for opening statements 320
28.5 Practical aspects of opening statements 321
28.6 Practical examples of opening statements 322
    28.6.1 Civil trial in High Court: opening address by counsel for plaintiff in motor accident case 322
    28.6.2 Criminal trial in High Court: opening address by prosecutor in fraud case 322

CHAPTER 29 EVIDENCE-IN-CHIEF **325**
29.1 Introduction 325
29.2 Legal basis for evidence-in-chief 325
29.3 Prohibition on leading questions during evidence-in-chief 326
29.4 Exceptions to the rule against leading questions 327
29.5 Procedure for evidence-in-chief 327
29.6 Practical aspects of evidence-in-chief 328
29.7 Practical examples of evidence-in-chief 330
    29.7.1 Civil trial in High Court: evidence-in-chief of plaintiff in motor accident case 330
    29.7.2 Criminal trial in High Court: evidence-in-chief of complainant in fraud case 331

CHAPTER 30 CROSS-EXAMINATION **335**
30.1 Introduction 335
30.2 Legal basis for cross-examination 336
30.3 Procedure for cross-examination 336
30.4 Practical examples of cross-examination 337
    30.4.1 Civil trial in High Court: cross-examination of defendant in motor accident case 337
    30.4.2 Criminal trial in High Court: cross-examination of complainant in fraud case 340

CHAPTER 31 RE-EXAMINATION **346**
31.1 Introduction 346
31.2 Legal basis for re-examination 346
31.3 Procedure for re-examination 347
31.4 Practical aspects of re-examination 347
31.5 Practical examples of re-examination 347
    31.5.1 Civil trial in High Court: re-examination of plaintiff in motor accident case 347
    31.5.2 Criminal trial in High Court: re-examination of complainant in fraud case 348

CHAPTER 32 CLOSING ADDRESS **350**
32.1 Introduction 350
32.2 Legal basis for the closing address 350
32.3 Practical aspects of the closing address 351
32.4 Practical example of a closing address 353
    32.4.1 Civil trial in High Court: closing address for the plaintiff in motor accident case 353

CHAPTER 33 OBJECTIONS **357**
33.1 Introduction 357
33.2 Legal aspects of objections 357

33.3	Practical aspects of objections	358
33.4	Practical example of objections	358
	33.4.1 Civil trial in High Court: objections during evidence-in-chief in motor accident case	358

CHAPTER 34   REFRESHING MEMORY — 360

34.1	Introduction	360
34.2	Consequences of refreshing memory	361
34.3	Refreshing memory before giving evidence	361
34.4	Adjourning to refresh memory	362
34.5	Refreshing memory while under oath	362

CHAPTER 35   PREVIOUS INCONSISTENT STATEMENTS — 365

35.1	Introduction	365
35.2	Procedure for dealing with previous inconsistent statements	365
35.3	Evidentiary consequences of previous inconsistent statements	366

CHAPTER 36   HOSTILE WITNESSES — 368

36.1	Introduction	368
36.2	Calling other witnesses to counter unfavourable evidence	368
36.3	Proving a previous inconsistent statement against our own witness	369
36.4	Declaration of hostility: cross-examining our own witness	370

PART SIX   EVALUATION OF EVIDENCE — 373

CHAPTER 37   EVALUATION OF EVIDENCE — 374

37.1	Introduction	374
37.2	The process of evaluation	374
	37.2.1 Factual basis	374
	37.2.2 A dispute of fact	375
	37.2.3 Resolving a dispute of fact	375
37.3	General principles for the evaluation of evidence	376
	37.3.1 Credibility	376
	37.3.2 Credibility and probabilities	376
	37.3.3 Piecemeal reasoning	377
	37.3.4 Further evaluation principles	379
	37.3.5 A practical example of the principles of evaluation	379

CHAPTER 38   CREDITWORTHINESS: CREDIBILITY AND RELIABILITY — 382

38.1	Introduction	382
38.2	The credibility of witnesses	382
38.3	Mendacity: assessing the evidence of the lying witness	384
38.4	Reliability of witnesses	385

CHAPTER 39   INHERENT PROBABILITIES — 388

39.1	Introduction	388
39.2	Probabilities	388

CHAPTER 40 CONTRADICTIONS AND DISCREPANCIES 391
40.1 Introduction 391
40.2 Contradictions 391

CHAPTER 41 THE CAUTIONARY RULE 394
41.1 Introduction 394
41.2 Status of the cautionary rule 395
41.3 Definition of the cautionary rule 395
41.4 Purpose of the cautionary rule 395
41.5 Compliance with the cautionary rule 395
41.6 Specific applications of the cautionary rule 396
    41.6.1 The risk of deliberate false evidence 396
        41.6.1.1 Participants (including accomplices) 396
        41.6.1.2 Other examples 398
    41.6.2 The cautionary rule applied to the single witness's evidence 398
    41.6.3 The cautionary rule applied to children's evidence 399
    41.6.4 The cautionary rule applied to evidence of identification 400
    41.6.5 *S v Jackson*: abolition of the cautionary rule in sexual offences 400
41.7 Conclusion 401

CHAPTER 42 CORROBORATION 404
42.1 Introduction 404
42.2 Meaning of corroboration 405
42.3 Process of corroboration 405
42.4 Characteristics of corroborating evidence 405
    42.4.1 Admissibility 405
    42.4.2 Independent source 405
42.5 Corroboration and the cautionary rule 406
42.6 Corroboration of confessions 406
42.7 Conclusion 407

CHAPTER 43 IDENTIFICATION: VISUAL AND VOICE 408
43.1 Introduction 408
43.2 Visual identification 408
43.3 Voice evidence 408
43.4 Legal rules applicable 408
    43.4.1 Visual identification 409
        43.4.1.1 Reliability of observation 409
        43.4.1.2 Recollection 409
        43.4.1.3 Narration 409
    43.4.2 Identification parades 410
    43.4.3 Dock identification 410
    43.4.4 Photographic identification 410
    43.4.5 Voice identification 410

CHAPTER 44 CIRCUMSTANTIAL EVIDENCE 412
44.1 Introduction 412
44.2 Circumstantial evidence in criminal proceedings 412

44.3 Circumstantial evidence in civil proceedings 414

CHAPTER 45 DEMEANOUR **416**
45.1 Introduction 416
    45.1.1 Appearance 416
    45.1.2 Manner of testifying 416
    45.1.3 Other factors 416
45.2 Legal rules applicable 417
    45.2.1 Fallibility of demeanour 417
    45.2.2 Trial court's observations 417

CHAPTER 46 ASSESSMENT OF MENDACITY **419**
46.1 Introduction 419
46.2 Means of assessing mendacity 419
46.3 Legal rules applicable 420

CHAPTER 47 FAILURE TO TESTIFY **422**
47.1 Introduction 422
47.2 Legal rules applicable 422
    47.2.1 Criminal proceedings 422
    47.2.2 Civil proceedings 424

CHAPTER 48 JUDICIAL NOTICE **426**
48.1 Introduction 426
48.2 Categories of judicial notice 427
    48.2.1 Notorious facts of general knowledge 427
    48.2.2 Facts of local notoriety 428
    48.2.3 Facts easily ascertainable 428
48.3 Examples of instances where courts may take judicial notice 428
    48.3.1 The nature of animals 428
    48.3.2 Political matters 428
    48.3.3 Maps and historical facts 429
    48.3.4 Words 429
    48.3.5 Scientific instruments 429
48.4 South African law 430
    48.4.1 Common law, legislation and customary international law 430
    48.4.2 Foreign law 430
    48.4.3 Customs and indigenous law 430
    48.4.4 Judicial notice by the Constitutional Court 431
48.5 Legal rules applicable to judicial notice 432

CHAPTER 49 PRESUMPTIONS **433**
49.1 Introduction 433
49.2 Irrebuttable presumptions of law 434
49.3 Rebuttable presumptions of law 434
49.4 Rebuttable presumptions of fact 435
49.5 Reverse onus statutory presumptions and the Constitution 436
49.6 Examples of presumptions 438

49.6.1	Rebuttable presumptions of law	438
49.6.2	Rebuttable presumptions of fact	438
49.6.3	Other examples of presumptions	438
49.6.4	Documents	438

CHAPTER 50 ADMISSIONS, POINTINGS OUT AND CONFESSIONS 440

50.1 Introduction 441
50.2 A brief history of developments on admissions, pointings out and confessions in criminal proceedings 442
50.3 Formal admissions in criminal proceedings 442
50.4 Informal admissions in criminal proceedings 444
    50.4.1 Definition of an informal admission 444
    50.4.2 The admissibility of informal admissions 445
    50.4.3 Vicarious admissions: co-perpetrators and authorisation 446
50.5 Pointings out 449
    50.5.1 Defining a pointing out 449
    50.5.2 The admissibility of pointings out 450
    50.5.3 The *Samhando* exception 450
50.6 Confessions 451
    50.6.1 Defining a confession 451
    50.6.2 The intention to make a confession 451
    50.6.3 Determining whether a statement contains a confession or an admission 452
    50.6.4 The admissibility of confessions 452
        50.6.4.1 The general test of admissibility of confessions 453
        50.6.4.2 Technical prerequisites in terms of section 217 of the Criminal Procedure Act, 1977 455
        50.6.4.3 Confessions: the State's burden of proof 456
        50.6.4.4 Confessions to lesser or related offences 456
        50.6.4.5 Confirmation of confessions: section 209 of the Criminal Procedure Act, 1977 456
50.7 Formal admissions in civil matters 459
    50.7.1 Introduction 459
    50.7.2 Intention to make a formal admission 460
    50.7.3 Withdrawal of a formal admission 460

PART SEVEN SCIENTIFIC FORENSIC EVIDENCE 463

CHAPTER 51 FINGERPRINTS AND BODY-PRINTS 464

51.1 Introduction 464
51.2 Fingerprints and body-prints 465
51.3 Footprints 466

CHAPTER 52 BLOOD TYPING AND DNA TESTING 468

52.1 Blood tests 468
    52.1.1 Criminal cases 468
    52.1.2 Civil cases 469
52.2 DNA testing 470
    52.2.1 How DNA testing works 470

52.2.2	Process of DNA testing	470
52.2.3	Probative value of DNA testing	471
52.2.4	Procedure for admitting DNA evidence	471
52.2.5	Chain of custody of DNA evidence	472
52.2.6	Pre-trial disclosure of DNA evidence	472

CHAPTER 53   POLYGRAPHS AND VOICE-STRESS ANALYSERS ... **474**

53.1   Polygraphs (lie-detectors) ... 474

     53.1.1   Scientific reliability of polygraph tests ... 474

     53.1.2   Admissibility of polygraph tests ... 475

     53.1.3   Unresolved issues in South Africa and the approach in the United States of America ... 476

     53.1.4   Arguments against admissibility of polygraph tests ... 476

         53.1.4.1   Collateral issues ... 477

         53.1.4.2   Unreliability ... 477

         53.1.4.3   Weight of opinion evidence ... 477

         53.1.4.4   Probative value versus practicality ... 477

         53.1.4.5   Probative value versus prejudice ... 477

         53.1.4.6   Admissibility of opinion evidence ... 478

53.2   Voice-stress analysers ... 478

CHAPTER 54   NEUROTECHNOLOGY AND NEUROLOGICAL EVIDENCE ... **480**

54.1   Introduction ... 480

54.2   How forensic brain scan analysis (FBSA) works ... 481

54.3   Testing methodology ... 482

54.4   The use of forensic brain scan analysis (FBSA) in criminal cases ... 483

54.5   Future application of forensic brain scan analysis (FBSA) ... 485

54.6   How functional magnetic resonance imaging (fMRI) works ... 485

54.7   The use of fMRI in court cases ... 485

54.8   Future application of fMRI ... 486

PART EIGHT   SPECIAL EVIDENTIARY PROCEDURES ... **489**

CHAPTER 55   THE TRIAL-WITHIN-A-TRIAL ... **490**

55.1   Introduction ... 490

55.2   Principles of a trial-within-a-trial ... 491

55.3   Procedure in a trial-within-a-trial ... 492

     55.3.1   When is a trial-within-a-trial held? ... 492

     55.3.2   Procedure ... 492

     55.3.3   Ruling ... 494

55.4   Burden of proof in a trial-within-a-trial ... 495

55.5   Appeal against the ruling in a trial-within-a-trial ... 495

CHAPTER 56   ESTOPPEL ... **498**

56.1   Introduction ... 498

56.2   Essential elements of estoppel ... 498

     56.2.1   A representation of a factual position ... 499

xxviii

56.2.2 The party must have relied on the representation 499
56.2.3 The representation must have induced a reasonable belief on the part of the party relying on estoppel 499
56.2.4 The party acted or failed to act to his or her detriment 500
56.2.5 The representation must have been the cause of the party's detrimental action 500
56.2.6 Can a representation be made negligently? 501
56.3 Legal rules applicable to estoppel 501
56.3.1 Defence of claim 501
56.3.2 In replication 501
56.4 Estoppel by judgment 502
56.4.1 Civil proceedings 502
56.4.2 Criminal proceedings 502

CHAPTER 57   THE PAROL EVIDENCE RULE **504**
57.1 Introduction 504
57.2 Requirements for the parol evidence rule 504
57.2.1 Single memorial 504
57.2.2 Intention of the parties 505
57.3 Exceptions to the parol evidence rule 505
57.3.1 Statutory restrictions 505
57.3.2 Rectification 505
57.3.3 Validity 505
57.3.4 Partial record 506

CHAPTER 58   CHILDREN'S EVIDENCE **508**
58.1 Introduction 508
58.2 Children and the oath 509
58.3 Evaluating the testimony of children 510
58.3.1 Evidence of previous consistent statements 511
58.3.2 Evidence of delay in reporting 511
58.3.3 Evidence of character and previous sexual history 511
58.3.4 Children's evidence and the cautionary rule 512

CHAPTER 59   EVIDENCE IN LABOUR MATTERS **514**
59.1 Introduction 515
59.2 The onus of proof in labour matters 515
59.2.1 The onus of proof in the Labour Relations Act, 1995 515
59.2.2 The onus of proof in the Employment Equity Act, 1998 516
59.2.3 The onus of proof in unfair labour practices 516
59.3 The standard of proof in labour disputes 516
59.4 Shifting the evidentiary burden in labour matters 517
59.4.1 The evidentiary burden in labour matters 517
59.4.2 The right to remain silent in labour hearings 517
59.5 The conduct of arbitrations held in terms of the Labour Relations Act, 1995 518
59.5.1 Oral evidence in arbitration hearings 518
59.5.2 Documentary evidence in arbitration hearings 518
59.5.3 Real evidence in arbitration hearings 518
59.5.4 Labour arbitration procedure 518

	59.5.5	Arbitrations as hearings *de novo*	520
	59.5.6	The duty to begin in arbitration hearings	520
59.6	Admissibility of evidence in arbitrations		520
	59.6.1	Discussions at conciliation proceedings	520
	59.6.2	Hearsay evidence in arbitrations	521
	59.6.3	Opinion evidence in arbitrations	523
	59.6.4	Illegally and improperly obtained evidence in labour matters	524
		59.6.4.1 Entrapment in labour matters	524
		59.6.4.2 Interception of communications in labour matters	524
		59.6.4.3 Admissibility of improperly obtained evidence in labour matters	525
	59.6.5	Monitoring and searches in labour matters	527
	59.6.6	Admissions and confessions in labour matters	527
	59.6.7	The parol evidence rule in labour matters	527
	59.6.8	Legal privilege in labour matters	528
	59.6.9	Evidence in earlier proceedings in labour matters	528
	59.6.10	Similar fact evidence in labour matters	528
59.7	Proof without evidence in labour matters		528
59.8	Evaluation of evidence in arbitrations		529
59.9	Internal disciplinary hearings		530
59.10	The Labour Court		530

CHAPTER 60   EVIDENCE OBTAINED BY MEANS OF ENTRAPMENT 533

60.1	Introduction	533
60.2	Cautionary approach to entrapment: section 252A of the Criminal Procedure Act, 1997	533
60.3	Procedure for challenging entrapment evidence	537

CHAPTER 61   EVIDENTIARY PROBLEMS WITH THE PREVENTION OF ORGANISED
CRIME ACT, 1998 (POCA) 538

61.1	Introduction	538
61.2	Section 1(2) and (3) of the POCA: knowledge, intention and negligence	538
61.3	Section 2(2) of the POCA: expansion of common law of evidence in racketeering cases	539

Annexure A: Civil trial process	543
Annexure B: Criminal trial process	544
Bibliography	545
Table of cases	549
Table of legislation	573
Glossary	581
Index	591

Preface

The general aim of this book

The law of evidence is based on numerous disparate rules of practice, common law principles, selected statutes and judicial precedents which have been adopted from a number of different sources at various times. It is rooted in the English common law – due to various residuary provisions, the common law of England as it was at 30 May 1961 still forms part of the current South African common law of evidence. However, it is applicable to a substantive body of law that is predominantly Roman-Dutch in origin, with the relatively recent overlay of constitutional supremacy, which itself has caused the law of evidence not only to develop in new and original ways, but has also mandated the inclusion of customary law and approaches adopted in foreign jurisdictions in these developments.

Probably the single factor that makes the law of evidence a difficult subject to grasp is that it is essentially a practical subject that can only be properly understood within the context of the practical application of civil and criminal procedure. Unfortunately, this practical experience is not available to students and new professionals, who are often not introduced to practical issues other than in the classroom.

This book therefore attempts to provide students and new lawyers with clear explanations and descriptions of the basic principles that they need to master in order to have a fundamental understanding of the law of evidence. The first step towards mastering the subject is an understanding of the relevant principles and how they are applied in practice. This book aims to equip students and new lawyers with this knowledge so that they are in a position to apply these principles and to recognise and deal with the complexities that inevitably arise in practice.

Logical sequencing

This book approaches evidence in a logical, sequential manner. Part One is devoted to the history of the South African law of evidence, including the impact of the Constitution, to place the present system in its proper context. Part Two is devoted to definitions and basic principles to give students a foundation for more advanced concepts.

Part Three describes the basic types of evidence and the methods most frequently used to present them in court, while Part Four describes the various rules that have developed over the years for excluding evidence. Part Five deals with the next step, namely the trial processes, and specifically the rules of evidence as they apply during a trial. Part Six then focuses on the evaluation of the evidence presented. Part Seven deals with the impact of scientific developments on the law of evidence. Finally, in Part Eight, we discuss special evidentiary procedures that apply in problematic areas of the law of evidence.

An additional feature is the extensive use of diagrams that set out the logical and sequential stages of various aspects of evidentiary procedures, providing a visual framework within which to contextualise the applicable rules and principles.

Clear language

This book describes, discusses, analyses and comments on the various topics in language that is clear and easy to follow, without deviating from established words, terms and phrases (be they Latin or otherwise) that are in common use daily in our courts, and that appear in reported cases on evidence. The editors feel that to replace these with translations or more accessible terms would be doing students a disservice as the book aims to prepare students for law as it is practised in our courts. To assist students, however, there is an extensive glossary of the terms and concepts that we refer to in the book.

The scope of this book

As the title of the book indicates, its objective is to be a guide to the basic principles of the South African law of evidence and it makes no claim to be definitive. Students are encouraged to refer to the various textbooks and other readings contained in the References at the end of the book. However, what this book does aim to do is to introduce students to all the necessary principles, laws, terms and concepts to enable them to master the subject.

Adrian Bellengère and Constantine Theophilopoulos
(Editors to the second edition)
Durban and Johannesburg
November 2018

List of authors

Adrian Bellengère (Editor)
BA LLB (Natal), LLM (Aberdeen)
Adrian Bellengère is a Senior Lecturer at the University of KwaZulu-Natal, Howard College campus, where he is a subject specialist in the law of evidence and civil procedure, and is an instructor at the LSSA School for Legal Practice in Durban. He is also an Attorney and a Conveyancer of the High Court of South Africa.

Constantine Theophilopoulos (Editor)
BSc LLB (Witwatersrand), LLM, LLD (South Africa)
Constantine Theophilopoulos is an Associate Professor in the School of Law at the University of the Witwatersrand. He is an admitted Attorney of the High Court of South Africa, with a professional interest in litigation. Constantine has published widely in local and international scholarly journals in the fields of evidence, civil and criminal procedure, and is a co-author of a number of books on procedural law. His other academic interests are in the fields of constitutional law, conflicts of law, legal history and jurisprudence. He is also the author of a scholarly book on the Anglo-American right to silence.

Robin Palmer (Editor)
BA LLB (Witwatersrand) PG Dip Maritime Law LLM (Natal)
Robin Palmer is a practising advocate of the High Court of South Africa, and Professor of Law in the Faculty of Law, University of Canterbury, New Zealand. He is also the Executive Director of the Institute for Professional Legal Training, affiliated to the University of KwaZulu-Natal, Durban, and Honorary Research Fellow in the School of Law, University of the KwaZulu-Natal, Durban.

Zakhele Hlophe
BA (Natal) MSc (Leicester) PhD (King's College London)
Zakhele Hlophe is strategy advisor to the National Assembly's Portfolio Committee on Justice and Correctional Services and the Standing Committee on Finance. He previously worked as a Lecturer at the UKZN School of Law where he taught criminal procedure, criminology theory and anti-money laundering law for the postgraduate diploma in Forensic Investigations and Criminal Justice. He also worked as a senior analyst for the National Prosecuting Authority's Directorate of Special Operations.

Thea Illsley
LLB (Pretoria), LLM (South Africa), LLM (McGill)
Thea Illsley is a Senior Lecturer in the Department of Procedural Law at the University of Pretoria's Faculty of Law. She teaches the law of evidence at undergraduate and postgraduate level, and is a specialist in alternative dispute resolution.

Neville John Melville
BA LLB (Natal), LLM (Natal)
Neville Melville is an Advocate of the High Court of South Africa and a former district/regional court prosecutor and state advocate. He is an Honorary Research Fellow in the School of Law, University of KwaZulu-Natal, Durban, author of and contributor to various books, and has published a number of articles in local journals.

Lesala Mofokeng
BA LLB (Natal) LLM (Georgetown)
Lesala Mofokeng is a senior lecturer and academic leader in the School of Law at the University of KwaZulu-Natal. His teaching and research interests include legal diversity, legal reasoning and legal pluralism. He is an Advocate of the High Court of South Africa and appears regularly in the superior courts in cases involving traditional leadership and customary marriages.

Bobby Naudé
B Iuris, LLB, LLD (South Africa)
Bobby Naudé is a Professor of criminal and procedural law in the Faculty of Law at the University of South Africa, where he lectures on the law of evidence. He is an Advocate of the High Court of South Africa and a former district court prosecutor. Bobby is a co-author of a casebook on the law of evidence, and has published a number of articles in local journals on matters dealing with evidence and criminal procedure.

Mathobela Shadrack Nkutha
BA LLB (Witwatersrand), LLM (Natal, Howard College)
Mathobela Shadrack Nkutha is a former Legal Resources Centre Fellow, Johannesburg Office (1991); a former National Specialist Monitor with the IEC (1994); became a member of Johannesburg Bar (December 1994); a former lecturer in criminal law, private international law, criminal procedure, law of evidence and criminal legal practice at Vista University, Rand Afrikaans University and University of Johannesburg and used to compile Students' Study Guides in various related subjects; practised in criminal law, medical negligence and malpractice; sat as an assessor on Circuit and Gauteng Local Division of the High Court; a former Researcher and External Examiner at LLM level with the Department of Criminal Law and Procedure at Nelson Mandela University. He is currently a Door Member of Johannesburg Society of Advocates.

Toni Palmer
LLB (UKZN) LLM (Cantab)
Toni is an Advocate of the High Court of South Africa and a member of the Society of Advocates of KwaZulu-Natal. Toni practises in all areas of public and private law.

Elizabeth Picarra
BA (Witwatersrand), LLB (Witwatersrand), LLM (Witwatersrand)
Elizabeth Picarra was a Senior Lecturer at the School of Law at the University of the Witwatersrand. She was formerly a practising Advocate with the Johannesburg Society of Advocates. Elizabeth has published articles in the field of gender law and virtual legal issues.

Shanta Reddy
BA LLB (Natal)
Shanta Reddy is a practising attorney of the High Court of South Africa. She runs her own practice and specialises in labour law. She is a CCMA-trained arbitrator and has acted as a Judge in the Labour Courts.

Les Roberts

BA, LLB (Rhodes), SC

After graduating from Rhodes University, Les Roberts spent 32 years in the prosecuting service, the last eight as Attorney-General/Director of Public Prosecutions of the Eastern Cape. He was appointed Senior Counsel in 1980. After taking early retirement, he lectured at Rhodes University Law Faculty for nine years, mainly in the field of criminal procedure and the law of evidence. After retiring from Rhodes University at the end of 2011, he continued lecturing in the law of evidence for two years. He is now fully retired.

Lee Swales

LLB (KwaZulu-Natal) LLM (Witwatersrand) PhD Candidate

Lee Swales is a lecturer at the School of Law, University of KwaZulu-Natal, Howard College campus, where he is a subject specialist in cyber law and the law of evidence. Lee is also a practising attorney and consultant at Thomson Wilks Incorporated, where he specialises in all aspects of technology-related law.

Annette van der Merwe

B Proc (Pretoria), LLB (South Africa), LLM (Pretoria), PhD (Rhodes)

Annette van der Merwe is a former prosecutor. She is currently an Associate Professor in the Faculty of Law, University of Pretoria. Annette teaches the law of evidence, criminal procedure, sentencing law and victims' rights.

Benita Whitcher

B Journ (Rhodes), LLB (UKZN), LLM (UKZN)

Benita Whitcher is a Judge in the Labour Court. She is a former labour law attorney and university lecturer.

Specialist contributors

The contributions offered by the following persons in the development of this work, warrant special acknowledgement. The publisher and editors express sincere appreciation for their valued support:

Ms Toni Palmer, LLB (UKZN), LLM (Cantab), Advocate of the High Court, for the significant role she performed in researching and updating various areas of content within this text.

Dr Kanagie Naidoo, BProc, LLM, LLD, Head of the Law Department, University of Zululand for kindly providing advice and lending her expertise and assistance during the process of editing this book.

Mr Jacques Matthee, LLB, LLM, Faculty of Law, North-West University, for the research and other valuable support he contributed during the development of the book, and for his authorship of the ancillary materials that augment the first edition of this book.

About the book

The Law of Evidence in South Africa: Basic Principles is a pedagogically rich learning resource, providing a clear, practical and innovative introduction to the law of evidence in South Africa. The text clarifies and explains a complex subject in a style that encourages understanding. Practical in its approach, it provides step-by-step guidance, with numerous case illustrations and practical examples. The text is supported, in addition, by diagrams, and a comprehensive glossary that defines the terms and concepts which appear in the book.

Brief description of features

Discussion boxes: These discussions consider the policy ramifications of the law; how it works in practice; its logic and consistency with other principles; possible alternatives, and other key issues. This feature instils a broader and deeper understanding of the subject matter. It stimulates discussion, supports independent thinking, and develops the ability to engage meaningfully with relevant issues.

Diagrams: The diagrams provide overviews and explain key concepts visually. This feature reinforces understanding, helps to clarify key concepts, and shows more clearly the interrelationship between distinct legal concepts and processes.

Chapter in essence: This feature at the end of each chapter summarises the key areas and core topics covered in the chapter in a succinct list of essential points.

Glossary: This resource contains explanations for the words and phrases that constitute the jargon, or terms of art, particular to the area of study covered in the book. Latin phrases, and many others phrases, are explained and contextualised in the glossary.

Bibliography: A list of reference works appears at the end of the book. The works cover the most important South African sources, including common law authorities, as well as relevant international and comparative sources.

Acknowledgements

South African Criminal Law Reports
48 quotes and extracts from *South African Criminal Law Reports* of Juta and Company (Pty) Ltd are reprinted by kind permission of Juta and Company (Pty) Ltd.

Chapter 2
Figure 2.1 on p. 5, Union of South Africa, 1911: Image # 120575674, World Atlas (Gallo Images).

Chapter 4
Quote on p. 19 from I Moodley *The Customary Law of Intestate Succession* (2012) PhD Thesis, University of South Africa. Reprinted with the author's permission; Quote on p. 24 from I Currie & J De Waal *The Bill of Rights Handbook* 6 ed (2103) Juta at 630; Quote on p. 24 from ES Nwauche 'Affiliation To A New Customary Law In Post-Apartheid South Africa' *PER/PELJ* 2015 (18)3 569 at 579 *Potchefstroom Electronic Law Journal/Potchefstroomse Elektroniese Regsblad (PER/PELJ)* https://www.ajol.info/index.php/pelj/article/view/127044; Quote on p. 26 from C Himonga and C Bosch 'The application of African Customary Law under the constitution of South Africa: Problems solved or just beginning?' 2000 117(2) *SALJ* 306 at 335 and 336, reprinted by permission of Juta and Company (Pty) Ltd; Quote on p. 27 from S Mnisi Weeks 'Securing women's property inheritance in the context of plurality: Negotiations of law and authority in Mbuzini customary courts and beyond' 2011 *Acta Juridica* 140 at 147, footnote 29, reprinted by permission of Juta and Company (Pty) Ltd; Quote on p. 32 from RB Mqeke 'Chiefs' civil court rules' 1983 *De Rebus* 1983(188) at 399, tel. (012) 366 8800, reprinted by permission of the editor; Quote on p. 38 from S Nkosi 'Customary marriage as dealt with in *Mxiki v Mbata in re: Mbata v Department of Home Affairs and Others* (GP) (unreported case no A844/2012, 23-10-2014)' 2015 *De Rebus* (549) at 67, reprinted by permission of the editor; Quote on p. 32 per Stubbs P in *Motaung v Dube* 1930 NAC (N & T) 9 (quoted by RB Mqeke 'Chiefs' civil court rules' 1983 *De Rebus* 1983(188) at 399–400), reprinted by permission of the editor; Quote on p. 34 from JC Rideout 'Storytelling, Narrative Rationality, and Legal Persuasion' 14 *Legal Writing: The Journal of the Legal Writing Institute* (2008) 53 at page 59, quoting A MacIntyre *After Virtue* (1984) at page 215; Quote on p. 35 from RM Cover (1983) 'The Supreme Court, 1982 Term – Foreword: Nomos and Narrative' Faculty Scholarship Series. FS Papers 2705, 4–68 at 4–5 http://digitalcommons.law.yale.edu/fss_papers/2705 or G Olson 'Narration and Narrative in Legal Discourse' at para 23 in P Hühn et al (eds) *The Living Handbook of Narratology* Hamburg, Hamburg University, http://www.lhn.uni-hamburg.de/article/narration-and-narrative-legal-discourse (accessed 1 May 2018); Quote on p. 36 from D Knapp van Bogaert and GA Ogunbanjo (2008) 'Post-birth Rituals: Ethics and the Law' *South African Family Practice* 50(2): 45–46 at 45, reprinted by permission of Prof. Ogunbanjo, editor of the journal; Quote on p. 37, footnote 124, referring to HJ Simons 'Customary unions in a changing society' (1958) *Acta Juridica* 320 at 322–325, reprinted by permission of Juta and Company (Pty) Ltd; Quote on p. 138 from S Nkosi 'Customary marriage as dealt with in *Mxiki v Mbata in re: Mbata v Department of Home Affairs and Others* (GP) (unreported case no A844/2012, 23-10-2014)' 2015 *De Rebus* (549) at 67, reprinted by permission of the editor.

Chapter 8

Quote on p. 71 from *R v Downey* 1992 (13) Cr 4th 129 (SCC) at 138, a judgment of the Supreme Court of Canada, published online by Lexum, https://scc-csc.lexum.com/scc-csc/scc-csc/en/item/879/index.do.

Chapter 14

Quote on p. 122 from United Nations Commission on International Trade Law 2017, http://www.uncitral.org/uncitral/en/uncitral_texts/electronic_commerce/1996Model_status.html; Quote on p. 139 from C Theophilopoulos 'The admissibility of data, data messages, and electronic documents at trial' (2015) 3 *TSAR* 461 at 477, Tydskrif vir die Suid-Afrikaanse Reg, reprinted by permission of Juta and Company (Pty) Ltd; Quote on p. 149 from JC Smith 'The Admissibility of Statements by Computer' 1981 *Criminal Law Review* 387 at 390, reproduced with permission of Thomson Reuters through PLSclear; Quote on p. 152 from *U-Haul Intern Inc. v Lumbermens Mut. Cas.Co* 576 F.3d 1040 (9th Cir. 2009) 1043 United States Court of Appeals, Ninth Circuit, https://www.courtlistener.com/opinion/1188880/u-haul-intern-inc-v-lumbermens-mut-cas-co,Creative Commons License Content licensed under a Creative Commons Attribution-NoDerivatives 4.0 International License; Quote on p. 152 from LJ Kemp '*Lorraine v. Markel*: An Authoritative Opinion Sets the Bar for Admissibility of Electronic Evidence (Except for Computer Animations and Simulations)' (2007) 9(3) NC *JOLT* at 16–29. *Carolina Journal of Law & Technology*: Content on this site is licensed under a Creative Commons Attribution 4.0 International license.

Chapter 15

Quote on p. 159 from *R v A* (No 2) [2002] 1 AC 45, ICLR Law Report Series, published by the ICLR; Quote on p. 163 from *R v Kilbourne* [1973] AC 729 at paras 756–757, Appeal Cases, *The Law Report Series*, published by the ICLR; Quote on p. 162 from *Lithgow City Council v Jackson* (2011) 244 CLR 352 at para 26, Commonwealth Law Reports, which report decisions of the High Court of Australia, reproduced with permission of Thomson Reuters (Professional) Australia Limited, https://legal.thomsonreuters.com.au/; Quote on p. 164 from *DPP v Kilbourne* [1973] AC 729 at 757–758, Appeal Cases, *The Law Report Series*, published by the ICLR.

Chapter 16

Quote on p. 177 from *R v Collins* (1987) 1 SCR 265 at para 35, Supreme Court Reports, Canada, published by the Canadian government, https://www.canlii.org/en/; Quote on p. 184 from *R v Grant* (2009) SCC 32 at para 76 (Supreme Court of Canada), a judgment of the Supreme Court of Canada, published online by Lexum, https://scc-csc.lexum.com/scc-csc/scc-csc/en/item/7799/index.do; Quote on p. 187 from D Ally (2012) Determining the effect (the social costs) of exclusion under the South African exclusionary rule: should factual guilt tilt the scales in favour of the admission of unconstitutionally obtained evidence?, *PER* 15(5) at 476, https://www.ajol.info/index.php/pelj/article/view/85961.

Chapter 17

Quote on p. 201 from *R v Bond* [1906] 2 KB 389 (CCR) at 424, Law Reports, King's Bench, published by the ICLR; Quote on p. 203 from *DPP v Boardman* [1975] AC 421 (HL) Law Reports, Appeal Cases, published by the ICLR.

Chapter 22
Quote on p. 247 from *Attorney-General v Hitchcock* (1847) 1 Exch 91 at 99, Exchequer Reports, published by the ICLR; Discussion 22.1 on p. 247 from R Palmer and D Mcquoid-Mason *Basic Trial Advocacy Skills* (2000) at 84–5, reprinted by permission of LexisNexis.

Chapter 30
Quote on p. 335 from E du Toit et al. Commentary on the Criminal Procedure Act (1987) at 22–79 (Revision service 59, 2017), University of Pretoria.

Chapter 38
Quote from p. 384 from HC Nicholas 'The credibility of witnesses' (1985) 102(1) *South African Law Journal* at 32. Reprinted by permission of Juta and Company (Pty) Ltd.

Chapter 46
Quote on p. 420 from HC Nicholas 'The credibility of witnesses' (1985) 102(1) *South African Law Journal* 32 at 35–36. Reprinted by permission of Juta and Company (Pty) Ltd.

Chapter 51
Quote on p. 465 from L Meintjes-Van der Walt 'Fingerprint evidence: Probing myth and reality' (2006) *South African Journal of Criminal Justice* 19(2): 152–172 at 156 note 26, reprinted by permission of Juta and Company (Pty) Ltd.

Chapter 52
Figure 52.1 on p. 471, DNA autoradiogram: Image # G2100964-DNA_autoradiogram-SPL (Science Photo Library).

Chapter 53
Figure 53.1 on p. 475, Polygraph: Image # 576877944 Polygraph from Jack Ruby (Photo © CORBIS/Corbis via Getty Images).

Chapter 54
Quote on p. 485 from JG Hakun et al 'Towards clinical trials of lie detection with fMRI' (2009) *Social Neuroscience* 4(6): 518–527, reprinted by permission of the publisher (Taylor & Francis Ltd, http://www.tandfonline.com); Quote on p. 485 from E Rusconi and T Mitchener-Nissen 'Prospects of functional magnetic resonance imaging as lie detector' (2013) *Frontiers in Human Neuroscience* 7 at 594, in CJ Kraft and J Giordano 'Integrating Brain Science and Law: Neuroscientific Evidence and Legal Perspectives on Protecting Individual Liberties' (2017) *Frontiers in Neuroscience* 11: 621, doi: 10.3389/fnins.2017.00621, copyright © 2017 Kraft and Giordano, distributed under the terms of the Creative Commons Attribution License (CC BY).

PART ONE

General introduction

CHAPTER 1   Defining evidence   2

CHAPTER 2   Brief history and sources of the South African law of evidence   4

CHAPTER 3   Systems of legal fact-finding   10

CHAPTER 4   Truth verification, fact finding and rules of evidence in African oral traditional law   18

CHAPTER 5   Impact of the Constitution on the law of evidence   44

Chapter 1

Defining evidence

We may broadly define **evidence** as *any information* that a court has *formally admitted* in civil or criminal proceedings, or at administrative or quasi-judicial hearings.

There is a wide variety of information that we may consider and rely on when we attempt to resolve disputes before the start of formal civil or criminal court proceedings. This also applies to proceedings before other tribunals, such as arbitration hearings or workplace disciplinary hearings. This information includes:

- written or computer-printed documents such as letters, memoranda and reports
- oral or written statements
- the contents of electronic mail (email) exchanges
- photographs, tape recordings and video recordings
- the observations of eyewitnesses to an incident
- the nature and characteristics of certain physical objects.

Whatever the nature of the information that may help to resolve the dispute, we cannot call it 'evidence' at this stage – only once this information has been formally admitted[1] into court can we label it evidence.[2] Therefore, during the process of attempting to have the information admitted by a court, this information is at most *potential evidence*. Note, however, that the general practice, in practice, is to call such information 'evidence' even at the pre-admission stage. This can be potentially confusing for newcomers to the field.

To complicate matters, the courts have created a category of information that is used during trial proceedings, but is not formally admitted by the court. The courts have called this type of information **evidentiary material**[3] to distinguish it from formally admitted evidence. The courts may nevertheless rely on this evidentiary material in coming to their decision. Examples of evidentiary material include:

- the contents of a criminal **accused**'s explanation of a plea statement made in terms of section 115 of the Criminal Procedure Act 51 of 1977[4]
- **presumptions**[5]
- **formal admissions** made in criminal proceedings[6]
- where the court takes **judicial notice** of something.[7]

For the sake of convenience, we refer to both properly admitted evidence and evidentiary material jointly as **probative material**.[8]

---

1. See ch 6 Admissibility and weight of evidence.
2. See Part Three: Kinds of evidence.
3. Sometimes also called probative material. See *S v Mjoli and Another* 1981 (3) SA 1233 (A).
4. *S v Mjoli and Another* 1981 (3) SA 1233 (A) and *S v De Ruiter* 2004 1 SACR 332 (W).
5. See *S v AR Wholesalers (Pty) Ltd and Another* 1975 (1) SA 551 (NC).
6. *S v Mokgeledi* 1968 (4) SA 335 (A).
7. See ch 48 Judicial notice.
8. See ch 7 Evidence and proof.

The **law of evidence**, also called 'rules' of evidence, governs:

- first, what requirements we must meet and what steps we must follow to render this information *admissible* in court as evidence or evidentiary material
- second, how the courts must *evaluate* admitted evidence to come to a decision.[9]

As we discuss below, the **common law** rules of evidence apply to all types of proceedings. These include criminal proceedings, civil proceedings, administrative hearings[10] and labour dispute resolution, for example in the Commission for Conciliation, Mediation and Arbitration (CCMA). These rules of evidence are also generally adhered to as guidelines in informal proceedings, such as workplace disciplinary hearings. Various statutes have also confirmed, supplemented and, in some cases, modified the common law rules of evidence. Examples here include the:

- Criminal Procedure Act, 1977[11]
- Civil Proceedings Evidence Act 25 of 1965
- Electronic Communications and Transactions Act 25 of 2002
- Law of Evidence Amendment Act 45 of 1988 ('Hearsay Amendment Act')
- Constitution of the Republic of South Africa, 1996.

Finally, the correct use of terminology will assist to avoid confusion. As mentioned above, prior to its admission by a court or tribunal, we, in this book, refer to information of whatever nature as *information,* an *evidentiary fact* or *potential evidence* rather than *evidence*. Further examples of the correct use of terminology are as follows:

- Evidence admitted under **oath** is called **testimony.**[12]
- Once evidence is admitted, the court *evaluates* it to establish its **weight.**[13]
- **Probative force** or **probative value** means the potential the information has to help prove an issue in order to establish **relevance** before the information is admitted.[14] Alternatively, it can mean the potential the admitted evidence has to tilt the probabilities in favour of one **party** to the litigation during the process of evaluating the evidence.[15]

THIS CHAPTER IN ESSENCE

1   Evidence refers to any information formally admitted by a court in all types of legal proceedings.
2   We can only label information tendered to help resolve a dispute as evidence once it has been formally admitted.
3   Evidentiary material refers to information received during trial proceedings, which is not formally admitted by the court, but which the court can nevertheless rely on in coming to its decision.
4   Probative material refers to both properly admitted evidence and evidentiary material.
5   The law of evidence is the branch of law governing:
    5.1   the requirements we must meet and the steps we must follow to render information admissible in court as evidence or evidentiary material
    5.2   the manner in which the courts must evaluate admitted evidence before coming to a decision.
6   The law of evidence is made up of various common law rules. In some cases, various specific statutes have also confirmed, supplemented and modified the common law rules.

---

9   See ch 6 Admissibility and weight of evidence.
10   In compliance with s 33 of the Constitution, 1996.
11   Particularly Chs 21, 22, 23 and 24 of the Criminal Procedure Act, 1977.
12   Oral evidence or evidence in the form of an affidavit, hence the verb, 'He *testified* ...'. See ch 10 Oral evidence.
13   See ch 6 Admissibility and weight of evidence.
14   See ch 15 The general test for relevance.
15   See Part Six: Evaluation of evidence.

Chapter 2

Brief history and sources of the South African law of evidence

2.1	Background: the reception of the English law of evidence in South Africa	4
2.2	The 30 May 1961 rule: the residuary sections	5
2.3	The impact of the interim (1993) and final Constitution, 1996	7
2.4	Overview of the main evidence statutes	7
2.5	The South African Law Reform Commission (SALRC) Project 126 *Review of the Law of Evidence*	8

2.1 Background: the reception of the English law of evidence in South Africa

After the British occupation of the Cape of Good Hope in 1806, the existing **Roman-Dutch** derived laws of the colony initially remained unchanged. However, in 1830 they were replaced with the Cape Evidence Ordinance, based on English law.[1]

This 1830 Cape Evidence Ordinance thereafter formed the basis for laws on evidence in various other parts of the southern African region, including the Evidence Proclamations of the Zuid-Afrikaanse Republiek (ZAR)[2] and the Orange River Colony.

After Britain annexed the ZAR in 1902, the Evidence Proclamation[3] was issued. This duplicated most of the provisions of the 1830 Cape Evidence Ordinance. In addition, it included a residuary section to deal with instances that the new proclamation did not cover. This residuary section provided that, in cases not covered by the proclamation, the law in force in the Supreme Court of Judicature in England[4] had to be followed.

The Evidence Proclamation for the Orange River Colony (the Orange Free State Province after 1910) was essentially a duplication of that of the ZAR. However, where the ZAR Proclamation mentioned the law of England, the Orange River Colony Proclamation referred to the law of the Cape of Good Hope.

---

1 Ordinance 72 of 1830.
2 Later to become the Transvaal Province after union in 1910.
3 Proclamation 11 of 1902.
4 The Judicature Acts of 1873 and 1875 completely reorganised the higher court system, which had existed since the Middle Ages. The old higher courts were abolished and a new Supreme Court of Judicature was created, consisting of the High Court of Justice and the Court of Appeal. The Appellate Jurisdiction Act of 1876 placed the role of the House of Lords as the highest court of appeal on a proper judicial footing by providing for the appointment of senior and experienced judges.

CHAPTER 2   BRIEF HISTORY AND SOURCES OF THE SOUTH AFRICAN LAW OF EVIDENCE

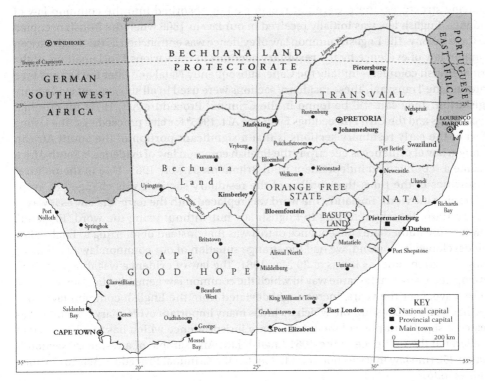

Figure 2.1 *Map of the Union of South Africa*

The development of the law of evidence in the Natal Colony (later the Natal Province and now KwaZulu-Natal) took a different route. Natal Colony Law 17 of 1859[5] states that the law as it is in England should be followed. This was followed by a list of topics on the law of evidence.

In 1910, the Union of South Africa[6] was formed from the Cape Colony, the ZAR, the Orange River Colony and the Natal Colony. The laws of evidence relating to criminal proceedings contained in the 1830 Cape Evidence Ordinance, the ZAR and Orange River Colony Proclamations, and the Natal Law 17 of 1859 were consolidated in the Criminal Procedure and Evidence Act 31 of 1917. This was later replaced by the Criminal Procedure Act 56 of 1955 and then by the Criminal Procedure Act 51 of 1977.

For civil proceedings, the colonial statutes remain in force for some purposes.[7] However, they have been mostly consolidated for the whole of South Africa by the Civil Proceedings Evidence Act 25 of 1965.

2.2   The 30 May 1961 rule: the residuary sections

The South African common law of evidence is derived almost exclusively from English law. Although rules relating to the resolution of disputes (including the leading and evaluation of evidence) in customary tribunals did exist and were in used in customary dispute

---
5   In s 1.
6   Comprising the Cape, Transvaal, Orange Free State and Natal Provinces.
7   But not all – see *Van der Linde v Calitz* 1967 (2) SA 239 (A) and DT Zeffertt and AP Paizes *The South African Law of Evidence* 2 ed (2009) at 13–14.

6 | THE LAW OF EVIDENCE IN SOUTH AFRICA

resolving structures, these were not recognised or absorbed into the common law of evidence. English law was initially received in our law in 1806 when the British occupied the Cape Colony. The English common law of evidence was entrenched as the South African common law of evidence by the **residuary sections** in the various Proclamations of the former British colonies – initially the Cape, subsequently Natal and later the Orange Free State and the Transvaal. These residuary sections were used in all subsequent evidentiary **legislation**. They can still be found in the Criminal Procedure Act, 1977[8] for criminal proceedings and the Civil Proceedings Evidence Act, 1965[9] for civil proceedings. The lasting effect of the early residuary sections is that a significant portion of the South African common law of evidence is effectively the English common law of evidence.[10] South Africa became a republic and independent from Britain on 31 May 1961. Due to the political sensitivities of the time, the wording of the residuary sections was changed to avoid mentioning the word 'England'. The word was replaced with the term 'the law as it was at 30 May 1961', thereby referring to English law but without using the word 'England'. However, the immediate consequence of this was that, instead of referring to English law as it developed in England, we had the strange situation of our common law of evidence being 'frozen in time' as it was at 30 May 1961. The law of evidence was thus unable to develop and evolve in the same way in which the common law generally did. However, our courts have, over the years, increasingly deviated from the English common law. This, together with the Constitution, which includes many important evidentiary principles, has created a significant postcolonial evidentiary jurisprudence which has to a large extent ameliorated the influence of pre-1961 English law. An example of a residuary section is section 252 (the law in cases not provided for) of the Criminal Procedure Act, 1977 which reads as follows:

> The law as to the admissibility of evidence, which was in force in respect of criminal proceedings on the thirtieth day of May 1961, shall apply in any case not expressly provided for by this Act or any other law.

To summarise the effect of the 30 May 1961 rule on the South African law of evidence:

- The general rule is that the South African common law of evidence is English law as it was at 30 May 1961.
- However, in most cases, it will not be necessary to research this old English common law as most of the applicable principles of our common law have been analysed and declared by the South African courts after 1961. In doing so, the courts' starting point will always be the residuary rule, in other words the English law as it was at 30 May 1961.
- As stated above, the effect of the residuary rule was extensively analysed in the **Appellate Division** case of *Van der Linde v Calitz*.[11] In summary, the effect of this case appears to be as follows:
  - *Decisions of the (UK) Supreme Court of Judicature*: This Court's decisions, as interpreted by the South African courts, are binding on all our courts except the Constitutional Court.
  - *Decisions of the (UK) Privy Council*: All **Privy Council** decisions taken before 1950, as interpreted by the South African courts, are regarded as decisions of South Africa's then-highest court (previously the Appellate Division of the Supreme Court – now

---

8 Ss 206 and 252.
9 S 42. See also Zeffertt and Paizes 2 ed (2009) at 14.
10 The residuary sections applied the law as it stood in the Supreme Court of Judicature in England.
11 1967 (2) SA 239 (A).

CHAPTER 2 BRIEF HISTORY AND SOURCES OF THE SOUTH AFRICAN LAW OF EVIDENCE

the Supreme Court of Appeal). Note, however, that this rule does not apply to the Constitutional Court.

- ♦ *Post-30 May 1961 English decisions not binding*: Court decisions on the law of evidence of all English courts handed down after 30 May 1961 do not bind South African courts, but as with any other foreign cases, they could be persuasive.
- The South African Constitutional Court is not bound by the residuary rule as the supremacy clause of the Constitution (section 2) empowers it to overrule any law, court decision (including pre-1961 English law or court decisions) or conduct (including any pre-1961 English rules of practice) should these not be in accordance with constitutional principles. Section 39(2) of the Constitution, in fact, obliges all courts to develop common law and customary law to conform to the principles in the **Bill of Rights** (sections 7–39 of the Constitution).

The obligation to apply this frozen-in-time law was ameliorated somewhat by the decision in *Van der Linde v Calitz*[12] in which the Appellate Division, now the Supreme Court of Appeal, held that it was entitled to deviate from English decisions if it felt that they were wrongly decided and by an increasing body of statutes governing various aspects of the law of evidence.[13] There is also the obligation contained in section 39(2) of the Constitution, when developing the common law, to '... promote the spirit, purport and objects of the **Bill of Rights**'.[14] In addition, the **South African Law Reform Commission (SALRC)** has reviewed the entire South African law of evidence[15] with the possible outcome being a recommendation to develop a comprehensive code of evidence, although none has yet been published.[16]

2.3 The impact of the interim (1993) and final Constitution, 1996

The so-called supremacy clause, section 2 of the Constitution, 1996, expressly states that 'law or conduct inconsistent with it is invalid, and the obligations imposed by it must be fulfilled'. This means that any common law rule or statutory provision of the law of evidence, or any evidentiary practice, has to comply with the Constitution and especially the Bill of Rights.[17]

2.4 Overview of the main evidence statutes

The main statutes dealing with the law of evidence are the:
- *Civil Proceedings Evidence Act (CPEA) 25 of 1965*: This Act deals with the law of evidence applicable to most aspects of civil proceedings.
- *Criminal Procedure Act (CPA) 51 of 1977*: Chapter 23 (Witnesses) and Chapter 24 (Evidence) of this Act make provision for procedures and related matters in criminal

---

12 1967 (2) SA 239 (A).
13 See 2.4 below.
14 In this case, applying the common law as it was on 30 May 1961 would be subject to those common law rules being in line with the Bill of Rights (ss 7–39 of the Constitution).
15 SALRC Project 126 *Review of the Law of Evidence: Hearsay and Relevance* Issue Paper 26. See also Issue Paper 27 *Electronic Evidence in Criminal and Civil Proceedings: Admissibility and Related Issues* (2008) and Discussion Paper 131. See 2.5 below.
16 Consolidating the various statutes applicable to the law of evidence and codifying common law rules and concepts.
17 See ch 5 Impact of the Constitution on the law of evidence.

proceedings. Note that section 222 of the CPA makes sections 33 to 38 of the CPEA that deal with **documentary evidence** also applicable to criminal proceedings.
- *Law of Evidence Amendment Act 45 of 1988 (Hearsay Amendment Act)*: This Act provides for the taking of judicial notice of the law of a foreign state and of indigenous law. It also codifies the South African law on hearsay.
- *Electronic Communications and Transactions Act (ECT Act) 25 of 2002*: This Act deals with the regulation of electronic communications and transactions, and repealed the Computer Evidence Act 57 of 1983.
- *Interpretation Act 33 of 1957*: This Act consolidates the laws relating to the interpretation of statutes in South Africa.

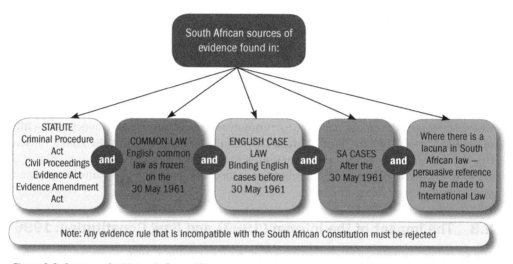

Figure 2.2 Sources of evidence in South Africa

2.5 The South African Law Reform Commission (SALRC) Project 126 *Review of the Law of Evidence*

The SALRC project commenced in 2002. It is tasked with reviewing all aspects of the South African law of evidence and making recommendations for reform. Two of the most important current sub-projects of this project are Discussion Paper 113 on *Hearsay and Relevance* and Issue Paper 27 on *Electronic Evidence,* together with the subsequent Discussion Paper 131 on the same topic.

Discussion Paper 113 on *Hearsay and Relevance* is an investigation arising out of a preliminary study conducted in 2002. This study identified areas of the law of evidence that may require reform. The preliminary investigation pointed out the necessity of taking into account the structural features of the courts. This includes looking at the limited role of lay assessors and the adversarial nature of the proceedings. Discussion Paper 113 expands on the implications of the structural features for the reform of the law of evidence. It reiterates the policy considerations identified in the preliminary survey and then examines **hearsay evidence** and relevance.

After research in this investigation had been completed, it transpired that the **admissibility** of electronic evidence, the provisions of the Electronic Communications and Transactions Act, 2002 and the provisions of the Law of Evidence Amendment Act, 1988

CHAPTER 2   BRIEF HISTORY AND SOURCES OF THE SOUTH AFRICAN LAW OF EVIDENCE   9

dealing with hearsay evidence cannot be considered in isolation. The SALRC stated that a report on hearsay evidence could not be finalised without considering the provisions of the Electronic Communications and Transactions Act, 2002 and the admissibility of electronic evidence in general. The SALRC decided to publish an issue paper exploring issues relating to the admissibility of electronic evidence in criminal and civil proceedings. It released Issue Paper 27 *Electronic Evidence in Criminal and Civil Proceedings: Admissibility and Related Issues* for general information and public comment by way of a media statement issued on 16 March 2010. In the case of criminal proceedings, Issue Paper 27 was particularly concerned with the relationship between Chapter Three of the Electronic Communications and Transactions Act, 2002 and the rule against hearsay.

These sub-projects have not yet been completed, but should eventually lead to significant statutory amendments.

THIS CHAPTER IN ESSENCE

1   The South African common law of evidence is based almost exclusively on the English common law of evidence. This was entrenched as the South African common law of evidence by the residuary sections in the various Proclamations of the former British colonies.

2   When South Africa became an independent republic in 1961, all references to the word 'England' in the residuary sections were changed to 'the law as it was at 30 May 1961'. As a result, the South African common law of evidence was 'frozen in time' and unable to develop and evolve as the common law generally does. However, this problem is somewhat ameliorated by:

2.1   the decision in *Van der Linde v Calitz*,[18] in which the Appellate Division, now the Supreme Court of Appeal, held that it was entitled to deviate from English decisions if it felt that they were wrongly decided

2.2   statutes governing various aspects of the law of evidence

2.3   the supremacy clause in the Constitution, which prescribes that any common law rule or statutory provision of the law of evidence, or any evidentiary practice, has to comply with the Constitution, especially the Bill of Rights

2.4   section 39(2) of the Constitution which obliges the courts to '... promote the spirit, purport and objects of the Bill of Rights' when developing the common law

2.5   Project 126 of the South African Law Reform Commission (SALRC), which is aimed at reviewing the entire South African law of evidence and possibly compiling a comprehensive code of evidence at some point in the future.

---

18   1967 (2) SA 239 (A).

Chapter 3

Systems of legal fact-finding

3.1	**Introduction**	**10**
3.2	**Different systems in use in Africa**	**11**
3.3	**Evidentiary differences between the adversarial and inquisitorial justice models in Africa**	**11**
	3.3.1 The adversarial system is jury-centred and an inquisitorial system is judge-centred	11
	3.3.2 A strict system versus a free natural system of evidence	11
	3.3.3 The difference in approach to evidence is particularly striking in criminal matters	12
	3.3.4 Other major differences between these two models	12
3.4	**The South African adversarial system**	**13**
3.5	**The basic jurisprudential principles of an adversarial trial**	**13**
3.6	**The basic rules of the South African adversarial trial system**	**14**
3.7	**The role of evidence in the South African adversarial system**	**15**
	3.7.1 The place of the law of evidence	15
	3.7.2 The scope of the law of evidence	15

3.1 Introduction

Every culture, society and legal system has a method, or methods, of resolving disputes between parties. While the details, processes and procedures may differ, there is nonetheless a core set of basic principles that lay the same foundation for every system. These include at the most basic level:

- the need to actually resolve disputes
- a forum in which the resolution of disputes takes place
- an orderly manner (or procedure) that is followed
- a person or system of adjudication or decision making.

And at a more complex level, they include:

- the desire to uncover or ascertain the truth
- the need to ensure that the process of doing so is fair, and is perceived to be fair
- the need to do so in a manner that balances efficiency with expediency
- the need to achieve all of the above in way that preserves and does not undermine the integrity of the system.

3.2 Different systems in use in Africa

Three broad categories of systems, all of which achieve these objectives to a greater or lesser extent, can be found throughout Africa. The customary systems that preceded the advent of colonisation, some of which are still in use, will be discussed in detail in a chapter dedicated to them. The colonially introduced systems, which can be broadly categorised into adversarial and inquisitorial systems, which still dominate, will be discussed here, with a particular focus on the systems in use in South Africa.

3.3 Evidentiary differences between the adversarial and inquisitorial justice models in Africa

The adversarial system is found in all African countries with a British colonial history whereas the inquisitorial system is found in African countries with a French, Spanish or Portuguese colonial heritage. The ultimate objective of both the adversarial and inquisitorial systems is to establish the truth. The adversarial system attempts to do this by setting the parties against each other, relying on the conflict between them to uncover the truth or reveal any falsehoods, while the inquisitorial system attempts to do it by eliciting information (through questioning) from those involved in the matter in dispute. The principal jurisprudential differences between these two jurisprudential models are twofold.

3.3.1 The adversarial system is jury-centred and an inquisitorial system is judge-centred

The adversarial, also called the accusatorial, system places the fact-finding and decision-making process on the shoulders of a layperson jury (selected randomly from a pool of ordinary persons without any legal experience). Consequently, an adversarial magistrate or judge is a passive, objective official primarily tasked with overseeing the conduct of a trial process in an administratively efficient and fair manner. In this regard, the South African adversarial trial is different from those in other Anglo-American jurisdictions as trial by jury was abolished in civil trials in 1927 and criminal trials in 1969. This means that judges oversee the conduct of the trial process and also are responsible for the fact-finding and decision-making process.

The inquisitorial process places the fact-finding and decision-making process on the shoulders of a professionally experienced judge. The judge is solely in control of the trial and decides which evidence to include or exclude in order to reach a final decision. The strict rules of evidence and procedure of an adversarial system generally limit the discretionary powers of a judge at trial, whereas a free system of evidence allows an inquisitorial judge wide-ranging discretionary powers at trial.

3.3.2 A strict system versus a free natural system of evidence

The adversarial system of evidence consists of a number of strict technical rules of evidentiary inclusion or exclusion. The adversarial determination of legal truth is made within strict procedural and evidentiary boundaries. The layperson, legally inexperienced jury in an adversarial process bases its decision making solely on a strictly selected quantum of relevant evidence admitted at trial in terms of these technical and somewhat artificial rules. The first concern of an adversarial lawyer is the question of the admissibility of evidence at the beginning of a trial; the second is the weight and cogency of such evidence. A free system of evidence applies in the inquisitorial process and the professional judge does not need to be guided by technical rules of admissible evidence. The inquisitorial determination of legal truth is made within a natural inquiry which is free of any evidentiary barriers. All evidence is potentially admissible; the judge decides which evidence to admit or reject and is solely responsible for assigning the correct probative weight to be attached to the evidence. In practice, an inquisitorial judge has no need of exclusionary categories such as hearsay, *res gestae*, similar fact evidence or prior consistent statements. However, common sense rules of privilege, judicial notice and witness competency do apply. An expert witness must lay a foundation for his or her expertise. While an adversarial party may include any number of expert witnesses in its witness list, an inquisitorial party has a limited ability or opportunity to call experts as these are usually appointed by the court.

3.3.3 The difference in approach to evidence is particularly striking in criminal matters

It is argued that an adversarial process emphasises the accused's procedural rights, individual autonomy and privacy. The presumption of innocence, the accused's right to silence and the witness privilege against self-incrimination are examples of constitutionally entrenched adversarial procedural protections. While these procedural protections are present in the inquisitorial process they are somewhat weak and do not provide the inquisitorial accused with the same adversarial level of protection. Therefore, an inquisitorial judge may freely adduce character, opinion evidence and the accused's history of previous convictions at trial. The adversarial lawyer's first ethical duty is to the client and not to the truth, while an inquisitorial process places the truth-seeking function before the accused's procedural autonomy. In the adversarial system, it is the duty of the prosecution to adduce sufficient evidence to establish a *prima facie* case and for the accused to rebut such a case, whereas in the inquisitorial system the *prima facie* case against the accused has already been established in the dossier before trial.

3.3.4 Other major differences between these two models

Table 3.1 Differences between the adversarial and inquisitorial model

Adversarial	Inquisitorial
Party control The adversarial parties are in control of a trial and must adduce sufficient evidence to prove or rebut a case. A party will only adduce evidence which is favourable to its case and ignore evidence which is not.	**Judicial control** The judge conducts an active judicial inquiry and determines the evidence to be admitted and the probative value to be attached to the admitted evidence. The judge has access to favourable and unfavourable evidence.
Legal representation Party control means that a party will usually employ a professional practitioner to conduct its case.	**Legal representation** Lawyers play a limited and largely subordinate role to that of the judge at trial. May suggest avenues of inquiry to the judge and follow judicial questioning with their own questioning in the interests of the client.
Judicial passivity In this process a judge plays a neutral but objective role. A judge decides procedural disputes and makes the final decision on the admissibility of evidence.	**Active judicial management and decision making** The judge controls the process whereby parties present their respective cases and actively questions witnesses; he or she may call witnesses and require witnesses to address specific points.

Adversarial	Inquisitorial
A right of party confrontation The opposing parties confront each other through a process of oral presentation of evidence and actively compete with each other to persuade a judge and jury of their unique case version.	**Judicial confrontation** In practice, the confrontation is between the judge and a party, or witness, in which the judge chooses, directs and controls the questioning.
Principle of orality Presentation of all evidence by way of party and witness participation. The orality principle is constitutionally guaranteed in s 35(3)(*i*) of the Constitution, 1996.	**Written record of evidence** The judge will usually rely on a written dossier. This dossier of evidence will have been collected over a series of pre-trial judicial hearings. Most inquisitorial judges rely on written witness depositions at trail.
Cross-examination Witness oral testimony is presented at trial by examination-in-chief and cross-examination. Leading questions are discouraged and a witness may be declared a hostile witness.	**No cross-examination** The witness is allowed to answer questions in a discursive narrative form. There are no formal rules as to how questions are put to the witness.
Burden of proof As a consequence of party control, there are rules for determining the onus of proof, the duty to begin and the evidentiary burden. These burdens must be determined at the beginning of a trial.	**No formal burden of proof** The judge assumes the burden for admitting evidence, questioning witnesses and the final decision making.
Standard of proof On a balance of probabilities (civil) and beyond a reasonable doubt (criminal).	**No formal standard of proof** Judicial decision making is based on the principle of *intime conviction*, or the inner reasonable and moral certainty of a judge.
Precedent A judge is bound by the decisions of higher courts on the same issues of law and fact.	**No precedent** Judges are free to make decisions independently on a case-by-case basis.

3.4 The South African adversarial system

The South African procedural system is primarily adversarial. However, it is not a pure adversarial one and there are a number of specific proceedings which incorporate inquisitorial rules. For example, the small claims court is an inquisitorial court which applies a free system of evidence, does not permit cross-examination and bars the use of legal representation. A free system of evidence applies to **bail** applications and formal rules of evidence are flexibly applied at a sentencing hearing after an accused is found guilty. Rules of evidence are flexibly applied in arbitration proceedings and through statutory tribunals such as the National Consumer Tribunal, etc.

3.5 The basic jurisprudential principles of an adversarial trial

The basic jurisprudential principles of an adversarial trial are as follows:
- An adversarial system is designed to provide for procedural and evidential rules to allow for reasonable access to justice and an administratively fair trial for the purpose of arriving at the legal truth.

- In order to settle a legal dispute between litigating or adversarial parties, the procedural presentation of facts at trial and the judgment of an adjudicator (usually a magistrate or a judge) must necessarily progress in an orderly and formulistic manner.
- A legal dispute must be fully ventilated or explored before a passive adjudicator who provides each party with an equal opportunity to present their respective cases.
- The **adversarial procedure** must allow for a reasonably efficient and effective implementation of substantive norms. These procedures must also be reasonably easy to understand and reasonably speedy in application in order to avoid excessive costs and time wastage. However, a reasonably speedy process should not be at the expense of truth-finding and may require reasonable postponements of the truth-finding process.

3.6 The basic rules of the South African adversarial trial system

The basic rules of the adversarial trial system in South Africa are as follows:
- The adversarial parties bear the **onus** of proving their respective cases through **oral argument (principle of orality)** and by way of a **forensic debate (based on a right of confrontation)** before a **neutral and objective adjudicator**.
- The adversarial structure also requires a formula for the determination of which party bears the **duty to begin** by presenting a *prima facie* case and which party must respond in rebuttal, hence the principle of *dominus litis* which fixes the **primary burden of proof** on the state in a criminal trial and usually, but not exclusively, on the plaintiff in a civil trial. In such a circumstance the accused in a criminal trial and the defendant in a civil trial would only be required to bear a burden of **evidentiary rebuttal**.
- The adversarial model makes a practical distinction between a **pre-trial stage** in which evidentiary facts are discovered and exchanged between parties in preparation for trial and a **trial stage** during which the discovered evidence is subject to forensic examination of its probative value.
- The South African criminal adversarial model has evolved in conjunction with the adjudicative principle of **trial with assessors**. The adversarial model makes a fundamental distinction between:
  - the **function of a witness** (to testify about identified facts in issue) and that of **an assessor** (to assess facts in issue on the basis of a witness's testimony); and
  - specific adjudicatory functions in which **an assessor** decides on matters of **fact** and a **judge** on matters of **law**.
- A fundamental distinction in an adversarial trial is that a **criminal judgment** of guilt or no-guilt is decided on an evidentiary standard of proof beyond a reasonable doubt and a **civil decision** on a finding for or against a plaintiff on the evidentiary standard of proof on a balance of probabilities.
- Recourse may be made to the **services of a legal practitioner** to assist the parties in this formal debate (hence the need for legal professional privilege) but this does not prevent a party from representing itself.
- An integral part of an adversarial model is the **doctrine of precedent** (i.e. *stare decisis*) based on a structural hierarchy of lower courts which are bound by the decisions made by the superior courts on matters of fact and law. Precedent influences the evidentiary rules of admissibility, relevance and the evaluation of evidence.

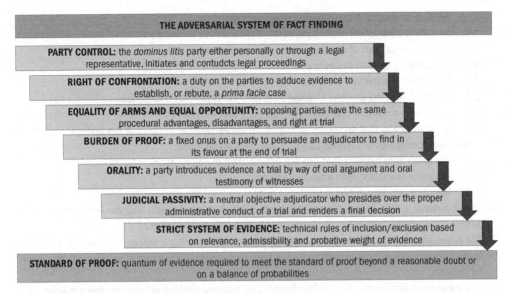

Figure 3.1 The adversarial system of fact-finding

3.7 The role of evidence in the South African adversarial system

The law of evidence may be defined by examining its place, scope and functions within the South African legal system.

3.7.1 The place of the law of evidence

The law of evidence (sometimes also referred to as **adjectival law**) is associated with criminal and **civil procedure** and forms part of the field of procedural law. South African procedural law, which regulates the procedures of the civil and criminal trial system, is partially governed by English common law as it was frozen on 30 May 1961 and partially by indigenous developments of that law, in particular legislation, including the Constitution. On the other hand, South African substantive law, which regulates the rights, duties and obligations of a litigating party or accused person, is governed by Roman-Dutch common law.

3.7.2 The scope of the law of evidence

The law of evidence (as a component of procedural law) gives practical effect to the rules of substantive law. The rules of evidence assist (together with civil or **criminal procedure**) in transforming substantive norms (rights, duties and obligations) into a quantifiable decision or judgment and subsequent enforceable court order. The South African system of evidence at trial is **fact driven** and the selected quantity of evidence admissible at trial is determined by nature of the substantive facts in issue. In other words, the law of evidence provides the evidentiary facts which serve to prove the substantive facts in issue which make up a civil dispute or a criminal offence.

THIS CHAPTER IN ESSENCE

1 Every culture, society and legal system has a method, or methods, of resolving disputes between parties with a core set of basic principles:
    1.1 The need to actually resolve disputes

16 THE LAW OF EVIDENCE IN SOUTH AFRICA

    1.2   A forum in which the resolution of disputes takes place
    1.3   An orderly manner (or procedure) that is followed
    1.4   A person or system of adjudication or decision making.

2   At a more complex level all systems also seek:
    2.1   to uncover or ascertain the truth
    2.2   to ensure that the process of doing so is fair, and is perceived to be fair
    2.3   to do so in a manner that balances efficiency with expediency
    2.4   to do so in way that preserves and does not undermine the integrity of the system.

3   Three broad categories of systems can be found throughout Africa:
    3.1   The customary systems that preceded the advent of colonisation
    3.2   The colonially introduced adversarial system
    3.3   The colonially introduced inquisitorial system.

4   The adversarial system is found in countries with a British colonial history and the inquisitorial system is found in countries with a French, Spanish or Portuguese colonial history.

5   The adversarial system pits the parties against each other in the hope that competition will reveal the truth, while the inquisitorial system seeks the truth by questioning those most familiar with the events in dispute.

6   The adversarial system places the fact-finding and decision-making process on the shoulders of a layperson jury so an adversarial magistrate or judge is a passive objective official primarily tasked with overseeing the conduct of a trial process in an administratively efficient and fair manner.

7   In South Africa trial by jury was abolished in civil trials in 1927 and criminal trials in 1969, which means that judges oversee the conduct of the trial process and also are responsible for the fact-finding and decision-making process.

8   The inquisitorial process places the fact-finding and decision making process on the shoulders of a professionally experienced judge.

9   The strict rules of evidence and procedure of an adversarial system limit the discretionary powers of a judge at trial, whereas a free system of evidence allows an inquisitorial judge wide-ranging discretionary powers at trial.

10   The adversarial system of evidence consists of a number of strict technical rules of evidentiary inclusion or exclusion:
    10.1   The first question is the admissibility of evidence at the beginning of a trial.
    10.2   The second question is to assess the weight and cogency of such evidence.

11   The inquisitorial system is free of any evidentiary barriers and all evidence is potentially admissible. There are no exclusionary categories such as hearsay, *res gestae*, similar fact evidence or prior consistent statements, but rules of privilege, judicial notice and witness competency do apply.

12   In criminal matters an adversarial process emphasises the accused's procedural rights, individual autonomy and privacy. These do not provide the inquisitorial accused with the same level of protection.

13   The adversarial lawyer's first ethical duty is to the client and not to the truth, while an inquisitorial process places the truth-seeking function before the accused's procedural autonomy.

14   In the adversarial system it is the duty of the prosecution to adduce sufficient evidence to establish a *prima facie* case, whereas in the inquisitorial system the *prima facie* case against the accused has already been established in the dossier before trial.

15   The adversarial parties are in control of a trial, whereas in an inquisitorial system the judge conducts the judicial inquiry.

16   In the adversarial system, a party will usually employ a professional lawyer whereas in an inquisitorial system, lawyers play a limited and largely subordinate role.

17   In the adversarial process a judge plays a neutral but objective role, whereas in an inquisitorial system the judge controls the process and actively questions witnesses.

CHAPTER 3   SYSTEMS OF LEGAL FACT-FINDING   17

18 In the adversarial system the opposing parties confront each other, whereas in an inquisitorial system the confrontation is between the judge and a party, or witness.
19 In the adversarial system presentation of all evidence is by way of party and witness participation, whereas in an inquisitorial system the judge relies on a written dossier collected over a series of pre-trial judicial hearings.
20 In the adversarial system oral testimony is presented at trial by examination-in-chief and cross-examination, whereas in an inquisitorial system there is no cross-examination and the witness is allowed to answer questions in a discursive narrative form.
21 In the adversarial system there are rules for determining the onus of proof, the duty to begin and the evidentiary burden, whereas in an inquisitorial system the judge assumes the burden for admitting evidence, questioning witnesses and the final decision making.
22 In the adversarial system the standard of proof is on a balance of probabilities (civil) and beyond a reasonable doubt (criminal), whereas in an inquisitorial system the decision is based on the principle of *intime conviction*, or the inner reasonable and moral certainty of the judge.
23 In the adversarial system a judge is bound by the decisions of higher courts, whereas in an inquisitorial system judges are free to make decisions independently on a case-by-case basis.
24 The South African procedural system is primarily, but not purely, adversarial and a number of specific proceedings incorporate inquisitorial rules, for example, the small claims court, bail applications, sentencing hearings and in arbitration proceedings and statutory tribunals.
25 An adversarial system is designed to provide for procedural and evidential rules to allow for reasonable access to justice and an administratively fair trial for the purpose of arriving at the legal truth.
26 The adversarial system fixes the primary burden of proof on the state in a criminal trial and usually, but not exclusively, on the plaintiff in a civil trial.
27 The adversarial system distinguishes between a pre-trial stage in which evidentiary facts are discovered and exchanged between parties and a trial stage during which evidence is subject to forensic examination.
28 The adversarial system makes a fundamental distinction between:
   28.1 the function of a witness (to testify about facts) and that of an assessor (to assess facts based on a witness's testimony).
   28.2 the adjudicatory function in which an assessor decides on matters of fact and a judge on matters of law.

Chapter 4

Truth verification, fact finding and rules of evidence in African oral traditional law

4.1	**Introduction**	**18**
4.2	**Verification of existence, and ascertainment of content, of customary law**	**20**
4.3	**Proof of existence, content and applicability of customary law by the litigant**	**21**
	4.3.1 No evidence required	21
	4.3.2 Evidence of existence	22
	4.3.3 Evidence of content	23
	4.3.4 Proof of affiliation to, or membership of, a traditional community	23
4.4	**The notion of a 'living version of customary law' and its relevance in evidence**	**25**
	4.4.1 Presiding officer's own knowledge: is it proof of 'living' customary law?	27
	4.4.2 Court assessors' opinions	31
4.5	**Rules of evidence in the courts of traditional leaders**	**31**
4.6	**Truth verification**	**33**
	4.6.1 Narrative methods of evidence presentation	33
	4.6.2 Rituals and customs as evidence of a juristic act	36
	4.6.3 Presumptions concerning hearsay	38
	4.6.4 Presumptions in sex and marriage matters	40

4.1 Introduction

Customary law is a sophisticated, values-centred system which prioritises the rights, interests and obligations of a defined group as opposed to individuals within the group.[1] This explains the framework and environment of many customary rules of law which are designed and developed as legal rules by the same group through usage and participation or dialogue. Similarly, in the law of evidence, fact finding or truth is determined by a group and in accordance with the shared values, philosophies and doctrines accepted by that group.[2]

---

1   We use the word 'group' to refer to either a family, clan or traditional community as recognised in terms of the provisions of the Constitution.

2   The basic African values are community participation, reconciliation, community or communal responsibility, and respect (which incorporates *Ubuntu*). For a discussion regarding these values, see CN Himonga (ed), RT Nhlapo (ed), IP Maithufi, S Mnisi-Weeks, LL Mofokeng and DD Ndima *African Customary Law in South Africa: Post-Apartheid and Living Law Perspectives* (2014) at 261.

CHAPTER 4   TRUTH VERIFICATION, FACT FINDING AND RULES OF EVIDENCE   **19**

For example, many disputes are resolved at a family level under the leadership of the family heads of the parties involved in the dispute. If a dispute cannot be resolved at a family level, African customary law makes provision for the involvement of the extended members of the group, namely clans (headmen councils), then chiefs' courts and then civil courts.[3] Litigation is often only seen as a last resort.

In its purest form, African customary law derives from the cultural usages and customs of a traditional African community.[4] Most of the rules are transmitted orally and are recorded in the languages of the African people. For a custom or usage to have the force of law it must be considered to be obligatory by the community concerned. Mere custom, as opposed to customary law, is not considered to be obligatory, although it may include some 'traditions, practices, moral or ethical codes and the rules ... adhered to by members of a [specific traditional] community'.[5]

Before the colonial era, the only system of law applied in South Africa was customary law. Through the eyes of the colonialists, African customary law was barbaric and uncivilised, to such an extent that it was rejected by colonial governments. Where it was accepted, it was considered as an exception to the then prioritised colonial law. Although courts had a discretion to apply customary law, legislation required, and still requires, that its existence and content be proved by the litigant seeking to rely on a customary rule. Thus the universal presumption that the court knows the law does not apply in respect of customary law in South Africa.

During the colonial era and up to the enactment of the Statute of Westminster in 1931 all law, including customary law, was subject to the British parliament determination. Under the Colonial Laws Validity Act[6] any principle of South African law, including customary law, could be invalidated by the British parliament. The consequence for customary law was that it was mostly considered to be contrary to public (colonial) policy.[7] This resulted in the non-development of almost all disciplines of customary law, including the law of evidence and procedure.

The fact that these customary procedural laws were ignored or were deliberately undermined does not mean that they did not exist, that they do not still exist and that they may not be in some way relevant to evidentiary issues that might arise. However, due to the fact that they were so efficiently sidelined, the first step in understanding their application is to establish their existence. This necessitates a brief discussion on how this is done. This chapter, therefore, will attempt to answer the following questions:

- First, how must the existence and content of customary law be proved in court? This will include a discussion on the law concerning the proof and ascertainment of customary law. This is necessary because legislation requires the litigant who relies on a customary law rule to prove its existence and content. Further, even if the rule of custom can be

---

3   See generally CN Himonga et al (ed) *African Customary Law in South Africa: Post-Apartheid and Living Law Perspectives* (2014) at 255–261.

4   Traditionally, chiefs, as individuals, could issue executive orders, but they could not make customary law because customary law was made by the group through consensus and the chief was only part of that group. This unique method of making customary law was endorsed and approved by the Constitutional Court in *Shilubana and Others v Nwamitwa* 2009 (2) SA 66 (CC).

5   I Moodley *The Customary Law of Intestate Succession* (2012) PhD Thesis, University of South Africa at 7.

6   Colonial Laws Validity Act, 1865 (Britain) (repealed).

7   According to Dugard, this law provided that 'there could be no competition between Westminster and a colonial legislature: any colonial law repugnant to an Act of British Parliament extending to that colony was null and void' J Dugard *Human Rights and the South African Legal Order* (1978) at 28.

proved to exist, legislation requires litigants to prove the applicability of such rule to the parties in the matter before the court.

- Second, which types of evidence are unique to customary law? The focus here will be on the nature and types of evidence recognised in terms of original[8] customary law and an attempt will be made restore the legitimacy of African customary law types of evidence, ignored by the courts for so long.
- Third, what are the distinctive rules of evidence in customary law? The answer will attempt to outline the various rules of evidence presentation and methods of fact or truth verification used by traditional African courts.

The Constitution fully recognises customary law[9] but, subject to the Bill of Rights, there is now a duty, firmly placed on our courts, to develop customary law, which includes the customary law of evidence. Considering this obligation and the powers of the courts, it likely that the courts will reinstate some of these rules of evidence in respect of customary law matters.

4.2 Verification of existence, and ascertainment of content, of customary law

Traditional law did not require a party to a dispute to prove the existence of a customary law rule even when the parties came from diverse backgrounds. The existence of the rules was common knowledge and a lived reality although the actual content of a rule would sometimes be interpreted by elders where required. Arguably because most South African judges have received a Western education and because legislation in South Africa has a colonial influence, the law still requires litigants to prove the existence of their own customary rules in disputes originating from such law. Section 1(1) of the Law of Evidence Amendment Act 45 of 1988[10] provides that:

> Any court may take judicial notice of the law of a foreign state and of indigenous law in so far as such law can be ascertained readily and with sufficient certainty: Provided that indigenous law shall not be opposed to the principles of public policy or natural justice: Provided further that it shall not be lawful for any court to declare that the custom of lobola or bogadi or other similar custom is repugnant to such principles.

The phrase 'readily ascertainable and with sufficient certainty' implies that the courts have a discretion to refuse to apply a customary law or rule if it cannot be proved to exist. Furthermore, even if it can be proved to exist, if it is not 'readily ascertainable' – or, even if ascertainable, it is not sufficiently certain – the court does not have to take judicial notice of

---

8 The word 'original' here is used to distinguish African customary law in its traditional, unwritten – i.e. oral – format prior to its codification or attempted codification. Codification, which was attempted in many regions and in many guises, was often incomplete, often reflected the interpretation of the codifier and often only reflected a 'snapshot' of any particular African customary law system at the time of codification – thereby undermining the flexible, constantly evolving nature of customary law.

9 See section 211 of the Constitution of South Africa, 1996.

10 Law of Evidence Amendment Act 45 of 1988. Note that the current version of this Act applies as from 1 April 1997, i.e. the date of commencement of the Justice Laws Rationalisation Act 18 of 1996 – to date. See Justice Laws Rationalisation Act 18 of 1996 – Government Notice 632 in *Government Gazette* 17129, dated 19 April 1996. Commencement date: 1 April 1997 [Proc. R23, Gazette No. 17849, dated 12 March 1997].

CHAPTER 4   TRUTH VERIFICATION, FACT FINDING AND RULES OF EVIDENCE   **21**

it.[11] However, if a rule is proved to exist, or if the parties to a dispute are in agreement concerning the existence of customary law applicable to their dispute, and if it is readily ascertainable and sufficiently certain, the court may still refuse to apply it if it is 'opposed to the principles of public policy or natural justice'. Currently, it is not clear what impact the provisions of the Constitution that require the courts to apply customary law 'when that law is applicable' will have on the provisions of section 1(1) of the Law of Evidence Amendment Act, 1988.

It is significant that the existence of a customary rule may not necessarily be in issue, but a party may argue that he or she is not a member of the community to which that law applies. This may require evidence to be presented that such person is or is not a member of that community. It is therefore important to understand how the existence, content and applicability of customary law is determined under the current law.

4.3   Proof of existence, content and applicability of customary law by the litigant

4.3.1   No evidence required

There are three methods of ascertaining the existence and content of a rule in customary law. The first method does not require the parties to present evidence to prove such existence or content. This is where the court will be satisfied that customary law has been 'ascertained readily and with sufficient certainty'.[12] The second and third methods require the party who relies on the rule to prove its existence and content by presenting necessary evidence.

With the first method, the court relies on primary and secondary sources to establish a customary law rule. This law is clearly codified or recorded in relevant precedents. Further, no evidence will be required where the parties do not dispute such existence or are in agreement concerning the existence and content of a customary law rule.

Further, it seems that the courts will not require evidence to be presented they are satisfied, based on argument, about the existence and content of the applicable rule. In *Ngcobo v Ngcobo*[13] the court said:

> If we were to insist on every usage and practice being proved by evidence, as we prove trade and other customs in our Courts, it may render the application of native usage and practice unworkable, for then native cases might become too expensive and too protracted.

Further, where a special court has been established by legislation to hear matters arising out of customary law (e.g. the court of traditional leaders), then the litigants may not be expected to prove the rule is customary law. This view was expressed in *Mosii v Motseoakhumo*[14] as follows:

> It is true that there are certain courts in which native custom need not be proved, but in the ordinary courts of law native custom must be proved in the same manner as any other custom.

---

11   Ironically, judicial notice exists to allow a court to accept a fact without the need to lead evidence, yet this statute specifically requires that a customary rule must first be established (by means of evidence) in order to be judicially noted by the court.

12   Section 1(1)–(2) of the Law of Evidence Amendment Act, 1988.

13   1929 AD 233 at 236 (per Wessels JA).

14   1954 (3) SA 919 (A) at 930C.

22 | THE LAW OF EVIDENCE IN SOUTH AFRICA

Similar views were expressed in *Ex parte Minister of Native Affairs: In re Yako v Beyi*[15] where Schreiner JA said:

> But one of the advantages of setting up native commissioners' courts is that cases involving native customs may be tried by experts who do not require the existence of a custom to be proved in each case; where the judicial officer has not the requisite knowledge, evidence of the custom must be given (see *Msonti v Dingindawo*, 1927 AD 531).

4.3.2 Evidence of existence

The second method requires evidence of the existence of the rule as well as its content. Normally, expert evidence must be adduced to prove the existence and content of the rule.[16] The word 'expert' should not be given a literal meaning because traditional leaders, community and family elders (matriarchs and patriarchs) were considered to be knowledgeable and proficient in customary law and are therefore regarded as experts. This was confirmed in *Sigcau v Sigcau*,[17] where the court said the following:

> ... But apart from making what use is possible of these scanty records [textbooks and reports of Native Appeal Courts], the only way in which the Court can determine a disputed point, which has to be decided according to native custom, is to hear evidence as to that custom from those best qualified to give it and to decide the dispute in accordance with such evidence as appears in the circumstances to be the most probably correct.

It is troubling that the Court in *Ex parte Minister of Native Affairs: In re Yako v Beyi*[18] held that the existence of customary law should be proved in the same way as the existence of 'trade custom' under civil law. The court said the following:

> Native customs would then be provable and would have effect according to the principles generally applicable to customs (see *van Breda and Others v Jacobs and Others*, 1921 AD 330).

It is submitted that the court erred by equating customary law with trade custom in the *Yako* matter. The essential requirements laid down in the case of *van Breda and Others v Jacobs and Others*,[19] which dealt with trade custom were as follows: 'first it must be immemorial, secondly it must be reasonable, thirdly it must have continued without exception since its immemorial origin, and fourthly it must be certain'.[20] Therefore, the *van Breda* decision dealt with a trade custom and not a rule of customary law.[21] It is therefore surprising that in *Yako* the court equated proof of existence of customary law to proof of the existence of a trade custom.

---

15 1948 (1) SA 388 (A) at 394–395 (per Schreiner JA).
16 *Ex Parte Minister of Native Affairs: In re Yako v Beyi* 1948 (1) SA 388 (A) at 396.
17 1944 AD 67 at 76.
18 1948 (1) SA 388 (A) at 394 (per Schreiner J.A).
19 1921 AD 330.
20 At 334.
21 Note that the decision was also criticised by Van der Westhuizen J in *Shilubana and Others v Nwamitwa and Others* 2009 (2) SA 66 (CC) as follows: '*Van Breda* dealt with proving custom as a source of law. It envisaged custom as an immemorial practice that could be regarded as filling in normative gaps in the common law. In that sense, custom no longer serves as an original source of law capable of independent development, but survives merely as a useful accessory. Its continued validity is rooted in and depends on its unbroken antiquity. By contrast, customary law is an independent and original source of law. Like the common law it is adaptive by its very nature. By definition, then, while change annihilates custom as a source of law, change is intrinsic to and can be invigorating of customary law'. At para 54.

4.3.3 Evidence of content

The third method also requires evidence, but this will be evidence concerning the content and not the existence of the rule. This is because customary law is a system of law that moves with the times as the mores of the community change and customs are modernised. For instance, the *lobola* property delivered for the marriage of a woman used to be in the form of livestock only, but in modern times the same property consists of money or a combination of livestock and money.

With this method, the court will rely on tertiary sources such as colonial Commissions Reports,[22] textbooks and old case law[23] to establish the existence of a customary rule, but will require evidence from a party relying on the custom to prove its content. The evidence must be required because customary law as recorded in tertiary sources may not necessarily be the same in present times as it was when was recorded in those sources.[24] The courts have used the term 'living version of customary law'[25] to refer to the modern content of customary law or customs that have been amended by usage. Therefore, any reliance on tertiary sources must be done with caution.

4.3.4 Proof of affiliation to, or membership of, a traditional community

Although by definition the term 'customary law' incorporates all customary laws in South Africa, there are differences and regional variations in respect of the customs of various traditional communities. Litigants may belong to different tribal groups and clan lineages, or may even live in different territorial jurisdictions. In addition to the existence and content of customary law, a litigant may be required to prove the cultural affiliation of the defending or opposing party – that is, the customary law which the court must apply in a particular case.

Traditionally, the court had to apply the law of the plaintiff (*moqusi* in Sotho or *ummangaleli* in Zulu). Legislation has, however, superseded traditional law in that section 1(3) of the Law of Evidence Amendment Act[26] provides that:

> In any suit or proceedings between Blacks who do not belong to the same tribe, the court shall not in the absence of any agreement between them with regard to the particular system of indigenous law to be applied in such suit or proceedings, apply any system of indigenous law other than that which is in operation at the place where the defendant or respondent resides or carries on business or is employed, or if two or more different systems are in operation at that place (not being within a tribal area), the court shall not apply any such system unless it is the law of the tribe (if any) to which the defendant or respondent belongs.

---

22 See the discussion on Commission Reports as a source of customary law in LL Mofokeng *Legal Pluralism in South Africa: Aspects of African customary, Muslim and Hindu Family Law* (2009) at 14. See also AJ Kerr Customary Family Law. *Family Law Service*, Issue 44, October at para G6.

23 *Bhe & Others v Magistrate, Khayelitsha & Others (Commission for Gender Equality as amicus curiae); Shibi v Sithole & Others; South African Human Rights Commission & Another v President of the Republic of South Africa & Another* 2005 (1) SA 580 (CC) at para 12.

24 See minority judgment of Ngcobo J in *Bhe & Others v Magistrate, Khayelitsha & Others (Commission for Gender Equality as amicus curiae); Shibi v Sithole & Others; South African Human Rights Commission & Another v President of the Republic of South Africa & Another* 2005 (1) SA 580 (CC) at para 152. For instance, the custom of lobola involved the transfer of animals and goods to the family of the prospective wife – in modern times, cattle and goods have been replaced with money and goods in urban areas.

25 See discussion of the decisions in *Mabena v Letsoalo* 1998 (2) SA 1068 (T) and *Hlophe v Mahlalela* 1998 (1) SA 449 (T).

26 45 of 1988.

This section has created evidentiary problems in respect of the application of customary law. In their private dealings and transactions, communities do not choose the law as provided for in this section. However, if their dispute ends in court, they are unfortunately bound by the provisions of the section. The only unlikely but ideal situation would be where the parties agree on the law to be applied to their dispute. In the absence of an agreement between the litigants, this section requires the following evidence to be presented to determine which law is applicable: proof of domicile or residence of the defendant or respondent, or proof of a place where he or she carries on business or is employed.

The customary law that exists in that area will then be applied by the court. This means that there is no need for the plaintiff to prove the cultural affiliation of the respondent or defendant and that the court will impose the law on the parties irrespective of their cultural membership or affiliation.

Where there is more than one system of customary laws in operation where the defendant resides, carries on business or is employed, the plaintiff must prove the cultural orientation of the defendant. It significant that original customary law did not require the plaintiff to prove the cultural orientation of the defendant because the plaintiff would base his or her action on his or her own customary law rules and traditional law required remedies to be in accordance with that law.

In addition to the above requirements, the Law of Evidence Amendment Act, 1988 requires the plaintiff to prove that the defendant is actually 'Black'. This requirement is highly controversial considering the Bill of Rights, but also because nothing in original customary law required the plaintiff to prove the race of the defendant. In fact, and stated above, the plaintiff was entitled to remedies in accordance with his own customary law, as an injured party. Customary law did not categorise people according to race, but only by ancestral lineages, affiliations and origins and this was purely for the purpose of personal identification and religious compliance. Currie and De Wet properly point out that:

> ... to prove membership of a cultural religious or linguistic community some concrete tie of affinity must be proved to exist between the individual and his community ... . A person belongs to one of section 31's communities because that person has historical associations with the community and has chosen to maintain those associations.[27]

A person's affiliation to a traditional group can happen only in two ways, none of which has an element of race as a requirement. First, affiliation to the community or group is by birth. As pointed out by Nwauche:

> ... cultural identities of parents are passed on to their children just as citizenship is also determined by birth.[28] Birth and blood descent determine ethnic affiliations, essentially foreclosing for many people the possibility of changing their ethnic affiliations.[29]

Further, affiliation of a person to a community or group may be by acceptance of that person into the group. A traditional community, clan or family may 'accept' a person as a member in accordance with custom. With smaller groups like clans and families, a ritual may be

---

27   I Currie and J De Waal *The Bill of Rights Handbook* 6 ed (2013) at 630. Quoted in ES Nwauche 'Affiliation To A New Customary Law In Post-Apartheid South Africa' *PER/PELJ* (2015) 18(3) 569 at 578.

28   Referring to section 2 of the South African Citizenship Act 88 of 1995.

29   ES Nwauche 'Affiliation To A New Customary Law In Post-Apartheid South Africa' *PER/PELJ* 2015 (18)3 569 at 579.

CHAPTER 4 TRUTH VERIFICATION, FACT FINDING AND RULES OF EVIDENCE

required to formalise or seal the acceptance of a person as a member of the group.[30] Obviously, after acceptance, the person will be required by the community to comply with the customs and culture of the group concerned. It has never been part of customary law to impose law on a person just because he or she is black. Under the current Constitution, this would violate the right to freedom of choice.

There is some advantage in the law that requires the litigants to prove the existence of customary law. If proved, the courts are likely to apply the living version of customary law. The contrary view is that litigation becomes expensive for the litigants.

4.4 The notion of a 'living version of customary law' and its relevance in evidence

In *Bhe*, the court described 'living customary law' as 'rules that are adapted to fit in with changed circumstances'.[31] In *Shilubana*, the court described the concept of living law by indicating that '[c]ustomary law must be permitted to develop, the enquiry must be rooted in the contemporary practice of the community in question'.[32] Apart from definitional difficulties concerning the living law notion, there is the problem of how to prove it. As was further noted by the court in *Bhe*, 'abuses of indigenous law are at times construed as a true reflection of indigenous law, and these abuses tend to distort the law and undermine its value. The difficulty is one of identifying the living indigenous law and separating it from its distorted version'.[33] This section discussed the methods which have been used to identify living customary law.

It was stated in *Sigcau v Sigcau*[34] that, to establish the existence of a customary law rule, it is best for the court to hear expert evidence. Ordinarily, experts are required to file their affidavits[35] or reports in court, or present oral evidence. Since the advent of democracy, the courts seem to prefer expert evidence concerning the actual content of living customary law[36] but may also accept combined evidence of experts and ordinary members of the community.[37]

The term 'living version of customary law' has been crafted by the courts in situations where they see the opportunity to develop customary law. According to Himonga and Bosch,[38] this new approach to the application of customary law was meant to avoid a too-positivist approach to the application of customary law in a constitutional framework.

---

30 See further discussion in 4.6.2 dealing with rituals and customs.

31 *Bhe & Others v Magistrate, Khayelitsha & Others (Commission for Gender Equality as amicus curiae); Shibi v Sithole & Others; South African Human Rights Commission & Another v President of the Republic of South Africa & Another* 2005 (1) SA 580 (CC) at para 87.

32 *Shilubana and Others v Nwamitwa* 2009 (2) SA 66 (CC) at para 55.

33 *Bhe* at para 154.

34 1944 AD 67.

35 See for instance the affidavit of a community elder, Hlanganani Mayimele in the case of *MM v MN and Another* 2013 (4) SA 415 (CC).

36 See generally *Mabena v Letsoalo* 1998 (2) SA 1068 (T); *Mabuza v Mbatha* 2003 (4) SA 218 (C); *Maluleke (in her capacity as representative of the estate of the late Dumakude Patrick Mtshali) and Others v Minister of Home Affairs and Another* (02/24921) [2008] ZAGPHC 129 (9 April 2008).

37 Spies noted the affidavits by Mbhazima Surprise Bungeni, Mamaila Rikhotso, Mkhatshane Daniel Shiranda and Khazamula Isaac Nkanyani, and an expert affidavit by Dr Mabalana Mhlaba, in the hearing of the Mayelane decision. See A Spies 'Relevance and importance of the amicus curiae participation in *Mayelane v Ngwenyama*' 2015 26(1) *Stell LR* 156.

38 Chuma Himonga and Craig Bosch 'The application of African Customary Law under the constitution of South Africa: Problems solved or just beginning?' 2000 117(2) *South African Law Journal* 306 at 335 and 336.

THE LAW OF EVIDENCE IN SOUTH AFRICA

They refer particularly to the cases of *Hlophe v Mahlalela and Another*[39] and *Mabena v Letsoalo*.[40] These authors make the following observation:

> The court had an opportunity to ascertain living customary law via two witnesses who claimed to be closely associated with the communities: the daughter of a Swazi chief who claimed personal knowledge of, and expertise in, Swazi culture and who was appointed by King Sobuza of Swaziland to assist in the revival of Swazi traditions; and an official of the government of Swaziland, who was not only responsible for information on Swazi law and custom, but was himself the son of a chief, claiming personal knowledge of Swazi law and custom.

Although the term 'living version' appears to be a new term, it has been long known by African people that the rules of custom are ambulatory.[41] Customary law usually amends and develops itself through usage and, where necessary, abrogates itself through disuse as its recollection fades away in the minds of the oldest living persons.[42]

The courts have not clarified how to reconcile the notion of living customary law with codified customary law (legislation), especially where the legislature had misconstrued customary law at the time of codification. It would seem that in such cases the court may either apply the relevant rules of statutory interpretation or exercise its constitutional mandate (to develop customary law) by ordering the legislature to make the necessary amendments.

The example of this can be found in the case of *MM v MN*[43] where the Constitutional Court interpreted the relevant provisions of the Recognition of Customary Marriages Act 120 of 1998. The issue was whether the Act or Tsonga customary law required a husband to obtain his first wife's consent in order to conclude a further marriage with another woman and, if the Act or Tsonga law did not, whether customary law must be developed to include this rule. Although the court found that the Act did contain such rule, it decided to develop Tsonga customary law to include the requirement. This decision was made after the court had heard the evidence of at least nine witnesses – experts and non-experts.[44] In taking into account their evidence, the court found that the living law of the baTsonga community required that the first wife must give consent to and be informed of her husband's subsequent marriages to other women.[45] These witnesses consisted of elders, advisors, traditional leaders and academic experts.[46] Therefore, in this case, the evidence of lived law came from the community itself and, despite the relevant legislation not having such a requirement, the court found it to be necessary to introduce it based on what the community did.

---

39 1998 (1) SA 449 (T).

40 1998 (2) SA 1068 (T).

41 See the opinion of O'Regan J in *MEC for Education, KwaZulu-Natal and Others v Pillay* 2008 (1) SA 474 (CC) at para 152 where she said: 'It is also important to remember that cultural, religious and linguistic communities are not static communities that can be captured in constitutional amber and preserved from change. Our constitutional understanding of culture needs to recognise that these communities, like all human communities, are dynamic. It is tempting as an observer to seek to impose coherence and unity on communities that are not, in the lived experience of those who are members of those communities, entirely unified.'

42 With reference to religious law, the court in *MEC for Education, KwaZulu-Natal and Others v Pillay* 2008 (1) SA 474 (CC) warned that the 'courts, as outsiders, must seek to avoid imposing a false internal coherence and unity on a particular cultural community', at para 153 (per O'Regan J).

43 2013 (4) SA 415 (CC).

44 L Mwambene 'The essence vindicated? Courts and customary marriages in South Africa' 2017 (1) *AHRLJ* 35 at note 44.

45 Ibid. at note 44.

46 Ibid. at note 99.

CHAPTER 4 TRUTH VERIFICATION, FACT FINDING AND RULES OF EVIDENCE 27

Another example can be found in the case of *Shilubana and Others v Nwamitwa*,[47] where the court confirmed that, under the provisions of the Constitution, traditional communities have the freedom to amend their customary law in order for those laws to comply with the Bill of Rights.

Generally, most African people believe that traditional leaders,[48] community matriarchs and patriarchs, and other elders are 'living archives' and custodians of African customary law. They are presumed to possess comprehensive and specialised knowledge of customary law. The matriarchs and patriarchs are also expected to guide their communities concerning matters of custom inclusive of any necessary deviations from usage. For instance, according to section 7 of the [Namibian] Traditional Authorities Act,[49] '[a] chief or head of a traditional community ... shall be the custodian of the customary law of the traditional community which he or she leads'.[50]

In South Africa, according to the provisions of section 18(1)(*a*) of the Traditional Leadership and Governance Framework Act, 2003,[51] the houses of traditional leaders are required to comment on any legislation pertaining to customary law proposed by Parliament.[52] Their comments are not only considered before legislation can be passed, but also their knowledge of customary law is presumed in this section, making them recognised experts in customary law.

It is important to note that apart from being community leaders, traditional leaders also have authority to establish their own courts and to apply customary law in those courts.[53] Further, under the provisions of section 20(1) of the Traditional Leadership and Governance Framework Act, 2003[54] national government or a provincial government may provide a role for traditional councils or traditional leaders through legislative measures in respect of roles such as, *inter alia*, the administration of justice. Therefore, the evidence of traditional leaders will likely be preferred in matters concerning proof of existence and content of customary law.

4.4.1 Presiding officer's own knowledge: is it proof of 'living' customary law?

During the apartheid era, only the so-called Bantu Affairs Commissioners (i.e. presiding officers in the Bantu Commissioners' Courts) were empowered to take judicial notice of customary law without the need to hear evidence proving its existence. This was based on the principle, or rather the assumption, that they were experts and had specialised

---

47 2007 (5) SA 620 (CC). See in particular the discussion in paragraphs 54 and 55.
48 S Mnisi Weeks 'Securing women's property inheritance in the context of plurality: Negotiations of law and authority in Mbuzini customary courts and beyond' 2011 *Acta Juridica* 140 at 147. At footnote 29, Mnisi Weeks says that 'we see this claim [that chiefs define customary law] embodied in the South African Law Reform Commission's Discussion Paper 82 Traditional Courts and the Judicial Function of Traditional Leaders Project 90 (1999) 1-3, where traditional leaders are deemed the custodians of customary law and African culture. See the treatise of traditional authority and its renegotiation by traditional leaders since 1994 by L Ntsebeza, Democracy Compromised: Chiefs and the Politics of Land in South Africa (2006).'
49 25 of 2000.
50 See section 7 of the Traditional Authorities Act 25 of 2000 (Namibia). See also the Namibian decision in *Hikumwah v Nelumbu* 2015 JDR 1202 (Nm).
51 41 of 2003.
52 The section provides that 'Any parliamentary Bill pertaining to customary law or customs of traditional communities must, before it is passed by the house of Parliament where it was introduced, be referred by the Secretary to Parliament to the National House of Traditional Leaders for its comments'.
53 See 4.5 below.
54 41 of 2003.

28 THE LAW OF EVIDENCE IN SOUTH AFRICA

knowledge of customary law.[55] The Commissioners' Courts were abolished by the Special Courts for Blacks Abolition Act[56] and their powers were transferred to the Magistrates' Courts. It is not clear whether the Magistrates' Court has the same powers to apply customary law without hearing evidence of the existence and content of customary law rules.[57]

As stated, the choice of whether or not to call for evidence to prove customary law depends mainly on whether or not customary is ascertainable readily and with sufficient certainty. The phrase 'ascertainable readily and with sufficient certainty' may also suggest that the presiding officer's own knowledge of customary law may suffice as proof of its existence. In the case of *S v Makwanyane and Another*,[58] the court interpreted the word '*Ubuntu*'[59] which appeared in the post-amble to the Interim Constitution of South Africa[60] with reference to traditional beliefs, culture and customs. Without the evidence of any expert witness, and after acknowledging that 'a number of references to *Ubuntu* have already been made in various texts,[61] but largely without explanation of the concept',[62] the court then gave content and meaning to the principle of *Ubuntu* without considering evidence of its content under customary law.[63] Mokgoro J defined and described the concept *Ubuntu* in detail without expert evidence, presumably relying on her own knowledge of and familiarity with the concept of *Ubuntu*.[64]

It significant that the Interim Constitution only used a single word – *Ubuntu* – as opposed to the whole maxim '*umuntu ngumuntu ngabantu*' or '*motho ke motho ka batho*'. The question is on what basis did the court conclude that *Ubuntu/botho* carries the same meaning as the maxim, other than relying on the judges' own knowledge of customary law legal maxims? Although the interpretation of *Ubuntu* as a constitutional value by the court in *Makwanyane* is welcome, it is submitted that it is necessary for the presiding officer to bring this 'knowledge' to the attention of the litigants, so as to allow them to make representations or to adduce evidence in support of, or to contradict, that knowledge. Some earlier decisions have developed the following rules of evidence in respect of both criminal and civil matters where the presiding officer does not call for evidence or proof of customary law.

---

55 See *Ex parte Minister of Native Affairs: In re Yako v Beyi* 1948 (1) SA 388 (A) where the Court said '... cases involving native customs may be tried by experts who do not require the existence of a custom to be proved in each case'. At 394–395.

56 34 of 1986.

57 See the discussion of the appeal jurisdiction of the Magistrates' Court in 4.5 below.

58 1995 (3) SA 391 (CC).

59 This part of the post-amble reads: 'These can now be addressed on the basis that there is a need for understanding but not for vengeance, a need for reparation but not for retaliation, a need for ubuntu but not for victimisation.'

60 Constitution of the Republic of South Africa, Act 200 of 1993.

61 Referring to the following literature: L Mbigi with J Maree 'UBUNTU – The Spirit of African Transformation Management' *Knowledge Resources* (1995) 1–16.

62 See Langa J at para 227.

63 Langa J said: 'An outstanding feature of *ubuntu* in a community sense is the value it puts on life and human dignity. The dominant theme of the culture is that the life of another person is at least as valuable as one's own. Respect for the dignity of every person is integral to this concept. During violent conflicts and times when violent crime is rife, distraught members of society decry the loss of *ubuntu*. Thus, heinous crimes are the antithesis of *ubuntu*. Treatment that is cruel, inhuman or degrading is bereft of *ubuntu*.' (para 225). Madala J added to this, saying: 'The concept "*ubuntu*" appears for the first time in the post-amble, but it is a concept that permeates the Constitution generally, and more particularly chap 3, which embodies the entrenched fundamental human rights. The concept carries in it the ideas of humaneness, social justice and fairness.' (para 237).

64 At para 308 Mokgoro J said: 'Generally, *Ubuntu* translates as "humaneness". In its most fundamental sense it translates as personhood and "morality". Metaphorically, it expresses itself in *umuntu ngumuntu ngabantu*, describing the significance of group solidarity on survival issues so central to the survival of communities. While it envelops the key values of group solidarity, compassion, respect, human dignity, conformity to basic norms and collective unity, in its fundamental sense it denotes humanity and morality. Its spirit emphasises respect for human dignity, marking a shift from confrontation to conciliation.'

CHAPTER 4 TRUTH VERIFICATION, FACT FINDING AND RULES OF EVIDENCE | 29

In criminal matters, according to the decision of the court in *S v Sihlani and Another*[65] the following two rules apply:[66]

- Where a presiding officer is entitled to take judicial notice of customary law principle, he or she should not make an adverse finding against an accused person based on his specialised knowledge, without first placing on record his intention to rely on such knowledge.[67]
- If the presiding officer is not familiar with the relevant principle or does not have specialised knowledge of customary law, he must bring this to the attention of the litigants so that they can call witnesses.[68] In the *Sihlani* case, the court emphasised the consequence of the disclosure by the presiding officer as follows:

> ... thus enabling the accused to deal with the correctness or otherwise of the magistrate's view of the custom in issue. Unless the magistrate makes it clear that his views of a particular custom differ from those contended for by an accused, or that he proposed to take cognisance of a custom which is adverse to the accused's case, there is a grave danger of prejudice to an accused who may be misled by the magistrate's silence into believing that it is not necessary for him to amplify or corroborate his own evidence relating to such custom.[69]

- In *R v Dumezweni*[70] the court considered the options available to the presiding officer when there is no dispute concerning the existence or nature of the customs before court. According to Steyn CJ, if the presiding officer is familiar with customary law there is no need to call witnesses, such presiding officer may rely on his or her specialised knowledge of customary law, but must first record reasons for not calling witnesses.[71] In creating this rule, the court said the following in *R v Dumezweni*:[72]

> Where such a rule or precept does in fact exist, there is no reason why a native commissioner should not take cognisance of it. Where there is a dispute as to the existence or nature of a law or custom, it would either not be well-established or well-known, or one of the parties would in honest or pretended ignorance or misunderstanding be contesting what is in fact well-established and well-known. In the former case the native commissioner would have to hear evidence. In the latter he may, where the law or custom is clear, decide without hearing evidence, relying on his own knowledge, but in such a case it would be necessary, for purposes of the record, and in giving reasons in an appeal from his decision, to note the contentions of the parties and his reasons for not hearing evidence. It would be open to a party aggrieved, to apply on appeal for the matter to be re-opened and evidence as to the law or custom to be heard.[73]

---

65 1966 (3) SA 148 (E).

66 *S v Sihlani & Another* 1966 (3) SA 148 (E) at 149. See also *Mosii v Motseoakhumo* 1954 (3) SA 919 (A) at 930C–D, 'It is true that there are certain courts in which Native custom need not be proved but in the ordinary courts of law Native custom must be proved in the same manner as any other custom'.

67 *S v Sihlani & Another* 1966 (3) SA 148 (E) at 149D.

68 1966 (3) SA 148 (E) at 149.

69 At 149D–F.

70 1961 (2) SA 751 (A).

71 *R v Dumezweni* 1961 (2) SA 751 (A). See also *Msonti v Dingindawo* 1927 AD 256.

72 1961 (2) SA 751 (A).

73 At 757.

THE LAW OF EVIDENCE IN SOUTH AFRICA

In civil matters, the general rule is that a party who alleges the existence of a customary rule must prove its nature and existence. Where the presiding officer relies on his or her knowledge of customary law, the same rule quoted from the case of *Dumezweni* (above)[74] applies. The case of *Dumezweni* cited with approval the procedure which was followed in the case of *Msonti v Dingindawo*.[75] Essentially, where there is a dispute concerning the existence or nature of customary law, 'one of the parties would in honest or pretended ignorance or misunderstanding' object to the existence of a customary law rule, the presiding officer may rely on his or her special knowledge of customary law without hearing evidence provided that that: he or she records and notes the contentions of the parties; and provides reasons for not hearing evidence. On **appeal**, the aggrieved party may apply for the matter to be re-opened and evidence concerning customary law to be heard.

Logically, if the presiding officer is not familiar with customary law, he must bring this to the attention of the litigants and must allow them or order them to present evidence to prove it. It is submitted that the presiding officer's knowledge of customary law should always be scrutinised or challenged by litigants so that a decision of the court is not based on limited knowledge of law. For instance in *Smit v His Majesty King Goodwill Zwelithini Kabhekuzulu*[76] the judge relied on his own previous (single) experience of Zulu customs and rituals without calling for any expert testimony. The **applicants** had brought an **application** *nomine officio* in their capacity as duly appointed and authorised trustees of the Animal Rights Africa Trust against King Goodwill Zwelithini Kabhekuzulu. The purpose of the application was to interdict the slaughtering of a bull or any animal at the annual *ukweshwama* festival (First Fruits Festival). After explaining the purpose of the festival, Van Der Reyden J, in what appears to be his own evidence of the custom and rituals associated with the *ukweshwama* practice, said the following:

> I personally have witnessed the ritual killing of a bull during the Ukweshwama ceremony. The bull was put to death in the usual way by twisting and breaking its neck in the complete absence of the type of mutilation and acts of cruelty the Applicants allege ... These acts have no place in Zulu culture and would not be tolerated for an instant ...[77] I reiterate the strongest terms that no acts of cruelty are part of the ceremony nor is barbaric and inhumane cruelty to animals a feature of Zulu culture although it appears that the Applicants suggest otherwise[78] ... Finally it is not correct that the ceremony had fallen into disuse prior to its "reintroduction" by the King. It has always been adhered to in Zulu culture to a greater or lesser extent but was elevated to its full spectacle once again after the King's new palace or 'town' had been built.[79]

In this case, it seems that the judge only brought his knowledge of a customary law rule to the attention of the litigants during the delivery of judgment and not before evidence was presented. Clearly, it was too late to challenge the knowledge of the judge at that time.

---

74 In *R v Dumezweni* 1961 (2) SA 751 (AD). Steyn CJ relied on the principle created in *Msonti v Dingindawo* 1927 AD 255 and applied the same principle in a criminal matter.
75 1927 AD 256. See in particular page 257.
76 2009 JDR 1361 (KZP).
77 At para 18.
78 At para 19.
79 At para 20.

4.4.2 Court assessors' opinions

Other than a judge's own knowledge of customary law, section 34 of the Magistrates' Courts Act 32 of 1944 allows the court to permit assessors to sit with the Magistrate who hears a matter and act 'in an advisory capacity'. The section reads as follows:

> In any action the court may, upon the application of either party, summon to its assistance one or two persons [of skill and experience in the matter to which the action relates] who may be willing to sit and act as assessors in an advisory capacity.[80]

During the colonial and apartheid eras, assessors were always used in the Commissioners' and Native Appeals Courts. Their duties included assisting the commissioners to ascertain the existence and content of customary laws. Usually, the commissioners accepted the assessors' opinions and applied those opinions in their judgments. The fact that these assessors essentially acted as 'sources' of the content of customary law was important because they usually influenced the recording of customary law in those authorities.

The assessors contemplated in the current legislation do not have the same powers – they merely assist the presiding officers when assessing the factual findings in a matter before the court. During the colonial era, these duties were not limited to the facts or merits of the case because the assessors could also assist the then Commissioners with their knowledge of customary law. The same approach was adopted in Lesotho before its independence in 1966 where the High Court used assessors to ascertain rules of customary law.[81] Usually, these assessors were experts in their respective areas and the 'evidence' concerning the existence of a customary rule was usually preferred by the courts. Although the Native courts were abolished in terms of the provisions of the Special Courts for Blacks Abolition Act,[82] the powers of the Commissioners of those courts were transferred to the Magistrate's Courts. This implies that the magistrates may allow the appointment of assessors and may also rely on the evidence of those assessors concerning the existence of a customary law rule.

4.5 Rules of evidence in the courts of traditional leaders

The courts of traditional leaders are recognised in the Constitution of South Africa[83] and in the provisions of the Black Administration Act.[84] With civil matters, these courts can adjudicate matters arising only out of customary law and not common law disputes.[85] They have a wider jurisdiction in respect of criminal matters.[86]

---

80 Note that section 34 has been substituted by section 1 of the Magistrates' Courts Amendment Act 67 of 1998, a provision which will be put into operation by proclamation.

81 L Berat 'Customary Law in a New South Africa: A Proposal' *Fordham International Law Journal*, Volume 15, Issue 1 (1991) 92 at 112.

82 34 of 1986.

83 Section 166(*e*) which refers to 'any other court established or recognised by an Act of Parliament' and section 16(1) of Schedule 6 of the Constitution is more direct in its recognition of traditional courts when it states that: 'every court, including courts of traditional leaders ... continues to function'.

84 38 of 1927.

85 According to section 12, 'The Minister may- (a) authorize any Black chief or headman recognized or appointed under subsection (7) or (8) of section two to hear and determine civil claims arising out of Black law and custom brought before him by Blacks against Blacks resident within his area of jurisdiction ... Provided that a Black chief, headman or chief's deputy shall not under this section or any other law have power to determine any question of nullity, divorce or separation arising out of a marriage.'

86 Section 20 provides that: 'The Minister may (a) by writing under his hand confer upon any Black chief or headman jurisdiction to try and punish any Black who has committed, in the area under the control of the chief or headman concerned- (i) any offence at common law or under Black law and custom other than an offence referred to in the Third Schedule to this Act; and (ii) any statutory offence other than an offence referred to in the Third Schedule to this Act, specified by the Minister.'

THE LAW OF EVIDENCE IN SOUTH AFRICA

The rules of evidence and procedure in traditional courts are governed by unwritten customary law[87] unless the provisions of the Chiefs and Headmen's Civil Courts Rules apply.[88] This is a set of rules of procedure and evidence peculiar to these courts which do not apply in any other court. Essentially, the traditional African customary rules of procedure and evidence were amended or supplemented by the Chiefs and Headmen's Civil Courts Rules only to the extent covered in those rules. The main problem with these amendments to the traditional African customary rules of evidence and procedure was identified by Mqeke as follows:

> Of the courts created by the Black Administration Act of 1927, the chief's court is the only court which finds itself torn between two worlds. This observation is made in the light of the provisions of the rules governing these courts. The rules as framed in GN R2082 of 1967 represent a confused mixture of Western and traditional norms.[89]

Originally, the rules of evidence and procedure in the traditional courts were not intended to be a mixture of the English, Roman-Dutch and traditional African customary law. The mixture was not only foreign to the courts for which it was intended, but also unexpectedly diluted many of the values-based African customary rules of evidence, resulting in great confusion. In *Motaung v Dube*,[90] Stubbs P expressed the view that:

> It was even suggested that the new court system was "designed to suit the psychology, habits and usages of the Bantu, creating as nearly as possible the atmosphere of the *Lekgotla*, to the arbitrament of which they have from time immemorial been accustomed to submit their disputes ..."[91]

As legal practitioners are not permitted in traditional courts,[92] the presentation of *viva voce* evidence follows the customary method of narration, discussed hereunder. If the decision of the traditional leader's court is appealed against, the traditional court must furnish reasons[93] for its judgment and cause a record of the proceedings of the court[94] to be delivered to the Magistrates' Court, which will hear the appeal.[95] On appeal in the Magistrates' Court,

---

87 Section 20(2) of the Black Administration Act 38 of 1927.
88 GG No 1929, GN. R2082 of 1967. According to the provisions of Rule 1 of the Chiefs and Headmen's Civil Courts Rules, the rules of civil procedure and evidence in these courts shall be in accordance with 'the recognised customs and laws of the tribe'.
89 RB Mqeke 'Chiefs' civil court rules' *De Rebus*, 1983, Volume 1983, Issue 188, Aug 1983, at 399.
90 1930 NAC (N & T) 9.
91 Per Stubbs P in *Motaung v Dube* 1930 NAC (N & T) 9 (quoted by RB Mqeke 'Chiefs' civil court rules' *De Rebus*, 1983, Issue 188, Aug 1983, p. 399-400.
92 See Rule 5. See also section 7(4)(*b*) of the Traditional Courts Bill which provides that 'No party to any proceedings before a traditional court may be represented by a legal practitioner acting in that capacity'.
93 See Rule 11.
94 See Rules 6 and 7.
95 Section 29A of the Magistrates' Court Act 32 of 1944 read with the provisions of section 12(4) of the Black Administration Act, 1927.
'Section 29A Jurisdiction in respect of appeals against decisions of Black chiefs, headmen and chiefs' deputies (1) If a party appeals to a magistrates' court in terms of the provisions of section 12(4) of the Black Administration Act, 1927 (Act 38 of 1927), the said court may confirm, alter or set aside the judgment after hearing such evidence as may be tendered by the parties to the dispute, or as may be deemed desirable by the court.
(2) A confirmation, alteration or setting aside in terms of subsection (1), shall be deemed to be a decision of a magistrates' court for the purposes of the provisions of Chapter XI.'
[S29A inserted by s2 of Act 34 of 1986.]
S22 has been substituted by s29A and s29B has been inserted by s23 of the Magistrates' Courts Amendment Act 120 of 1993, provisions which will be put into operation by proclamation. See PENDLEX.

CHAPTER 4   TRUTH VERIFICATION, FACT FINDING AND RULES OF EVIDENCE | **33**

the matter will be heard ***de novo*** (almost like a retrial) and all evidence must again be presented by the litigants.[96]

It is not clear what the magistrate hearing the appeal is supposed to do with the reasons and record furnished to him or her, but it appears that he or she may take the record as evidential material. On appeal, the rules of evidence followed in the traditional court will not be followed in the Magistrates' Court. The problem presented by the mixture of rules of evidence concerning customary law matters can be highlighted with reference to the following points,

First, the Magistrates' Court can hear any customary law matter as a court of first instance, where the matter is first instituted in the Magistrates' Court.[97] In such a case, the ordinary rules of evidence in terms of civil law must be followed by the litigants, despite the fact that the matter arises out of customary law[98] and there is no rule that prevents the litigant from simultaneously instituting the same action in a traditional court.[99]

Second, a Magistrates' Court can act as a court of appeal against a decision of the court of the traditional leaders and, despite the fact that the matter was dealt with in terms of the customary law rules of evidence in the court *a quo*, on appeal the magistrate is required to hear the matter *de novo*. Although the magistrate is required to consider the reasons furnished by the traditional leader for his decision, the customary law rules of evidence[100] are not applied on appeal. Clearly, the rules of evidence applied in these two fora differ and it is therefore unlikely that all evidence that was admissible in the court of traditional leader will be admissible in the Magistrates' Court.

Third, under the provisions of section 29A of the Magistrates' Court Act, 1944, on appeal the magistrate has the power to confirm, alter or set aside the judgment of the traditional leader, but only after hearing evidence presented by the litigants. Further, a decision of a Magistrates' Court for the purposes of this provision is considered to be the judgement of the magistrate which means that the decision may be further appealed against in a superior court.

4.6   Truth verification

4.6.1   Narrative methods of evidence presentation

Narrative evidence is a form of oral evidence presented *viva voce* by a witness. Both African and Western legal systems recognise *viva voce* presentation of evidence. The difference lies in the manner in which such evidence is extracted from a witness. When a witness is called in a traditional court, he or she is required to tell a story about an incident without being questioned by any other person, including attorneys or presiding officers. This does not

---

96 See sections 12 and 20 of the Black Administration Act 38 of 1927 and section 29A(1)–(2) of the Magistrates' Courts Act 32 of 1944 which provides that: 'If a party appeals to a magistrates' court in terms of the provisions of section 12(4) of the Black Administration Act, 1927 (Act 38 of 1927), the said court may confirm, alter or set aside the judgment *after hearing such evidence as may be tendered by the parties to the dispute*, or as may be deemed desirable by the court. (2) A confirmation, alteration or setting aside in terms of subsection (1), shall be deemed to be a decision of a magistrates' court for the purposes of the provisions of Chapter XI.' (emphasis added). See also section 309A(1) of the Criminal Procedure Act 51 of 1977: 'In hearing any appeal to him under the provisions of section 20 of the Black Administration Act, 1927 (Act 38 of 1927), the magistrate *shall hear and record such available evidence as may be relevant* to any question in issue ...' (emphasis added).

97 In terms of section 211 of the Constitution of South Africa, 1996, all courts, including Magistrates' Courts, are required to apply customary law when that law is applicable, but subject to the Bill of Rights.

98 *Nombona v Mzileni* and Another 1961 NAC 22 (S).

99 *Mdumane v Mtshakule* 1948 NAH (C20) 28.

100 *Nombona v Mzileni* and Another 1961 NAC 22 (S).

34 | THE LAW OF EVIDENCE IN SOUTH AFRICA

mean that the witness will not be questioned at all during the trial. The questioning is simply delayed until the narration is over, whereafter the presiding officer has a duty to elicit all the additional necessary facts through questions.[101]

The disadvantage of narrative testimony is that the opposing party cannot challenge the admissibility of the testimony at the time when it is narrated. In matters arising out of customary law, this does not necessarily present a problem because orality is a foundation and a major component of the African way of life, including traditional African jurisprudence. Similarly to Western systems, traditional African judges are expected to 'gauge the witness's demeanour and thereby draw conclusions as to the credibility of the witness.'[102] However, this seemingly similar process may lead to very different conclusions, for instance in an adversarial system a judge may interpret the avoidance, or lack, of eye contact on the part of a witness as an indication of lack of credibility[103] whereas in African courts it actually shows respect to the elders in the courtroom.

Further, unlike in adversarial systems, conclusions drawn by the court from narrative testimony are not drawn from 'the disjointed parts of some possible narrative'[104] as may often result from the evidence of a witness who has been constantly interrupted and guided on how to tell his or her version of the facts of the case. The involvement of lawyers, more specifically the disruptions caused by their guidance while questioning witnesses, disrupts natural chronological logic, coherence and the sequence of the story as was grasped by the witness in the context of their cultural background.

There are numerous reasons why the South African courts should be sympathetic to the narrative methods of oral evidence presentation in matters involving customary law, especially when a question about the demeanour of a witness arises or a finding on demeanour has to be established. First, African patriarchal and matriarchal systems have generated the value concept of *hlompho* (Sotho) or *inhlonipho* (Zulu) which literally means 'respect'. In the context of public speaking, the essence of this concept requires, in the first instance, the careful use and choice of words, as well as the use of acceptable body language when addressing people who are considered to be elders of the speaker.

Second, during the narration of evidence, most African traditions prohibit direct eye contact between the witness and anybody who may be considered an elder. In this instance, adherence to the traditional narrative method allows witnesses to tell their stories in the form and manner which is most appropriate for the event, and in a manner that does not appear to violate the traditional rule relating to respect.

Third, Africans are expected by tradition to use only euphemistic language when addressing elders. This means that although African languages may have certain words and expressions which provide direct and unambiguous meanings, custom does not allow the use of some of those expressions or words which are considered offensive to elders in public spaces. The words chosen in such circumstances are undoubtedly ambiguous. For instance, the courts have cautioned that certain African words may result in a miscarriage of justice where presiding officers accept these words without proper clarity or explanation from a witness.[105] In this instance, adherence to the traditional narrative methods allow witnesses

---

101 *Nkala v Nkosi* 1975/77 AC 227 (NE); *Kutoone v Stofile* 1971 BAC 142 (C); *Phalandira v Moloi* 1978/80 AC 97 (C); *Mokoena v Mokoena* 1972/74 AC 382 (C); *Hlabathi v Nkosi* 1970 BAC 51 (C).
102 *S v Adendorff* 2004 (2) SACR 185 (SCA).
103 See generally SA Beebe (2009) 'Eye Contact: A Nonverbal Determinant of Speaker Credibility' *The Speech Teacher* Vol 23:1 pages 21–25 (1974) DOI. K James 'The Importance of Eye Contact' *Plaintiff* (Magazine) November 2008.
104 J Christopher Rideout 'Storytelling, Narrative Rationality, and Legal Persuasion' 14 Legal Writing: *J. Legal Writing Inst.* (2008) 53 at page 59 quoting A MacIntyre *After Virtue* (1984) at page 215.
105 *Madubula v Mahlangu* 1972/74 AC 449 (C).

CHAPTER 4 TRUTH VERIFICATION, FACT FINDING AND RULES OF EVIDENCE 35

to tell their stories in the language which is most appropriate for the event and the context of their testimony.

Some examples of such expressions include 'sleeping together'[106] as opposed to sexual intercourse. Further, the words 'my child' do not necessarily mean one's own child.[107] Furthermore, the word 'house' means both a physical structure and a 'family' unit of human beings – that is, a wife and her children and sometimes even the rights and duties of the wife and her children.[108]

DISCUSSION 4.1 **Inquisitorial narrative**

Customary law is essentially inquisitorial in nature and so the inquisitorial system is used to elicit all the necessary evidence from a witness.[109] Based solely only cogency, all such evidence is admissible with the emphasis being placed on the varying weight to be attached to it. Technicalities concerning admission or non-admission of such evidence are irrelevant. Cover, one of the proponents of narrative evidence, wrote:

> No set of legal institutions or prescriptions exists apart from the narratives that locate it and give it meaning. [...] Once understood in the context of the narratives that give it meaning, law becomes not merely a system of rules to be observed, but a world in which we live.[110]

Brooks argues that in most cases the courtroom evidence presentation implicitly recognises narrative methods through 'formulas by which the law attempts to impose form and rule on stories.'[111] Should the South African civil courts (i.e. courts other than courts of traditional leaders) use narrative methods of evidence presentation?

The seTswana maxim *ntho eatlholwa kekgosi* may be used to illustrate the manner in which oral testimony is dealt with. The maxim literally means that 'a wound (due to assault) is judged by the chief.'[112] According to the maxim, the chief who presides over a case must gauge the demeanour of a witness to draw reasonable inferences, but only after having considered the opinions of his council (people invited to

---

106 Ibid.

107 See for instance the definition of 'child' concerning the law of intestate succession under customary law as partly codified in section 4(2) of the Reform of Customary Law of Succession and Regulation of Related Matters Act, 2009. The section reads as follows: 'Any reference in the will of a woman referred to in subsection (1) to her child or children and any reference in section 1 of the Intestate Succession Act to a descendant, in relation to such a woman, must be construed as including any child— (a) born of a union between the husband of such a woman and another woman entered into in accordance with customary law for the purpose of providing children for the first-mentioned woman's house; or (b) born to a woman to whom the first-mentioned woman was married under customary law for the purpose of providing children for the first-mentioned woman's house.'

108 See the definition of 'house' in section 1 of the Reform of Customary Law of Succession and Regulation of Related Matters Act, 2009 which reads as follows: '"house" means the family, property, rights and status which arise out of the customary marriage of a woman.' See also the definitions of the various houses in Zulu polygamous marriages under the provisions of section 1 of the Natal Code of Zulu Law GG No 10966, Proc R.151 of 1987.

109 SE Van der Merwe 'Accusatorial and Inquisitorial Procedures and Restricted and Free Systems of Evidence' in AJGM Sanders (ed) (1981) Southern Africa in Need of Law Reform: Proceedings of the Southern African Law Reform Conference, Sun City, Bophuthatswana, 11–14 August 1980.

110 RM Cover (1983) 'The Supreme Court, 1982 Term – Foreword: Nomos and Narrative' Faculty Scholarship Series. FS Papers 2705, 4–68 at pages 4–5 http://digitalcommons.law.yale.edu/fss_papers/2705 or G Olson 'Narration and Narrative in Legal Discourse' paragraph 23 in P Hühn et al (eds) *The Living Handbook of Narratology* Hamburg: Hamburg University, http://www.lhn.uni-hamburg.de/article/narration-and-narrative-legal-discourse (accessed 1 May 2018).

111 P Brooks (1996). 'The Law as Narrative and Rhetoric.' P Brooks & P Gewirtz (eds) *Law's Stories: Narrative and Rhetoric in the Law*. New Haven: Yale UP, 14–22. G Olson 'Narration and Narrative in Legal Discourse' paragraph 7 in P Hühn et al (eds) *The Living Handbook of Narratology* Hamburg: Hamburg University, http://www.lhn.uni-hamburg.de/article/narration-and-narrative-legal-discourse (accessed 1 May 2018).

112 A translation of the seTswana phrase.

participate in the proceedings, usually chiefs' deputies and community elders) who are present in court.

Custom permits the chief's council members to cross-examine the witnesses on both sides of the dispute, but only after the witness has 'narrated' his or her evidence. The most obvious effect of the narrative method is that the court will hear all evidence, including evidence that would normally be objected to by the opposing party. It is the duty of the presiding officer to determine how much weight to assign to the evidence, after hearing the evidence. Of course the anomaly that arises is that because admissibility is an absolute *sine qua non* in the adversarial system (unlike the inquisitorial system where it is largely irrelevant) narrative evidence, while inquisitorial in nature and thus theoretically automatically admissible, is subjected to an unnecessary and inappropriate adversarial admissibility threshold when the matter is heard in any court other than the courts of traditional leaders.

Counterpoint: in the state of California in the United States of America, narrative testimony is permitted and may even be required where appropriate. An example of where the narrative method is required is when an attorney is aware that the witness is likely to commit perjury during his or her testimony. Although the context in *People v. Johnson*[113] was different in that the court was dealing with a law relating to possible perjured evidence, the Californian court recognised the importance of narrative testimony by saying:

> None of the approaches ... is perfect. Of the various approaches, we believe the narrative approach represents the best accommodation of the competing interests of the defendant's right to testify and the attorney's obligation not to participate in the presentation of perjured testimony since it allows the defendant to tell the jury, in his own words, his version of what occurred, a right which has been described as fundamental, and allows the attorney to play a passive role.[114]

We believe that narrative evidence is designed to fit in with, and is integral to, the oral culture of the litigants in customary law.

4.6.2 Rituals and customs as evidence of a juristic act

A ritual may be defined as a series of words or a sequence of activities which are uttered or performed in accordance with prescribed rules and in the same manner, indicating a particular formality. Rituals govern almost every aspect of a traditional person's life and these rituals are associated with either medical,[115] religious,[116] cultural[117]

---

113 62 Cal.App.4th 608 at 629 (per Kremer, PJ).

114 Ibid.

115 See for instance Knapp van Bogaert and Ogunbanjo who state that 'placental rituals and other birth-by rituals are common in various societies. These rituals often include culturally determined behavioural sequences which operate as anxiety-releasing mechanisms and they serve to offer a spiritual means of 'control' over the future health and welfare of mother, child, and even the community. As long as such rituals do not cause harm, they should be respected for the role that they play and be left alone.' D Knapp van Bogaert and GA Ogunbanjo (2008) 'Post-birth Rituals: Ethics and the Law' *South African Family Practice* 50:2, 45–46 at 45 (abstract).

116 For instance, the ritual slaughtering of animals to feed or communicate with ancestral spirits.

117 For instance, initiation and circumcision rituals.

or legal[118] objectives or a combination of any of these rituals and their objectives.[119] There is always a meaning behind, and a consequence of, every African ritual because all rituals are performed in contemplation of one of the above objectives.[120] For instance, marriage rituals not only signify the severance of a woman's legal affiliation with her biological family or her ancestral line of birth and her joining of her husband's family and ancestral lineage, but also symbolise the consummation of a valid marriage.[121]

The relevance of rituals in the customary law of evidence has not been dealt with adequately in literature and judicial precedent. Amoah and Bennett[122] argue that 'law-makers paid scant regard to traditional beliefs' and this is evident in the South African Law Reform Commission's report on Christian, Islamic, Hindu and Jewish marriages which hardly mentions African religions. Accordingly, they argue that 'nearly all of the parties involved in the legislative process assumed that recognition of customary marriages rested exclusively on the right to culture' and not on the right to religious freedom.

Further, they argue, correctly, that 'in this respect, the Commission was following a pattern of thinking already well established in the courts'. For example in the case of *Sila & Another v Masuku*,[123] the court rejected evidence of rituals in deciding whether an African customary marriage was valid or not. The court said that the 'religious element' of a customary marriage was to be construed as 'mere custom' and that it produced no greater consequence than 'music, singing or a wedding.'[124] It seems therefore that the courts assumed that customary law contained no religious elements. It is submitted that rituals, although they may appear to be purely religious, have significant legal relevance.

Despite the decision in *Sila & Another v Masuku*,[125] the courts have endorsed some rituals as evidence of a fact in dispute or as evidence of compliance with the requirements of the relevant African customary law principles.

First, in respect of adoption of children, the courts have accepted that the sacrifice of an animal for that purpose serves as evidence of such adoption. In *Maswanganye v Baloyi N.O. and Another*[126] the court, quoting previous decisions[127] said the following:

> In *Kewana*, the facts were briefly these. The father of the child in that case had died. His mother became mentally ill. The child was cared for by the relatives, who decided

---

118 Note that in *Smit v His Majesty King Goodwill Zwelithini Kabhekuzulu* 2009 JDR 1361 (KZP) at para 16, the court in describing the Zulu *ukweshwama* festival (The First Fruit Ceremony) stated, 'ceremony is of a ritualistic nature and sacrifice plays an important role as in most agricultural societies worldwide. Apart from being mere rituals, such ceremonies take into consideration the other natural effect of food. It also alerts the community against the wrong use of food, such as the necessity to wait until it is properly ripened and prepared.' The words 'mere rituals' here should be construed to mean 'with no legal consequence.'

119 Note that most rituals involve the ritual sacrifice of animals. Where animal sacrifices are made, there may be a combination of objectives of the sacrifice. For instance, in respect of a wedding, the blood of the animal is presumed to be a method of communication with ancestral spirits of both families; the meat is used to feed the guests and the exchange of organs or carcasses between the families symbolises their union in marriage.

120 See for example the acceptance by court of certain rituals which supported the testimony of a witness in *Venevene v Hlandlini* 1972/74 AC 109 (S) (Elliotdale).

121 For example, the smearing of red ochre on the bride's face (*libovu*) in terms of Swazi law; the slaughtering of an ox (*tlhabiso*) in seSotho law (the families swop half of the carcasses as a sign of unity between the ancestors and the parties and their families); the bride drinking sour milk (*ukutyis' amasi*) for the same purpose in Xhosa law and the Zulu exchange of compulsory gifts (*umabo*).

122 J Amoah and T Bennett 'The freedoms of religion and culture under the South African Constitution: Do traditional African religions enjoy equal treatment?' 2008 8(2) *AHRLJ* 357 at 359, also note 5.

123 1937 NAC (N&T) 121 at 123.

124 Referring to HJ Simons 'Customary unions in a changing society' (1958) *Acta Juridica* 320 at 322–325.

125 1937 NAC (N&T) 121 at 123.

126 (62122/2014) [2015] ZAGPPHC 917 (4 September 2015) at para 10.

127 *Kewana v Santam Insurance Co. Ltd* 1993 (4) SA 771 (TkA) at 776B. See also *Metiso v Padongelukfonds* 2001 (3) SA 1142 (T).

38 | THE LAW OF EVIDENCE IN SOUTH AFRICA

that the deceased should adopt the child. The deceased agreed. A traditional ceremony was held attended by the deceased's family, the local chief and neighbours. A male relative was present as the 'eye' of the family, and he informed the gathering that the purpose of the ceremony was that the child was accepted and recognised as the child of the deceased. A sheep was slaughtered for the enjoyment of the guests and a goat was slaughtered 'to give the occasion the significance and solemnity of an act being done in accordance with tribal customs.' The deceased was present at the ceremony.

Second, in respect of African customary marriages, the courts have recognised, as evidence of a marriage, the rituals concerning the handing over of the wife to the family group of her new husband,[128] and the rituals concerning her acceptance and integration (*imvume*) as a newlywed woman and as a member of her husband's extended family (and ancestral line).[129]

Third, the courts have recognised rituals concerning initiation and coming of age thereby declaring a person as having full legal capacity to perform juristic acts under customary law.[130]

Fourth, rituals concerning piercing and scarification of some bodily parts have been recognised by the courts as not merely serving aesthetic roles but as being a form of identification as members of a group.

In the majority of cases, the interpretation or the establishment of the meaning and relevance of a ritual will require the services of an expert in the relevant field of African customary law.

4.6.3 Presumptions concerning hearsay

The Supreme Court of Appeal held that vicarious admissions[131] are generally not admissible because they constitute hearsay evidence.[132] Despite this, the courts may still admit vicarious hearsay evidence if the relevant requirements of the Law of Evidence Amendment Act, 1988

---

128 An example of the isiSwazi marriage ritual of *ukumekeza* was considered in the case of *Mabuza v Mbatha* 2003 (4) SA 218 (C) at 225. The ritual 'involves the bride appearing naked in front of the female elders of the groom's family.' S Nkosi 'Customary marriage as dealt with in *Mxiki v Mbata in re: Mbata v Department of Home Affairs and Others* (GP) (unreported case no A844/2012, 23-10-2014)' *De Rebus* January 2015 Issue 549 p 67. Although the court in *Mabuza v Mbatha* 2003 (4) SA 218 (C) rejected the ritual of *ukumekeza* as a requirement for the validity of a customary marriage on the basis that the parties can 'waive' this ritual by agreement, the judgment implies that the ritual could be regarded as evidence of conclusion of a marriage. Hlophe J held, at para 25, that 'In my judgment, there is no doubt that *ukumekeza*, like many other customs, has somehow evolved so much . ..it is inconceivable that *ukumekeza* has not evolved and that it cannot be waived by agreement between the parties and/or their families in appropriate cases.'

129 *Maluleke and Others v The Minister of Home Affairs and Another* (02/24921) [2008] ZAGPHC 129 (9 April 2008). The court had to decide whether a valid customary marriage existed between the deceased and a woman who had registered a marriage after the man's death. The deceased had paid *lobolo* in full for their proposed marriage but died before the custom of *imvume* (literally 'acceptance') a form of integration of the woman into the husband's family through a celebration or by agreement. The court found that the date for *imvume* was fixed by agreement before the death of the deceased; the deceased was an adult man and a divorcee; the deceased and the respondent were permanently cohabiting at the time of his death; the family of the deceased regarded the respondent as his wife; and that the deceased and the respondent had 'agreed that they were husband and wife' (para 16).

130 For example, the Xhosa and Sotho people practise *ulwaluko* and *lebollo* respectively. Young men take part in a coming of age initiation where they are first circumcised without anaesthetic, they are then sent away from their village and into the bush with minimal supplies so that they can fend for themselves for up to six months. Upon completion of the initiation period, they attain the status of legal majority and are legally emancipated. Other examples are rituals performed during the birth of children and the deaths of family heads, rituals associated with a change of personal legal status and rituals performed during religious and cultural events.

131 For example the hearsay admissions of witnesses who have express or implied authority or power to act as agents, partners, representatives, referees etc.

132 *Mdani v Allianz Insurance Ltd* 1991 (1) SA 184 (A). See also *S v Litako and Others* 2014 (2) SACR 431 (SCA) and *Mhlongo v S; Nkosi v S* 2015 (2) SACR 323 (CC).

CHAPTER 4 TRUTH VERIFICATION, FACT FINDING AND RULES OF EVIDENCE

are met. In most matters arising out of customary law, the family head will testify in his capacity as a representative of the family and his testimony would be regarded as a vicarious admission where admissions are made by him on behalf of the family. Section 9 of the Law of Evidence Amendment Act, 1988 has repealed sections 216 and 223 of the Criminal Procedure Act, 1977, which provided for hearsay rules and dying declarations respectively in criminal law. The new rule concerning hearsay is found under section 3 which defines and lays down requirements for the admissibility of hearsay evidence, namely that:

> [s]ubject to the provisions of any other law, hearsay evidence shall not be admitted as evidence at criminal or civil proceedings, unless the court, having regard to
> (i)   the nature of the proceedings;
> (ii)   the nature of the evidence;
> (iii)   the purpose for which the evidence is tendered;
> (iv)   the probative value of the evidence;
> (v)   the reason why the evidence is not given by the person upon whose credibility the probative value of such evidence depends;
> (vi)   any prejudice to a party which the admission of such evidence might entail; and
> (vii)   any other factor which should in the opinion of the court be taken into account, is of the opinion that such evidence should be admitted in the interest of justice.

As a general rule, and due to the oral nature of African customary law, hearsay evidence is generally admissible. For instance, an event or fact is recorded orally and then handed down to future generations through metaphors, idioms, proverbs, maxims, deathbed declarations[133] and orders, etc. Usually, such hearsay must be corroborated to carry weight, usually through exhibits (*intlonze*[134]) and/or opinion evidence of another person.[135]

DISCUSSION	The recognition of narrative evidence
4.2	Canadian law recognises oral historical statements of the aboriginal people as evidence in land-related matters and such evidence is considered as exception to the hearsay rule.[136] During 1982, Canada amended its Constitution to recognise 'the rights of First Nation peoples.'[137] Australia followed the Canadian example in the 1990s, but with a much more advanced approach to the recognition of aboriginal rules of evidence. Section 29(2) of the Australian Evidence Act, 1995 recognises this method of fact finding: 'A court may, on its own motion or on the application of the party that called the witness, direct that the witness give evidence wholly or partly in narrative form'. The Act goes even further and states explicitly: 'The hearsay rule does not apply to evidence of a representation about the existence or non-existence, or the content, of the traditional laws and customs of an Aboriginal or Torres Strait Islander group.'[138]

---

133 R Slovenko 'Deathbed Declarations' *The Journal of Psychiatry & Law* (1996) 24(3) 469–484.
134 *Maqutu v Sancizi* 1936 NAC (C & O) 86; *Myataza v Macasa* 1952 NAC (S) 28.
135 JH Soga *The AmaXosa: Life and Customs* (1932).
136 HM Babcock '"[This] I Know from My Grandfather": The Battle for Admissibility of Indigenous Oral History as Proof of Tribal Land Claims' (2012) 37(19) *Am. Indian L. Rev.* 19 at 22.
137 HM Babcock '"[This] I Know from My Grandfather": The Battle for Admissibility of Indigenous Oral History as Proof of Tribal Land Claims' (2012) 37(19) *Am. L. Rev.* 19 at 21. Constitution Act, 1982, s 35(1), being Schedule B to the Canada Act, 1982, c. 11 (U.K.) (entitled 'Rights of the Aboriginal Peoples of Canada', and provides as follows: 'The existing aboriginal and treaty rights of the aboriginal peoples of Canada are hereby recognized and affirmed.'). See note 9 of p. 21 in Babcock's article supra.
138 Section 72 of the Evidence Act, 1995 (Australia).

40 | THE LAW OF EVIDENCE IN SOUTH AFRICA

In *Mnyama v Gxalaba and Another*[139] the applicant, the eldest brother of the second respondent's deceased husband who died intestate on 24 June 1989 and to whom the second respondent was married by customary law, brought an urgent application for an order interdicting the first respondent (an undertaker in possession the body of the deceased) and the second respondent from proceeding with the burial arrangements of the deceased and sought an order to have the deceased's body handed over to him to enable him (the applicant) to bury his brother's body.

The second respondent opposed this application on the basis of an oral wish expressed by the deceased to her that she should attend to his burial in Cape Town and not in the Transkei. It was **common cause** that the second respondent, as partner of the deceased in a customary union, was not in Xhosa customary law the deceased's heir and that she had no rights other than those which might have been conferred by the orally expressed wishes of the deceased.

The court considered the 'death-bed wishes' of a deceased person and concluded that the statements made by the deceased to the applicant constituted an exception to the old (pre-statutory) hearsay rule and that under the provisions of section 3(1)(*c*) of the Law of Evidence Amendment Act, 1988, the court has the discretion to admit hearsay evidence in the interest of justice. The court found that in exercising 'this immense discretion', it had to take into account that the type of disputed hearsay in this matter had traditionally been accepted as an exception to the hearsay rule even before the Act was enacted. The court seems thus to have recognised the aspect of customary law wherein a deceased person tells members of his family how he wishes his estate to devolve upon his death and how succession to his status should be dealt with.

4.6.4 Presumptions in sex and marriage matters

In all matters relating to the seduction of women, there is a rebuttable presumption that all never-married women are virgins. In the absence of proof indicating otherwise, a man is held liable to compensate the mother of a woman whom he has alleged to have seduced. In these circumstances, proof of sexual intercourse is enough to prove the act of seduction. This presumption has been criticised by some academics who argue that these presumptions are 'infused' with gender prejudices.[140] Although corroboration of a woman's evidence is not required in cases involving illicit intercourse, such corroboration is required where the woman refuses to testify or where she is colluding with the wrongdoer. In such a case, the testimony of a third party (such as a family head) will provide corroboration.

Further, there is a presumption that people who share the same paternal name (surname) are related to each other by blood. The racial or tribal connection of the persons is immaterial, because the inference leads to the conclusion that the two people with the same paternal name share a common ancestor. With some communities, the same rules apply to persons who share the same maternal name. The proof of how people are related to each other is found in the name itself. It is significant that there are customary rules which prohibit sexual relations between people who are related to each other by blood or affinity. For instance, section 3(6) of the Recognition of Customary Marriages Act, 1998 provides that: 'The prohibition of a customary marriage between persons on account of their relationship by blood or affinity is determined by customary law.'

---

139 1990 (1) SA 650 (C).

140 TW Bennett, C Mills and G Munnick 'The anomalies of seduction: A statutory crime or an obsolete, unconstitutional delict?' 2009 25(2) *SAJHR* 330 at 335.

CHAPTER 4   TRUTH VERIFICATION, FACT FINDING AND RULES OF EVIDENCE   **41**

Furthermore, even if it is common knowledge that persons are not related to each by blood or affinity, the presumption still applies. For instance, a child may be 'accepted' in accordance with customary law by any person, and once accepted, the child will be deemed to be related to its biological as well as the accepting parents. An example of this relationship can be found in the definition of a 'descendant' under the provisions of section 1(*a*) of the Reform of Customary Law of Succession and Regulation of Related Matters Act[141] which defines descendant as:

> **a person who is not a descendant in terms of the Intestate Succession Act, but who, during the lifetime of the deceased person, was accepted by the deceased person in accordance with customary law as his or her own child.**

Proof of 'acceptance' 'in accordance with customary law' depends on the rituals performed by the parties indicating an act of acceptance.

THIS CHAPTER IN ESSENCE

1   Customary law is a sophisticated, values-centred system which prioritises the rights, interests and obligations of a defined group as opposed to individuals within the group.

2   African customary law makes provision for the involvement of the extended members of the group, namely clans (headmen councils), then chiefs' courts and then civil courts.

3   Most of the rules are transmitted orally and are recorded in the languages of the African people.

4   Legislation requires that the existence and content of customary law be proved by the litigant seeking to rely on a customary rule.

5   The Constitution fully recognises customary law, but subject to the Bill of Rights there is now a duty, firmly placed on our courts, to develop customary law, which includes the customary law of evidence.

6   Traditional law did not require a party to a dispute to prove the existence of a customary law rule even when the parties came from diverse backgrounds. Section 1(1) of the Law of Evidence Amendment Act allows any court to take judicial notice of indigenous law if it can be readily ascertained with sufficient certainty.

7   There are three methods of ascertaining the existence and content of a rule in customary law.

  7.1   The first method does not require the parties to present evidence – the court relies on primary and secondary sources to establish a customary law rule.

  7.2   The second method requires evidence of the existence of the rule as well as its content. Normally expert evidence must be adduced to prove the existence and content of the rule.

  7.3   The third method also requires evidence, concerning the content and not the existence of the rule.

8   There are differences and regional variations in respect of the customs of various traditional communities.

9   Traditionally, the court had to apply the law of the plaintiff but section 1(3) of the Law of Evidence Amendment Act provides that in the absence of any agreement, courts must apply the law in operation at the place where the defendant or respondent resides or carries on business or is employed, or the law of the tribe (if any) to which the defendant or respondent belongs.

10   The plaintiff must also prove that the defendant is actually 'Black'.

11   Customary law did not categorise people according to race, but only by ancestral lineages, affiliations and origins, and a person's affiliation to a traditional group can happen only in two ways:

  11.1   Affiliation to the community or group is by birth

  11.2   By acceptance of that person into the group in accordance with custom.

---

141   Act 11 of 2009.

42 THE LAW OF EVIDENCE IN SOUTH AFRICA

12 'Living customary law' is customary law adapted to fit in with the contemporary practice of the community in question.

13 To establish the existence of a customary law rule, it is best for the court to hear expert evidence.

14 Where living customary law is in conflict with codified customary law the court may either apply the relevant rules of statutory interpretation or exercise its constitutional mandate (to develop customary law) by ordering the legislature to make the necessary amendments.

15 Generally, most African people believe that traditional leaders, community matriarchs and patriarchs, and other elders are 'living archives' and custodians of African customary law.

16 The Traditional Leadership and Governance Framework Amendment Act recognises traditional leaders as experts in customary law.

17 Traditional leaders also have authority to establish their own courts and to apply customary law in those courts.

18 During the apartheid era, presiding officers in the Bantu Commissioners' Courts were empowered to take judicial notice of customary law without the need to hear evidence proving its existence.

19 The Commissioners' Courts were abolished and their powers transferred to the Magistrates' Courts but it is not clear whether the Magistrates' Court have the same powers to apply customary law without hearing evidence of the existence and content.

20 The presiding officer's own knowledge of customary law may suffice as proof of its existence but the following rules of evidence have developed in criminal and civil matters where the presiding officer does not call for evidence or proof of customary law:

   20.1 A presiding officer should not make an adverse finding against an accused person based on his specialised knowledge, without first placing on record his intention to rely on such knowledge.

   20.2 Where there is no dispute concerning the existence or nature of the customs before court and the presiding officer is familiar with customary law, there is no need to call witnesses; the presiding officer may rely on his or her specialised knowledge of customary law, but must first record reasons for not calling witnesses.

   20.3 In civil matters, the general rule is that a party who alleges the existence of a customary rule must prove its nature and existence.

   20.4 On appeal, the aggrieved party may apply for the matter to be re-opened and evidence concerning customary law to be heard.

21 If the presiding officer is not familiar with the relevant principle or does not have specialised knowledge of customary law, he or she must bring this to the attention of the litigants so that they can call witnesses.

22 During the colonial and apartheid eras, assessors were always used in the Commissioners' and Native Appeals Courts, *inter alia* to assist the commissioners to ascertain the existence and content of customary laws.

23 Section 34 of the Magistrates' Court Act allows the court to permit assessors to sit with the magistrate who hears a matter and act 'in an advisory capacity' but they do not have the same powers. However, the powers of the Commissioners of the Native Courts were transferred to the Magistrates' Courts which implies that assessors may assist in ascertaining the existence of a customary law rule.

24 The courts of traditional leaders are recognised in the Constitution of South Africa and in the Black Administration Act. With civil matters, these courts can adjudicate matters arising only out of customary law and not common law disputes. They have a wider jurisdiction in respect of criminal matters.

25 The rules of evidence and procedure in traditional courts are governed by unwritten customary law unless the provisions of the Chiefs and Headmen's Civil Courts Rules apply.

26 This is a set of rules of procedure and evidence peculiar to these courts and they are a confused mixture of Western and traditional rules.

27 Legal practitioners are not permitted in traditional courts and the presentation of *viva voce* evidence follows the customary method of narration.

CHAPTER 4 TRUTH VERIFICATION, FACT FINDING AND RULES OF EVIDENCE 43

28 On appeal in the Magistrates' Court, the matter will be heard *de novo* and the rules of evidence followed in the traditional court will not be followed in the Magistrates' Court.

29 The mixture of rules of evidence is problematic in that:

29.1 The Magistrates' Court can hear any customary law matter as a court of first instance, and the ordinary rules of evidence must be followed despite the fact that the matter arises out of customary law.

29.2 There is no rule that prevents the litigant from simultaneously instituting the same action in a traditional court.

29.3 A Magistrates' Court can act as a court of appeal and the customary law rules of evidence applied in the court *a quo* are not applied on appeal.

29.4 A decision of a Magistrates' Court on appeal is considered to be the judgement of the magistrate which means that it may be further appealed against in a superior court.

30 Narrative evidence is a form of oral evidence and requires a witness to tell a story about an incident without been questioned by any other person, including attorneys or presiding officers.

31 Questioning is delayed until the narration is over, whereafter the presiding officer has a duty to elicit all the additional necessary facts through questions.

32 Traditional African judges are expected to gauge the witness's demeanour and thereby draw conclusions as to the credibility of the witness.

33 Unlike in adversarial systems, conclusions drawn by the court from narrative testimony are not drawn from a constantly interrupted and guided narrative which disrupts the natural chronological logic, coherence and sequence of the story.

34 Narrative methods of oral evidence presentation also involve:

34.1 the value concept of *hlompho* (Sotho) or *inhlonipho* (Zulu) which means 'respect' and the careful use and choice of words and acceptable body language when addressing elders.

34.2 a prohibition on direct eye contact between the witness and an elder which allows witnesses to tell their stories in a manner that does not violate the rule relating to respect.

34.3 the use of euphemistic language when addressing elders which means witnesses can tell their stories in the language which is most appropriate for the event and the context of their testimony.

35 Rituals, which are a series of words or a sequence of activities uttered or performed in accordance with prescribed rules, have largely been ignored by the courts, although they have significant legal relevance.

36 However, some courts recognised some rituals as evidence of a fact in dispute or as evidence of compliance with the requirements of the relevant African customary law principles, for example:

36.1 the sacrifice of an animal as evidence of an adoption.

36.2 rituals concerning the handing over of the wife to the family group of her new husband and the rituals concerning her acceptance and integration (*imvume*) as evidence of a marriage.

36.3 rituals concerning initiation and coming of age as evidence of a person having full legal capacity to perform juristic acts under customary law.

36.4 rituals concerning piercing and scarification of some bodily parts as being a form of identification as members of a group.

37 As a general rule, and due to the oral nature of African customary law, hearsay evidence is generally admissible but must be corroborated to carry weight, usually through exhibits (*intlonze*) and/or opinion evidence of another person.

38 In most matters arising out of customary law, the family head will testify in his capacity as a representative of the family and his testimony would be regarded as a vicarious admission where admissions are made by him on behalf of the family.

39 Certain presumptions apply in sex and marriage matters:

40.1 In matters relating to the seduction of women, there is a rebuttable presumption that all never-married women are virgins.

40.2 There is a presumption that people who share the same paternal name (surname) are related to each other by blood.

Chapter 5

Impact of the Constitution on the law of evidence

5.1 Introduction **44**

5.2 The impact of the Constitution on the law of evidence in criminal matters **45**
    5.2.1   General fundamental rights and specific legal protections 45
    5.2.2   Reverse onus clauses 46
    5.2.3   Docket privilege 47
    5.2.4   The admissibility of unconstitutionally obtained evidence 48

5.3 The impact of the Constitution on the law of evidence in civil matters in general **48**

5.1 Introduction

On 27 April 1994 the Constitution of the Republic of South Africa Act 200 of 1993, referred to as the interim Constitution, came into operation. It transformed the South African legal system from one of parliamentary sovereignty to one in which the Constitution was supreme. It also introduced the concept of a bill of rights into South African law. The interim Constitution was followed by the Constitution of the Republic of South Africa Act 108 of 1996 (the Constitution) which came into operation on 4 February 1997.

Chapter 1, section 2 of the Constitution provides that the Constitution 'is the supreme law of the Republic' and that 'law or conduct inconsistent with it is invalid, and the obligations imposed by it must be fulfilled'. This section clearly imposes a duty to view, evaluate and apply all laws, legal rules and procedures through the lens of the provisions of the Constitution. This has had a discernible impact on the law and rules of evidence.

The Bill of Rights contained in Chapter 2 of the Constitution[1] is of particular relevance to the law of evidence because it contains several rights that affect the gathering or obtaining of evidence as well as the admissibility of such evidence in legal proceedings. In some instances, what were previously rules of evidence have been strengthened to the status of rights. These rights cannot now be infringed unless the infringement is justifiable in terms of the limitation clause set out in section 36 of the Constitution.[2] 'The Bill of Rights applies to all law, and binds the legislature, the executive, the judiciary, all organs of State'[3] as well as all natural and **juristic persons** with reference to the nature and duty imposed by the

---

1 Ss 7–39.
2 S 36(1). 'The rights in the Bill of Rights may be limited only in terms of law of general application to the extent that the limitation is reasonable and justifiable in an open and democratic society based on human dignity, equality and freedom, taking into account all relevant factors ...'.
3 S 8(1).

CHAPTER 5   IMPACT OF THE CONSTITUTION ON THE LAW OF EVIDENCE   45

particular right in question.[4] Therefore, the Bill of Rights is applicable vertically between the State and natural or juristic persons. Depending on the nature and duty imposed by the particular right,[5] it is also applicable horizontally between natural or juristic persons and other natural or juristic persons. The implication of the vertical, and in some instances horizontal, applicability of the Bill of Rights[6] is thus relevant to the law of evidence in respect of both criminal and civil matters.

5.2   The impact of the Constitution on the law of evidence in criminal matters

5.2.1   General fundamental rights and specific legal protections

When it comes to criminal matters, many pre-existing common law, statutory, procedural and evidentiary rights of a criminal accused, arrested person and detainee have been elevated to justiciable constitutional rights.[7] As noted in chapter 1, the rights contained in section 35 of the Constitution merely entrench most of the pre-existing common law procedural and evidentiary rights. These pre-existing rights are complimentary to, and have not been replaced by, section 35. For example, in terms of section 35(1)(*b*) of the Constitution, an arrested person must be informed of the *consequences* of not remaining silent after his or her arrest. The Constitution does not, however, define these consequences. They were originally to be found in the **Judges Rules**, which state that anything that an arrested person says can be taken down and used in evidence against him or her. Subsequent case law has recognised the incorporation of this wording as part of the South African common law.[8] They oblige an arresting police official to warn the person being arrested that anything he or she says may be taken down in writing and used in evidence against him or her.[9]

In addition to the general fundamental rights applicable to all persons, section 35 of the Constitution provides for extensive specific legal protections for arrested, accused and detained persons. These include:

- the right to remain silent
- the right not to testify at trial
- the right to adduce and challenge evidence in criminal proceedings[10]
- the right to legal representation[11]
- the right to be presumed innocent.[12]

---

4   S 8(2).

5   S 8(2).

6   S 8(2).

7   S 35.

8   The Judges Rules are a set of rules that were formulated at a judges' conference in 1931 in Cape Town. They set out procedural safeguards for suspects and arrested and accused persons in criminal matters. The police authorities subsequently adopted the Judges Rules as administrative directions and these have, over the years, been widely recognised by the courts. They have, arguably, now become part of the common law.

9   PJ Schwikkard and SE van der Merwe *Principles of Evidence* 3 ed (2009) Appendix C, Rule 8. The Judges Rules are now seldom referred to as the principles they espouse have been elevated, through their application by our courts, to the status of constitutionally protected rights.

10   S 35(3)(*i*).

11   S 35(3)(*f*) and (*g*).

12   S 35(3)(*h*).

THE LAW OF EVIDENCE IN SOUTH AFRICA

These constitutionally entrenched rights have, in many cases, had a significant impact on the law of evidence. For example, the right of an accused person to be presumed innocent places a burden on the prosecution to prove the guilt of that accused beyond a reasonable doubt.[13] Although this was always the case, the entrenchment of this right in the Bill of Rights means that we can now challenge legislation that undermines this right as being in conflict with the Constitution.

5.2.2 Reverse onus clauses

A provision in a statute that requires an accused to prove or disprove an element of an offence on a balance of probabilities is known as a *reverse onus clause*. In a number of instances, the Constitutional Court has held reverse onus clauses to be in violation of the right to be presumed innocent at trial.

In the first judgment of the Constitutional Court, *S v Zuma and Others*,[14] the Court declared unconstitutional the reverse onus provision contained in section 217(1)(*b*)(ii) of the Criminal Procedure Act 51 of 1977 as it conflicted with the right to be presumed innocent in section 25 of the interim Constitution. The section placed a burden of proof on the accused, in specified circumstances, to prove on a balance of probabilities that his or her **confession** was *not* freely and voluntarily obtained. The Court held unanimously that the presumption of innocence will be infringed in circumstances where the accused could be convicted despite not having been proven guilty beyond a reasonable doubt.

In contrast, in the case of *Scagell and Others v Attorney-General, Western Cape and Others*,[15] the Court considered whether various sections of the Gambling Act 51 of 1963, particularly section 6(3), violated the constitutional right to be presumed innocent. This section of the Act provided that if certain items relating to gambling were found on the premises, they 'shall be *prima facie* evidence' that the person in control or in charge of the premises had permitted gambling to take place. The Court held that section 6(3) created an **evidentiary burden** only and not a reverse onus. Nevertheless, the Court held this section to be unconstitutional as it could lead to convictions against an accused where there was no evidence other than *prima facie* evidence to support a conviction.

In the case of *S v Bhulwana; S v Gwadiso*,[16] the Court considered the presumption that a person in possession of an amount of dagga exceeding 115 grams would be considered a dealer in terms of section 21(1)(*a*)(i) of the Drugs and Drug Trafficking Act 140 of 1992. The Court held that this presumption violated the right to be presumed innocent and declared this section unconstitutional.

In *S v Coetzee and Others*,[17] the Court (per Langa J) stated the general rule to apply when considering the constitutionality of reverse onus clauses and similar provisions, namely, that:

> if a provision is part of the substance of the offence, and the statute is formulated in a way which permits a conviction despite the existence of a reasonable doubt in regard to that substantial part, the presumption of innocence is breached.[18]

---

13 See *S v Zuma and Others* 1995 (2) SA 642 (CC); *S v Coetzee and Others* 1997 (3) SA 527 (CC); *S v Boesak* 2001 (1) SA 912 (CC).
14 1995 (2) SA 642 (CC).
15 1997 (2) SA 368 (CC).
16 1996 (1) SA 388 (CC).
17 1997 (1) SACR 379 (CC).
18 1997 (1) SACR 379 (CC) at para 38.

The cases below are further examples of where the Constitutional Court has found reverse onus clauses to be in violation of the right to be presumed innocent at trial.

Osman and Another v Attorney-General, Transvaal

The Court in *Osman and Another v Attorney-General, Transvaal*[19] assessed the constitutionality of section 36 of the General Law Amendment Act 62 of 1955. This section deems criminally liable 'any person who is found in possession of any goods ... in regard to which there is a reasonable suspicion that they have been stolen and is unable to give a satisfactory account of such possession'. Madala J, in a unanimous judgment, rejected the argument that an unwillingness to give an explanation would lead to a finding that the accused was unable to give an explanation, thereby infringing on the right to be presumed innocent, on the ground that it is the inability and not the unwillingness that is specified in this section. The inability was nothing other than an element of the offence and the burden rested on the State throughout the trial to prove it.

S v Manamela and Another (Director-General of Justice Intervening)

Similarly, in *S v Manamela and Another (Director-General of Justice Intervening)*,[20] the Court held that section 37 of the General Law Amendment Act, 1955 violated the presumption of innocence. The section considered it an offence to acquire stolen goods otherwise than at a public sale without having reasonable cause to believe that the person disposing of the goods was authorised or entitled to do so.

S v Singo

The Court in *S v Singo*[21] considered a challenge to the validity of section 72(4) of the Criminal Procedure Act, 1977. This section allows for summary proceedings when an accused fails to appear in court on a fixed date unless the accused can satisfy the court that the failure to appear was not his fault. The Court held that section 72(4) limited the right to remain silent and the right to be presumed innocent. It held that the limitation of the right to remain silent was justifiable in terms of section 36 of the Constitution, but that the limitation on the presumption of innocence was not justified. The Court accordingly ordered that section 72(4) be read as requiring the accused to raise only a *reasonable possibility* that the failure was not his fault, thus ensuring that the accused does not bear a reverse onus.

5.2.3 Docket privilege

In addition, the right to be presumed innocent and the right of access to information[22] have changed the limits of **state privilege**, in particular **police docket privilege**.[23] In the case of *Shabalala and Others v Attorney-General, Transvaal and Another*,[24] the Constitutional Court substituted the previous so-called blanket privilege applicable to police dockets with a flexible test that permitted the accused person access to the contents of the police docket and state witnesses where such access was required for a fair trial. However, different rules apply insofar as access to the docket for purposes of the bail applications are concerned.[25]

---

19 1998 (4) SA 1224 (CC).
20 2000 (3) SA 1 (CC).
21 2002 (4) SA 858 (CC).
22 S 32 of the Constitution.
23 *Shabalala and Others v Attorney-General, Transvaal and Another* 1995 (2) SACR 761 (CC).
24 1995 (2) SACR 761 (CC).
25 *S v Dlamini, S v Dladla and Others; S v Joubert; S v Schietekat* 1999 (4) SA 623 (CC) and *S v Josephs* 2001 (1) SACR 659 (C) and section 60(14) of the CPA.

5.2.4 The admissibility of unconstitutionally obtained evidence

Finally, the accused's right to have **unconstitutionally obtained evidence** excluded from court if its admission would render the trial unfair or would otherwise be detrimental to the **administration of justice**[26] has created a secondary admissibility test for virtually all criminal admissibility tests.[27]

5.3 The impact of the Constitution on the law of evidence in civil matters in general

The impact of the Constitution on the law of evidence extends to civil trials too.

Section 34 of the Constitution provides that:

> Everyone has the right to have any dispute that can be resolved by the application of law decided in a *fair public hearing* before a court or, where appropriate, another independent and impartial tribunal or forum.[28]

A fair public hearing must include the right to a fair trial in both civil and criminal matters.[29] Prior to the enactment of the Constitution, South African courts had already confirmed that they had a discretion to exclude **illegally obtained evidence**.[30] Section 34 of the Constitution has strengthened this common law position. In a number of cases, the courts have also held that, in certain circumstances, unconstitutionally obtained evidence may be excluded in civil cases as well.[31]

Furthermore, Section 33(1) of the Constitution provides that 'everyone has the right to administrative action that is lawful, reasonable and procedurally fair.'[32] As all administrative action is enforced through civil proceedings, the necessary implication of this section is that civil proceedings enforcing administrative action must likewise be procedurally fair. The Constitution has thus not only entrenched the right to fair administrative action but has also had an impact on how that action occurs.

THIS CHAPTER IN ESSENCE

1   The Constitution, which superseded the interim Constitution, replaced the system of parliamentary sovereignty with one of constitutional supremacy and also introduced the concept of a bill of rights into South African law.

2   The supremacy clause in the Constitution imposes a duty on courts to view, evaluate and apply all laws, legal rules and procedures subject to the provisions of the Constitution, in particular the Bill of Rights contained in the Constitution. This has had a discernible impact on the law of evidence as the Bill of Rights contains several rights that affect the gathering or obtaining of evidence as well as the admissibility of such evidence in legal proceedings. In addition, what were previously rules of evidence

---

26   In terms of s 35(5) of the Constitution.
27   See ch 16 Unconstitutionally obtained evidence.
28   Our emphasis.
29   Therefore, all civil litigants – plaintiffs and defendants – and criminal litigants – the state and the defence – are entitled to a fair trial. Note that s 35(3) expressly entrenches an accused's right to a fair trial with reference to a number of specific sub-rights.
30   *Lenco Holdings Ltd and Others v Eckstein and Others* 1996 (2) SA 693 (N).
31   See also 15.4.2 The discretion to exclude evidence in civil cases.
32   As all administrative action is enforced through civil proceedings, the necessary implication of this section is that civil proceedings enforcing administrative action must likewise be procedurally fair.

have now have been strengthened to the status of substantive rights that can only be infringed if it is justifiable in terms of the Constitution.

3   Section 35 of the Constitution provides for extensive specific legal protections for arrested, accused and detained persons and entrenches most of the pre-existing common law procedural and evidentiary rights in criminal matters. These pre-existing rights are complimentary to, and have not been replaced by, section 35.

4   Reverse onus provisions, which permit the conviction of an accused despite no proof of his or her guilt beyond reasonable doubt, have been held to be unconstitutional as they infringe the constitutional right to be presumed innocent.

5   The limits of state privilege, particularly that pertaining to police docket privilege, have changed due to the right to be presumed innocent and the right of access to information.

6   The accused's right to have unconstitutionally obtained evidence excluded from court now serves as a secondary admissibility test for virtually all criminal admissibility tests.

7   The impact of the Constitution in criminal trials extends to civil trials in a similar manner.

PART TWO

Basic concepts

CHAPTER 6   Admissibility and weight of evidence 52

CHAPTER 7   Evidence and proof 61

CHAPTER 8   *Prima facie*, conclusive and
sufficient proof 69

CHAPTER 9   Evidence: substantive or procedural law? 74

Chapter 6

Admissibility and weight of evidence

6.1   **Introduction** **52**

6.2   **Admissibility** **54**
    6.2.1   Relevance 54
    6.2.2   Determination of admissibility 55
           6.2.2.1   The issues to be proved 55
           6.2.2.2   Collateral issues 55
           6.2.2.3   Potential weight 56
           6.2.2.4   Unreliable evidence 56
           6.2.2.5   Prejudice versus probative value 56
           6.2.2.6   Precedent 56
           6.2.2.7   Completeness 56
    6.2.3   Procedure to determine admissibility 57

6.3   **Weight** **57**
    6.3.1   Fundamental principles 57
           6.3.1.1   Evidence weighed as a whole 57
           6.3.1.2   Inferences versus speculation 57
    6.3.2   Factors 57
           6.3.2.1   Corroboration 58
           6.3.2.2   Credibility 58
           6.3.2.3   Direct or circumstantial evidence 59

6.1 Introduction

The concepts of admissibility and weight are fundamental to the law of evidence. They are often regarded as separate topics but we shall see that they are closely related to one another and that they do, at times, overlap. To explore these concepts fully, we will give a brief overview of where they fit into the law of evidence as a whole.

We present evidence to a court to try to persuade the court of the veracity of our case, or to prove a particular fact, or even to undermine an opponent's case. However, we may only present evidence if it complies with certain rules. This means that not all potential evidence is actually allowed. Therefore, the first step is to establish whether we are permitted to lead the evidence we are hoping to present. The rules governing this are referred to as *rules regulating the admissibility of evidence.*

If evidence is regarded as admissible, we can present it in court where the opposing party, and to a lesser extent the court, will test and examine it. The court will then analyse the evidence to see how influential it may be. In other words, the court will decide how much weight to give to the evidence.

CHAPTER 6 ADMISSIBILITY AND WEIGHT OF EVIDENCE

From the above description we can see that the concepts of admissibility and weight are closely related and that they occur sequentially. We deal first with admissibility. Then, once the court has admitted the evidence, and once it has been tested, it assesses the weight of this evidence. Evidence therefore cannot be weighed if it is not admissible. For this reason, admissibility is seen as a ***sine qua non*** (a condition without which something else is not possible) for weight.

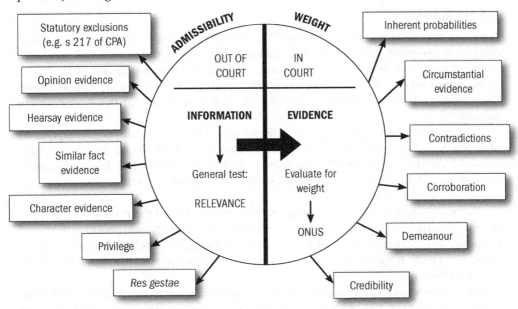

Figure 6.1 Admissibility versus weight

DISCUSSION 6.1

Is a single evidentiary system of adjudication better than a two-stage evidentiary system?

The system of a two-stage process where we first consider the admissibility of potential evidence and then the weight of the evidence once it is admitted is not the only system of regulating the reception of evidence. The **Continental system**, also known as the **civil law system** or **inquisitorial system**, follows a different approach. Because only a judge (with no tradition of a jury system) presides over trials, there are minimal admissibility requirements for evidence. Nearly all relevant evidence is admitted. The complex range of evidentiary admissibility rules, typical of the current South African law of evidence, is absent. The presiding judge controls proceedings, questions the witnesses and allocates weight to evidence presented. The role of lawyers is typically limited to the leading of witnesses and the presentation of evidence. This emphasis on the general admissibility of evidence is typical of inquisitorial trial proceedings.

The method of adjudication in South Africa's Small Claims Courts is essentially inquisitorial. Many argue that inquisitorial adjudication should be extended to all our civil and criminal courts to reduce the disproportionate influence, symptomatic of adversarial court proceedings, that trial lawyers have on the administration of justice.

What are the advantages and disadvantages of the single evidentiary system versus the two-stage evidentiary system?

6.2 Admissibility

Admissibility is often referred to as an *absolute test* in the sense that evidence is either admissible or it is not. If evidence is considered admissible, then it is allowed. If not, it cannot be presented to the court. Therefore, the question that arises is how precisely do we determine admissibility?

6.2.1 Relevance

There are several rules relating to the admissibility of evidence. If summarised, these rules comprise one foundational rule (with several variations and limitations). Evidence is admissible if it is relevant to an issue in the proceedings. Evidence must be relevant to be admitted.[1] It follows, therefore, that irrelevant evidence is inadmissible. Determining relevance is therefore probably the most important step in any evidentiary enquiry.[2]

This rule of relevance is stated in two different ways. First, there is the positive expression of the statement: 'Evidence is admissible if it is relevant.' Second, there is also the negative expression of the statement: 'No evidence ... shall be admissible which is irrelevant or immaterial ...'.[3] The positive form is the position in terms of the common law, while the negative expression is found in statutes.[4]

The term 'relevance' itself is the subject of much debate and there are several ways to describe it. A piece of evidence is considered relevant if it might help to prove (or disprove) the probable existence (or non-existence) of a fact in issue. This has been phrased in many ways.[5] Essentially, if a piece of evidence might assist the court in establishing a fact in issue, then it is relevant.

Deciding whether a piece of evidence will assist the court, that is, whether it is relevant, is the task of the presiding officer. Schreiner JA describes determining relevance as 'based on a blend of logic and experience'.[6] Lord Steyn states, 'The question of relevance is typically a matter of degree to be determined, for the most part, by common sense and experience.'[7] This may be oversimplifying things, however, as complex inductive reasoning is seldom as simple as it seems and exercising this common sense, logic and experience is restricted to a certain extent as presiding officers must take several factors or guidelines into account.[8]

Before we analyse these factors, note that relevance alone is not the sole determinant of admissibility as evidence may be deliberately excluded for other reasons. If evidence is found to be relevant (logically relevant), it does not mean that it is automatically legally admissible. The term 'legally relevant' is often incorrectly used to describe logically relevant evidence

---

1 See ch 15 The general test for relevance.
2 For a more detailed analysis of the concept of relevance, see ch 15.
3 'No evidence as to any fact, matter or thing shall be admissible which is irrelevant or immaterial and which cannot conduce to prove or disprove any point or fact in issue in criminal proceedings.' S 210 of the Criminal Procedure Act 51 of 1977. See also s 2 of the Civil Proceedings Evidence Act 25 of 1965.
4 S 210 of the Criminal Procedure Act, 1977 and s 2 of the Civil Proceedings Evidence Act, 1965.
5 'The word "relevant" means that any two facts to which it is applied are so related to each other that according to the common course of events one either taken by itself or in connection with other facts proves or renders probable the past, present, or future existence or non-existence of the other.' JF Stephen *Digest of the Law of Evidence* 12 ed (1914) Art 1. 'Evidence is relevant if it is logically probative or disprobative of some matter which requires proof.' *DPP v Kilbourne* [1973] AC 729 at 756.
6 *R v Matthews and Others* 1960 (1) SA 752 (A) at 758.
7 *R v Randall* [2004] 1 WLR 56 (HL) at para 20.
8 See ch 15 The general test for relevance.

CHAPTER 6 ADMISSIBILITY AND WEIGHT OF EVIDENCE | **55**

which is excluded by a legal rule.[9] There are several other limitations. For example, logically relevant evidence may be inadmissible if:

- it was illegally obtained
- it is highly prejudicial (if its prejudicial effect outweighs its probative value)
- if it is privileged
- if it was obtained in breach of the Constitution.

In other words, relevant evidence is inadmissible if its use is precluded by another law.[10] Irrelevant evidence is excluded for several reasons. The most obvious reason is that admitting irrelevant evidence will unnecessarily prolong the duration of the trial, thus wasting time and increasing the costs. In addition, the presentation of irrelevant evidence obscures the actual issues in dispute. This causes parties to lose focus on relevant matters as well as requiring them to spread their resources more thinly than necessary. It also has the potential to prejudice a party, both by causing this loss of focus and because it may '... prejudice the court against a party'.[11]

6.2.2 Determination of admissibility

The court alone decides if evidence is relevant to proceedings and it will often be called on to do so when any of the parties dispute admissibility. There are many factors[12] that the court will take into account when determining relevance. We will discuss some of these below.

6.2.2.1 The issues to be proved

The first step when deciding whether evidence is relevant to an issue is to establish exactly what the issues in dispute are. Only then can the court consider the relevance of a piece of evidence.[13] This applies to the essential elements that must be proved, called the *facta probanda*, and also to any issues that are relevant to the essential issues, called the *facta probantia*.[14]

6.2.2.2 Collateral issues

A logical consequence of this first step is for the court also to consider not admitting evidence if the evidence relates only to collateral or peripheral issues. These are issues that do not add any value to the resolution of the issues in dispute. These issues would also simply result in parties spending time and resources exploring matters that would not be of any value or assistance to the court in determining the points in dispute before it.[15]

---

9   Of course, if it is not logically relevant, then no questions of legal relevance arise. 'Logical relevance is a *sine qua non* of admissibility.' J McEwan *Evidence and the Adversarial Process: The Modern Law* 2 ed (1998) at 33–34.

10 '... any evidence which is relevant is admissible unless there is some other rule of evidence which excludes it.' *R v Schaube-Kuffler* 1969 (2) SA 40 (RA) at 50B.

11 P Murphy *A Practical Approach to Evidence* 10 ed (2008) at 25.

12 See PJ Schwikkard and SE van der Merwe *Principles of Evidence* 3 ed (2009) at 47–57 for a more complete list and analysis of factors.

13 *Lloyd v Powell Duffryn Steam Coal Co Ltd* 1914 AC 733 at 738.

14 In holding that the credibility of a witness, if it is related to the issues in dispute, may itself be an issue that may warrant evidence being led, the Court stated that evidence should not be excluded '... whether it is relevant to the issue or to issues which are themselves relevant to the issue but strictly speaking not in issue themselves'. *S v Mayo and Another* 1990 (1) SACR 659 (E) at 661F–G.

15 In *Land Securities plc v Westminster City Council* [1993] 4 All ER 124 at 128H the Court summed up such a situation when deciding on the admissibility of a piece of evidence. It stated that the evidence was considered to have 'insufficient weight to justify the exploration of otherwise irrelevant issues which its admissibility would require'.

6.2.2.3 Potential weight

To determine whether a particular piece of evidence is relevant or not, the court will look at the **potential weight** that the piece of evidence may carry. The court considers potential weight to establish whether the evidence is of sufficient quality or relevance to enable it to draw **inferences** from it. Inferences are essentially interim conclusions which are relied on in ultimately reaching a decision on the main issue. If so, the evidence is more likely to be admitted. If the evidence is unlikely to help the court draw inferences, then admitting it will be of little practical use. Thus, although the court can only weigh the evidence once it has been admitted, it must make a preliminary assessment of the potential weight of the evidence before it can be admitted.

6.2.2.4 Unreliable evidence

This factor simply requires a court to be aware that certain types of evidence are easy to manufacture and that this undermines their usefulness to the court. Accordingly, evidence where there is a high risk of manufacture is often not admitted. The best example of this is the general rule that **previous consistent statements** by a witness are excluded because they are easy to fabricate and thus have 'no probative value'.[16]

6.2.2.5 Prejudice versus probative value

Prejudice in this context means that a party to proceedings will suffer a procedural disadvantage if certain evidence is admitted. 'Prejudice' in this context does not mean that the evidence itself will result in a finding of fact against that party – this is not considered prejudicial. In certain circumstances, the admission of particular evidence may cause so much prejudice to a party that the evidence should not be admitted despite the fact that the evidence may be relevant and useful. However, if the evidence is of significant importance, this will be balanced against the possible prejudice to determine its admissibility.

6.2.2.6 Precedent

Previous judgments are a useful guide in deciding whether evidence is relevant and therefore admissible. However, the determination of relevance is so intrinsically linked to the facts and issues of every individual case that it is rare that any two cases will be comparable in this respect. For this reason, **precedent** can only be a guideline and can never be a determinant of weight.

6.2.2.7 Completeness

Even irrelevant evidence is admissible if its purpose is to fill the gaps in a witness's testimony on relevant issues so as to present a complete picture.[17] The term '*res gestae*' is sometimes used (unhelpfully) in this context to describe such evidence. Although the same term is used in a number of different circumstances, in this context it simply means that 'evidence of facts may be admissible as part of the *res gestae* if these facts are so closely connected in time, place and circumstances with some transaction which is at issue that they can be said to form part of that transaction'.[18] In other words, facts that are irrelevant may be admitted if bound up with relevant facts or facts in issue.

---

16 *S v Scott-Crossley* 2008 (1) SACR 223 (SCA) at para 17.
17 See *Palmer v Minister of Safety and Security* 2002 (1) SA 110 (W) at 115D–E which states that the necessity of having a complete picture may require the reception of facts that are neither in issue nor relevant.
18 A Choo *Evidence* 3 ed (2012) at 292.

6.2.3 Procedure to determine admissibility

The procedure adopted to determine whether a particular piece of evidence is admissible is often referred to as the **trial-within-a-trial**[19] process. If at any point in proceedings a party disputes the admissibility of evidence, the court suspends proceedings and conducts a mini-trial. Both sides put forward evidence and argument as to the admissibility or otherwise of the evidence. The court will then decide whether the evidence is admissible. If so, the trial will resume and the evidence will then be led. If not, the trial will resume without the evidence being presented.

6.3 Weight

It is the court's role to evaluate evidence to assess its weight. However, prudent practitioners should be mindful of the process that the court will adopt in doing so as it may well influence the amount, type and nature of the evidence that they will use and method that they will adopt when presenting such evidence.

6.3.1 Fundamental principles

There is no exhaustive analysis of the process of evaluation but several guidelines have developed over time. There are two fundamental guiding principles:
- First, the court must weigh up all the evidence as a whole rather than on a piece-by-piece basis.
- Second, the court must draw proper inferences (conclusions based on facts found to be proved) and must avoid conjecture and speculation (conclusions based on 'what if' hypothetical scenarios).

6.3.1.1 Evidence weighed as a whole

Evaluating evidence as a whole requires that the court must weigh all the evidence presented together. Although it may analyse individual aspects separately, it cannot ignore how a particular piece fits into the overall picture. It would also be incorrect to reject individual pieces of evidence without taking into account how they affect the complete body of evidence.[20]

6.3.1.2 Inferences versus speculation

The court must first establish which facts it finds are proved before drawing inferences. Once these facts are established, then the court may draw conclusions based on these facts. If a fact is not proved, a conclusion that takes the supposed fact into account may not be drawn. Any finding made or conclusion reached based on a fact that has not been found proved is tantamount to speculation[21] and is not allowed.

6.3.2 Factors

In weighing the evidence, the court will apply coherent, logical thought to an objective analysis of the evidence. It will be guided by experience and will refer to several factors that

---

19 See ch 55 The trial-within-a-trial.

20 See *S v Trainor* 2003 (1) SACR 35 (SCA) at para 9 where the court condemned a 'compartmentalised and fragmented approach' adopted by a magistrate as 'illogical and wrong'.

21 See *De Wet and Another v President Versekeringsmaatskappy Bpk* 1978 (3) SA 495 (C) at 500F–G. 'If there are no positive proved facts from which the inference can be made, the method of inference fails and what is left is mere speculation or conjecture.' See also *S v Ndlovu* 1987 (1) PH H37 (A) at 68. The court 'is not entitled to speculate as to the possible existence of other facts.'

58 THE LAW OF EVIDENCE IN SOUTH AFRICA

may be of relevance to that particular trial. These factors include, but are not limited to, those listed below.

6.3.2.1 Corroboration

Independent corroboration of an aspect, or aspects, of the evidence presented is of significant importance. In evidentiary terms, **corroboration** means that a piece of evidence is supported or confirmed by another piece of evidence from a different source. It is therefore clear that the repetition of a piece of evidence by the same witness cannot amount to corroboration. This merely shows that the witness has been consistent. This may be important for other reasons[22] but it does not mean that the story is any more likely to be true merely because it has been repeated.

Corroboration must come from an independent source and a witness cannot corroborate himself or herself. This is often referred to as the rule against **self-corroboration**.[23] The distinction can be subtle because a witness's oral testimony may be corroborated by real evidence. For example, evidence of a physical injury to the witness's own body constitutes real evidence that corroborates the witness's **oral testimony** of an assault. This cannot therefore be considered inadmissible self-corroboration.[24]

6.3.2.2 Credibility

When analysing evidence the court will first look at the source of the evidence. With oral testimony this means the court will assess the **credibility** (believability) of the witnesses. Evidence from a credible source is likely to carry more weight than evidence from a witness who is not believable. In assessing credibility the court will look at several things.[25] Chief among these is the demeanour of the witness. **Demeanour** refers to the witness's behaviour, manner of testifying, personality and the general impression that he or she creates.[26] This means that the court takes into account details such as hesitation when answering questions, evasiveness, a reluctance to answer and, sometimes, physical indicators like a nervous twitch. There are, however, certain limitations to this and it is not to be considered an infallible guide, particularly because witnesses in a witness box are usually nervous.[27]

Other factors besides demeanour are also relevant. Was the witness present in court before testifying, thereby giving the witness foreknowledge of the evidence and affording the person the opportunity to tailor his or her own evidence to suit what he or she heard?[28] Is the witness from that category of witnesses that the courts traditionally, as a result of experience, distrust?[29] Was the witness clearly lying about one aspect of the evidence and what impact, if any, will this have on the rest of his or her testimony? Was the evidence inconsistent with other proven facts, or earlier parts of the witness's own testimony?

---

22 For example, to rebut an allegation of a recent fabrication.

23 See *Director of Public Prosecutions v Kilbourne* [1973] 1 All ER 440 at 456.

24 Some authors appear to treat this, erroneously and automatically, as self-corroboration.

25 For a summary of several of the factors taken into account, see *Hees v Nel* 1994 (1) PH F11 (T) at 32.

26 A witness's demeanour constitutes real evidence in that it is a tangible piece of evidence observable by the court.

27 For a list of limitations, see Schwikkard and Van der Merwe 3 ed (2009) at 535–536.

28 In criminal cases, if the accused was present before testifying, the court is entitled to 'draw such inference from the accused's conduct as may be reasonable in the circumstances'. S 151(1)(*b*)(ii) of the Criminal Procedure Act, 1977.

29 This is referred to as the cautionary rule and it requires the court to be (a) consciously careful and (b) to seek some kind of safeguard when assessing evidence presented by witnesses from this category. This category traditionally includes witnesses who are suspected of deliberately giving false evidence. These include witnesses who may have a motive to lie, for example co-accused; identification evidence, which is notoriously unreliable; child witnesses, although the rule is no longer automatically applied; and single witnesses.

CHAPTER 6   ADMISSIBILITY AND WEIGHT OF EVIDENCE   59

6.3.2.3 Direct or circumstantial evidence

The nature of the evidence also influences its weight. It is important to determine whether the evidence is direct or circumstantial.[30]

Direct evidence is evidence given by witnesses who have made direct assertions with regard to a fact in dispute.[31] **Circumstantial evidence** is evidence where there are no direct assertions about a fact in dispute. Instead, evidence is presented about other facts from which a conclusion can be drawn. Thus, circumstantial evidence is evidence that requires a court to draw inferences or conclusions. It furnishes indirect proof.

Note that the fact that evidence may be circumstantial does not in any way render it less useful or reliable than direct evidence. In many instances, several pieces of circumstantial evidence may present a much more compelling case than an item of direct evidence. This is especially the case when we consider the cumulative effect of several pieces of circumstantial evidence. Individually, each piece may easily be dismissed, but, when considered together, they are irrefutable.[32]

However, when dealing with circumstantial evidence, the court is required to draw conclusions. Thus, clear rules regarding the drawing of inferences from circumstantial evidence have been developed. In respect of *criminal cases*, these rules were set out most clearly in *R v Blom* where they are referred to as the 'two cardinal rules of logic'[33] that cannot be ignored.

The *first rule* is that the inference we seek to draw must be consistent with all the proved facts. If the inference is not consistent with the facts, then it cannot be drawn.[34] Simply put, if a conclusion does not match all the proved facts, the conclusion must be rejected.

The *second rule* is linked to the standard of proof in criminal cases, that is, proof beyond reasonable doubt. It states that the proved facts must exclude every reasonable inference except the inference we seek to draw.[35] The logic here is obvious – if there is another reasonable inference that we can draw from the facts, then reasonable doubt exists as to the correctness of the first inference. This rule is often, but not without some debate,[36] expressed as requiring the inference to be the only reasonable inference.

In *civil cases*, the first rule in *R v Blom* applies as it is an inherently logical rule applicable in all circumstances. However, the second rule does not apply as the standard of proof in civil cases is based on a balance of probabilities. This an express recognition that, in civil matters, the court is charged with choosing the *most* probable, not the *only* probable, explanation as there are often competing inferences arising out of the same facts.[37]

THIS CHAPTER IN ESSENCE

1   The concepts of admissibility and weight are closely related and, at times, overlap.

2   Parties may only present evidence to the court if it complies with the rules regulating the admissibility of evidence. Parties must therefore first establish whether they are permitted to lead the evidence they were hoping to present.

---

30   See ch 44 Circumstantial evidence.

31   Schwikkard and Van der Merwe 3 ed (2009) at 21.

32   *R v De Villiers* 1944 AD 493 at 509.

33   1939 AD 188 at 202–203.

34   'The inference sought to be drawn must be consistent with all the proved facts. If it is not, then the inference cannot be drawn.' *R v Blom* 1939 AD 188 at 202–203.

35   'The proved facts should be such that they exclude every reasonable inference from them save the one sought to be drawn.' *R v Blom* 1939 AD 188 at 202–203.

36   See DT Zeffertt and AP Paizes *The South African Law of Evidence* 2 ed (2009) at 101.

37   *Katz and Another v Katz and Others* [2004] 4 All SA 545 (C) at 95 and *AA Onderlinge Assuransie-Assosiasie Bpk v De Beer* 1982 (2) SA 603 (A). See also the discussion in ch 34 Circumstantial evidence.

3 Once evidence is regarded as *admissible*, the party can present it in court where the opposing party, and to a lesser extent the court, will test and examine it. Afterwards, the court will determine how much *weight* to give to the evidence.

4 Evidence is admissible if it is relevant to an issue in the proceedings. Irrelevant evidence is, therefore, inadmissible.

5 Evidence is considered relevant if it might help to prove (or disprove) the probable existence (or non-existence) of a fact in issue. The presiding officer is solely responsible for deciding whether a piece of evidence will assist the court. In doing so, the presiding officer will take into account the following factors or guidelines:

5.1 the exact issues in dispute between the parties

5.2 collateral issues which do not add value to the resolution of the issues in dispute or would result in a waste of time or resources

5.3 the potential weight of the evidence, in other words, whether the evidence is of sufficient quality or relevance to enable a court to draw inferences from it

5.4 the fact that certain types of evidence are easy to manufacture and would therefore undermine their usefulness to the court

5.5 the possibility that a party to proceedings will suffer a procedural disadvantage if certain evidence is admitted

5.6 previous judgments, although they can never be a determinant of weight as it is rare that two cases will be exactly the same

5.7 irrelevant evidence may be admitted if it is bound up with relevant facts or facts in issue.

6 Relevant evidence is, however, inadmissible if its use is precluded by another law.

7 Whenever the admissibility of evidence is placed in dispute during proceedings, the proceedings are suspended and a trial-within-a-trial is held to determine the admissibility of the evidence.

8 Although there is no exhaustive analysis of the process courts follow to determine the weight to give to evidence, the courts should be guided by the following two fundamental principles:

8.1 Evidence must be weighed as a whole and not on a piece-by-piece basis.

8.2 The court must first establish which facts it finds are proved before drawing inferences rather than relying on speculation.

9 Also, in determining the weight to be attached to the evidence, the court will apply coherent, logical thought to an objective analysis of the evidence, will be guided by experience and will refer to the following factors:

9.1 whether there is independent corroboration of an aspect of the evidence presented which is of significant importance

9.2 whether the evidence came from a credible source

9.3 whether the evidence is direct (direct assertions with regard to a fact in dispute) or circumstantial (evidence about other facts that are not in dispute). If the evidence is circumstantial, the court decides what inferences to draw from it.

Chapter 7

Evidence and proof

7.1	**Introduction**	**61**
7.2	**The pursuit of truth**	**62**
7.3	**Evidence and proof**	**63**
7.4	**Burden of proof**	**63**
	7.4.1 General principles applicable to criminal and civil cases	64
	7.4.2 Criminal cases	64
	7.4.3 Civil cases	65
7.5	**Evidentiary burden**	**65**
	7.5.1 Criminal cases	66
	7.5.2 Civil cases	67
7.6	**Duty to begin**	**67**
	7.6.1 High Court Rule 39 and Magistrates' Courts Rule 29	67

7.1 Introduction

Before discussing the notion of proof, we first need to look at the purpose of leading evidence – what are we trying to achieve? Twining describes the overall objective as '[t]he pursuit of truth as a *means* to justice under the [common] law'.[1] More specifically, through the mechanism of the courts, we are simply trying to win our case. However, to succeed in a hearing, we need to prove certain facts. The facts that we have to prove to win our case are considered to be the essential elements of our case and are called the *facta probanda* (singular: *factum probandum*). The various pieces of information we present to court in the form of evidence to prove the *facta probanda* are called the *facta probantia* (singular: *factum probans*). In other words, the *facta probantia* are the facts we rely on to convince the court of our argument. The distinction between *facta probanda* and *facta probantia* is important. The *facta probanda* are **substantive** in nature or origin while the *facta probantia* are regulated by **procedural law**.[2]

---

1 W Twining *Theories of Evidence: Bentham and Wigmore* (1985) at 16.
2 See *King's Transport v Viljoen* 1954 (1) SA 133 (C).

7.2 The pursuit of truth

Truth verification by way of testing evidence in trial[3] is the best method currently available. As the reliability of scientific truth verification technology[4] is established and eventually accepted in the notoriously slow and conservative legal environment, judges and other presiding officers may place less and less reliance on the assessment of evidence.[5] This will lead to more certain truth verification and fewer errors.

The current methodology used in trials to try to establish the truth is relatively flawed. The court, usually long after the event, hears and considers evidence presented by the parties to the dispute. It then has to make a reconstructive finding about what happened based on the evidence presented to it. This finding – in effect, the court's finding of what *probably* happened – is called the **formal truth**. Depending on the quality of the evidence, and sometimes the quality of the legal representation as well, this formal truth may be far removed from what actually happened – also called the **material truth**.

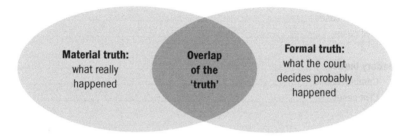

Figure 7.1 Formal versus material truth

As no more reliable truth verification method is available, the formal truth is then deemed to be the truth for the purposes of the justice system, whether erroneous or not.[6] Such assessment errors could have devastating consequences, especially in criminal cases and the execution of innocent people in death penalty cases.[7]

DISCUSSION 7.1	The formal versus the material truth
	The material truth is what *really* happened. The formal truth is what the court *decides probably* happened after conducting a hearing or a trial. Figure 7.1 indicates that there may be a large overlap between the material truth and the formal truth. However, a court's reconstruction of what happened, based on fallible evidence, will seldom *exactly* reflect the material truth. Sometimes, the court's decision may be completely wrong and the circles do not overlap at all. The problem is that once the court has made its finding on the evidence, the formal truth is *deemed* to be the truth for all purposes. In cases of error, a party's only hope then is a successful appeal.

---

3   Whether by way of adversarial or inquisitorial procedures.
4   See Part Seven: Scientific forensic evidence. See, in general, RH Underwood 'Truth verifiers: From the hot iron to the lie detector' (1995–6) 84(3) *Kentucky Law Journal* 597.
5   See ch 6 Admissibility and weight of evidence.
6   The appeal process provides some safeguard as does the requirement to prove criminal cases beyond a reasonable doubt, but these safeguards are not foolproof.
7   See Innocence Project at: www.innocenceproject.org.

7.3 Evidence and proof

Once we understand the need to establish particular facts in a trial, then it follows that the information we present to court to establish these facts can generally be termed 'evidence'. We sometimes also refer to it as 'probative material', a term describing everything presented to court. Although probative material is a broader term than evidence, the term includes both evidence and other forms of information. Evidence is thus a sub-set of probative material.

We usually present evidence (or probative material to use the broader term) to court through witnesses, documents, real objects, oral testimony, photographs, audio tapes or files and a number of other ways. At this stage, the evidence is merely information that we have presented to court. Once the court has heard all the evidence from all the parties, it will weigh it up and assess it. If the court decides that a particular fact is the truth, in other words, that the fact has been proved, it means that the evidence presented was good enough to convince the court. We can now say that the evidence is, or has become, **proof**. In other words, once evidence has been admitted and assessed, and has been relied on to establish a *factum probans*, it can be called proof. Therefore, no attorney or client can ever claim to have proof of something – they merely have evidence of it. Only the court can turn evidence into proof.

7.4 Burden of proof

Thus the word 'proof' in the term 'burden of proof' relates to the concept of presenting evidence that the court can rely on. However, we often use the term 'burden of proof' to refer to two distinct concepts.

The first is the question of which party has to prove their case in order to win. In other words, on whom does the burden of proving his or her case rest? Strictly speaking, this is the correct use of the term[8] and we will focus on this use in this chapter. It is sometimes referred to as the **onus of proof** and can be defined as 'the obligation to persuade the court, by the end of the trial, of the truth of certain allegations'. Alternatively, as specified by precedent, the burden of proof is 'the duty which is cast upon the particular litigant, in order to be successful, of finally satisfying the court that he is entitled to succeed on his claim or defence'.[9]

The second is the question: what is the standard of proof required in a particular case? We will refer to this as the standard of proof to distinguish it from the first usage of the term 'burden of proof'. We may also refer to the standard of proof as the quantum of proof. The standard of proof does not have any impact on the burden of proof – it merely determines the lengths to which we must go to persuade the court.

In any court case there is an applicable standard or level of proof that we must achieve. This differs between criminal and civil cases. In civil cases, we must prove our case on *a balance of probabilities*. In criminal cases, the State must prove its case *beyond reasonable doubt*. The civil standard is essentially comparative in nature. The side bearing the onus (in the first sense of the term) must persuade the court that their case is more probable than that of their opponent. There is no absolute test because the question of whether they have discharged this onus will often depend on the relative strength of their opponent's case.

---

8 The 'true and original sense'. *Pillay v Krishna and Another* 1946 AD 946 at 952.
9 *South Cape Corporation (Pty) Ltd v Engineering Management Services (Pty) Ltd* 1977 (3) SA 534 (A) at 548.

THE LAW OF EVIDENCE IN SOUTH AFRICA

In criminal cases, however, the test is absolute as the State must prove its case beyond reasonable doubt and this assessment is made on the strength of the State's case. The defence may, and often does, raise a reasonable doubt, which would result in the State being unsuccessful. This is not the same as a court weighing up the relative merits of two competing arguments as it does in civil cases.

There are several general principles when deciding who has to prove their case. There are, however, also some additional principles that are specifically applicable to criminal or civil cases. As a result, the party on whom the burden rests may differ between criminal and civil cases.

7.4.1 General principles applicable to criminal and civil cases

We sometimes refer to the burden of proof as the 'risk of non-persuasion'[10] – if we do not persuade the court of the merits of our case, we run the risk of losing it. The burden of proof is determined at the beginning of a case and remains on the same party throughout the proceedings. In other words, the burden of proof does not shift between the parties during the trial depending on the circumstances of the case. It is fixed at the outset and remains fixed throughout the trial.[11]

We may determine the burden of proof in a number of ways. Zeffertt and Paizes argue that the incidence (on whom the burden rests) is a matter of substantive law in the sense that substantive law defines what must be proved and, in so doing, also determines who must prove it.[12] There are, however, general principles underlying these substantive law rules that are useful in helping to decide where the onus lies and also in understanding why the onus rests on a particular party. Policy (societal) or procedural considerations are therefore instrumental in locating the incidence of the onus of proof.

7.4.2 Criminal cases

The incidence of the onus of proof in criminal cases is an example of policy (societal) considerations at work. A direct consequence of the presumption of innocence – that all are presumed innocent until proven guilty – is that if a person is accused of a crime, the State has the burden of proving it. This is the position at common law where the presumption of innocence is a cornerstone of the Anglo-American **adversarial system** and is also constitutionally endorsed in the Bill of Rights.[13]

This means that the State must prove every element that is in dispute relating to the crime of which a person is accused. This includes:

- the **actus reus** or the action or conduct which is a constituent element of a crime
- the **mens rea** or the mental state of the accused
- the identity of the accused
- the unlawfulness of the act
- the absence of any defence[14] raised by the accused.

---

10   JH Wigmore *Wigmore on Evidence* 3 ed (1940) at para 2485.

11   'The onus can never shift from the party upon whom it originally rested.' *South Cape Corporation (Pty) Ltd v Engineering Management Services (Pty) Ltd* 1977 (3) SA 534 (A) at 548. This fixed onus in both civil and criminal matters is sometimes called the **primary onus of proof**.

12   Zeffertt and Paizes 2 ed (2009) at 45–46.

13   S 35(3)(*h*) of the Constitution.

14   The accused has a common law responsibility to introduce his or her defence, either at the pleading stage, for example in a statement made in explanation of a plea, or during cross-examination of the state witnesses to enable the State to focus only on the defence raised by the accused and to save the State from proving the absence of all defences. Statute, s 107 of the Criminal Procedure Act 51 of 1977, requires this in criminal defamation cases.

CHAPTER 7 EVIDENCE AND PROOF | 65

In practice, the State does not always have to do this as the accused may formally admit many of these elements, thus limiting the issues that the State needs physically to prove. Although the onus remains on the State in respect of these admitted issues, the accused's admission is regarded as amounting to sufficient proof of the issue admitted.[15]

There are, however, exceptions to the above, the most common of which is the issue of mental incapacity. In terms of the common law, everyone is presumed to be of sound mind. This has been codified by statute: 'Every person is presumed not to suffer from a mental illness or intellectual disability so as not to be criminally responsible.'[16] This means that the State does not need to prove that the accused was sane at the time of the **offence**. Instead, the onus is on the accused, who alleges that he or she was not of sound mind, to prove such an allegation on a balance of probabilities.[17]

7.4.3 Civil cases

As mentioned above, in civil cases the area of substantive law within which we are litigating usually determines the incidence of the onus. For example, in a **delict** case, the laws of delict – as interpreted by case law and established in the body of precedent – determine who bears the onus of proving the essential elements of **negligence**, causation, wrongfulness and so on. If, however, this is not the case, then we apply the general, fundamental principle that 'he who asserts, must prove'. In other words, 'the onus is on the person who alleges something'.[18] Thus, in any particular civil matter where either side makes several allegations with regard to an element or elements, it may well occur that the onus of proof in respect of each item falls on a different party. For example, the plaintiff will bear the onus in respect of the issues or elements alleged in the pleadings, but the **defendant** may bear the onus in respect of a special defence that he or she has raised.[19]

7.5 Evidentiary burden

The evidentiary burden differs from the burden of proof. We can best define it as the duty or burden that rests on a party at any particular point in a trial to lead enough evidence to force the other side to respond. In other words, we must lead enough evidence to make out a case that is sufficiently strong to create the risk for our opponent that, if they do nothing, they could lose. This has been phrased in several ways in case law, the most succinct being that of Corbett JA who defined the evidentiary burden as 'the duty cast upon a litigant to adduce evidence in order to combat a ***prima facie* case** made by his opponent'.[20]

We can establish a number of important features of the evidentiary burden from this definition:

* First, it is a concept that is entirely procedural in nature. It exists purely to regulate the order of the presentation of evidence in trials and has no basis in substantive law.
* Second, it is clear that the evidentiary burden can rest on either side in a trial. For example, the evidentiary burden can rest on the plaintiff to lead enough evidence to force the other party to respond. It can also rest on the defendant to lead enough evidence to

---

15 Zeffertt and Paizes 2 ed (2009) at 45.
16 S 78(1A) of the Criminal Procedure Act, 1977.
17 S 78(1B) of the Criminal Procedure Act, 1977 states that 'the burden of proof with reference to the criminal responsibility of the accused shall be on the party who raises the issue'.
18 *Pillay v Krishna and Another* 1946 AD 946 at 951–952, quoting with approval, Voet, and locating the source of the principle in the *Corpus Juris Civilis* at D 22.3.21 and D 4.1.1.
19 For a critique of this approach, see Zeffertt and Paizes 2 ed (2009) at 57–60.
20 *South Cape Corporation (Pty) Ltd v Engineering Management Services (Pty) Ltd* 1977 (3) SA 534 (A) at 548A.

66 THE LAW OF EVIDENCE IN SOUTH AFRICA

rebut the plaintiff's *prima facie* case (*prima facie* evidence will be discussed in detail in chapter 8).

- Third, we often refer to the evidentiary burden in the context of establishing a *prima facie* case and we must thus remain mindful of the meaning of this concept.
- Finally, it raises the following questions: who does the evidentiary burden rest on first and when does it shift?

At the outset, the evidentiary burden usually rests on the party seeking to establish their case. This means that initially it is often aligned with the onus of proof although it may be altered by admissions. If this occurs, or if the burden has been discharged by the presentation of sufficient evidence, then the evidentiary burden passes to the other party as they are now the party at risk of losing if they do nothing. The other party now bears the burden to produce enough evidence to rebut the case established against them. Thus, the evidentiary burden will move to and fro between the parties depending on the circumstances of the case.

7.5.1 Criminal cases

In most cases the evidentiary burden initially rests on the State. This because, as with the burden of proof, the presumption of innocence places the overall onus of establishing guilt on the State. The State must also produce enough evidence to build a *prima facie* case against the accused. This means that it must lead enough evidence to build a case, which, on the face of it, looks solid. If the State does this, the evidentiary burden will then shift to the accused who runs the risk of being convicted if he or she does nothing. If the accused feels that the State has not discharged its evidentiary burden, that is, it has not established a case that compels a response, the accused may apply for a discharge in terms of section 174 of the Criminal Procedure Act, 1977.[21] This is one of the few occasions when the court is called on to adjudicate whether the evidentiary burden has been discharged. The court will do so by applying the test whether there is 'evidence on which a reasonable man might convict?'[22] If not, the accused will be discharged.[23]

If there is more than one accused, however, and there are reasonable grounds for concluding that a co-accused may incriminate the accused, the court retains a discretion. In *S v Nkosi and Another*[24] the Supreme Court of Appeal held that where there are co-accused, there must be reasonable grounds for concluding that the co-accused might implicate the accused who has applied for a discharge. When an application for a discharge in terms of section 174 of the Criminal Procedure Act, 1977 is considered, the credibility of witnesses should not play a part in the court's assessment. The credibility of witnesses is to be provisionally assumed, unless the witness is found to be so unreliable that his or her evidence must be left out of consideration.[25]

---

21 S 174 of the Criminal Procedure Act, 1977. 'If ... the court is of the opinion that there is no evidence that the accused committed the offence referred to in the charge or any offence of which he may be convicted on the charge, it may return a verdict of not guilty.'

22 *S v Shuping and Others* 1983 (2) SA 119 (B) at 120 and *S v Lubaxa* 2001 (4) SA 1251 (SCA).

23 In the past, the test was twofold. The second part was that if there was a possibility that if the accused gave evidence, it would supplement the State's case, then the application for discharge would be refused. This is no longer sustainable in terms of the Constitution. See *S v Mathebula and Another* 1997 (1) SACR 10 (W), *S v Jama and Another* 1998 (2) SACR 237 (N) and *S v Lubaxa* 2001 (4) SA 1251 (SCA).

24 2011 (2) SACR 482 (SCA).

25 *S v Agliotti* 2011 (2) SACR 437 (GSJ).

7.5.2 Civil cases

In civil matters substantive law determines the onus of proof as well as the 'he who alleges must prove' principle. The pleadings therefore usually determine the evidentiary burden. This means that the plaintiff typically bears the evidentiary burden unless there are sufficient admissions made in the pleadings for the burden to have shifted to the defendant.[26] Once the plaintiff has produced enough evidence to build a *prima facie* case against the defendant, the evidentiary burden will shift to the defendant who runs the risk of losing his or her case if he or she does nothing. If the defendant feels that the plaintiff has not discharged his or her evidentiary burden, the defendant may apply for absolution from the instance. The test applied is 'whether there is evidence upon which a court, applying its mind reasonably to such evidence, could or might (not should, nor ought to) find for the plaintiff.'[27]

7.6 Duty to begin

In criminal cases, the **duty to begin** always rests on the State. In civil cases, however, the situation is slightly more complex. The rules of court determine who has the right or bears the obligation to commence leading evidence at trial.

7.6.1 High Court Rule 39 and Magistrates' Courts Rule 29

The duty to begin tends to follow the burden of proof. High Court Rule 39(5) states:

> **Where the burden of proof is on the plaintiff he ... may briefly outline the facts intended to be proved and the plaintiff may then proceed to the proof thereof.**

High Court Rule 39(9) provides that if the burden of proof is on the defendant, then the defendant has the same rights as the plaintiff in terms of Rule 39(5). If neither party is satisfied with this, then, in terms of Rule 39(11), either party may apply to court for a ruling on the onus of adducing evidence.[28]

High Court Rule 39(13) deals with situations in which there is an evidentiary burden on both parties in respect of different issues. In this case, the plaintiff commences with regard to those issues where the burden rests on him or her and the defendant will follow. Of course, the pleadings will determine precisely which issues are in dispute and on whom the evidentiary burden rests. Therefore, the rules, together with the topography of the case as defined by the pleadings, will determine who will start.

Although the wording in the Magistrates' Courts Rule[29] differs from the High Court Rule,[30] the principles are essentially the same.

THIS CHAPTER IN ESSENCE

1. To succeed in a hearing, we have to prove the essential elements of the case (*facta probanda*) by presenting certain information to the court (*facta probantia*).

---

26 *HA Millard and Son (Pty) Ltd v Enzenhofer* 1968 (1) SA 330 (T).

27 *Claude Neon Lights SA (Ltd) v Daniel* 1976 (4) SA 403 (A) at 409 G–H.

28 Also see S Peté, D Hulme, M du Plessis, R Palmer O Sibanda and T Palmer *Civil Procedure: A Practical Guide* 3 ed (2017) at 299.

29 Specifically Rules 29(7), (8), (9) and (10).

30 The Magistrates' Courts Rule refers to 'burden of proof' whereas the High Court Rule refers to 'onus of adducing evidence'. In *HA Millard and Son (Pty) Ltd v Enzenhofer* 1968 (1) SA 330 (T), the Court interpreted the phrase 'burden of proof' in this context to mean the 'duty to adduce evidence'.

2 Probative material refers to all the evidence presented to the court. This evidence will only be considered to be proof once it has been admitted, assessed and relied on to establish a *factum probans*.

3 The question of who has the burden of proving his or her case, called the burden of proof, is determined at the beginning of each trial. The burden of proof does not shift between the parties during the trial. In criminal cases, the State has the burden of proving each and every element of the crime and must do so beyond reasonable doubt. In civil cases, the burden of proof rests generally on the person who alleges something although it may be determined by the area of substantive law applicable to a particular case. Furthermore, the party who has the burden of proof in a civil case must prove his or her case on a balance of probabilities.

4 The evidentiary burden differs from the burden of proof. Evidentiary burden refers to the burden that rests on a party to lead enough evidence to force his or her opponent to respond. The evidentiary burden usually rests on the party seeking to establish the case, but may shift between the parties during trial.

5 In a criminal matter, the evidentiary burden initially rests on the State which must produce enough evidence to build a *prima facie* case against the accused. Once the State has established a *prima facie* case, the evidentiary burden will shift to the accused who runs the risk of being convicted if he or she does nothing. However, if the accused feels that the State has not established a case that compels a response, he or she may apply for a discharge in terms of section 174 of the Criminal Procedure Act, 1977.

6 In a civil matter, the question of who bears the evidentiary burden depends largely on who bears the onus of proof and is usually determined by the pleadings. The evidentiary burden usually rests on the plaintiff. Once the plaintiff has established a *prima facie* case, the burden then shifts to the defendant. If the defendant feels that the plaintiff has failed to discharge the evidentiary burden, he or she may apply for absolution from the instance.

7 In criminal matters, the State has the duty to lead evidence first. In civil matters, the duty to begin can rest on either the plaintiff or the defendant, or they may apply to court for a ruling on who may commence.

Chapter 8

Prima facie, conclusive and sufficient proof

8.1	**Introduction**	**69**
8.2	***Prima facie* proof**	**69**
	8.2.1 *Prima facie*: the term	69
	8.2.2 A *prima facie* case	70
	8.2.3 *Prima facie* proof	71
	8.2.4 Frequently occurring examples of *prima facie* evidence	71
8.3	**Conclusive proof**	**72**
8.4	**Sufficient proof**	**72**

8.1 Introduction

We have now seen:
- first, that there is a technical difference between the words 'evidence' and 'proof'
- second, precisely what that difference is
- third, what both words mean.

However, there are still more commonly used phrases that use the word 'proof'. We need to know the meaning of these phrases to understand what we are aiming at in any particular scenario in which evidence is led. The most common of these phrases are *prima facie* proof, **conclusive proof** and sufficient proof.

8.2 *Prima facie* proof

We will discuss the concept of *prima facie* in detail below.

8.2.1 *Prima facie*: the term

Before we can discuss the concept of *prima facie* proof, we must first understand the often-used term '*prima facie*'. Holmes JA has used the term to describe the following situation in a criminal case: if the State has led *prima facie* evidence implicating an accused and if the accused fails to take action to contradict this evidence, then 'his failure to give evidence, whatever his reason may be for such failure, in general *ipso facto* tends to strengthen the State case, because there is then nothing to gainsay it and therefore less

70 | THE LAW OF EVIDENCE IN SOUTH AFRICA

reason for doubting its credibility or reliability'.[1] This, of course, is more an example than a definition. Therefore, drawing from this example, we can formulate a definition as follows: *prima facie* in this context means superficially compelling with the potential to become conclusive, but still subject to the possibility of being challenged. Schwikkard and Van der Merwe describe it thus: '*prima facie* proof implies that proof to the contrary is [still] possible'.[2]

8.2.2 A *prima facie* case

Therefore, the term 'a ***prima facie case***' means a case where, on the face of it, there seems to be enough evidence to find for the plaintiff in civil cases or to find for the State, that is, to convict the accused, in criminal cases. In other words, a particular party presents enough evidence on every essential element to allow the court to find in that party's favour if the other side does nothing about it. Thus, establishing a *prima facie* case places the other side under pressure to respond. The other side may do this in a number of ways, including, in certain instances, making the tactical choice of not responding at all. Generally speaking, if the other side fails to respond or does so inadequately, a *prima facie* case will become a conclusive one.

Thus, when referring to establishing a *prima facie* case, the term implies that there is an obligation on a litigant – the plaintiff in civil cases or the State in criminal cases – to build a *prima facie* case. The plaintiff, or the State, must therefore present sufficient evidence to establish a case against the defendant, or the accused, that will require a response. In other words, a *prima facie* case is one which will not result in absolution from the instance being granted at the end of the plaintiff's case in civil cases, or the accused being discharged at the end of the State's case in criminal cases.

We can say that the plaintiff in civil cases or the State in criminal cases has discharged their evidentiary burden in establishing a *prima facie* case. By leading enough evidence to discharge the evidentiary burden, a party has, in fact, built a *prima facie* case.

Arguably though, according to Zeffertt and Paizes,[3] and it is a fine distinction, describing a *prima facie* case as discharging, and thus shifting, the evidentiary burden may be an over-simplification. The learned authors argue that a simple *prima facie* case merely places a tactical burden on the other side to respond. They maintain that there are instances where the *prima facie* case created is sufficiently compelling, due to the nature of the case, the evidence led or admissions made, to require the other side to lead evidence. If the other side fails to do so, they will face conviction. This places an evidentiary, not merely a tactical, burden on the other side to lead evidence.

The most important point to note with regard to a *prima facie* case is that there is still an opportunity to contradict it or to challenge it. It is not a case that has already been decided, although, admittedly, there is a hint as to which way it may go. If there is no response, that is, if the other side fails to answer the *prima facie* case, then, and only then, will the court decide the matter. For example, the other side may make a tactical decision not to respond or does not discharge the evidentiary burden that was shifted onto them. Most often, but not always, in such a situation, the *prima facie* case will become final. We then say it has hardened into a conclusive case.

---

1 *S v Mthetwa* 1972 (3) SA 766 (A) at 769.
2 PJ Schwikkard and SE van der Merwe *Principles of Evidence* 3 ed (2009) at 20.
3 Zeffertt and Paizes 2 ed (2009) at 130–132.

8.2.3 *Prima facie* proof

Following on from this, ***prima facie* proof** is proof which we use to establish a *prima facie* case, but which can still be challenged or contradicted. If such *prima facie* proof remains unchallenged or uncontradicted, then it will, in all likelihood, become conclusive proof.

The words '*prima facie* evidence' are often also used in this context, particularly by the legislature. Although there is technically a subtle distinction between *prima facie* proof and *prima facie* evidence, they tend to be used interchangeably. Stratford JA, in an often-quoted passage, states:

> *Prima facie* evidence in its usual sense is used to mean *prima facie* proof of an issue, the burden of proving which is upon the party giving that evidence. In the absence of further evidence from the other side, the *prima facie* proof becomes conclusive proof and the party giving it discharges his onus.[4]

***Prima facie* evidence** is thus evidence that looks compelling, invites a response and, in the absence of such response, will probably be found by the court to constitute proof.

8.2.4 Frequently occurring examples of *prima facie* evidence

In practice, there are instances where particular scenarios occur often. Eliot describes these instances as 'frequently recurring examples of circumstantial evidence.'[5] These examples have resulted over time in the formulation of certain rules that allow courts to make certain presumptions. We often refer to these examples as **presumptions of fact**. However, Wigmore emphatically states, '... the term "presumption of fact" should be discarded as [worthless] and confusing.'[6] In fact, presumptions of fact are restatements of the substantive law phrased in such a way as to allow courts to take a shortcut to a *prima facie* conclusion. The court is entitled, on proof of a fact, to presume, infer or conclude that another fact exists. The so-called presumptions can be regarded as examples of *prima facie* evidence that allow the court to assume something until such time as it may be rebutted. Obviously, this will have an impact on the evidentiary burden. If the court accepts a piece of evidence or a fact as *prima facie* evidence of a state of affairs, there is going to be pressure on the other side to respond to this *prima facie* conclusion.

The precise impact on the other side will depend on the strength of the presumption. It may be informal. In this case, the more accurate term 'permissive inference'[7] better encapsulates the notion that the court, on proof of a fact, may draw an inference but is not compelled to do so. The effect of this is to place a tactical burden on the other party to present evidence to contradict this inference.

If the presumption is more strongly stated, then the court is obliged to draw the relevant conclusion. An example of stating the presumption more strongly is legislation that states that 'in the absence of evidence to the contrary, the court must ...' or '... constitutes *prima facie* evidence/proof of ...'. In effect, this means that the legislation has created a mechanism whereby proof of a fact will result in a *prima facie* case being established and the evidentiary burden is consequently shifted to the other party, who now must lead evidence in rebuttal.

---

4 *Ex parte Minister of Justice: In re R v Jacobson and Levy* 1931 AD 466 at 478. See also *Trust Bank of Africa Ltd v Senekal* 1977 2 SA 587(W) at 592H where Nestadt J held: 'There is I consider, no material difference in the present context between "*prima facie* evidence" and "*prima facie* proof".

5 DW Elliott *Elliott and Phipson Manual of the Law of Evidence* 12 ed (1987) at 89.

6 JH Wigmore *Wigmore on Evidence* 3 ed, Vol 9 (1940) at para 2491, p. 289.

7 *R v Downey* 1992 (13) Cr 4th 129 (SCC) at 138.

72 THE LAW OF EVIDENCE IN SOUTH AFRICA

Some examples of *prima facie* evidence are the following:

- *Possession of recently stolen goods*: If we prove that someone is in possession of recently stolen property, we may infer that he or she is the person who stole it or that he or she received the property knowing that it had been stolen.
- *Paternity of children born out of wedlock*: Section 36 of the Children's Act 38 of 2005 states, 'If ... it is proved that [a] person had intercourse with the mother of the child at any time when that child could have been conceived, that person is, in the absence of evidence to the contrary which raises a reasonable doubt, presumed to be the biological father of the child.' Therefore, proof of intercourse at the relevant time is *prima facie* evidence, or proof, of fatherhood. It clearly establishes a *prima facie* case and shifts the evidentiary burden onto the man.
- *Defects in recently purchased goods*: If a defect is found in a recently purchased item, the court is entitled to infer that it was defective at the time of the sale and that the seller is liable for the latent defect.
- *Driving a vehicle and being employed to do so*: If the driver of a vehicle is not the owner, the court is entitled to infer that he or she was driving within the course and scope of the authorisation given by the owner.

8.3 Conclusive proof

If the court has assessed, analysed and evaluated the evidence presented to it and has found that the evidence proves a fact, we can say that the evidence is proof of that fact. In other words, the fact has been proved by the evidence.

Conclusive proof is simply evidence which has become proof and which can no longer be contradicted. The opportunity for contradicting or challenging the evidence has come and gone without it being challenged. Alternatively, the evidence has been challenged, but the court has nonetheless found it to be true or the court has found the fact to be proved and it can no longer be contradicted. As seen in the discussion of *prima facie* proof above, generally *prima facie* cases become conclusive when uncontradicted. Conclusive proof means that rebuttal is no longer possible.[8]

8.4 Sufficient proof

The term 'sufficient proof' is of specific relevance to criminal proceedings and is to be found in section 220 of the Criminal Procedure Act 51 of 1977. This section regulates the making of formal admissions, something for which the common law does not make provision. Section 220 states that any formal admission made by the defence of any fact in issue in a criminal matter 'shall be sufficient proof of such fact'. Formal admissions are intended to dispense with the need to prove the fact or issue admitted.[9] However, the term 'sufficient', not 'conclusive', is used. We therefore cannot interpret this term to mean that formal admissions are conclusive and cannot be rebutted.[10] Consequently, there is a debate about the status of a fact formally admitted.[11] It has been argued that this absolves the State of the need to prove such a fact,[12] which is correct.

---

8 Schwikkard and Van der Merwe 3 ed (2009) at 20. *S v Moroney* 1978 (4) SA 389 (A).
9 *R v Fouche* 1958 (3) SA 767 (T).
10 *S v Mjoli and Another* 1981 (3) SA 1233 (A) at 1247A–B.
11 Some commentators are of the opinion that although s 220 of the Criminal Procedure Act, 1977 refers to 'sufficient proof', 'conclusive proof' was intended. See A Kruger Hiemstra's *Criminal Procedure* (2008) at 24–73.
12 *S v Seleke en 'n Ander* 1980 (3) SA 745 (A) at 746A–B.

CHAPTER 8 *PRIMA FACIE*, CONCLUSIVE AND SUFFICIENT PROOF | **73**

However, sufficient proof does not mean conclusive proof as the fact is still open to rebuttal by the accused during the course of the trial. In other words, the accused may, at some point during the trial, lead evidence that contradicts the formal admission made. Of course, if the accused does not do this and the formal admission remains uncontradicted, then sufficient proof will become conclusive proof.[13]

THIS CHAPTER IN ESSENCE

1   A *prima facie* case is one where a party has provided enough evidence on every essential element of the case so that the court can find in favour of either the plaintiff in civil cases or the State in criminal cases.
2   The plaintiff in civil cases or the State in criminal cases has discharged their evidentiary burden once they have established a *prima facie* case against the defendant in civil cases or the accused in criminal cases. The defendant or accused can, however, still contradict or challenge a *prima facie* case. If the defendant or accused does not respond to the *prima facie* case, it will become a conclusive case. This means that it can no longer be challenged or contradicted, and the court can make a decision on the matter.
3   We use *prima facie* proof to establish a *prima facie* case. Like a *prima facie* case, the other side can still challenge or contradict this evidence. If they do not challenge or contradict the *prima facie* proof, it becomes conclusive proof and can no longer be challenged or contradicted.
4   The most frequently occurring examples of *prima facie* evidence are presumptions of fact. These presumptions allow the court to assume something until it has been rebutted.
5   Conclusive proof is evidence which has become proof and which can no longer be contradicted.
6   Formal admissions made by the accused in terms of section 220 of the Criminal Procedure Act, 1977 are considered to be sufficient proof, possibly conclusive proof, of a particular fact. However, the accused can still challenge or contradict formal admissions. If the accused does not challenge or contradict the formal admissions, the sufficient proof will become conclusive proof.

---

13   If a party wishes to withdraw a formal admission, it must do so by means of an application to court. It cannot be left to the court to infer that the admission has been withdrawn by virtue of the fact that contradictory evidence has been led. *S v Seleke en 'n Ander* 1980 (3) SA 745 (A).

Chapter 9

Evidence: substantive or procedural law?

9.1 Introduction **74**

9.2 The importance of distinguishing between substantive and procedural law **74**

9.3 Problem areas **75**
    9.3.1 Burden of proof 75
    9.3.2 Irrebuttable presumptions 76
    9.3.3 Estoppel 76
    9.3.4 Parol evidence rule 77

9.1 Introduction

By way of a general overview, we can divide the law into several areas. One of these areas is substantive law, which generally contains a person's rights, duties, obligations and entitlements. A second area is procedural law, which is the area of law that regulates how we go about enforcing our rights and performing our duties. There are other areas of the law. For example, jurisprudence is concerned with a number of areas of study but primarily deals with the philosophical theories underlying the need for a system of laws, or justifications or criticisms thereof. Jurisprudence often includes the study of the historical and sociological aspects of legal systems. However, when discussing the law of evidence, the focus is on the categories of substantive and procedural law. The law of evidence, although primarily procedural, does not always fit neatly into this category.

9.2 The importance of distinguishing between substantive and procedural law

The categorisation of the law into the areas of substantive and procedural law is largely an irrelevant process because in day-to-day practice the laws applicable to a particular situation are usually inherently determined by that situation. However, in South Africa our legal system has a mixed pedigree. South African common law is essentially and primarily Roman-Dutch and therefore our substantive law is Roman-Dutch in origin. South African court structures, however, are closely modelled on English judicial structures and principles. Thus, our procedural law tends to be English in origin. On the one hand, Roman-Dutch principles determine the issues we need to establish to succeed in a delictual dispute, a contractual dispute or a matter relating to the law of persons (substantive areas of law). On the other hand, a system of rules that is largely, and sometimes specifically and

CHAPTER 9   EVIDENCE: SUBSTANTIVE OR PROCEDURAL LAW?   **75**

expressly,[1] based on English law regulates which court to use (**jurisdiction**), what process to follow (procedure), what evidence is needed or permitted, and who must present the evidence.

It is therefore of vital importance to know which area of law we are dealing with as this will influence where we look for the answers to any issues or problems that may arise. It will also determine which system of rules will apply. Different consequences may result from the same set of facts depending on whether we apply English or **Roman-Dutch law** precedent. Most of these situations have already been subject to judicial scrutiny and adjudication, and a body of precedent exists which covers most instances. We shall see that not all of this is necessarily correct, resulting in a blurring of the borders between procedural and substantive law, especially with regard to the law of evidence.

9.3   Problem areas

As a result of the dichotomy of legal sources to refer to when seeking clarity on issues that are theoretically substantive or potentially procedural, there are several areas of law where the distinction has become blurred. We will briefly discuss a few of the more commonly occurring examples below.

9.3.1   Burden of proof

Perhaps the best example of the consequences of having to choose between English and Roman-Dutch law to resolve a legal issue is to be found in the case of *Tregea and Another v Godart and Another*.[2]

This case involved determining the validity of a will. The Court needed to decide whether the onus was on the plaintiff, who was challenging the validity of a will, to prove the will was invalid, or whether it was on the defendant, who was seeking to rely on the will, to prove it was valid. In Roman-Dutch law, the will was presumed valid and the onus rested on the person alleging invalidity to prove his or her claim. In English law, the person seeking to rely on a will needed to establish its validity. The question of where the onus lay became a choice between two systems. If the question of onus was a substantive issue, Roman-Dutch law was to be followed, whereas if it were a procedural issue, English law would prevail. Stratford CJ stated that 'substantive law lays down what has to be proved in any given issue and by whom, and the rules of evidence relate to the manner of its proof.'[3] Thus, the Court decided that determining 'by whom' a matter must be proved was a substantive issue and applied Roman-Dutch law.

According to this precedent, wills are presumed valid and the onus to prove their invalidity rests on the persons challenging them. However, the most important aspect of this precedent is not its impact on the law of succession. Rather, substantive law and not procedural law determines the means of establishing on whom the burden of proof in any particular matter rests. We can argue that this is incorrect as the burden of proof is not an element of any matter or claim, either civil or criminal, but relates purely to the procedural aspects of a dispute even though it may be influenced by, but not determined by, the issues in dispute.[4]

---

1   There are several statutory provisions, called residuary clauses, expressly providing that, if there is no South African law on a topic, we must seek the answers in English law or, to be more precise, the law in effect in South Africa on 30 May 1961, in other words English law. See ch 2 Brief history and sources of the South African law of evidence.

2   1939 AD 16.

3   *Tregea and Another v Godart and Another* 1939 AD 16 at 30.

4   PJ Schwikkard and SE van der Merwe *Principles of Evidence* 3 ed (2009) at 34.

9.3.2 Irrebuttable presumptions

As seen in chapter 8, presumptions of fact are actually statements of substantive law. Similar confusion has arisen around irrebuttable presumptions. **Irrebuttable presumptions** arise when proof of a certain fact carries a consequence that cannot or, more accurately, may not be disproved. In other words, once we have proved a certain fact, the court is obliged to reach a particular conclusion and no evidence is admissible to prove the contrary.

For example, in terms of the common law, once we have proved that the perpetrator of a crime, or of a delict or other civil wrong, is under the age of seven, that child is irrebuttably presumed *doli* and *culpa incapax* and therefore cannot be held criminally or civilly liable.[5] As with presumptions of fact, this is actually a rule of substantive law, not procedural law. However, confusion has arisen because the rule is often phrased as follows: 'No evidence may be led (or is admissible) to show that a **child** understood the consequences of his or her actions and formulated the intention to commit a crime.' The use of the words 'no evidence is admissible' results in the mistaken impression that this is an evidentiary rule and is thus part of procedural law. As O'Regan J remarked in *Scagell and Others v Attorney-General of the Western Cape and Others*, 'The legal character of an irrebuttable presumption is not that it is a rule of evidence, but that it is a rule of substantive law.'[6] Note, however, that with regard to criminal liability, the Child Justice Act 75 of 2008 has changed the common law position. The position now is that children under the age of 10 lack criminal **capacity**.[7]

9.3.3 Estoppel

The law of **estoppel** also falls into the category of substantive law masquerading as procedural law but with an additional twist. Estoppel, as applied in South Africa, has been adopted from English law. It provides that a person who has made a false representation to another party, which the other party has believed and which induced the other party to act to their detriment or prejudice, is prevented from denying the truth of their representation. In other words, this person is not allowed to prove the falseness of his or her representation. They are estopped from denying its veracity. This has often been described as a rule of evidence and phrased in the following way: 'No evidence is admissible to prove the falseness of the representation.' However, this is not the case at all. It is true that no evidence is admissible, not because the rule of estoppel prevents it (a procedural rule), but merely because it is irrelevant to proceedings as the rule of estoppel (a substantive rule) renders it thus.

Estoppel is, thus, an English law concept that is not part of our Roman-Dutch-based common law. It has, nevertheless, been adopted as part of the South African common law. However, it has been incorrectly regarded as being part of the procedural law of evidence because it is regulated by English law. In other words, estoppel is a substantive rule, which means it should be Roman-Dutch in origin. However, as discussed, we know it is English in origin. For this reason, many believe it is procedural, but it is not procedural at all. It is simply an anomaly and illustrates clearly the confusion that arises from having hybrid sources of law.

---

5   The common law rule that children under the age of seven are *doli* and *culpa incapax* applied to both the criminal law as well as civil law. The Child Justice Act 75 of 2008 has raised the age of criminal capacity for children to 10, but the age of capacity for children for purposes of civil litigation remains unchanged. For an overview of the legal position pertaining to the age of capacity of children for purposes of criminal law, see G Kemp, S Walker, R Palmer, D Baqwa, C Gevers, B Leslie, A Steynberg *Criminal Law in South Africa* (2012) at 156–158. For purposes of civil procedure, see S Peté, D Hulme, M du Plessis, R Palmer, O Sibanda and T Palmer *Civil Procedure – A Practical Guide* 3 ed (2017) at 39.

6   *Scagell and Others v Attorney-General of the Western Cape and Others* 1997 (2) SA 368 (CC) at para 30.

7   S 7(1) of the Child Justice Act, 2008.

9.3.4 Parol evidence rule

The **parol evidence rule** is most commonly found in the law of contract.[8] Provided that its application is agreed on in the written contract, the parol evidence rule states that any terms that are not embodied in the contract, often called extraneous terms or terms extrinsic to the contract, are irrelevant when interpreting the contract. Thus, it is clearly a rule of substantive law. We often call it the *integration rule* as it means that all the relevant contractual terms are integrated into the contract.

However, due to the way the parol evidence rule is often formulated, it is frequently regarded as an evidentiary rule. For example, when it comes to a written contract, '... the writing is in general regarded as the exclusive memorial of the transaction and ... no evidence to prove its terms may be given ...'.[9] It is easy to see why people make this mistake as it seems to be a rule regarding the admissibility of evidence. It has been seen this way for a sufficiently long period that it is regarded as being part of procedural law, therefore English in origin and following English precedent. It seems unlikely that this will change despite a recognition that the rule is substantive in nature,[10] despite the fact that it has no place in our law of evidence and despite the fact that it has been diluted or even rejected in England.[11]

There are limitations on the parol evidence rule. First, it is only applicable if its application is an express term of the agreement. Thus, a contract in which the parties agree that 'this contract constitutes the whole agreement between the parties and no other terms or representations are admissible' is subject to the parol evidence rule. If this is not a term of the agreement, the rule is not applicable.

The rule also does not apply to the admissibility of evidence designed to illuminate the true underlying nature of a contract. Nor does it apply to evidence led to establish a material fact relating to the contract that is not part of its terms, for example the legibility of a signature or the capacity of one of the parties.

In addition, evidence is admissible to establish whether the contract is valid. Therefore, this rule does not exclude evidence relating to whether the contract is **void** by reason of mistake, fraud, lack of consensus, impossibility of performance or non-fulfilment of a suspensive condition.

Finally, we should look at the solution adopted to deal with instances where a contract does not correctly reflect the terms that the parties orally agreed it would. This is not a rule of procedural law or evidence, but is closely related to the parol evidence rule. Even though the parol evidence rule may be applicable in a specific instance, our courts have held that this cannot be a bar to rectification.

The two cases of *Standard Bank of SA Ltd v Cohen*[12] illustrate this clearly. In these cases, arising out of the same cause of action, the Court held in the first judgment that oral terms alleged to have been agreed on in a suretyship agreement could not be relied on due to the parol evidence rule. However, in the second case, the Court held that the oral terms had been agreed on and, thus, the contracts had to be rectified to reflect correctly the intention of the parties.

---

8 The parol evidence rule is also found when dealing with wills, negotiable instruments and court orders.

9 *Union Government v Vianini Ferro-Concrete Pipes Pty (Ltd)* 1941 AD 43 at 47.

10 *De Klerk v Old Mutual Insurance Co. Ltd* 1990 (3) SA 34 (E) at 39D–E.

11 See the reasoned critique of the South African situation in DT Zeffertt and AP Paizes *The South African Law of Evidence* 2 ed (2009) at 350.

12 *Standard Bank of SA Ltd v Cohen* (1) 1993 (3) SA 846 (SE) and *Standard Bank of SA Ltd v Cohen* (2) 1993 (3) SA 854 (SE).

THIS CHAPTER IN ESSENCE

1   Substantive law contains the rights, duties, obligations and entitlements of all individuals while procedural law regulates the way in which we enforce these rights and perform our duties.
2   The area of law applicable to a particular situation determines the system of rules to be applied as well as the consequences thereof. It is, therefore, vitally important to determine the applicable area of law at the outset of any type of proceedings.
3   There are, however, areas of law where the distinction between substantive and procedural law is not quite clear. These areas pertain to the burden of proof, irrebuttable presumptions, estoppel and the parol evidence rule.

PART THREE

KINDS OF EVIDENCE

CHAPTER 10   Oral evidence   80

CHAPTER 11   Documentary evidence   99

CHAPTER 12   Real evidence   110

CHAPTER 13   Forms of analogue evidence   116

CHAPTER 14   Electronic and cyber evidence   119

Chapter 10

Oral evidence

10.1 Introduction 80

10.2 Testimony must be given on oath or affirmation 81

10.3 Exceptions 82
    10.3.1 Unsworn evidence 82
    10.3.2 The intermediary 82
        10.3.2.1 The role of intermediaries when examining and cross-examining
                child witnesses 82
        10.3.2.2 Principles to consider when appointing an intermediary 84
    10.3.3 Closed-circuit television and other electronic media 85
    10.3.4 Evidence on commission 85
    10.3.5 Interrogatories 86
    10.3.6 Testimony by way of affidavit 86
        10.3.6.1 Types of affidavits 87
        10.3.6.2 The use of affidavits in civil application proceedings 88
        10.3.6.3 The form and content of civil affidavits 88
        10.3.6.4 Inadmissible evidence in affidavits 90
        10.3.6.5 The court's powers in application proceedings 91
        10.3.6.6 Perjury: the consequences of being untruthful in affidavits 93

10.4 When is oral evidence used? 93
    10.4.1 Criminal trials 94
    10.4.2 Civil matters 94

10.5 Method and procedure of presenting oral evidence 95
    10.5.1 Criminal trials 95
    10.5.2 Civil matters 96
    10.5.3 Precognition versus putting words in the witness's mouth 96
    10.5.4 Use of interpreters 96
    10.5.5 Perjury 96

10.1 Introduction

Oral evidence is the first-hand account of events as provided by witnesses.[1] As a general rule in both criminal and civil matters, when parties present oral evidence, it must be done under oath, in court and in the presence of all the parties to the court proceedings.

---

1 For further reading, see PJ Schwikkard and SE van der Merwe *Principles of Evidence* 3 ed (2009) at 362–418.

CHAPTER 10   ORAL EVIDENCE   81

This general rule falls within the ambit of the *audi alteram partem* principle. This principle requires that parties have the right to be heard by presenting evidence. In addition, the parties must have an opportunity to challenge the evidence presented by the witnesses testifying against them[2] by way of cross-examination. Parties have a right to do this in a setting that allows not only them, but also the court, to gauge a witness's demeanour and thereby draw conclusions as to the credibility of the witness.[3]

We refer to the process by which a party adduces oral evidence as the **examination-in-chief**. The court may elicit further evidence through examination. Oral evidence is challenged by **cross-examination**.[4] Although we may not use **re-examination** to adduce new evidence, it is useful to correct errors and tidy up the evidence presented during the examination-in-chief and to repair damage done during cross-examination.

A witness in criminal proceedings should give oral or *viva voce* evidence as stipulated by section 161 of the Criminal Procedure Act 51 of 1977.[5] Sign language by deaf and speech-impaired witnesses falls within the concept of *viva voce* for purposes of testimonial evidence, as do non-verbal expressions if the witness is under the age of 18 years.[6] Section 42 of the Civil Proceedings Evidence Act 25 of 1965 contains a similar provision that requires oral testimony in civil proceedings. An exception is the permissibility of written testimony – that is, **affidavits** – in certain limited circumstances.[7]

There are, however, further exceptions to the general rule requiring oral testimony, for example permitting evidence to be received by way of commission, interrogatories or affidavits, which we will discuss below.

10.2   Testimony must be given on oath or affirmation

Before a witness is permitted to give oral evidence, he or she must take an oath or **affirmation** which has to be administered by the judge, registrar or presiding officer.[8] The oath, the form of which appears in section 162 of the Criminal Procedure Act, 1977, reads, 'I swear that the evidence that I shall give, shall be the truth, the whole truth and nothing but the truth, so help me God'.

A witness sometimes has an objection to taking the oath – there may be religious reasons for his or her objections or the witness may not subscribe to a religion at all. In such a circumstance, section 163 of the Criminal Procedure Act, 1977 allows for a witness to make an affirmation instead whereby the witness affirms that he or she will speak only the truth.[9]

Both the oath and the affirmation have the same legal effect in that the witness may be charged with **perjury** or statutory perjury if it is later discovered that he or she was untruthful in the witness box.

Sections 39, 40 and 41 of the Civil Proceedings Evidence Act, 1965 make similar provisions for witnesses in civil proceedings.

---

2   S 35(3)(*i*) of the Constitution confirms this common law principle. This section states that in criminal cases all accused have the right to 'challenge evidence'.

3   *S v Adendorff* 2004 (2) SACR 185 (SCA).

4   See Part Five: The rules of trial.

5   Unless the Criminal Procedure Act, 1977 or any other law expressly provides for evidence to be received in a non-oral form.

6   S 161(2) of the Criminal Procedure Act, 1977.

7   See para 10.3.6 below.

8   S 162 of the Criminal Procedure Act, 1977.

9   S 163(1)(*a–d*).

10.3 Exceptions

10.3.1 Unsworn evidence

There may be instances when a witness does not understand what the oath or affirmation is or what the implications of taking an oath or making an affirmation are. An example is a young child or someone who lacks the necessary capacity or level of sophistication to understand. In such an instance, section 164 of the Criminal Procedure Act, 1977 and section 41 of the Civil Proceedings Evidence Act, 1965 allow such a witness to testify without taking an oath or affirmation. Instead, the presiding officer or judge is required to admonish the witness to speak the truth. The admonishment has the same legal effect as an oath or affirmation in that a witness who gives false testimony after having been admonished to speak the truth faces the possibility of perjury or statutory perjury charges being laid against him or her.

10.3.2 The intermediary

10.3.2.1 The role of intermediaries when examining and cross-examining child witnesses

Previously, child witnesses were examined and cross-examined in the same manner as adult witnesses. This was especially difficult for child witnesses in matters such as rape or sexual abuse cases. This led the South African Law Commission (SALC) to state in its report of April 1989 that the adversarial trial procedure was insensitive and unfair to child witnesses.[10] This, and subsequent reports, led to the introduction of intermediaries through the insertion of section 170A into the Criminal Procedure Act, 1977.

Section 170A(1) provides for the appointment of an **intermediary** whenever criminal proceedings are pending before a court and it appears to the court that a child under the age of 18 will be a witness and by testifying will be exposed to 'undue mental stress or suffering'. The court may appoint an intermediary in any criminal proceeding, not only those dealing with sexual offences with child victims. However, intermediaries have, almost exclusively, been used only in sexual offences cases.

Although the intermediary is a court official, he or she is not a lawyer. The intermediary is usually a social worker or psychologist although the class of people from which intermediaries may be appointed is wider.[11] The intermediary is accorded the status of a court official. This imposes an obligation on the intermediary to be impartial and unbiased.

In practice, the child witness is not in the presence of the parties, but is placed in a separate room. Face-to-face confrontations between the child witness and all other parties, especially the accused, are limited by using electronic or other devices. The parties therefore do not have direct access to the child witness. They must convey their questions to the intermediary who will then relay them to the child witness for his or her response. The child witness gives all evidence through the intermediary. This includes examination-in-chief, cross-examination and re-examination. The court may pose questions directly to the child but all other parties must pose their questions to the child through the intermediary.

The intermediary's role is largely that of a conduit between the parties and the child witness. The intermediary therefore cannot initiate a particular line of questioning or

---

10 SALC Project 71 Working Paper 28 *The Protection of the Child Witness* (1989).

11 The list is determined by the Minister of Justice by notice in the *Government Gazette*. See *GG* R 22435, GN 597 of 2 July 2001.

CHAPTER 10   ORAL EVIDENCE | **83**

formulate answers to any question. However, section 170A(2)(b) of the Criminal Procedure Act, 1977 does allow the intermediary some flexibility to reformulate a question so that it is appropriate in the particular circumstances of the case. However, the reformulated question must convey the purport of the original question. The intermediary is, therefore, not constrained to using the exact wording of questions conveyed to him or her by the parties.

Section 170A(3)(b) provides that when an intermediary is appointed, the child witness may be placed where he or she does not have to see anyone who may upset him or her. This includes the accused.[12] The constitutionality of this section has thus been challenged[13] on the basis that it infringes the accused's right to challenge evidence. However, section 170A(3)(c) requires the court to direct that the evidence must be given in a place 'which enables the court and any person whose presence is necessary at the relevant proceedings to see and hear, either directly or through the medium of any electronic or other devices, that intermediary as well as that witness during his or her testimony.' This provision goes some way towards ameliorating the possible limitations that section 170A poses on the right to confront and challenge oral testimony in a public forum.

Precisely such a challenge was first made in *K v The Regional Court Magistrate NO and Others*.[14] This challenge was founded on the premise that the separation of the witness from the courtroom violated the right to a public trial. The Court found that the parties are still in control of the examination-in-chief, cross-examination and re-examination of the witness through the conduit of the intermediary. Since the intermediary is restricted merely to conveying questions, albeit possibly in different words, to the witness, parties still retain their ability to restrict witnesses or to probe a particular aspect of a case just as they would in the usual adversarial environment of a public forum. Accordingly, the Court held that section 170A did not violate the right to a public trial simply because the witness is allowed to be in a different room to the parties. Similarly, it also stated that section 170A did not infringe the right to cross-examine. By reaching the conclusion that section 170A was not unconstitutional, the Court found it unnecessary to go further and to decide whether the infringement was reasonable and justifiable in terms of section 36 of the Constitution.

Unfortunately, presiding officers have applied section 170A inconsistently. Some presiding officers have considered the stress to which a child witness is subjected to be part and parcel of the stress of testifying and therefore not undue stress at all. They have thus declined to appoint intermediaries in some cases.[15]

Section 170A has thus also been challenged on the basis that it does not do enough to protect child witnesses. In *S v Mokoena; S v Phaswane*,[16] section 170A was challenged using section 28(2) of the Constitution. The section stipulates that '[a] child's best interests are of paramount importance in every matter concerning the child.' The Court found that because section 170A gives a presiding officer a discretion to appoint an intermediary only if a child witness has been exposed to 'undue mental stress or suffering', it fails to comply with section 28(2). Thus, it found section 170A(1) to be unconstitutional.[17]

The order of invalidity in respect of section 170A(1) went to the Constitutional Court for confirmation but it was not upheld. Ngcobo CJ found that section 170A(1) was intended to

---

12   S 170A(3)(b).
13   The constitutionality of s 170A was challenged in the matter of *K v The Regional Court Magistrate NO and Others* 1996 (1) SACR 434 (E) and its constitutionality was confirmed.
14   1996 (1) SACR 434 (E).
15   *S v F* 1999 (1) SACR 571 (C).
16   2008 (2) SACR 216 (T).
17   2008 (2) SACR 216 (T) at para 185.

84 THE LAW OF EVIDENCE IN SOUTH AFRICA

protect child complainants from being exposed to undue mental stress or suffering caused by giving evidence in court and that it succeeded in doing so by providing for the intermediary process. Furthermore, on a proper interpretation of section 170A(1), the State should have the child witness assessed prior to testifying to determine whether an intermediary should be appointed or not. Where the State fails to do so, then the court must enquire into the need to appoint an intermediary and may do so *mero motu*. Therefore, Ngcobo CJ ruled that section 170A(1), properly construed, fulfils its purpose and is therefore constitutional.[18]

10.3.2.2 Principles to consider when appointing an intermediary

As we can see from the above cases, there is considerable debate about intermediary proceedings. In *S v Stefaans*,[19] Mitchell AJ provided a succinct set of guidelines that courts should consider when exercising their discretion as to whether to appoint an intermediary. The most important of these guidelines are as follows:

1. A court faced with an **application** for the provisions of section 170A to be invoked should be mindful of the dangers that are inherent in the use of an intermediary which might prejudice the right of the accused to a fair trial. These are:
   1.1 that cross-examination through an intermediary may be less effective than direct cross-examination of a witness
   1.2 that an accused *prima facie* has the right to confront his or her accusers and be confronted by them
   1.3 that human experience shows that it is easier to lie about someone behind his or her back than to do so to his or her face.
2. The provisions of the section will find application more readily in cases involving a physical or mental trauma or insult to the witness than in other types of cases.
3. The giving of evidence in court is inevitably a stressful experience. To find application, the section requires the court to be satisfied that such stress will be 'undue', in other words something in excess of the ordinary stresses. In this regard, it seems fair to say that the younger and more emotionally immature the witness is, the greater is the likelihood that such stress will be 'undue'.
4. A witness who is known to the accused and who knows the accused and is still prepared to testify is less likely to be unduly stressed by the need to testify before the accused than a witness who is unknown to the accused and may fear intimidation. This factor, of course, needs to be balanced by the factor referred to in point 3 above.
5. If the application to invoke the section is not opposed, it may be more readily granted.
6. The presiding officer should carefully explain to an unrepresented accused his or her right to oppose the application. As in the case of a plea of guilty, if any doubt exists as to the accused's understanding of the matter, the application should be treated as opposed.
7. If the application is opposed, the presiding officer should require that appropriate evidence be adduced to enable him or her to exercise a proper discretion as to whether the section should be invoked or not. In the case of a younger witness in a matter clearly involving mental or physical trauma, such evidence may consist of nothing more than evidence of the nature of the charge and the age of the witness. In other matters, evidence

---

18 *Director of Public Prosecutions, Transvaal v Minister of Justice and Constitutional Development, and Others* 2009 (4) SA 222 (CC).
19 1999 (1) SACR 182 (C).

CHAPTER 10   ORAL EVIDENCE | **85**

of a suitably qualified expert, whether a social worker, psychologist or psychiatrist, may be necessary.

8. If the section is invoked, the presiding officer should be aware of the risk that the efficacy of cross-examination may be reduced by the intervention of the intermediary. The judicial officer should be alert to this and should be prepared to intervene to ensure that the exact question, rather than the import thereof, is conveyed to the witness.

10.3.3   Closed-circuit television and other electronic media

Section 158(2)(*a*) of the Criminal Procedure Act, 1977 allows a court, either on its own initiative or on application by the public prosecutor, to order that a witness or an accused may give evidence by means of closed-circuit television or other such electronic media. This can only be done if the witness or accused consents to such an order.

A court may only make an order in terms of section 158(2)(*a*) if the facilities are readily available or obtainable, and if it appears to the court that to do so would:

*   prevent unreasonable delay
*   save costs
*   be convenient
*   be in the interest of the security of the State, public safety or in the **interests of justice** or the public
*   prevent the likelihood that prejudice or harm might result to any person if he or she testifies or is present at such proceedings.[20]

In the case of *S v Domingo*,[21] the Court found that a disjunctive approach is required in applying section 158(3). In other words, not all the considerations set out in section 158(3) have to be met to bring section 158(2) into operation.

In civil proceedings, a procedure to testify via video link has been approved by the High Court in several recent cases[22] on the basis that it was convenient and in the interests of justice to vary the general trial procedure and receive the evidence of witnesses from abroad via video link.

10.3.4   Evidence on commission

Situations may arise where criminal proceedings are pending and it is in the interests of justice that a witness be examined in court, but there are difficulties in obtaining the presence of the witness. Such difficulties in obtaining the witness's presence could result in an undue delay, increased costs or inconvenience. Where the witness is resident in South Africa, the State or the accused may make an application to court for evidence to be led on commission in terms of section 171(1)(*a*) of the Criminal Procedure Act, 1977. If granted, the court issues a commission to a magistrate in the district where the witness resides.

The magistrate can either go to where the witness is or summon the witness to appear before him or her. The examination takes place before the specific magistrate. The witness must first take the oath or make an affirmation. The magistrate asks a set of questions prepared beforehand by both parties. Alternatively, counsel can go to the commission and pose the questions personally. The examination is recorded and read back to the witness,

---

20   S 158(3) of the Criminal Procedure Act, 1977.
21   2005 (1) SACR 193 (C).
22   *Uramin (Incorporated in British Columbia) t/a Areva Resources Southern Africa v Perie* 2017 (1) SA 236 (GJ). See also I Knoetze 'Virtual evidence in courts – a concept to be considered in South Africa' 2016 (October) *De Rebus* 30. *MK v Transnet Ltd t/a Portnet* Case no A105/2004 [2018] ZAKZDHC 39 (20 August 2018). The Courts have utilised their inherent jurisdiction to deviate from standard procedure to allow this form of evidence.

THE LAW OF EVIDENCE IN SOUTH AFRICA

who must then sign it, as must the magistrate. Once signed, the recorded examination is returned to the court that issued the commission where it will form part of the court record. However, as the court is unable to observe the demeanour of the witness when evidence is given on commission, it may attach less weight to such evidence.

High Court Rule 38(3) and section 53 of the Magistrates' Courts Act 32 of 1944 provide for **evidence on commission** in civil proceedings.

It is accepted that a court's inability to observe the demeanour of a witness under examination where commissions are granted lessens the weight of evidence on commission in both civil and criminal proceedings. Nonetheless, while commissions are granted sparingly,[23] the courts' general view is that it is better to have evidence on commission before the court than not to have the evidence at all.

10.3.5 Interrogatories

Interrogatories are similar to commissions in both procedure and the principles underlying their application. In interrogatories, however, the parties compile a list of specific questions, with the court being entitled to add questions of its own. The list is then sent to a court in the witness's jurisdiction. A court in the jurisdiction summons the witness, puts the questions to him or her and records the answers. The record is then returned to the court that issued the interrogatories and read as evidence at the trial to form part of the evidence to be considered.

High Court Rule 38(5) and section 39 of the Superior Courts Act 10 of 2013 provide for interrogatories for civil proceedings in the High Court if it is in the interests of justice. Similarly, section 52 of the Magistrates' Courts Act, 1944 makes provision for interrogatories in Magistrates' Courts.

Section 40 of the Superior Courts Act 10 of 2013 sets out the manner in which courts must deal with commissions *rogatoire*, letters of request and documents for service originating from foreign countries.

10.3.6 Testimony by way of affidavit

There are instances where evidence may be received in both criminal and civil proceedings by way of written affidavits. Affidavits are essentially a method whereby written evidence can be presented under oath or affirmation. The evidence contained in an affidavit is thus oral evidence which does not strictly comply with all the requirements for oral testimony – primarily in that it is not given *viva voce*. This has certain negative consequences the most significant being that the witness (called a deponent in an affidavit) cannot be cross-examined and the court cannot assess his or her demeanour. For these reasons, among others, the use of affidavits, although convenient, time and cost saving, is strictly regulated and is often only allowed for formal or uncontested evidence, or in matters where there is no **dispute of fact**.

Section 17 of the Civil Proceedings Evidence Act, 1965 allows for documents duly 'certified or purporting to be certified by the registrar or clerk of the court or other officer having the custody of the records of the court where such conviction or acquittal took place' to be received as proof of trial and conviction or acquittal of any person.

Similarly, sections 22(1) and 25 of the Civil Proceedings Evidence Act, 1965 provide for evidence to be received by affidavit in specific instances. Section 22(1) refers to affidavits that verify the institution to which a scientific expert, who is involved in ascertaining facts by examination or processes requiring specific skills, is in service. Certain affidavits are

---

23 *S v Hassim and Others* 1973 (3) SA 443 (A) at 453.

admissible on production if they relate to evidence about biology, chemistry, physics, anatomy and pathology. Section 25 pertains to a presumption of death of a soldier. In civil cases, a party must deliver a copy of the affidavit to their opponent seven days prior to the hearing and the court may on application order the **deponent** to give evidence.

Sections 212 and 212A of the Criminal Procedure Act, 1977 provide for the reception of affidavits and certificates as evidence in criminal proceedings in certain circumstances. The State or the accused usually uses affidavits for formal evidence in cases where calling the witness would be inconvenient. These affidavits most commonly contain evidence given by state departments, provincial administrations, courts, banks, or any facts established by means of an examination requiring a special skill. Section 212(4)(a) provides a list of such instances which include any examination involving skill in biology, physics, chemistry, astronomy, geography, geology, mathematics, statistics, computer science, anatomy, biochemistry, metallurgy, pathology, toxicology, ballistics and fingerprints. This covers evidence about:

- the mass and nature of precious stones
- the finding, lifting and identification of fingerprints
- the identity and condition of a deceased's body
- the receipt, custody, packing and delivery of specimens
- the consignment of goods by rail
- compliance with regulations relating to measuring equipment like speed cameras
- syringes and blood receptacles
- acts and transactions in foreign banks.

Such affidavits are considered to be *prima facie* proof of the facts stated in them. However, just because evidence is admitted by way of affidavit does not mean that the other party is unable to challenge it as the court has a discretion[24] to call the witness who deposed to the affidavit to give oral evidence at the trial. This means that an accused, for example, will always be able to challenge the evidence contained in an affidavit if he or she so wishes. Thus, the sections allowing for affidavit evidence, which is technically hearsay evidence, cannot be said to be unconstitutional.[25]

10.3.6.1 Types of affidavits

In our law, affidavits can generally be used for three purposes:
- To enhance the legal consequences of any written statement, for use by the police and in everyday interactions, by confirming the statement under oath or affirmation before a **commissioner of oaths**[26]
- To convert a written statement made by a person into an affidavit for the purpose of handing the affidavit into court in a civil or criminal matter in lieu of giving oral evidence in that matter[27]
- In special format to be used as legal documents in civil application proceedings.[28]

---

24 S 212(12). This discretion must be exercised on proper, and not spurious, grounds: see *S v Rululu* 2013 (1) SACR 117 (ECG).

25 *S v Van der Sandt* 1997 (2) SACR 116 (W). In formulating and presenting certificates and affidavits, the State must follow the correct procedures and drafting. In this regard, see *S v Ross* 2013 (1) SACR 77 (WCC) where the state provided a J88 certificate and not an affidavit as required by s 212. See also *S v Hlongwa* 2002 (2) SACR 37 (T).

26 Thereby converting a statement into a sworn statement (another name for an affidavit) or affidavit. This is governed by the Justices of the Peace and Commissioners of Oaths Act 16 of 1963.

27 Complying with s 222 of the Criminal Procedure Act 51 of 1977 and ss 33–38 of the Civil Proceedings Evidence Act 25 of 1965.

28 In terms of the High Court and Magistrates' Courts Rules.

88 THE LAW OF EVIDENCE IN SOUTH AFRICA

Our focus is on the third type of affidavit mentioned above – that is, affidavits that serve as written evidence in civil court proceedings. Keep in mind, however, that witness affidavits may also be used in criminal matters, especially at bail proceedings[29] and sometimes during sentencing proceedings. Section 212 of the Criminal Procedure Act 51 of 1977 also provides for various categories of evidence in criminal proceedings to be proved by affidavit only.[30]

10.3.6.2   The use of affidavits in civil application proceedings

The application procedure is one of two main ways in which a party may approach a court of first instance (as opposed to a court of appeal) for relief. Unlike action proceedings – in which witnesses give oral evidence at a trial – the court decides applications on the papers placed before it. All the evidence that a party wishes to put forward in support of his or her claim must be included in his or her application papers.

Application papers consist of a **notice of motion** (the court document containing the order the applicant wishes the court to grant) and an affidavit, known as a founding affidavit.[31] In certain cases there will be more than one affidavit, in which case there will be a notice of motion, a founding affidavit and a number of supporting affidavits. There may also be supporting documentation attached to the affidavits in the form of various annexures to the affidavits. The affidavits, together with the annexures, contain not only a summary of the main facts of the claim being made, in other words the cause of action, but also the evidence which is being put forward in support of the claim. The respondent issues an answering affidavit in which he or she deals with the various averments in the founding affidavit and in which his or her version is recorded. The applicant then has an opportunity to respond to the respondent's answering affidavit with a replying affidavit.

10.3.6.3   The form and content of civil affidavits

An affidavit is a statement given under oath,[32] also called a sworn statement, which the deponent[33] signs before a commissioner of oaths[34] who administers the oath to the deponent. The oath is administered to convert the contents of the affidavit into admissible evidence in the same way that a witness taking the witness stand in action proceedings has to take the oath or affirmation.

As far as the formalities relating to the affidavits are concerned, an affidavit will usually take the following form:

I the undersigned, JOE SOAP,

do hereby state under oath that: [statement follows]

---

29   Permitted by s 60(11B)(b) of the Criminal Procedure Act, 1977.

30   This is an exception to the general rule in criminal procedure that evidence must be given orally in open court, and is aimed at expediting the presentation of evidence which is of a formal, technical and usually uncontentious nature.

31   All the legal elements of the applicant's case must be contained in the founding affidavit – the applicant stands or falls by his or her founding affidavit. See *M & V Tractor & Implement Agencies Bk v Venootskap DSU Cilliers en Seuns en Andere* 2000 (2) SA 571 (N).

32   Persons who do not wish to take an oath may affirm their statements. An affirmation has the same legal effect as an oath.

33   The person who makes and signs the statement is called the deponent. The act of taking the oath and signing an affidavit is referred to as deposing to an affidavit.

34   A person, such as a police official or attorney, who has been appointed a commissioner of oaths in terms of the Justices of the Peace and Commissioners of Oaths Act, 1963.

The first paragraph of the affidavit sets out the identity of the deponent. The affidavit is then divided into numbered paragraphs, each paragraph containing a separate factual averment or allegation. If it is necessary to make more than one averment in a paragraph, the paragraph should then be divided into numbered sub-paragraphs. The purpose of this numbering is to enable the opponent to respond point by point to the averments contained in the affidavit. This makes the opponent's written responses to the allegations made in the affidavit easy to follow. The statements made in the paragraphs of the affidavits may further be supported by additional documents, for example invoices and receipts, which are attached as annexures to the affidavits and cross-referenced in the relevant paragraphs. Finally, the deponent signs the affidavit. After administering the oath to the deponent, the commissioner of oaths also signs the affidavit.

The conclusion of the affidavit may look something like this:

Signature of deponent JOE SOAP

Sworn to before me at Johannesburg on this   day of   2018, the deponent having acknowledged that:

1. He knows and understands the contents of this affidavit.
2. He has no objection to taking the prescribed oath.
3. He considers the prescribed oath to be binding on his conscience.

Signature of Commissioner of Oaths
Commissioner of Oaths [Full details]

The oath which the deponent swears will take the following form:

I swear that the contents of this declaration are true, so help me God.[35]

If the deponent objects to taking the prescribed oath, or does not consider it binding on his or her conscience, he or she will be asked to make the following affirmation:

I truly affirm that the contents of this declaration are true.[36]

In such a case, the wording at the beginning and end of the affidavit set out above must be amended to reflect the fact that the affidavit has been affirmed rather than sworn to.

The deponent and the commissioner of oaths must initial each page of the affidavit, as well as any additions or alterations that have been made to the affidavit. Note that the attorney acting for the deponent, or any member of his or her firm, may not act as a commissioner of oaths in the deponent's matter.

A deponent may only testify in an affidavit with respect to facts that are within his or her personal knowledge. Testifying on facts that are not within his or her knowledge would amount to hearsay evidence. Therefore, if a deponent is not personally aware of certain facts, his or her affidavit must be supported by an affidavit made by another deponent. These are

---

35 Regulation 1(1) of the regulations promulgated under s 10 of the Justices of the Peace and Commissioners of Oaths Act, 1963 – GN R1258 GG 3619 of 21 July 1972 (Reg Gaz 1949), as amended by GN R1648 GG 5716 of 10 August 1977 (Reg Gaz 2516), GN R1428 GG 7119 of 11 July 1980 (Reg Gaz 3030) and GN R774 GG 8169 of 23 April 1982 (Reg Gaz 3411).
36 Ibid. Regulation 1(2).

90 THE LAW OF EVIDENCE IN SOUTH AFRICA

referred to as supporting affidavits, or sometimes as confirmatory or verifying affidavits. They are usually much shorter, the deponent merely confirming, under oath, that the averments in the founding affidavit, insofar as they relate to the deponent of the supporting affidavit, are true and correct.

10.3.6.4 Inadmissible evidence in affidavits

This section discusses some of the kinds of inadmissible evidence that founding and supporting affidavits may not contain.

10.3.6.4.1 Hearsay

The affidavits may not contain hearsay evidence.[37] Where a deponent includes in his or her affidavit facts of which he or she does not have first-hand knowledge, the deponent must annex to the affidavit a supporting affidavit (here called a verifying affidavit) by someone who does have first-hand knowledge of these facts.

10.3.6.4.2 Privileged communications

Privileged communications are communications that are privileged from disclosure in all circumstances and which are accordingly inadmissible in affidavits as well. These include statements made or written 'without prejudice', communications between attorney and client, communications between husband and wife, and state privilege.[38]

10.3.6.4.3 Scandalous, vexatious or irrelevant matter

In terms of High Court Rule 6(15), affidavits may not contain matter which is scandalous, vexatious or irrelevant. These matters may be defined as follows:
- Scandalous matter: Allegations that may or may not be relevant but that are so worded as to be abusive or defamatory
- Vexatious matter: Allegations that may or may not be relevant but are so worded as to convey an intention to harass or annoy
- Irrelevant matter: Allegations that do not apply to the matter in hand and do not contribute to the making of a decision in the matter.[39]

There is no specific provision dealing with this kind of exclusion in the Magistrates' Courts Rules, but drafters of affidavits in Magistrates' Court practice use the High Court Rules as a guide.

10.3.6.4.4 Inadmissible new matter

The applicant's case stands or falls by the contents of the founding affidavit. No information or issues that have not been included in the founding affidavit may be raised in a replying affidavit. The purpose of the replying affidavit is to rebut issues raised by the respondent in his or her answering affidavit. A replying affidavit does not constitute an opportunity to include issues or information that the applicant forgot to include in his or her founding

---

37 See *Pountas' Trustee v Lahanas* 1924 WLD 67; *Levin v Saidman* 1930 WLD 256; *Cash Wholesalers Ltd v Cash Meat Wholesalers* 1933 (1) PH A24 (D) and *Hlongwane and Others v Rector, St Francis College and Others* 1989 (3) SA 318 (D).
38 See ch 26 Privilege.
39 *Vaatz v Law Society of Namibia* 1991 (3) SA 563 (Nm).

CHAPTER 10   ORAL EVIDENCE   91

affidavit. All the facts necessary to support a claim for relief must be set out in the founding affidavit, and new issues may only be raised in limited circumstances.[40]

10.3.6.4.5   Matter excluded by the use of inherent jurisdiction

The High Court may also use its **inherent jurisdiction**[41] to exclude other matter in order to grant relief where High Court Rule 6(15) is silent.[42]

The following are examples: (note that the Magistrates' Courts do not have inherent jurisdiction powers and are therefore confined to the powers they have in terms of the rules of court):

- Irrelevant attacks on credibility: An attack on the credibility of a person is permissible in circumstances where it is relevant and not otherwise excluded by the laws of evidence. However, to embark on a personal attack on someone's trustworthiness with regard to a matter unrelated to the case is not allowed.[43]
- Argumentative matter: Only the facts of the matter should be stated and parties should not embark on an argument on paper in relation to the facts or the law. In other words, the affidavits should not contain any legal arguments attempting to convince the court to reach the conclusion that the facts given by the other side are wrong or that there is no legal basis for the claim or relief.[44]

10.3.6.5   The court's powers in application proceedings

When a matter comes before the court in application proceedings, the court has a number of options. The most appropriate option is almost always determined by the nature and quality of the evidence contained in (or omitted from) the affidavits presented. Furthermore, the option settled on by the court may have a further evidentiary impact. For these reasons they will be briefly listed below.

10.3.6.5.1   If no real dispute of fact has arisen on the papers

If no real dispute of fact is apparent on the papers and the applicant's papers are in order (they set out a valid cause of action supported by the evidence necessary to prove it), the court will simply grant the order as prayed in the notice of motion.

A court will not readily infer that a dispute of fact has arisen. If at all possible, the court will decide the matter on the affidavits of the parties themselves, if necessary, by applying the **Plascon-Evans rule** discussed below.

DISCUSSION	The Plascon-Evans rule: *Plascon-Evans Paints Ltd v Van Riebeeck Paints (Pty)*
10.1	*Ltd* **1984 (3) SA 623 (A)**
	In the Plascon-Evans case, the Court stated that if disputes of fact become apparent on the affidavits, a final order (or relief with a final effect) may only be granted if the

---

40   See High Court Rules 6(5)(*d*) and (*e*). The inclusion of new matter in the replying affidavits will inevitably result in the need for the respondent to respond with a further set of affidavits, and the court will have to be approached to use its discretion under Rule 6(5)(*e*) to provide the requisite permission.

41   Inherent jurisdiction is a discretionary power held by the High Courts, the Supreme Court of Appeal and the Constitutional Court. It enables these courts to avoid procedural injustices from occurring by either overriding the rules of court or providing some procedural remedy where none exists.

42   *Titty's Bar and Bottle Store (Pty) Ltd v ABC Garage (Pty) Ltd and Others* 1974 (4) SA 362 (T).

43   *Duchen v Flax* 1938 WLD 110.

44   *SAR v Hermanus Municipality* 1931 CPD 184.

allegations in the applicant's affidavits which have been admitted by the respondent, considered together with the allegations made by the respondent, justify such an order.

In this case, the applicant alleged that the respondent's use of the product name 'Mikacote' was an infringement of the applicant's trademark 'Micatex'. The factual dispute was whether the product name was used as a trademark or whether it was simply a product name. The respondent's affidavits contained evidence of how it was being used. This evidence, although aimed at showing that it was being used only as a product name, actually showed that it was being used as a trademark.

This evidence, together with the admitted facts that 'Micatex' was a registered trademark and that the respondent did not have the applicant's authority to use that mark, were enough for the Court to find that the respondent had infringed on the applicant's trademark. The Court granted a final interdict on the application papers alone.

The Court approved the *Room Hire*[45] decision and held that if a denial does not raise a real, genuine or **bona fide** dispute of fact, then the applicant's averments can be accepted.

10.3.6.5.2   If a real dispute of fact has arisen on the papers

If a real dispute of fact[46] is apparent on the papers, the court may deal with the matter in one of four different ways, discussed below.

10.3.6.5.2   (i) The court may decide the matter on the affidavits alone

Unless one of the parties requests the court to refer the matter for oral evidence or for trial, the court will not usually do so of its own accord, but will deal with the matter on the basis of the undisputed facts.[47] If the undisputed facts in the applicant's affidavits are not sufficient to persuade the court on a balance of probabilities that it is entitled to the relief sought, the court will dismiss the application.

10.3.6.5.2   (ii) The court may refer the matter to oral evidence

Referral to oral evidence is usually only done where the disputed facts are restricted to a narrow range of issues.[48] These issues may be referred for oral evidence. This will happen when one fact, or only a few disputed facts, cannot be decided on the affidavits, when the issues are comparatively simple and clearly defined, and when the evidence in question has a narrow scope. However, the court will not refer a matter to oral evidence when complicated issues are involved and it is not possible to know how wide a field of evidence the disputed issues will cover.[49] Also, where the court has doubts about the credibility of a deponent, it may order the opponent to appear for cross-examination.[50]

---

45   *Room Hire Co (Pty) Ltd v Jeppe Street Mansions (Pty) Ltd* 1949 (3) SA 1155 (T).

46   A dispute between parties to litigation regarding a material fact or set of facts. Where a party decides to initiate court proceedings against another party and foresees that a 'real dispute of fact' will arise between the parties, it is necessary for that party to proceed by way of action as opposed to application so that oral evidence can be presented with regard to the fact in dispute.

47   This is known as the Plascon-Evans rule: *Plascon-Evans Paints Ltd v Van Riebeeck Paints (Pty) Ltd* 1984 (3) SA 623 (A).

48   High Court Rule 6(5)(g).

49   *Standard Bank of SA Ltd v Neugarten and Others* 1987 (3) SA 695 (W) at 699D–E.

50   *Klep Valves (Pty) Ltd v Saunders Valve Co Ltd* 1987 (2) SA 1 (A).

CHAPTER 10 ORAL EVIDENCE 93

10.3.6.5.2 (iii) The court may refer the matter to trial

If the disputed facts cover a broad range of issues or are relatively complicated, the court will usually refer the matter to trial.[51]

10.3.6.5.2 (iv) The court may dismiss the matter with costs

If a real dispute of fact should have been foreseen by the applicant, the court may dismiss the application with costs.[52] This dismissal is a final order, which means that the same application may not be brought again.[53] If, however, the applicant's negligence is not clear-cut, the court will usually refer the matter to oral evidence or to trial.[54]

10.3.6.5.2 (v) In certain cases, the court may decide to make no order

The court may decline to make any order on the application itself and give the applicant leave to renew the application on the same papers.[55] The court will usually indicate the shortcomings of the pending application so that the applicant knows what evidence to obtain to supplement the existing affidavits. The effect of this order (or rather, the lack of an order) is that the applicant may bring the application again, but costs will normally be awarded to the respondent.[56]

10.3.6.6 Perjury: the consequences of being untruthful in affidavits

Just as is the case with oral testimony under oath, statements made in affidavits must be the truth. Although a deponent is unlikely to be cross-examined on the contents of his or her affidavit, if it is found that the deponent was untruthful in the affidavit, he or she can be prosecuted for perjury. Sometimes legal practitioners have to depose to affidavits as well. If it is found that a practitioner was untruthful in an affidavit, not only can he or she be prosecuted for perjury, he or she can also be struck off the roll of attorneys or struck from the **bar**.

10.4 When is oral evidence used?

As mentioned above, the primary method that witnesses use to testify (in other words, to give evidence under oath or affirmation) in civil or criminal matters is to give oral testimony. Also mentioned above is a second method, which is to present evidence by affidavit, in other words written evidence given under oath or affirmation. The decision about which method to use will be influenced primarily by the type of proceedings at which witnesses present the evidence, as well as several other factors, which will be examined below. In civil and criminal trials, the method used is primarily oral testimony, while in civil application proceedings, affidavit evidence is the norm.

---

51 See High Court Rule 6(5)(g) and *Pressma Services (Pty) Ltd v Schuttler and Another* 1990 (2) SA 411 (C). In referring a matter for trial, the court may order that the founding affidavit should stand as the summons and will give directions regarding the further exchange of pleadings. It will often treat the three sets of affidavits as pleadings.

52 *Room Hire Co (Pty) Ltd v Jeppe Street Mansions (Pty) Ltd* 1949 (3) SA 1155 (T) at 1162; *Conradie v Kleingeld* 1950 (2) SA 594 (O) at 597; *Winsor v Dove* 1951 (4) SA 42 (N); *Blend and Another v Peri-Urban Areas Health Board* 1952 (2) SA 287 (T) at 291H–292B.

53 *Purchase v Purchase* 1960 (3) SA 383 (N).

54 *Pressma Services (Pty) Ltd v Schuttler and Another* 1990 (2) SA 411 (C) at 419J–420A. The court may still show its disapproval of the applicant's lack of diligence by awarding costs in favour of the respondent; see *Van Aswegen and Another v Drotskie and Another* 1964 (2) SA 391 (O).

55 This procedure is similar to absolution from the instance at the end of the trial in action proceedings.

56 High Court Rule 6(6) and see *African Farms and Townships Ltd v Cape Town Municipality* 1963 (2) SA 555 (A).

10.4.1 Criminal trials

In criminal matters, all relevant direct and circumstantial evidence must be presented to the court. The facts that need to be proved, and thus in respect of which evidence needs to be led, in any particular criminal case are established before the trial in the charge sheet to which the accused pleads, either orally or in a section 112[57] or a section 115 statement.[58] If an accused pleads not guilty, the State must establish the factual and legal basis on which it alleges the accused is guilty.[59] Therefore, in criminal trials, oral evidence is required in almost every circumstance. The **complainant**, the investigating officer and all relevant witnesses should testify. Once the State has closed its case, the defence is afforded an opportunity to present its evidence. As with the State's case, the defence uses oral evidence from relevant witnesses. However, unlike the State's case, there is no obligation on the defence to do so and the defence may elect to close its case without presenting any oral evidence at all.

10.4.2 Civil matters

Unlike criminal matters, civil matters can take the form of either action or motion proceedings. Whether a civil matter proceeds by way of action or motion will have an impact on whether oral evidence is required.

Actions proceedings are used in circumstances where there is a dispute of material fact between the parties.[60] Evidence, especially oral evidence, is thus required to enable the court to decide on the disputed fact or facts. Oral testimony is therefore important as it allows for a proper examination of the merits of the evidence and for the opportunity to observe the demeanour and assess the credibility of the witnesses.

Action proceedings are commenced by way of a summons and involve the use of pleadings to define the ambit of the dispute. All the issues in dispute are set out in the pleadings and no new issues can be raised during the trial if they were not set out in the pleadings. Pleadings contain only the *facta probanda* – the essential elements and allegations forming the basis of the dispute between the parties. They do not contain any of the evidence that parties will later present to the court. The pleadings therefore constitute an important stage in pre-trial preparation as they narrow down the issues in dispute and thereby define precisely what evidence will be required. If it is apparent from the pleadings that certain facts are agreed or regarded as common cause, it follows, then, that evidence is not required in respect of those facts. Evidence is also not required when a pleaded version is not denied or when there are clear and unequivocal admissions of certain facts.[61] Therefore, the pleadings,[62] together with any pre-trial documents,[63] create a framework that determines what a party needs to present and when the party needs to present it. They also provide an overview of how all the pieces of oral evidence fit together.

If there is no dispute of material fact between the parties,[64] motion proceedings may, or should, be used. Because there is no material fact in dispute, the court is not called on to

---

57 A plea of guilty in terms of s 112 of the Criminal Procedure Act 51 of 1977.
58 A plea of not guilty in terms of s 115 of the Criminal Procedure Act, 1977.
59 In accordance with the fundamental principle of the presumption of innocence.
60 They are also used in certain other circumstances, for example where action proceedings are prescribed by statute or common law, such as divorce matters or claims for damages.
61 See ch 50 for more on admissions in civil and criminal matters.
62 Pleadings in civil matters include summonses and particulars of a claim, pleas, replies and replications in ordinary civil courts, and statement of claim and response in specialised courts like the Labour Courts.
63 The pre-trial documents contain additional and more detailed information about the dispute and include pre-trial notices, the pre-trial minute, expert witness notices, subpoenas, discovery affidavits and various trial bundles comprising a range of items including documents, expert opinions and sometimes photographs.
64 Or if statute specifically authorises the use of motion proceedings, for example for sequestrations and liquidations.

CHAPTER 10   ORAL EVIDENCE   95

adjudicate on the existence or non-existence of any facts and thus has no need to observe any witness or to assess any oral evidence on the facts. Thus no oral evidence is required. Therefore, in motion proceedings, parties use affidavits to present the evidence. In certain limited circumstances, once motion proceedings have commenced, an unforeseen factual dispute may arise. The court has the discretion to require that oral evidence be presented to it on the disputed fact to enable it to decide the matter.

10.5   Method and procedure of presenting oral evidence

10.5.1   Criminal trials

In criminal trials, the State commences and calls all its witnesses sequentially. Each witness presents his or her oral evidence through the process of examination-in-chief, and is subject to cross-examination by the accused and then to possible re-examination by the State if necessary.[65] If the State is able to establish a *prima facie* case, the accused then has an opportunity to present oral evidence. This is both a right and an obligation.

Section 35(3)(*i*) of the Constitution specifies that '[e]very accused person has a right to a fair trial, which includes the right to adduce and challenge evidence'. The accused cannot thus be refused an opportunity to present oral evidence. There are, however, certain procedural regulations which govern the method and procedure through which this is done. Because the accused has a right to be present at his or her trial,[66] he or she is entitled to be in court during the testimony of any of the defence witnesses. Therefore, the convention is for the accused to testify first so that the accused does not have an opportunity to tailor his or her evidence depending on what he or she heard the other witnesses say.[67] However, because the accused has a right to remain silent[68] and not to testify,[69] he or she may elect not to give oral evidence. The accused is entitled to change his or her mind once other defence witnesses have testified and can subsequently elect to testify notwithstanding that he or she has observed the testimony of the other defence witnesses. However, section 151(1)(*b*)(ii) of the Criminal Procedure Act, 1977 specifically provides that if the accused does this, the court is entitled to draw any reasonable inference as may be appropriate in the circumstances. This would include drawing an inference that the accused has tailored his or her evidence as a result of having observed the evidence of the other defence witnesses.

The obligation that rests on an accused to testify is not a legal obligation, but is created by the factual circumstances of each case. If the State has established a *prima facie* case, the evidentiary burden shifts to the accused. The evidentiary burden may have been discharged by cross-examination of the State witnesses, or it may be discharged by calling defence witnesses other than the accused, but in some cases the accused may need to testify. If the accused elects not to, as is his or her right, his or her silence cannot prevent the court drawing such inferences as may be appropriate from the State's case in the absence of evidence to the contrary by the accused.[70]

---

65   See chs 29 to 31 for a detailed discussion of this process.
66   S 35(3)(*e*) of the Constitution.
67   S 151(1)(*b*)(i) of the Criminal Procedure Act, 1977 specifically provides for this.
68   S 35(1)(*a*) of the Constitution.
69   S 35(3)(*h*) of the Constitution.
70   *S v Brown en 'n Ander* 1996 (2) SACR 49 (NC) at 61I–63C.

10.5.2 Civil matters

As with criminal matters, each witness, once sworn in, will give evidence-in-chief[71] where his or her version is elicited through open-ended questions such as, 'Please tell us what happened on the day in question.'

The other side is then entitled to cross-examine[72] the witness, usually by using leading questions in an attempt to elicit favourable evidence or to undermine the witness's evidence-in-chief. After cross-examination, a party may re-examine a witness if necessary. Re-examination is meant to cure problems, misinterpretations or defects that the other side elicited during cross-examination. It cannot be used to plead an entirely different version, to rehash issues which have been properly canvassed, or to introduce new or irrelevant issues.[73]

10.5.3 Precognition versus putting words in the witness's mouth

Legal practitioners should tread carefully when preparing a witness for testimony. This process is called **precognition**. A legal practitioner may advise a witness as to why his or her evidence is relevant and what, in summary, is expected of his or her testimony. A legal practitioner may also advise a witness as to what issues may arise and what he or she is likely to be cross-examined on. However, a legal practitioner cannot tell a witness what to say when in the witness box. This is unethical and such evidence will also carry no weight as it is no longer the witness's own evidence. There is also a risk that should the cross-examination become too much to bear for the witness, he or she may justify an answer by stating, 'My lawyer told me to say that!'

10.5.4 Use of interpreters

Witnesses can give evidence in any language, but a sworn interpreter must interpret it. A sworn interpreter is an officer of the court and must therefore remain completely impartial in his or her interpretation of the witness's evidence.

10.5.5 Perjury

Any oral testimony given under oath must be the truth. Although the taking of the oath itself is no longer a complete deterrent, the fact that a witness is likely to be cross-examined means that he or she runs the risk of having any false statements uncovered. If it is found that the witness was untruthful when presenting evidence under oath, he or she can be prosecuted for perjury.

Figures 10.1 and 10.2 summarise the principles of oral evidence.

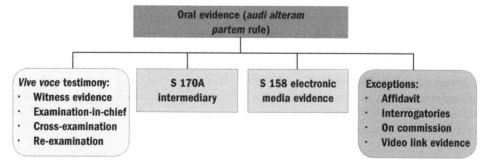

Figure 10.1 A summary of oral evidence

---

71 See ch 29 Evidence-in-chief.
72 For a more detailed discussion of cross-examination, see ch 30.
73 For greater detail about examination-in-chief, cross-examination and re-examination, see Part Five: The rules of trial.

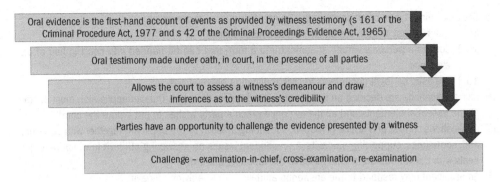

Figure 10.2 Oral evidence principles

THIS CHAPTER IN ESSENCE

1 Generally, when parties present oral evidence, it must be done under oath or affirmation in court and in the presence of all the parties to the court proceedings. The presiding officer can admonish a witness who does not understand the oath or affirmation to speak the truth.
2 Oral evidence is adduced through examination-in-chief and challenged through cross-examination. Thereafter, a party can use re-examination to fix errors and tidy up evidence given during examination-in-chief. However, the party may not adduce new evidence during re-examination.
3 Previously, child witnesses testified in the same manner as adult witnesses. Today, however, child witnesses under the age of 18 in criminal proceedings can testify through an intermediary if it appears to the court that the child witness will be exposed to undue mental stress and suffering.
4 A court may only order that a witness or an accused give evidence by means of closed-circuit television or other electronic media if such media is readily available or obtainable. Also, the court must be convinced that it would prevent unreasonable delay, save costs, be convenient, be in the interest of security and prevent prejudice to any person who testifies at such proceedings.
5 If it is in the interests of justice that a witness be examined in court but there are difficulties in obtaining the presence of the witness, evidence can be led on commission. A magistrate in the district where the witness resides can then either go to the witness or summon the witness to appear before him or her.
6 Witnesses can testify either orally (*viva voce* evidence) in court or in writing by affidavit.
7 In criminal trials, oral evidence is required in almost every circumstance.
8 In civil trials, oral evidence is presented almost exclusively in action proceedings, while affidavits are used to present evidence in motion proceedings.
9 An accused has a constitutional right to adduce and challenge evidence and to be present during his or her trial.
10 An accused may refuse to testify. However, if an accused elects to testify, he or she should testify first. The accused may testify after hearing the testimony of other defence witnesses, but if the accused does so, a court can draw any reasonable inference as may be appropriate in the circumstances.
11 A legal practitioner is allowed to prepare a witness for testimony (precognition). It is, however, unethical to tell a witness what to say.
12 Witnesses can give evidence in any language provided that it is done through a sworn interpreter.
13 A witness who lies under oath can be prosecuted for perjury.
14 In certain cases evidence may be received in both criminal and civil proceedings by way of written affidavits. These are considered to be *prima facie* proof of the facts stated in them.

15 There are three types of affidavits in the South African law – those which:
    15.1 enhance any written statement's legal consequences
    15.2 convert a person's written statement into a form that can be handed into court in lieu of oral evidence
    15.3 are used as legal documents in civil application proceedings.

16 Civil applications are decided on the papers placed before the court. Thus an application must contain all the essential elements and all the evidence which a party wishes to put before the court.

17 Applications consist of a notice of motion, a founding affidavit by the applicant together with annexures and, sometimes, supporting affidavits. A respondent issues an answering affidavit in which he or she deals with the various averments made in the founding affidavit.

18 An applicant may respond to the answering affidavit with a replying affidavit.

19 Affidavits are made under oath before a commissioner of oaths.

20 There are specific rules regulating precisely what affidavits must and must not contain.

21 Where no real dispute of fact is apparent on the papers and the applicant's papers are in order, the court will grant the order as prayed in the notice of motion.

22 Where a real dispute of fact is apparent on the papers, the court may decide the matter on the affidavits alone, refer the matter to oral evidence, refer the matter to trial, dismiss the matter with costs or make no order.

23 Deponents who are untruthful in their affidavits can be prosecuted for perjury.

Chapter 11

Documentary evidence

11.1	**Introduction**	**99**
11.2	**Categories of documents**	**100**
11.3	**Admissibility**	**101**
	11.3.1 Inspection and discovery	102
	11.3.2 The production of the original document	102
	11.3.2.1 The best evidence versus secondary evidence	102
	11.3.2.2 Admissibility of secondary evidence	103
	11.3.3 Proof of authenticity	105
	11.3.4 Current applicability of the Stamp Duties Act, 1968	107
11.4	**The procedural steps in admitting a document in civil proceedings**	**108**

11.1 Introduction

R v Daye[1] gives the common law definition of a document as 'any written thing capable of being evidence'. Section 33 of the Civil Proceedings Evidence Act 25 of 1965 ('CPEA') expands on this definition to include any 'book, map, plan, drawing or photograph'. Section 221 of the Criminal Procedure Act 51 of 1977 ('CPA') states that the term 'documentary evidence' may comprise any device by which information is stored or recorded. The current term 'document' also covers data messages, computer discs, flash drives, tape recordings and microfilms.[2]

To be admissible at trial as evidence, documents must meet the common law requirements of relevance,[3] **originality** and **authenticity**. The essential evidentiary difference between admitting a document at trial as documentary evidence or as real evidence lies in the purpose for which the document is admitted. Where the contents of a document are at issue before the court, the document must be admitted as documentary evidence, but where the document is admitted merely to prove its existence as an object,

---

1 [1908] 2 KB 333 at 340; *Seccombe and Others v Attorney-General and Others* 1919 TPD 270 at 277, 'everything that contains the written or pictorial proof of something'. The Oxford Dictionary defines a document as something written which furnishes evidence or information upon any subject, including any inscriptions on tombstones, coins, etc.

2 *S v Harper and Another* 1981 (1) SA 88 (D) at 95. S 236(5) of the Criminal Procedure Act defines a document as including a recording or transcribed computer printout produced by any mechanical or electronic device and any device by means of which information is recorded or stored.

3 See ch 15 The general test for relevance.

THE LAW OF EVIDENCE IN SOUTH AFRICA

then it may be admitted as an item of real evidence.[4] For example, a copy of a typed contract will constitute documentary evidence where it is admitted to establish the terms of the contract. However, it will constitute real evidence if it is admitted for the purpose of proving the existence of the written contract in the circumstance where one of the parties denies that a written contract was ever created.

11.2 Categories of documents

All documents fall into two general categories and may be labelled as either private or public documents. The category of public documents further includes a sub-category of official documents. Private or public documents may also be labelled as ancient documents when they are 20 years or older and have been correctly and properly archived. Foreign documents are documents drafted and executed in a foreign country and certified in terms of High Court Rule 63 for use in a South African court. In terms of section 1 of the Electronic Communications and Transactions Act 25 of 2002, an electronic document that exists in a digitalised form is referred to as a data message where data is defined as 'electronic representations of information in any form'.[5]

A public document is positively defined as a document drafted by a public official (i.e. a state, provincial or local municipal official) in the execution of a public duty, intended for public use and to which a member of the public has a common law and constitutional right of access.[6] The public official's duty is twofold: (i) to ensure that the contents of the public document are truthful and accurate, and (ii) that the document is properly maintained as a permanent record for public use.

A legal distinction is also drawn between a public document and an official document. Section 19(1) of the CPEA defines an official document as being 'in the custody or under the control of any state official by virtue of his/her office'. The principal distinguishing feature of an official document is that it is drafted for state administrative use and placed in the custody of a designated state official and may only be accessed or made public on the instruction of a designated senior departmental official mandated to do so in civil proceedings or a director of public prosecutions in criminal proceedings.[7]

A private document is legally defined in negative terms as 'any document which is not a public document'. A private document must comply with the requirements of the hearsay rule as defined in section 3 of the Law of Evidence Amendment Act 1988 when adduced at trial, whereas a public document may be adduced at trial as an exception to the hearsay rule.[8] All documents are subject to privilege and may not be adduced at trial when falling within the ambit of either private or public privilege.[9]

---

4 See ch 12 Real evidence.
5 See ch 14 Electronic and cyber evidence.
6 *Northern Mounted Rifles v O'Callaghan* 1909 TS 174 at 177.
7 *S v Mpumlo and others* 1987 (2) SA 442 (SE) at 445.
8 See ch 25 Hearsay evidence.
9 See ch 26 Privilege.

DISTINCTION BETWEEN PUBLIC AND PRIVATE DOCUMENTS	
Public documents	**Private documents**
Public documents are drafted for administrative purposes and public use, and are controlled by a State official in terms of a public duty.	Private documents are negatively defined as 'all documents which are not public documents'.
Are an exception to the hearsay rule. Are subject to a claim of public privilege.	Must comply with the hearsay rule when the document's contents are in issue. Are subject to a claim of private privilege.
The original may not be produced at trial without the permission of the State official in whose custody it is.	In terms of the best evidence rule the original must be produced and authenticated in order to be admissible at trial.
True copies or extracts may be admitted at trial in terms of a number of statutory exceptions when certified by a State official entrusted with the custody of the document.	Secondary evidence or a true copy may be admitted at trial on good cause shown either in terms of a *bona fide* common law reason or statutory law exception.
A public or private document is defined as an ancient document when it is older than 20 years and has been properly archived and maintained.	
A public or private document is defined as a foreign document when executed or created abroad and authenticated for use in a South African court in terms of High Court Rule 63.	

Figure 11.1 Distinction between public and private documents

11.3 Admissibility

Three formal common law requirements must be met before documentary evidence is admissible at trial:
- *Relevance*: the statement or document must be relevant.
- *Originality*: the original document must be produced in court.
- *Authenticity*: the authenticity of the document must be proved.

In addition to these formal requirements and before a relevant, original and authenticated document may be admitted at trial it must first be identified, discovered to the opposing party and produced for inspection. In civil matters there are specific formal procedures of identification, discovery, inspection and production which must be met before a document may be adduced at trial. There are no formal rules of discovery in criminal matters although the prosecution is obliged to provide further particulars in writing to an accused. The accused is constitutionally entitled to access a police docket subject to the rules of privilege.

The purpose for which the documentary evidence is to be admitted must also be established. Where a party intends adducing documentary evidence to prove the truth of the contents of the document, then such documentary evidence falls within the parameters of documentary hearsay. The requirements of section 3 of the Law of Evidence Amendment Act 45 of 1988, Part VI of the CPEA, or other statutory provisions dealing with documentary hearsay will also have to be met in addition to the above requirements in order to admit a document.

11.3.1 Inspection and discovery

In order to establish which particular documents may be relevant to a proposed civil litigation, a number of formal pre-trial discovery procedures are set out in the High Court and Magistrates' Courts Rules.[10] During the preparation for trial stage of civil proceedings, the opposing parties are obliged to list all relevant documents by way of a discovery affidavit and to produce for inspection all documents (including any plans, maps, X-rays, CTA scans, written medical examinations and summaries of expert opinions) in their possession or control intended to be used as evidence at trial.[11] A subpoena *duces tecum* may be used to oblige a third party to produce any document at trial where the document is in possession or control of a third party. A document which has not been formally identified and discovered may not be adduced at a civil trial.

In criminal proceedings there are no formal rules of discovery, but an accused may in terms of section 87(1) of the CPA request further particulars in writing from the prosecution and may also access any part of the police docket subject to police docket privilege.

11.3.2 The production of the original document

A party must produce the original document in court where the contents of the document are themselves in issue or where the contents serve as evidence of other issues. The reason for this is that errors may be made in subsequent copies or documents may be falsified. The requirement that the original must be produced avoids these potential dangers.[12]

Multiple originals such as carbon copies and initialled copies may also be admitted as if they are originals.[13] When a document is made in duplicate, both copies are considered to be original. The same applies to photostat copies.[14] Each part of a counterpart copy, where a document is made in duplicate and a different person signs each copy, will be admissible as evidence against the person who signed it. This occurs frequently when one party signs a document and faxes or emails it to another party who then prints and signs it.

11.3.2.1 The best evidence versus secondary evidence

The best evidence rule holds that no evidence may be admitted at trial to prove the contents of a document except the original document itself (i.e. the best or primary evidence).[15] In terms of this rule, primary evidence in the form of an original document is preferable to secondary evidence in the form of a copy of the document because it is the best evidence available. *Primary evidence* is evidence that tends to suggest that there is no better evidence available. *Secondary evidence* is evidence that tends to suggest that there is better evidence available.[16] An example of secondary evidence is a copy of a person's identity document. The actual identity document itself is primary evidence. The best evidence rule has largely

---

10 High Court Rule 35 and Magistrates' Courts Rule 23.

11 See C Theophilopoulos, CM van Heerden and A Boraine *Fundamental Principles of Civil Procedure* 3 ed (2015) ch 18.

12 *R v Regan* (1887) 16 Cox CC 203, if a party wants to use a telegram as documentary evidence against the person who sent it, then the party must produce the original, which is the form that the person completed and handed in at the post office.

13 *Herstigde Nasionale Party van Suid-Afrika v Sekretaris van Binnelandse Sake en Immigrasie* 1979 (4) SA 274 (T).

14 *S v Mbovana and others* 1985 (1) SA 224 (C) at 229.

15 *Standard Merchant Bank Ltd v Rowe and Others* 1982 (4) SA 671 (W) at 674B.

16 The court in *Transnet Ltd v Newlyn Investments (Pty) Ltd* 2011 (5) SA 543 (SCA) stated that there are no degrees of secondary evidence and, although production of a photocopy would be more reliable than oral evidence, and failure to produce a photocopy may be cause for comment, this goes to weight and not admissibility.

CHAPTER 11 DOCUMENTARY EVIDENCE | **103**

fallen into disuse but it has some limited utility in the context of documentary evidence.[17] The Appeal Court in *R v Amod & Co (Pty) Ltd and Another*[18] held that the best evidence rule only applies when the contents of a document are in dispute, in which case the original document must be produced. Secondary evidence or a copy of a document is acceptable where the dispute merely concerns the existence of a document.

The distinction between primary and secondary evidence is best explained by an example from case law. In *R v Pelunsky*,[19] sheep traders were required to keep tickets recording the correct number of sheep taken to market to indicate how much tax should be levied. To prove that the accused had written the incorrect number on his tickets, the State sought to have the counterfoils of the tickets admitted. The State did not adduce the original tickets. The Appeal Court held that the counterfoils were secondary evidence and inadmissible because the State offered no explanation as to why it did not adduce the originals into evidence.

There are instances where producing the original document may not be necessary. Where a party can provide the court with a satisfactory explanation as to why it cannot produce the original, then it may be allowed to admit a copy or some other form of secondary evidence. Arguably, if the original has been destroyed the remaining copy becomes the best evidence available. Furthermore, if the party can prove a fact-in-issue by evidentiary means other than the document, then it will not have to meet the primary or best evidence rule.[20] The following circumstances do not require the production of an original document at trial:

- *Where the existence of a relationship or status flowing from a document is in dispute.* For example, where proof of marriage is required but there is no marriage certificate available, the marriage may still be proved by producing other evidence such as evidence of cohabitation or that a marriage ceremony took place. The existence of a partnership may be proved without producing the written partnership agreement.
- *Where oral testimony instead of documentary evidence will suffice.* For example, the purchase price of an object in a shop may be proved by an eyewitness without producing the invoice. The appearance of a person may be proved by oral evidence without producing a photograph.

11.3.2.2 Admissibility of secondary evidence

Secondary evidence of a document is admissible if there is an acceptable explanation for the non-availability of the original. Any secondary copy is acceptable, even the oral evidence of a person who can remember the contents of a document. Where a statute requires a particular form of a copy (usually in the form of a certified copy), a party may not adduce other secondary evidence unless the party has a reasonable explanation for the absence of the original or the statutorily required copy. Secondary evidence is admissible where:

- the existence of the document rather than its contents is a fact in issue. For example, if the dispute is whether a contract was concluded between two parties and not about the actual terms of the contract, then a copy will suffice to prove the contract's existence.

---

17 *Welz and Another v Hall and Others* 1996 (4) SA 1073 (C) at 1079C–E per Conradie J, 'as far as the best evidence rule is concerned, it is a rule that applies nowadays only in the context of documents and then only when the content of a document is directly in issue'. See also PJ Schwikkard and SE van der Merwe *Principles of Evidence* 3 ed (2009) ch 2.

18 1947 (3) SA 32 (A).

19 1914 AD 360; *R v Zungu* 1953 (4) SA 660 (N) at 661–662.

20 In *R v Lombard and Another* 1957 (2) SA 42 (T), the State needed to prove that the accused was a retail butcher in a controlled area, but it could not produce a registration certificate showing this. The Court held that the State could prove its case without producing the certificate by adducing other evidence.

- it can be shown that the original has been destroyed and a diligent search has failed to locate the original.[21] However, where the original has been intentionally destroyed by a party in contemplation of litigation, that party will not be allowed to rely later on secondary evidence in the form of a copy. However, a copy is admissible where the original has been destroyed in the ordinary course of business or where it can be proved that lack of physical storage space resulted in the destruction of the original and its replacement with a recorded copy (i.e. a digital or microfilm record).[22]
- the production of the original may result in a criminal charge.[23] For example, it would be an illegal act to produce a document whose contents are protected by statute (i.e. State privileged documents that pose a threat to national security if disclosed in open court).
- the production of the original is impossible. For example, the document in question may be in the form of defamatory statements spray-painted on the external walls of a 10-storey building, making it impossible to produce the original spray-painted statements in court.
- the original is in the possession of an opposing party who has been given notice to produce it and has failed to do so.[24]
- the original is in the possession of a third party who refuses to produce it, despite being served with a subpoena *duces tecum*, on the basis of privilege or that the person resides outside the court's jurisdiction.

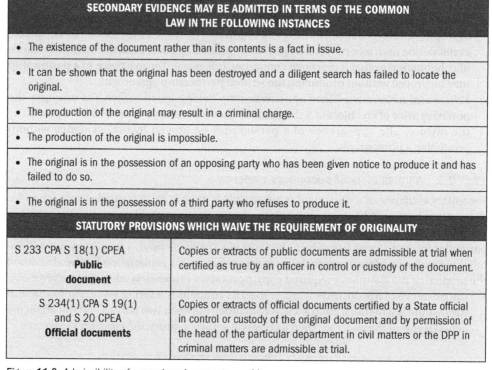

Figure 11.2 Admissibility of secondary documentary evidence

---

21 *S v Tshabalala* 1980 (3) SA 99 (A) at 103.
22 *Barclays Western Bank Ltd v Creser* 1982 (2) SA 104 (T).
23 *R v Zungu* 1953 (4) SA 660 (N).
24 *Singh v Govender Brothers Construction* 1986 (3) SA 613 (N) at 617–618.

There are also a large number of statutory provisions which allow the contents of documents to be proved by secondary evidence without the need to produce the original. Examples of some of these statutory provisions are:

- Section 233(1) of the CPA and section 18(1) of the CPEA: copies or extracts of public documents are admissible at trial when signed or certified as true by an officer in whose custody the original document is entrusted.
- Section 234(1) of the CPA and sections 19(1) and 20 of the CPEA: copies or extracts of official documents certified by the State official in control of the original document or the head of the particular department are admissible at trial. Note that the original official document itself may not be produced without an order from the Director of Public Prosecutions (DPP) in criminal matters or the head of the department to whom the original document has been entrusted in civil matters.[25]

11.3.3 Proof of authenticity

A document must be original and authentic in order to be admitted at trial especially where the contents of the document are in dispute. Evidence must be led to prove the authenticity of the document (i.e. the authenticity of a document is proved by establishing the authorship of the document).[26] Authenticity may be proved in a number of ways depending on the circumstances. A document may be authenticated by the following persons:

1. The author, executor or other signatory.
2. A witness who signed the document.
3. Any person who can identify the signature.
4. An attested document (i.e. a will or testamentary writing) is signed in front of witnesses able to testify that the author has signed the document and has done so before their very eyes as confirmed by their signatures as witnesses in terms of section 36 of the CPEA.
5. Any person who has lawful control and custody of the document.
6. A handwriting expert may make handwriting comparisons to prove authenticity in terms of s 228 of the CPA.
7. A notary public is a good example of a reliable witness to a signature.
8. In civil proceedings, authenticity of a document may be confirmed by serving a notice in terms of High Court Rule 35(9) on an opposing party requiring the party to admit that the identified document was properly executed and authenticated.

Where the contents of a document are in dispute, calling the author, signatory or a person who witnessed the signing of a document to the witness box serves two evidentiary purposes. Firstly, it serves to avoid an objection based on hearsay as the witness may testify as to the trustworthiness of the document's contents. Secondly, the witness may also testify as to the authenticity of the document. Where a document cannot be authenticated, it cannot be used in evidence or for the purpose of cross-examination.[27] A document need not be authenticated for the purpose of adducing it in civil proceedings when the following procedural rules are adhered to.[28] The document:

- has been produced in court as part of the pre-trial discovery process
- has been produced in court under a subpoena *duces tecum*

---

25 *S v Mpumlo and others* 1987 (2) SA 442 (SE).
26 Note that proof of authentication of a document does not also constitute evidence of the truth of the contents of the document.
27 *S v Swanepoel en 'n Ander* 1980 (1) SA 144 (NC); *Carpede v Choene NO and Another* 1986 (3) SA 445 (O) at 445.
28 *Howard & Decker Witkoppen Agencies & Fourways Estates (Pty) Ltd v De Souza* 1971 (3) SA 937 (T) at 940.

- is part of an interlocutory affidavit
- has been handed up from the bar.

In addition to these procedural rules, the requirement of authenticity may be waived where:
- the court takes judicial notice of the document
- the opposing party to a dispute acknowledges its authenticity
- s 34(1) and (2) of the CPEA applies in civil matters[29]
- foreign documents have been authenticated in their country of origin by the signature or seal of the head of a South African diplomatic mission in terms of High Court Rule 63(1)-(5) read with Rule 27(3).[30] Rule 63 is merely directory and the authenticity of a foreign document may be proved or disproved in the normal course of trial proceedings by direct or circumstantial evidence.[31]

A number of statutory provisions which waive the requirement of producing the original at trial and allow instead for the admission of a certified copy also waive the evidentiary requirement of authenticity. Examples of these statutory provisions, in addition to those mentioned above, are briefly discussed below:
- *Section 231(a) and (b) of the CPA*: a document that has the signature of a public official and an official seal or stamp of the department in which that public official is employed will be deemed *prima facie* proof that the particular public official did sign the document.
- *Section 222 of the CPA and section 37 of the CPEA*: ancient documents proved to be not less than 20 years old and which have been properly and securely archived are presumed to have been duly executed if there is nothing to suggest the contrary.[32] For example, a contract signed 21 years ago and secured in a lawyer's office throughout this period will be presumed to have been duly executed unless evidence is produced to dispute its proper custody in the lawyer's office.
- *Section 236 of the CPA and sections 27–32 of the CPEA*: entries in bank accounting records or documents are *prima facie* regarded as authentic on the production of an affidavit deposed to by a person in the service of a bank that the entries or records have been made in the ordinary course of business and are under the control and custody of the bank.
- *Section 246 of the CPA*: any document (including books, letters, lists, records, etc.) on the premises of an incorporated or unincorporated association or in the control of any office-bearer shall be admissible on its mere production.

---

29 S 34(1) of the CPEA reads 'in any civil proceedings where direct oral evidence of a fact would be admissible, any statement made by a person in a document and tending to establish that fact shall on production of the original document be admissible as evidence of that fact.' Note the section is silent on the need for authenticity of the admitted document.

30 These officials include consuls, consular agents, formally appointed foreign notaries, officers of the SANDF and documents authenticated in terms of the Hague Convention Abolishing the Requirement of Legislation for Foreign Public Documents.

31 Note High Court Rule 27(3) allows for non-compliance with the Rule 63 requirements where good cause can be shown. See *Blanchard, Krasner & French v Evans* 2004 (4) SA 427 (W) at 432; *Stocks & Stocks Properties (Pty) Ltd v City of Cape Town* 2003 (5) SA 140 (C) at para 14.

32 The common law defined an ancient document as being 30 years old but this time period was reduced to 20 years by s 5 of the repealed Evidence Act of 1962.

STATUTORY PROVISIONS WHICH WAIVE THE REQUIREMENT OF AUTHENTICITY	
S 231 CPA	Documents which have the signature of a public official and an official seal or stamp of the department in which that public official works, will be deemed *prima facie* proof that the particular public official did indeed sign the document.
S 222 CPA S 37 CPEA	Ancient documents proved to be not less than 20 years old and which have been properly and securely archived are presumed to have been duly executed if there is nothing to suggest the contrary.
S 236 CPA S 27 CPEA	Entries in bank accounting records or documents are *prima facie* regarded as authentic on the production of an affidavit deposed to by a person in the service of a bank that the entries or records have been made in the ordinary course of business and are under the control and custody of the bank.
S 246 CPA	Any document (including books, letters, lists, records, etc.) on the premises of an incorporated or unincorporated association or in the control of any office-bearer, shall be admissible on its mere production.
RULES OF COURT WHICH WAIVE THE REQUIREMENT OF AUTHENTICITY	
HCR 35 MCR 23 S 87 CPA	Documents produced in court as part of the pre-trial discovery process in civil matters Documents and the police docket requested from the prosecution in criminal matters
<ul><li>Documents produced in court under a subpoena *duces tecum*</li><li>Documents which are part of an interlocutory affidavit</li><li>Documents handed up from the bar</li><li>Documents the court takes judicial notice of</li></ul>	
HCR 63	Foreign documents which have been authenticated in their country of origin by the signature or seal of the Head of a South African diplomatic mission.

Figure 11.3 *Waiver of proof of authenticity*

11.3.4 Current applicability of the Stamp Duties Act, 1968

Section 12 of the Stamp Duties Act 77 of 1968 provided that certain instruments, as defined in the Act, could not be used in evidence or made available in any court unless the instrument concerned had been stamped as required by the Act. This requirement applied only to civil and not criminal proceedings.[33] Unstamped instruments could nevertheless be admitted in court if they were stamped prior to admission and the requisite monetary penalties, as provided for in the proviso to section 12 of the Stamp Duties Act, 1968 had been paid.[34]

Section 103 of the Revenue Laws Amendment Act 60 of 2008, which came into operation on 1 April 2009, repealed the Stamp Duties Act, 1968. The repeal of the Stamp Duties Act, 1968 is not retrospective and stamp duties are still payable on documents and other instruments created or signed before 31 March 2009.

---

33 See s 261 of the CPA.

34 See *Steyn v Gagiono en 'n Ander* 1982 (3) SA 562 (NC) and *Gleneagles Farm Dairy v Schoombee* 1947 (4) SA 66 (E).

11.4 The procedural steps in admitting a document in civil proceedings

There are 10 practical steps that must be taken by a legal practitioner when adducing a document as evidence in a civil trial. These are:

1. Identify all relevant documents intended to be used as evidence.
2. Determine whether the document is an original or a copy.
3. Discover all relevant documents not covered by privilege.
4. Allow for the inspection and examination of these documents by the opposing party.
5. Determine whether there are any common law or statutory exceptions to the admissibility of the original and/or any exceptions to the requirement of authenticity.
6. Serve a notice in terms of High Court Rule 35(9) or Magistrates' Courts Rule 23(10) on all other parties to the litigation requiring them to admit the authenticity of the documents intended to be used at trial.
7. Avoid the hearsay trap by subpoenaing all witnesses capable of testifying or proving the originality and/or authenticity of a relevant document.
8. Provide *bona fide* reasons why the original document has been lost and why only a secondary copy is being admitted as evidence.
9. Provide for expert witness testimony where necessary.
10. Determine whether a document is intended to be admitted for the probative value of its contents (i.e. as documentary evidence) or merely to prove its existence as an object (i.e. as real evidence).

THIS CHAPTER IN ESSENCE

1 Documentary evidence refers to a written or electronic document categorised as private, public, official, ancient or foreign.

2 Where documentary evidence is adduced to prove the truth of the contents of a private document, then such documentary evidence may fall within the parameters of documentary hearsay. Section 3 of the Law of Evidence Amendment Act, 1988, Part VI of the Civil Proceedings Evidence Act, 1965 or other statutory provisions dealing with documentary hearsay will govern its admissibility.

3 Public and official documents may be adduced at trial as an exception to the hearsay rule.

4 Where documentary evidence is adduced to prove what the private document contains, but not necessarily the truth of those contents, the common law and certain statutory provisions will govern its admissibility.

5 Documentary evidence will only be admissible if the original document is produced in court and the authenticity of the document is established, and where the content of the document is relevant to the facts-in-issue.

6 A distinction is drawn between the best evidence rule (i.e. primary evidence), which requires the production of the original document at trial, and secondary evidence. Primary evidence is evidence that suggests that there is no better evidence available. Secondary evidence is evidence that suggests that there is better evidence available.

7 The best evidence rule does not apply when:
   7.1 the existence of the document rather than its contents is a fact-in-issue
   7.2 the existence of a relationship or status flowing from the document is to be proved.

8 Secondary evidence may be admissible where:
   8.1 the original document has been destroyed or cannot be located

CHAPTER 11   DOCUMENTARY EVIDENCE   **109**

8.2   the production of the original would result in criminal charges being laid

8.3   the production of the original is impossible

8.4   the original is in the possession of a third party or an opposing party who refuses to produce it.

9   The originality and authenticity of a document is usually proved by subpoenaing a person who witnessed the creation of the document such as an author, executor or signatory. However, in certain instances the requirement of originality and/or proof of authenticity may be required as specific High Court Rules, common law and statutory provisions waive these requirements.

Chapter 12

Real evidence

12.1	Introduction	110
12.2	Immediate versus reported real evidence	111
12.3	Appearance of persons	111
12.4	Tape recordings	112
12.5	Fingerprints	112
12.6	Handwriting	113
12.7	Blood tests, tissue typing and DNA	113
12.8	Inspections *in loco*	114

12.1 Introduction

Real evidence is an object which, on proper identification, becomes evidence of itself.[1] Real evidence is, therefore, any tangible thing that we produce for the court to inspect so as to enable the court to draw a conclusion as to any fact in issue.[2] Examples of real evidence include:

- the appearance of persons
- tape recordings
- fingerprints
- handwriting samples
- blood tests
- weapons used in the commission of a crime
- photographs
- films
- video recordings
- documents
- any other thing that we can see or hear.

---

1 *S v M* 2002 (2) SACR 411 (SCA) at para 31.
2 See PJ Schwikkard and SE van der Merwe *Principles of Evidence* 3 ed (2009) at 395–403; DT Zeffertt and AP Paizes *The South African Law of Evidence* 2 ed (2009) at 849–863.

The admissibility requirement for real evidence is that the piece of real evidence must be relevant to proceedings. There are also the standard requirements that the real evidence must, like all evidence, be properly identified and must not be excluded by any other rule of evidence.

The weight a court affords to an item of real evidence is largely dependent on the testimony associated with it. This testimony is usually given by a witness who can clarify or explain what the item of real evidence is and what it is being used to demonstrate. For example, in a murder trial where the deceased was shot, a gun presented as evidence in court will have no weight unless a witness links it to the crime. A ballistics expert will testify that the fatal shot was fired from that particular gun. Likewise, there is no point in entering fingerprints into evidence unless a fingerprint expert explains the similarities of the fingerprints found to those of the accused.

The court may make its own observations in respect of real evidence admitted, provided that no specialist or expert knowledge is required to do so. Where the court's interpretation of real evidence requires more than ordinary knowledge or skill, the evidence of an expert will be necessary and such **expert evidence** should be received. Thus, a court may measure an item such as footprints,[3] but would need an expert lip reader to testify as to what a person is saying in a soundless video recording.[4]

12.2 Immediate versus reported real evidence

Immediate real evidence refers to a situation where we produce the item of real evidence in court for inspection in conjunction with oral testimony by a witness. The witness identifies the real evidence, describes it, or offers an explanation as to its relevance as evidence in the proceedings. With *reported real evidence*, a witness gives oral testimony in court describing the real evidence but we do not present the real evidence itself in court for inspection. This does not render the real evidence inadmissible. The weight the court gives to such evidence may be affected if the real evidence is available but the party relying on the real evidence elects not to produce it. It may even, in some instances, have an adverse effect on the case of the party concerned.[5]

> As noted previously, the list of what is considered to be real evidence is a relatively open-ended one. However, it is useful to consider the most common types of real evidence and how the courts have considered their admission.[6]

12.3 Appearance of persons

A person's physical appearance and characteristics may be relevant to a matter and, as such, will be real evidence that a court may wish to inspect. Where a party wants to present a person's physical appearance and characteristics as real evidence, they may do so either by having the individual in court where the person can be observed or by presenting photographs and so on into evidence. Instances where the appearance of persons is necessary include:

---

3 *R v Makeip* 1948 (1) SA 947 (A).
4 *R v Luttrell* [2004] 2 Cr App R 31 (CA).
5 *S v Mosoinyane* 1998 (1) SACR 583 (T) at 598 E–G.
6 See Schwikkard and Van der Merwe 3 ed (2009) at 396. This distinction was first discussed by Phipson, SL "'Real' evidence' (1920) 29 *Yale Law Journal* 705 at 706 as referred to by Schwikkard and Van der Merwe *Principles of Evidence* 4 ed (2016) at 396 note 8.

112 | THE LAW OF EVIDENCE IN SOUTH AFRICA

- where the court wishes to examine wounds or injuries sustained by a person
- where a party wishes to establish the identity of a person
- where a party wishes to establish a person's size, strength, dexterity or to examine identifying features such as tattoos or scars
- where a party wishes to show parentage (evidence of the child's appearance compared with that of the alleged parent is of limited value. It may be of greater value when dealing with a situation where there are apparent differences in ethnicity between parents or between a parent and an alleged child[7] but this method has been superseded by significant advances in technology that are more reliable and accurate)
- where a party wishes to establish ethnic origins
- where a party wishes to estimate the approximate age of that individual (section 337 of the Criminal Procedure Act 51 of 1977 allows a court to consider a person's physical appearance and characteristics to do this, but section 337(*b*) excludes such estimations where the precise age of the accused is an element of the offence)
- where a court wishes to establish competency to testify (a court may observe a witness's mental abilities to determine his or her competency to testify[8]).

12.4 Tape recordings

Tape recordings may be admissible as real evidence providing:
- the tape recording is shown to the court's satisfaction to be *prima facie* original
- the tape recording is sufficiently intelligible
- evidence is led which identifies the speakers in the tape recording[9] either by testimonial evidence of witnesses who heard the speech or conversation that was recorded or by inference drawn from what was said in the recording[10]
- any accompanying transcript of the tape recording is identified by the person who transcribed it.[11]

12.5 Fingerprints

A fingerprint is an impression left by the friction ridges of a human finger. A friction ridge is a raised portion of the skin on the fingers and toes. Sweat or any other substance which may be on the fingers or toes at the time the print is made leave impressions of these ridges behind on a surface. Fingerprints are unique to an individual. No two people will ever have the same fingerprints, not even identical twins. Thus, fingerprint evidence found at the scene of a crime has strong probative value in linking the accused to the crime.

DISCUSSION	A short history of fingerprinting
12.1	Fingerprints have been used as a means of positively identifying people for many years. In ancient Babylon, in the second millennium BC, fingerprints were used as signatures to protect against forgery. In 1880, a Scottish doctor in Tokyo, Dr Henry Faulds, published an article in which he discussed the use of fingerprints as a means of

---

7   *S v Mavundla and Another; S v Sibisi* 1976 (2) SA 162 (N).
8   *S v Katoo* 2005 (1) SACR 522 (SCA) at para 13.
9   *R v Behrman* 1957 (1) SA 433 (T).
10 *S v Peake* 1962 (4) SA 288 (C).
11 Refer to ch 13 Forms of analogue evidence for a detailed discussion on both audio and video tape recordings.

CHAPTER 12 REAL EVIDENCE **113**

> identification. In 1891, Juan Vucetich, an Argentinian policeman, initiated a system whereby criminals were fingerprinted. Today, law enforcement bodies throughout the world use the system and science of fingerprinting. For example, in the United States of America, the FBI manages a fingerprint identification system and database that holds the fingerprints and criminal records of over 51 million criminal record subjects and over 1,5 million civil fingerprint records.

We gather fingerprint evidence by taking an exemplar of the suspect's fingerprints and comparing it to fingerprints found at the scene of the crime or on an object pertinent to the crime. If there are seven points of similarity between the exemplar fingerprints and those found at the crime scene, this is sufficient to prove beyond doubt that the same person made the prints.[12] An expert in dermatoglyphics, the science of fingerprints, will make the comparison. If the court is satisfied as to his or her expertise, it will accept the evidence.[13] The evidence of the comparison may be given orally or by way of affidavit in terms of section 212(4) and (6) of the Criminal Procedure Act, 1977.

12.6 Handwriting

Handwriting is unique in that an ordinary layperson, the court itself or an expert witness can make handwriting comparisons. In terms of section 228 of the Criminal Procedure Act, 1977 and section 4 of the Civil Proceedings Evidence Act 25 of 1965, whenever the veracity of a particular handwriting is in dispute, a genuine handwritten sample may be compared to the disputed piece of handwriting. Both the disputed piece and the genuine sample are items of real evidence.

A handwriting expert, known as a questioned document examiner, may give evidence concerning the comparison. A layperson can also give evidence provided that he or she knows the writing being compared. A court is not bound by the expert's opinion[14] and may even draw its own conclusions from its own comparisons.[15]

12.7 Blood tests, tissue typing and DNA

Blood tests are often used in litigation. In criminal matters, blood alcohol levels are pertinent in cases such as driving with excessive blood alcohol levels. In civil matters, blood tests are used, for example, where paternity is in issue. In criminal matters, a person is obliged to submit to a blood test. However, in civil matters, it is not clear whether a person may be ordered to submit to blood or tissue typing tests. Where paternity is at issue, section 37 of the Children's Act 38 of 2005 provides:

> If a party to any legal proceedings in which the paternity of a child has been placed in issue has refused to submit himself or herself, or the child, to the taking of a blood sample in order to carry out scientific tests relating to the paternity of the child, the court must warn such party of the effect which such refusal might have on the credibility of that party.

---

12 *S v Nala* 1965 (4) SA 360 (A).
13 *R v Nksatlala* 1960 (3) SA 543 (A).
14 *R v Smit* 1952 (3) SA 447 (A).
15 *S v Boesak* 2000 (1) SACR 633 (SCA) at para 57.

114 | THE LAW OF EVIDENCE IN SOUTH AFRICA

It may also be possible to argue that, in terms of section 28 of the Constitution, a party to a paternity dispute can be forced to submit to such tests in the 'best interests' of the child.[16]

There are three tests that may be performed to prove paternity. The first and oldest test is based on an analysis of the red blood cells. An antiserum is used to identify the blood groups of the mother, the alleged father and the child. The blood group of the parents determines the blood group to which their biological child will belong. This test is of limited value because it can only conclusively prove that an alleged father is not the father. It cannot be used to prove conclusively who the father actually is.

The second test is based on an analysis of white blood cells and is known as the **HLA system of tissue typing**. By determining the haplotype of the child as well as of both parents, it can be determined whether the child has indeed inherited one haplotype from each of the adults. This test can positively identify the natural father of the child concerned to a degree of probability of 99,9%.

The third and the most conclusive test for determining paternity and for identification, used in both criminal and civil matters, is that of DNA fingerprinting. DNA or genetic coding may be identified from cells taken from skin, bone, blood, hair follicles and bodily fluids such as saliva, sweat or semen. Every individual's DNA is unique although, unlike fingerprints, identical twins will have identical DNA. An individual's DNA will also resemble that of both his or her parents. It is thus useful for identifying human remains and for establishing paternity and familial connections.

Whichever tests are done, the results will be received as real evidence if they were performed and recorded properly. The results are sometimes submitted by way of affidavit, but an objective scientist or expert, usually the person who conducted the tests, can give verifying testimonial evidence orally in court.[17]

12.8   Inspections *in loco*

Section 169 of the Criminal Procedure Act, 1977, High Court Rule 39(16)(*d*) and Magistrates' Courts Rule 30(1)(*d*) all allow for inspections *in loco* to be held in both criminal and civil matters. An **inspection *in loco*** occurs where a court and both parties inspect a particular location which is relevant to the matter being heard. They may also go to inspect an object or objects that could not practically be brought to court. Inspections *in loco* are generally held in the presence of both parties to a matter. An inspection *in loco* attended by one party only is irregular. The court may *mero motu* raise the issue of an inspection *in loco* or one of the parties may apply for one to be held. However, it is up to the court to exercise its discretion as to whether to grant such an application or not.

An inspection *in loco* may be useful as it can facilitate the court's ability to follow the oral evidence with greater clarity. It also affords the court an opportunity to observe real evidence that is additional to the oral evidence adduced in court.

If an inspection *in loco* is held:
- observations by the court should be recorded
- parties should be given an opportunity to make submissions and lead evidence where they consider the observations to be incorrect
- witnesses who are present at the inspection and who point out items and/or places during it should be called, or recalled if they have already testified, to give oral evidence in court on what they pointed out at the inspection.

---

16   *YM v LB* 2010 (6) SA 338 (SCA).

17   *S v Maqhina* 2001 (1) SACR 241 (T). See also ch 52 Blood typing and DNA testing.

CHAPTER 12   REAL EVIDENCE   **115**

THIS CHAPTER IN ESSENCE

1   Real evidence refers to tangible evidence we produce for the court to inspect so as to enable the court to draw a conclusion as to any fact in issue. There are various types of real evidence, each with its own requirements.

2   For real evidence to be admissible, it must be relevant to the proceedings at hand. The evidence must also be properly identified and not excluded by any other rule of evidence. Furthermore, the weight afforded to an item of real evidence depends largely on the testimony associated with it.

3   Where the interpretation of real evidence requires more than ordinary knowledge or skill, a court is obliged to hear the testimony of an expert on the particular real evidence.

4   Immediate real evidence refers to real evidence produced in court together with oral testimony which identifies the real evidence, describes it or explains its relevance as evidence in the proceedings.

5   Real evidence of a person's physical appearance and characteristics can be presented by either having the individual in court or by presenting photographs. There is a variety of instances where this would be necessary, for example where a court wishes to examine a person's wounds or injuries.

6   Tape recordings may be admissible as real evidence if:

6.1   they are shown to be *prima facie* original

6.2   they are sufficiently intelligible

6.3   evidence regarding the identity of the speakers on the tape recording is led

6.4   accompanying transcripts of the tape recordings are identified by the persons who made them.

7   Fingerprint evidence has strong probative value as no two people have the same fingerprints. Therefore, if seven points of similarity exist between exemplar fingerprints and those found at, for example, the scene of the crime, they are sufficient proof that the prints were made by the same person.

8   A layperson, the court or an expert witness can make handwriting comparisons by comparing a genuine handwriting sample to the disputed piece of handwriting. However, for purposes of such a comparison, both pieces of handwriting must be submitted as real evidence.

9   In criminal proceedings, a person is obliged to submit to a blood test should one be required. It is unclear whether the same rule applies to civil matters. However, where paternity is at issue in a civil matter, it may reflect negatively on a party's credibility should he refuse to submit to a blood test. Furthermore, section 28 of the Constitution also opens up the possibility of forcing a person to submit to a blood test in the 'best interest' of the child.

10   If, for practical reasons, it is not possible to bring a particular piece of real evidence, which is relevant to a matter, before the court, an inspection *in loco* of such evidence can be done in the presence of the court and both parties.

Chapter 13

Forms of analogue evidence

13.1 Introduction 116

13.2 Cinematographic films and photographs 116

13.3 Video and audio tape recordings 117

13.1 Introduction

The exact location of photographs, video tapes and audio tapes within the defined traditional categories of types of evidence has been the subject of much judicial debate. In some instances, their usage is clear. For example, if a photograph has been stolen and then recovered, the actual photograph would constitute an item of real evidence to be produced for the court to inspect (along with its frame). If, however, a court seeks to draw inferences from the content of the photograph, it is documentary evidence. This has consequences when deciding precisely what steps we need to take to render the photograph or tape admissible.

Although, strictly speaking, photographs, cinematographic films, video tapes and audio tapes form a subset of both real and documentary evidence, we have gathered them together as the courts are not consistent in their application of the rules relating to real and documentary evidence to these forms of evidence and certain *sui generis* rules relating to their admission have developed over time.

Furthermore, their prevalence is rapidly being overtaken by technological developments as most forms of analogue evidence are being replaced by digital (electronic) evidence. This chapter will therefore deal with those forms of analogue evidence that do not always fit neatly into the traditional categories and which are also being rapidly superseded by technological advances.

Increasing legislative reform of the rules of evidence and its possible eventual codification will no doubt see various new categories of evidence being formalised as part of the South African law of evidence, in much the same manner that has occurred with electronic or digital evidence.[1]

13.2 Cinematographic films and photographs

The difficulties facing photographic evidence are compounded when dealing with cinematographic (celluloid) films. Such films are regarded as being a series of photographs on a celluloid strip and thus the rules pertaining to photographic evidence apply in the same manner to films. The same difficulties occur with microfilms.

---

1 For example, the Electronic Communications and Transactions Act 25 of 2002 and see SALRC Project 126 *Review of the Law of Evidence.*

CHAPTER 13   FORMS OF ANALOGUE EVIDENCE   **117**

Section 232 of the Criminal Procedure Act 51 of 1977 allows for the production of photographs as evidence. In terms of section 33 of the Civil Proceedings Evidence Act 25 of 1965, a photograph is also a document. A photograph may therefore be admissible in both criminal and civil matters provided that the photographer acknowledges in writing that he or she is responsible for its accuracy. If the photographer does not do so, then we must lead evidence to show that the photograph is a true likeness of the thing shown, in other words, that it has not been doctored. The situation has become further complicated because in modern terms a 'photograph' is now almost always a digital image, not a celluloid film. Thus, new developments in the laws of evidence covering digital, electronic and computer-generated evidence have become applicable. Notwithstanding this, the traditional requirement that the authenticity of the photograph (i.e. that the photograph is a true likeness) remains applicable.

13.3   Video and audio tape recordings

However, our courts have taken different approaches in different jurisdictions where parties have sought to admit video and tape (audio) recordings into evidence.

In *S v Singh and Another*,[2] the Court held that tape recordings are real evidence. They therefore have to be shown to be the original recordings to be admitted into evidence. If their originality is disputed and if sufficient doubt is raised indicating that it is unlikely that they are the originals, then the Court has no alternative but to reject them.

In *S v Mpumlo and Others*,[3] it was held that a video film is not a document but is real evidence. If it is relevant, it can be produced subject to any dispute as to authenticity and interpretation.

In *S v Ramgobin and Others*,[4] the Court held that there is no difference in principle between audio tapes and video recordings. In respect of both audio tape recordings and video tape recordings, the State must prove the following to have them admitted:

- The recordings are original.
- No reasonable possibility exists of 'some interference' with the recordings.
- The recordings relate to the occasion to which it is alleged they relate.
- The recordings are faithful – a witness must testify to having witnessed the event purportedly recorded on the tape and that it accurately portrays that event.
- The recordings prove the identity of the speaker.
- The recordings are sufficiently intelligible to be put before the Court.

In *S v Baleka and Others (1)*,[5] the Court held that a video recording is not a document or a photograph or a cinematographic film. Tape audio recordings and tape video recordings (and a combination of the two) are real evidence to which the rules of evidence relating to documents are not applicable. Thus, the requirements for admissibility of real evidence apply. In other words, it must be relevant to be admissible. The authenticity of the video recording affects the weight given to such evidence and not its admissibility.

---

2   1975 (1) SA 330 (N).
3   1986 (3) SA 485 (E).
4   1986 (4) SA 117 (N).
5   1986 (4) SA 192 (T).

118 | THE LAW OF EVIDENCE IN SOUTH AFRICA

In *S v Nieuwoudt*,[6] the Court took cognisance of the differing approaches and stated:

> **Even if it is accepted that proof of authenticity is a prerequisite for the admissibility of a tape recording, the recording cannot be excluded from evidence solely on the grounds that interferences ... appear in it.**

The Court went on to say that the weight given to the evidence would be affected by the irregularities. The Court, however, failed to provide a clear precedent as to which of the competing approaches is to be preferred and there is thus no clear binding precedent at a national level.[7]

THIS CHAPTER IN ESSENCE

1 Photographs may be admissible in both criminal and civil matters provided that the photographer acknowledges their accuracy in writing. If this requirement is not met, then we must lead evidence to show that the photograph was not doctored. The same rules apply to films.
2 There is no uniform rule pertaining to the admissibility of video and tape (audio) recordings as the South African courts have taken different approaches in different jurisdictions.

---

6 1990 (4) SA 217 (A) at 220B.
7 See the discussion in A Kruger *Hiemstra's Criminal Procedure* (2008) at 28–42.

Chapter 14

Electronic and cyber evidence

14.1 Introduction **120**

14.2 History of electronic evidence in South Africa **121**
    14.2.1 Background and context 121
    14.2.2 History of electronic evidence in South Africa 121
        14.2.2.1 Position prior to the Electronic Communications and
                Transactions Act 25 of 2002 121
        14.2.2.2 Background to the Electronic Communications and
                Transactions Act 25 of 2002 122
        14.2.2.3 Functional equivalence 123

14.3 Electronic Communications and Transactions Act, 2002 .... **123**
    14.3.1 Overview 123
    14.3.2 Data messages 124
    14.3.3 Legal recognition of data messages 124
    14.3.4 Writing 124
    14.3.5 Original 125
    14.3.6 Electronic signature 126
    14.3.7 Production of document or information 126

14.4 Admissibility and evidential weight of electronic evidence **127**
    14.4.1 Overview of Section 15 of the Electronic Communications and Transactions Act 127
    14.4.2 Section 15(1) of the Electronic Communications and Transactions Act 127
    14.4.3 Best evidence rule 128
    14.4.4 Hearsay electronic evidence 128
        14.4.4.1 Business records exceptions – section 15(4) of the Electronic
                Communications and Transactions Act 128
        14.4.4.2 Can electronic evidence (a data message) constitute hearsay within
                the meaning of section 3 of the Law of Evidence Amendment Act? 130
        14.4.4.3 The interaction between the statutory exceptions to hearsay contained
                in the Electronic Communications and Transactions Act, the Law of
                Evidence Amendment Act, the Civil Proceedings Evidence Act and the
                Criminal Procedure Act in the context of hearsay electronic evidence 131
        14.4.4.4 Data messages as real evidence 133
        14.4.4.5 Requirements for a data message to be admissible 136
    14.4.5 Evidential weight of data messages 136

14.5 Distinctions between civil and criminal proceedings **137**
    14.5.1 Criminal Procedure Act 138
    14.5.2 Cybercrimes and Cybersecurity Bill 138

14.6 Presumption of reliability	**139**
14.6.1 Background	139
14.6.2 A presumption of reliability or regularity?	140
14.7 Overview of search and seizure of electronic evidence	**141**
14.7.1 Search and seizure in criminal cases (South Africa)	141
14.7.2 Search and seizure in criminal cases (foreign)	142
14.7.3 Search and seizure in civil cases	143
14.8 Overview of forensic science	**144**
14.9 Overview of the South African Law Reform Commission's review of electronic evidence	**145**
14.10 Overview of foreign law in respect of electronic evidence	**148**
14.10.1 England and Wales	148
14.10.2 Canada	149
14.10.3 The United States of America	151
14.11 Conclusion	**153**

14.1 Introduction[1]

Technology is an indispensable part of modern life. Globally, it continues to develop at a rapid pace. Its ubiquitous and pervasive nature results in the frequent production of electronic evidence in all forms of judicial and administrative proceedings.[2] New technological capabilities and the dynamic nature of communication present several challenges to established and traditional concepts in the South African law of evidence.[3]

Internet penetration – in South Africa and around the world – continues to increase, and technology is more accessible and affordable than ever before. So, electronic evidence will play a significant role in most, if not all, forms of legal and administrative proceedings – now and in the future.[4] As a result, the legislative environment governing electronic evidence, both in South Africa and worldwide, has already seen significant change and will continue to see more change as we progress further into the 21st century.[5]

---

1 This chapter is based on a portion of the author's ongoing PhD study.

2 South African Law Reform Commission, Discussion Paper 131, Project 126, *The Review of the Law of Evidence: Discussion Paper on the Review of the Law of Evidence* (2014) at 27.

3 See, for example, A Bellengere and L Swales 'Can Facebook ever be a substitute for the real thing? A review of *CMC Woodworking Machinery (Pty) Ltd v Pieter Odendaal Kitchens* 2012 5 SA 604 (KZD) 27(3) *Stellenbosch Law Review* at 454. See also *S v Miller and Others* 2016 (1) SACR 251 (WCC); *S v Brown* 2016 (1) SACR 206 (WCC); and *S v Meyer* 2017 JDR 1728 (GJ).

4 For example, see *Trustees for the Time Being of the Delsheray Trust and Others v ABSA Bank Limited* [2014] JOL 32417 (WCC) at para 18, where it was held that 'modern technological developments have brought about a revolution in the way that information, including legal information, is captured and disseminated.' See also *Heroldt v Wills* 2013 (2) SA 530 (GSJ) at para 8 where it was noted that 'the pace of the march of technological progress has quickened to the extent that the social changes that result therefrom require high levels of skill not only from the courts, which must respond appropriately, but also from the lawyers who prepare cases such as this for adjudication.'

5 South African Law Reform Commission, Discussion Paper 131, *Review of the Law of Evidence* (2014) at 22–23 where the SA Law Reform Commission proposes three options to reform the current regulatory landscape.

CHAPTER 14   ELECTRONIC AND CYBER EVIDENCE | 121

Currently, however, the primary legislative instrument regulating electronic evidence is the Electronic Communications and Transactions Act 25 of 2002.[6]

14.2   History of electronic evidence in South Africa

14.2.1   Background and context

There is no *sui generis* category for electronic evidence in South Africa – depending on the form it takes, or the purpose it will serve, evidence will be admitted to court in the form of oral evidence from a witness, documentary evidence in the form of a document, or real evidence in the form of a tangible thing: the 'traditional' categories of evidence. Typically, for the short to medium term at least, electronic evidence is admitted to court as a document, or as a tangible thing.[7]

14.2.2   History of electronic evidence in South Africa

14.2.2.1   Position prior to the Electronic Communications and Transactions Act 25 of 2002

The first computer arrived in South Africa in the 1950s,[8] but the statutory evolution of electronic evidence can be traced to the decision in *Narlis v South African Bank of Athens* (*Narlis*).[9]

In *Narlis*, the key issue before the court was the existence of a principal debt owed by surety and co-principal debtor, *Narlis*, to the South African Bank of Athens. The decisive evidence was electronic in nature – computerised versions of bank statements and ledgers.

At the time, the Civil Proceedings Evidence Act 25 of 1965 regulated evidentiary issues pertaining to civil matters – it did not provide expressly for electronic evidence. An amended version of the legislation is still in effect in 2018, and it still does not expressly recognise electronic evidence.

In *Narlis*, the lower court ruled that the electronic evidence was admissible and decided in favour of the bank. However, the Appellate Division found that, as a 'person' had not made a 'statement', as provided for in section 34 of the Civil Proceedings Evidence Act, 1965, the evidence was therefore inadmissible. The Appeal Court ultimately held that the legislation at the time provided no basis for any discretionary admissibility of electronic evidence – it famously noted: 'a computer, perhaps fortunately, is not a person.'[10]

Clearly, there was a need for legislative reform, so the South African Law Commission suggested the promulgation of a separate statute.[11] In the interim, in *S v Harper and Another*[12] the court was concerned with the meaning of the word 'document' in the context of a criminal trial where the admissibility of a computer printout was at issue. In the absence of

---

6   Read together with the Law of Evidence Amendment Act 45 of 1988 insofar as hearsay is concerned, and the Civil Proceedings Evidence Act 25 of 1965, together with the Criminal Procedure Act 51 of 1977 in the context of civil and criminal proceedings respectively.

7   South African Law Reform Commission, Discussion Paper 131, *Review of the Law of Evidence* (2014) at 29.

8   YG-M Lulat *United States Relations with South Africa: A Critical Overview from the Colonial Period to the Present* (2008) at 73; J Hofman and J de Jager 'South Africa' in Mason S (ed) *Electronic Evidence* 3 ed (2012) at 761 and Mybroadband 2015 https://mybroadband.co.za/news/hardware/132408-south-africas-first-computers.html all state the year as 1959.

9   1976 (2) SA 573 (A); DP van der Merwe et al *Information and Communications Technology Law* (2016) at 111.

10   *Narlis v South African Bank of Athens* 1976 (2) SA 573 (A) at 577(h).

11   South African Law Commission Project 6 *Report on the Admissibility in Civil Proceedings of Evidence Generated by Computers, Review of the Law of Evidence* 1982.

12   1981 (1) SA 88 (D).

THE LAW OF EVIDENCE IN SOUTH AFRICA

specific governing legislation, the court held that, in terms of section 221 of the Criminal Procedure Act 51 of 1977, the word 'document' in section 221(5), in its ordinary grammatical sense, was wide enough to include printouts from a computer. However, the court held that the computer itself, and the information thereon, could not fall under the wider definition of the word 'document'.

Following the South African Law Commission's recommendation, the Computer Evidence Act 57 of 1983 came into operation on 1 October 1983 and was South Africa's first attempt at legislating rules and norms for computer and electronics-based evidence. It only applied to civil proceedings,[13] and was criticised by a variety of academics[14] and even courts[15] for being overly technical and for ignoring the regulation of electronic evidence in criminal matters. The understandably cautious approach was based on the general belief that alterations (or manipulation) of electronic data were far harder to detect than alteration(s) made to a paper-based document.[16]

A limited number of courts dealt with the Computer Evidence Act,[17] but in *Ex parte Rosch*[18] the court tried to bypass the cumbersome[19] nature of the admissibility provisions by interpreting the statute to be facilitating, not restricting.[20] The Computer Evidence Act notwithstanding, the Law Reform Commission continued investigating evidence – in particular, computer or electronic evidence – through the 1980s[21] and into the 2000s.[22]

14.2.2.2 Background to the Electronic Communications and Transactions Act 25 of 2002

In response to modern trends involving computers and various new forms of communication, in 1996 the United Nations Commission on International Trade Law published the Model Law on Electronic Commerce ('the UN 1996 Model Law').[23]

The broader goal of the UN Commission is to facilitate and encourage international trade. Consequently, the UN 1996 Model Law is intended to serve as a guide for member states regarding e-commerce and related issues (such as electronic evidence). But for two sections,[24]

---

13 DT Zeffertt and AP Paizes The South African Law of Evidence 2 ed (2009) at 843; South African Law Reform Commission Issue Paper 27 *Electronic Evidence in Criminal and Civil Proceedings: Admissibility and Related Issues* (2010) at 19–21.

14 PJ Schwikkard and SE van der Merwe *Principles of Evidence* 4 ed (2016) at 440; D Van der Merwe et al *Information and Communications Technology Law* 2 ed (2016) at 112; South African Law Reform Commission Issue Paper 27 *Electronic Evidence in Criminal and Civil Proceedings: Admissibility and Related Issues* 2010 at para 4.5; J Hofman and J de Jager 'South Africa' in Mason S (ed) *Electronic Evidence* 3 ed (2012) at 763.

15 *Ndlovu v Minister of Correctional Services and Another* [2006] 4 ALL SA 165 (W) at 171 where the court noted that the Computer Evidence Act had two major shortcomings: firstly, that it was 'cumbersome' to comply with its provisions, and secondly, that it only applied to civil proceedings; see also *S v Brown* (CC 54/2014) [2015] ZAWCHC 128 (17 August 2015) at para 16, where it was stated that the Computer Evidence Act 'was generally considered to have failed to achieve its purpose'.

16 C Theophilopoulos 'The admissibility of data, data messages, and electronic documents at trial' (2015) 3 *TSAR* 461 at 467–468.

17 See *S v Ndiki and Others* [2007] 2 ALL SA 185 (Ck) at para 2 and *Ndlovu v Minister of Correctional Services and Another* [2006] 4 ALL SA 165 (W) at 171.

18 [1998] 1 All SA 319 (W).

19 [1998] 1 All SA 319 (W) at 327–328; see also South African Law Reform Commission Issue Paper 27 *Electronic Evidence in Criminal and Civil Proceedings: Admissibility and Related Issues* 2010 at 20–21.

20 [1998] 1 All SA 319 (W) at 327.

21 South African Law Commission Project 6 *Review of the Law of Evidence* 1982.

22 SALRC Discussion Paper 99 Project 108; Project 126; Project 113 and Discussion Paper 113.

23 United Nations 1996 Model Law on Electronic Commerce with Guide to Enactment 1996 http://www.uncitral.org/pdf/english/texts/electcom/05-89450_Ebook.pdf accessed 20 February 2016

24 United Nations Commission on International Trade Law 2017 http://www.uncitral.org/uncitral/en/uncitral_texts/electronic_commerce/1996Model_status.html, which states that South Africa is largely compliant '... except for the provisions on certification and electronic signatures'.

CHAPTER 14 ELECTRONIC AND CYBER EVIDENCE | **123**

dealing with certification and electronic signatures, the Electronic Communications and Transactions Act 25 of 2002 is based entirely on the United Nations guidance.

14.2.2.3 Functional equivalence

The UN 1996 Model Law and the Electronic Communications and Transactions Act 25 of 2002 both seek to follow a functionally equivalent approach that remains technologically neutral.[25] With the fluidity of the internet platform and technology in mind, and the increasing amounts of commerce conducted via electronic means, electronic commerce laws should ideally seek to remain neutral in so far as technology is concerned – this will ensure that South Africa has the ability to keep abreast with technological developments while recognising the difference in characteristics between data messages and paper.

This approach seeks to give effect to what the parties intended without over-prescribing methodology and technology. In *Ketler Investments CC t/a Ketler Presentations v Internet Service Providers' Association*,[26] the court noted that the Electronic Communications and Transactions Act 'recognises both the economic and social importance of electronic communications as well as the need to promote technology neutrality in the application of legislation'.

Briefly, the principle of functional equivalence demands that, as far as possible and practical, electronic evidence should be treated the same as traditional forms of evidence. The United Nations[27] states that a functional equivalent approach is 'based on an analysis of the purposes and functions of the traditional paper-based requirement with a view to determining how those purposes or functions could be fulfilled through electronic-commerce techniques'.

Primarily, this approach seeks to provide or facilitate an electronic equivalent for written, signed and original documents.[28] The Electronic Communications and Transactions Act facilitates this modern methodology in South Africa by recognising data messages as the functional equivalent of paper. This approach has been endorsed by various decisions,[29] and technological neutrality is codified as one of the objects of the Electronic Communications and Transactions Act 25 of 2002.[30]

14.3 Electronic Communications and Transactions Act, 2002

14.3.1 Overview

The Electronic Communications and Transactions Act repealed[31] the Computer Evidence Act entirely when it commenced operation on 30 August 2002. It is the primary legislative

---

25 For more detail, see JAE Faria 'E-commerce and international legal harmonization: Time to go beyond functional equivalence?' 2004 16(4) *SAMLJ* at 529–555.

26 2014 (2) SA 569 (GJ) at para 30.

27 United Nations 1996 http://www.uncitral.org/pdf/english/texts/electcom/05-89450_Ebook.pdf at para 16.

28 SA Law Reform Commission Discussion Paper 131 *Review of the Law of Evidence* (2015) at 57. See also Hofman J 'Electronic Evidence in Criminal Cases' (2006) 19(3) *SACJ* at 257-275; JAE Faria 'E-commerce and international legal harmonization: Time to go beyond functional equivalence?' (2004) 16(4) *SAMLJ* at 529–555.

29 *S v Miller and Others* 2016 (1) SACR 251 (WCC) at para 52; *La Consortium & Vending CC t/a LA Enterprises v MTN Service Provider (Pty) Ltd* 2011 (4) SA 577 (GSJ) at paras 12–13; *Ndlovu v Minister of Correctional Services and Another* [2006] 4 All SA 165 (W) at 165. See also *S v Ndiki and Others* 2008 (2) SACR 252 (Ck) where, although the term is not specifically used, the analysis performed by the court (para 53) uses similar logic; and the South African Law Reform Commission in Discussion Paper 131 *Review of the Law of Evidence* (2015) at para 4.67.

30 Section 2(f).

31 Section 92.

124 | THE LAW OF EVIDENCE IN SOUTH AFRICA

instrument regulating electronic evidence and, although not expressly stated, applies to both civil and criminal proceedings[32] – addressing one of the primary flaws of the Computer Evidence Act. It seeks comprehensively to regulate all aspects of electronic commerce, including electronic evidence, and primarily follows the guidance provided by the UN 1996 Model Law.

14.3.2 Data messages

Computer or machine-related evidence is often referred to as electronic evidence, digital evidence, ESI evidence (electronically stored information), computer evidence,[33] or ICT evidence. None of these terms exist in South African statute – rather, the terms *data message*[34] or *data*[35] are used. South Africa drew this definition from the UN 1996 Model Law.[36]

The current definition in the Electronic Communications and Transactions Act reads as follows:

> "data message" means data generated, sent, received or stored by electronic means and includes–
>
> (a) voice, where the voice is used in an automated transaction; and
>
> (b) a stored record

14.3.3 Legal recognition of data messages

Section 11 provides legal recognition for data messages. In *Jafta v Ezemvelo KZN Wildlife*,[37] the Labour Court found that the Electronic Communications and Transactions Act is consistent with global law,[38] and that section 11 gives legal effect to agreements or juristic acts performed via or with a data message. As a result, even though SMS, messaging applications such as WhatsApp, and e-mail often contain colloquial or relaxed language, 'treating them [data messages] as having no legal effect would be a mistake'.[39]

14.3.4 Writing

Section 12 provides that data messages will constitute a document and be considered in *writing* for legal purposes, provided certain requirements are satisfied. The section reads as follows:

---

32 Section 4 of the Electronic Communications and Transactions Act states that it applies in respect of any electronic transaction or data message. See the general discussion in South African Law Reform Commission Issue Paper 27 *Electronic Evidence in Criminal and Civil Proceedings: Admissibility and Related Issues* (2010) paras 3.2–3.4, 6.3–6.5 where the South African Law Reform Commission also concludes that the Electronic Communications and Transactions Act applies to both civil and criminal proceedings; see also C Theophilopoulos 'The admissibility of data, data messages, and electronic documents at trial' (2015) 3 *TSAR* at 461.

33 The term used by Van Zyl J in *S v Ndiki and Others* 2008 (2) SACR 252 (Ck) at para 4.

34 See the sections containing definitions (section 1) in both the Electronic Communications and Transactions Act 25 of 2002, and the Cybercrimes and Cybersecurity Bill B6 of 2017. The term 'electronic evidence' does not exist. The term used is 'data message'; see also South African Law Reform Commission Discussion Paper 131 *Review of the Law of Evidence* (2015) at para 3.2.

35 The term 'data' is defined in the Electronic Communications and Transactions Act 2002 as 'electronic representations of information in any form'. See also C Theophilopoulos 'The admissibility of data, data messages, and electronic documents at trial' (2015) 3 *TSAR* 461 at 462–463 where the admissibility requirements for an electronic document to be presented at a trial are discussed.

36 United Nations 1996 http://www.uncitral.org/pdf/english/texts/electcom/05-89450_Ebook.pdf; see also South African Law Reform Commission Discussion Paper 131 *Review of the Law of Evidence* (2015) at para 3.2.

37 (2009) 30 ILJ 131 (LC).

38 [2008] ZALC 84 at paras 62–99.

39 [2008] ZALC 84 at para 78.

CHAPTER 14   ELECTRONIC AND CYBER EVIDENCE   **125**

12. Writing.—A requirement in law that a document or information must be in writing is met if the document or information is—

(*a*)   in the form of a data message; and

(*b*)   accessible in a manner usable for subsequent reference.

Consequently, a data message must be accessible in a manner that is usable in the future for it to be considered to be in writing. In *Sihlali v South African Broadcasting Corporation Ltd*,[40] the Labour Court held that the SMS message 'quit with immediate effect' was *in writing* for purposes of a resignation.[41]

Moreover, in *Makate v Vodacom (Pty) Ltd*[42] the South Gauteng High Court held that a data message is a document for purposes of Rule 35 of the Uniform Rules of Court. In addition, in *Spring Forest Trading CC v Wilberry (Pty) Ltd t/a Ecowash and Another*[43] the Supreme Court of Appeal found that e-mail communication will be regarded as reduced to writing for the purposes of commercial agreements.[44]

14.3.5   Original

Section 14 provides that a data message can be regarded as an *original* for legal purposes if the information can be displayed or produced, and if the integrity of the information in the data message has been assessed in terms of section 14(2). The section reads as follows:

14. Original.—**(1) Where a law requires information to be presented or retained in its original form, that requirement is met by a data message if—**

(*a*)   **the integrity of the information from the time when it was first generated in its final form as a data message or otherwise has passed assessment in terms of subsection (2); and**

(*b*)   **that information is capable of being displayed or produced to the person to whom it is to be presented.**

(2) For the purposes of subsection 1(a), the integrity must be assessed—

(*a*)   **by considering whether the information has remained complete and unaltered, except for the addition of any endorsement and any change which arises in the normal course of communication, storage and display;**

(*b*)   **in the light of the purpose for which the information was generated; and**

(*c*)   **having regard to all other relevant circumstances.**

Consequently, the data message must be shown to be authentic. In S v Brown,[45] the court found that certain images contained on a mobile phone were admissible in evidence after complying with the requirements set out in section 14 of the Electronic Communications and Transactions Act. Moreover, in *S v Meyer*,[46] the court confirmed that authenticity of a data message is critical, and held that section 14 requires:

that the integrity of the information contained in the data message be assessed: has it remained complete and unaltered except for the addition or endorsements or changes which arise in the normal course of communication, storage or display

---

40   (2010) 31 ILJ 1477 (LC).

41   (2010) 31 ILJ 1477 (LC) at para 18. See also DP Van der Merwe et al *Information and Communications Technology Law* 2 ed (2016) at 115.

42   2014 (1) SA 191 (GSJ).

43   2015 (2) SA 118 (SCA).

44   2015 (2) SA 118 (SCA) at para 17.

45   (CC 54/2014) [2015] ZAWCHC 128 (17 August 2015) at paras 22–24.

46   2017 JDR 1728 (GJ) at para 302.

(S14(2)). The EFT Act also requires that the information be capable of being displayed or produced to the person to whom it is to be presented (S14(1)(b)).

14.3.6 Electronic signature

Section 13 deviates from the UN 1996 Model Law by creating two distinct types of digital signature. The first is an electronic signature[47] which is, according to section 1 of the Electronic Communications and Transactions Act, 'data attached to, incorporated in, or logically associated with other data and which is intended by the user to serve as a signature.'

This type of electronic signature is one that most computer users will create on a regular basis – a typed name at the end of an e-mail, for example. Section 13(2) provides further legal recognition for electronic signatures, stating that 'an electronic signature is not without legal force and effect merely on the grounds that it is in electronic form.'

The second type of electronic signature is an advanced electronic signature, which results from a process which has been authorised by an accreditation authority.[48] In terms of section 13(4), an advanced electronic signature is rebuttable proof that a person has validly and properly signed an electronic document.

Moreover, in terms of section 13(1), where 'the signature of a person is required by law', only an advanced electronic signature will suffice. This refers to instances where legislation specifically requires a signature, for example, in a will or an agreement for the sale of immoveable property. It does not, however, refer to instances where parties impose obligations on themselves, such as in a commercial agreement where parties are expected to 'sign' a document – in this latter instance, an electronic signature will suffice.[49]

Where parties to an electronic transaction have not specified the type of electronic signature to be used, or where the parties themselves decide to impose an obligation upon themselves, an 'electronic signature' will exist and suffice if, according to section 13(3)(a), a method is used to identify the person and to indicate the person's approval of the information communicated; and in terms of section 13(3)(b), one must have regard to the circumstances used, and whether it was appropriately reliable for the purpose for which the information was communicated.

Consequently, and as explained by the Supreme Court of Appeal in *Spring Forest Trading 599 CC v Wilberry (Pty) Ltd t/a Ecowash*,[50] the Act distinguishes between instances where the law requires a signature and those in which the parties to a transaction impose this obligation upon themselves. In this case, the SCA found that a typed name at the end of an e-mail constituted a signature (an electronic signature) for purposes of cancelling an agreement.

14.3.7 Production of document or information

In terms of section 17, where a person is required to produce a document or information, a person may produce it via data message if the data message is reliable (its integrity can be demonstrated) and is readily accessible for subsequent use. In *S v Meyer*,[51] the court interpreted section 17 as follows:

---

47 S Eiselen 'Fiddling with the ECT Act – Electronic Signatures' (2014) 17(6) *PELJ* at 2804–2820; Y Mupangavanhu 'Electronic signatures and non-variation clauses in the modern digital world: The case of South Africa' (2016) *South African Law Journal* 133(4) at 853–873; L Swales 'The Regulation of Electronic Signatures: Time for Review and Amendment' (2015) 132(2) *South African Law Journal* at 257–270.

48 Section 13, read together with section 1 and section 37 of the Electronic Communications and Transactions Act.

49 *Spring Forest Trading CC v Wilberry (Pty) Ltd t/a Ecowash and Another* 2015 (2) SA 118 (SCA) at paras 16–29.

50 2015 (2) SA 118 (SCA) at paras 17–18.

51 2017 JDR 1728 (GJ) at para 301.

CHAPTER 14 ELECTRONIC AND CYBER EVIDENCE | **127**

In the case of private electronic documents, admissibility can only be achieved through proving: (a) production: The use of data messages as documents is permitted by Section 17(1) provided that certain conditions are met namely: that the method of generating the electronic form of that document provided a reliable means of assuring the maintenance of the integrity of the information contained in that document S17(1)(a); and that it was reasonable to expect that the information contained in the data message would be readily accessible so as to be usable for subsequent reference S17(1)(b).

14.4 Admissibility and evidential weight of electronic evidence

14.4.1 Overview of Section 15 of the Electronic Communications and Transactions Act

Section 15 regulates the admissibility and evidential weight of data messages. Section 15(1) deals with admissibility, while section 15(2) and section 15(3) provide guidance insofar as assessing evidential weight is concerned; finally, section 15(4) creates a further statutory exception[52] to the hearsay rule by introducing an exception for business records.

14.4.2 Section 15(1) of the Electronic Communications and Transactions Act

Section 15(1) reads as follows:

15. Admissibility and evidential weight of data messages.—(1) In any legal proceedings, the rules of evidence must not be applied so as to deny the admissibility of a data message, in evidence—

(*a*) on the mere grounds that it is constituted by a data message; or

(*b*) if it is the best evidence that the person adducing it could reasonably be expected to obtain, on the grounds that it is not in its original form.

Importantly, section 15(1) seeks to facilitate[53] the admissibility of data messages, and follows an inclusionary rather than an exclusionary approach. It prohibits the exclusion of evidence on the mere grounds that it is generated by a computer and not by a natural person;[54] and further prohibits the exclusion of evidence on the grounds that it is not original – if the evidence is the best evidence reasonably available.[55]

Section 15(1), as noted by the Supreme Court of Appeal in *Firstrand Bank Ltd v Venter*, can be summarised as facilitating the use of and reliance on data messages.[56]

---

52 In addition to the exceptions created in section 34 of the Civil Proceedings Evidence Act 25 of 1965, section 222 of the Criminal Procedure Act 51 of 1977 and section 3 of the Law of Evidence Amendment Act 45 of 1988.

53 *Ndlovu v Minister of Correctional Services and Another* [2006] 4 All SA 165 (W) at 165–166; *LA Consortium & Vending CC t/a LA Enterprises v MTN Service Provider (Pty) Ltd* 2011 (4) SA 577 (GSJ) at para 17; *S v Meyer* 2017 JDR 1728 (GJ) at paras 300–310; *S v Brown* (CC 54/2014) [2015] ZAWCHC 128 (17 August 2015) at para 17.

54 Section 15(1)(*a*); *Ndlovu v Minister of Correctional Services and Another* [2006] 4 All SA 165 (W) at 172; LA Consortium and Vending CC t/a LA Enterprises v MTN Service Provider (Pty) Ltd 2011 (4) SA 577 (GSJ); *S v Ndiki and Others* 2008 (2) SACR 252 (Ck); *Firstrand Bank Limited v Venter* [2012] JOL 29436 (SCA); *Maseti v S* [2014] 1 ALL SA 420 (SCA); *S v Brown* [(CC 54/2014) [2015] ZAWCHC 128 (17 August 2015); *S v Miller and Others* 2016 (1) SACR 251 (WCC); *S v Meyer* 2017 JDR 1728 (GJ).

55 Section 15(1)(*b*); *Ndlovu v Minister of Correctional Services and Another* [2006] 4 All SA 165 (W) at 172; *MTN Service Provider (Pty) Ltd v LA Consortium & Vending CC t/a LA Enterprises and Others* [2009] JOL 23394 (W) at 18 10; *Maseti v S* [2014] 1 ALL SA 420 (SCA) at para 33.

56 [2012] JOL 29436 (SCA) at para 16.

14.4.3 Best evidence rule

Section 15(1)(*b*) provides that in any legal proceedings the rules of evidence must not be applied so as to deny the admissibility of a data message *if it is the best evidence that the person adducing it could reasonably be expected to obtain.*

Ultimately, if the electronic evidence – digital images, e-mail messages, SMS messages etc. – satisfies section 14 (it can be produced and its integrity is not in question), then it will generally be regarded as an original, and further, the evidence will in most circumstances be regarded as the best evidence reasonably available if that is indeed factually the case.[57]

In *Maseti v S*,[58] the court noted that 'the best evidence rule seems everywhere to be in retreat' – however, the court warned that in the context of electronic evidence, there is a 'need for caution'.[59] Further, before data messages are admissible, a court must be satisfied that they had been generated, stored and communicated in a reliable manner, and that their integrity was maintained in a reliable manner.

14.4.4 Hearsay electronic evidence

Section 15 does not seek to override the normal principles applicable to hearsay[60] – data messages must be treated the same as any other evidence and the admissibility thereof must follow the ordinary rules applicable to the South African law of evidence, except where concessions are made in the Electronic Communications and Transactions Act – for example, *inter alia*, with the concepts of an original and writing, and with the statutory exception to the hearsay rule created in section 15(4) for verified business records.[61] However, what is as yet unclear is exactly what constitutes hearsay in a data message. Clearly the probative value of some data messages relies on the credibility of another person, which renders them hearsay but, equally clearly, the probative value of other data messages which are not the agency of human invention or intervention cannot be said to depend on the credibility of another person – after all, according to the SCA in *Narlis v South African Bank of Athens*, 'a computer ... is not a person'.[62]

14.4.4.1 Business records exceptions – section 15(4) of the Electronic Communications and Transactions Act

Section 15(4) provides an exception to the hearsay rule for data messages created in the ordinary course and scope of business, and creates a rebuttable presumption that the information contained in the data message is correct. It reads as follows:

> A data message made by a person in the ordinary course of business, or a copy or printout of or an extract from such data message certified to be correct by an officer in the service of such person, is on its mere production in any civil, criminal, administrative or disciplinary proceedings under any law, the rules of a self

---

57 *Maseti v S* [2014] 1 ALL SA 420 (SCA) at para 33; *S v Brown* [2015] ZAWCHC 128 at paras 22–24.

58 2014 (2) SACR 23 (SCA) at para 33.

59 PJ Schwikkard and SE van der Merwe *Principles of Evidence* 4 ed (2016) at 438 and J Hofman and J de Jager 'South Africa' in Mason S (ed) *Electronic Evidence* 3 ed (2012) 761 at 762 where South African decisions relating to electronic evidence are described as 'conservative' and 'cautious' respectively.

60 *LA Consortium & Vending CC t/a LA Enterprises v MTN Service Provider (Pty) Ltd* 2011 (4) SA 577 (GSJ) at para 13; *Ndlovu v Minister of Correctional Services and Another* [2006] 4 All SA 165 (W) at 172–173; *S v Ndiki and Others* 2008 (2) SACR 252 (Ck) at para 31; *S v Meyer* 2017 JDR 1728 (GJ) at paras 299–301. See also PJ Schwikkard and SE van der Merwe *Principles of Evidence* 4 ed (2016) at 442–443.

61 J Hofman and J de Jager 'South Africa' in Mason S (ed) *Electronic Evidence* 3 ed (2012) 761 at 772–773.

62 1976 (2) SA 573 (A) at 577H. See para 14.4.5.3 below for an extension of this debate which is articulated in the question whether a data message is documentary or real evidence.

CHAPTER 14 ELECTRONIC AND CYBER EVIDENCE | 129

regulatory organisation or any other law or the common law, admissible in evidence against any person and rebuttable proof of the facts contained in such record, copy, printout or extract.

In *LA Consortium & Vending CC t/a LA Enterprises v MTN Service Provider (Pty) Ltd*, section 15(4) was described as 'controversial'.[63] The South Gauteng High Court further held that:

despite the very wide words of s 15(4), any hearsay contained in a data message must pass the criteria set out in s 3 of the Law of Evidence Amendment Act 45 of 1988.[64]

That notwithstanding, in *Absa Bank Ltd v Le Roux and Others* the Western Cape High Court noted:

Section 15(4) has a twofold effect. It creates a statutory exception to the hearsay rule and it gives rise to a rebuttable presumption in favour of the correctness of electronic data falling within the definition of the term 'data message'.[65]

Earlier, in what appears to be the first case dealing with section 15(4), *Golden Fried Chicken (Proprietary) Limited v Yum Restaurants International (Proprietary) Limited*,[66] the court held that:

In terms of section 15(4) of that Act a printout of a data message can constitute *prima facie* proof if the data message was made by a person in the ordinary course of business and if the printout is certified to be correct by 'an officer in the service of such person'.[67]

In *Trend Finance (Pty) Ltd and another v Commissioner for SARS and Another*, the court pointed out that a party seeking to rely on section 15(4) must show that the document 'sought to be admitted is a printout of information existing in electronic form'.[68]

The Supreme Court of Appeal has had limited opportunity to consider the provision. In *Sublime Technologies (Pty) Ltd v Jonker and Another*,[69] the court merely describe the section as 'controversial', referring to the at-the-time unreported full bench decision of the South Gauteng High Court in *LA Consortium & Vending CC t/a LA Enterprises v MTN Service Provider (Pty) Ltd*.

In *Firstrand Bank Ltd v Venter* the court only referred to the section in passing, and noted that it 'lays down minimum requirements for admissibility'.[70]

As a result, notwithstanding the literal interpretation of the section,[71] the decision of *LA Consortium & Vending CC t/a LA Enterprises v MTN Service Provider (Pty) Ltd* means that the precise meaning of section 15(4) is not entirely settled. However, most recent cases decided after *LA Consortium* appear to ignore the interpretation set out by Malan J, and appear to accept the literal interpretation of section 15(4) of the Electronic Communications and Transactions Act; that is, if properly authenticated, section 15(4) provides a valid exception to the hearsay rules (presumably, on the basis that this type of 'business records'

---

63 2011 (4) SA 577 (GSJ) at para 12; *Sublime Technologies (Pty) Ltd v Jonker and Another* 2010 (2) SA 522 (SCA) at para 21.
64 At para 19.
65 2014 (1) SA 475 (WCC) at para 19.
66 (1243/2004) [2005] ZAGPHC 311 (22 August 2005).
67 [2005] ZAGPHC 311 at 6.
68 [2005] 4 All SA 657 (C) at 678–679.
69 [2009] JOL 24639 (SCA) at para 21.
70 (829/11) [2013] ZASCA 117 (14 September 2012) at para 16.
71 J Hofman and J de Jager 'South Africa' in Mason S (ed) *Electronic Evidence* 3 ed (2012) 761 at 772–773.

130 | THE LAW OF EVIDENCE IN SOUTH AFRICA

exception is the globally accepted norm, and that section 15(4) appears to be an intentional step by South Africa's legislature to subjugate the hearsay rule).

For example, in *Diniso v African Bank Limited*[72] the court did not refer to *LA Consortium* or its concerns over section 15 being controversial and – correctly, in our view – held as follows:

> Section 15 (4) of the ECT Act provides for data messages, or copies or printouts thereof or extracts from such data messages, duly certified to be correct by an officer to be admissible in evidence on its mere production in civil proceedings and constitutes rebuttable proof of the facts contained in such record, copy, printout or extract.

Similarly, in *ABSA Bank Limited v Le Roux and Others*,[73] Binns-Ward J summarised section 15(4) as follows: '[it] has a twofold effect. It creates a statutory exception to the hearsay rule and it gives rise to a rebuttable presumption in favour of the correctness of electronic data falling within the definition of the term "data message"'.[74]

14.4.4.2 Can electronic evidence (a data message) constitute hearsay within the meaning of section 3 of the Law of Evidence Amendment Act?

Section 3 of the Law of Evidence Amendment Act regulates the admissibility of any hearsay evidence and provides judicial officers with a general discretion to admit hearsay if it proves to be in the interests of justice.[75]

Does this legislation apply to data messages? According to the prevailing view of the courts, it seems that it does, in the sense that 'any hearsay contained in a data message must pass the criteria set out in s 3 of the Law of Evidence Amendment Act 45 of 1988'.[76] Moreover, in *S v Meyer*,[77] the court held as follows:

> Section 15(1) does not, however make all data messages automatically admissible. According to the Electronic Communications and Transactions Act data messages are the functional equivalents of documents and therefore, except where the Act specifically provides for exceptions, the ordinary common law requirements for the admissibility of documents must be adhered to.

Earlier, in *Ndlovu v Minister of Correctional Services and another*,[78] the court held that 'there is no reason to suppose that section 15 seeks to override the normal rules applying to hearsay evidence'.[79] In *S v Brown*, it was held that '[section] 15(1)(a) does not render a data message admissible without further ado. The provisions of [section] 15 certainly do not exclude our common law of evidence'.[80]

As a result, a court will always be vested with the overall discretion to admit hearsay evidence (whether in data message or otherwise) in terms of section 3 of the Law of Evidence Amendment Act and, notwithstanding the academic and judicial debate on the precise meaning of section 15(4) discussed above, a court will ultimately be able to receive hearsay

---

72 2017 JDR 0120 (ECG) at para 19.
73 2014 (1) SA 475 (WCC) at para 19.
74 See also *Liberty Group Limited v K & D Telemarketing CC* 2015 JDR 1846 (GP) at para 33.
75 Section 3(1)(c) of the Law of Evidence Amendment Act.
76 *LA Consortium & Vending CC t/a LA Enterprises v MTN Service Provider (Pty) Ltd* 2011 (4) SA 577 (GSJ) at para 13.
77 2017 JDR 1728 (GJ) at 299.
78 [2006] 4 All SA 165 (W) at 165–166.
79 [2006] 4 All SA 165 (W) at 172–173.
80 *S v Brown* 2016 (1) SACR 206 (WCC) at para 18.

CHAPTER 14 ELECTRONIC AND CYBER EVIDENCE | 131

electronic evidence via section 15(4) of the Electronic Communications and Transactions Act, via the general discretion to admit in terms of section 3 of the Law of Evidence Amendment Act, or via the existing statutory exceptions created in section 34 of the Civil Proceedings Evidence Act 25 of 1965, and sections 221 and 222 of the Criminal Procedure Act 51 of 1977.

Finally, with the principle of functional equivalence in mind, if electronic evidence were to be exempt from the rules regulating hearsay, the net effect of this approach would be to favour electronic evidence over other forms of evidence. This could lead to forum or format shopping and would undoubtedly abolish any form of functional equivalence. Ideally, any form of electronic evidence must be treated in the same way as traditional evidence – the functional equivalent as far as possible and practical.

14.4.4.3 The interaction between the statutory exceptions to hearsay contained in the Electronic Communications and Transactions Act, the Law of Evidence Amendment Act, the Civil Proceedings Evidence Act and the Criminal Procedure Act in the context of hearsay electronic evidence

The South African Law Reform Commission suggests that the current position regulating hearsay electronic evidence may lead to 'inefficiency or potential confusion'.[81] It requires the potential review of several statutes – section 15(4) of the Electronic Communications and Transactions Act; section 3 of the Law of Evidence Amendment Act; Part VI of the Civil Proceedings Evidence Act; and sections 221, 222 and 236 of the Criminal Procedure Act.

14.4.4.3.1 The Civil Proceedings Evidence Act

The three primary exceptions created by the Civil Proceedings Evidence Act (in the context of data messages) relate to bankers' books, business records and a general exception where the author of a data message is not available. The promulgation of the Civil Proceedings Evidence Act took place when data messages were not fully contemplated or developed, but there is no reason these exceptions should not apply to electronic evidence if they are appropriate.[82]

Section 34(1)(*a*)(i) creates an exception for situations where the author of the data message had personal knowledge of the statements made therein, but is not available to testify.

Moreover, section 34(1)(*a*)(ii), the wording of which is certainly not a model of clarity, creates a further exception where a document was created by someone who was recording another (which recording is continuous and in the ordinary course of duty), and the person who was being recorded had personal knowledge of the statement.

Although these exceptions are still applicable, they have been largely nullified by the Law of Evidence Amendment Act and section 15(4) of the Electronic Communications and Transactions Act.

14.4.4.3.2 The Criminal Procedure Act

The Criminal Procedure Act also creates an exception for business records in terms of section 221.[83] If the conditions of section 221(1) are satisfied, any statement contained in the document that establishes a fact will be admissible on the mere production thereof.

---

81 South African Law Reform Commission, Discussion Paper 131, *Review of the Law of Evidence* (2014) at 65.

82 J Hofman and J de Jager 'South Africa' in Mason S (ed) *Electronic Evidence* 3 ed (2012) at 771.

83 Sections 221 and 222 of the Criminal Procedure Act 51 of 1977. See also J Hofman 'Electronic Evidence in Criminal Cases' (2006) 19(3) *SACJ* at 266.

The conditions for admissibility in terms of section 221 are: the compilation of the document must have taken place in the ordinary course of business; and someone who can be reasonably presumed to have knowledge of the matters dealt with therein must supply it. Further, the person who supplied the information must be dead, outside the Republic, or unable to testify due to mental or physical ailments.

In addition, section 222 of the Criminal Procedure Act incorporates sections 33 to 38 of the Civil Proceedings Evidence Act, making them applicable to all forms of criminal proceedings. In the present context, that means that the exception created by section 34 of the Civil Proceedings Evidence Act (for the admissibility of a data message where the author is not available) is also applicable to criminal proceedings.

Finally, sections 236 and 236A of the Criminal Procedure Act create an exception for banking records (both local and international banks) where an employee of the bank certifies the accuracy of the record and confirms that the capture thereof took place in the ordinary course of business.

14.4.4.3.3 The Law of Evidence Amendment Act

The Law of Evidence Amendment Act changed the law of evidence by introducing a statutory definition for hearsay, and including several exceptions to the exclusionary hearsay rule. The three exceptions created by section 3(1) are as follows:

- In terms of section 3(1)(*a*) where the party against whom the hearsay evidence is to be adduced agrees to its admission
- In terms of section 3(1)(*b*) where the person upon whose credibility the probative value of the hearsay evidence depends testifies
- In terms of section 3(1)(*c*) where a court has a wide discretion to admit hearsay evidence if the court deems it to be in the interests of justice to admit such evidence after considering a list of factors.

Consequently, even if a court takes a conservative approach and classifies a data message as documentary hearsay evidence, then it will still have the discretion to admit the hearsay data message if it is of the view that the interests of justice demand its admission into evidence.

Therefore, where a court is in doubt as to the classification of a data message, it may classify it as documentary hearsay and still have the ability to receive it into evidence via the broad discretion vested in a court via the Law of Evidence Amendment Act.

14.4.4.3.4 Electronic Communications and Transactions Act and the interaction between the various exceptions

As noted above, section 15(4) creates an exception to the hearsay rule for data messages created in the ordinary course and scope of business. Further, data messages accepted into court in terms of section 15(4) are rebuttable proof of the information contained therein. The exceptions contained in section 15(4) relate broadly to business records – as do the exceptions in both the Criminal Procedure Act and the Civil Proceedings Evidence Act. The Law of Evidence Amendment Act, however, relates to hearsay evidence in any context.

In addition to the cases discussed above, in *Director of Public Prosecution v Modise and Another*[84] the court categorised section 15(4) of the Electronic Communications and Transactions Act as follows:

---

84   2012 (1) SACR 553 (GSJ).

[It is] designed to ... allow evidence in the form of the facts and opinions contained in a document which complies with [section 15(4)] to be admitted in evidence at a trial notwithstanding that the person who listed the facts and formed the opinions in the document is not called as a witness.[85]

Lamont J seemed to indicate that, notwithstanding some of the concerns with the section, it is an intentional step by South Africa's legislature to subjugate the hearsay rule:

[Section 15(4) is] specifically designed to enable [persons] to avoid the need to lead the evidence of a witness by way of producing him and then leading viva voce evidence. The facts and matters in a document are the evidence. The evidence is admissible if the provisions of this section are complied with. Nothing more is required. The section enables [persons] to easily produce evidence which will generally be of a formal and uncontested nature and to place same in documentary form before a court without the need to call the witness... [A person] ... does not have to send its experts to a variety of courts countrywide to give evidence which generally is uncontested with the concomitant waste of money and time. In addition the expert becomes free to perform other work. These sections allow limited resources to be properly and adequately used.[86]

As noted elsewhere,[87] this exception appears to go further than previous statutory iterations, and arguably may favour evidence in the form of a data message if in a business context. Moreover, if a person is able to comply with the statutory provisions of section 15(4) – which simply require certification from an employee that the printout of a data message is correct – then those facts are rebuttably presumed true. This position may be problematic in criminal matters and may create a reverse onus, which is unconstitutional.

Finally, as noted by the South African Law Reform Commission, the current position (regulating hearsay electronic evidence) with potential interaction between several statutes when dealing with hearsay data messages is 'complex', creates 'unnecessary confusion' and requires 'greater alignment'.[88]

14.4.4.4   Data messages as real evidence

The question of whether a data message is a document (documentary evidence) or an object (real evidence) can be pivotal in determining whether evidence is admissible or inadmissible (due to hearsay), and will further dictate the hurdles to be overcome in its reception to court.

Real evidence is not subject to the hearsay rules for the simple reason that it is what it purports to be.[89] However, real evidence (traditionally, in any event) is typically only meaningful when supplemented by witness testimony – that is, someone to explain its relevance.[90]

---

85   2012 (1) SACR 553 (GSJ) at 557.
86   2012 (1) SACR 553 (GSJ) at 557.
87   J Hofman 'Electronic Evidence in Criminal Cases' (2006) 19(3) *SACJ* 257 at 267–268; DS De Villiers 'Old "documents", "videotapes" and new "data messages" - a functional approach to the law of evidence (part 2)' (2010) 4 *TSAR* 720 at 729–734. See also *S v Miller and Others* 2016 (1) SACR 251 (WCC) at paras 52–53 where the controversy regarding section 15(4) is mentioned briefly, but the court held that 'it is not necessary for the purposes of this ruling to go into any detail of the discussion on that score'.
88   South African Law Reform Commission Discussion Paper 131 *Review of the Law of Evidence* 2014 at paras 3.17 and 4.104.
89   J Hofman and J De Jager 'South Africa' in Mason S (ed) *Electronic Evidence* 3 ed (2012) at 776; *S v Ndiki and Others* 2008 (2) SACR 252 (Ck) at para 31; *Ndlovu v Minister of Correctional Services and Another* [2006] 4 All SA 165 (W) at 173.
90   DT Zeffertt and AP Paizes *The South African Law of Evidence* 2 ed (2009) at 849.

134 | THE LAW OF EVIDENCE IN SOUTH AFRICA

Consequently, as real evidence, a data message would not need to be admitted to court under one of the various hearsay exceptions and, technically, is evidence in and of itself which a court must accord appropriate weight (even without oral testimony – although, without oral testimony the evidence is likely to have little evidentiary weight). Therefore, if evidence is real in nature, it should not be subject to a hearsay enquiry.[91]

In *Ndlovu v Minister of Correctional Services*, the court found that data messages could be either real evidence or documentary evidence, depending on the nature of the evidence by holding as follows:

> Where the probative value of the information in a data message depends upon the credibility of a (natural) person other than the person giving the evidence, there is no reason to suppose that section 15 seeks to override the normal rules applying to hearsay evidence. On the other hand, where the probative value of the evidence depends upon the 'credibility' of the computer (because information was processed by the computer), section 3 of the Law of Evidence Amendment Act 45 of 1988 will not apply, and there is every reason to suppose that section 15(1), read with sections 15(2) and (3), intend for such 'hearsay' evidence to be admitted, and due evidential weight to be given thereto according to an assessment having regard to certain factors.[92]

In *S v Ndiki and Others*,[93] the court followed similar logic to that used in *Ndlovu* by finding that a data message will be considered real evidence if its credibility depends on the reliability of a computer, by holding that:

> Evidence on the other hand that depends solely upon the reliability and accuracy of the computer itself and its operating systems or programs, constitutes real evidence. What section 15 of the ECT Act does, is to treat a data message in the same way as real evidence at common law. It is admissible as evidence in terms of subsection (2) and the Court's discretion simply relates to an assessment of the evidential weight to be given thereto.

However, the court in *S v Ndiki* did express reservations about the reliability of computer-based evidence and *obiter* expressed the view[94] that all computer-based evidence should be hearsay.[95] However, the court did not deem it necessary to finally determine this issue and left the question open.

In *LA Consortium & Vending CC t/a LA Enterprises v MTN Service Provider (Pty) Ltd*, the South Gauteng High Court supported the distinction created in both *Ndlovu* and *Ndiki* by finding that evidence in the form of computer printouts was real evidence by stating that 'this is real evidence the probative value of which depends on the reliability and accuracy of the computer and its operating systems'.[96]

---

91 See also the discussion in DS De Villiers 'Old "documents", "videotapes" and new "data messages" – a functional approach to the law of evidence (part 2)' (2010) 4 *TSAR* 720 at 723–724 where the treatment of data messages as real evidence is consistent with the position in the United Kingdom – see further below at para 14.10 for a discussion on the foreign position.

92 [2006] 4 ALL SA 165 (W) at 173.

93 2008 (2) SACR 252 (Ck) at para 7.

94 Para 33; J Hofman and J De Jager 'South Africa' in Mason S (ed) *Electronic Evidence* 3 ed (2012) 761 at 777, where the reservations expressed in Ndiki are based on the misgivings noted in the *Annual Survey of South African Law* by Bilchitz where the view espoused is that all computer-based evidence is subject to credibility of natural person and should therefore be regarded as hearsay. This view should be rejected as it is inconsistent with recent case law, the international position and South Africa's common law on real evidence.

95 This view is only *obiter*, and Van Zyl J did not feel it necessary to decide this point.

96 *La Consortium & Vending CC t/a LA Enterprises v MTN Service Provider (Pty) Ltd* 2011 (4) SA 577 (GSJ) at para 22.

CHAPTER 14   ELECTRONIC AND CYBER EVIDENCE | **135**

The court went further to state that 'the data messages relied upon in this case are not only real evidence but includes hearsay'.[97] Perhaps the court meant to say that there was both real evidence and documentary hearsay evidence (as was the case in *Ndiki*). This is not clear from the judgment and it appears the court was referring to the printouts as being both real and documentary in nature. This classification is problematic as, conceptually, real evidence cannot be subject to a hearsay analysis – if the evidence is real in nature, it is therefore what it purports to be. It cannot be subject to the credibility of a person'; it is in theory subject to the credibility of a computer.

In *S v Brown*, Bozalek J took a conservative approach (although the court did endorse the decision in *Ndiki*), and found that, even though the admissibility of photographs (stored via electronic means) was more akin to being real evidence, photographs were ultimately classified as documentary evidence. The court found that:

> Given the potential mutability and transient nature of images such as the images in this matter which are generated, stored and transmitted by an electronic device I consider that they are more appropriately dealt with as documentary evidence rather than '*real evidence*'. I associate myself, furthermore, with the approach followed in *S v Ndiki and others* [2007] 2 All SA 185 (CK) where Van Zyl J expressed the view that the first step in considering the admissibility of documentary evidence is to examine the nature of the evidence in issue in order to determine what kind of evidence one was dealing with and what the requirements for its admissibility are.[98]

The as yet unresolved question, therefore, is: when should data messages be considered documentary evidence and when should they be considered real evidence? Finally, and to add a further nuance, is it possible for electronic evidence to be both real and documentary at the same time – or, at the very least, to exhibit characteristics of both real and documentary evidence?

The solution is a relatively simple one: consider the nature[99] of the data message, its purpose and the requirements of the relevant legislation.[100] As noted in *Ndiki*:

> It is an issue that must be determined on the facts of each case having regard to what it is that the party concerned wishes to prove with the document, the contents thereof, the function performed by the computer and the requirements of the relevant section relied upon for the admission of the document in question.[101]

It may be that a data message exhibits characteristics of both real and documentary evidence – this was the case in both *Ndiki* and *LA Consortium*, and the distinction between whether a data message is real or documentary can certainly be difficult at times. Moreover, as many have noted (sometimes with more concern than necessary in an advancing digital age), it is certainly possible to amend, alter or surreptitiously edit data messages. These concerns and apparent difficulties notwithstanding, it must not mean all data messages are treated as documentary evidence – this would be short-sighted, conceptually incorrect, and ignoring the common law. If the data message relies substantially on a computer, then that evidence should be real in nature. To guard against manipulation, a court must satisfy itself that the

---

97   *La Consortium & Vending CC t/a LA Enterprises v MTN Service Provider (Pty) Ltd* 2011 (4) SA 577 (GSJ) at para 12.
98   *S v Brown* (CC 54/2014) [2015] ZAWCHC 128 (17 August 2015) at para 20.
99   *S v Brown* (CC/54/2014) [2015] ZAWCHC 128 (17 August 2015) at para 20; *S v Ndiki and Others* 2008 (2) SACR 252 (Ck) at paras 20–21.
100   *S v Ndiki and Others* 2008 (2) SACR 252 (Ck) at paras 20–21.
101   *S v Ndiki and Others* 2008 (2) SACR 252 (Ck) at paras 20–21.

THE LAW OF EVIDENCE IN SOUTH AFRICA

evidence is authentic (reliable, accurate) – i.e.: that it is what it purports to be. Furthermore, a court has a discretion when deciding what weight to give the evidence.

This issue can be controversial,[102] and arguably requires law reform – the South African Law Reform Commission states that:[103]

> The South African Law Reform Commission supports the maintenance of a distinction between automated data messages and data messages "made by a person" and proposes statutory reform ... to guide the production and proof of both types of evidence in court. In addition, [we] support the development of a handbook on obtaining and producing electronic evidence that will provide clarity, to practitioners and judicial officers, on the legal position and advice on technical aspects of producing electronic evidence in court to avoid unnecessary confusion.

14.4.4.5 Requirements for a data message to be admissible

Given the various possible combinations of software applications and hardware systems that may be required to read or display a relevant data message, it will normally be presented to court as a document. An electronic communication in the form of a document, in order to be admissible, must be: relevant, produced, original and authentic[104] (subject to concessions provided in the Electronic Communications and Transactions Act regarding production and originality).[105]

As noted in *Ndlovu v Minister of Correctional Services*:[106]

> For documentary evidence to be admissible, the statements contained in the document must be relevant and otherwise admissible; the authenticity of the document must be proved; and the original document must normally be produced.

If the evidence is classified as real in nature, then as long as it is relevant it should be admissible, subject to any disputes regarding its authenticity.[107]

14.4.5 Evidential weight of data messages

Once evidence is admitted, its evidentiary weight must be assessed. Section 15(2) states that 'information in the form of a data message must be given due evidential weight.'

In addition, guidance in assessing weight is provided in section 15(3), which reads as follows:

---

102 See DT Zeffertt and AP Paizes *The South African Law of Evidence* 2 ed (2009) at 432–433 where the authors disagree with the proposition that a computer can produce real evidence and rely on Bilchitz to support their position. This position is not consistent with modern international practice and does not accord with the South African common law in relation to real evidence – as a result, the proposition that computers cannot produce real evidence should be rejected – as appears to be the case in most of the recent South Africa judgments dealing with the issue. See *S v Ndiki and Others* 2008 (2) SACR 252 (Ck); *Ndlovu v Minister of Correctional Services and Another* [2006] 4 All SA 165 (W); *La Consortium & Vending CC t/a LA Enterprises v MTN Service Provider (Pty) Ltd* 2011 (4) SA 577 (GSJ) and *S v Brown* (CC/54/2014) [2015] ZAWCHC 128 (17 August 2015). See also the discussion of selected foreign jurisdictions below in para 14.10.

103 South African Law Reform Commission Discussion Paper 131 *Review of the Law of Evidence* 2014 at para 4.104.

104 *S v Meyer* 2017 JDR 1728 (GJ) at para 300; *Ndlovu v Minister of Correctional Services and Another* [2006] 4 All SA 165 (W) at 165–166.

105 C Theophilopoulos 'The admissibility of data, data messages, and electronic documents at trial' (2015) 3 *TSAR* at 461–481; also PJ Schwikkard and SE van der Merwe *Principles of Evidence* 4 ed (2016) at 431–435.

106 *Ndlovu v Minister of Correctional Services and Another* [2006] 4 All SA 165 (W) at 165–166.

107 *S v Ndiki and Others* 2008 (2) SACR 252 (Ck) at paras 7–8, 18–22; *La Consortium & Vending CC t/a LA Enterprises v MTN Service Provider (Pty) Ltd* 2011 (4) SA 577 (GSJ) at para 16; *Ex Parte Rosch* [1998] 1 All SA 319 (W) at 321.

CHAPTER 14 ELECTRONIC AND CYBER EVIDENCE | **137**

(3) In assessing the evidential weight of a data message, regard must be had to—

    (*a*)   the reliability of the manner in which the data message was generated, stored or communicated;

    (*b*)   the reliability of the manner in which the integrity of the data message was maintained;

    (*c*)   the manner in which its originator was identified; and

    (*d*)   any other relevant factor.

As noted by the Supreme Court of Appeal in *Firstrand Bank Limited v Venter*[108] the purpose of section 15(3) is to deal with 'the assessment of the evidential weight' of data messages. Based on the court's analysis,[109] each of the four factors above must be considered holistically when determining the weight to be accorded to evidence, and no one factor should be over-emphasised.

In coming to a decision with regards to the weight to be accorded to a data message, a court will in all likelihood rely on expert evidence, although this is not mandatory and a court will retain the ultimate discretion. In *LA Consortium & Vending CC t/a LA Enterprises v MTN Service Provider (Pty) Ltd*, the court relied on evidence as to the reliability of the manner in which the data message was generated, stored or communicated; the reliability of the manner in which the integrity of the data message was maintained; and the manner in which its originator was identified[110] and found that a software package that creates detailed accounting and procurement data was reliable and trustworthy in the circumstances, particularly where the **appellant** did not challenge the reliability or otherwise of the system.[111]

Further, in *Jafta v Ezemvelo KZN Wildlife*,[112] in one of the first reported decisions dealing with the Electronic Communications and Transactions Act, the court relied on expert evidence to determine issues relating to the conclusion of a contract via data message.

The weight to be accorded to a data message will of course be dependent upon the facts of the particular case; consequently, while the four factors above should be holistically considered, and while no one factor should be over-emphasised, a court ultimately retains a discretion when deciding on the appropriate weight to be accorded to any data message that is admissible.

14.5   Distinctions between civil and criminal proceedings

The major distinguishing factor between criminal and civil matters relates to the onus of proof. That aside, the regulatory frameworks and applicable common law governing electronic evidence is overwhelmingly similar.

---

108 [2012] JOL 29436 (SCA) at paras 16–18, where the court also correctly noted the overlap between the factors listed in s 3(1)(*c*) of the Law of Evidence Amendment Act, and the factors listed in section 15(3) of the Electronic Communications and Transactions Act.

109 PJ Schwikkard and SE van der Merwe *Principles of Evidence* 4 ed (2016) at 437–446.

110 Paras 15–16. See also *Maseti v S* [2014] 1 All SA 420 (SCA) at para 33.

111 See *also Ndlovu v Minister of Correctional Services and Another* [2006] 4 All SA 165 (W) at 175 and *S v Ndiki and Others* [2007] 2 All SA 185 (Ck) where both courts perform a similar, holistic analysis of all four factors in light of the particular circumstances of each case.

112 (2009) 30 ILJ 131 (LC) at paras 17–29 where experts from both sides produced a substantially agreed set of facts regarding e-mail usage and Google Mail.

138 | THE LAW OF EVIDENCE IN SOUTH AFRICA

In addition to the common law, the Constitution, the Law of Evidence Amendment Act[113] and the Electronic Communications and Transactions Act[114] apply to both civil and criminal matters. The primary distinction from a legislative perspective is that in criminal matters the Criminal Procedure Act[115] will find application, as opposed to the Civil Proceedings Evidence Act in civil matters.

Further, and as noted above, in criminal matters, section 222 of the Criminal Procedure Act incorporates sections 33 to 38 of the Civil Proceedings Evidence Act, making those sections applicable to all forms of criminal proceedings.

14.5.1 Criminal Procedure Act

Chapter 24 (sections 208–253) of the Criminal Procedure Act deals with evidence. Section 210, titled irrelevant evidence inadmissible, repeats the common law, albeit phrased in the negative – the basic rationale being that only relevant evidence will be admissible.

The principal sections in the CPA relevant to electronic evidence are sections 221, 222 and 236, read together with sections 246 and 247.[116] Primarily, these sections create an exception to the hearsay rule in the form of business records (duly authenticated), as well as making the Civil Proceedings Evidence Act applicable to criminal proceedings (insofar as documentary evidence is concerned).

However, insofar as electronic evidence is concerned, section 221(5) of the Criminal Procedure Act defines a document as 'any device by means of which information is recorded or stored'. This was one of the central issues in *S v Harper and Another*,[117] where the court found that a computer could not be a document for purposes of the Criminal Procedure Act, but that a printout by a computer could be a document.

Conversely, in civil proceedings, a document is defined in Section 33 as 'any book, map, plan, drawing or photograph'.

On the face of it, the definition of document in the Civil Proceedings Evidence Act is not wide enough as it currently stands to include a data message. Moreover, and strangely, it appears that the definition of document for civil proceedings is more restrictive (and narrow) than the definition contained in the Criminal Procedure Act, which is not a sustainable position.

Consequently, there are different definitions for the word 'document' in civil and criminal proceedings, and it is an area that concerns the South African Law Reform Commission.[118]

14.5.2 Cybercrimes and Cybersecurity Bill

According to a discussion document[119] in relation to the Cybercrimes and Cybersecurity Bill B6-2017 released by the Department of Justice in January 2017:

---

113 Section 3(1), dealing with hearsay evidence, expressly states that it applies to both civil and criminal proceedings.

114 Section 4 of the Electronic Communications and Transactions Act, 2002 states that it applies in respect of any electronic transaction or data message. See also the general discussion in South African Law Reform Commission Issue Paper 27 *Electronic Evidence in Criminal and Civil Proceedings: Admissibility and Related Issues* (2010) paras 3.2 to 3.4 and 6.3 to 6.5, where the Commission also concludes that it applies to both civil and criminal proceedings. See also C Theophilopoulos 'The admissibility of data, data messages, and electronic documents at trial' (2015) 3 *TSAR* at 461.

115 Act 51 of 1977.

116 *S v De Villiers* 1993 (1) SACR 574 (Nm) at 575–580; *S v Harper and Another* 1981 (1) SA 88 (D) at 260.

117 1981 (1) SA 88 (D) at 95C.

118 South African Law Reform Commission Discussion Paper 131 *Review of the Law of Evidence* 2014 at 83–88.

119 Department of Justice and Constitutional Development 2017 http://www.justice.gov.za/legislation/bills/CyberCrimesDiscussionDocument2017.pdf.

> The laws dealing with electronic evidence are, in general, sufficient for the purposes of criminal proceedings. However, certain improvements can be made to cater for new technologies.

The perception that the current position insofar as electronic evidence is adequate is further borne out by the marked difference in the evidentiary provisions in the two versions of the Cybercrimes and Cybersecurity Bill released for public comment. In the B-2015 version, Chapter 8, Evidence,[120] contained three comprehensive sections dealing with evidence: section 61 (admissibility of affidavits); section 62 (admissibility of evidence obtained as result of direction requesting foreign assistance and cooperation); and section 63 (admissibility of evidence).

Conversely, the new version of the Bill, B6-2017, contains only one section under the heading Chapter 8, Evidence – section 51 (proof of certain facts by affidavit). As it stands, the section appears to have a built-in condition making it only applicable to criminal proceedings or civil proceedings as contemplated in Chapter 5 or 6 of the Prevention of Organised Crime Act 121 of 1998.

The only inference one can draw is that the legislature appears satisfied with the current position regarding electronic evidence in criminal trials, and that it is adequately regulated by the Electronic Communications and Transactions Act, the common law, the Law of Evidence Amendment Act and the Criminal Procedure Act and/or the Civil Proceedings Evidence Act.

14.6 Presumption of reliability

14.6.1 Background

In the context of data messages and electronic communications, a presumption of reliability is a presumption that electronic equipment was working and reliable at the relevant time, unless there is evidence to the contrary.[121] For example, an e-mail server with typical commercially available software that routinely functions and facilitates the exchange of e-mail messages will, under a presumption of reliability, be presumed to be working and in order: the primary rationale being expediency – to save time, and avoid proving the obvious.[122] This type of presumption is consistent with international best practice in the context of electronic evidence.[123]

---

120 These were predominantly applicable to criminal proceedings. Department of Justice and Constitutional Development 2015 http://www.justice.gov.za/legislation/invitations/CyberCrimesBill2015.pdf or http://cybercrime.org.za/docs/Cybercrimes_and_Cybersecurity_Bill_2015.pdf

121 *Trustees for the time Being of the Delsheray Trust and Others v ABSA Bank Limited* [2014] 4 All SA 748 (WCC) at paras 40–41. See also DS De Villiers 'Old "documents", "videotapes" and new "data messages" – a functional approach to the law of evidence (part 2)' (2010) 4 *TSAR* 720 at 722–734 where the presumption is discussed in the broader context of electronic evidence; C Theophilopoulos 'The admissibility of data, data messages, and electronic documents at trial' (2015) 3 *TSAR* 461 at 477 where the author discusses courts taking judicial notice of the 'integrity and reliability of the operation of electronic hard drive systems and software programs'.

122 S Mason 'Mechanical Instruments: the presumption of being in order' in Mason S (ed) *Electronic Evidence* 3 ed (2012)149 at 149.

123 [2014] 4 All SA 748 (WCC) at para 40 where the court refers to PM Storm 'Admitting Computer Generated Records: A presumption of Reliability' 18(1) 1984 *John Marshall Law Review* 115, which reviews the position in the United States supporting such a presumption. See also the United Kingdom case of *Castle v Cross* [1984] 1 WLR 1372, [1985] 1 All ER 87 which supports such a presumption.

14.6.2 A presumption of reliability or regularity?

In *Trustees for the time being of the Delsheray Trust and Others v ABSA Bank Limited*,[124] the court discussed a presumption of reliability and concluded that, although the presumption is not applied in name, it is established and applied in form and substance in South Africa.[125] The court further refers to The Law Commission of the United Kingdom, which refers to case of *Castle v Cross*[126] and describes the presumption of reliability as follows:

> In the absence of evidence to the contrary, the courts will presume that mechanical instruments were in order at the material time.

The presumption of reliability is often closely linked to a presumption of regularity.[127] A presumption of regularity has been described as our general observation of life based on statistical probabilities[128] – for example, if something regularly works without any incident, it should be presumed that the process or machine was working and reliable at the relevant time. Further, it can be categorised as a rebuttable presumption that events or acts which occur regularly will likely occur again. It is often referred to in conjunction with the Latin maxim *omnia praesumuntur rite esse acta donec probetur in contrarium* – which roughly translates to 'all are presumed to be done until the contrary is proved'.[129]

The presumption of reliability, which is also found in foreign law,[130] often occurs in context of government officials and their duties. For example, in *United States v Chemical Foundation Inc.* it was held that 'the presumption of regularity supports the official acts of public officers, and, in the absence of clear evidence to the contrary, courts presume that they have properly discharged their official duties'.[131]

In the United Kingdom matter of *R v Minors; R v Harper*[132] (also referred to with approval in *Trustees for the time Being of the Delsheray Trust v ABSA Bank Limited*),[133] the court noted as follows:

> ...in a great many cases the necessary evidence could be supplied by circumstantial evidence of the usual habit or routine regarding the use of the computer. Sometimes this is referred to as the presumption of regularity. We prefer to describe it as a common sense inference.

Moreover, in *Trustees for the time Being of the Delsheray Trust v ABSA Bank Limited*, the court noted:

> There is clearly a significant degree of overlap between this presumption and the presumption of reliability discussed above. This is understandable as the reliable operation of a computer also depends upon the quality of the human input. It seems

---

124 [2014] 4 All SA 748 (WCC).
125 [2014] 4 All SA 748 (WCC) at para 41 where the court refers to a presumption in the context of drug trafficking in *S v Mthimkulu* 1975 (4) SA 759 (A).
126 [1984] 1 WLR 1372, [1985] 1 All ER 87.
127 *Byers v Chinn and Another* 1928 AD 322. See also the useful discussion in M Dendy *Law of South Africa Presumptions* 18(3) para 242 and the cases quoted therein in footnotes 1–3.
128 M Dendy *Law of South Africa Presumptions* 18(3) para 242.
129 DT Zeffertt and AP Paizes *The South African Law of Evidence* 2 ed (2009) at 212.
130 For example, see *Castle v Cross* [1985] 1 All ER 87. See also the discussion in S Mason 'The presumption that computers are "reliable"' in S Mason and D Seng (eds) *Electronic Evidence* 4 ed (2017) at 101–185 where the authors are critical of this type of presumption.
131 272 U.S. 1, 14-15 (1926). See also *Latif v Obama* 666 F.3d 746 (D.C. Cir. 2011) where the presumption was approved.
132 [1989] 1 WLR 441 CA.
133 [2014] 4 All SA 748 (WCC) at para 50.

CHAPTER 14   ELECTRONIC AND CYBER EVIDENCE | **141**

> to us therefore that the arguments in favour of the application of the presumption
> of reliability in this case, mentioned in para [32] above, applies mutatis mutandis to
> the application of the presumption of regularity.[134]

Consequently, whether referred to as a presumption of reliability or a presumption of
regularity,[135] there is a long history of authority, in South Africa and abroad, in support of
this type of presumption in the context of electronic evidence. However, it should be noted
that some argue that the presumption is too 'crude' to apply to computers,[136] and that the
presumption is so wide and vague that it is meaningless.[137]

Be that as it may, in the context of electronic evidence, the recent matter of *Trustees for
the time Being of the Delsheray Trust and Others v ABSA Bank Limited*[138] illustrates that a
presumption of reliability is established in South African law.

14.7   Overview of search and seizure of electronic evidence

As at 30 June 2016, approximately 52 per cent of the South African population (about 28 580 290
people)[139] were internet users and so the likelihood that electronic evidence will be used in
a legal dispute is very high. For this reason, among others, the means by which such evidence
may legitimately be obtained are important.

14.7.1   Search and seizure in criminal cases (South Africa)

The primary regulatory mechanism for the search and seizure of electronic evidence is
the Criminal Procedure Act 51 of 1977, particularly Chapter 2 dealing with search warrants,
entering of premises, forfeiture and disposal of property, and seizure.[140] In addition,
sections 82 and 83 the Electronic Communications and Transactions Act provide wide-
ranging search and seizure powers to Cyber Inspectors. However, these sections of the
Electronic Communications and Transactions Act, and the entire Chapter XII (sections
80–84) are effectively defunct for one simple reason: a Cyber Inspector has never been
appointed. In *S v Miller and Others*[141] the court correctly described Cyber Inspectors as
'non-existent'.[142] Chapter 3 of the Regulation of Interception of Communications and
Provision of Communication-Related Information Act 70 of 2002 also provides for warrants
and direction insofar as communication-related data is concerned.

The Criminal Procedure Act was created at a time when a data message was not envisaged
and was created for the search and seizure of physical objects in a tangible world.[143] However,

---

134   [2014] 4 All SA 748 (WCC) at para 51.

135   In general, see DT Zeffertt and AP Paizes *The South African Law of Evidence* 2 ed (2009) at 212–222.

136   S Mason 'Mechanical Instruments: the presumption of being in order' in Mason S (ed) *Electronic Evidence* 3 ed (2012)
149 at 176.

137   S Mason 'The presumption that computers are "reliable"' in S Mason and D Seng (eds) *Electronic Evidence* 4 ed (2017) 101–185.

138   [2014] 4 All SA 748 (WCC).

139   Internet World Stats 'South Africa' available at http://www.internetworldstats.com/af/za.htm.

140   For further detail, see VM Basdeo et al 'Search for and Seizure of Evidence in Cyber Environments: A Law Enforcement
Dilemma in South African Criminal Procedure' *JLSD* (2014) 1(1) 48–67; VM Basdeo 'The legal challenges of search and
seizure of electronic evidence in South African criminal procedure: A comparative analysis' (2012) 25(2) *SACJ* 195;
GP Bouwer 'Search and seizure of electronic evidence: Division of the traditional one-step process into a new two-step
process in a South African context' (2014) 27(2) *SACJ* 156–171.

141   [2015] 4 All SA 503 (WCC).

142   [2015] 4 All SA 503 (WCC) at para 56.

143   GP Bouwer 'Search and seizure of electronic evidence: Division of the traditional one-step process into a new two-step
process in a South African context' (2014) 27(2) *SACJ* 156–171. See also South African Law Commission Discussion Paper
99 Project 108 *Computer related crime: Preliminary proposals for reform in respect of unauthorised access to computers,
unauthorised modification of computer data and software applications and related procedural aspects* (2001) quoted therein.

142 | THE LAW OF EVIDENCE IN SOUTH AFRICA

as demonstrated in *Thint (Pty) Ltd v NDPP and Others; Zuma v NDPP and Others*,[144] electronic evidence can be seized (then copied and searched off-site) via sections 20 and 21 of the Criminal Procedure Act.

Importantly, the search warrant must be as specific as possible – it should provide clarity as to which offence is suspected. In *Van der Merwe and Others v Additional Magistrate, Cape Town and Others*[145] the court set aside several warrants on the basis that they were overly broad (they did not contain details of the alleged offence). The court reviewed the legal framework and noted with approval the judgment in *Powell NO and Others v Van Der Merwe NO and Others*[146] where it was held that the common law position has developed as follows:

- **The terms of a search warrant must be construed with reasonable strictness. Ordinarily there is no reason why it should be read otherwise than in the terms in which it is expressed.**
- **A warrant must convey intelligibly to both searcher and searched the ambit of the search it authorises.**
- **If a warrant is too general, or if its terms go beyond those the authorising statute permits, the Courts will refuse to recognise it as valid, and it will be set aside.**
- **It is no cure for an overbroad warrant to say that the subject of the search knew or ought to have known what was being looked for: The warrant must itself specify its object, and must do so intelligibly and narrowly within the bounds of the empowering statute.[147]**

Consequently, although the current legislative matrix was developed for a physical world, the current regime can still adequately regulate the search and seizure of electronic evidence.[148]

Be that as it may, the imminent promulgation of the Cybercrimes and Cybersecurity Bill B6-2017[149] will ensure that the position is comprehensively regulated. Chapter 5 (sections 24–43) provides exhaustive powers to investigate, search and seize that are consistent with the Criminal Procedure Act, 1977. Provision is made for, *inter alia*, application to a High Court Judge or a Magistrate to issue a warrant to search and seize electronic evidence; oral application to a High Court Judge or Magistrate to issue a warrant to search and seize electronic evidence; search and seizure with consent; search and seizure without a warrant; and preservation of evidence orders.

Further, standard operating procedures for law enforcement agencies will be adopted in terms of section 24 and section 25 of the Cybercrimes and Cybersecurity Bill B6-2017.

14.7.2 Search and seizure in criminal cases (foreign)

The International Co-operation in Criminal Matters Act 75 of 1996 aims to facilitate the provision of evidence, the execution of sentences in criminal cases, and the confiscation and transfer of the proceeds of crime between South Africa and foreign states. Simply put, it

---

144 2009 (1) SA 1 (CC).

145 2010 (1) SACR 470 (C).

146 2005 (1) SACR 317 (SCA).

147 2005 (1) SACR 317 (SCA) at para 59.

148 *Beheersmaatschappij Helling I NV and Others v Magistrate Cape Town and Others* 2007 (1) SACR 99 (C). See also DP Van der Merwe et al *Information and Communications Technology Law* 2 ed (2016) at 87, as well as the discussion at para 2.5 of the South African Law Commission Discussion Paper 99 Project 108 *Computer related crime: Preliminary proposals for reform in respect of unauthorised access to computers, unauthorised modification of computer data and software applications and related procedural aspects* (2001).

149 Bill B6-2017, available at https://www.gov.za/documents/cybercrimes-and-cybersecurity-bill-b6-2017-21-feb-2017-0000.

CHAPTER 14   ELECTRONIC AND CYBER EVIDENCE | 143

regulates the law in respect of mutual legal assistance. It provides, *inter alia*, for the issuing of a request to a foreign state for assistance in obtaining evidence that is located outside the borders of South Africa.[150]

In addition, the Council of Europe's Convention on Cybercrime,[151] which South Africa has signed but not ratified,[152] provides guidance on measures to be taken at a national level and general principles relating to international cooperation.[153]

The Cybercrimes and Cybersecurity Bill B6-2017 will ensure that South Africa is fully compliant in the future with its international law obligations in electronic communications and transactions in the cybercrime context.[154]

14.7.3   Search and seizure in civil cases

In civil proceedings, it may happen that certain electronic evidence is required to prove a cause of action; but the applicable evidence may be in the possession or control of another person – perhaps even the person or entity that is about to be sued. Consequently, a real danger exists that the evidence may be destroyed before trial; accordingly, one may approach a court, on an *ex parte* basis, to ensure the critical evidence is preserved for future use through the process of an Anton Piller order.[155]

Moreover, in civil proceedings, although Uniform Rule 35 (Discovery, Inspection and Production of Documents) does not specifically refer to data messages, 'document' has been interpreted to include 'electronic matter' and data messages. In *Makate v Vodacom (Pty) Ltd*,[156] the court found that a data message is a document for purposes of discovery. Moreover, in *Le Roux and Others v Viana NO and Others*,[157] the Supreme Court of Appeal in the context of section 69 of the Insolvency Act 24 of 1936 (referring to the Concise Oxford English Dictionary, 10th edition revised) found that a document is 'a piece of written, printed or *electronic matter* that provides information or evidence or that serves as an official record'. It found further that the court should take judicial notice of 'the technological advancements regarding electronic data creation, recording and storage'.[158]

In *Metropolitan Health Corporate (Pty) Ltd v Neil Harvey and Associates (Pty) Ltd and Another*[159] the court confirmed that, for purposes of Rule 35 and discovery, a backup of source code is a document. Consequently, until such time as the Uniform Rules of Court are amended, electronic evidence will be received in discovery in terms of the broader definition of 'document'.[160]

---

150 *Beheersmaatschappij Helling I NV and Others v Magistrate Cape Town and Others* 2007 (1) SACR 99 (C). See further M Watney 'A South African perspective on mutual legal assistance and extradition in a globalized world' 2012 *PELJ* 15(2) at 291.

151 23.XI.2001, also known as the Budapest Convention of Cybercrime.

152 See https://www.coe.int/en/web/conventions/full-list/-/conventions/treaty/185/signatures?p_auth=S71vDc4w.

153 Chapter II.

154 For example, see chapter 6 (sections 44–49) dealing with mutual assistance. See also the explanatory memorandum published by the Department of Justice on 19 January 2017 together with the Bill, where the following is stated: 'Current procedures for mutual assistance between South Africa and foreign countries in the investigation of cybercrimes do take into account the transient nature of electronic evidence and the need to act expeditiously'. Available at http://www.justice.gov.za/legislation/bills/CyberCrimesDiscussionDocument2017.pdf at 3.

155 *Shoba v Officer Commanding, Temporary Police Camp, Wagendrift Dam* 1995 (4) SA 1 (A). See also the United Kingdom case of *Anton Piller KG v Manufacturing Processes Ltd and Others* [1976] 1 All ER 779.

156 2014 (1) SA 191 (GSJ) at para 38.

157 2008 (2) SA 173 (SCA).

158 Ibid. at para 10.

159 (10264/10) [2011] ZAWCHC 358 (19 August 2011).

160 See also *Uramin (Incorporated in British Columbia) t/a Areva Resources Southern Africa v Perie* 2017 (1) SA 236 (GJ) where technology was 'simply another tool for securing effective access to justice' in the context of evidence being led via video link (at para 35).

144 | THE LAW OF EVIDENCE IN SOUTH AFRICA

In addition, Rule 23 (discovery) of the Rules of the Magistrates' Courts of South Africa, amended in 2010, makes specific provision for electronic evidence, and provides as follows:

> 23. (1) (a) Any party to any action may require any other party thereto, by notice in writing, to make discovery on oath within 20 days of all documents and tape, *electronic, digital* or other forms of recordings relating to any matter in question in such action, whether such matter is one arising between the party requiring discovery and the party required to make discovery or not, which are or have at any time been in the possession or control of such other party.

14.8 Overview of forensic science

Digital forensics is the process of gathering, analysing and interpreting digital information to be used in legal proceedings.[161] The International Organization on Computer Evidence,[162] working together with the United States Federal Bureau of Investigation's Scientific Working Group on Digital Evidence,[163] has developed international principles for the standardised recovery of computer-based evidence as follows:

- Upon seizing digital evidence, actions taken should not change that evidence.
- When it is necessary for a person to access original digital evidence, that person must be forensically competent.
- All activity relating to the seizure, access, storage, or transfer of digital evidence must be fully documented, preserved, and available for review.
- An individual is responsible for all actions taken with respect to digital evidence while the digital evidence is in their possession.
- Any agency that is responsible for seizing, accessing, storing, or transferring digital evidence is responsible for compliance with these principles.

Further, the International Organization on Computer Evidence recommends:

- Forensic competency and the need to generate agreement on international accreditation and the validation of tools, techniques, and training;
- Issues relating to practices and procedures for the examination of digital evidence; and
- The sharing of information relating to hi-tech crime and forensic computing, such as events, tools, and techniques.

Consequently, section 24 of the Cybercrimes and Cybersecurity Bill B6-2017 will be critical in this regard. It currently reads as follows:

> Standard Operating Procedures
> 24. (1) The Cabinet member responsible for policing, in consultation with the National Director of Public Prosecutions and the Cabinet member responsible for the administration of justice must, after following a process of public consultation,

---

161 TJ Holt, AM Bossler AM and KC Seigfried-Spellar *Cybercrime and Digital Forensics: An Introduction* (2015) at 322.

162 Founded by the Organization of American States, which claims to be the world's oldest regional organisation, dating back to the First International Conference of American States held in Washington from October 1889 to April 1890 – see more on http://www.oas.org/.

163 https://archives.fbi.gov/archives/about-us/lab/forensic-science-communications/fsc/april2000/swgde.htm#IOCEInternationalPrinciples.

CHAPTER 14   ELECTRONIC AND CYBER EVIDENCE | **145**

within six months of the commencement of this Chapter, issue Standard Operating Procedures which must be observed by—

(a) the South African Police Service; or

(b) any other person or agency who or which is authorised in terms of the provision of any other law to investigate any offence in terms of any law, in the investigation of any offence in terms of Chapter 2 or section 16, 17 or 18 or any other offence which is or was committed by means of or facilitated by the use of an article.

(2) The Standard Operating Procedures referred to in subsection (1) and any amendment thereto must be published in the Gazette.

In *S v Mthethwa*,[164] it was held that:

> In South Africa there are no clear technical guidelines with regard to the authentication of video evidence such as CCTV footage. In the UK, best practices were adopted in respect of digital evidence including the creation of audit trails to authenticate it. Notwithstanding the recommended best practice, the rule of evidence in UK remains that digital evidence should not be inadmissible solely because it does not conform to specific technological requirements.

Consequently, an important task within the first six months of the promulgation of the Cybercrimes and Cybersecurity Bill B6-2017 will be to prepare the guidelines and submit them for public comment.

14.9   Overview of the South African Law Reform Commission's review of electronic evidence

The South African Law Reform Commission has been reviewing electronic evidence and related issues for an extended period. The latest document is the Discussion Paper 131 Project 126 *Review of the Law of Evidence*.[165] Although comment closed in 2015, the proposals put forward by the Commission[166] have yet to be implemented, and it remains to be seen whether any further action will result from this comprehensive research.

In summary, the Commission recommends three possible options for law reform:[167]

* Option 1: 'retention of current regulatory landscape with possible minor reform', where the Commission states:

> The advantage of such an approach is that fewer changes would be required – which would be minimally disruptive to the legal profession, and changes would likely be introduced more quickly than if more substantive regulatory reform is undertaken. However, this conservative approach would mean that multiple laws would still apply; the disadvantages of this scenario include the likelihood that confusion would continue to exist around certain laws and principles, including the following: hearsay as it applies to automated electronic evidence (and the seeming hesitance to treat electronic evidence as real evidence); the authentication of electronic evidence; the admissibility of business records in terms of section 15(4) of the ECT Act; and the interaction between, and applicability of, the various laws which regulate exceptions to the hearsay rule.

---

164   2017 JDR 0551 (WCC) at para 78.

165   2014. Available at http://www.justice.gov.za/salrc/dpapers/dp131-prj126-ReviewLawOfEvidence.pdf.

166   See Chapter 5, 83–87

167   See note 165 above at 22. The recommendations are set out on pp. 86–88.

146 THE LAW OF EVIDENCE IN SOUTH AFRICA

- Option 2: 'largely retain the current regulatory framework, with minor statutory reform'. However, it would introduce additional legislation or regulations to existing legislation, which:

  > ...would be more detailed than the current section 15 of the ECT Act, specifically to address the admissibility of electronic evidence (with a focus on issues such as authentication and reliability).

- Option 3: 'extensive overhaul of the regulatory framework for hearsay and certain types of documentary evidence'.

Consequently, the Commission sees the following issues as problematic insofar as electronic evidence is concerned:

- *Regular review of the Electronic Communications and Transactions Act required and revision of the data message definition.* The promulgation of the proposed B6-2017 version of the Cybercrimes and Cybersecurity Bill in its current form will lead to the term data message having conflicting definitions. The current definition in the Electronic Communications and Transactions Act reads as follows:

  > "data message" means data generated, sent, received or stored by electronic means and includes-
  > (a) voice, where the voice is used in an automated transaction; and
  > (b) a stored record

- The Cybercrimes and Cybersecurity Bill B6-2017 defines the term as:

  > "data message'" means data generated, sent, received or stored by electronic means, where any output of the data is in an intelligible form

- According to section 61 of the Cybercrimes and Cybersecurity Bill B6-2017, the definition of 'data message' contained within the Electronic Communications and Transactions Act is not due to be repealed or amended – this misnomer, although a minor oversight and of little practical effect, should be corrected as soon as possible.

- *Admissibility of data messages as evidence in legal proceedings in the context of hearsay.*[168] In light of the principle of functional equivalence, it cannot be that section 15 of the Electronic Communications and Transactions Act automatically prescribes that all data messages are admissible. As a result, South African courts have consistently found that the Electronic Communications and Transactions Act does not override the normal rules applicable to hearsay.[169]

  The position promoted in *Ndiki obiter* (that all data messages should be treated as documentary hearsay)[170] should be avoided. It will conflict with the internationally accepted position and, arguably, it would not be conceptually correct in light of the

---

168 South African Law Reform Commission Discussion Paper 131 *Review of the Law of Evidence* 2014 issue 6 at 62; see also paras 4.66–4.76.

169 See *S v Brown* at para 18; *S v Ndiki* at para 31; *S v Meyer* at para 299; *LA Consortium & Vending CC t/a LA Enterprises v MTN Service Provider (Pty) Ltd* at para 13.

170 *S v Ndiki and Others* 2008 (2) SACR 252 (Ck) at para 33. The court relies on the opinion of Bilchitz to form the view that all data messages should be treated as hearsay. Although the argument of Bilchitz is noted (that all computer-based evidence relies on some human intervention or input), it is in my view semantics and outdated in 2018. As with the international position, if a data message relies substantially on a computer for its 'credibility', then that evidence must be treated as real in nature. A court will always have the discretion to give the evidence very low weight if there are doubts about accuracy and/or reliability.

South African law of evidence.[171] Moreover, simply because the distinction between real evidence and documentary evidence in the context of data messages can be difficult, it should not mean sacrificing conceptual clarity. If a court is unsure (whether evidence is real or documentary) it can err on the side of caution and classify the evidence as documentary hearsay.[172] This will mean subjecting the data message to a hearsay enquiry where, in terms of the Law of Evidence Amendment Act, the court will in any event have the discretion to admit the evidence if the interests of justice demand that to be the case.

As with other issues in the Discussion Paper, there is no consensus from the comments received,[173] and there is support for data messages to be admissible if relevant and authentic (regardless of hearsay),[174] as well as support for the position that all data messages constitute hearsay.[175]

The Commission supports the view that hearsay evidence in a data message should be treated in the same way as a paper-based document (in line with the principle of functional equivalence).[176] Ultimately, however, the Commission proposes a Law of Evidence Amendment Bill to clarify the distinction between various types of electronic evidence (real or documentary) and to clarify the interaction between the statutory exceptions to the hearsay rule.

- *Distinguishing between various types of electronic evidence.*[177] The determination as to whether a data message is real evidence or documentary evidence will dictate the admissibility requirements applicable and, importantly for present purposes, will determine whether a hearsay enquiry is necwessary. The South African Law Reform Commission supports a distinction between automated data messages and data messages made by a person.[178] Moreover, recent cases in the form of *Ndlovu, Ndiki* and *LA Consortium*, amongst others, all endorse this approach.

- *Statutory exceptions to the hearsay rule.* 'Confusing' and 'complicated' are two common descriptions of the statutory exceptions to the hearsay rule.[179] This is because, potentially, a legal practitioner must consider multiple sources of law,[180] and a variety of (at times) conflicting and conceptually grey cases when determining whether a hearsay exception applies – this is less than ideal and leads to misunderstanding and inconsistent application.

  In addition, the exception created by section 15(4) of the Electronic Communications and Transactions Act has received severe academic criticism.[181] Moreover, in comments received by the Law Reform Commission, the South African Police Services and Legal

---

171   J Hofman and J De Jager 'South Africa' in Mason S (ed) *Electronic Evidence* 3 ed (2012) at 777 and particularly footnote 3 thereof.

172   However, where the evidence is clearly automated and depends upon the credibility of a computer (or as Theophilopoulos puts it: an information system automatically generated data message which does not require the input of a human mind) then it must be treated as real evidence and cannot be subjected to a hearsay enquiry.

173   South African Law Reform Commission Discussion Paper 131 *Review of the Law of Evidence* 2014 at para 4.67–4.77.

174   Ibid. at para 4.73.

175   Ibid. at para 4.72.

176   Ibid. at para 4.89.

177   Ibid. at para 3.26–3.38.

178   Ibid. at para 4.104.

179   Ibid. at para 3.17.

180   The Law of Evidence Amendment Act, the Civil Proceedings Evidence Act, the Criminal Procedure Act and the Electronic Communications and Transactions Act.

181   J Hofman and J de Jager 'South Africa' in S Mason (ed) *Electronic Evidence* 3 ed (2012) at 771–772.

THE LAW OF EVIDENCE IN SOUTH AFRICA

Aid submit that, in the context of criminal proceedings, the section unjustly shifts the onus of proof and may well be unconstitutional.[182]

Be that as it may, if the Amendment Bill proposed by the Commission is promulgated in its current form it will seek to repeal section 3 of the Law of Evidence Amendment Act; section 15(4) of the Electronic Communications and Transactions Act; sections 27–38 of the Civil Proceedings Evidence Act and sections 221, 222 and 236 of the Criminal Procedure Act. It will be replaced by a far better, single piece of legislation which will facilitate a more coherent, less fragmented approach.[183]

In the event that only minor reform is adopted (as opposed to the proposed Amendment Bill), this area will require amendment to provide clarity.

14.10 Overview of foreign law in respect of electronic evidence

What follows is a consideration of several foreign jurisdictions – not as a comprehensive comparative study of international law, but as a basis for information on other possible interpretations regarding electronic evidence in South Africa.

14.10.1 England and Wales

The English law of evidence (upon which significant portions of the South African law of evidence is based), has been referred to as being founded on **exclusionary rules**, which contain two fundamental guiding principles – the best evidence rule and the hearsay rule.[184] Evidence will be admissible if relevant to an issue in dispute, subject to a number of exceptions.[185] Moreover, much like South Africa, one of the core concerns insofar as computer evidence is concerned has been in relation to the hearsay rule.[186]

In England,[187] the position is the same as in South Africa – that is, if the production of data occurs without human intervention, it is real evidence (there is thus no hearsay enquiry). Conversely, if the data is a record of human assertions, then it is hearsay.

The key, as with many jurisdictions around the world, is to determine whether the credibility of the data relies on a person or a computer (automated process) – and this distinction often leads to 'confusion' and has acted as a 'brake' on the introduction of new technology.[188]

However, even if the data is documentary in nature, and therefore subject to the exclusionary hearsay rules, there are several statutory exceptions, including those found in the Criminal Justice Act 2003 and the Civil Evidence Act 1995[189] which allow for its admission.

In the fourth and most recent edition of *Electronic Evidence*[190] the authors of the chapter on hearsay appear critical of the 'complex' rules one must consider. With this complexity in mind, it is beyond the scope of this chapter to analyse the regulatory framework of hearsay

---

182 South African Law Reform Commission Discussion Paper 131 *Review of the Law of Evidence* 2014 at para 4.120–4.121.

183 Ibid. at paras 87–88 where the Commission state the proposed bill is reflective of practice in several commonwealth countries, and consistent with the UN Model Law, 1996.

184 Leroux (2004) *International Review of Law, Computers & Technology* at 202.

185 Mason, Freedman and Patel 'England & Wales' in Mason S and Seng D (eds) *Electronic Evidence* 4 ed (2017) at 347.

186 Ibid. at 363.

187 For a comprehensive view of the English position, see Tapper C *Cross and Tapper on Evidence* 12 ed (2010).

188 Reed C 'The Admissibility and Authentication of Computer Evidence – A Confusion of Issues' in 5th Annual British and Irish Legal Education Technology Association Conference (1990) at 3–5.

189 For a detailed analysis of this legislation, see Tapper C *Cross and Tapper on Evidence* at 586–621; see also 551–581 for a discussion on hearsay in general.

190 Gallavin and Mason 'Hearsay' in Mason S and Seng D (eds) *Electronic Evidence* 4 ed (2017) at para 4.43–4.45.

CHAPTER 14   ELECTRONIC AND CYBER EVIDENCE | 149

evidence in England, other than to note that an approach whereby data messages are classified as real evidence (if they rely on the credibility of a computer) is possible (and preferred) in England.[191] For example, in *R (on the application of O) v Coventry Justices*,[192] automated transactions (involving a credit card and a pornography website) were regarded as real evidence, and admissible.

Earlier, in *R v Spiby*,[193] where an automated process (a computer) monitored telephone calls, this evidence was regarded as real evidence because there was no human intervention in the production of the data and, accordingly, it was not hearsay evidence.[194]

A quote from an early academic article[195] by Smith by the court in *R v Spiby*[196] sums up and articulates why certain printouts should be real evidence:

> **Where information is recorded by mechanical means without the intervention of a human mind the record made by the machine is admissible in evidence provided, of course, it is accepted that the machine is reliable. An elementary example is a maximum and minimum thermometer. This records two items of information in the course of 24 hours and there is no doubt that a witness could give evidence of the reading he took from it if that was relevant to the issue before the court. *A fortiori*, the instrument itself could be produced, if it were possible to do so, if it still bore the relevant readings. It would not be necessary to call a professor of physics to prove how a thermometer works because that is, surely, such a matter of common knowledge as to be judicially noticed. The same is true of a camera which photographs an event or a tape recorder which records a conversation where the event or conversation is in issue or is relevant to the issue before the court. A radar speedmeter similarly makes a record of an event – the speed of a passing vehicle – and it is no different in legal principle from the thermometer.**

The key point to take from the English position is that electronic evidence can be classified as either real evidence (not subject to the hearsay rules), or it can be classified as documentary evidence (subject to the hearsay rules). The classification of the evidence will depend on its nature and purpose in court. Simply, though, it appears from the cases reviewed above that if the data is subject to human intervention in its production, it will be classified as hearsay documentary evidence. Conversely, if the data is not subject to any human intervention, it will be real evidence.

14.10.2   Canada

The Canadian law of evidence is primarily based on English common law (except in Quebec),[197] and electronic evidence is subject to the same evidentiary regime as traditional (paper-based) evidence. The electronic evidence must be (as with all other forms of

---

191   Reed C 'The Admissibility and Authentication of Computer Evidence – A Confusion of Issues' in 5th Annual British and Irish Legal Education Technology Association Conference (1990) at 2–6.

192   [2004] All ER (D) 78.

193   [1990] 91 Cr App R 186.

194   See also *Castle v Cross* [1985] 1 All ER 87 where a printout (from a computer or device) of what is displayed or recorded on a mechanical measuring device is real evidence.

195   Smith 1981 *Criminal Law Review* 387 at 390.

196   (1990) 91 Cr App R 186.

197   N Boyd *Canadian Law: An Introduction* 5 ed (2011) at 87–105; see also Central Intelligence Agency 2017 https://www.cia.gov/library/publications/the-world-factbook/fields/2100.html.

150 | THE LAW OF EVIDENCE IN SOUTH AFRICA

evidence) material and relevant to the issues, and must not be subject to any other exclusionary rule.[198]

The primary legislative instruments regulating electronic evidence are: the Canada Evidence Act, 1985 and the Uniform Electronic Evidence Act, 1999. Canada has departed from the Model Law by using the term 'electronic record' instead of 'data message' or 'computer evidence'. In *R v Mondor*,[199] the Ontario Court of Justice, referring to academic authors,[200] confirmed that electronic evidence (much like the position in South Africa and England) can take the form of real evidence or documentary evidence. The court found that:

> Where the electronically stored data is recorded electronically by an automated process, then the evidence is real evidence. Where, however, the electronically stored information is created by humans, then the evidence is not real evidence, and is not admissible for its truth absent some other rule of admissibility.

As with many other jurisdictions, Canada also has a business records hearsay exception,[201] and the court in *Mondor* was tasked with determining whether hearsay electronic evidence (documentary evidence that is subject to human intervention) would be admissible in terms of the Canadian hearsay exception.[202]

Using similar logic to the South African decisions in *Ndlovu* and *Ndiki*, the Canadian court in *Mondor* found that:

> [The Canada Evidence Act] does not allow for the admission of hearsay evidence contained within an electronic document just because it is in electronic form. The applicant must first establish that the hearsay is admissible either under section 30 or some other mechanism.

Ultimately, after analysing previous cases dealing with hearsay electronic evidence,[203] the court found the evidence to be 'inadmissible for the truth of their contents'.[204]

In *Saturley v CIBC World Markets Inc.*,[205] the Nova Scotia Supreme Court set out the position as follows (essentially the same as the position in South Africa):

> Electronic information may be considered either real or documentary evidence. If it is real evidence, it simply needs to be authenticated and the trier of fact will then draw their own inferences from it. Examples of real evidence include photographs and physical objects.[206]
>
> If electronic information is determined to be real evidence, the evidentiary rules relating to documents, such as the best evidence and hearsay rules, will not be applicable.[207]

The court went on further to note that the real issue lies in deciding 'when electronic information should be treated as real evidence, rather than documentary'.[208] Ultimately,

---

198 In general, for a comprehensive overview and discussion of the Canadian law of evidence, see Paciocco DM and Stuesser L *The Law of Evidence* 7 ed 2015.
199 2014 ONCJ 135 at para 17.
200 Underwood and Penner *Electronic Evidence in Canada* at para 12.2
201 See discussion above at para 14.4.4.1.
202 Section 30 and 31 of the Canada Evidence Act, 1985.
203 2014 ONCJ 135 at paras 34–39 where previous Canadian cases dealing with hearsay electronic evidence are discussed.
204 2014 ONCJ 135 at para 43.
205 2012 NSSC 226.
206 2012 NSSC 226 at para 11.
207 2012 NSSC 226 at para 13.
208 2012 NSSC 226 at para 14.

CHAPTER 14   ELECTRONIC AND CYBER EVIDENCE | **151**

and as with the position in England and South Africa, electronic evidence will be real evidence when its production is 'without human intervention'.[209] This position has received further judicial support, including in *R v McCulloch*,[210] where the admission of telephone records were introduced to court as real evidence because of the automated nature of the data.

Moreover, in *R v Hall*,[211] the court found that automated billing records were real evidence (although they also in this case fell under the hearsay business records exception). In this matter, the Canadian court referred with approval to the English case of *R v Spiby*[212] where the English court found that an automated process monitoring phone calls was also real evidence and thus not subject to hearsay rules.

Consequently, as with South Africa and England, the classification of electronic evidence as real or documentary is important as it guides the admissibility enquiry. Consequently, a critical determination is to establish whether the data produced (and on which a litigant relies) was created with or without human intervention.

14.10.3   The United States of America

It is almost impossible to summarise concisely the legal position on any legal issue in the United States, primarily because of the federal system – each state has its own independent judiciary, and applies its own procedural and evidentiary rules.[213]

However, the legal system of the United States is predominantly a common law system based on English common law (at a federal level).[214] Moreover, and as a general position, the United States adopts a similar stance in relation to hearsay electronic evidence. The United States adopts a business records hearsay exception,[215] and distinguishes between computer-generated records (no human intervention and thus real evidence) and computer-stored records (human intervention and thus documentary hearsay).[216]

In terms of the Federal Rules of Evidence, hearsay is not admissible as evidence,[217] but this is subject to several exceptions.[218]

The basis for considering the admissibility of electronic evidence in the United States is similar to that in South Africa – the evidence must be relevant, authentic, must not be hearsay, must be the best evidence available, and its probative value must outweigh any prejudicial effect.[219]

For example, in *U-Haul Intern Inc. v Lumbermens Mut. Cas.Co*,[220] the United States Court of Appeals for the Ninth Circuit dealt with computer-generated summaries of

---

209   2012 NSSC 226 at para 21.
210   [1992] B.C.J. 2282 at para 18.
211   [1998] B.C.J. No. 2515.
212   [1990] 91 Cr App R 186.
213   Schwerha, Bagby and Esler 'United States of America' in Mason S and Seng D (eds) *Electronic Evidence* 4 ed (2017) at para 19.03.
214   LM Friedman and GM Hayden *American Law: An Introduction* (2017) at 35–55; see also Central Intelligence Agency 2017 https://www.cia.gov/library/publications/the-world-factbook/fields/2100.html.
215   Schwerha, Bagby and Esler 'United States of America' in Mason S and Seng D (eds) *Electronic Evidence* 4 ed (2017) at 797–835.
216   Seng and Chakravarthi 2003 https://www.agc.gov.sg/DATA/0/Docs/PublicationFiles/Sep_03_ComputerOutput.pdf.
217   Fed. R. Evid. 802. See also Fed. R. Evid. Article VIII – Hearsay, and sections 801–807.
218   Fed. R. Evid. 803. See also Fed. R. Evid. Article VIII – Hearsay, and sections 801–807.
219   LJ Kemp '*Lorraine v. Markel*: An Authoritative Opinion Sets the Bar for Admissibility of Electronic Evidence (Except for Computer Animations and Simulations)' (2007) 9(3) *NC JOLT* at 16–29; JD Frieden and LM Murray 'The Admissibility of Electronic Evidence under the Federal Rules of Evidence' (2011) 17(2) *Rich J L & Tech* at 1–40.
220   576 F.3d 1040 (9th Cir. 2009).

THE LAW OF EVIDENCE IN SOUTH AFRICA

payments made on insurance claims and found that, in the context of the business records hearsay exception, 'Rule 803(6) provides that records of regularly conducted business activity meeting ... criteria constitute an exception to the prohibition against hearsay evidence.'[221]

In *Telewizja Polska USA Inc. v Echostar Satellite Corp*,[222] the court found that images and text (that purported to show what a website looked like at a point in time) were not statements for purposes of the federal hearsay rules (akin to real evidence in South Africa).

Moreover, in *United States v Rollins*[223] the court found that computer-generated evidence (without human intervention) was admissible without requiring admissibility in terms of hearsay rules.

Furthermore, in the seminal matter of *Lorraine v Markel American Insurance Company*[224] the court delivered a comprehensive 101-page opinion outlining the admissibility of electronically stored information. One submission from a practitioner in the United States suggests that the court set the admissibility bar unnecessarily high,[225] but the lengthy opinion canvasses all relevant United States law (insofar as electronic evidence is concerned) and may well be a point of departure if American electronic evidence is at issue.

In summary, the court comprehensively reviewed the applicable statutory regime for admissibility of electronic evidence (at a federal level) – and found that, if evidence is generated by a computer, it cannot be subject to hearsay as it is not produced by a person.[226] In the context of hearsay electronic evidence, the court found that:[227]

> **When an electronically generated record is entirely the product of the functioning of a computerized system or process, such as the "report" generated when a fax is sent showing the number to which the fax was sent and the time it was received, there is no "person" involved in the creation of the record, and no "assertion" being made. For that reason, the record is not a statement and cannot be hearsay.**

In a similar vein, in *United States v Lizarraga-Tirado*[228] the Ninth Circuit Court of Appeals found that machine-generated evidence (without any substantial human intervention) is not hearsay. In this case, the court found that a 'pin' from Google Earth (satellite image software) was not an assertion by a person, and was therefore not hearsay. The court stated: 'we join other circuits that have held that machine statements aren't hearsay.'[229]

Consequently, the key issue in the United States as far as computer-generated evidence and hearsay is concerned is to determine whether the evidence is subject to input, assertions or conclusions by a person. If so, it is hearsay. If not, and the evidence is automatically generated, then subject to the other evidential conditions being satisfied

---

221 576 F.3d 1040 (9th Cir. 2009) 1043.
222 2004 WL 2367740.
223 2004 WL 26780.
224 241 F.R.D. 534.
225 BW Esler '*Lorraine v Markel*: Unnecessarily Raising the Standard for Admissibility of Electronic Evidence' (2007) 4 *DEESLR* at 80–82.
226 Similar logic was used in the South African cases of *Ex Parte Rosch* and *Narlis*.
227 *Lorraine v. Markel American Insurance Company* 241 F.R.D. 534 (D. Md. 2007). See also LJ Kemp '*Lorraine v. Markel*: An Authoritative Opinion Sets the Bar for Admissibility of Electronic Evidence (Except for Computer Animations and Simulations)' (2007) 9(3) NC JOLT at 16–29.
228 (9th Cir. 2015) F 3d. 2015 WL 3772772.
229 (9th Cir. 2015) F 3d. 2015 WL 3772772 at 7–8.

CHAPTER 14   ELECTRONIC AND CYBER EVIDENCE | 153

(relevance, authenticity, best evidence and the probative value outweighing prejudicial effect), the evidence will be admissible. Of course, as with South Africa and other jurisdictions, even if the evidence is hearsay in nature, then it may still be admissible under one of the statutory exceptions contained in the Federal Rules of Evidence or in an applicable State statute.

14.11   Conclusion

A data message is not automatically admissible. It must be considered in light of the relevant facts, and in light of the sections of the Electronic Communications and Transactions Act discussed above in order to determine conclusively whether it is admissible. Only after it is found to be admissible will a court determine the weight the evidence should carry. As pointed out in *S v Meyer*, '[e]vidence is either admitted or not admitted. It should conceptually not be confused with to what degree weight is given to evidence'.[230]

Moreover, a data message is not exempt from the rules regulating hearsay, must be treated in the same way as any other traditional forms of evidence, and the admissibility thereof must follow the ordinary rules applicable to the South African law of evidence – except where concessions are made in the Electronic Communications and Transactions Act.

The admissibility and weight of data message evidence does not require drastic overhaul.[231] Common law principles – read together with the Electronic Communications and Transactions Act and recent case law dealing therewith – are largely adequate for the time being. South Africa needs to ensure that new forms of technology remain admissible in evidence and that, when assessing admissibility and weight of evidence – whether electronic or otherwise – the judiciary should retain a discretion, rather than over-legislating or adopting a rigid approach.

SECTION 1 DEFINITIONS	
Data:	Electronic representations of information in any form
Data message:	Data generated, sent, received or stored by electronic means, including voice, where the voice is used in an automated transaction; and a stored record
Electronic signature:	Data attached to, incorporated in, or logically associated with other data and which is intended by the user to serve as a signature'
Advanced electronic signature:	An electronic signature which results form a process which has been accredited by the Authority as provided for in s 37
Electronic communication:	A communication by means of data messages

---

230 2017 JDR 1728 (GJ) at para 310 referring to PJ Schwikkard and SE van der Merwe *Principles of Evidence* 4 ed (2016) at 20.

231 However, law reform is desirable in at least the following areas: the definition of 'data message'; the definition of 'document' in the statutes applicable to hearsay exceptions; a distinction between types of electronic evidence insofar as computer generated evidence with human intervention and without human intervention is concerned; and more cohesion and alignment with the statutory exceptions.

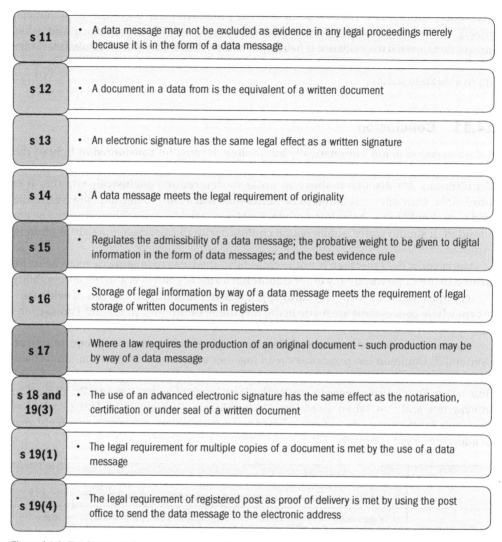

Figure 14.1 The Electronic Communications and Transactions Act

THIS CHAPTER IN ESSENCE

1. New technology and methods of communication present challenges to the traditional concepts of evidence.
2. The primary legislative instrument regulating electronic evidence is the Electronic Communications and Transactions Act 25 of 2002.
3. As there is no category for electronic evidence, it will be admitted to court in the form of oral, documentary, or real evidence.
4. In *Narlis v South African Bank of Athens* the Appellate Division held that the legislation at the time provided no basis for any discretionary admissibility of electronic evidence and so the Computer Evidence Act 57 of 1983 was enacted.
5. This only applied to civil proceedings and was heavily criticised.

CHAPTER 14 ELECTRONIC AND CYBER EVIDENCE

6 In 1996, the United Nations Commission on International Trade Law published the Model Law on Electronic Commerce.

7 The Electronic Communications and Transactions Act 25 of 2002 is based entirely on the United Nations guidance.

8 Both seek to follow a functionally equivalent approach which means that, as far as possible and practical, electronic evidence should be treated in the same way as traditional forms of evidence.

9 The Electronic Communications and Transactions Act facilitates this methodology by recognising data messages as the functional equivalent of paper.

10 The Electronic Communications and Transactions Act repealed the Computer Evidence Act entirely and applies to both civil and criminal proceedings.

11 Computer or machine-related evidence is often referred to as electronic evidence, digital evidence, ESI evidence (electronically stored information), or ICT evidence.

12 South Africa uses the terms 'data message' or 'data' drawn from the UN 1996 Model Law.

13 A 'data message' means data generated, sent, received, or stored by electronic means and includes (i) voice, where the voice is used in an automated transaction; and (ii) a stored record.

14 Section 11 provides legal recognition for data messages.

15 Section 12 provides that data messages will constitute a document and be considered *in writing* for legal purposes, provided it is accessible in a manner that is usable in the future.

16 A data message is considered to be a document for purposes of Rule 35 of the Uniform Rules of Court.

17 Section 14 provides that a data message can be regarded as an *original* for legal purposes if the information can be displayed or produced, and if the integrity of the information in the data message has been assessed in terms of section 14(2), which essentially requires that it must be shown to be authentic.

18 Section 13 creates two types of digital signature – an electronic signature (an electronic indication intended to be a signature) and an advanced electronic signature (authorised by an accreditation authority).

19 Where a person's signature is required by law, only an advanced electronic signature will suffice. Where parties impose obligations, an electronic signature will suffice.

20 In terms of section 17, if a person is required to produce a document or information, they may do so via data message if the data message is reliable and is readily accessible.

21 Section 15(1) prohibits the exclusion of evidence on the mere grounds that it is generated by a computer and not by a natural person, and further prohibits the exclusion of evidence on the grounds that it is not original – if the evidence is the best evidence reasonably available.

22 Section 15 does not seek to override the normal principles applicable to hearsay, but it is not yet clear exactly what constitutes hearsay in a data message.

23 Section 15(4) provides an exception to the hearsay rule for data messages created in the ordinary course and scope of business, but the precise meaning of section 15(4) is not entirely settled.

24 Section 3 of the Law of Evidence Amendment Act applies to data messages so courts can use their discretion to admit hearsay evidence.

25 The South African Law Reform Commission suggests that the current position regulating hearsay electronic evidence may lead to inefficiency or confusion and that it should be reviewed.

26 Whether a data message is a document or an object (real evidence) can be pivotal in determining whether evidence is admissible or inadmissible as real evidence is not subject to the hearsay rules.

27 Data messages can be either real evidence or documentary evidence. They are real if their probative value depends on the credibility of a computer and they are documentary if their probative value depends on the credibility of a person.

28 Some data messages may exhibit characteristics of both real and documentary evidence, and the distinction between whether a data message is real or documentary can be difficult.

29 A data message is normally presented to court as a document and must be relevant, produced, original and authentic.

30 However, if the evidence is classified as real, it should be admissible as long as it is relevant.

31 Section 15(2) states that data messages must be given due evidential weight and provides the following guidelines for assessing weight, stating that regard must be had to:

31.1 the reliability of the manner in which the data message was generated, stored or communicated;

31.2 the reliability of the manner in which the integrity of the data message was maintained;

31.3 the manner in which its originator was identified; and

31.4 any other relevant factor.

32 A court may rely on expert evidence in assessing weight.

33 The Cybercrimes and Cybersecurity Bill proposes improvements that can be made to cater for new technologies.

34 A presumption of reliability, namely that electronic equipment was working and reliable at the relevant time, applies in South Africa and is consistent with international best practice.

35 The primary regulatory mechanism for the search and seizure of electronic evidence is Chapter 2 of the Criminal Procedure Act 51 of 1977.

36 Sections 82 and 83 the Electronic Communications and Transactions Act provide wide-ranging search and seizure powers to Cyber Inspectors; none have been appointed.

37 Chapter 3 of the Regulation of Interception of Communications and Provision of Communication-Related Information Act 70 of 2002 provides for warrants and direction insofar as communication-related data is concerned.

38 The Cybercrimes and Cybersecurity Bill proposes to regulate search and seizure of electronic evidence and will also ensure that South Africa is fully compliant with its international law obligations in electronic communications and transactions in the cybercrime context.

39 It will also be responsible for the development of standard operating proceedings for digital forensics, which is the process of gathering, analysing and interpreting digital information to be used in legal proceedings.

40 Existing procedures, like Anton Piller orders or Rule 35 (Discovery, Inspection and Production of Documents) have been interpreted to regulate to the acquisition of electronic evidence in civil matters.

41 The South African Law Reform Commission has been reviewing electronic evidence for an extended period and has made several proposals, which have yet to be implemented.

42 In English law, if the production of data occurs without human intervention, it is real evidence, but if the data is a record of human assertion, it is hearsay.

43 In Canada, electronic evidence is subject to the same evidentiary regime as traditional (paper-based) evidence and electronic evidence can take the form of real evidence or documentary evidence.

44 The United States of America also distinguishes between computer-generated records (no human intervention and thus real evidence), and computer-stored records (human intervention and thus documentary hearsay) and adopts a similar test for admissibility – the evidence must be relevant, authentic, must not be hearsay, must be the best evidence available, and its probative value must outweigh any prejudicial effect.

PART FOUR

RULES FOR EXCLUDING EVIDENCE

CHAPTER 15   The general test for relevance 158

CHAPTER 16   Unconstitutionally obtained evidence in criminal
cases: section 35(5) of the Constitution 174

CHAPTER 17   Similar fact evidence 197

CHAPTER 18   Opinion and expert evidence 207

CHAPTER 19   Character evidence 222

CHAPTER 20   Evidence in sexual offences cases 235

CHAPTER 21   Self-corroboration 244

CHAPTER 22   Collateral evidence 246

CHAPTER 23   *Res gestae* 250

CHAPTER 24   Previous consistent statements 256

CHAPTER 25   Hearsay evidence 264

CHAPTER 26   Privilege 280

Chapter 15

The general test for relevance

15.1 The relationship between relevance and admissibility 158

15.2 The practical meaning of relevance 159
    15.2.1 The general test of relevance 160

15.3 The inquiry into logical relevance 162
    15.3.1 The facts in issue 162
        15.3.1.1 Identify the facts in issue 162
        15.3.1.2 Establish the relationship between the evidentiary fact and the issue 162
    15.3.2 The closeness or remoteness of the logical connection 163

15.4 The inquiry into admissibility 164
    15.4.1 Admissibility and the degree of probative value: a cost–benefit analysis 164
    15.4.2 The use of the term 'legal relevance' 166
    15.4.3 The meaning of procedural prejudice 167

15.5 Exclusion or inclusion of relevant evidence for policy or constitutional reasons 168
    15.5.1 Exclusion of relevant evidence 168
    15.5.2 Exclusion in terms of the Constitution 168
    15.5.3 Inclusion of immaterial evidence 168
    15.5.4 Inclusion of evidence not connected to a material fact in issue 168
    15.5.5 Precedent 169

15.6 The practical application of relevance 169
    15.6.1 Basic functional elements 169
        15.6.1.1 Relevance is a relational question of fact 169
        15.6.1.2 Multiple relevance and admissibility 169
        15.6.1.3 Provisional or conditional relevance 170
    15.6.2 The practical test of relevance 170

15.7 The court's general discretion to exclude relevant evidence 171
    15.7.1 The discretion to exclude evidence in criminal cases 171
    15.7.2 The discretion to exclude evidence in civil cases 172

15.1 The relationship between relevance and admissibility

Relevance is a foundational concept of the law of evidence as it forms the basis for the admissibility of all kinds of evidence in court proceedings. Any information that a party intends to admit at a court or tribunal proceedings must be shown to be relevant as a precondition for admission. The relationship between relevance and admissibility can be broadly explained as follows:

In order to be admissible an item of information (i.e. evidentiary facts or the *facta probantia*) must be relevant – this means that a logical connection must be established between the item of information and a material issue before a court (i.e. the facts in issue or the *facta probanda*).

In essence the concept of relevance may be summarised as follows: 'Information in the form of *facta probantia* will be relevant where it has the potential to assist the court in drawing a reasonable inference about a fact in issue or the *facta probanda*.'

Where a court determines that an item of information has this potential, it will be admissible in court but is now labelled as an evidentiary fact.

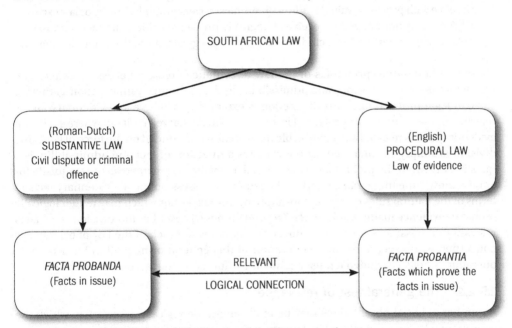

Figure 15.1 The relationship between facta probanda and facta probantia

15.2 The practical meaning of relevance

According to the English case *Hollington v E Hewthorn & Co Ltd*,[1] the general principle is that relevant evidence is admissible (expressed in its positive form) or irrelevant evidence is inadmissible (expressed in its negative form) at trial. Relevant evidence is usually admissible because it serves to prove, or disprove, the issues in dispute between opposing parties. Irrelevant evidence is inadmissible because it has no effect on the disputed issues.

In order to assess whether an evidentiary fact is relevant to a civil dispute or a criminal offence according to *R v Mathews*,[2] a judge must apply a 'blend of common sense, judicial

---

1 [1943] KB 587 at 594.
2 *R v Mathews and Others* 1960 1 SA 752 (A) at 758; *R v A (No 2)* [2002] 1 AC 45, per Lord Steyn 'to be relevant the evidence need merely have a tendency in logic and common sense to advance the proposition in issue'; *R v Cloutier* (1979) 48 C.C.C. (2d) 1 'relevance is assessed in context ... It requires a determination whether, as a matter of human experience and logic, the existence of a particular fact, directly or indirectly, makes the existence or non-existence of a material fact more probable than it would be otherwise'.

160 | THE LAW OF EVIDENCE IN SOUTH AFRICA

experience and logic lying outside the law'. The common law concept of relevance is measured in terms of logic and where an evidentiary fact is found in terms of logic to be relevant it is referred to as 'a logically relevant evidentiary fact'. This concept of relevance is a unique construction of adversarial jurisprudence and it does not exist in the same degree of complexity in any other legal system.[3] Relevance as a practical concept in the law of evidence is grounded upon two fundamental principles:[4]

1. The first principle in its negative form states 'no evidentiary fact is to be received at trial which is not logically probative of a fact-in-issue requiring to be proved'. A court cannot receive any information or potential evidence which has not been assessed in terms of the natural rules of logic.

2. The second principle in its positive form states that 'logically relevant evidence (i.e. evidence with probative value) is admissible, unless a clear ground of policy or law excludes it'.[5] A court is not obliged to receive all logically probative evidentiary facts and may in terms of certain legal rules exclude certain kinds of logically probative evidentiary facts.

These two foundation principles of the law of evidence create a necessary conceptual distinction between relevance and admissibility at the preliminary information-gathering stage of legal proceedings. This distinction is explained as 'where an evidentiary fact is rejected on the ground of irrelevance it is the rules of logic that rejects it but where a relevant evidentiary fact is rejected as inadmissible the rejection is grounded on the force of law'. The division is simply summarised as: relevance is a question of fact and admissibility is a question of law. At the preliminary stage of trial, relevance is regarded as a prerequisite for admissibility – meaning that a court is obliged first to assess potential evidentiary facts in terms of the natural rules of logic before applying any legal rules which may render logically probative evidence inadmissible. In *R v Trupedo*,[6] Innes CJ describes this division as 'all facts relevant to the issue in legal proceedings may be proved. Much of the law of evidence is concerned with exceptions to the operation of this general principle [...] but where its operation is not so excluded it must remain as the fundamental test of admissibility'.

15.2.1 The general test of relevance

A number of initial observations may be made about the logical framework in which the concept of relevance is analysed in order to assist in properly explaining it:

1. Relevance is assessed in terms of logic and tested by way of probability (hence the term 'logically relevant evidence').

2. Relevance is also a matter of common sense and judicial experience.

3. Relevance cannot be assessed in a vacuum – it may only be explained in terms of the relationship between an item of factual evidence and a substantive fact forming a material element of a civil dispute or a criminal offence.

In terms of this framework it is a mistake to attempt a formal, rigid definition of relevance but it is possible to formulate a functional test of how relevance is applied by the courts.

---

3 For example, in the inquisitorial system of justice the professional judge does not need to be guided by technical rules of admissible evidence. The inquisitorial natural inquiry is free of most evidentiary barriers, except common sense ones. All evidence is potentially admissible; the inquisitor decides on which evidence to admit or reject and is solely responsible for assigning the correct probative weight to be attached to the evidence.

4 JB Thayer *A Preliminary Treatise on Evidence at the Common Law* (rev 1969) at 264.

5 Ibid. at 530.

6 1920 AD 58 at 62.

A distinction must be drawn between direct and circumstantial evidence. A direct testimonial item of evidence, where reliable, is always relevant and serves to resolve a fact in issue directly. The issue of relevance generally only arises in respect to circumstantial evidence which requires the drawing of a reasonable inference in order to determine the relevance of the circumstantial item of evidence.

In all adversarial jurisdictions that apply a strict system of evidence, the general test of relevance may be understood as consisting of a three-legged inquiry:

1. The first inquiry is a test of logic and inferential reasoning based on probability in order to determine whether an evidentiary fact is relevant or irrelevant (i.e. the inquiry into logical relevance).
2. The second inquiry is to establish the extent to which the reception of a relevant evidentiary fact is procedurally undesirable. This requires balancing a number of procedural considerations. If an evidentiary fact is likely to cause prejudice or confusion, or to result in any other material disadvantage, a court will require that it possesses a substantially sufficient degree of probative value before it will admit it (i.e. it is an inquiry into admissibility of evidence and is based on a cost-benefit analysis – probative value versus prejudicial effect).[7]
3. The third inquiry is based on legal rules of exclusion. A relevant evidentiary fact may be excluded by reason of certain policy considerations (e.g. privilege) or for an unjustifiable infringement of the Constitution (i.e. the inquiry into illegally obtained evidence).

Summarised, these three steps, each a *sine qua non* for the step that follows, focus on establishing logical factual relevance, weighing potential procedural prejudice against probative value and whether the evidence is specifically excluded by law.

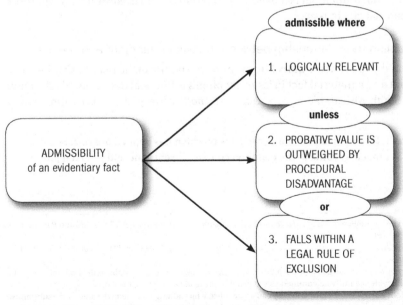

Figure 15.2 Admissibility of an evidentiary fact

---

[7] DT Zeffertt and AP Paizes *The South African Law of Evidence* 2 ed (2009) 238–241; AAS Zuckerman *The Principles of Criminal Evidence* (1992) at 51 'the admissibility test is therefore a composite test made of a mesh of considerations of logical probabilities and of practical utility'.

15.3 The inquiry into logical relevance

15.3.1 The facts in issue

Relevance cannot be determined in isolation, nor does it exist in a vacuum, and must be assessed by examining the totality of the unique combination of factual circumstances which make up each individual case. According to *S v Zuma*,[8] the first question is always, 'What are the issues?' Relevance cannot be divorced from the disputed facts of a particular case before a court. These unique sets of factual circumstances vary on a case by case basis and the concept of relevance cannot be easily reduced to a single abstract legal theory. Smalberger JA in *Van der Berg v Coopers & Lybrand Trust (Pty) Ltd and Others*[9] understood the assessment of relevance as 'having its foundation in the facts, circumstances and principles governing each particular case'. In other words, relevance is not an inherent characteristic of any item of evidence, the determination of its existence cannot be found in a void, and it finds its existence only as a common sense relationship between an evidentiary fact and a substantive fact in issue. The meaning of relevance now begins to take shape – fundamentally, relevance is a question of fact and inferential logic, and not a matter of law.

15.3.1.1 Identify the facts in issue

The first step in any coherent relevance inquiry is to identify the substantive facts of the dispute before the court. Common sense dictates that an item of evidence (i.e. an evidentiary fact) is selected to be a part of the legal-truth seeking process because it has a logical connection to a primary or even a secondary material fact in issue. Evidence that has a logical connection to an immaterial fact in issue is superfluous and irrelevant for the purpose of proving the material fact in issue.[10]

15.3.1.2 Establish the relationship between the evidentiary fact and the issue

The second step in the relevance inquiry is to examine the nature of the relationship between an evidentiary fact and a material fact in issue. Stephen's influential definition of relevance, as adopted into South African law by *R v Katz and Another*,[11] explains this relationship as follows:[12]

> [T]he word 'relevant' means that any two facts to which it is applied are so related to each other that according to the common course of events one, either taken [on

---

8   2006 (2) SACR 191 (W) at 199F; see also *Lloyd v Powell Duffryn Steam Coal Co Ltd* [1914] AC 733 at 738 and *R v Dhlamini* 1960 (1) SA 880 (N) at 881.

9   2001 (2) SA 242 (SCA) at para 26; see also *S v Letsoko and Others* 1964 (4) SA 768 (A) at 774–775 and *R v Sole* 2004 (2) SACR 599 (Les) at 660–661.

10   P Murphy *P Murphy on Evidence* (2008) 10 ed at 25: '... the purpose of evidence is to establish the probabilities of the facts-in-issue and evidence must be confined to the proof of these facts-in-issue. The proof of supernumerary or unrelated facts does not assist the court and may cause prejudice while adding no probative value to the substantive issues before it.' *R v Yaeck* (1991) 68 C.C.C. (3d) 545 at 565: 'all ... irrelevant [evidence] or insufficiently relevant [evidence] should be excluded'; *Lithgow City Council v Jackson* (2011) 244 CLR 352 at para 26: 'where the effect of the evidence is so ambiguous that it could not rationally affect the assessment of the fact-in-issue, the evidence is irrelevant'; *Smith v The Queen* (2001) 206 CLR 650 at paras 7, 12.

11   1946 AD 71 at para 78.

12   JF Stephen *A Digest of the Law of Evidence* 12 ed (1936) art 1. Also approved of by *R v Nethercott* [2002] 2 Cr App R 117.

CHAPTER 15   THE GENERAL TEST FOR RELEVANCE | **163**

its own], or in connection with other facts, *proves or renders probable the past, present or future existence or non-existence of the other.* [Emphasis added].[13]

Lord Simon in *DPP v Kilbourne*[14] reworks Stephen's definition in terms of probative value as follows: 'evidence is relevant if it is logically probative or disprobative of some matter which requires proof [...] relevant evidence (i.e. logically probative or disprobative) evidence is evidence which makes the matter which requires proof more or less probable'. Section 210 of the Criminal Procedure Act[15] codifies the South African common law relationship between an evidentiary fact and a fact in issue as follows:

> [N]o evidence as to any fact, matter or thing shall be admissible which is irrelevant or immaterial and which cannot *conduce* to prove or disprove any point or fact-at-issue. [Emphasis added]

Section 210 is merely a copy of Stephen's definition and simply means that there must be a logical relationship between the *facta probantia* (i.e. the evidentiary facts) and the *facta probanda* (i.e. the material substantive facts in issue) from which an inference may be drawn in order to demonstrate the probable existence or probable non-existence of a particular fact in issue.

15.3.2   The closeness or remoteness of the logical connection

The threshold test of relevance is an inquiry based on inferential logic about the relationship between an evidentiary fact and the probable existence, or non-existence, of a fact in issue. The common sense logical relationship between an evidentiary fact and a fact in issue may be a close one or it may be a remote one. Where the relationship is a close one, an evidentiary fact renders the existence of the fact in issue probable (i.e. the evidentiary fact has a high degree of probative value) and the evidentiary fact is said to be logically relevant. But where the relationship is remote, the existence of the fact in issue becomes improbable (i.e. the evidentiary fact has no probable value) and the evidentiary fact is rendered irrelevant. Clearly a threshold must be drawn between a relevant evidentiary fact and one which is irrelevant. The question of where such a line is to be drawn will depend on the circumstances of a particular case. The line will generally be drawn where inferential logic and common sense give way to mere conjecture and speculation. *R v Mpanza*[16] explains the logical connection between an evidentiary fact and a fact in issue as allowing for an inference to be drawn from the existence of the evidentiary fact about the probable existence of the fact in issue which cannot be based on mere speculation or conjecture.[17]

---

13   Rule 401 of the USA Federal Rules of Evidence similarly defines relevant evidence as 'evidence having any tendency to make the existence of any fact (i.e. fact-in-issue) more probable or less probable than it would be without the evidence'. The Canadian and English definitions are to the same effect: *R v Cloutier* 1979 48 C.C.C. (2d) 1 'relevance requires a determination whether, as a matter of human experience and logic, the existence of a particular fact, directly or indirectly, makes the existence or non-existence of a material fact more probable than it would otherwise be'; *R v Sims* (1946) 31 Cr App R 158 at 164 'we start with the general principle that evidence is admissible if it is logically probative ...'.

14   *DPP v Kilbourne* [1973] AC 729 at 756–757.

15   S 2 of the Civil Proceedings Evidence Act is to the same effect.

16   1915 AD 348 at 352–353.

17   *Hollingham v Head* (1858) 27 LJCP 241 at 242; 140 ER 1135 at 1136: 'it is not easy in all cases to draw the line, and to define with accuracy where probability ceases and speculation begins.' The line is generally drawn where considerations of fairness and convenience require it to be drawn – see DT Zeffertt and AP Paizes *The South African Law of Evidence* 2e (2009) supra note 7 at 238.

15.4 The inquiry into admissibility

15.4.1 Admissibility and the degree of probative value: a cost–benefit analysis

Relevance is not only a contextual test of logical probability, but may also be explained in terms of its probative value. Probative value may be generally defined as the weight of the evidentiary fact in proving or disproving a fact in issue. This value depends on the strength or weakness of the logical relationship between an evidentiary fact and a fact in issue, along with many other factors such as the importance of the issue, the extent to which the fact is challenged by the opposing party, and whether it is outweighed by other countervailing factors. Specifically, a logically relevant evidentiary fact of middling or average probative value may be excluded from trial for a variety of procedural reasons,[18] most importantly where:

1. Its probative value is outweighed by the procedural disadvantage of receiving it at trial;
2. Its admission is contrary to certain policy considerations irrespective of its probative value; or
3. It is an unjustifiable limitation of a constitutional right.

The primary practical reason advanced for these admissibility exclusionary rules is that there must be a reasonable limit on the amount of evidence adduced at trial.

DPP v Kilbourne[19] stated that 'all relevant evidence is *prima facie* admissible' but relevant evidence may be inadmissible 'because it's logically probative significance is considered to be grossly outweighed by its prejudice to the accused, so that a fair trial is endangered if it is admitted'.

An evidentiary fact is either logically relevant or it has no logical relevance. Between these two parameters lie evidentiary facts which, although possessing logical relevance, are inadmissible because their degree of probative value is outweighed by certain material procedural disadvantages inherent in such evidence – in the sense that the evidentiary fact will have a material adverse impact on the trial process. Therefore, logically relevant evidentiary facts with marginal probative value – but which are likely to cause material procedural prejudice resulting in undue delay, or unnecessary expense, or result in a lengthy investigation into collateral side issues, or raise problematic questions of credibility – are inadmissible at trial simply because these material procedural disadvantages do not warrant the reception of such flawed evidence.

DISCUSSION　　**Going to the dogs?**

15.1　　*R v Trupedo*[20] is authority that the material procedural prejudice of admitting tracker dog evidence far outweighed whatever little relevant probative value could be attached

---

18 JH Wigmore *A Treatise on the Anglo-American System of Evidence in Trials at Common Law* (rev 1983) 3 ed Vol. I at § 29a, 978–979: 'a fact may be logically relevant, and thus admissible, and yet be excluded by reason of the auxiliary principles of policy, particularly confusion of issues, unfair surprise or undue prejudice'.

19 *DPP v Kilbourne* [1973] AC 729 at 757–758; *R v Gordon* (1995) 2 Cr App R 61 at 64; *R v Edwards* (1991) 93 Cr App R 48 at 59.

20 1920 AD 58 at 62–63; *R v Katz* 1946 AD 71 at 78 '... the legal admissibility of a fact is not entirely determined by its relevance to an issue before the court because facts which may be regarded as logically relevant ... are sometimes excluded by the rules of evidence'. Facts are excluded because of little probative value and are likely to cause prejudice if admitted. See also *S v Mavuso* 1987 3 SA 499 (A) at 505B–C; *Holtzhausen v Roodt* 1997 (4) SA 766 (W) at 776–777; *S v M* 2003 (1) SA 341 (SCA) at para 17.

to it. The police, on investigating a break-in at a house and discovering two bare footprints outside the house, brought in a tracker dog to follow the scent trial left by the alleged thief. The tracker dog sniffed its way to a nearby building occupied by a disparate number of individuals sleeping together in the same room and began barking at a particular individual, who was then arrested by the police. The Appeal Court (now the SCA) overturned the trial court's conviction on the reasoning that in certain circumstances tracker dog evidence could have probative value,[21] but that in this particular circumstance no reasonable inference could be drawn from a tracker dog's behaviour in respect to the identity of the thief. Drawing such an inference would simply be based on conjecture and uncertainty, and its reception would result in prejudice as the jury[22] would be inclined to give it an exaggerated importance.

In *S v Shabalala*,[23] the Appeal Court held that it was bound by the *Trupedo* precedent and somewhat vaguely indicated that a tracker dog's identification was untrustworthy and therefore inadmissible, stating when the probative value of evidence is 'so inconsequential and relevance accordingly so problematic there would be little point in receiving the evidence'. The cogency of tracker dog evidence *in casu* was not such as to remove it from the realm of conjecture but where untrustworthiness could be sufficiently reduced the actions of a tracker dog could possibly become relevant and admissible.

Remember, however, that we no longer use juries and so the rationale underpinning the *Trupedo* judgment is actually irrelevant in a South African context. The Appeal Court in *Shabalala* was thus probably wrong to hold that it was bound by *Trupedo* as the rationale underlying *Trupedo* is no longer relevant. Is it now time to for the dog to have its day?

According to *Delew v Town Council of Springs*,[24] a high degree of probative value is required before a court will admit an evidentiary fact which is likely to cause procedural prejudice or confusion, or involve a complex investigation into collateral issues.

The number and kind of countervailing procedural considerations are generally identified by way of a cost–benefit analysis of what evidentiary facts should be admitted or excluded at trial in order to provide justice to the accused or litigant as fairly, speedily and as accurately as possible.[25] The New Zealand High Court in *R v Wilson* makes a clear distinction between the inquiry of logical relevance in the form of probability/likelihood and the inquiry into countervailing considerations.[26]

---

21 *R v Trupedo* supra at 63: for example, probative value could be attached to the habit of a dog to resent the entrance of a stranger at night to its master's room by barking. This behaviour is independent of instruction or experience and is based on the instinct of self-preservation.

22 South Africa no longer uses juries.

23 1986 (4) SA 734 (A) at 742–743.

24 1945 TPD 128 at 131.

25 *R v Mohan* [1994] 2 S.C.R 9: a cost–benefit analysis is not used in its traditional economic sense but rather in terms of its impact on the trial process. The factors to be balanced against probative value include (i) an excessive procedural burden on the court, (ii) unfair surprise, (iii) confusion of issues, (iv) material procedural prejudice, (iv) unrestrained collateral side issues, (v) manufactured evidence, and (vi) excessive time wastage. In certain circumstances other well-established common law rules of evidence may serve to exclude a relevant evidentiary fact. *R v Schaube-Kuffler* 1969 (2) SA 40 (RA) at 50B: 'the general rule ... under common law is that any evidence which is relevant is admissible unless there is some other rule of evidence which excludes it'.

26 [1991] 2 NZLR 707 at 711, from which the quotes about the foundational and second characteristics of relevance are taken.

166 | THE LAW OF EVIDENCE IN SOUTH AFRICA

The foundational characteristic of relevance is described as follows:
- '[L]ack of relevance can be used to exclude evidence not because it has absolutely no bearing upon the likelihood or unlikelihood of a fact-in-issue but because the connection is considered to be too remote.'

The second characteristic is summarised as:
- 'Once it [*relevance*] is regarded as a matter of degree, competing policy considerations can be taken into account. These include the desirability of shortening trials, avoiding emotive distractions,[27] or marginal significance, protecting the reputations of those not represented before the courts. [ ] None of these matters would be determinative if the evidence in question were of significant probative value'. [28]

It must be noted that section 210 of the Criminal Procedure Act does not make such a clear distinction: 'no evidence as to any fact, matter or thing shall be admissible which is irrelevant or immaterial and which cannot *conduce to prove or disprove any point or fact-at-issue*' [emphasis added]. The section requires giving the words 'conduce to prove or disprove any point or fact-in-issue' a wide enough interpretation in order to justify the necessity for excluding logically relevant facts on the bases of established exclusionary rules of evidence.[29]

15.4.2 The use of the term 'legal relevance'

The design of relevance as set out above in *R v Trupedo*, *DPP v Kilbourne* and *R v Wilson* simply states that relevance is primarily a matter of logic and only secondarily a question of law. Wigmore[30] was of the opposite view and argued that relevance could be interpreted as a question of law and that logical relevance could be distinguished from legal relevance. According to Wigmore, an evidentiary fact is logically relevant if it tends to make the existence of a fact in issue more probable – but, in addition, it must be legally relevant in the sense that its probative value must exceed its prejudicial effect. To be legally relevant and admissible, a logically relevant evidentiary fact should also possess a 'plus value' in the form of additional probative value in order to outweigh any possible material procedural disadvantage its reception would cause at trial. Logical relevance is insufficient – it only establishes a bare minimum of probative value. To be admissible, logically relevant evidence requires an additional legal content of sufficiency. This view of relevance is also referred to as the test of sufficient relevance and is set out in the formula:

Legal Relevance (sufficiency) = Logical Relevance + Plus Value

The test of legal relevance has been the subject of vigorous criticism because it blurs the distinction between the inquiry into relevance and the separate inquiry about procedural

---

27   The factor of avoiding emotive distraction does not apply in a South African courtroom. This cost-aggravating factor refers to the effect certain evidentiary facts would have in a trial system where a layperson jury, and not a professionally trained judge, is the final decision maker.

28   The USA Federal Rules of Evidence make the same clear distinction between the test of logical relevance in Rule 401 and Rule 403, which provide for a general discretion to exclude logically relevant evidence based on substantial prejudice. See supra at note 13.

29   See DT Zeffertt and AP Paizes *The South African Law of Evidence* 2 ed (2009), note 7, the summary at 243.

30   Wigmore supra note 18 at § 28, p. 969: 'the judge in his efforts to prevent a jury from being satisfied by matters of slight value, capable of being exaggerated by prejudice ... has constantly seen fit to exclude matter which does not rise to a clearly sufficient degree of value ... legal [reasoning] denotes ... *something more than a minimum of probative value*. Each single piece of evidence must have a plus value'. C Boyle, MT MacCrimmon, D Martin *The Law of Evidence: Fact Finding, Fairness, and Advocacy* (1999) at 45 'to be admissible the evidence must be legally relevant, not subject to an exclusionary rule or fall to be excluded on any other policy grounds'.

CHAPTER 15 THE GENERAL TEST FOR RELEVANCE | **167**

disadvantages at trial (i.e. for confusing relevance with admissibility).[31] The concept of 'plus value' is simply an imprecise way of stating that the probative value of relevant evidence must outweigh any procedural disadvantage (i.e. prejudice) likely to result from its admission at trial.[32] In addition, the requirement of 'plus value' or an additional legal sufficiency over and above logical relevance simply confuses relevance with the evaluation of probative weight at the proof stage of a trial. Despite these criticisms, the use of the legal relevance concept persists in part in South African law.[33] However, whether or not an evidentiary fact is rendered inadmissible on the ground of a discretionary exclusionary rule (i.e. the common law approach) or through the application of the test of legal relevance (i.e. the Wigmore approach), the practical effect is much the same.

15.4.3 The meaning of procedural prejudice

Procedural prejudice does not refer to the damage caused to an accused's defence or a defendant's case by the admission of logically relevant evidence, nor does it refer to unfair bias or influence on the mind of a judge – it is simply a uniform catch-all for any procedural harm caused to any party in a trial. Therefore, the general term 'procedural prejudice' refers to a situation where certain kinds of logically relevant evidentiary facts with marginal probative value are inadmissible because their reception may unfavourably impact on the trial process.

The term 'procedural prejudice' must always be qualified by materiality and not by unfairness, as is sometimes mistakenly done. All prejudice is unfair but it is the materiality of the prejudice which must be weighed against the probative value of logically relevant evidence. Admitting procedurally prejudicial evidence may result in added court costs, wasted court time, an unreasonable burden being placed on one party or the other, or possible confusion and duplication of issues, etc.

There is no *closed list* of logically relevant evidentiary facts which are inadmissible because their reception would result in material procedural prejudice to the trial process.[34] Examples of some of the traditional classes of evidence which are considered to be inherently procedurally disadvantageous are the following:

1. Admitting a logically relevant evidentiary fact with marginal probative value may result in a time-consuming investigation into collateral or subsidiary side issues, thereby diverting the court's attention from the material facts in issue. For example, an inquiry into the reliability and scientific validity of lie-detector tests, brain-scan testing, behaviour modification therapy, hypnosis therapy and some psychiatric evaluations would entangle the court in a time-consuming investigation with few useful probative results.[35]

---

31 W Twining *Theories of Evidence: Bentham & Wigmore* (1985) at 152–155.
32 R Lempert and S Salzburg *A Modern Approach to Evidence: Text, Problems, Transcripts and Cases* 2 ed (1982) at 153 '... the concept of plus value is confusing...it is probably a less precise way of acknowledging, as modern courts do, that even relevant evidence may be excluded if it seems likely to be prejudicial, misleading or time-consuming'; GF James 'Relevancy, Probability and the Law' (1941) Vol. 29(6) *Calif.L.Rev* 689, 701–2 'logical relevancy ... defies definition. No statement ... of probative value higher than logical relevancy can be made precise enough for use without excluding much evidence [in daily use]'.
33 See the South African Law Reform Commission, Discussion Paper 113, Project 126 *Review of the Law of Evidence* ch 3, 15–18; *R v Matthews and Others* 1960 (1) SA 752 (A) at 758; *S v Nel* 1990 (2) SACR 136 (C) at 142–143; cf DT Zeffertt and AP Paizes *The South African Law of Evidence* 2 ed (2009) at 239–240.
34 For example, an accused's personal motive in committing a crime may be relevant for the purpose of establishing intent or identity. In certain cases the probative value of motive outweighs the risk of introducing potential collateral issues; see PJ Schwikkard and SE van der Merwe *Principles of Evidence* 3 ed (2009) at 52–54; *R v Kumalo & Nkosi* 1918 AD 500 at 504.
35 PJ Schwikkard and SE van der Merwe *Principles of Evidence* 3 ed (2009) at 49–52; *Delew v Town Council of Springs* 1945 TPD 128; *Holtzhauzen v Roodt* 1997 (4) SA 766 (W); *S v Nel* 1990 (2) SACR 136 (C).

168 | THE LAW OF EVIDENCE IN SOUTH AFRICA

2. Hearsay is logically relevant but is inadmissible because it is untrustworthy and prejudicial, and the danger of admitting hearsay evidence may place an unfair procedural burden on an opposing party. However, hearsay is statutorily admissible in terms of section 3 of the Evidence Amendment Act when it is in the interest of justice to admit it.
3. The assessment of the trustworthiness and reliability of tracker dog identification may waste the court's time.[36]
4. Similar fact evidence, character evidence, laypersons' opinion and evidence of previous convictions are generally regarded as procedurally prejudicial and irrelevant but these classes of evidence may become exceptionally admissible in certain circumstances.[37]
5. Previous consistent statements and other kinds of easily manufactured evidence are usually irrelevant and inadmissible[38] – although it must be noted that a previous consistent statement can never be relevant to a material fact in issue and may only be exceptionally admitted to establish credibility and to rebut a charge of recent fabrication made by an opposing party.[39]

15.5 Exclusion or inclusion of relevant evidence for policy or constitutional reasons

15.5.1 Exclusion of relevant evidence

Privileged evidence is logically relevant evidence with a high probative value which is inadmissible for certain policy reasons. All relevant evidence which falls under the private or State categories of privilege are usually inadmissible unless a party freely and voluntarily waives the right to privilege. Relevant admissions, confessions and pointings out may also be inadmissible when involuntarily induced from an accused.

15.5.2 Exclusion in terms of the Constitution

Similarly, any logically relevant evidentiary fact which is obtained by way of an unjustifiable violation of an accused's constitutional right to a fair trial as defined in section 35(5) or illegally obtained by unjustifiably infringing a party's procedural rights as defined in section 35(1)–(3), including the rights to dignity or privacy, will be inadmissible.

15.5.3 Inclusion of immaterial evidence

In terms of the *res gestae* principle of completeness it may be necessary in certain instances to admit an irrelevant fact because it forms part of a continuous transaction or it will allow a court to understand a witness's testimony properly. A witness may be allowed to introduce immaterial facts of time, place and context in order to fill in the gaps when testifying in order to give coherent testimony (commonly referred to as completing the whole picture).

15.5.4 Inclusion of evidence not connected to a material fact in issue

Section 210 of the Criminal Procedure Act and section 2 of the Civil Proceedings Evidence Act refer not only to facts in issue but also to any fact, point or thing. Evidentiary facts which are not relevant to a fact in issue may be admitted because they are relevant and cogent to

---

36 *S v Trupedo* supra; *S v Shabalala* supra.
37 *R v Straffen* [1952] 2 QB 911; *DPP v Boardman* [1975] AC 421; *S v Nieuwoudt* 1990 (4) SA 217 (A); *R v Rowton* [1865] 169 ER 1497.
38 *S v Scott-Crossley* 2008 (1) SACR 223 (SCA) at para 17.
39 *S v Bergh* 1976 (4) SA 857 (A); *S v Moolman* 1996 (1) SACR 267 (A).

CHAPTER 15   THE GENERAL TEST FOR RELEVANCE   169

another fact only indirectly related to a fact in issue. For example, evidence may be adduced which goes to the credibility of a witness, an expert witness being asked to show evidence of expertise, and evidence adduced to show that a confession was made freely and voluntarily is always relevant and admissible.

15.5.5   Precedent

As explained above by the Appeal Court in *S v Shabalala*, the precedent established by the previous judgment in *R v Trupedo* is binding on it and determines the relevance and admissibility of a certain kind of evidence – the uniform thread in both cases was the irrelevance and inadmissibility of untrustworthy tracker dog identification evidence. However, it must be noted that the determination of relevance is entirely based on the existence of a unique set of facts present in each particular case and it is rare that the facts of two cases are always exactly the same. Therefore, precedent should serve only as a useful guideline in determining relevance, and not as an inflexible rule.[40]

15.6   The practical application of relevance

15.6.1   Basic functional elements

Before relevance may be properly set out as a practical test, a number of points about the functional nature of relevance must be illustrated.

15.6.1.1   Relevance is a relational question of fact

The relevance of an evidentiary fact must be assessed by its logical relational connection to a particular material fact in issue. Furthermore:
1.   As new material facts in issue arise or are identified during the course of a trial, so previously irrelevant evidentiary facts may become relevant and admissible.[41]
2.   The logical connection between an evidentiary fact and a fact in issue may be found not only in respect to primary facts in issue but also in respect to secondary facts in issue.[42]
3.   The material facts in issue also determine the form of potential evidentiary facts which may be relevant (i.e. in the form of oral, written, electronic or physical evidence).

15.6.1.2   Multiple relevance and admissibility

Depending on the given set of factual circumstances, evidence may be inadmissible for one purpose but admissible for another.[43]

---

40   James supra note 32 at 702, 'a precedent is of no value save in another case substantially identical in all its particulars. Treated more broadly its tendency will be to mislead subsequent judges'.
41   *R v Solomons* 1959 (2) SA 352 (A) at 362.
42   *S v Mayo and Another* 1990 (1) SACR 659 (E) at 661–662 'it is not in the interest of justice that relevant material should be excluded from the court, whether it is relevant to the issue or to issues which are themselves relevant to the issue but strictly speaking not in issue themselves ...'.
43   For example, evidence of character (i.e. propensity evidence) is inadmissible for the direct purpose of establishing guilt, but where an accused adduces evidence of his or her good character, the door is open for the prosecution to adduce bad character evidence for the purpose of rebuttal (s 197(*a*) of the Criminal Procedure Act). Similarly, evidence of previous convictions is inadmissible for the direct purpose of establishing guilt but where the accused is charged with receiving stolen property, evidence of previous convictions, or bad character, may be received (s 197(*c*) of the Criminal Procedure Act).

15.6.1.3 Provisional or conditional relevance

An isolated item of evidence may appear to be irrelevant but when assessed together with another item of evidence its relevance becomes apparent. Where there is a problem in adducing the second item of evidence before the first item, a court may provisionally allow the admission of the first item subject to the subsequent admission of the second item.

Once these functional elements of relevance have been understood, a practical test of relevance for the day-to-day use by the average legal practitioner may be attempted. The practical test is based on three simple inquiries and is flexible enough to apply to any circumstance or combination of circumstances. Note that the test offered below does not amount to a definition of relevance. Relevance is conceived of and takes its form within a particular set of circumstances; as circumstances change from case to case, so does relevance, which means that relevance cannot be reduced to a single unifying abstract theory.

15.6.2 The practical test of relevance

Step 1 (inquiry 1): Determining logical relevance
- Identify the material substantive facts in issue which make up a civil or criminal matter.
- Collect all the potential evidentiary facts and sift through these facts in order to establish which of these potential evidentiary facts are logically related to the material facts in issue:
  - Where a strong inference can be drawn about the probable existence or non-existence of the fact in issue – the evidentiary fact is relevant and admissible.
  - Where no inference can be drawn about the probable existence or non-existence of the fact in issue – the evidentiary fact is irrelevant and inadmissible.
  - Where only a weak inference can be drawn about the probable existence or non-existence of the fact in issue – the evidentiary fact is relevant but possesses marginal probative value and may or may not be admitted.

Step 2 (inquiry 2): Determining admissibility – weighing logically relevant evidence with marginal probative value against procedural disadvantage
- In order to establish the admissibility of a logically relevant evidentiary fact with a marginal probative value, make a discretionary cost–benefit weighing of such marginal probative value against the possible procedural prejudice which may result from its reception at trial:
  - Where the probative value of a relevant evidentiary fact outweighs its procedural prejudicial impact at trial – it will be admissible.
  - Where the procedural prejudicial impact of receiving a relevant evidentiary fact at trial outweighs its probative value – it will be inadmissible.

Step 3 (inquiry 3): Other rules of exclusion or inclusion
- Exclusion of logically relevant evidentiary facts in terms of policy considerations:
  - State and private privileged relevant evidence is inadmissible.
  - Involuntarily obtained relevant admissions, confessions and pointings out are inadmissible.
- Constitutional exclusions:
  - Relevant, illegally obtained evidence obtained by unjustifiably infringing section 35(5) of the Bill of Rights is inadmissible.
  - Relevant evidence obtained by unjustifiably infringing the rights to dignity and privacy of the Bill of Rights is inadmissible

CHAPTER 15 THE GENERAL TEST FOR RELEVANCE | **171**

- Inclusion by way of precedent:
  - ◆ Any evidentiary fact admitted by way of precedent.
- Inclusion of irrelevant evidentiary facts:
  - ◆ *Res gestae* evidence as to time and place in order to establish narrative coherence of witness testimony is admissible.
- Inclusion of relevant evidence by judicial notice:
  - ◆ Notoriously well-known facts are admissible without proof.

15.7 The court's general discretion to exclude relevant evidence

15.7.1 The discretion to exclude evidence in criminal cases

The common law rule in criminal cases is that the courts have discretion to exclude potential evidence even if the potential evidence is relevant and was obtained lawfully and constitutionally.[44] In *Kuruma, son of Kaniu v R*,[45] the High Court held that in a criminal case the judge always has discretion to disallow evidence where the strict rules of admissibility would operate unfairly against the accused.[46] The court will usually exercise its discretion to exclude where the court is satisfied that the evidence would be materially prejudicial and procedurally detrimental to the accused.[47] In some cases, the concept of prejudice has been extended beyond mere procedural prejudice to include the likelihood of undue delay or inordinate financial expense.[48] The court may respond to an application by the accused to exclude such prejudicial evidence or may decide *mero motu* to exclude after submissions on the issue from the State and defence.[49]

There is no closed list of factors which justify the exclusion of evidence on the ground of potential prejudice. Prejudicial factors include:

- the likelihood of wasting the court's time by admitting the evidence in circumstances where the potential evidentiary weight of the proposed evidence is limited
- the duplication of evidence already before the court
- the danger of confusion of issues

---

44 See ch 16 Unconstitutionally obtained evidence. Prior to the advent of the Constitution, the general approach of the courts was that all evidence relevant to the matters in issue was admissible and the court did not concern itself with how the evidence was obtained (whether lawfully, unlawfully, improperly or unfairly).

45 [1955] AC 197 (PC). See *S v Forbes and Another* 1970 (2) SA 594 (C); *S v Mushimba en Andere* 1977 (2) SA 829 (A) at 839–840.

46 Note that the discretion to exclude here is based on whether the effect of admitting the evidence will operate 'unfairly' against the accused – the test is not whether the evidence was unfairly obtained. Thus, even unfairly obtained evidence was admissible if relevant, as was unlawfully or improperly obtained evidence, but the court nevertheless retained a discretion to exclude this evidence if admitting it would operate unfairly against the accused

47 See the discussion in PJ Schwikkard and SE van der Merwe *Principles of Evidence* 3 ed (2009) at 52: '"Prejudice" in this context does not mean that the evidence must be excluded simply because the party against whom the evidence stands to be adduced will be incriminated or implicated. It means that incrimination or implication will take place in circumstances where the party concerned may be procedurally disadvantaged, or otherwise exposed to a lengthy trial involving issues which, though logically relevant, are legally too remote to assist the court in its ultimate decision on the merits.'

48 That is, prejudice in the sense that the accused's ability to prepare for his or her trial, or to conduct his or her defence effectively, has been compromised in some way, for example crucial witnesses may be missing or dead, or documents may be lost or destroyed.

49 In *S v Hammer and Others* 1994 (2) SACR 496 (C) the court used its common law discretion to exclude evidence obtained by the police in circumstances where they had promised to pass a note from a detained minor to his mother but had instead kept the note to use at trial against him.

172 | THE LAW OF EVIDENCE IN SOUTH AFRICA

- the delay and expense resulting from trying to procure the potential evidence; and
- the likelihood that the admission of evidence that is arguably only relevant to collateral issues will blur the focus on the *facta probanda* of the case.[50]

15.7.2 The discretion to exclude evidence in civil cases

The common law rule in civil cases is that the only test for the admissibility of evidence is relevance. However, in *Shell SA (Edms) Bpk en Andere v Voorsitter, Dorperaad van die Oranje-Vrystaat en Andere*,[51] the Free State High Court recognised a discretion to exclude **improperly obtained evidence**. The High Court in other provincial divisions subsequently also recognised the existence of such discretion.[52] For example, in *Fedics Group (Pty) Ltd and Another v Matus and Others, Fedics Group (Pty) Ltd and Another v Murphy and Others*,[53] the court relied on section 39(2) of the Constitution to hold that the duty on the courts to promote the spirit, purport and objects of the Bill of Rights[54] empowered courts to exclude relevant evidence in civil cases. However, the Appeal Court in *Janit and Another v Motor Industry Fund Administrators (Pty) Ltd and Another*[55] declined to decide whether such discretion was part of South African law.

THIS CHAPTER IN ESSENCE

1   Any information that a party intends to admit in court must be shown to be relevant as a precondition for admission.

2   Relevance is based on a logical connection between the item of information and a material fact in issue before a court.

3   The general principle is that relevant evidence is admissible (expressed in its positive form) or irrelevant evidence is inadmissible (expressed in its negative form) at trial.

4   Relevance expressed in its negative form states that 'no evidentiary fact is to be received at trial which is not logically probative of a fact-in-issue requiring to be proved'.

5   Relevance expressed in its positive form states that 'logically relevant evidence (i.e. evidence with probative value) is admissible, unless a clear ground of policy or law excludes it'.

6   The division between relevance and admissibility of evidence is simply summarised as follows: relevance is a question of fact and admissibility is a question of law.

7   Relevance is assessed in terms of logic and tested by way of probability (hence the term 'logically relevant evidence').

8   Relevance is not an inherent characteristic of any item of evidence, the determination of its existence cannot be found in a void, and it finds its existence only as a common sense relationship between an evidentiary fact and a substantive fact in issue.

---

50   See DT Zeffertt and AP Paizes *The South African Law of Evidence* 2 ed (2009) at ch 18.
51   1992 (1) SA 906 (O).
52   See *Motor Industry Fund Administrators (Pty) Ltd and Another v Janit and Another* 1994 (3) SA 56 (W); *Lenco Holdings Ltd and Others v Eckstein and Others* 1996 (2) SA 693 (N).
53   1998 (2) SA 617 (C).
54   Sections 7–39 of the Constitution.
55   1995 (4) SA 293 (A). But see *Waste Products Utilisation (Pty) Ltd v Wilkes and Another* 2003 (2) SA 515 (W) at 550F which held that the courts retain a discretion to admit tape recordings into evidence notwithstanding the commission of an offence or the infringement of a constitutional right in obtaining the recording. This decision is unlikely to be followed as it is in violation of the constitutional obligation in s 39(2) to promote the spirit, purport and objects of the Bill of Rights.

CHAPTER 15   THE GENERAL TEST FOR RELEVANCE   **173**

9   In other words, 'relevant' means that any two facts to which it is applied are so related to each other that, according to the common course of events, one, either taken on its own or in connection with other facts, proves or renders probable the past, present or future existence or non-existence of the other.

10   A logically relevant evidentiary fact of middling or average probative value may be inadmissible at trial for a variety of procedural reasons where:

10.1   Its probative value is outweighed by the procedural disadvantage of receiving it at trial;

10.2   Its admission is contrary to certain policy considerations irrespective of its probative value; or

10.3   It is an unjustifiable limitation of a constitutional right.

11   Relevance is conceived of and takes its form within a particular set of circumstances. As circumstances change from case to case, so does relevance, which means that relevance cannot be reduced to a single unifying abstract theory.

12   The common law rule in criminal cases is that the courts have discretion to exclude potential evidence even if the potential evidence is relevant and was obtained lawfully and constitutionally.

13   The common law rule in civil cases is that the only test for the admissibility of evidence is relevance.

Chapter 16

Unconstitutionally obtained evidence in criminal cases: section 35(5) of the Constitution

16.1 Introduction 174

16.2 Theoretical basis for excluding unconstitutionally obtained evidence 175
    16.2.1 Rationales for excluding unconstitutionally obtained evidence 176
        16.2.1.1 The condonation rationale 176
        16.2.1.2 The deterrence rationale 177
        16.2.1.3 The corrective justice rationale 177
    16.2.2 Some critiques of the rationales for excluding unconstitutionally
        obtained evidence 178
    16.2.3 Rationales used by the courts to exclude unconstitutionally
        obtained evidence 179
    16.2.4 Implications of excluding unconstitutionally obtained evidence 179

16.3 Overview of section 35 of the Constitution 180

16.4 The section 35(5) test for excluding unconstitutionally obtained evidence 181
    16.4.1 First leg of the test: whether admission would render a trial unfair 182
    16.4.2 Second leg of the test: whether admission would be detrimental to the
        administration of justice 186

16.5 Procedural issues 189
    16.5.1 Section 35(5): onus of proof 190
    16.5.2 Section 35(5): *locus standi* 191
    16.5.3 Section 35(5): trial-within-a-trial 193

16.6 A section 35(5) case study of *S v Van Deventer and Another* 193
    16.6.1 Background 193
    16.6.2 Facts of the case 193
    16.6.3 The admissibility test to be applied in terms of section 35(5) of the Constitution 194
    16.6.4 Applying this test in terms of section 35(5) to the facts of this case 194

16.1 Introduction

This chapter focuses on the treatment of unconstitutionally obtained evidence in criminal matters under South African law. This discussion is comparatively informed as South African law, jurisprudence and scholarly literature generally draws from the Canadian and US approaches to unconstitutionally obtained evidence. South Africa's jurisprudence

CHAPTER 16 UNCONSTITUTIONALLY OBTAINED EVIDENCE IN CRIMINAL CASES 175

post-apartheid is influenced by the Constitution, specifically the Bill of Rights.[1] Under the current constitutional dispensation, the courts have a qualified duty to exclude relevant unconstitutionally obtained evidence, particularly if the admission of such evidence will lead to an unfair trial or will otherwise be detrimental to the administration of justice. Previously, the courts were not preoccupied so much with how evidence was procured, but rather with whether it was relevant or not.[2] In the Interim Constitution of 1993, there was also no specific provision for the exclusion of **unlawfully obtained evidence** although the courts relied on the right to a fair trial to deal with instances of illegally obtained evidence.[3]

16.2 Theoretical basis for excluding unconstitutionally obtained evidence

In 1968, Herbert Packer published a seminal paper entitled *Two Models of the Criminal Process*[4] in which he conceptualised the competing models of the criminal process as the 'crime control' and 'due process' models. The 'crime control' model described a criminal justice process which, among other things, prioritised the speedy finalisation of criminal cases based on the 'factual guilt' of an accused person as opposed to 'legal guilt', with scant or no regard to the rights of such persons.[5] On the other hand, the 'due process' model described a criminal process which operates as an 'obstacle course' to the finalisation of criminal cases as it prioritised the observance of the rights of accused persons.[6]

The constitutional safeguards in the criminal process of South Africa lean squarely to the due process model, as opposed to the crime control model which was prevalent under apartheid, as the rights of accused, arrested and detained persons, and even criminal suspects, have become more central and elevated in the criminal process. This has been done in order to provide due process rights protection and to mark a break with the unfortunate past. The exclusion of unconstitutionally obtained evidence seeks to protect the rights of accused, arrested and detained persons against any possible abuse of power and process by the State, particularly the police, prosecutors and the courts to the extent that they have done so in the past. This includes stricter rules for the collection of evidence by law enforcement agencies and for the admission of such evidence by the courts in criminal trials.

The general rule is that all relevant evidence is admissible in criminal matters. However, section 35(5) of the Constitution compels the courts to exclude unconstitutionally obtained evidence under certain circumstances, even when such evidence is relevant. It provides that:

> Evidence obtained in a manner that violates any right in the Bill of Rights must be excluded if the admission of that evidence would render the trial unfair or otherwise be detrimental to the administration of justice.

This provision also gives judicial officers an oversight role over the work of the police and prosecution authorities. Primarily, though, it orders courts to exclude any evidence if it is collected or procured in a manner that violates rights enshrined in the Bill of Rights. In order

---

1 Sections 7–39 of the Constitution
2 De Vos, W Le R. 2011(2) 'Illegally or unconstitutionally obtained evidence: a South African perspective' TSAR 268
3 De Vos (2011) at 269. See also *Gumede v S* (800/2015) [2016] ZASCA 148; [2016] 4 ALL SA 692 (SCA); 2017(1) SACR 253 (SCA) (30 September 2016) at para 19.
4 Packer, HL (1964) 'Two models of the criminal process' *University of Pennsylvania Law Review* 113(1) 1.
5 See Packer (1964).
6 See Packer (1964).

176 | THE LAW OF EVIDENCE IN SOUTH AFRICA

to do this, the courts need to determine whether unconstitutionally obtained evidence, if admitted, would render the trial unfair. If not, they still need to determine whether admission of the evidence would otherwise be detrimental to the administration of justice or not. Courts and academics have interpreted section 35(5) of the Constitution and some rich jurisprudence and literature is developing. However, there still appears to be no Constitutional Court interpretation of section 35(5) to settle a number of contradictions, which will be seen below. In interpreting section 35(5) of the Constitution, our courts have relied on foreign law, particularly on judgments emanating from the Canadian Courts.[7] Section 39(1)(c) of the Constitution empowers them to consider foreign law when interpreting the Bill of Rights.

The basic mischief that section 35(5) seeks to remedy is the abuse of power and process by law enforcement agencies against accused, arrested and detained persons and so section 35(5) protection only accrues to accused, arrested and detained persons as opposed to anyone else, including suspects.[8] However, when unconstitutionally obtained evidence is excluded, in many instances an accused is not convicted, especially if the police relied on such evidence to convict. The unintended consequences and implications of exclusions on the broader societal objectives of controlling crime and preserving public order, and on the victims of crime, are also important to emphasise. Let us look at the rationales for excluding unconstitutionally obtained evidence.

16.2.1 Rationales for excluding unconstitutionally obtained evidence

Unconstitutionally obtained evidence can be defined as evidence that is obtained through the violation of any of the rights contained in the Bill of Rights. However, it is also possible for law enforcement agencies to collect evidence without violating any of the rights contained in the Bill of Rights, but through violation of other laws, rules and principles.[9] The latter would best be defined as improperly, illegally or unlawfully obtained evidence where the law enforcement officers fail to abide by the rules of evidence when collecting the evidence. There is, however, a thin line between them as unconstitutionally obtained evidence is also improperly or illegally obtained.

Previously, at common law, in South Africa and abroad, there was no duty on the courts to exclude relevant evidence even when obtained in an improper, illegal, unlawful or unconstitutional manner.[10] However, over the past decades this position has changed in many jurisdictions, particularly with the advent of the 'exclusionary rule' from the United States of America and from Canadian law. There are three main rationales that have been advanced in literature for the exclusion of unconstitutionally obtained evidence. These are the '**condonation**', 'deterrence' and 'corrective justice' rationales.[11]

16.2.1.1 The condonation rationale

This rationale, also referred to as the 'judicial integrity rationale',[12] is based on the reasoning that the courts should not, and should not be seen to, condone police misconduct of using

---

7   Canadian Charter of Rights and Freedoms, Part I of the Constitution Act 1982.
8   Jerome Wells 'The admissibility of real evidence in the light of the Constitution of the Republic of South Africa, 1996'. Submitted in accordance with the requirements for the degree of Doctor of Laws at the University of South Africa. Supervisor: Professor SS Terblanche (November 2013) at 44.
9   De Vos (2011).
10   S Penney 'Taking deterrence seriously: excluding unconstitutionally obtained evidence under section 24 (2) of the Charter' (2003) 49(1) *McGill Law Journal*, 105–139.
11   Penney (2003) at 110.
12   Wells (2013) at 30.

CHAPTER 16 UNCONSTITUTIONALLY OBTAINED EVIDENCE IN CRIMINAL CASES 177

unconstitutional means to obtain evidence.[13] The courts should dissociate themselves from the violation of constitutional rights. The objective is to protect the integrity of the judiciary and the criminal process.[14] It is argued that courts become accomplices to police misconduct if they admit evidence that was illegally acquired.[15] It is not only the integrity of the judiciary that this rationale speaks to, it is also the integrity of the criminal justice system as a whole. By refusing to be accomplices, it is hoped that this will help to reform police behaviour and improve compliance with the dictates of the law. In this way the condonation rationale complements the deterrence rationale as it also seeks to impact on the behaviour of police officers.

16.2.1.2 The deterrence rationale

The 'deterrence' rationale seeks to discourage or deter law enforcement agencies from collecting evidence through unconstitutional means.[16] The objective of excluding evidence under this rationale is to discipline the police who have collected such evidence and to deter future misconduct.[17] This rationale focuses on past conduct, which the courts cannot undo except by excluding evidence, and on preventing future similar violations. It seeks to safeguard substantive and procedural due process rights of the criminal process. Ally has argued that to achieve effective deterrence, constitutional violations must lead to an automatic exclusion of evidence.[18] However, this would seem to be more a normative position than reality, as many jurisdictions give courts a discretion to decide.

16.2.1.3 The corrective justice rationale

The 'corrective justice' rationale, also referred to as the 'remedial imperative', justifies the exclusion of unconstitutionally obtained evidence on the basis that the police should not benefit from the wrongfulness of their actions – the constitutional violations they have committed when collecting evidence.[19] Unconstitutionally obtained evidence under this rationale is therefore excluded on the basis of restoring the status quo before the rights were violated. This is seen as compensating the accused in that evidence collected through the violation of their rights is not used against them. Penney argues that excluding evidence under this rationale makes it more likely that factually guilty defendants will go unpunished.[20] The justification for this rationale is that the condonation and deterrence rationales are inadequate. Courts must go further to vindicate and uphold the rights of suspects by excluding unconstitutionally obtained evidence.

---

13 Penney (2003) at 110.
14 Wells (2013) at 30.
15 Wells (2013) at 31.
16 Ibid. See also J Wells (2013) The admissibility of real evidence in the light of the Constitution of the Republic of South Africa 1996, University of South Africa, at 17–32. Dressler and Michaels succinctly capture the essence of this view: 'The exclusionary rule is meant to deter unconstitutional police conduct by promoting professionalism within the ranks, specifically by creating an incentive for police departments to hire individuals sensitive to civil liberties, to better train officers in the proper use of force, to keep officers updated on constitutional law, and to develop internal guidelines that reduce the likelihood of unreasonable arrests and searches'. J Dressler and AS Michaels *Understanding Criminal Procedure* 4 ed (2006) at 378.
17 Wells (2013) at 20.
18 Ally, D (2012) Determining the effect (the social costs) of exclusion under the South African exclusionary rule: should factual guilt tilt the scales in favour of the admission of unconstitutionally obtained evidence, *PER* 15(5) at 476. See also Wells (2013) at 20.
19 Penney (2003), Wells (2013).
20 Penney (2003) at 112.

16.2.2 Some critiques of the rationales for excluding unconstitutionally obtained evidence

Penney has argued that it is only the deterrence rationale that the courts should seek to follow as the other rationales are superfluous. He contends in respect of the condonation rationale, for instance, that excluding relevant evidence of guilt, even if it was obtained unconstitutionally, is much more likely to bring the justice system into disrepute than admitting such evidence would.[21] He further argues that admitting unconstitutionally obtained evidence does not condone police misconduct but merely recognises that the violation cannot be undone.[22] It also recognises that the exclusion of such evidence will not prevent future misconduct by the police and that it would serve no purpose to suppress reliable evidence of guilt.[23]

With regards to the corrective justice rationale, Penney argues that excluding evidence simply to compensate for the breaches suffered by the accused disproportionately compensates them for the wrongs that were committed against them. The benefits of exclusion (which accrue to the accused) greatly outweigh their social costs (the violations by law enforcement agencies when collecting evidence).[24] According to him, this rationale could be rescued only in rare cases where the rights violations against the accused are extreme and 'the consequences of a conviction are unusually benign'.[25]

There are also disagreements among scholars as to whether the exclusion of evidence actually assists in changing police behaviour and achieving the deterrence objectives.[26] Some scholars believe it does not, some argue that it should surely influence both individual and institutional behaviour as convictions are lost or set aside.[27] They argue that individual performance of police officers is affected when they lose cases based on their misconduct. Institutional performance is also affected, leading to individual behavioural change and institutional measures being put in place to comply with the legal requirements.[28]

Penney observes that excluding evidence on the basis of the deterrence rationale is hard to assess for effectiveness, but empirical studies conducted in the US show that the introduction of the exclusionary rule in *Mapp v Ohio* (367 U.S. 643 (1961)) led to an increase in warrant searches as opposed to warrantless searches.[29] Surveys conducted in the US with police officers and other justice officials have also shown that exclusion does impact on their behaviour as it affects their individual performance and their career advancement.[30] No studies have been conducted in South Africa to assess the effectiveness of exclusion on police conduct. However, jurisprudence from the Supreme Court of Appeal shows that many convictions are being set aside on appeal. There are also many decisions from the High Courts which have applied the section 35(5) remedies.

---

21 Penney (2003) at 111.
22 Ibid.
23 Ibid.
24 At 113 Penney argues strongly that the compensation for victims of investigatory abuses should rather be monetary damages or other appropriate remedies than the exclusion of evidence.
25 Penney (2003) at 112.
26 See discussion of this in Wells supra, n 23.
27 Wells (2013) at 23.
28 Wells (2013) at 23.
29 Penney (2003) at 115.
30 At 115.

16.2.3 Rationales used by the courts to exclude unconstitutionally obtained evidence

South African courts have tended to favour all these rationales (condonation, deterrence and corrective justice) in justifying their exclusion of unconstitutionally obtained evidence.[31] This trend is similar to that adopted by the Canadian courts,[32] whereas the US courts tend exclusively to favour the deterrence rationale.[33] In *S v Hena and Another*[34] the court justified its decision on the condonation rationale. The court reasoned that when judicial officers take the oath of office, they swear or affirm to uphold and protect the Constitution and the rights entrenched in it, and to administer justice without fear, favour or prejudice, and Judges should therefore guard against condoning constitutional abuses.

In *S v Pillay and Others*[35] and *S v Mthembu*[36] exclusion was premised on the deterrence rationale. In *S v Pillay*, the accused appellant contested the admission of evidence which was obtained through illegal monitoring of telephone conversations and the court held that including evidence so obtained will encourage the police to violate the rights of accused persons. In *Mthembu*,[37] the SCA referred violations by police officers to their supervisor for possible disciplinary, administrative or criminal action.[38] While this does not happen in all the cases where violations occur, other judges could follow suit and refer such cases of misconduct by police officers and impact on deterrence.

16.2.4 Implications of excluding unconstitutionally obtained evidence

As much as there are benefits to the accused persons and the long-term objectives of the constitutional order for excluding unconstitutionally obtained evidence, there are also social costs.[39] The obvious social cost is that factually guilty defendants often go unpunished for their crimes when such evidence is excluded or convictions are overturned following an appeal or a review.

Arguably, society would not condone the non-accountability of anyone for the offences they have committed, but for the illegal manner in which the relevant evidence against such a person was collected. This therefore has implications for the administration of justice in that the criminal justice system ends up failing to hold criminal suspects and accused persons accountable for their criminal conduct.

This could affect public confidence where a large number of cases are lost due to the exclusion of tainted evidence. It could result in communities taking the law into their own hands, under some circumstances, where this phenomenon of exclusion is prevalent or, in some sensitive cases, where society is deeply offended. It could also send a wrong message to the victims of crime, that their rights and protections by the State are subordinate to those of accused persons who are factually guilty but are set free because legal guilt cannot be sustained – as evidence is excluded. And, of course, a factually guilty criminal is released

---

31 Wells (2013) at 17–34.
32 Penney (2003) at 110.
33 Wells (2013) at 197.
34 *S v Hena and Another* 2006 (2) SACR 33 (SE) at 41–42. In this case evidence showed that policing functions had been assumed by street committees who were found to have taken the law into their own hands without any political or administrative supervision. The court found that this undermined the Constitution and the integrity of the criminal justice system and held that the evidence that had been acquired should be excluded. See also Wells (2013) at 32.
35 *S v Pillay and Others* 2004 (2) SACR 419 (SCA) cited in Wells (2013) at 21.
36 2008 (2) SACR 407 (SCA).
37 2008 (2) SACR 407 (SCA) at para 39.
38 Wells (2013) at 23.
39 See Ally, D (2012) supra for more discussion on these social costs.

180 THE LAW OF EVIDENCE IN SOUTH AFRICA

into society, which is thereby unprotected against further criminal action by the acquitted criminal.

As we examine section 35 (5) of the Constitution, we highlight the balance that this section seeks to strike between the competing interests of accused persons on the one hand, and society at large and victims of crime on the other.

16.3 Overview of section 35 of the Constitution

In criminal cases, evidence must be excluded in terms of section 35(5) of the Constitution if it was obtained in a manner that violates any right in the Bill of Rights and if the admission of that evidence would render the trial unfair or would otherwise be detrimental to the administration of justice. From the wording of section 35(5) it is apparent that a causal relationship is envisaged between a Bill of Rights violation and the procurement of evidence. *S v Tandwa* confirms that there needs to be a 'causal connection' between a rights violation and the subsequent procurement of incriminating evidence from the accused.[40] In other words, it must be shown that the evidence was obtained in violation of a right protected in the Bill of Rights.[41] Where this link is not established, the accused may not be entitled to the exclusionary remedy.[42]

There are a number of pre-trial and trial rights of accused persons in the Bill of Rights. The more important ones in relation to section 35(5) are those that may, when violated, lead to the state unconstitutionally acquiring evidence from or against an accused person. These are the right to remain silent (section 35(1)(*a*)); the right to remain silent and not testify in the proceedings (s 35(3)(*h*)); the right not to be compelled to give self-incriminating evidence such as a confession or admission (section 35(1)(*c*) and 35(3)(*j*)) and the right to legal representation (s 35(3)(*f*) and (*g*)). The latter is of great importance as legal representatives are expected to be better placed to advise accused persons in their interaction with the criminal justice system.

Some of these rights are relatively old compared to our current constitutional dispensation. They have been part of statutory and common law, in one form or the other, for many decades. The rights to remain silent, legal representation and privilege against self-incrimination were part of common law applicable in South Africa prior to the present constitutional dispensation. However, due to apartheid and racial discrimination, these rights were not consistently upheld for all. In some instances where these rights were violated and evidence was procured, the courts would exercise their common law discretion to exclude such evidence.[43] However, the courts did not have a duty and were not obliged to exclude such impugned evidence as provided for now in section 35(5).

There are other statutory provisions which are linked to certain constitutional rights which may be infringed in collecting evidence, for example the right to privacy. For instance, the police use statutory provisions to intercept communications and to search for and seize evidence and so an infringement of these statutory provisions means that a right in the Bill of Rights has been infringed, rendering the evidence liable to exclusion. Some fundamental

---

40 2008 (1) SACR 613 (SCA).

41 At para 117. See also Wells (2013) at 46–49.

42 Wells (2013) at 46. Wells argues that our courts have not been consistent in interpreting the phrase 'obtained in a manner', which establishes the causal connection, in section 35(5). Some have adopted a direct causal connection (using a 'but for' test), as in *S v Orrie and Another* 2005 (1) SACR 63 (C) and others an indirect/temporal connection – where a violation is followed by the discovery of evidence as in *S v Pillay and Others* 2004 (2) SACR 419 (SCA), *S v Soci* 1998 (2) SACR 275 (E) and *S v Ntlantsi* [2007] 4 All SA 941 (C).

43 See De Vos (2011). See also Wells (2013) at 4.

CHAPTER 16   UNCONSTITUTIONALLY OBTAINED EVIDENCE IN CRIMINAL CASES | 181

rights in the Bill of Rights, such as the right to privacy and the right to freedom of movement, are already limited by a law of general application, particularly the search and seizure and arrest provisions in the Criminal Procedure Act 51 of 1977 (CPA). For instance, an arrested person has already had their right to freedom of movement curtailed. A person whose house has been searched has already had their right to privacy infringed. Section 35 rights therefore serve to protect persons whose other fundamental rights might already have been infringed, albeit lawfully, through laws of general application. Such rights provided for by section 35 of the Constitution could arguably be waived only by the accused, for an example, where she or he elects to testify, make a confession or an admission, or plead guilty.

Section 35(5) provides that evidence collected in violation of any right in the Bill of Rights (sections 7 to 39 of the Constitution) should be excluded if its admission would render the trial unfair or otherwise be detrimental to the administration of justice. However, where such a right is limited by a law of general application (statutory or common law), as per section 36 of the Constitution, and all the legal procedures were followed to limit such a right legitimately, such an infringement would not constitute a violation as envisaged in section 35(5), unless a statute or legal provision used or applicable common law rule limiting the right is itself unconstitutional. For instance, search and seizure provisions in the CPA, which is a law of general application, permit the limitation of the right to privacy. Where the police follow all the legal prescripts in gathering evidence against the accused as prescribed by the CPA, that search would be legal.

This does not mean, however, that a legal search and seizure operation does not infringe on a person's right to privacy. It does, albeit lawfully. However, where the police conduct an unjustifiable and illegal search and seizure operation, this would constitute an unconstitutional violation of the right to privacy (section 12) protected by the Bill of Rights. The accused would then be able to seek the protection accorded by section 35(5). Only after an unlawful constitutional infringement has been shown must the court substantively consider whether admission of the evidence would render the trial unfair – the first leg of the test – or whether admission would otherwise be detrimental to the administration of justice – the second leg of the test.

16.4   The section 35(5) test for excluding unconstitutionally obtained evidence

As stated above, once it has been established that the evidence was unconstitutionally obtained,[44] the court must next consider whether its admission would render the trial unfair or whether admission would otherwise be detrimental to the administration of justice. This appears to be an either/or test which does not require that both legs of the enquiry be satisfied before tainted evidence is excluded. In other words, evidence could be excluded based on the unfair trial grounds or on the integrity of the administration of justice imperative. Although the two legs overlap, they are generally treated as separate enquiries. Each step of the test has its own factors that need to be considered.

Schwikkard and Van der Merwe[45] point out that to establish whether the admission of unconstitutionally obtained evidence would have one of the undesirable consequences

---

44   That is, a causal link has been established. This may be done by way of a trialwithinatrial or by the State admitting that the evidence in dispute was unconstitutionally obtained.

45   PJ Schwikkard and SE van der Merwe *Principles of Evidence* 3 ed (2009) at 215.

182 | THE LAW OF EVIDENCE IN SOUTH AFRICA

indicated above, a court must make a value judgment[46] that takes all the facts of a specific case into account. This includes fair trial principles and considerations of public policy. Cachalia JA, in *S v Mthembu*,[47] explained what is meant by the term public policy in this context:

> [Public policy] ... is concerned not only to ensure that the guilty are held accountable; it is also concerned with the propriety of the conduct of investigating and prosecutorial agencies in securing evidence against criminal suspects. It involves considering the nature of the violation and the impact that evidence obtained as a result thereof will have, not only on a particular case, but also on the integrity of the administration of justice in the long term. ... Public policy therefore sets itself firmly against admitting evidence obtained in deliberate or flagrant violation of the Constitution. If on the other hand the conduct of the police is reasonable and justifiable, the evidence is less likely to be excluded – even if obtained through an infringement of the Constitution.

As discussed below, section 35(5) has been interpreted by our courts in a manner that attempts to strike a balance between the competing due process and crime control values. This is an involved process of public policy considerations and an analysis of a number of factors in assessing the admissibility of unconstitutionally obtained evidence. As per Cachalia JA above, public policy is not only about holding accused persons accountable, but it is also about upholding their due process rights throughout the criminal process. He explains that in instances where police conduct in obtaining evidence improperly is reasonable and justifiable, such evidence would more likely be admitted. However, to arrive at such a determination, the courts must consider the nature of the violation and the impact that the admission or exclusion of such evidence will have on the case and the administration of justice.

16.4.1   First leg of the test: whether admission would render a trial unfair

The Court in *S v Soci*[48] said that a court may examine the type of evidence that was unconstitutionally obtained when considering whether a trial would be rendered unfair if such evidence were admitted. It may draw a distinction between evidence such as admissions and confessions (testimonial evidence), and real evidence (physical evidence).[49] If real evidence was obtained in a manner that unjustifiably violated a constitutional right, it would not necessarily mean that such evidence should be automatically excluded – the court would still need to consider whether its admission would render the trial unfair. However, the admission of unconstitutionally obtained testimonial evidence (admissions or confessions) will automatically render the trial unfair.[50]

---

46 See *S v Tandwa and Others* 2008 (1) SACR 613 (SCA) at para 116 discussed in 16.5.3 below. Also see in this regard *S v Lottering* 1999 (12) BCLR 1478 (N) at 1483B; *S v Pillay and Others* 2004 (2) SACR 419 (SCA) at para 92; *S v Nell* 2009 (2) SACR 37 (CPD) at 42J–43B.

47 2008 (2) SACR 407 (SCA) at para 26.

48 1998 (2) SACR 275 (E) at 293.

49 In *R v Stillman*, the Supreme Court of Canada warned against distinguishing between real and testimonial evidence and noted that real evidence could be bodily fluids or tissue, hair and teeth imprints. Instead Cory J said that it may be more accurate to distinguish between evidence acquired through the accused's participation (conscriptive or autoptic evidence) and evidence gathered without the participation of an accused (non-conscriptive evidence). *R v Stillman* 1997 42 CRR (2d) 189 (SCC); 1997 1 SCR 607.

50 *S v Naidoo and Another* 1998 (1) SACR 479 (N).

In determining whether the admission of evidence would deprive the accused of his or her constitutional right to a fair trial, the court must consider the facts of each case and take into account factors such as the nature and extent of the constitutional breach, the presence or absence of prejudice to the accused, the interest of society, and public policy.[51] In this context, the right to a fair trial cannot be interpreted in the abstract, but must be applied to the particular circumstances of the case. The court should look at each case on its own merits and look at the way in which the evidence is question was procured.

The section 35(3) right to a fair trial also encompasses some pre-trial rights contained in s 35(1). The exclusionary rule in section 35(5) flows directly from the specific rights of accused (and arrested and detained) persons, which are pre-trial rights, and the right to a fair trial. In *S v Zuma and Others*,[52] the court stated that the right to a fair trial 'embraces a concept of substantive fairness' and that it is up to the criminal courts 'to give content' to the basic fairness and justice that underlie a fair trial.

In *S v Dzukuda and Others; S v Thilo*,[53] the Constitutional Court gave an exposition of the general right to a fair trial. It stated that the right to a fair trial is a comprehensive and integrated right and that the content thereof will be established on a case-by-case basis. Although it is possible to specify certain inherent elements (see section 35(3) of the Constitution), it may also contain certain unspecified elements. The Court explained that:

> An important aim of the right to a fair criminal trial is to ensure adequately that innocent people are not wrongly convicted, because of the adverse effects which a wrong conviction has on the liberty, and dignity (and possible other) interests of the accused. There are, however, other elements of the right to a fair trial such as, for example, the presumption of innocence, the right to free legal representation in given circumstances, a trial in public which is not unreasonably delayed, which cannot be explained exclusively on the basis of averting a wrong conviction, but which arise primarily from considerations of dignity and equality.[54]

In *S v Tandwa and Others*,[55] the Supreme Court of Appeal said that when considering the exclusion of unconstitutionally obtained evidence, the relevant factors for purposes of determining trial fairness would include:

> [T]he severity of the rights violation and the degree of prejudice, weighed against the public policy interest in bringing criminals to book. Rights violations are severe when they stem from the deliberate conduct of the police or are flagrant in nature ... There is a high degree of prejudice when there is close causal connection between the rights violation and the subsequent self-incriminating acts of the accused ... Rights violations are not severe, and the resulting trial not unfair, if the police conduct was objectively reasonable and neither deliberate nor flagrant.

The reasoning expressed in *Tandwa* is similar to that expressed in the Canadian case *R v Collins*,[56] where Lamer J summarised the factors for determining trial fairness as follows:

---

51 See Schwikkard and Van der Merwe 3 ed (2009) at 227.
52 1995 (1) SACR 568 (CC) at para 16.
53 2000 (2) SACR 443 (CC).
54 At para 11.
55 2008 (1) SACR 613 (SCA) at para 117.
56 (1987) 1 SCR 265 at para 35.

184 THE LAW OF EVIDENCE IN SOUTH AFRICA

As Le Dain J. wrote in *Therens*, at 652:

> 'The relative seriousness of the constitutional violation has been assessed in the light of whether it was committed in good faith, or was inadvertent or of a merely technical nature, or whether it was deliberate, wilful or flagrant. Another relevant consideration is whether the action which constituted the constitutional violation was motivated by urgency or necessity to prevent the loss or destruction of the evidence.'

> I should add that the availability of other investigatory techniques and the fact that the evidence could have been obtained without the violation of the Charter tend to render the Charter violation more serious. We are considering the actual conduct of the authorities and the evidence must not be admitted on the basis that they could have proceeded otherwise and obtained the evidence properly. In fact, their failure to proceed properly when that option was open to them tends to indicate a blatant disregard for the Charter, which is a factor supporting the exclusion of the evidence.

This jurisprudence seems to indicate that the aim of the right to a fair trial is to ensure that, among others, no one is wrongfully convicted. Evidence obtained through a deliberate and flagrant violation of constitutional rights would impact negatively on public confidence in the criminal justice system and would point towards exclusion. However, evidence collected through inadvertent or minor rights violation would, consequently, hardly be excluded as it might not undermine public confidence. For instance, the need to prevent the disappearance of evidence by law enforcement officers may provide for extenuating circumstances and attenuate the seriousness of a violation.[57] In instances where police officers make errors in good faith, the court may be persuaded not to distance itself from their unfortunate conduct. However, where they are grossly negligent or are wilfully blind, such conduct cannot be seen as good faith.

The extent to which a rights violation actually undermines the interests protected by the right violated is also an important consideration. The impact of a particular violation may only be technical or fleeting, but it can also be 'profoundly intrusive'.[58] It is important to look at the interests engaged by the infringed right and to consider the degree to which the violation had an impact on those interests.[59] Ultimately, however, as Kriegler J stated in *Key v Attorney-General, Cape Provincial Division and Another*:

> In any democratic criminal justice system there is a tension between, on the one hand, the public interest in bringing criminals to book and, on the other, the equally great public interest in ensuring that justice is manifestly done to all, even those suspected of conduct which would put them beyond the pale. To be sure, a prominent feature of that tension is the universal and unceasing endeavour by international human rights bodies, enlightened legislatures and courts to prevent or curtail excessive zeal by state agencies in the prevention, investigation or prosecution of crime. ... But none of that means sympathy for crime and its perpetrators. Nor does it mean a predilection for technical niceties and ingenious legal stratagems. What the Constitution demands is that the accused be given a fair trial. Ultimately, as was held in *Ferreira v Levin*, fairness is an issue which has to be decided upon the facts

---

57   See *R v Grant* (2009) SCC 32 at para 75.
58   Compare *R v Grant* (2009) SCC 32 at para 76.
59   *R v Grant* (2009) SCC 32 at para 77.

CHAPTER 16   UNCONSTITUTIONALLY OBTAINED EVIDENCE IN CRIMINAL CASES   185

of each case, and the trial judge is the person best placed to take that decision. ... At times fairness might require that evidence unconstitutionally obtained be excluded. But there will also be times when fairness will require that evidence, albeit obtained unconstitutionally, nevertheless be admitted.[60]

It is important to emphasise that regarding the first leg of the test for exclusion, there are many factors that influence the courts in determining whether unconstitutionally obtained evidence would render the trial unfair. Many of these factors would be engaged separately or simultaneously in the assessment process based on the facts of a particular case under consideration, and could include the nature and extent of a constitutional violation when the evidence was collected, the presence or absence of prejudice to the accused, the interests of society and public policy considerations.

DISCUSSION	Section 35(5): should it be one test or two?
16.1	Some commentators have suggested that there is essentially only one test in section 35(5), namely whether the admission of evidence would be detrimental to the administration of justice. They argue that the test of whether the admission of the evidence would render the trial unfair is just a specific aspect of the wider enquiry into whether the admission would be detrimental to the administration of justice. This is because any unfair trial would automatically be detrimental to the administration of justice. However, because section 35(5) has created two tests, these should be kept separate as the rules applicable to each test may differ.[61]

What, then, is the better view? Is the criterion of whether the trial will be rendered unfair by the admission of unconstitutionally obtained evidence effectively merely a subcategory of the second criterion of undermining the administration of justice, or is it conceptually better to separate the two tests? For example, if a person is arrested and, without being threatened or influenced in any way, voluntarily confesses his or her crime, this would speed up the trial and ensure that justice is swiftly done. In these circumstances, the fact that this person was not informed of his or her section 35(1) right to remain silent would clearly not render the trial unfair. However, the admission of the arrested person's statement, without informing the person of his or her section 35 rights, could encourage the police to continue with the practice of not informing arrested persons of their rights to ensure quick and easy convictions. This practice would undermine adherence to the Constitution and would therefore be detrimental to the administration of justice.

Arguably, therefore, there are circumstances where the procedural fairness of the trial would not be affected by the failure to comply with the Constitution but the administration of justice would nevertheless be detrimentally affected. In essence, the unfair trial test is a fact-based enquiry and the second leg of the test – the detrimental to the administration of justice test – is a policy-based enquiry.

Is there merit in persisting with the two-test approach or should a single 'detrimental to the administration of justice' test, as proposed by Steytler, be preferred?

---

60   1996 (2) SACR 113 (CC) at para 13.
61   For more details on this viewpoint, see N Steytler *Constitutional Criminal Procedure* (1998) at 36.

16.4.2 Second leg of the test: whether admission would be detrimental to the administration of justice

Generally one proceeds to the second leg of the test where the court finds that the admission of the evidence would not render the trial unfair. It has been argued that unconstitutionally obtained evidence may in some instances not lead to an unfair trial, but where it does such evidence would also automatically be detrimental to the administration of justice. In *S v Tandwa*, Cameron JA stated that

> ... admitting impugned evidence could damage the administration of justice in ways that would leave the fairness of the trial intact: but where admitting the evidence renders the trial itself unfair, the administration of justice is always damaged ... evidence must be excluded in all cases where its admission is detrimental to the administration of justice.[62]

A close reading of this dictum by Cameron JA suggests that there might be no need to carry on to the second leg of the inquiry once a court has determined that tainted evidence would lead to an unfair trial, as that evidence automatically damages the administration of justice. However, in instances where the court determines that such evidence would not render the trial unfair, the court must then apply itself to the second leg of the inquiry and if the court is satisfied that its admission would be detrimental to the administration of justice it must be excluded. The courts consider several factors in determining whether the admission of evidence would be detrimental to the administration of justice. These factors can be summarised as follows: the public interest of society to see those who commit crime held to account, public opinion or the public mood, the seriousness of the rights violation when the state collected such evidence, and the seriousness of the offence committed by the accused.[63] In *S v Mphala and Another*,[64] Cloete J said that:

> So far as the administration of justice is concerned, there must be a balance between, on the one hand, respect (particularly by law enforcement agencies) for the Bill of Rights and, on the other, respect (particularly by the man on the street) for the judicial process. Overemphasis of the former would lead to acquittals on what would be perceived by the public as technicalities, whilst overemphasis of the latter would lead at best to a dilution of the Bill of Rights and at worst to its provisions being negated.

This approach addresses the issue of creating a balance between due process rights and crime control imperatives. Where a serious offence was committed and evidence is technically excluded by the courts, this offends the public interest and brings the administration of justice into disrepute, especially when the public and victims of crime feel that the law is protecting the factually guilty. Instructive perhaps are comments by Combrinck J, in *S v Ngcobo*,[65] about the exclusion of incriminating evidence:

---

62 *S v Tandwa* 2008 (1) SACR 613 (SCA) at para 116.
63 See D Ally (2012) at 482–501 on the discussion of these factors. Ally notes that the case of *Pillay and others v S* 2004 (2) BCLR 158 (SCA) introduced the two-leg admissibility assessment and the second leg focused on two sets of factors. These are factors relating to the seriousness of a constitutional infringement and the effect that exclusion of unconstitutionally obtained evidence may or would have on the integrity of the administration of justice.
64 1998 (1) SACR 654 (W) at 657G–H.
65 1998 JDR 0747 (N) at 11, emphasis added.

CHAPTER 16 UNCONSTITUTIONALLY OBTAINED EVIDENCE IN CRIMINAL CASES | 187

> At best of times but particularly in the current state of endemic violent crime in all parts of our country it is unacceptable to the public that such evidence be excluded. Indeed the reaction is one of shock, fury and outrage when *a criminal* is freed because of the exclusion of such evidence.

Equally, it offends the administration of justice when the state procures evidence through serious infringements of the accused's rights. The Court, in *S v Tandwa*,[66] remarked that:

> [I]n this country's struggle to maintain law and order against the ferocious onslaught of violent crime and corruption, what differentiates those committed to the administration of justice from those who would subvert it is the commitment of the former to moral ends and moral means. We can win the struggle for a just order only through means that have moral authority. We forfeit that authority if we condone coercion and violence and other corrupt means in sustaining order. Section 35(5) is designed to protect individuals from police methods that offend basic principles of human rights.

The courts therefore have a very difficult balancing act in ensuring that the criminal justice system is not seen as protecting those who commit crime while also ensuring that those who are charged with investigating and prosecuting crime on behalf of society do not abuse their powers. In *S v Tandwa*, the Court said that central to the second leg of the test for exclusion is the public interest. The public interest is what society desires or wants which, in this context, is the combatting of crime and ensuring that those who commit crime are brought to book.[67] It is however in the interest of society that police officers respect the law and constitutional rights of accused persons. Holding accused persons to account cannot be done at all costs, even where it damages the administration of justice if they are not.[68]

In *S v Mankwanyane and Another*,[69] the court reasoned that the reason for establishing the new constitutional order is to protect the rights of all including 'social outcasts'.[70] Chaskalson P said that 'it is only if there is a willingness to protect the worst and the weakest amongst us, that all of us can be secure that our own rights will be protected'.[71] It is therefore also a public interest goal to ensure that law enforcement agencies comply with the prescripts of the law. This is therefore a difficult balancing exercise.

Public opinion is also a major consideration in the second leg of the test.[72] With regards to public opinion, Chaskalson P cautioned in *S v Makwanyane and Another*[73] that in interpreting the Bill of Rights, the courts should not follow public opinion blindly or rigidly or, as Ally puts it, become 'slaves to it'.[74] This is particularly true in a cosmopolitan society with polarised views. In *Makwanyane*, the Constitutional Court ruled that the death sentence was unconstitutional despite the assumption that there was overwhelming public support for it.[75]

---

66 2008 (1) SACR 613 (SCA) at 649F–G.
67 2008 (1) SACR 613 (SCA).
68 This approach was cited with approval by the Supreme Court of Appeal in *S v Tandwa and Others* 2008 (1) SACR 613 (SCA) at para 118 and in *S v Pillay and Others* 2004 (2) SACR 419 (SCA) at 447I–J.
69 1995 (3) SA 391 (CC).
70 At para 88.
71 At para 88.
72 See D Ally (2012) for a detailed discussion on the second leg of this test, particularly on public opinion considerations.
73 1995 (3) SA 391 (CC).
74 D Ally (2012) at 483.
75 1995 (3) SA 391 (CC) at paras 87–88.

188 | THE LAW OF EVIDENCE IN SOUTH AFRICA

However, with regards to section 35(5), the courts have said that public opinion constitutes an important element of the inquiry.[76] Many judgments suggest is that although public opinion or mood is an important consideration, the courts must not be overwhelmed by it and lose sight of their duty to interpret the law and find a balance between competing interests. In *S v Melani*,[77] Froneman J argued that due to the perceived high levels of crime in South Africa, 'a public opinion would probably show that a majority of our population would ... be quite content if the courts allow evidence at a criminal trial, even if it was unconstitutionally obtained'. He cautioned that while the courts should be accountable to the public, they should exercise some restraint and 'not seek public popularity'. In *S v Nombewu*,[78] Erasmus J said that some value must be given to public opinion. He said that the role of the court in that regard should be educative. Where evidence is excluded for rights violations, the courts have a duty to educate citizens that the Constitution does not seek to protect criminals but to protect all citizens from official abuse.

Further judgments have contributed to the developing jurisprudence in this area. Elements that are possibly detrimental to the administration of justice include, in *S v Naidoo and Another*,[79] evidence obtained by the State as a result of a deliberate and conscious violation of the constitutional rights of an accused person – while in *S v Gumede and Others*,[80] the Court held that the test must not consider whether the manner of the procurement of the evidence is detrimental to the administration of justice but rather whether the admission of the unconstitutionally obtained evidence will be detrimental to the administration of justice.

South Africa's jurisprudence and literature has drawn lessons from the Canadian courts in interpreting section 35(5) due to its similarities with the Canadian Charter, particularly section 24(2).[81] The Canadian courts have suggested various factors that should be considered when deciding on the integrity of the administration of justice. In *R v Grant*, one of the main questions was whether the 'truthseeking function of the criminal trial process would be better served by admission of the evidence, or by its exclusion'.[82] The Supreme Court of Canada said that the court should, therefore, consider the negative impact on the administration of justice if the evidence is admitted as well as the impact of failing to admit the evidence.[83]

Another important factor to consider under the second leg of the test is the seriousness of the offence. Sachs J, in *S v Coetzee and Others*,[84] pointed out that:

---

76 *Pillay and Others v S* 2004 (2) BCLR 158 (SCA) at para 126.
77 1996 (1) SACR 335 (E) at 352D–E.
78 1996 (2) SACR 396 (E) at para 648a–c. See also *S v Soci* 1998 (2) SACR 275 (E).
79 1998 (1) SACR 479 (N).
80 1998 (5) BCLR 530 (D).
81 See D Ally (2012) at 479.
82 *R v Grant* (2009) SCC 32 at para 79.
83 The Court in *R v Grant* (2009) SCC 32 at para 82 noted that the concern for truthseeking is only one of the considerations and the view that reliable evidence is admissible regardless of how it was obtained is inconsistent with their Charter's affirmation of rights. Such a notion is also inconsistent with the wording of their exclusionary rule that requires an enquiry into all the circumstances and not just into the reliability of the evidence. The reliability of the evidence remains, however, an important factor to consider. The Court notes at para 82: 'The fact that evidence obtained in breach of the Charter may facilitate the discovery of the truth and the adjudication of a case on its merits must therefore be weighed against factors pointing to exclusion, in order to "balance the interests of truth with the integrity of the justice system": *Mann*, at para 57, per Iacobucci J. The court must ask "whether the vindication of the specific Charter violation through the exclusion of evidence exacts too great a toll on the truthseeking goal of the criminal trial". *R v Kitaitchik* (2002), 166 CCC (3d) 14 (Ont. CA) at para 47, per Doherty J.A.'
84 1997 (1) SACR 379 (CC) at para 220.

CHAPTER 16 UNCONSTITUTIONALLY OBTAINED EVIDENCE IN CRIMINAL CASES 189

> **There is a paradox at the heart of all criminal procedure, in that the more serious the crime and the greater the public interest in securing convictions of the guilty, the more important the constitutional protections of the accused become.**

The Canadian courts have remarked, in this regard, that it is the longterm repute of the justice system that is important, not the seriousness of the immediate crime being tried:

> **As pointed out in *Burlingham*, the goals furthered by section 24(2) 'operate independently of the type of crime for which the individual stands accused' (para. 51) ... The short-term public clamour for a conviction in a particular case must not deafen the section 24(2) judge to the longer-term repute of the administration of justice. Moreover, while the public has a heightened interest in seeing a determination on the merits where the offence charged is serious, it also has a vital interest in having a justice system that is above reproach, particularly where the penal stakes for the accused are high.[85]**

It is important to note that all the factors that the courts take into account in determining the second leg of the enquiry overlap. For instance, when considering the seriousness of the offence, a court may also look at the public interest and public opinion and the impact that the admission or exclusion will have on the administration of justice. What has, however, been emphasised is the long-term repute of the criminal justice system, rather than the short-term repute of losing a conviction in a particular case. This then points towards both the condonation and the deterrence rationale objectives for excluding evidence. The public may have an interest in seeing a case decided on its merits, but this has to be balanced with the public's interest in a criminal justice system that is beyond reproach.

In assessing whether the admission would be detrimental to the administration of justice, Canadian courts have employed the 'shock the public' test.[86] This test asks what will shock the public more; is it including the evidence and condoning an infringement of the rights of the accused or excluding it and letting a factually guilty accused go free?

DISCUSSION 16.2

What will shock the public more?

In deciding whether to admit or exclude unconstitutionally obtained evidence, the Canadian courts ask the question: what will shock the public more: admitting unconstitutionally obtained evidence and by doing so condoning the unconstitutional conduct in obtaining the evidence, or excluding the evidence and by doing so possibly allowing an alleged criminal to go free? Would this test work as a test for determining whether admitting unconstitutionally obtained evidence would be detrimental to the administration of justice for the purposes of section 35(5) of the Constitution?

16.5 Procedural issues

The two-legged test above mainly addresses the substantive aspects of the exclusionary rule. However, there are a number of practical procedural issues that have emerged with the enactment of the exclusionary rule. These procedural aspects, or what have been referred to as the threshold requirements, include issues such as: who bears the onus of proof? Does

---

85 *R v Grant* (2009) SCC 32 at para 84.
86 *R v Campbell* [1999] 1 SCR 565.

THE LAW OF EVIDENCE IN SOUTH AFRICA

the accused have standing to challenge the admission of evidence that was collected as result of a violation of a third party's constitutional rights? Can suspects claim section 35(5) protections? When, during the criminal process, and how can the accused challenge the admissibility of evidence?

16.5.1 Section 35(5): onus of proof

The question of who bears the onus of proof when the admissibility of evidence is challenged has been subject to debate by courts and scholars alike. The question is: who bears the onus of proving that there was indeed a violation of the constitutional rights during the procurement of the evidence and that the reception of the evidence will render the trial unfair or be detrimental to the administration of justice? Section 35(5) of the Constitution does not say who should bear this onus of proof and our courts have taken contradictory approaches when determining where the onus of proof lies. One approach is that the accused should prove the violation of his or her constitutional rights. The other approach is that the prosecution must prove that the evidence was not collected through a violation of rights. A third position is that the accused needs to prove a violation of his or her rights, whereafter the prosecution should prove that admission will not lead to an unfair trial nor be detrimental to the administration of justice.

In *S v Gumede and Others*[87] and *Director of Public Prosecutions, Transvaal v Viljoen,*[88] the courts held that the onus of proof rests with the party wishing to exclude the evidence on constitutional grounds, while in *S v Mfene and Another,*[89] the courts held that once an accused is able to prove the evidence was unconstitutionally obtained, the onus is then on the State to prove that this does not render the evidence inadmissible. According to the latter approach the accused must still prove that the evidence was unconstitutionally obtained. *S v Mgcina,*[90] on the other hand, held that held that the prosecution bears the onus of proving that the evidence had not been obtained unconstitutionally.

In Canada, it is the accused that bears the onus of proving, on a balance of probabilities, that his or her constitutional rights were violated in the procurement of evidence[91] and our courts, in *S v Gumede and Others*[92] and *DPP, Transvaal v Viljoen,*[93] adopted this Canadian approach.[94] However, South African scholars tend to favour the *S v Mgcina* approach that the State should, upon being challenged by the accused that his or her rights were violated in the collection of evidence, prove beyond a reasonable doubt that the evidence was collected lawfully.[95]

Like many other issues regarding the interpretation of section 35(5), this issue of the onus of proof has not been settled by the Constitutional Court. What is also not clear is exactly what needs to be proved: is it that the constitutional rights were violated (where the accused bears the onus) or not violated (where the State bears the onus)? Does the onus carry further to proving that although rights were violated, the admission of evidence would not lead to an unfair trial or be detrimental to the administration of justice?

---

87   1998 (5) BCLR 530 (D).
88   2005 (1) SACR 505 (SCA).
89   1998 (9) BCLR 1157 (N).
90   2007 (1) SACR 82 (T).
91   See Ally D (2010) Constitutional exclusion under s 35(5) of the Constitution: should an accused bear a 'threshold burden' of proving that his or her constitutional right has been infringed? *SACJ* 23(1) 22 at 23. See also Wells (2013) at 37.
92   1998 (5) BCLR 530 (D).
93   2005 (1) SACR 505 (SCA).
94   Which is attributed to *R v Collins.*
95   See Ally (2010), Wells (2013).

CHAPTER 16 UNCONSTITUTIONALLY OBTAINED EVIDENCE IN CRIMINAL CASES | 191

In the case of *S v Soci*,[96] it was pointed out that there is no onus on the state to disprove an alleged violation of an accused's rights under the Constitution. The defence must allege that an infringement occurred but need not prove that there was indeed an infringement. The defence must also allege that such infringement calls for the exclusion of the evidence obtained as a result of the infringement. During the trial-within-a-trial purely factual matters must be distinguished from matters of judgment and value. The accused must get the benefit of the doubt in factual matters that the State failed to prove beyond reasonable doubt. Once the factual findings have been made and it is indeed concluded that there was a breach of a constitutional right, the court must exercise its discretion and make a value judgment on whether the admission of the evidence will be detrimental to the administration of justice or bring it into disrepute.

In *S v Gumede and Others*,[97] the court held that the onus of proof rests on the party wishing to exclude the evidence on constitutional grounds. On the other hand, in *S v Mfene and Another*[98] the court held that once the accused has proved that the evidence was unconstitutionally obtained the onus is then on the State to prove that the admission of the evidence will not render the trial unfair and that the evidence should not be declared as inadmissible.

16.5.2 Section 35(5): *locus standi*

What happens if the rights of a third party, but not those of the accused, were violated in collecting evidence? Can the accused challenge the admission of such evidence even though it did not violate his or her rights, but those of somebody else? This question arises because there are instances where the rights of a third person, other than the accused, are violated when collecting evidence and the incriminating evidence is then produced against the accused. Does section 35(5) protect an accused when the violation of third party constitutional rights leads to the discovery of evidence against him or her? In *S v Mthembu*,[99] the court held that evidence procured in violation of the rights of a third party may be rejected in circumstances that warrants its exclusion. It may be that evidence obtained from a third party does not lead to an unfair trial against the accused (as it is not his or her rights which were violated), but it might be excluded based on the damage its admission would have on the administration of justice.

DISCUSSION 16.3

Evidence obtained in violation of someone other than the accused's rights

How should the courts deal with a situation where someone other than the accused's rights were violated in obtaining certain evidence? Can an accused argue for exclusion even where another person's rights were violated in the obtaining of the evidence?

In *S v Mthembu*,[100] evidence against an accused had been illegally obtained, through torture, from a third party and had been used against the accused. At no point were the accused's rights directly violated. However, the Supreme Court of Appeal explained that principle and policy require the exclusion of improperly obtained evidence from any person, not only from a particular accused.[101] Evidence

---

96   1998 (2) SACR 275 (E).
97   1998 (5) BCLR 530 (D).
98   1998 (9) BCLR 1157 (N).
99   2008 (2) SACR 407 (SCA).
100 2008 (2) SACR 407 (SCA).
101 At para 27.

> unconstitutionally obtained from a third party may, therefore, be excluded where the circumstances of a particular case warrant it:
>
> **A plain reading of section 35(5) suggests that it requires the exclusion of evidence improperly obtained from any person, not only from an accused.**[102]
>
> It would be impossible to draw up a closed list of factors that will play a role in determining whether evidence should be excluded because it was obtained in violation of a third person's rights. The decision in S v Mthembu at least makes it clear that evidence obtained in a deliberate or flagrant violation of the Constitution will be inadmissible and even more so when such a violation coincides with police violence.

The question of standing also extends to the categories of persons who can claim protection under section 35(3). Section 35(5) applies specifically to accused, arrested or detained persons[103] and so only these persons are clearly accommodated by section 35(5). It is a group whose fundamental rights have already been curtailed through being criminally charged (accused), arrested or detained. However, some courts have extended this to criminal suspects as well.[104]

The police have a general power to investigate crime, including questioning suspects and accused persons.[105] Once the police consider someone to be a suspect, however, he or she must be properly warned of his or her rights prior to being questioned. This includes being warned of the right to remain silent, to legal representation and not to self-incriminate.[106] These rights should also be explained clearly.[107] Where a person is not warned of his or her status as a suspect and he or she makes an incriminating statement which leads to criminal charges, he or she has recourse to the protection offered by section 35(5) of the Constitution, even if he or she made those statements before being arrested or charged. In *S v Orrie and Another*,[108] Bozalek J, citing *S v Sebejan and Others*,[109] reasoned that if criminal suspects are not accorded pre-trial rights:

> investigating authorities could simply leave potentially accused persons in the category of '*suspect*', thus enabling themselves to collect evidential material from the '*unwary*', '*unsilent*', '*unrepresentative*' and unwarned suspect.[110]

Other court judgments have disputed that suspects are entitled to section 35(5) protection since they are not accused, arrested or detained persons.[111] However, the there is a strong consensus in case law and literature that suspects are also protected by section 35(5).

---

102 At para 27.

103 Wells (2013) at 44.

104 See Wells (2013) at 44 for more discussion on this.

105 See section 41 of the Criminal Procedure Act, 1977.

106 See section 35(3) of the Constitution.

107 *S v Orrie and Another* 2005 (1) SACR 63 (C).

108 2005 (1) SACR 63 (C).

109 1997 (1) SACR 626 (W) at 635G.

110 *S v Orrie and Another* 2005 (1) SACR 63 (C), where Bozalek J cites with approval the *obiter dictum* in *S v Sebejan and Others* 1997 (8) BCLR 1806 (T).

111 The judgments that have not followed *S v Sebejan and Others* on this issue are *S v Langa and Others* 1998 (1) SACR 21 (T), *S v Mthethwa* 2004 (1) SACR 449 (E), *S v Ngwenya and Others* 1998 (2) SACR 503 (W), among others.

16.5.3 Section 35(5): trial-within-a-trial

An accused may challenge the admissibility of certain evidence prior to the trial (as happens in the US and Canada).[112] However, more often an accused will challenge the admissibility of evidence during the trial. As soon as the accused alleges that particular rights were violated in the collection of particular evidence, whether testimonial or real evidence, the court would hold a trial-within-a-trial to determine the admissibility of such evidence, unless the prosecution concedes to the accused allegations, in which case there would be no need for a trial-within-a-trial process.

A trial within a trial is, as the name denotes, a process that is quite separate from the main trial. The purpose is to determine the truth about how the evidence was collected. It culminates in a ruling by the court on the admissibility of the disputed evidence. However, this decision is interlocutory and is subject to review at the end of the trial. The advantage of this process for the accused is that it allows him or her to testify freely about the admissibility of evidence without being exposed to cross-examination about issues of guilt.[113] This means that the accused could testify during this process and elect to remain silent during the main trial. During a trial-within-a-trial the parties are to lead evidence limited to proving the admissibility or inadmissibility of the disputed evidence only, and no evidence regarding the merits of the case should be led at this stage of the proceedings.

16.6 A section 35(5) case study of *S v Van Deventer and Another*

16.6.1 Background

In *S v Van Deventer and Another*,[114] Mr van Deventer and Mr van der Merwe were convicted on 7 September 2003 in the regional court on the following:
1. 767 counts of fraud
2. one count of contravening section 58(*c*) of the ValueAdded Tax Act 89 of 1991
3. 10 counts of contravening section 58(*d*) of the ValueAdded Tax Act, 1991.

Mr van der Merwe was also convicted on one count of contravening section 58(*a*) of the Value Added Tax Act, 1991. On 7 May 2004, Mr van Deventer was sentenced to four years' imprisonment in terms of section 276(1)(*i*) of the Criminal Procedure Act 51 of 1977. Mr van der Merwe was sentenced to three years' imprisonment in terms of section 276(1)(*i*) of the Criminal Procedure Act, 1977. Both men appealed against their convictions and sentences.

16.6.2 Facts of the case

Mr van Deventer and Mr van der Merwe, the appellants, were allegedly adding VAT to the invoices they issued for the entity, Markman Depot. Markman Depot was not registered for VAT and VAT charged and paid to them was not handed over to SARS.

During the course of the investigation, a search warrant was issued in terms of the Income Tax Act 58 of 1962. The appellants contended that the search warrant was invalid in that it should have been issued in terms of the ValueAdded Tax Act, 1991 and also because Mr van der Merwe and the entity Markman Depot were not mentioned in the warrant as possible offenders.

---

112 Wells (2013).
113 Wells (2013) at 39.
114 2012 (2) SACR 263 (WCC).

194 | THE LAW OF EVIDENCE IN SOUTH AFRICA

On appeal, the Court held that the documents seized during the investigation, and in terms of the warrant, were valuable evidence to establish the existence and extent of the income tax evasion of Markman Depot and so fell within the ambit of the warrant. Further, the relevant provisions of the Income Tax Act, 1962 were identical to the ValueAdded Tax Act, 1991, which meant that the appellants could not argue that they were prejudiced in any way.

It was further held that even if the search for, and seizure of, the documentation was unlawful, the evidence would still be admissible in terms of section 35(5) of the Constitution. This is because the admission of the evidence would not have violated the appellant's right to a fair trial and would not have been detrimental to the administration of justice.

16.6.3 The admissibility test to be applied in terms of section 35(5) of the Constitution

The applicable legal test is contained in *S v Tandwa and Others*,[115] where the Court held the following:

> The notable feature of the Constitution's specific exclusionary provision is that it does not provide for automatic exclusion of unconstitutionally obtained evidence. Evidence must be excluded only if it (*a*) renders the trial unfair; or (*b*) is otherwise detrimental to the administration of justice. This entails that admitting impugned evidence could damage the administration of justice in ways that would leave the fairness of the trial intact: but where admitting the evidence renders the trial itself unfair, the administration of justice is always damaged. Differently put, evidence must be excluded in all cases where its admission is detrimental to the administration of justice, including the subset of cases where it renders the trial unfair. The provision plainly envisages cases where evidence should be excluded for broad public policy reasons beyond fairness to the individual accused.

In determining whether the trial is rendered unfair, courts must take into account competing social interests. The court's discretion must be exercised by weighing the competing concerns of society on the one hand to ensure that the guilty are brought to book against the protection of entrenched human rights accorded to accused persons on the other hand.[116]

As we have pointed out, although admitting evidence that renders the trial unfair will always be detrimental to the administration of justice, there may be cases when the trial will not be rendered unfair, but admitting the impugned evidence will nevertheless damage the administration of justice. Central in this enquiry is the public interest.[117]

16.6.4 Applying this test in terms of section 35(5) to the facts of this case

Factors present that supported the conclusion that the admission of the evidence would not be unfair to the appellants or otherwise detrimental to the administration of justice include:[118]

> (i) The evidence had been obtained without any compelled participation by or conscription of the appellants – the evidence had been discovered in the course of the execution of a search warrant which itself was valid.

---

115   2008 (1) SACR 613 (SCA) at para 116.
116   See *S v Tandwa and Others* 2008 (1) SACR 613 (SCA) at para 117.
117   See *S v Mphala and Another* 1998 (1) SACR 654 (W) at 657G–H.
118   *S v Van Deventer and Another* 2012 (2) SACR 263 (WCC) at 265A–D.

(ii) [T]he violation of the appellants' rights was of a technical nature and not flagrant at all – the warrant itself was lawful and authorised the SARS investigators to enter the premises and seize documents relating to contraventions of the Income Tax Act. The relevant provisions of the VAT Act were identical to those of the Income Tax Act, which meant that the appellants were not prejudiced in any way by the omission of any reference to the VAT Act in the warrant, nor did SARS derive any benefit therefrom. The omission of a reference to the VAT Act in the warrant was due to a mistake.
(iii) [T]he SARS officers had acted bona fide.
(iv) [T]he 'no difference principle' favoured the admission of the invoices as evidence, that is, if the evidence would in any event have been discovered by lawful means, the exclusion thereof would generally be detrimental to the administration of justice, and in the present case the Markman Depot invoices would have been discovered if a lawful warrant had been issued, and the appellants could not have done anything lawful to prevent it.

Therefore the appeal against the convictions failed.

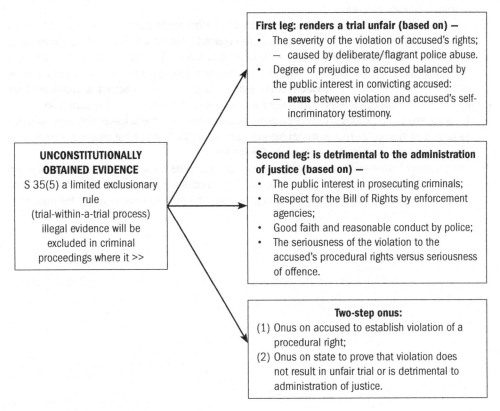

Figure 16.1 Unconstitutionally obtained evidence

THIS CHAPTER IN ESSENCE

1 Since the enactment of the Constitution, evidence obtained improperly, unfairly, illegally or unlawfully is classified as unconstitutionally obtained evidence despite the fact that it may be relevant to the case at hand.

2   In criminal cases, unconstitutionally obtained evidence must be excluded in terms of section 35(5) of the Constitution if the admission of such evidence would violate any right in the Bill of Rights, render the trial unfair or would otherwise be detrimental to the administration of justice.

3   There are a number of rationales that are used by the Courts to justify the exclusion of unconstitutionally obtained evidence. These include the condonation rationale, which seeks to distance the judiciary from police misconduct; the deterrence rationale, which seeks to prevent future abuses of power and influence legal compliance by law enforcement agencies in the collection of evidence; and the corrective justice rationale, which seeks mainly to vindicate and uphold the rights of an accused person through excluding tainted evidence.

4   The test to determine whether unconstitutionally obtained evidence is admissible is twofold: first, the court must consider whether the admission of such evidence will render the trial unfair and, second, whether the admission of such evidence would otherwise be detrimental to the administration of justice. The test requires a court to make a value judgment based on all the facts of a particular case.

5   The South African courts have tried to interpret section 35(5) of the Constitution in manner that seeks to find a balance between due process rights enshrined in the constitution and the interest of society to ensure that those who commit crime are held to account for their criminal conduct. This has been a delicate balance to strike.

6   The South African courts have taken contradictory approaches to the question of who bears the onus of proving that the reception of unconstitutionally obtained evidence will render the trial unfair or be detrimental to the administration of justice. There seems, however, to be a popular view emerging from some judgments and the literature that the accused needs only to allege a violation and the State needs to prove beyond a reasonable doubt that evidence was not collected in violation of the constitutional rights of the accused or anyone else – as the circumstances hold in each case.

7   There are also contradictions in case law regarding the treatment of crime suspects. There are questions as to whether they should receive similar pre-trial rights as accused, arrested or detained persons since they are not mentioned in section 35 of the Constitution.

8   The question of admissibility of unconstitutionally obtained evidence is settled in a trial-within-a-trial in order to give an accused an opportunity to testify on questions of admissibility without having to be cross-examined on questions of guilt, thus negating his or her right to remain silent in the main trial.

Chapter 17

Similar fact evidence

17.1	Meaning of similar fact evidence	197
17.2	Purpose of similar fact evidence	197
17.3	Admissibility and evidentiary aspects of similar fact evidence	198
17.4	Evolution of the similar fact rule	199
	17.4.1 The *Makin* formulation	199
	17.4.2 Criticism of the *Makin* formulation	200
	17.4.3 Explaining the similarity away as mere coincidence	201
	17.4.4 Further categories of similar fact evidence	202
17.5	Similar fact evidence: the present-day rule	203
	17.5.1 The test in *DPP v Boardman*	203
	17.5.2 Extension of the *Boardman* test	203
17.6	Other supporting evidence	204
17.7	Additional examples	204
17.8	An example of the non-admittance of similar fact evidence	205

17.1 Meaning of similar fact evidence

In simple terms, **similar fact evidence** is evidence that a person, who has been charged with a particular crime, has behaved in a similar way on other occasions. In evidentiary terms, similar fact evidence is evidence of illegal or immoral conduct by a person in circumstances that are logically connected or substantially similar to that person's conduct in a circumstance that is the subject of the charge or dispute.[1] Similar fact evidence therefore consists of two sets of facts:

- Those facts that are in issue before the court
- Those facts that are similar to the facts in issue but are themselves not in issue.

17.2 Purpose of similar fact evidence

The purpose of similar fact evidence is to show that a person has on other occasions acted in a similar manner to the circumstances presently before the court in order to support the

---

1 See DT Zeffertt and AP Paizes *The South African Law of Evidence* 2 ed (2009) at 271–308; PJ Schwikkard and SE van der Merwe *Principles of Evidence* 3 ed (2009) at 70–82.

198 THE LAW OF EVIDENCE IN SOUTH AFRICA

allegation that the person has again behaved in a particular manner. As the person is not actually on trial for his or her behaviour on other occasions, the use of similar fact evidence has the potential to be highly prejudicial to such a person. There are, therefore, several rules or principles guiding its use.

17.3 Admissibility and evidentiary aspects of similar fact evidence

Some of the most important characteristics of similar fact evidence are as follows:
- It is generally inadmissible, but may be admitted in civil as well as criminal proceedings in certain circumstances.
- The most important evidentiary aspect of similar fact evidence is that there must be a connection, referred to as a link or nexus, between the similar fact and the fact in issue. This connection must be more than a mere similarity. In other words, the similar fact must be relevant to the fact in issue to be admissible.
- Similar fact evidence may sometimes amount to character evidence, in which case it must also conform to the evidentiary requirements of character evidence.
- It should be treated as circumstantial evidence from which a reasonable inference must be drawn which assists in establishing a *prima facie* case especially when there is no direct evidence available.[2]
- The similar conduct may amount to a crime or a delict, or it may simply be some form of immoral conduct.
- Similar fact evidence is commonly used in criminal cases by the prosecution against an accused. However, an accused may use similar fact evidence to establish a defence.
- Similar conduct previous to, as well as subsequent to, the facts in issue may be admissible.

The most common kind of similar fact evidence used in criminal cases relates to serial offenders. For example, if an accused is charged with shoplifting and has shoplifted before, the prosecutor will try to admit the previous counts of shoplifting. The previous counts will be similar fact evidence.

The primary reason for the development of the rule against using similar fact evidence was to prevent juries from being prejudicially influenced by such evidence. The accused's previous acts of bad conduct or bad character may unfairly prejudice a jury. The jury may decide that, as the accused had behaved in a particular way in the past, he or she must be guilty of doing so again even if there is insufficient evidence to prove the present crime.

South Africa has abolished the jury system and so the ongoing existence of such a rule has been questioned as it is unlikely that a judge would be prejudicially influenced by an accused's previous conduct when reaching a decision. However, the rule remains in place and similar fact evidence is therefore considered inadmissible for the following reasons:
- It is usually irrelevant because it does not relate directly to the issue before the court.
- It is procedurally inconvenient because it raises many collateral issues that are distracting, expensive and time-consuming to investigate.

---

2   Zeffertt and Paizes 2 ed (2009) at 272–274 and 279–280.

CHAPTER 17 SIMILAR FACT EVIDENCE | **199**

- Using similar fact evidence may take an accused by surprise and will add an additional prejudicial burden to the defence – the accused may have to defend him- or herself not only against the present charge, but also against his or her previous bad acts.
- If similar fact evidence is freely admitted, it may encourage inefficient and poor police investigation. A police force may be tempted to focus on a suspect's previous record of bad conduct, in other words, to search for and arrest 'the usual suspects'[3] instead of searching for the real criminal. In addition, a past offender is vulnerable because police can apply pressure on an offender with a record to induce an involuntary confession.

A similar fact does not usually assist a court in drawing a reasonable inference with respect to the fact in issue. For example, the mere fact that an accused has committed three previous acts of shoplifting is of little assistance to a court in determining whether an accused has committed another act of shoplifting as alleged in the charge. Mere similarity, coincidence or correspondence between a similar fact and a fact alleged in the charge is insufficient. There must be a relevant connection or nexus between the similar fact and the fact alleged in a charge. This connection has been explained in a number of ways. Stephen explains it as follows:

> You are not to draw inferences from one transaction to another which is not specifically connected with it merely because the two resemble each other. They must be linked together by the chain of cause and effect in some assignable way before you can draw your inference.[4]

According to Zeffertt and Paizes, the rational connection, link, nexus or the chain of cause and effect simply means that, to be admissible, similar fact evidence must be *relevant* to a fact in issue. First, the probative value of a similar fact lies in the reasonable inferences that a judge may draw from such a fact in reaching a decision about the charge or dispute. Second, a similar fact must have relevance other than one based solely on character.[5] Finally, the relevance of a similar fact will also depend on what the facts in issue are, as well as the strength of all the other evidence available to the court.[6]

17.4 Evolution of the similar fact rule

This section will discuss the evolution of the similar fact rule starting with its early formulation in the case of *Makin v Attorney-General New South Wales*.[7] We then follow the various ways in which it has been expressed in subsequent case law, culminating in its present expression as set out in *DPP v Boardman*.[8]

17.4.1 The *Makin* formulation

In *Makin v Attorney-General New South Wales*[9] in 1894, an Australian couple were charged with the murder of their foster child after the child's skeleton was found buried in the back

---

3 J Epstein, PR Epstein and H Koch *Casablanca* (1942).
4 JF Stephen *Digest of the Law of Evidence* 12 ed (1914) note VI; art 10, 11 and 12.
5 Zeffertt and Paizes 2 ed (2009) at 271; *S v Zuma* 2006 (2) SACR 191 (W).
6 Zeffertt and Paizes 2 ed (2009) at 284; Schwikkard and Van der Merwe 3 ed (2009) at 78. In civil proceedings, the facts in issue are identified from the pleadings. In criminal matters, the facts in issue are usually apparent from the nature of the crime and also from when the accused specifically answers to the charge.
7 [1894] AC 57 (PC); [1891–1984] All ER 24 (PC).
8 [1975] AC 421 (HL); [1974] 3 All ER 887 (HL).
9 [1894] AC 57 (PC); [1891–1984] All ER 24 (PC).

200 | THE LAW OF EVIDENCE IN SOUTH AFRICA

garden of their rented home. They pleaded not guilty and argued that the child had died of natural causes. The prosecution attempted to lead two important pieces of evidence:

- First, evidence of other baby skeletons buried in the gardens of houses previously rented by the couple
- Second, testimony by four women who had handed over their children, with money, to the Makins for foster care. All these children had disappeared.

This evidence is similar fact evidence and, as can be seen, would have been highly prejudicial to the accused.

The Court held that this similar fact evidence was inadmissible to show that the Makins had a propensity or disposition to kill babies and therefore to infer that they had murdered the child. However, the Court did admit the evidence to show the statistical improbability, that is, the extreme unlikelihood, that the child had died of natural causes. In other words, the similar fact evidence was relevant and admissible to rebut the Makins' defence that the child had died accidentally.

The presiding judge, Lord Herschell, set out two general principles with regard to the admission of similar fact evidence:[10]

- It is not competent for the prosecution to adduce evidence tending to show that the accused had been guilty of criminal acts other than those covered by the charge for the purpose of reasoning that the accused is a person likely from such criminal conduct or bad character to have committed the offence. In other words, similar fact evidence cannot be admitted merely to show that the accused has the propensity to commit the offence for which he or she is charged.[11]
- Evidence that shows the commission of other crimes is admissible if it is relevant to an issue before the court. It may be relevant if it bears on the question whether the acts alleged to constitute the crime charged were designed or accidental, or to rebut a defence open to the accused. In other words, similar fact evidence is admissible either to rebut a defence or to show that the crime was designed, not accidental.

17.4.2 Criticism of the *Makin* formulation

There have been several criticisms of the principles set out in *Makin v Attorney-General New South Wales*. The first principle has been criticised because the accused's propensity to act in a particular way has been found to be relevant in certain circumstances. In *R v Straffen*,[12] the accused's propensity to act in a particular way was admitted to show the identity of the accused.

A criticism of the second principle is that the list of instances when similar fact evidence can be used is too limited as other circumstances may arise where it is relevant. The practical consequence of such an approach is that it results in the exclusion of relevant similar fact evidence simply because it does not fit into a recognised category or the reception of irrelevant similar fact evidence simply because it does.[13] The categorisation approach was rejected in *Harris v DPP*[14] where the Court held that it is an error to draw up a closed list of cases which act as exceptions. As a result of the above criticism of the *Makin* formulation,

---

10 Ibid. at 65.

11 *R v Davis* 1925 AD 30; *R v Simon and Another* 1925 TPD 297; *S v Zuma* 2006 (2) SACR 191 (W) at 211–212.

12 [1952] 2 QB 911 (CCA). See also *R v Ball* [1911] AC 47 (HL); *Thompson v R* [1918] AC 221 (HL).

13 *R v Straffen* [1952] 2 QB 911 (CCA).

14 [1952] AC 694 (HC) at 705.

Zeffertt and Paizes have suggested, as a proviso, that in cases where **disposition** or propensity is highly relevant to a fact in issue, such evidence should be admissible.[15] However, this only deals with the first problem and so, over time, courts have attempted to find other ways to deal with the limitations of the *Makin* formulation.

Previously, South African courts followed the reasoning of Lawrence J in *R v Bond*,[16] who explained that 'in proximity of time, in method or in circumstance there must be a nexus between the two sets of facts, otherwise no inference can be safely deduced therefrom'. In other words, there must be a connection, link or nexus between the similar fact and a fact in issue. This, in essence, means no more than the standard requirement that the evidence must bear some relevance to an issue before the court.[17]

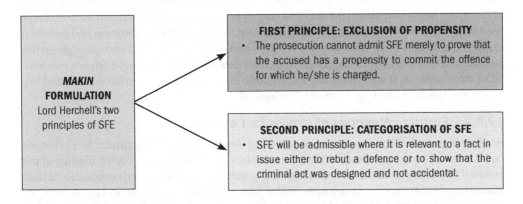

Figure 17.1 The Makin *formulation*

17.4.3 Explaining the similarity away as mere coincidence

However, the difficulty with similar fact evidence lies in determining exactly what constitutes a sufficient nexus. To establish a nexus or link, some courts examined whether the similarity could be explained away as being a mere coincidence. Similar fact evidence will have no relevant probative value if the connection between the similar fact evidence and a fact in issue can be explained away as a coincidence.[18] However, similar fact evidence will be relevant and admissible if the connection goes beyond mere coincidence. The nexus thus

---

15 For more detail, see Zeffertt and Paizes 2 ed (2009) at 279.
16 [1906] 2 KB 389 (CCR) at 424. See also *S v Green* 1962 (3) SA 886 (A) at 894.
17 According to Zeffertt and Paizes, the nexus requirement is simply another way of saying that similar fact evidence must be relevant to the issue of guilt. Alternatively, similar fact evidence has relevant probative value and is admissible when it gives rise to a reasonable inference which may assist in deciding a fact in issue. Zeffertt and Paizes 2 ed (2009) at 279.
18 J McEwan *Evidence and the Adversarial Process: The Modern Law* 2 ed (1998) at 58-59.

202 | THE LAW OF EVIDENCE IN SOUTH AFRICA

lies in the extreme unlikelihood of coincidence. The cases of *R v Smith* and *R v Bond* discussed below provide good examples of this.

In *R v Bond*,[19] the accused was charged with procuring an abortion for his girlfriend. He admitted using surgical instruments suitable for an abortion but claimed that the abortion had occurred accidentally during the course of a medical examination. The Court admitted the evidence of another woman who testified that the accused had intentionally procured an abortion for her. Both women had been living in the accused's house before their abortions and both had been made pregnant by him. The accused had also told her that he had 'put dozens of girls right'.

In *R v Smith*,[20] the accused was charged with the murder of a woman, to whom he was bigamously married, by drowning her in the bath. The Court admitted evidence of the deaths of two other women to whom the accused had also been bigamously married. In both cases the women had drowned in their baths. The accused claimed that each woman had drowned during an epileptic fit. In each case the accused had taken out life insurance policies on the women and stood to benefit financially from their deaths. The similar fact evidence was held to be admissible as it was extremely improbable or unlikely that all three deaths, and the circumstances surrounding them, could reasonably be explained as coincidence.

17.4.4 Further categories of similar fact evidence

Another approach taken by courts was to extend the categories where similar fact evidence could be used. Courts thus have allowed similar fact evidence to establish the identity of the accused. The issue of identity is, of course, inseparable from a person's disposition and thus admitting similar fact evidence to establish identity often was a way to circumvent the restrictions established by the *Makin* rule. The cases of *R v Straffen* and *Thompson v R* discussed below provide good examples of this, as is the more recent case of *S v Nduna*.

In *R v Straffen*,[21] the accused was charged with the murder of a young girl. The Court allowed the admission of evidence that the accused had killed two other girls in the same way, on earlier occasions, by strangling them without sexually molesting them. The accused had been declared insane and had been committed to an institution, but had escaped. It was while he was an escapee that the present murder had occurred. The similar fact evidence was thus admitted to establish the identity of the accused although it is arguable that it was, in fact, admitted to show that he had the propensity to kill.

In *Thompson v R*,[22] the accused was charged with committing indecent acts with two little boys. After committing the indecent acts, the accused had arranged to meet the boys three days later. The police arrested the accused on the basis of the identification of the accused by one of the boys when he arrived at the arranged place. The accused's defence was that the boys were mistaken and that the wrong man had been identified. Indecent photographs and 'powder puff' were found in the accused's possession. This similar fact evidence was held to be admissible because it established the accused's homosexual propensity which was relevant to the issue of identity.

In *S v Nduna*,[23] the accused was charged with two counts of armed robbery. The appeal concerned whether the fingerprint evidence which formed the basis for the conviction was admissible. The only evidence linking the accused to both charges against him was his

---

19 [1906] 2 KB 389 (CCR).
20 (1915) 11 Cr App Rep 229.
21 [1952] 2 QB 911 (CCA). See also *R v Ball* [1911] AC 47 (HL).
22 [1918] AC 221 (HL); [1918] All ER 521 (HL).
23 2011 (1) SACR 115 (SCA) at 120H–121E.

CHAPTER 17   SIMILAR FACT EVIDENCE | 203

fingerprints which were found on the two vehicles involved in the two armed robberies. The Court allowed the similar fact evidence as it found that it was highly unlikely that two robberies, committed in the same fashion (by armed men of a complainant who had just drawn cash from a bank, as he returned to his business premises), where the fingerprints of one of the accused were found on the different vehicles, would be entirely unconnected. The coincidence, especially when regard is had to the fact that the fingerprints of the appellant were lifted in each case from a vehicle proven to have been involved in each robbery, is explicable only on the basis that the appellant participated in each robbery.

17.5   Similar fact evidence: the present-day rule

17.5.1   The test in *DPP v Boardman*

Matters thus remained unsettled until a much clearer formulation of the rule was set out in *DPP v Boardman*.[24] Lord Wilberforce stated:

> Similar fact evidence as an item of circumstantial evidence is exceptionally admissible when its probative value, in respect to a fact in issue, outweighs its prejudicial effect.[25]

The reasonable inferences to be drawn from the similar fact evidence must thus be sufficiently relevant in a specific case to warrant its admissibility despite any prejudice it may cause. The formulation in *DPP v Boardman*, weighing up the probative value of the evidence against its prejudicial effect, is simply a restatement as a general rule of the notions of relevance weighed against propensity inherent in the original *Makin* formulation. The Supreme Court of Appeal in South Africa has endorsed this formulation in the case of *S v D*.[26]

In essence, this test provides the underlying basis of any test for admissibility with regard to any area of evidence where there are competing interests. It requires the courts to balance the usefulness of the evidence against the potential prejudice to the accused. In cases involving similar fact evidence, the court will, therefore, take into account issues such as the lack of coincidence, whether propensity is relevant, identity, the accused's defence and many others. The court will balance these against the prejudice that the accused may suffer.

17.5.2   Extension of the *Boardman test*

The rule, and its development over time, has, however, resulted in the application of the principles involved in similar fact evidence to a broader array of evidence. In terms of the similar fact rule, evidence may be admissible if considered relevant, and thus of significant probative value, and if it is so similar that it could not possibly be a coincidence. This provides the link, the relevance and the probative value. However, circumstances may arise where evidence, while not similar at all, may be so closely linked that it also could not possibly be a coincidence and thus becomes admissible.

---

24   [1975] AC 421 (HL); [1974] 3 All ER 887 (HL), accepted in South Africa by *S v D* 1991 (2) SACR 543 (A) at 546. See also *S v Sole* 2004 (2) SACR 599 (Les).

25   *DPP v Boardman* [1975] AC 421 (HL); [1974] 3 All ER 887 (HL) at 444 and 896C argues that the admissibility of similar fact evidence is exceptional and requires a strong degree of probative force. This probative force is derived from the similarity of circumstances that the facts bear to each other This similarity is so striking that the facts must, when judged by experience and common sense, either be true or have arisen from pure coincidence. See also *DPP v P* [1991] 2 AC 447 (HL) at 460; *S v M* 2003 (1) SA 341 (SCA); *S v Wilmot* 2002 (2) 3ACR 145 (SCA) at 157.

26   1991 (2) SACR 543 (A) at 543.

THE LAW OF EVIDENCE IN SOUTH AFRICA

This is precisely what occurred in *S v D*[27] where an alleged serial rapist, arrested on a charge of rape, was found to have in his possession the house keys of a previous rape victim. Although not similar in any way to the matter before the Court as he did not take the keys of the present victim, it could not have been a coincidence that he had the keys of a previous victim in his possession and the Court held that this evidence was admissible.

DISCUSSION 17.1	**The Zeffertt and Paizes 'similar test' formulation**
	The Zeffertt and Paizes formulation is a further clarification of the *Boardman* approach. The assessment of the probative value of similar fact evidence is determined by the reasoning that similar conditions are likely to produce similar results. There must be a degree of similarity between a person's conduct on other occasions and the occasion that is the subject of the court's enquiry. However, a mere rational connection between the similar facts and the facts in issue is not enough – it is the degree of relevance that counts.
	As a result, the admissibility of similar fact evidence in both civil and criminal matters is an exception to the general rule. Therefore, because of its practical and prejudicial disadvantages, similar fact evidence must have sufficient probative force to overcome these disadvantages in order to warrant its reception.[28]

Similar fact evidence should only be admitted when it is relevant to a fact in issue and is not prejudicial or unfair to the other side, and also when the other side has had sufficient notice of the similar fact evidence and is able to prepare for it.[29]

17.6   Other supporting evidence

The case of *S v D*[30] above illustrates another important consideration when dealing with an assessment of the admissibility of similar fact evidence which is to look at any other evidence that tends to support or corroborate the similar fact evidence in dispute. In *S v D*, quite apart from the fact that the accused having the keys of a previous rape victim in his possession could not possibly be a coincidence, what this fact also shows is that other evidence (in this case the real evidence of the keys) supports the similar fact evidence (the manner of the rape, the circumstances surrounding it and the identification of the accused) thereby rendering it more plausible, more reliable and thus more likely to be admitted and, once admitted, more likely to carry significant weight.

17.7   Additional examples

Other examples in which the courts have admitted similar fact evidence are described below.
- *Sexual passion:* In *R v Ball*,[31] a brother and sister were charged with incest. Similar fact evidence of previous cohabitation as man and wife was admitted to confirm other evidence that suggested that sexual intercourse had taken place between them.

---

27   1991 (2) SACR 543 (A).
28   See DT Zeffertt and AP Paizes *Essential Evidence* (2010) at 89.
29   *Omega, Louis Brandt et Frere SA and Another v African Textile Distributors* 1982 (1) SA 951 (T).
30   1991 (2) SACR 543 (A).
31   [1911] AC 47 (HL).

CHAPTER 17 SIMILAR FACT EVIDENCE | **205**

- *Motive:* In *R v Matthews and Others*,[32] the accused, a gang member, was charged with the murder of a rival gang member. Similar fact evidence was admitted to show a violent rivalry between the two gangs to establish a motive for the murder.
- *Proximity in place and time:* In *R v Dhlamini*,[33] the accused's alibi was rebutted by admitting similar fact evidence that he had stabbed another woman at more or less the same time and place.
- *Knowledge:* In *R v Keller and Parker*,[34] the accused were charged with selling pieces of glass as diamonds. Similar fact evidence was admitted to show that they had previously attempted to sell glass as diamonds to rebut a defence that they had honestly thought they were selling diamonds.
- *Innocent association:* In *R v Sims*,[35] the accused was charged with sodomy with four men complainants. The accused denied that any indecent acts had occurred. Similar fact evidence was admitted to show that the association that the accused had had with these men was a guilty one and not an innocent one as alleged.
- *Innocent possession:* In *R v Armstrong*,[36] the accused was charged with the murder of his wife by arsenical poisoning. He alleged that his wife had committed suicide. Similar fact evidence that he had tried to poison someone else eight months after his wife's death was admitted to rebut his defence of innocent possession of the poison.
- *Proving the* actus reus*:* In *R v Ball*, see the first example, similar fact evidence was introduced to prove the *actus reus* that incestuous sexual intercourse had taken place.

17.8 An example of the non-admittance of similar fact evidence

In *Laubscher v National Foods Ltd*,[37] the plaintiff, a pig farmer, claimed damages for the deaths of his pigs which he alleged died as a result of eating contaminated pig food sold by National Foods. He attempted to admit similar fact evidence of other pig farmers whose pigs had also died as a result of eating National Foods products. The Court rejected this evidence as insufficiently similar and therefore irrelevant for three reasons:

- First, the evidence did not show that the other farmers' pig food was bought at the same time as that of the plaintiff.
- Second, it did not show that all the farmers' pigs had died within the same space of time after eating the foodstuff.
- Finally, the evidence did not show that the conditions on all the pig farms were the same and that all the farmers took the same care of their pigs.

THIS CHAPTER IN ESSENCE

1   Similar fact evidence is tendered with the aim of showing that a person charged with a particular crime has, on other occasions, acted in a manner similar to the circumstances presently before the court to support the allegation that the person has again behaved in that particular manner.

2   Similar fact evidence is generally inadmissible, save for certain exceptions.

---

32   1960 (1) SA 752 (A).
33   1960 (1) SA 880 (N).
34   1915 AD 98. See also *R v Lipsitch* 1913 TPD 652.
35   [1946] 1 KB 531 (CCA). See also *Harris v DPP* [1952] AC 694 (HC) at 709–710.
36   [1922] 2 KB 555.
37   1986 (1) SA 553 (ZS).

206 | THE LAW OF EVIDENCE IN SOUTH AFRICA

3   For similar fact evidence to be admissible, there must be a connection between the similar fact evidence and the fact in issue.

4   Similar fact evidence sometimes amounts to character evidence, in which case it must meet the evidentiary requirements for character evidence.

5   Similar fact evidence should be treated as circumstantial evidence from which a reasonable inference can be drawn.

6   The similar conduct referred to in the evidence may amount to a crime, delict or immoral conduct.

7   Both the prosecution and the accused can rely on similar fact evidence.

8   Similar conduct previous to, as well as subsequent to, the facts in issue may be admissible.

9   The present-day formulation of the test applicable to the admissibility of similar fact evidence set out in *DPP v Boardman* states that similar fact evidence as an item of circumstantial evidence is exceptionally admissible when its probative value in respect to a fact in issue outweighs its prejudicial effect.

Chapter 18

Opinion and expert evidence

18.1 Introduction	**207**
18.2 Basis of the opinion rule	**208**
18.3 Admissibility of opinion evidence	**209**
18.3.1 Admissibility of a layperson's opinion	209
18.3.2 Admissibility of an expert's opinion	210
18.3.2.1 Introduction	210
18.3.2.2 The expert witness	211
18.3.2.3 Procedure for leading expert evidence	217
18.4 The opinion of a court and the *Hollington* rule	**218**

18.1 Introduction

The word 'opinion' has three distinct meanings that occur frequently in a legal context:

- First, when used in the context 'in my opinion', it amounts merely to a personal belief about a fact in question.
- Second, when used in the context 'that is a matter of opinion', it simply means that there is a reasonable doubt about a fact in question. Both these two forms of opinion are always irrelevant and inadmissible.
- However, in its third form, and in exceptional circumstances, a witness's opinion, which consists of a summary of the inferences or conclusions that a witness draws from an observed event, may be relevant and admissible.[1] This is particularly true in circumstances where the witness is regarded as an expert in the field in respect of which he or she is testifying.

The general rule is that the opinion of a witness is irrelevant because it is a function of the court to draw inferences and to form its own opinion from the facts. Witnesses must confine themselves to giving testimony as to the facts and a court will form its opinions as to those facts. However, such reasoning is based on a fallacious distinction between facts and inferences. In reality, all testimony as to an observed fact amounts to an opinion since the observer is drawing a conclusion about the fact based on his or her mental impressions and collective prior experiences.[2]

---

1 HC Nicholas 'Some aspects of opinion evidence' in C Visser (ed) *Essays in Honour of Ellison Kahn* (1989) at 225.
2 DT Zeffertt and AP Paizes *South African Law of Evidence* 2 ed (2009) at 310; PJ Schwikkard and SE van der Merwe *Principles of Evidence* 3 ed (2009) at 85–87.

208 | THE LAW OF EVIDENCE IN SOUTH AFRICA

In certain circumstances, a court will admit a witness's opinion, or a summary of inferences, to save time and to allow the witness to give testimony in a coherent and consistent manner. Where the court draws the line between irrelevant and relevant **opinion evidence** depends on the circumstances of each case and is often arbitrary and unpredictable. According to Zeffertt and Paizes, the true enquiry is to what extent a witness may give an opinion, in a form of a summary of his or her inferences, and whether such a summary will assist the court and is not prejudicial to the parties before the court.[3]

18.2 Basis of the opinion rule

A witness's objective statement of fact about a directly observed event is relevant and admissible. However, a witness's opinion, that is, the witness's summary of inferences about such an event, is irrelevant and thus inadmissible. Opinion evidence has no probative value and cannot assist the court in proving a fact in issue. The court can draw its own opinion from the received facts and does not need to rely on the witness's opinion.[4] Opinion evidence is therefore irrelevant and inadmissible because it is superfluous or supererogatory evidence.[5]

The central notion that the opinion rule protects the fact-finding function of a court is sometimes referred to as the *ultimate issue doctrine*. This doctrine states that only a court, and not a witness, can express an opinion about an ultimate fact in issue. However, in certain circumstances and with regard to certain facts in issue, a witness's opinion may assist a court in arriving at a conclusion. When a witness's opinion can assist a court in determining an issue, then the opinion is no longer superfluous and may be admitted because of its probative value.

The specific opinion rule is as follows: The opinion evidence of laypersons and experts is irrelevant and inadmissible when it is superfluous and cannot assist the court because a court can form its own opinion or inferences about a fact in issue. However, the opinion evidence of laypersons and experts is relevant and admissible when the witness is in a better position to form an opinion than the court and such an opinion will assist the court in determining a fact in issue. For example, in *R v Vilbro and Another*,[6] the Appellate Division held that the opinion of a layperson, a school inspector, was admissible as it was based on his knowledge and experience of the South African school system and would therefore be of appreciable assistance to the Court. Similarly, in *S v Mlimo*,[7] the opinion of a police officer, who had no higher education qualifications, on an issue of ballistics was admissible because the officer's practical experience of ballistics was of assistance to the Court. In *Holtzhauzen v Roodt*,[8] the opinion of a clinical psychologist that the defendant had been telling the truth when she claimed that she had been raped was held to be irrelevant and inadmissible as the Court was capable of reaching such a conclusion by itself. In this case, however, the Court admitted the opinion of certain laypersons who worked with abused women as these

---

3 Zeffertt and Paizes 2 ed (2009) at 310; Schwikkard and Van der Merwe 3 ed (2009) at 85–87.

4 *Hollington v F Hewthorne & Co Ltd* [1943] 2 All ER 35 (CA) at para 40 and *Helen Suzman Foundation v President of the Republic of South Africa and Others* 2015 (2) SA 1 (CC) at para 30.

5 JH Wigmore *Wigmore on Evidence* 3 ed, Vol. 7 (1940) at paras 1918–1920; D Zeffertt 'Opinion evidence' (1976) 93(3) *South African Law Journal* 275.

6 1957 (3) SA 223 (A) at 228, usually referred to as the Vilbro-Wigmore formulation. See also *Ruto Flour Mills Ltd v Adelson (1)* 1958 (4) SA 235 (T) at 237 and *Gentiruco AG v Firestone SA (Pty) Ltd* 1972 (1) SA 589 (A) at 616–619.

7 2008 (2) SACR 48 (SCA) at 52–53.

8 1997 (4) SA 766 (W) at 776–779. See also *S v Kleynhans* 2005 (2) SACR 582 (W) at para at 10 where the opinion of a social worker who was also a probation officer about the personal family circumstances of the accused was held inadmissible; *S v Engelbrecht* 2005 (2) SACR 41 (W) where the opinion of a clinical psychologist was admissible for the Court to understand why an abused woman had killed her abuser.

CHAPTER 18 OPINION AND EXPERT EVIDENCE | 209

persons, as a result of their work-related experience, were in a better position than the Court to draw inferences about the emotional behaviour of sexual assault victims.

18.3 Admissibility of opinion evidence

Opinion evidence becomes relevant and admissible when it can assist the court in deciding on a fact in issue.[9] There are two instances in which opinion evidence becomes relevant and admissible:

- First, the opinion of a layperson is relevant and admissible on certain issues which fall within the competence and experience of laypersons generally.
- Second, expert opinion evidence in the form of an appropriately qualified expert, or an experienced and skilled layperson, is always admissible to assist the court in determining facts in issue that require specialist knowledge not available to the court.

However, a witness cannot give an opinion as to the legal merits of a case. A witness may not give an opinion that results in a conclusion of law[10] or that interprets the meaning of words in a statute.[11] An opinion on the interpretation of a document is a matter of law belonging exclusively to the court.[12] The opinion of a witness in these matters is accordingly superfluous and inadmissible.

18.3.1 Admissibility of a layperson's opinion

A layperson's opinion must be shown to be based on the layperson's own observations of a fact in issue before the court. It is sometimes difficult for a witness to separate statements of facts from inferences based on opinion, that is, an opinion based on a summary of factual data as perceived by the witness. In this case, the court will allow the witness's observations to be conveniently communicated to the court in the form of an opinion.[13]

The witness's opinion will be admissible when it can assist the court on a fact in issue and inadmissible when the court is in the same position as the witness to decide on a fact in issue. For example, a witness may testify by giving an opinion that the driver of a motor vehicle was intoxicated because he staggered, slurred his voice and his breath smelt of liquor. This type of opinion is relevant because it falls within the observational competence and experience of the witness and assists the court. However, a witness may not give an opinion that the driver was incapable of exercising proper control over his vehicle. In respect of this fact in issue, it is the responsibility of the court to decide whether or not the driver's ability to drive was impaired. Similarly, a layperson may express an opinion on the speed at which a vehicle was travelling before an accident, but not on whether the accident was caused by the negligence of the driver.

Layperson opinion has been received in respect of the following categories, among others:

- the age of a person – whether a person was young, middle-aged or old
- the value of articles – cheap or expensive

---

9 Zeffertt and Paizes 2 ed (2009) at 310–321; Schwikkard and Van der Merwe 3 ed (2009) at 87–92.
10 *S v Haasbroek* 1969 (2) SA 624 (A).
11 *Association of Amusement and Novelty Machine Operators and Another v Minister of Justice and Another* 1980 (2) SA 636 (A).
12 *International Business Machines SA (Pty) Ltd v Commissioner for Customs and Excise* 1985 (4) SA 852 (A) at 874.
13 *Herbst v R* 1925 SWA 77 at 80. It is not always possible wholly to separate a statement of opinion from a statement of fact. Consequently, on the grounds of necessity, experience has evolved a rule that the opinions and beliefs of witnesses who are not experts are in certain circumstances admissible.

210 THE LAW OF EVIDENCE IN SOUTH AFRICA

- whether an article is new or second-hand
- the state of the weather during a particular event – cold, hot, rainy or clear
- whether a person was tall, short, fat or thin.

Another example is that a layperson may give an opinion on another's handwriting which is familiar to the layperson. Thus, a secretary may give an opinion on the genuineness of a senior's handwriting.[14] Note also that a witness may be cross-examined and re-examined on his or her reasons for reaching an opinion.

18.3.2 Admissibility of an expert's opinion

18.3.2.1 Introduction

Expert evidence is a sub-category of opinion evidence because it is evidence given by an expert in which he or she expresses his or her expert opinion on an issue before the court. However, expert opinion evidence is distinguishable from the opinion of an ordinary witness, both in the circumstances in which it can be used and in the procedural steps required to render it admissible. The opinion of an ordinary witness is generally inadmissible. The court will, however, receive expert opinion evidence on issues that cannot be decided without expert guidance.[15] For this reason, the expert opinion then becomes relevant to the matter in dispute. According to *Gentiruco AG v Firestone SA (Pty) Ltd*,[16] the opinion of expert witnesses is relevant and admissible because experts, as a result of their specialist, technical skills or knowledge, are better qualified than a court to draw proper inferences on certain facts in issue.[17] The expert can provide the court with specialist knowledge which falls outside the competence and experience of a court.[18]

However, courts have been cautioned against elevating expert evidence to such heights as to lose sight of their own capabilities and responsibilities.[19] Satchwell J stated that expert opinion would be relevant in instances where it would be 'of assistance to the court' and 'helpful':

> ... It would be unwise and it would be irresponsible for myself as a judicial officer, who is lacking in special knowledge and skill, to attempt to draw inferences from facts which have been established by evidence, without welcoming the opportunity to learn and to receive guidance from an expert who is better qualified than myself to draw the inferences which I am required myself to draw.[20]

Expert opinion will generally be received when the facts in issue before a court relate to chemistry, medicine, psychology, psychiatry, ballistics, banking, tool marks, fingerprints, body-prints, handwriting and other related identification marks, DNA samples, accountancy and many other scientific fields where expert opinion will assist a court. There are no closed categories.[21]

---

14 S 4 of the Civil Proceedings Evidence Act 25 of 1965 and s 228 of the Criminal Procedure Act 51 of 1977 allow a layperson to identify handwriting where the person is familiar with that handwriting.
15 PJ Schwikkard and SE van der Merwe *Principles of Evidence* 3 ed (2009) at 83.
16 1972 (1) SA 589 (A) at 616H. The true test of the admissibility of the opinion of a skilled witness is whether or not a court can obtain appreciable help on a particular issue.
17 Zeffertt and Paizes 2 ed (2009) at 321–9; Schwikkard and Van der Merwe 3 ed (2009) at 93–102.
18 For example, in *Jacobs and another v Transnet Ltd t/a Metrorail and Another* 2015 (1) SA 139 (SCA) the court relied on expert witnesses to provide evidence on the safe speed for a train to be travelling at in a particular set of circumstances.
19 *Holtzhauzen v Roodt* 1997 (4) SA 766 (W) at 772E–F.
20 At 778H.
21 See A Bellengère and D Spurrett 'A discordant note: *Kievits Kroon Country Estate (Pty) Ltd v Mmoledi and Others* (2014) 35 ILJ 406 (SCA), (2015) 132(3) *South African Law Journal* 483 in respect of the approach of the courts to evidence provided by traditional healers.

CHAPTER 18   OPINION AND EXPERT EVIDENCE | **211**

Expert evidence will not be received in determining the meaning of languages as the court will have access to authoritative dictionaries. However, in certain circumstances, the court may use an expert translator.

Section 1(1) of the Law of Evidence Amendment Act 45 of 1988 permits a court to take judicial notice of foreign law insofar as it can be readily ascertained and with sufficient certainty. However, a party is not prevented from admitting expert evidence about a rule of foreign law where the foreign law is not readily ascertainable.[22] Similarly, in *Alexkor Ltd and Another v Richtersveld Community and Others*,[23] the Court held that indigenous law may be proved by reference to writers on indigenous law and other authoritative sources, and may include the evidence of witnesses where necessary.

18.3.2.2   The expert witness

(a) Requirements to qualify as expert witness

Before a court will accept a witness as an expert, there is a need to establish his or her credentials:[24]

- An expert must have specialist training, knowledge, skill or experience. Formal qualifications are not always essential and in many instances the practical experience of the witness may be decisive. Thus, an experienced stock farmer may be called to render an expert opinion on the value of cattle. Also, formal qualifications without any practical experience may not be sufficient to qualify a witness as an expert. Thus, a candidate accountant with an accounting degree but no experience may not be qualified to render an expert opinion on the financial practices of a company.
- The witness must be an expert in the area in which he or she has been called to state his or her opinion, as illustrated in the case below. The question is whether the expert witness can speak authoritatively on the particular issue in the case. The fact that he or she is an expert in one field does not enable him or her to express an opinion in another matter.[25] For example, an experienced general medical practitioner who holds an ordinary medical degree cannot be called to testify authoritatively on the specialist procedures used in open-heart surgery. For the purpose of obtaining a reliable expert opinion, an experienced cardiologist must be called.

Mahomed v Shaik

In *Mahomed v Shaik*,[26] the Court held that an ordinary general medical practitioner was not qualified to give an expert opinion on the conclusions reached in a pathologist's report about the fertility of semen.

AB and Another v Minister of Social Development

In *AB and Another v Minister of Social Development*[27] the Minister relied on an expert witness in a matter relating to the possible psychological effect of not knowing one's origins. It was noted in the minority judgment of the Constitutional Court that:

---

22   Section 1(2) of the Law of Evidence Amendment Act, 1988.

23   2004 (5) SA 460 (CC) at 480.

24   Schwikkard and Van der Merwe 3 ed (2009) at 95–96; C Fortt 'Child sexual abuse and the UK expert witness' (2001) *Solicitors Journal* 3.

25   *AB and Another v Minister of Social Development* 2017 (3) SA 570 (CC), discussed below, illustrates the need to ensure that an expert is actually an expert in the field in respect of which they are testifying.

26   1978 (4) SA 523 (N).

27   2017 (3) SA 570 (CC).

THE LAW OF EVIDENCE IN SOUTH AFRICA

> Prof van Bogaert opines that knowledge of one's 'genetic origins' – in the case of donor-conceived children knowledge of the identity of the gamete donors – is an important part of one's 'self-identity'. Prof van Bogaert's opinion is denied – first, because Prof van Bogaert has no expertise in psychology; secondly, because her opinion suffers from a lack of intellectual rigor, objectivity and integrity.[28]

An expert witness called by the applicant concluded '... that Professor van Bogaert is not qualified to express expert opinions in the field of psychology, intimating further that she would initiate an investigation and disciplinary action against Professor van Bogaert on the basis that her testimony is "an attempt to mislead the Court, and is unethical"'.[29]

The facts on which the witness expresses an opinion must have a bearing on the case and must be capable of being reconciled with all the other evidence in the case.

(b) Providing reasons for expert opinion and its probative value

Expert witnesses are required to support and substantiate their opinions with valid reasons based on proper research. They should remain objective in their conclusions and not ignore matters that are inconvenient to their conclusions.[30] The expert must be able to explain to a court why he or she has drawn a particular inference with respect to a particular fact. The probative value of an expert's opinion will be substantially strengthened by an expert who properly explains the conclusions he or she is drawing, the reasoning on which the conclusions are based and the premises which support these conclusions. This is referred to as the need to lay a foundation for an expert opinion, as illustrated in the case below.

> ### Coopers (SA) (Pty) Ltd v Deutsche Gesellschaft Fur Schadlingsbekampfung MBH
> In *Coopers (SA) (Pty) Ltd v Deutsche Gesellschaft Fur Schadlingsbekampfung MBH*,[31] the Court held that an expert's bare or bald statement of an opinion is not of any assistance to a court. The opinion must be based on a disclosure in court by the expert of the processes of reasoning which result in his or her conclusions.

The court must be satisfied that the expert has the required specialist expertise and can, on the basis of these skills, assist the court in arriving at a conclusion with respect to a fact in issue.[32] Similarly, an expert's opinion will be inadmissible when it is based on a hypothetical situation that is inconsistent or has no connection with the facts in issue.

In circumstances where the court is unable to follow the reasoning of the expert as a result of the highly technical nature of the expert's evidence, the court must be guided by the reputation and professionalism of the expert witness, as illustrated in *R v Nksatlala* below.[33] The expert must testify in a neutral and unbiased manner and the expert opinion must carry the stamp of objective professionalism, as illustrated in *Schneider NO and Others v AA and Another* below.[34] The court still has to make the final decision after careful analysis of the expert opinion, as illustrated in *S v O* below.[35]

---

28 2017 (3) SA 570 (CC) at para 200.
29 2017 (3) SA 570 (CC) at para 201.
30 C Fortt 'Child sexual abuse and the UK expert witness' available online at: http://www.expertsearch.co.uk/articles/fortt.htm.
31 1976 (3) SA 352 (A) at 371.
32 *Menday v Protea Assurance Co Ltd* 1976 (1) SA 565 (EC) at 569.
33 1960 (3) SA 543 (A) at 546.
34 2010 (5) SA 203 (WCC).
35 *S v O* 2003 (2) SACR 147 (C) at 164F.

CHAPTER 18 OPINION AND EXPERT EVIDENCE 213

R v Nksatlala

In *R v Nksatlala*,[36] the Court stated that a court should not blindly accept the evidence of an expert witness. However, once satisfied, a court should give effect to the conclusions of the witness even if its own observations do not positively confirm these conclusions.

Schneider NO and Others v AA and Another

In *Schneider NO and Others v AA and Another*,[37] the Court stated that an expert must not assume the role of an advocate but must give an unbiased opinion on matters within his expertise. When a particular issue falls outside his expertise, he must say that his opinion is provisional if he has not fully researched it. If his opinion on an issue requires qualification, he must say so.

S v O

In *S v O*,[38] the Court called a social worker from the Department of Correctional Services who was based at Pollsmoor Prison. However, this witness was, in the end, unable to be of any real assistance to the Court regarding the prison programme for sex offenders. He had no specific information about the number of sex offenders participating in the programme or any data on the success rate thereof. His evidence was found not to be impressive.

An expert witness is not restricted to relying on his or her own perceptions, or even his or her own reasoning. Experts may, and must, rely on the general body of knowledge that constitutes their field.[39] However, this is an area of contention and one in which the courts have indicated their scepticism regarding this type of evidence, as illustrated in *S v O* below.

S v O

In *S v O*,[40] the judge seemed unconvinced by a clinical social worker's testimony regarding the appellant which was presented without having consulted with the appellant. The expert witness stated that, based on the circumstances of the case, '(it) would suggest that the accused is a multiple sex offender with exaggerated risk for recidivism'. He questioned the basis for this which the social worker had called 'a body of [research literature]'.

Experts in different fields may sometimes rely on each other's expertise to assist the court. For example, an industrial psychologist or occupational therapist will rely on the report of an orthopaedic surgeon to project a career path for an injured individual in a third-party claim for damages.

The court will normally receive all reports compiled by experts, but it will determine the weight of their evidence at a later stage. Expert witnesses generally testify under oath and thereafter submit their written reports. They read out the report and are then cross-examined on its contents. However, the cross-examiner might be faced with the same problem the judicial officer faces during evaluation, that is, a lack of knowledge about the particular field of expertise which thus limits his or her ability to conduct an effective cross-examination.

---

36 1960 (3) SA 543 (A) at 546.

37 2010 (5) SA 203 (WCC) at 211.

38 2003 (2) SACR 147 (C) at 164F.

39 L Meintjes-Van der Walt *Expert Evidence in the Criminal Justice Process: A Comparative Perspective* (2001) at 70. The cases of *Holtzhauzen v Roodt* 1997 (4) SA 766 (W) and the American case *S v Kinney* 171 Vt 239, 762 A 2d 833 (2000) are examples of cases where profile or syndrome evidence was admitted to explain and therefore assist the Court in understanding the behaviour of certain categories of people – even without a personal interview with the person in question.

40 2003 (2) SACR 147 (C) at 163I–J.

Only in cases where the report does not contain any information detrimental to the accused or where it is not disputed by any of the parties will it simply be handed in. However, in such a case, the danger still exists that issues that are not fully explained or matters that are open to interpretation cannot then be clarified, as illustrated in the case below. Such documentary evidence may thus carry less weight in the end.

S v S

For example, in S v S[41] an issue was the suitability of imprisonment for effective treatment. The expert witness explained why the appellant could, despite his acute anxiety and claustrophobia, cope with the film developing room as well as his classroom. Apparently, the appellant did not feel trapped in these environments and therefore did not suffer from his usual anxiety.

In the event of contradictory expert evidence, the proper approach for the court to follow is to assess the evidence of the expert witnesses in light of credibility, reliability and probabilities.[42] The SCA in *Buthelezi v Ndaba* provides some useful guidance in this regard stating that when choosing 'between the opposing views of two expert witnesses ... the court's determination must depend on an analysis of the cogency of the underlying reasoning which led the experts to their conflicting opinions'.[43]

(c) Duties of the expert witness

In *Schneider NO and Others v AA and Another*,[44] the issue was whether it would be in the best interests of two brothers to continue with home schooling as advocated by their mother. She called an educational psychologist as an expert witness. The Court expressed certain concerns regarding the expertise and the mandate of the expert. It highlighted the following duties of an expert witness (referring to the judgment of Creswell J in an English case, *National Justice Compania Naviera SA v Prudential Assurance Co Ltd*[45]):

- Expert evidence presented to the court should be, and should be seen to be, the independent product of the expert, uninfluenced as to form or content by the exigencies of litigation.
- An expert should provide independent assistance to the court by way of objective, unbiased opinion in relation to matters within his or her expertise. An expert should never assume the role of an advocate.
- An expert witness should state the facts or assumptions on which his or her opinion is based. He or she should not omit to consider material facts that could detract from his or her concluded opinion.
- An expert should make it clear if a particular question falls outside his or her field of expertise.
- If the expert opinion is not properly researched because he or she considers that insufficient data is available, then this must be stated with an indication that the opinion is no more than a preliminary report.

---

41 1977 (3) SA 830 (A) at 836H.

42 *Louwrens v Oldwage* 2006 (2) SA 161 (SCA).

43 2013(5) SA 437 (SCA) at para 14.

44 2010 (5) SA 203 (WCC).

45 *National Justice Compania Naviera SA v Prudential Assurance Co Ltd* (*'The Ikarian Reefer'*) [1993] 2 Lloyd's Rep 68 at 81–82. See also H Lerm 'Beware the hired gun' – are expert witnesses unbiased? *De Rebus*, May 2015 Issue 552 at 36.

CHAPTER 18 OPINION AND EXPERT EVIDENCE | 215

Davis J then proceeded to summarise the role and duty of an expert witness as follows:

> In short, an expert comes to court to give the court the benefit of his or her expertise.
> Agreed, an expert is called by a particular party, presumably because the conclusion
> of the expert, using his or her expertise, is in favour of the line of argument of the
> particular party. But that does not absolve the expert from providing the court with
> as objective and unbiased opinion, based on his or her expertise, as is possible. An
> expert is not a hired gun who dispenses his or her expertise for the purposes of a
> particular case. An expert does not assume the role of an advocate, nor gives
> evidence which goes beyond the logic which is dictated by the scientific knowledge
> which that expert claims to possess.[46]

The duty of the expert witness is to the court. Unlike jurisdictions such as England, Wales
and Australia, South African courts do not require a prior ethical undertaking from an expert
in this regard. In *Holtzhauzen v Roodt*,[47] the Court held that the expert witness should also
not take over the function of the court by making findings on credibility. However, it accepted
the opinion of the second expert, which was of a general nature:

> If there are particular reasons, known only or particular to those who work with rape
> survivors and who have experience in this field, why rape survivors do frequently
> not use the first opportunity to make known the rape or seek help – the court should
> take the opportunity to gain better understanding from an available expert.

DISCUSSION
18.1

The failure to follow expert advice

Unfortunately our courts are not consistent in their approach to the use of expert
evidence, with some courts electing not to take the opportunity to gain a better
understanding from an available expert. The Constitutional Court in *AB and Another v
Minister of Social Development*[48] demonstrated the problems inherent in, and
consequences of, ignoring expert evidence. This case concerned a woman who wanted
to have a child through surrogacy. Given her infertility, she could not contribute her own
egg cells for the purpose of conceiving a child and so she was excluded from using
surrogacy, as the Children's Act requires that a surrogacy parent must use only his or
her own genetic material for the conception of the surrogacy child. She challenged the
constitutionality of this requirement and although the High Court[49] agreed that the
requirement was indeed unconstitutional the Minister persisted in her opposition in
the Constitutional Court hearing. Argument centred on whether having a genetic link
with one's parents is in the best interests of the child. Although the extensive
psychological expert opinions filed in this case all agreed that a genetic link with one's
parents is not essential for a child's well-being, the majority of the Constitutional Court
brushed away all the expert evidence before it and decided that the best interests of
a child requires that a child should know its genetic origins. The majority made no
reference to any expert evidence in its judgment, instead quoting a proverb as

---

46 *Schneider NO and Others v AA and Another* 2010 (5) SA 203 (WCC) at 211–212. Reiterated in *S v M* 2018 (1) SACR 357
(GP) at para 160.
47 1997 (4) SA 766 (W) at 774E–F.
48 2017 (3) SA 570 (CC).
49 *AB and Another v Minister of Social Development* 2016 (2) SA 27 (GP).

> authority.[50] Essentially, the justices of the majority of the Constitutional Court replaced expert opinion evidence with their own personal opinions.[51]

(d) The expert and hearsay

When an expert bases his or her opinion on a specialist statement made by another person not called as a witness, such an opinion is based on hearsay. However, the expert may sometimes be allowed to rely on information or statements that technically amount to hearsay for a number of reasons:

- First, the courts should not set impossible standards. For example, the court should not reject an expert surgeon's evidence simply because the expert bases an opinion on surgical procedures developed by another authoritative surgeon not called to the witness box as this would be to ignore accepted methods of professional work and to insist on impossible standards as illustrated in *S v Kimimbi* below.[52]
- Second, many experts rely on textbooks written by authors who are not called to the witness box. The courts will allow the use of textbooks, which technically amounts to hearsay, if a number of conditions are adhered to by the expert witness.

An expert who relies on authoritative textbooks written by others to formulate an opinion must satisfy the court of the following:

- That the expert can, by reason of his or her own training, affirm the correctness of the statements taken from the textbook – this must be done under oath
- That the textbook relied on has been written by persons of established repute or proved experience in that field as illustrated in *Menday v Protea Assurance* below.[53]

S v Kimimbi

In *S v Kimimbi*,[54] the Court stated that an expert's knowledge does not have to be drawn from personal experience. It may be drawn from studying textbooks and other literature. For example, expert opinions on scientific matters usually involve references to scientific experimentations and data provided by other scientists.

Menday v Protea Assurance

In *Menday v Protea Assurance Co Ltd*,[55] the Court held that an expert must have personal knowledge and experience in the special field on which he or she testifies. Alternatively, the expert must rely on the knowledge and experience of others who are accepted as experts in that field.

(e) Experts for sentencing purposes

The sentencing phase is a separate trial during which new issues of a psychological nature become important. Questions posed here relate to the accused's degree of culpability, his

---

50 2017 (3) SA 570 (CC) at para 294: 'Here, the substance below the surface is the need for a genetic link between a child and at least one parent. The importance of this genetic link is affirmed in the adage "ngwana ga se wa ga ka otla ke wa ga katsala" (loosely translated the adage means "a child belongs not to the one who provides but to the one who gives birth to the child").'
51 See DW Thaldar 'Post-truth jurisprudence: the case of *AB v Minister of Social Development*' (2018) *SAJHR* 34(2).
52 1963 (3) SA 250 (C) at 252.
53 *Menday v Protea Assurance Co Ltd* 1976 (1) SA 565 (EC) at para 569. See also *S v Jones* 2004 (1) SACR 420 (C).
54 1963 (3) SA 250 (C) at 252.
55 1976 (1) SA 565 (E) at 569.

CHAPTER 18   OPINION AND EXPERT EVIDENCE | 217

or her dangerousness, the harm experienced by the victim, the chances of the accused's rehabilitation and the suitability of treatment programmes.[56] To obtain the relevant information, the court needs the expertise of behavioural scientists. In principle, the court has the discretion, except in a case where correctional supervision is imposed,[57] to decide what evidence to receive to impose a proper **sentence**. In some cases, the court itself will obtain expert evidence in addition to the expert evidence presented by the State and/or defence.[58] Expert evidence in mitigation or aggravation is of little value if it is not related to the accused and the particular crime, and to the facts found to be proved in the judgment.[59]

Evidence by an expert is referred to as a pre-sentence report and is usually requested with regard to the accused as a person. For example, with a sex offender or drug, alcohol or gambling addict, the report may examine factors such as his or her character, motive for the crime and possible future crimes, his or her risk of further offending and possible treatment. The pre-sentence report not only contains information regarding the offender but can also, based on social science research, correct incorrect perceptions about 'typical human behaviour' under certain conditions.[60] In addition, it can also provide the court with advice by making a recommendation as to the appropriate sentence. The court is not bound by these recommendations but should it decide not to follow the expert's advice, it should give reasons.[61] By calling experts from both sides the adversarial contest between the parties continues and, in the case of sentencing, this usually revolves around the question of imprisonment.

18.3.2.3   Procedure for leading expert evidence

(a) Civil litigation: expert evidence

In an accusatorial-adversarial legal system, a party is not entitled to prior knowledge of the oral evidence that will be adduced by their opponent.[62] However, the contrary is true when it comes to expert evidence because it is necessary for a party's legal representative to acquaint him- or herself with the opinion of an expert to prepare for trial.[63]

A party must give their opponent 15 days' notice prior to trial that they will be making use of an expert.[64] The party must then deliver a summary of the expert's evidence within 10 days prior to trial.[65] The same rules apply for the plaintiff and the defendant. However, if the defendant wants the plaintiff to be examined by their own expert witnesses, they must give the plaintiff 15 days' notice[66] that he or she must subject him- or herself to a medico-legal examination.[67] This notice must contain the following information:

- The person on whom the notice is served is required to submit him- or herself for a medico-legal examination

---

56 *Rammoko v Director of Public Prosecutions* 2003 (1) SACR 200 (SCA); *S v Abrahams* 2002 (1) SACR 116 (SCA).

57 When the sentencing option of correctional supervision in terms of section 276(1)(*h*) and (*i*) of the Criminal Procedure Act, 1977 is imposed on a sex offender, the court has no discretion with regard to a pre-sentence report. It is a statutory requirement that a report by either a probation officer or a correctional officer must be obtained.

58 *S v O* 2003 (2) SACR 147 (C) at 153G.

59 E du Toit, FJ de Jager, A Paizes, A St Q Skeen and S van der Merwe *Commentary on the Criminal Procedure Act* (1987) (Service Issue 60, 2018) at 28–6D-1.

60 J Monahan and L Walker 'Social frameworks: A new use of social science in law' (1987) 73(3) *Virginia LR* 559.

61 SS Terblanche *A Guide to Sentencing in South Africa* 2 ed (2007) at 106.

62 C Theophilopoulos, A Rowan, C van Heerden and A Boraine *Fundamental Principles of Civil Procedure* (2006) at 284.

63 Ibid.

64 High Court Rule 36(9)(*a*) and Magistrates' Courts Rule 24(9)(*a*).

65 High Court Rule 36(9)(*b*) and Magistrates' Courts Rule 24(9)(*b*).

66 High Court Rule 36(2) and Magistrates' Courts Rule 24(?)(*a*).

67 High Court Rule 36(1) and (2) and Magistrates' Courts Rule 24(1) and (2)(*a*) and (*b*).

218 | THE LAW OF EVIDENCE IN SOUTH AFRICA

- The nature of the examination required
- The person or expert who will be conducting the medical examination
- The date, time and place of the examination
- The person on whom the notice is served has the right to have his or her own medical adviser present.

If the notice informing a party to attend a medico-legal examination is defective or unsuitable,[68] then the aggrieved party should object to the notice. A party will have five days to object in the High Court[69] and 10 days in the Magistrates' Court.[70] A party who submitted to a medico-legal examination can request that the medical records, X-rays and so on relevant to the assessment be produced. The party that ordered the examination must submit the documents within 10 days in the High Court[71] and 15 days in the Magistrates' Court.[72] A party who attended a medico-legal examination called for by his or her opponent can request the report from his or her opponent.[73]

(b) Criminal litigation: expert evidence

In criminal proceedings, an expert witness must be subpoenaed to appear in court. However, in certain circumstances and provided good cause is shown, it is permissible to receive expert testimony by way of affidavit or certificate.[74] When an expert witness is physically present in court, it is sometimes acceptable for the expert to sit in on the trial proceedings before being called to the witness box. This is to allow the expert to assess the nature of the case and to understand the issues being presented in court. The expert will then be in a better position to give an expert opinion and to relate his or her testimony to the facts in issue.

In criminal cases, prior discovery of expert reports can be obtained on constitutional grounds and they should normally be discovered.[75] It is practice that the defendant can obtain expert reports from the prosecutor prior to the hearing. No concrete rules exist regarding the discovery of expert opinions. However, the courts have laid down guidelines about access to the police docket and the reports contained in them. These stipulate clearly that, unless there is a compelling reason not to disclose them, all such reports should be made available to the defence before the commencement of trial.

18.4   The opinion of a court and the *Hollington* rule

The rule that opinion evidence is admissible only if of appreciable assistance to a court has certain consequences that at first glance seem illogical. An example of this is the situation that arises when a court is faced with a judgment on the same set of facts that are before it, by another court. The judgment of the first court is considered to be merely an 'opinion' in the legal sense of the word. Thus, if a subsequent court is in a position to examine all the same evidence, then the 'opinion' of the previous court is of no assistance and is, therefore, inadmissible.

---

68 For example, the nature of the examination is vague or wrong, the plaintiff is not satisfied with the person conducting the examination or a problematic date, time and place of examination is stipulated, and so on.
69 High Court Rule 36(3).
70 Magistrates' Courts Rule 24(3)(*a*).
71 High Court Rule 36(4).
72 Magistrates' Courts Rule 24(4).
73 High Court Rule 36(8) and Magistrates' Courts Rule 24(8).
74 Section 212 of the Criminal Procedure Act, 1977.
75 *Shabalala and Others v Attorney-General Transvaal and Another* 1995 (2) SACR 761 (CC) at para 72.

CHAPTER 18 OPINION AND EXPERT EVIDENCE | 219

On occasion, an act can have both civil and criminal consequences. For example, an assault can result in the prosecution of the person perpetrating the assault. In addition, the victim may have a civil claim against the person who assaulted him or her based in delict on compensation for damages suffered as a result of the assault. If the criminal case is finalised first and the accused is found guilty, it means that the court found, beyond reasonable doubt, on the evidence, that the accused did indeed assault the victim. In the subsequent civil case, the burden of proof on the plaintiff (victim) is of a lower standard and the plaintiff only has to prove on a balance of probabilities that he or she was assaulted. One would think that the criminal case would establish this.

However, there is a common law rule that the judgment and conviction of an accused in a criminal trial is not admissible to prove any of the facts in issue in any subsequent civil proceedings. This was established in *Hollington v F Hewthorn & Co Ltd*[76] where the Court explained that the judgment of a previous criminal tribunal amounts to the opinion of that tribunal and was, therefore, irrelevant and inadmissible before a civil tribunal. The civil tribunal is capable of reaching its own opinion based on the evidence.

In England, the common law rule has been abolished by sections 11–13 of the Civil Evidence Act of 1968, which makes the judgments of a previous tribunal admissible in certain circumstances.[77] However, South Africa is bound by English law as it stood up to 30 May 1961, which means that South Africa is still bound by the common law rule and not by the English statutory abolition. In addition, the Constitutional Court in *Prophet v National Director, Public Prosecutions*[78] appears to have tacitly confirmed the rule in *Hollington v F Hewthorn*.

However, the absurdity of the rule has been criticised and Rumpff CJ in *S v Khanyapa*[79] expressed doubt about the correctness of the rule. Academics have called for the statutory abolition of this rule.[80]

The ***Hollington* rule** nonetheless remains applicable, but its effect has been somewhat ameliorated in South African law by the following:

- The Constitutional Court in *Prophet v National Director, Public Prosecution* has confined the rule to civil proceedings as defined in the Civil Proceedings Evidence Act, 1965. However, in *Hassim (also known as Essack) v Incorporated Law Society, Natal*,[81] the Court held that a previous conviction or judgment should at least be *prima facie* proof of the facts on which it is based in subsequent proceedings which are neither civil nor criminal in nature, for example in proceedings to strike a legal practitioner from the roll.
- The law of evidence allows for the admission of previous convictions by way of similar fact evidence in both civil and criminal proceedings.
- Finally, the rule should be strictly limited to civil proceedings and must not be extended to criminal proceedings in the opinion of Rumpff CJ in *S v Khanyapa*[82] although the question was left open by Hefer J in *S v Mavuso*.[83] In addition, sections 197(*d*) and 211

---

76 [1943] 2 All ER 35 (CA), an action for damages arising from the collision of two motor vehicles.
77 P Murphy *A Practical Approach to Evidence* (1980) at 261–265.
78 2007 (6) SA 169 (CC) at 187 where a criminal conviction was held to be irrelevant and superfluous in a civil trial concerning a forfeiture of assets. See also *Leeb and Another v Leeb and Another* [1999] 2 All SA 588 (N) where it was held that a spouse's murder conviction for killing her husband was inadmissible in a civil trial concerned with the division of the joint estate; *Du Toit v Grobler* 1947 (3) SA 213 (SWA) at 215 where the defendant's conviction on theft was inadmissible in a civil action to recover the stolen money; *S v Mavuso* 1987 (3) SA 499 (A) at 505.
79 1979 (1) SA 824 (A).
80 Zeffertt and Paizes 2 ed (2009) at 343.
81 1979 (3) SA 298 (A).
82 1979 (1) SA 824 (A).
83 1987 (3) SA 499 (A) at 505F.

220 | THE LAW OF EVIDENCE IN SOUTH AFRICA

of the Criminal Procedure Act, 1977 allow for the use of previous convictions in subsequent criminal proceedings in specific circumstances.

Table 18.1 Opinion and expert evidence

Opinion evidence	Expert evidence
• Inadmissible and irrelevant • Does not assist the court in reaching a decision • Is supererogatory and superfluous • Layperson witness must limit his or her testimony to the facts relevant to an issue and cannot give an opinion about the facts	• Admissible and relevant • Assists the court on issues requiring specialist knowledge or skills outside the experience or competence of the court • Expert better qualified to draw skilled inferences and opinions than the court
Layperson may give an opinion: • where a layperson witness cannot separate facts from opinion when being questioned at trial – court may allow opinion in order to save time	Expert may give an opinion on: • matters beyond the competence of the court no closed list (science, medicine, forensic and genetic evidence, accountancy, business, economics, etc.)
Layperson may give opinion on facts directly observed about: • identification of persons – young or old • condition or appearance – new or second-hand • speed of a car – fast or slow • value of things – cheap or expensive • weather – clear or rainy	Expert must lay a foundation for reception of expert opinion: • Satisfy the court as to qualifications, skills or training in respect of a specific fact in issue • Expert's opinion must be based on expert's personal knowledge or on expert facts proved by other experts • Expert may rely on authoritative textbooks written by other experts – expert exception to hearsay rule • Where experts conflict, the court must be guided by logical reasoning and analysis of the testimony given by conflicting experts • Expert must give unbiased, objective testimony about the expert facts within his or her expertise • Must state when a particular fact falls outside his or her expertise
Layperson cannot give an opinion on: • legal matters or general merits of a case • whether international law is part of domestic law • common law • interpretation of statutes • interpretation of documents	

THIS CHAPTER IN ESSENCE

1 Generally, opinion evidence is irrelevant and therefore inadmissible as it has no probative value and cannot assist the court in proving a fact in issue.

2 Opinion evidence will, however, be relevant and therefore admissible when a witness (layperson or expert) is in a better position to form an opinion than a court and the opinion will assist the court in determining a fact in issue.

CHAPTER 18   OPINION AND EXPERT EVIDENCE   221

3   Witnesses may not give opinions as to the legal merits of a case.

4   Generally, a court will receive expert opinion evidence on issues that cannot be decided without expert guidance by an expert witness.

5   Before a court will accept a witness as an expert, he or she will have to show that:

   5.1   he or she has specialist training, knowledge, skill or experience

   5.2   he or she is an expert in the area in which he or she has been called on to state an opinion.

6   The facts on which the expert witness expresses an opinion must have a bearing on the case and must be capable of being reconciled with all the other evidence in the case.

7   An expert opinion must be supported by valid reasons and based on proper research as this will substantially strengthen the probative value of the opinion.

8   Experts should remain objective in their conclusions and should not ignore matters inconvenient to their conclusions.

9   Should the court not be able to follow the reasoning of the expert due to the highly technical nature of his or her evidence, the court should let itself be guided by the reputation and professionalism of the expert witness.

10 Experts may and must rely on the general body of knowledge that constitutes their field.

11 In the event of contradictory expert evidence, the court must assess the evidence of the expert witnesses in light of credibility, reliability and probabilities.

12 An expert witness has the duty to:

   12.1 remain independent and uninfluenced

   12.2 provide an objective, unbiased opinion in relation to matters within his or her expertise

   12.3 never assume the role of an advocate

   12.4 state the facts or assumptions on which his or her opinion is based

   12.5 make it clear if a particular question falls outside his or her field of expertise

   12.6 indicate that an opinion is no more than a preliminary report if the opinion is not properly researched because he or she considers the available data to be insufficient.

13 An expert may from time to time be allowed to rely on information or statements that amount to hearsay.

14 When an expert relies on authoritative textbooks to formulate an opinion, he or she must satisfy the court that:

   14.1 the expert can, by reason of his or her own training, affirm the correctness of the statements taken from the textbook

   14.2 the textbook was written by persons of established repute or proven experience in that field.

15 A court itself can, for purposes of sentencing, obtain its own expert evidence in addition to that presented by the State and/or defence. However, expert evidence in mitigation, or aggravation, is of very little value if it does not relate to:

   15.1 the accused and the particular crime

   15.2 the facts found to be proved in the judgment.

16 Prior notice of the intention to use expert evidence must be given to a party in civil litigation. Such notice must be given within a specified time period and must contain certain information.

17 In criminal proceedings, an expert witness must be subpoenaed to appear in court. In circumstances where good cause is shown, expert testimony can also be received by way of an affidavit or certificate. Also, prior discovery of expert reports can be obtained on constitutional grounds.

18 The *Hollington* rule, which is still applicable today, and which concurs with the common law rule, entails that the previous judgment of a criminal court amounts to the opinion of that tribunal and is therefore irrelevant and inadmissible before a civil court adjudicating on the same matter. However, its effect has been somewhat ameliorated by case law and statute.

Chapter 19

Character evidence

19.1 Introduction: what is character evidence? 222

19.2 Admissibility of character evidence in the common law 223

19.3 Character evidence: admissibility in criminal cases 224
    19.3.1 The accused 224
        19.3.1.1 The State's power to present evidence of an accused's bad character:
            the common law 224
        19.3.1.2 Admissibility of previous convictions: section 211 of the Criminal
            Procedure Act, 1977 225
        19.3.1.3 The express provision in section 241 of the Criminal Procedure Act,
            1977: evidence of previous conviction on charge of receiving
            stolen property 227
        19.3.1.4 Lifting the shield: proving previous convictions, previous charges or bad
            character in terms of section 197 of the Criminal Procedure Act, 1977 228
        19.3.1.5 Proving previous convictions for purposes of sentencing 231
    19.3.2 The character of the complainant in criminal cases 231

19.4 The character of the plaintiff and defendant in civil cases 231

19.5 Character of witnesses: credibility 232

19.1 Introduction: what is character evidence?

A person's character comprises a variety of character traits or characteristics such as honesty, deceitfulness, integrity, trustworthiness, violent tendencies (in the sense that someone has a tendency to carry out acts of violence), and the like. **Character evidence** is, therefore, evidence about these characteristics, also referred to as a person's disposition.[1]

A distinction must be drawn between two main types of character evidence, namely a person's general reputation[2] and a person's disposition to think and act in a particular way. In the old English common law, evidence of general reputation as a means of establishing character was preferred to evidence of a person's disposition. However, the modern law does not reflect this preference.[3] The better view appears to be that character consists essentially

---

1 Stated differently, a person's character traits will predispose him or her to act in certain ways in certain circumstances, hence the term 'disposition'.
2 *R v Rowton* 1865 Le and CA 520; 169 All ER 1497. General reputation refers to a person's reputation in the community which he or she lives.
3 See C Tapper *Cross and Tapper on Evidence* 11 ed (2007) at 352.

of a person's disposition, in other words the summary of all his or her character traits, but that a person's reputation should nevertheless be considered as part of his or her general character assessment. This view was summarised in *R v Malindi*[4] where the Court, considering what the meaning of character was, quoted Viscount Simon, LC, in *Stirland v Director of Public Prosecutions*,[5] with approval:

> There is perhaps some vagueness in the use of the term 'good character' in this connection. Does it refer to the good reputation which a man may bear in his own circle, or does it refer to the man's real disposition as distinct from what his friends and neighbours may think of him? In *Reg v Rowton*, (1865) 10 Cox C.C. 25, on a re-hearing before the full Court, it was held by the majority that evidence for or against a prisoner's good character must be confined to the prisoner's general reputation, but Erle, C.J., and Willes, J., thought that the meaning of the phrase extended to include actual moral disposition as known to an individual witness, though no evidence could be given of concrete examples of conduct. In the later case of *Rex v Dunkley*, (1927) 1 K.B. 323, the question was further discussed in the light of the language of the section, but not explicitly decided. I am disposed to think that in para. (f) (where the word 'character' occurs four times) both conceptions are combined.

The central question relating to character evidence is this: in what circumstances may a witness be permitted to be led or cross-examined regarding, first, the character of one of the parties to the dispute, second, the character of another witness and, finally, the character of the witness him- or herself? In answering this question it will become apparent that the principles governing character evidence may, to a certain extent, overlap with those principles dealing with other types of evidence, such as the rules applicable to similar fact evidence. For example, a situation that frequently arises in practice is where a witness testifies that an accused has previously committed another crime. This evidence reflects on the character of the accused, but it may nevertheless be admissible as similar fact evidence.

19.2 Admissibility of character evidence in the common law

As a general rule of the common law, character evidence is inadmissible because of its low probative value as well as its high potential for prejudice. Character evidence has a low probative value because the mere fact that a person displays a certain characteristic does not necessarily help to prove a fact in issue. Further, character evidence is generally inadmissible because it has a high potential to prejudice the outcome of the case. The objectivity of the presiding officer may be tainted where the presiding officer is made aware of a certain bad character trait of an accused person. This is, of course, unlikely, but the rule makes more sense when one considers that it was developed when jury trials were more prevalent. It was indeed possible that the objectivity of a jury might have been tainted had the jurors been made aware of a certain bad character trait of an accused person.

To determine whether character evidence will be admissible, it is essential to establish that the evidence about a person's character is relevant to the facts in issue. On the one hand, if the character evidence cannot assist in proving a fact in issue, in other words if it

---

4   1966 (4) SA 123 (PC).
5   [1944] AC 315 at 324–325.

224 THE LAW OF EVIDENCE IN SOUTH AFRICA

cannot help to determine whether the fact in issue is more or less likely, it will not be admissible. On the other hand, if character evidence is relevant[6] to a fact in issue, it may be admissible.

Character evidence may be relevant, and therefore admissible, in two particular instances:

- In the first instance, where a characteristic or character trait of a party to the dispute is relevant to the facts of the dispute, such evidence will be admissible. In a criminal case, evidence regarding the character of the accused or the complainant may be relevant and admissible. In a civil case, the character of the plaintiff or the defendant may, in specific cases, be relevant and therefore admissible.
- In the second instance, evidence regarding the character of a specific witness may shed light on the credibility of such a witness. In particular, evidence that a witness is a dishonest, untruthful or deceitful person may be relevant.

We will examine these two broad categories of character evidence in more detail below.

19.3 Character evidence: admissibility in criminal cases

19.3.1 The accused

As a general rule in criminal cases, accused persons are allowed to lead evidence about their good character,[7] provided, of course, that this evidence is relevant to an issue before the court. The State, however, as a general rule, is not allowed to lead evidence of an accused's bad character, although there are certain exceptions to this rule.

In practice, the accused will lead evidence about his or her conduct from which inferences about his or her good character may be drawn because merely averring that he or she has good character traits, for example stating, 'I am an honest person,' will not meet the test for relevance.

The defence may present evidence about the good character of the accused in general, provided that the character evidence and the crime with which the accused is charged are sufficiently connected. For instance, it may be possible for an accused, who is charged with indecent assault, to call a witness to testify about the accused's moral values.

The danger for the accused in leading evidence about his or her good character is that the 'gate is then opened' for the State to present evidence it has at its disposal about the same accused's bad character.

Both the common law and the Criminal Procedure Act 51 of 1977[8] determine the extent to which the State may present evidence about the character of an accused person.

19.3.1.1 The State's power to present evidence of an accused's bad character: the common law

Section 252 of the Criminal Procedure Act, 1977 (the so-called residuary rule)[9] provides as follows:

---

6 See ch 15 The general test for relevance.
7 By testifying about their good character themselves or calling witnesses to do so: *R v Gimingham* 1946 EDL 156.
8 Sections 211 and 197.
9 See ch 2.

The law as to the admissibility of evidence, which was in force in respect of criminal proceedings on the thirtieth day of May 1961, shall apply in any case not *expressly* provided for by this Act or any other law. [Emphasis added]

Section 252 is therefore a 'catch-all' provision which makes the English common law as it was at 30 May 1961 applicable to all law of evidence matters not *expressly* provided for in the Criminal Procedure Act, 1977 itself or in any other statute.

In terms of the common law, evidence regarding the bad character of the accused will not be allowed if its only relevance is to show that he or she is the kind of person who may have committed the crime in question. This type of character evidence is often described as **propensity evidence** because it is aimed at showing that the accused is the kind of person who is inclined or predisposed to act in a certain manner. As a general rule, the use of character evidence for this purpose is not permitted in most Anglo-American legal systems. The following quote from *R v Solomons*[10] sums up the general rule in this regard:

> It is clear that evidence of criminal actions other than those laid in the indictment is inadmissible against an accused merely to show a criminal propensity. But it is, I think, equally well established – albeit seldom free from difficulty of application in any particular case – that evidence which is relevant to an issue before the court is not rendered inadmissible merely because it tends to show the commission by the accused of other crimes.[11]

However, if an accused does lead evidence of his or her good character, which can be done by testifying or by calling a character witness, the prosecution is then allowed to present evidence of the accused's bad character.[12] The prosecution can do this by cross-examining the accused, by cross-examining the accused's character witness or by leading the evidence of State witnesses of the accused's bad character.

If the accused does not lead evidence of his or her good character, but merely attacks the character of a State witness, in cross-examination for example, then the prosecution may cross-examine the accused with regard to his or her bad character only and may not lead bad character evidence.[13] Therefore, it is important for accused persons to avoid leading evidence of their good character if they wish to avoid having aspects of their bad character exposed.

19.3.1.2 Admissibility of previous convictions: section 211 of the Criminal Procedure Act, 1977

The two statutory provisions that deal specifically with evidence regarding the bad character of the accused are sections 211 and 197 of the Criminal Procedure Act, 1977.

Section 211 of the Criminal Procedure Act, 1977, reads as follows:

> Evidence during criminal proceedings of previous convictions
> Except where otherwise expressly provided by this Act ... or except where the fact of a previous conviction is an element of any offence with which an accused is charged, evidence shall not be admissible at criminal proceedings in respect of any offence to prove that an accused at such proceedings had previously been

---

10 1959 (2) SA 352 (A).
11 At 361–362.
12 S 197 of the Criminal Procedure Act, 1977.
13 *R v Butterwasser* [1948] 1 KB 4, [1947] 2 All ER 415 (CCA).

226 | THE LAW OF EVIDENCE IN SOUTH AFRICA

> convicted of any offence, whether in the Republic or elsewhere, and no accused, if called as a witness, shall be asked whether he or she has been so convicted.

Section 211 states the general principle that evidence regarding previous convictions of the accused is not admissible. It then also sets out two exceptions to this general rule in terms of which such evidence will indeed be admissible.

The first exception is where other provisions of the Criminal Procedure Act, 1977 *expressly*[14] make evidence of previous convictions admissible. The applicable express provisions in the Criminal Procedure Act, 1977 are section 197 (privileges of an accused when giving evidence);[15] section 241 (evidence of previous conviction on a charge of receiving stolen property);[16] and section 271 (proof of previous convictions after the conviction of the accused).[17]

DISCUSSION	**Is section 252 an 'express provision' for the purposes of section 211 of the**
19.1	**Criminal Procedure Act, 1977?**

There does not appear to be clarity in our law as to whether section 252 (the residuary provision that effectively makes the English common law as it was at 30 May 1961 the common law of South Africa) is an 'express provision' for the purposes of section 211 or not. If section 252 *is* regarded as an express provision, it opens the back door for the admission of an accused's previous convictions in criminal proceedings for various purposes, including using previous convictions as a basis for establishing similar fact evidence. Following a more restrictive approach, the phrase 'expressly provided for' would limit the admissibility of evidence of previous convictions to those cases expressly and specifically provided for in the Criminal Procedure Act, 1977, such as the exceptions contained in sections 197, 241 and 271 of the Criminal Procedure Act, 1977.

The issue, therefore, turns on the correct interpretation of the phrase 'expressly provided for' and there does not appear to be any case law directly in point.

What is your opinion of the correct interpretation? Take into account:

- the potential prejudice of disclosing previous convictions prior to a decision on the merits of the case
- the correct interpretation of section 252, considering that this section itself refers to its applicability only in cases not 'expressly provided for' by the Criminal Procedure Act, 1977 or any other Act
- whether the admissibility of an accused's previous convictions during the trial on the merits by applying section 252 to admit common law exceptions would potentially violate the accused's right to a fair trial in terms of section 35(3) of the Constitution and finally, whether following the interpretation that section 252 can

---

14 The words 'expressly provided for' in s 211 must, in our view, mean that only where the Criminal Procedure Act, 1977 specifically mentions particular exceptions, such as in ss 197 and 241, is the disclosure of an accused's previous convictions permitted. The disclosure of previous convictions prior to conviction has the potential to be extremely prejudicial to the accused, requiring a restrictive interpretation. We therefore respectfully disagree with the view of some authors (see DT Zeffertt and AP Paizes 2 ed (2009) at 249–51 and PJ Schwikkard and SE Van der Merwe 3 ed (2009) at 64) that the residuary provision contained in s 252 of the Criminal Procedure Act, 1977 is itself a provision that 'expressly' permits the application of common law admissibility exceptions, such as the admission of an accused's previous convictions as similar fact evidence. (See Discussion 19.1: Is section 252 an 'express provision' for the purposes of section 211 of the Criminal Procedure Act, 1977?)

15 Discussed below in 19.3.1.4.

16 Discussed below in 19.3.1.3.

17 Discussed below in 19.3.1.5.

> be regarded as an express provision effectively undermines most of the protections envisaged in section 211 of the Criminal Procedure Act, 1977.

The second exception provided for in section 211 provides, *inter alia*, that, '... where the fact of a previous conviction is an *element of any offence with which an accused is charged ...*' [emphasis added], then evidence that the accused has the relevant previous conviction will be admissible. An example here is the use of previous convictions when attempting to prove charges of **racketeering** in terms of the Prevention of Organised Crime Act 121 of 1998 (POCA).[18] To obtain a conviction on any of the racketeering offences contained in section 2(1) of the POCA, the prosecution has to prove, as one of the elements of racketeering, that the accused conducted an illegal enterprise 'through a pattern of racketeering activity'. To establish this 'pattern of racketeering activity', the State has to prove that the accused had previously committed two or more of the offences contained in Schedule 1 of the POCA.[19] The obvious way to prove the commission of these offences is, of course, by proving that the accused has previous convictions for the offences. The proof of these previous convictions against the accused would then be admissible in terms of section 211 of the Criminal Procedure Act, 1977 as they form part of the elements of the offence of racketeering.

19.3.1.3 The express provision in section 241 of the Criminal Procedure Act, 1977: evidence of previous conviction on charge of receiving stolen property

Section 241 reads as follows:

> If at criminal proceedings at which an accused is charged with receiving stolen property which he knew to be stolen property, it is proved that such property was found in the possession of the accused, evidence may at any stage of the proceedings be given that the accused was, within the five years immediately preceding the date on which he first appeared in a magistrates' court in respect of such charge, convicted of an offence involving fraud or dishonesty, and such evidence may be taken into consideration for the purpose of proving that the accused knew that the property found in his possession was stolen property: Provided that not less than three days' notice in writing shall be given to the accused that it is intended to adduce evidence of such previous conviction.

Section 241 must be read in conjunction with section 240 of the Criminal Procedure Act, 1977, which states, *inter alia*, that:

> ... at criminal proceedings at which an accused is charged with receiving stolen property which he knew to be stolen property, evidence may be given at any stage of the proceedings that the accused was, within the period of twelve months immediately preceding the date on which he first appeared in a magistrates' court in respect of such charge, found in possession of other stolen property ...

For the purposes of obtaining a conviction on the charge of receiving stolen property, an accused's previous convictions may only be used in the circumstances set out expressly in

---

18 S 2(1).
19 For the purposes of the racketeering charge, these offences are known as the underlying or predicate offences.

228 THE LAW OF EVIDENCE IN SOUTH AFRICA

section 241 of the Criminal Procedure Act, 1977. The State may prove that the property received for the purposes of section 240 was in fact stolen property using any means barring the production of the accused's previous convictions.[20] Should the State wish to use proof of the accused's previous convictions for any offence involving fraud and dishonesty to facilitate a conviction on a charge of receiving stolen property, then the requirements for section 241 must be strictly adhered to.

Sections 240 and 241 are applicable when the accused is charged with receiving stolen property. However, a difficulty arises when the accused is charged with other offences jointly such as theft.

In the English case of *R v Davies*,[21] which dealt with a case on similar English provisions, the Court held that the sections were applicable when the charge was 'substantially' one of receiving stolen property, but not if the prosecution were asking for a conviction on another charge as well. If the charges are theft and receiving stolen property as alternatives, it would be excessively technical to require the theft charge to be formally withdrawn since the accused could, in any case, be convicted of theft on the charge of receiving stolen property. This would mean that the prosecution need not formally withdraw the other charges before being able to use sections 240 and 241.

19.3.1.4 Lifting the shield: proving previous convictions, previous charges or bad character in terms of section 197 of the Criminal Procedure Act, 1977

In criminal proceedings, an accused person shall not be asked or required to answer any question which may show that he or she has previous convictions, previously been charged with another offence or that he or she is of bad character unless the requirements of section 197 of the Criminal Procedure Act, 1977 have been complied with. The full wording of section 197 reads as follows:

> **Privileges of accused when giving evidence**
> An accused who gives evidence at criminal proceedings shall not be asked or required to answer any question tending to show that he has committed or has been convicted of or has been charged with any offence other than the offence with which he is charged, or that he is of bad character, unless –
> (a) he or his legal representative asks any question of any witness with a view to establishing his own good character or he himself gives evidence of his own good character, or the nature or conduct of the defence is such as to involve imputation of the character of the complainant or any other witness for the prosecution;
> (b) he gives evidence against any other person charged with the same offence or an offence in respect of the same facts;
> (c) the proceedings against him are such as are described in section 240 or 241 and the notice under those sections has been given to him; or
> (d) the proof that he has committed or has been convicted of such other offence is admissible evidence to show that he is guilty of the offence with which he is charged.

This section of the Criminal Procedure Act, 1977 applies to the situation where an accused, testifying in his or her own defence, is cross-examined by the prosecution or questioned by

---

20 This is because s 240 does not *expressly* permit the use of previous convictions as required by s 211 of the Criminal Procedure Act, 1977. The one exception is where the accused has been given the requisite three days' notice to answer questions about whether he or she has been convicted or charged with being in possession of stolen property in terms of s 197(*c*) of the Criminal Procedure Act, 1977.

21 [1953] 1 QB 489, [1953] 1 All ER 341.

CHAPTER 19 CHARACTER EVIDENCE | 229

the court. In this situation, the accused should not be asked and does not have to answer questions relating to his or her previous convictions. There are, however, four exceptions to this rule.

In summary, the exceptions, which are contained in section 197(*a*)–(*d*), permit questions to establish an accused's previous convictions, previous charges or bad character, where:

1. the accused presents evidence of his or her own good character
2. the accused gives evidence against another accused
3. the proceedings relate to receiving stolen property (with reference to sections 240 and 241 of the Criminal Procedure Act, 1977)
4. the accused may legally be questioned on his or her previous convictions because a previous conviction forms part of or is very closely related to the charge the accused is facing.

The purpose of section 197 is to protect the accused against an attack on his or her character during cross-examination by the prosecution. The courts will not too readily infer that an accused person should be deprived of his or her section 197 protections merely because the accused has asked a witness relevant questions that coincidentally amount to an attack on that witness's character. For example, in *S v V*,[22] the complainant alleged that the accused was the only person with whom she had had intercourse. The accused cross-examined the complainant about her sexual relations with other men and, in fact, called a witness to testify that he, the witness, had also had intercourse with the complainant. The Court held that although his questions cast serious imputations on the complainant's character, they did not deprive the accused of his protection against cross-examination as to his bad character.

Section 197 provides the accused with protection (a shield) against having to answer certain questions. Not only is the accused allowed to refuse to answer such questions, but the prosecution is prohibited from asking these questions in the first place. Four types of questions are prohibited. These are questions specifically aimed at showing that the accused:

- has committed any offence other than the offence in the current charge; or
- has been charged with any offence other than the offence in the current charge; or
- has been convicted of any offence other than the offence in the current charge; or
- is of bad character.

In practice, only the fourth type of question seems to present difficulties when it comes to the interpretation of the provision. A question tends to show bad character if it suggests that the accused has a disposition to commit the offence in the current charge or even if it suggests that he or she has a tendency to behave in a certain criminal way.

Note that the shield does not protect the accused against questions relevant to an issue before court. Counsel may ask questions which are sufficiently probative of, in other words have the ability to prove, the question of the guilt of the accused in relation to the present charge even if they reveal that the accused had previously committed another offence.

There are four instances where the shield protecting the accused may be lifted. Subsections (*a*), (*b*), (*c*) and (*d*) of section 197 deal with these instances. We will now look at each of the four exceptions.

Subsection 197(*a*) provides that the shield is lifted where:

- the accused 'gives evidence of his own good character'[23]

---

22 1962 (3) SA 365 (E).
23 S 197(*a*) of the Criminal Procedure Act, 1977.

230 | THE LAW OF EVIDENCE IN SOUTH AFRICA

- the accused 'asks any question of any witness with a view to establishing his own good character',[24] which includes calling witnesses or cross-examining State witnesses to extract good character evidence
- 'the nature or conduct of the defence is such as to involve imputation of the character of the complainant or any other witness for the prosecution'.[25] Thus, if the accused attacks the character of the complainant or any State witness, he or she will lose the protection offered by section 197.

If a witness, while testifying for the defence, gives good character evidence about the accused out of his or her own free will, such evidence, called an *unsolicited statement*, will not cause the protective shield to fall away. Disclosing good character evidence in response to questions by the prosecution, under cross-examination, will also not cause the shield to fall away. Also, if disclosing good character evidence is an essential part of the accused's defence, the protection afforded by section 197 will remain in place.[26]

Subsection 197(*b*) provides that the shield is also lifted when the accused 'gives evidence against any other person charged with the same offence', in other words a co-accused, 'or an offence in respect of the same facts', [27] in other words an accomplice. This loss of protection will occur irrespective of the accused's intentions in giving such evidence.

DISCUSSION	Lifting the shield
19.2	For example, two accused are charged with dealing in dagga. Accused A testifies that he received a packet with unknown contents from accused B to keep for accused B. He avers he had no knowledge of the contents and thus places the entire blame squarely on accused B. In terms of section 197(*b*) the prosecution is permitted to present evidence that accused A has been convicted for possession and dealing in dagga on two previous occasions. By relying on section 197(*b*), the State can therefore lead evidence of accused A's previous convictions, despite the protection usually afforded by section 211 because his evidence implicates accused B, a co-accused.

Subsection 197(*c*) specifically excludes procedures under sections 240 and 241 of the Criminal Procedure Act, 1977 from the protection of section 197.

Sections 240 and 241 deal with instances where an accused is charged with receiving stolen property while knowing the goods to be stolen. Both sections allow the State to ask questions regarding the accused's possession of stolen goods on a previous occasion to prove that an accused knew the goods were stolen. Although intended to allow character questions only on aspects relevant to sections 240 and 241, the subsection does not directly express such a limitation, thus allowing for questioning on broader aspects of bad character.[28]

Subsection 197(*d*) allows the State to question the accused regarding a previous conviction if the purpose of the evidence (or the question aimed at extracting the evidence) is to show that the accused is guilty of the offence he or she is charged with in the present

---

24 S 197(*a*) of the Criminal Procedure Act, 1977.
25 S 197(*a*) of the Criminal Procedure Act, 1977.
26 Schwikkard and Van der Merwe 3 ed (2009) at 63 note 27, referring to *R v Hendrickz* 1933 TPD 451, *Spencer v R* 1946 NPD 696, *R v Persutam* 1934 TPD 253 and *S v V* 1962 (3) SA 365 (E).
27 S 197(*b*) of the Criminal Procedure Act, 1977.
28 Zeffertt and Paizes 2 ed (2009) at 262 and see 19.3.1.3 above.

case. According to section 197(*d*), an accused may be cross-examined as to previous offences if the purpose of such evidence is to 'show that he is guilty of the offence with which he is charged'. This provision usually applies to a situation where the accused has already been convicted of an offence and more serious consequences of that offence have come to light. An example of this is where an accused has been convicted of seriously assaulting the complainant and the complainant then dies as a result of complications of his or her injuries. In such a case the accused may be charged again, the charge in the second instance being murder or **culpable homicide**. Since the previous conviction of assault will form part of the necessary evidentiary matter on the murder charge, the prosecution will be permitted to ask the accused questions relating to the previous conviction.

This subsection effectively allows for the admission of similar fact evidence. In other words, the prosecution is entitled to cross-examine the accused to extract evidence of previous convictions if the previous convictions are of such a nature that they would be admissible in terms of the rules of similar fact evidence.[29]

19.3.1.5 Proving previous convictions for purposes of sentencing

In terms of section 271 of the Criminal Procedure Act, 1977 the previous convictions of an accused who has been convicted may be proved against the accused. The purpose of doing so at this stage is because previous convictions are an important factor that a court must take into account in imposing a suitable sentence. This is not controversial.

19.3.2 The character of the complainant in criminal cases

In theory, a complainant who testifies as a witness is in exactly the same position as any other witness in that evidence about his or her character is only admissible if it has a bearing on his or her credibility. However, in practice, the accused may want to prove that the complainant is an untruthful witness, due to the very fact that the complainant is alleging that he or she has been harmed by the accused's conduct. In instances where questions are allowed under cross-examination regarding the credibility of the complainant, they will be permitted only if they have a bearing on the general creditworthiness of the complainant, and not if they refer to specific instances where the complainant is alleged to have lied to the court. Questions about specific instances of untruthfulness have the potential to give rise to a 'fishing expedition' by the defence, which may turn into an investigation of collateral issues (something to be avoided).

A particularly contentious type of character evidence is evidence about the previous sexual experience of a complainant in a case of a sexual nature. Due to the complexity of this type of evidence, it is discussed in a separate section.[30]

19.4 The character of the plaintiff and defendant in civil cases

The character of a party in a civil case, whether plaintiff or defendant, is generally not relevant to the facts in issue. A party simply cannot attempt to prove a fact in issue by presenting evidence about either his or her own character or that of his or her opponent.

---

29 Although the methodology in deciding what evidence will be admissible under s 197(*d*) is similar to that used for determining the admissibility of similar fact evidence, this subsection must nevertheless be interpreted on its own merits, keeping in mind the danger of unnecessarily prejudicing the accused. See *S v Wilmot* 2002 (2) SACR 145 (SCA); *S v January* 1995 (1) SACR 202 (O); *S v Mthembu and Others* 1988 (1) SA 145 (A); *S v Mavuso* 1987 (3) SA 499 (A); *S v Mokoena* 1967 (1) SA 440 (A); *R v Lipschitz* 1921 AD 282; *R v Rorke* 1915 AD 145.

30 See ch 20 Evidence in sexual offences cases.

232 THE LAW OF EVIDENCE IN SOUTH AFRICA

However, there are exceptions to this general rule that apply if the character of a specific party is a fact in issue. A party to a matter does not necessarily need to testify, but where a party to a matter is called as a witness, the principles set out in 19.5 below apply.

Note, however, that the character of parties in civil matters may be relevant to the facts in issue in certain circumstances. For example, in defamation cases, the damage caused to the character of a plaintiff, including his or her reputation, is always a fact in issue. Also in seduction, breach of promise and adultery cases, the character of the parties may be facts in issue. In certain circumstances, the character of defendants in divorce cases may also be relevant although the focus in proving grounds for divorce will be on the conduct of the defendant and not on his or her character *per se*.

19.5 Character of witnesses: credibility

When assessing the evidence of a witness, a court will always make a finding on the credibility of the witness. Credibility, in the legal sense, is a term describing the believability of a witness. The character of a witness, to the extent that it has an impact on the witness's credibility, is therefore a factor that a court will take into account when deciding whether to rely on the witness's testimony. An opposing party, while cross-examining a witness, cannot ordinarily lead evidence of facts which are not relevant to the matter before the court, but which are relevant only to show that the witness is an untruthful person. A party's case can often depend on whether the court accepts or believes an important witness's testimony, and this can depend on the witness's credibility.[31] Therefore, to the extent that it affects credibility, the character of a witness is usually relevant.

One of the objectives of cross-examination may be to attack the credibility of the opponent's witnesses and, by doing so, to diminish the value of the evidence presented by them. As a result, a party (or the legal practitioner representing them) is generally allowed to ask questions aimed at achieving this. Some examples of questions asked during cross-examination in order to attack the credibility of a specific witness follow below:

- 'Is it correct that you were not wearing your glasses on the night in question and that you cannot see further than two metres without your glasses?' (The question highlights the physical or psychological characteristics of the witness, which may affect his or her credibility).
- 'I put it to you that you are a close friend of the accused and that you would be willing to say anything to ensure that he is found not guilty?' (The question is aimed at showing bias or partiality of the witness, which may undermine his or her credibility).
- 'Did your mother tell you to say to the policeman that the accused touched your private parts?' (This question is aimed at indicating that the witness is susceptible to manipulation and, as a result, is giving untruthful evidence).
- 'I have a witness who will testify that he overheard a conversation where the plaintiff offered to pay you a large sum of money if you pretend that you cannot remember the events of the evening.' (The purpose of this question is to show that the witness has been bribed to testify in a certain manner.)

However, questions attacking the credibility of a witness may not be so far removed from the facts in issue that they allow the cross-examiner to venture into collateral issues. These

---

31 See Part Six for more on credibility and its importance.

are issues that are not sufficiently related to the facts in issue for questions about them to be relevant and, therefore, admissible.[32]

Table 19.1 Character evidence

Principles defining character evidence in criminal proceedings	
Character evidence consists of:	• Disposition (a person's character traits) • Reputation (as perceived by a person's peers)
S 252 CPA incorporates the CL as at 30 May 1961	Character inadmissible because it has low probative value and high prejudice: • Criminal propensity: character inadmissible where it merely shows that an accused has a propensity to commit a crime; but • It is exceptionally admissible where it is relevant to a fact in issue (relevant to the issue of credibility as well as guilt).
Previous convictions: S 211 read with ss 240 and 241 CPA	Previous convictions are inadmissible except where the accused: • is charged with receiving stolen property (s 240 and 241) • is charged with an offence where the previous conviction is relevant to a fact-in-issue of the offence.
Lifting the accused's shield: S 197(a)–(b) CPA	The State may not lead evidence of an accused's bad character at trial except where the accused is called as a witness and: • gives evidence of good character; or • gives character evidence against a co-accused; or • is charged with receiving stolen property; or • is charged with an offence where a previous offence is relevant to a fact-in-issue of the offence The State may adduce evidence of, or cross-examine the accused on, character if any of these four exceptions apply.
The sexual history of the accused and/or complainant in sexual offences: S 227(2) CPA	No evidence of previous sexual history of any person shall be directly adduced, or adduced through cross-examination, where an accused has been charged with a sexual offence unless: • the court grants leave to adduce such evidence; • the evidence has been introduced by the prosecution. Sexual history evidence may only be adduced where it is relevant to a fact in issue and in the interests of justice.

THIS CHAPTER IN ESSENCE

1   Character evidence is evidence about a variety of a person's character traits, also referred to as a person's disposition.
2   Generally, character evidence is inadmissible because of its low probative value and high potential for prejudice.
3   Character evidence may be relevant and admissible in the following two particular instances:
  3.1   Where a characteristic or character trait of a party to the dispute is relevant to the facts of the dispute

---

[32] See Part Five for more on cross-examination and ch 22 in this Part for more on collateral evidence.

3.2 Where evidence regarding the character of a specific witness sheds light on the credibility of such a witness.

4 In criminal matters, the defence may present evidence regarding the good character of the accused provided that the character evidence is relevant to an issue before the court.

5 In terms of the common law, the State may not present propensity evidence because this type of evidence only shows that the accused is the kind of person who is inclined or predisposed to act in a certain manner. However, if the accused leads evidence of his or her good character, the prosecution is allowed to present evidence of the accused's bad character.

6 In terms of section 211 of the Criminal Procedure Act, 1977, evidence regarding previous convictions of the accused is not admissible, save for two exceptions:
   6.1 Where other provisions of the Criminal Procedure Act, 1977 make it admissible
   6.2 Where the previous conviction forms part of the crime of which the accused is charged in the current instance.

7 In terms of section 241, read with section 240, of the Criminal Procedure Act, 1977, evidence of previous convictions on charges of receiving stolen property is admissible.

8 Section 197 of the Criminal Procedure Act, 1977 protects an accused against propensity evidence, but not against questions regarding his or her character that are relevant for another purpose. However, this protection may be lifted in certain circumstances, which are outlined in subsections (a)–(d).

9 In terms of section 271 of the Criminal Procedure Act, 1977 it is permissible to prove the previous convictions of an accused who has been convicted for sentencing purposes.

10 Questions posed to the complainant under cross-examination regarding his or her credibility will only be permitted if they have a bearing on the general creditworthiness of the complainant.

11 Generally, character evidence of a party in a civil case is not relevant and therefore inadmissible. However, such evidence may be relevant and admissible if the character of a specific party is a fact in issue.

12 When deciding whether or not to rely on a witness's testimony, a court will take the character of a witness, to the extent that it has an impact on the witness's credibility, into account.

Chapter 20

Evidence in sexual offences cases

20.1	**Introduction**	**235**
20.2	**Previous consistent statement**	**235**
	20.2.1 Common law position	236
	20.2.1.1 The victim should make the complaint voluntarily	236
	20.2.1.2 The victim should make the complaint at the first reasonable opportunity	236
	20.2.1.3 The complainant must testify	237
	20.2.2 Statutory position	237
20.3	**Evidence regarding previous sexual history**	**238**
	20.3.1 Common law position	238
	20.3.2 Statutory position	239
	20.3.2.1 1989 amendments	239
	20.3.2.2 2007 amendments	240
20.4	**Cautionary rule**	**241**
	20.4.1 Common law	241
	20.4.2 Judicial abolition of the cautionary rule	241
	20.4.3 Statutory abolition of the cautionary rule	242

20.1 Introduction

Several specific, although not uncontroversial, rules have developed with regard to evidence in sexual offences cases. This chapter will discuss the three most important ones which are:

- the rule regarding the admissibility of a previous consistent statement by a complainant
- the rule regarding the admissibility of the sexual history of a complainant
- the cautionary rule as it was applicable to a complainant in cases of a sexual nature.

20.2 Previous consistent statement

One of the rules dealing with the exclusion of evidence, referred to as the rule against previous consistent statements, provides that a witness may not use a statement that he or she made on a previous occasion to strengthen or corroborate a statement which he or she is presently making in court. The reason for this rule is that the previous statement is considered to be irrelevant because it does not add anything of value to the witness's current testimony. It is simply a repetition of it. This rule has also been called the rule against self-corroboration because it prevents a situation arising where a witness corroborates his or her

THE LAW OF EVIDENCE IN SOUTH AFRICA

own evidence by referring to something that he or she said on a previous occasion. Repeating the same statement does not necessarily increase the truth of the statement as a lie can be repeated just as easily as the truth. Allowing such statements would merely give a witness the opportunity to fabricate or manufacture evidence designed to make his or her present testimony in court seem more truthful.

However, there are a number of exceptions to this rule. One such exception is the rule with regard to a recent complaint in cases of a sexual nature. The rule has traditionally been regulated by the common law, but legislation in the form of the Criminal Law (Sexual Offences and Related Matters) Amendment Act 32 of 2007 (hereafter referred to as the Sexual Offences Act, 2007) brought about changes to the common law rule.

20.2.1 Common law position

The rule regarding the admissibility of a previous consistent statement in a case of a sexual nature has been inherited from the English law and has a somewhat peculiar history. In the Middle Ages, it was of vital importance that a victim of rape should raise a hue and cry if she was to have any success in having the accused tried for rape. This meant that the victim was expected to:

> go with hue and cry, to the neighbouring townships and there show the injury done her to men of good repute, the blood and clothing stained with blood, and her torn garments ...[1]

The law thus specifically required the victim of a sexual assault to make a statement at the time of the sexual assault which would then be consistent with the evidence given later in court. The law developed somewhat and evidence of a previous statement is no longer required, but remains permissible. It thus creates an exception to the rule that generally does not allow such statements.

For this exception to the rule against previous consistent statements to apply, a number of conditions have to be met.

20.2.1.1 The victim should make the complaint voluntarily

This requirement gives rise to the problem of determining whether the statement was, in fact, a complaint or whether it could rather be seen as a mere conversation. It is obviously difficult to lay down exact rules as to when the statement will amount to a complaint and when it will merely form part of a conversation. This could be avoided if the law were to refer to a 'report' of the incident instead of a 'complaint'.

Complaints elicited by questions of an intimidating, inducing or leading nature would be inadmissible. This was confirmed in *S v T*[2] where a complaint was excluded as it was elicited as a result of threats of force made to the victim by the victim's mother. It is difficult to determine what amount of prompting would be acceptable so as to keep within the required parameters of voluntariness. It is a matter that only the presiding officer can decide after proper consideration of all the relevant circumstances.

20.2.1.2 The victim should make the complaint at the first reasonable opportunity

This requirement is the aspect of the rule that is most closely related to the old, discredited hue and cry rule. The expectation is that a complaint should be made 'at the

---

1   H de Bracton *On the Laws and Customs of England* Vol. 1 (1968) at 415.
2   1963 (1) SA 484 (A).

CHAPTER 20   EVIDENCE IN SEXUAL OFFENCES CASES | **237**

earliest opportunity'[3] to the first appropriate person. This aspect of the rule has been largely discredited.[4] A number of other factors which mitigate against reporting the assault at the first opportunity are now also taken into account, including the absence of any person the victim may have spoken to, whether the victim realised the immoral nature of the assault and psychological reasons for not reporting the matter.[5] This aspect is also decided on a case-by-case basis, the presiding officer taking into account all the relevant factors.

20.2.1.3   The complainant must testify

This requirement flows from the fact that the present rule is not an exception to the hearsay rule. If the complainant does not him- or herself give evidence, any reference to the complaint would amount to an infringement of the hearsay rule and would be inadmissible. Not only would the contents of the complaint be inadmissible, but so would the fact that the complaint was made at all.[6]

20.2.2   Statutory position

Sections 58 and 59 of the Sexual Offences Act, 2007 are applicable. Evidence that a complainant reported the alleged sexual offence to another person neither proves the crime against the accused nor the content of the complaint. It only proves that the complainant has been consistent in his or her version of the events.

However, where the complainant did not make a complaint or only did so a considerable time after the alleged attack, then 'the defence usually succeeds with an argument that a negative inference should be drawn about the credibility of the complainant'.[7] The basis for this defence is that if the rape really had happened, the complainant would have reported it and would have done so earlier. This argument clearly has a detrimental effect on the State's case.

The South African Law Commission (SALC) notes in its report that this position 'reflects assumptions about the psychological effects of rape and other sexual offences ... that are not borne out by recent empirical advances'.[8] The report also acknowledges the findings in several empirical studies regarding the psychological effects of rape. These studies indicate that complainants in cases of a sexual nature may refrain from reporting a sexual crime or may do so only after a considerable time for reasons that have nothing at all to do with their credibility. In accordance with the suggestions of the SALC report, sections 58 and 59 of the Sexual Offences Act, 2007 contain specific provisions regarding previous consistent statements in cases of a sexual nature.

Section 58 states that evidence regarding a relevant previous consistent statement by a complainant in a sexual offence will be admissible. This means that if all the other requirements for relevance are met, then such a statement will remain admissible. The important change brought about by this section, however, is its provision that a court may not draw a negative inference from the fact that no previous statement has been made.

---

3   *R v C* 1955 (4) SA 40 (N) at 41H.
4   *R v Valentine* [1996] 2 Cr App R 213 at 224 and *S v M* 1999 (1) SACR 664 (C) at 669F–H.
5   *S v Cornick and Another* 2007 (2) SACR 115 (SCA). A period of 19 years lapsed between the incident and the report.
6   *R v Wallwork* [1958] 42 Cr App R 153.
7   SALC Project 107 Discussion Paper 102 *Sexual offences: Process and procedure* (2002) at para 34.4.1.1.
8   Discussion Paper 102 at para 34.4.2.1.

THE LAW OF EVIDENCE IN SOUTH AFRICA

Therefore, this provision applies to a situation where a complainant did not complain at all regarding the alleged attack.[9]

Section 59 provides that 'the court may not draw [a negative] inference only from the length of any delay between the alleged commission of such offence and the reporting thereof'. This means, in essence, that the detrimental effect of the common law rule has now been removed.

Although a detailed discussion of the effect of these two sections is beyond the scope of this chapter, note the following points:

- The legislation does not remove the requirement that the victim should make the complaint voluntarily. A complaint obtained by coercion, violence or a threat of violence will lack reliability. A complaint obtained in such a manner may also be inadmissible in terms of section 35(5) of the Constitution.
- The common law requirement that the complainant him- or herself must testify has also not been altered by the amendment. If the complainant fails to testify, the evidence about the complaint will be hearsay evidence and, unless it is admitted as an exception in terms of section 3 of the Law of Evidence Amendment Act 45 of 1988, it will be inadmissible.
- The effect of the legislative provisions is that the absence of a complaint (section 58) or the delay between the alleged attack and the complaint (section 59) is just one of the factors that the court may take into account and should not be the only factor. The court must still decide whether the evidence against the accused, considered in its totality, gives rise to reasonable doubt.[10]
- There is no longer a statutory time limit on prosecuting cases of sexual assault.[11]

20.3 Evidence regarding previous sexual history

Evidence about a witness's sexual history is regarded as character evidence. As a general rule, the complainant in a sexual case is an ordinary witness and, therefore, evidence regarding his or her character should, theoretically, not be admissible. However, specific common law rules have developed regarding evidence about the previous sexual history of the complainant. These rules are the subject of much controversy and dispute and some amendments to the common law rules were brought about by legislation. However, the situation remained unsatisfactory and further legislative amendments, which were enacted in 2007, were considered necessary.

20.3.1 Common law position

Historically, in common law, evidence regarding the past sexual activities of the complainant with the accused was admissible. Evidence regarding his or her sexual acts with other people was not admissible during evidence-in-chief. However, questions about this area were

---

9   See Du Toit [Service Issue 52, 2014] 23–21 where he expresses the view that section 58 now permits previous consistent statements to be admissible only for the purposes of proving consistency, not as independent evidence of the act alleged. This appears to have been the approach adopted by the Supreme Court of Appeal in *S v Kruger* (612/13) [2013] ZASCA 198 (unreported, SCA case, 2 December 2013).

10 For a detailed discussion of the effects of ss 58 and 59 on the common law position, see PJ Schwikkard and SE van der Merwe *Principles of Evidence* 3 ed (2009) at 108–119.

11 In *Levenstein and Others v Estate of the Late Sidney Lewis Frankel and Others* 2018 ZACC 16 the Constitutional Court confirmed the 'declaration of constitutional invalidity of section 18 of the Criminal Procedure Act 51 of 1977' (para 89), which placed a time limit of 20 years on the prosecution of sexual offence cases (other than rape in respect of which there is no time limit).

CHAPTER 20   EVIDENCE IN SEXUAL OFFENCES CASES | 239

admissible during cross-examination as such evidence was regarded as relevant to the issue of consent.

The use of evidence about the sexual history of a complainant for the purpose of proving consent on the part of the complainant in the present rape trial was often criticised because it was said to be based on a stereotypical view that an unchaste woman[12] is more likely to consent to sexual intercourse. The second purpose for which this type of evidence was used was to attack the credibility of the complainant by implying that an unchaste woman had a propensity for dishonesty and was more likely to lie under oath, making her less worthy of belief.

The common law position was severely criticised on a number of grounds, not least of which were:

- that evidence of sexual history is largely irrelevant
- that such evidence is inadmissible in other cases
- that it subjects the complainant to a traumatic and humiliating experience.[13]

20.3.2   Statutory position

Until the common law position was first amended by the Criminal Law and Criminal Procedure Law Amendment Act 39 of 1989, the statutory provisions in the Criminal Procedure Act[14] regulating the admissibility of sexual history evidence corresponded with the common law position as set out above and was, therefore, subject to the same shortcomings. The section was subsequently amended twice, first in 1989 and again in 2007.

20.3.2.1   1989 amendments

Section 227 was amended in 1989 to the extent that evidence regarding the complainant's sexual experience with the accused remained relevant and as such admissible. However, the defence had to make a special application to the court to tender evidence about the complainant's sexual history with other men. This application had to be made *in camera* and relevance was the sole criterion according to which a court could decide to grant such an application. Section 227(2) thus provided that an application had to be made and that the court had a discretion to admit or deny such evidence.

The SALC in its *Women and Sexual Offences Report*[15] acknowledged that this rule, even in its amended form, was based on outdated views from an era when public morals dictated that no decent woman had sexual intercourse outside of marriage. Another significant problem with the rule was that its application also had the effect of humiliating and intimidating the complainant. This, in turn, discouraged victims from laying charges. Unfortunately, the changes to section 227 which flowed from the SALC's recommendations did not do much to alleviate the position of rape complainants regarding evidence of their past sexual history.

---

12 This discussion is intended to be inclusive of men and women, but for the sake of convenience the complainant in a sexual case will be referred to as a woman hereafter. It is more common that the complainant in a sexual case is a woman than a man.

13 In *S v Staggie and Another* 2003 (1) BCLR 43 (C) the High Court articulated its concern that greater assistance should be provided to those who report rape and other sexual offences. Sarkin AJ reasoned that if such complainants saw that they were spared public humiliation and embarrassment, they might be more willing to lay charges and to be witnesses in sexual offences cases. This is imperative, he held, as the success of the legal system depends, in part, on the cooperation of the community.

14 S 227 of the Criminal Procedure Act 51 of 1977.

15 SALC *Women and Sexual Offences in South Africa Report* (1985).

240 | THE LAW OF EVIDENCE IN SOUTH AFRICA

In *S v M*,[16] the appellant had been convicted in a regional court of the rape of his six-year-old daughter. He appealed to the High Court and also applied to lead evidence of two further witnesses. One witness would testify that he had had a sexual relationship with the complainant and the other would testify that the complainant had admitted to being influenced by her mother and grandmother to incriminate the accused.

Section 227 came under vigorous attack from the Supreme Court of Appeal. The Court specifically noted that:

> (t)he members of this Court are not aware of any instance where section 227(2) has been applied in this country. It seems likely that it is more honoured in the breach than in the observance.[17]

The Court then set out a number of guidelines for the admissibility of such evidence, several of which were subsequently incorporated in the 2007 amendment of section 227.

20.3.2.2 2007 amendments

The proposals of the South African Law Reform Commission[18] regarding the amendment of section 227 were enacted on 16 December 2007 when the Sexual Offences Act, 2007 came into force. The Act brought about significant changes to section 227 although it retained some similarities.

The similarities are as follows:

- The new section retains a judicial discretion as the mechanism for determining whether the evidence about the previous sexual conduct of the complainant is admissible.
- The basis of the court's discretion remains relevance as it was in the previous version of the section. This means that a court may only allow the evidence if the evidence is relevant to a fact in issue.

The most important difference between the current section 227 and the previous one is that the provision now sets out a number of factors which a court must consider when it determines if the evidence is relevant. These factors are contained in section 227(5) which provides that:

> (5) In determining whether evidence or questioning ... is relevant to the proceedings pending before the court, the court shall take into account whether such evidence or questioning –
> (a) is in the interests of justice, with due regard to the accused's right to a fair trial;
> (b) is in the interest of society in encouraging the reporting of sexual offences;
> (c) relates to a specific instance of sexual activity relevant to a fact in issue;
> (d) is likely to rebut evidence previously adduced by the prosecution;
> (e) is fundamental to the accused's defence;
> (f) is not substantially outweighed by its potential prejudice to the complainant's personal dignity and right to privacy; or

---

16 2002 (2) SACR 411 (SCA).

17 *S v M* 2002 (2) SACR 411 (SCA) at para 17(6) at 422H. In *S v Mkhize* (CC55/11 D) [2011] ZAKZDHC 62; 2012 (2) SACR 90 (KZD) (8 December 2011) the Court handled an application in terms of section 227 to cross-examine and question the complainant on an incident of a sexual nature which is alleged to have occurred a week or two after the arrest of the accused and the alleged rape of the complainant.

18 SALC Project 107.

CHAPTER 20 EVIDENCE IN SEXUAL OFFENCES CASES

(g) is likely to explain the presence of semen or the source of pregnancy or disease or any injury to the complainant, where it is relevant to a fact in issue.

Section 227(6) goes on to provide that a court is not to grant a section 227(2) application if the purpose of the application is to lead evidence to show, first, that the complainant is more likely to have consented to the offence, or second, is less credible.

DISCUSSION 20.1

Is section 227 constitutional?

It is possible that the amended section 227 may be subjected to a constitutional challenge related to the accused's right to a fair trial contained in section 35(3) of the Constitution, in particular the right to adduce and challenge evidence in section 35(3) (*i*). Experience from other jurisdictions, specifically Canada[19] and the United Kingdom,[20] indicates that such a challenge may arise in South Africa as well.

In both these jurisdictions an accused in a sexual offence case challenged the constitutionality of legislation that excluded evidence regarding the previous sexual conduct of the complainant. The basis of the challenge was that the exclusion of such evidence infringed the right of the accused to present evidence that may prove his innocence.

Commentator Du Toit, however, submits that the section is not unconstitutional as the first of these factors, the 'interests of justice', as well as the common law test for relevance, would require a proper ventilation of the evidence (i.e. this would allow the accused to adduce and challenge evidence).[21]

20.4 Cautionary rule

The cautionary rule, as it is applicable to complainants in cases of a sexual nature, is discussed below.[22]

20.4.1 Common law

Evidence of the complainant in a case of a sexual nature was one instance where, in terms of the common law, the court was required to apply a cautionary approach. The rule required a court to exercise caution when evaluating the evidence of a complainant in a sexual case and to seek some safeguard before relying on it.

20.4.2 Judicial abolition of the cautionary rule

The cautionary rule regarding evidence of complainants in sexual offences was abolished by the Supreme Court of Appeal in *S v Jackson*.[23] In this landmark judgment, Olivier JA stated that this rule was based on outdated and unjust stereotypes about complainants in sexual

---

19 *R v Seaboyer; R v Gayme* (1991) 83 DLR (4th) 193; [1991] 2 SCR 577.

20 *R v A (No 2)* [2001] UKHL 25; [2002] 1 AC 45 (HL). For an analysis of the European position under the European Convention on Human Rights, see B Emmerson, A Ashworth and A MacDonald *Human Rights and Criminal Justice* 2 ed (2007) at 151–152.

21 E du Toit, FJ de Jager, A Paizes, A St Q Skeen and S van der Merwe *Commentary on the Criminal Procedure Act* (1987) [Service Issue 49-2012] 24-100E.

22 See ch 41 The cautionary rule.

23 1998 (1) SACR 470 (SCA).

cases. While a cautionary approach may be called for in a specific case, a general cautionary rule in cases of this nature should be rejected.

20.4.3 Statutory abolition of the cautionary rule

The judicial abolition of the cautionary rule regarding the evidence of the complainant in cases of a sexual nature was confirmed by section 60 of the Sexual Offences Act, 2007 which provides as follows:

> Notwithstanding any other law, a court may not treat the evidence of a complainant in criminal proceedings involving the alleged commission of a sexual offence pending before that court, with caution, on account of the nature of the offence.

It is important to note here that the legislative provision does not prevent the court from applying a cautionary rule on a basis other than the nature of the offence. Where a cautionary approach is called for because the witness is a single witness, for example, the court may still approach the evidence with caution. In most cases where the alleged offence is one of a sexual nature, the complainant is indeed a single witness and thus a cautionary approach may sometimes be necessary. However, it is no longer the case that the rule will automatically apply in cases of a sexual nature.

Furthermore, it should always be kept in mind that the application of a cautionary approach must be in line with the overall duty of the court to decide whether the evidence against the accused establishes his guilt beyond reasonable doubt and care must be taken not to apply a stricter test inadvertently.

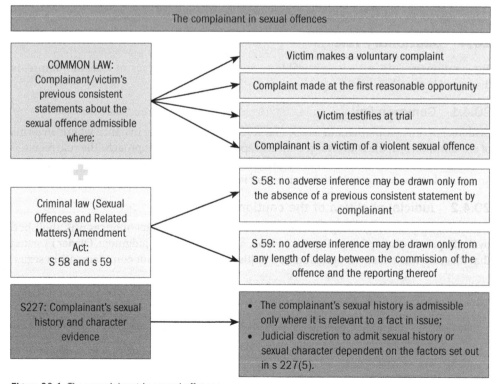

Figure 20.1 The complainant in sexual offences

CHAPTER 20 EVIDENCE IN SEXUAL OFFENCES CASES

THIS CHAPTER IN ESSENCE

1 In terms of the common law, evidence of a previous consistent statement is not required in sexual offence cases, but may be permissible if the following conditions are met:
   1.1 The previous consistent statement should have been made voluntarily.
   1.2 The previous consistent statement should have been made at the first reasonable opportunity.
   1.3 The complainant must testify him- or herself.
2 Section 58 of the Sexual Offences Act, 2007 provides that evidence regarding a relevant previous consistent statement by a complainant in sexual offence cases will be admissible.
3 Section 59 of the Sexual Offences Act, 2007 provides that the court may not draw any negative inference from the delay between the commission of the crime and when it was reported by the victim.
4 The provisions in the Sexual Offences Act, 2007 have not changed the first two common law requirements above. However, they have affected the third requirement in that the absence of a complaint or the delay between the alleged attack and the complaint is just one of the factors that the court may take into account and should not be the only factor.
5 Previously, in terms of the common law, evidence regarding the past sexual activities of the complainant with the accused was admissible. However, this position was severely criticised and subsequently amended by way of statute, first in 1989 (section 227(2) of the Criminal Law and Criminal Procedure Amendment Act 39 of 1989) and again in 2007.
6 The effect of the 1989 amendment was that evidence regarding the complainant's sexual experience with the accused remained relevant and admissible. However, the defence had to make a special application to the court to tender evidence about the complainant's sexual history with other partners.
7 The 2007 amendment provides that, when determining whether the evidence in sexual cases is relevant, a court must consider whether the evidence is:
   7.1 in the interests of justice
   7.2 in the interest of society in encouraging the reporting of sexual offences
   7.3 relates to a specific instance of sexual activity relevant to a fact in issue
   7.4 likely to rebut evidence previously adduced by the prosecution
   7.5 fundamental to the accused's defence
   7.6 not substantially outweighed by its potential prejudice to the complainant's personal dignity and right to privacy
   7.7 likely to explain the presence of semen, the source of pregnancy or disease or any injury to the complainant where it is relevant to a fact in issue.
8 A court may now not grant a section 227(2) Criminal Law and Criminal Procedure Law Amendment Act, 1989 application if its only purpose is to lead evidence to show that either the complainant is more likely to have consented to the offence or is less credible.
9 At common law, the courts were required to apply a cautionary approach when dealing with evidence of the complainant in cases of a sexual nature. This rule was, however, abolished in S v Jackson 1998 (1) SACR 470 (SCA). This abolition was confirmed by section 60 of the Sexual Offences Act, 2007.

Chapter 21

Self-corroboration

21.1 Introduction 244

21.2 Basis of the rule against self-corroboration 244

21.3 Purpose of the rule against self-corroboration 244

21.4 Scope and ambit of the rule against self-corroboration 245

21.1 Introduction

An important characteristic of corroborating evidence[1] is that it must originate from an independent source. In other words, it must not be from the same source as the evidence that requires corroboration. This rule is known as the *rule against self-corroboration*.[2]

21.2 Basis of the rule against self-corroboration

The rule against self-corroboration is based on the same evidentiary principle as the rule against the admissibility of previous consistent statements. This principle states that evidence regarding what a witness said on a previous occasion cannot be led to support something which the witness is currently saying in court. This is because a lie can be as easily repeated or self-corroborated as the truth. The rule against self-corroboration is also referred to as the *rule against narrative or the rule against self-serving statements*. It is not embodied in statutory law and is consequently governed by common law principles.

21.3 Purpose of the rule against self-corroboration

The rule against self-corroboration is aimed both at the admissibility of evidence and at the weight or probative value of the evidence.

Because of its strong connection with the rule against previous consistent statements, this rule has the effect of rendering self-corroborating evidence irrelevant. Such evidence does not help to prove a fact in issue as mere repetition does not make a statement more truthful.

The rule against self-corroboration also has bearing on the weight of evidence. It prohibits evidence emanating from a specific witness being used to bolster or strengthen

---

1 See ch 42 Corroboration. The Supreme Court of Appeal endorsed the Appellate Division authorities in *S v Scott-Crossley* 2008 (1) SACR 223 (SCA) at para 17.

2 See also ch 24 Previous consistent statements.

the credibility of that same witness. The credibility of certain witnesses plays an important role in determining the weight or probative value of the evidence presented by those witnesses so, in this sense then, the rule against self-corroboration also has an impact on the process of weighing up evidence.

21.4 Scope and ambit of the rule against self-corroboration

The rule against self-corroboration, however, is limited to the oral or written statements made by the specific witness only. This rule does not affect real evidence. For example, the physical injuries of a victim of an alleged assault may be admissible as real evidence to corroborate his or her later oral testimony regarding his or her injuries. Communications, whether oral or in writing, that originate from a witness may be self-serving in the sense that the witness may have made the statements or communications to use them at a later stage as corroboration. Evidence of injuries, however, does not emanate from the victim unless, of course, they are self-inflicted. As such, this evidence is admissible as an exception to the rule against self-corroboration.

THIS CHAPTER IN ESSENCE

1 Evidence regarding something a witness said on a previous occasion cannot be led to support something that the witness is currently saying in court. Self-corroborating evidence is therefore irrelevant and inadmissible.

2 The rule against self-corroboration applies to the oral or written statements of a witness and does not apply to real evidence.

Chapter 22

Collateral evidence

22.1 Introduction 246

22.2 Legal rules applicable to collateral evidence 247
    22.2.1 Questions as to credit 247
        22.2.1.1 Previous convictions 248
        22.2.1.2 Bias 249

22.1 Introduction

The admissibility of evidence depends on its relevance.[1] The exclusionary rule contained in section 210 of the Criminal Procedure Act 51 of 1977 specifies:

> No evidence as to any fact, matter or thing shall be admissible which is irrelevant or immaterial and which cannot conduce to prove or disprove any point or fact at issue in criminal proceedings.

Therefore evidence, or a question aimed at extracting evidence, that is not relevant to an issue before the court is generally inadmissible. The rationale for this is that it will waste both time and money pursuing something that is of no assistance to the court in deciding the matter before it. Although this rule seems, on the face of it, to be absolute, there is a type of evidence that does not relate directly to a point or a fact in issue but is nevertheless admissible – this is collateral evidence.

Collateral evidence or collateral fact evidence, as it is sometimes called, is evidence of facts that are, on the face of it, not connected to the issue or matter in dispute. The general rule is that collateral evidence is inadmissible. However, there are circumstances where it is admissible because it relates to an issue that is, or becomes, relevant.

Let us consider a practical example. In a case involving a traffic offence, the traffic officer who gave evidence against the accused and who had confronted the accused at the scene of the offence was exceptionally tall. The case was adjourned so that the accused driver could call a witness in his defence. After the witness corroborated the accused's version in his evidence-in-chief, the prosecutor asked only two questions:

Q: Did you notice anything unusual about the physical characteristics of the traffic officer?

A: No.

Q: Can you describe how tall he was?

A: Yes. He was of medium height.

This last answer relating to the height of the witness, a matter entirely unconnected to the offence, indicated either that the witness's powers of observation or recollection

---

1 Relevance is discussed in detail in ch 15 The general test for relevance.

CHAPTER 22   COLLATERAL EVIDENCE | 247

were lacking or that he was lying and was not at the scene at all. It often happens that where a witness is coached as to what to testify in favour of a party, the person is not filled in on background matters.

22.2   Legal rules applicable to collateral evidence

Evidence may be admitted where it affects the cogency of other evidence although it does not itself relate to a fact that must be proved or disproved by either of the parties. Thus, collateral evidence is admissible if it relates to the credibility of a witness or to the question of whether certain other evidence is admissible, such as evidence relating to whether or not a confession was voluntary.

22.2.1   Questions as to credit

In cross-examination, questions that relate to the credibility of the witness are called *questions as to credit*. Where a cross-examiner asks such questions, the rule is that the witness's answers to the question are final and no other evidence may be led by the cross-examiner to contradict the reply given.[2] For example, in *S v Zwane and Others*,[3] the cross-examiner asked a witness if he had been disbelieved in other court proceedings and he denied it. The Court ruled that the cross-examiner could then not put portions of the record to the witness to contradict him.

This rule is aimed at preventing endless collateral issues from arising. However, it is difficult to decide what constitutes a collateral issue. For this purpose, the test from *Attorney-General v Hitchcock*[4] is used to decide what a collateral issue is:

> If the answer of a witness is a matter which you would be allowed on your own part to prove in evidence – if it had such a connection with the issues, that you would be allowed to give it in evidence – then it is a matter on which you may contradict him.

Of course, the test for what 'you would be allowed on your own part to prove in evidence' is whether the evidence is relevant to an issue. Therefore, whether collateral evidence is admissible depends, ultimately, on whether it is relevant. 'Relevance to the issue before the court determines whether or not evidence is collateral ...'.[5]

DISCUSSION	Collateral evidence: the music of Frank Sinatra[6]
22.1	Mr Smith, a witness in an assault case that took place in a tavern one night was suspected of fabricating his version. If counsel for the defence suspects that Mr Smith had not been in the tavern at all on the day of the incident and had memorised the incident as narrated to him by the plaintiff, he could test this theory by using collateral evidence. In this case, the music of Frank Sinatra was the only music played the whole night in the tavern as a tribute to the singer following his recent death. Everyone who had been present in the tavern that evening would have known this. The fact that Sinatra's music was played the whole evening, including at the time of the assault, is of no assistance to prove or disprove the elements of assault. It is therefore collateral

---

2   *S v Damalis* 1984 (2) SA 105 (T) at 110D–E.
3   1993 (1) SACR 748 (W).
4   (1847) 1 Exch 91 at 99.
5   *S v Zwane and Others* 1993 (1) SACR 748 (W) at 750G.
6   Extract from R Palmer and D Mcquoid-Mason *Basic Trial Advocacy Skills* (2000) at 84–85.

THE LAW OF EVIDENCE IN SOUTH AFRICA

> evidence. However, this collateral fact can be used to show that Mr Smith was not present at the time of the assault and is an untruthful witness.
>
> If Mr Smith has been pre-briefed by the plaintiff to give a false version, the briefing would have covered the assault incident in detail but would most probably not have included a briefing on what background music had been playing at the time of the assault.
>
> The cross-examination of Mr Smith:
>
> Counsel: Mr Smith, on your evidence-in-chief, you arrived at the tavern at 7.30 pm and stayed until midnight. Is that correct?
>
> Mr Smith: Yes
>
> Counsel: And the assault took place at about 10pm?
>
> Mr Smith: That's right.
>
> Counsel: Was any music played in the tavern that evening?
>
> Mr Smith: Well, yes, I think so.
>
> Counsel: You're not sure?
>
> Mr Smith: I'm pretty sure background music was played.
>
> Counsel: What kind of background music?
>
> Mr Smith: The usual kind of stuff.
>
> Counsel: What is 'the usual kind of stuff'?
>
> Mr Smith: A lot of rock, pop – just a selection.
>
> Counsel: You don't remember the music of any specific singer or band?
>
> Mr Smith: No, not really.
>
> Magistrate: Counsel, what is the relevance of these questions? Is this not collateral evidence?
>
> Counsel: Your Worship, the evidence may appear to be collateral at this stage but I can assure the court the relevance will become apparent, Your Worship, that this series of questions is relevant to the witness's credibility. This will become apparent if the court will bear with me for a while.
>
> When every subsequent witness confirmed, without hesitation, that the music of Frank Sinatra was played during the entire evening in question, the inference was clear that Mr Smith could not have been in the tavern that evening due to his lack of knowledge of this fact. The court therefore found that Mr Smith had presented a fabricated version to the court and all his evidence could be rejected as false.

There are two exceptions to the rule against the finality of answers to collateral questions – previous convictions and bias.

22.2.1.1 Previous convictions

Based on English law,[7] in criminal and civil proceedings it is permitted to cross-examine a witness about his or her previous convictions and to prove them.[8] However, in criminal cases,

---

7 Section 6 of the Criminal Procedure Act of 1865.

8 This cannot be done with a witness who is the accused as he or she is entitled to both common law and statutory protection.

if the accused did this it would, of course, result in the accused losing the protection of sections 197 and 211 of the Criminal Procedure Act, 1977.

22.2.1.2 Bias

A witness may be cross-examined about his or her bias or attempts to affect the outcome of the case. This may include questions about whether the witness was schooled in his or her evidence,[9] was bribed by the other party, or if a relationship existed between the witness and the party calling the witness to testify.[10] The rationale for allowing this exception is that bias of a witness affects the credibility of the witness and the credibility of witnesses is always relevant to proceedings.

THIS CHAPTER IN ESSENCE

1   As a general rule collateral evidence is inadmissible. It is, however, admissible if it relates to the credibility of a witness or to the question of whether certain other evidence is admissible.
2   A witness's answers to collateral questions are considered to be final unless the questions relate to the witness's previous convictions or bias.

---

9   In *R v Mendy* (CA) (1976) 64 Cr App R 4 someone in court was seen taking notes of the cross examination of certain witnesses. They were later seen passing these notes on to a witness (the husband of the accused) who had not yet testified. When he did testify he was asked if he had seen the notes. He denied having seen them. Although this would ordinarily be a final answer to a question on a collateral issue, the court in this instance allowed evidence to rebut his denial.

10   *Thomas v David* 1836 (7) C&P 350. One of the plaintiff's witnesses was asked under cross examination whether she was the mistress of the plaintiff. The court was of the view this was relevant to the facts in issue (the witness might be biased) and allowed evidence to contradict her denial.

Chapter 23

Res gestae

23.1 Definition of *res gestae* 250

23.2 Kinds of evidence forming part of the *res gestae* 251
    23.2.1 Statements that accompany and explain a relevant act 251
    23.2.2 Spontaneous statements 252
    23.2.3 Statements that prove state of mind 253
    23.2.4 Statements of physical sensations 254

23.1 Definition of *res gestae*

Res gestae is the term used to describe an ambiguously defined and *ad hoc* collection of common law evidentiary facts and discrete legal concepts.[1] In Latin, the phrase means 'a transaction' or 'things done'. Tapper defines *res gestae* as follows:

> The common law *res gestae*
> ... the doctrine is mainly concerned with the admissibility of statements made contemporaneously with the occurrence of some act or event into which the court is inquiring ... .[2]

An evidentiary fact will be included in the *res gestae* if it forms a part of a legal story. In other words, an evidentiary fact forming part of the *res gestae* will be admissible because:
- it is an integral part of the same continuous transaction, that is, the fact in issue; or
- it is relevant to a transaction; or
- it throws light on the transaction by reason of its proximity in time, place or circumstance; or
- it forms a part of the complete picture, which allows for a better understanding of the transaction.[3]

For example, in *Cape Coast Exploration Ltd v Scholtz and Another*,[4] a number of telegrams were sent over a certain period of time. These telegrams were relevant to the cancelling of a certificate, the fact in dispute, and were, therefore, admissible as part of the *res gestae*. In *S v Moolman*,[5] a police officer made written entries in a pocket book, which recorded certain events that occurred over a period of time. A particular fact in issue concerned a number of events that occurred on a specific day. The court held that the entries in the pocket book that

---

1 See, in general, DT Zeffertt and AP Paizes *The South African Law of Evidence* 2 ed (2009) at 457–473; GL Peiris 'The rule against hearsay and the doctrine of *res gestae*: A comparative analysis of South African, English and Sri Lankan Law' (1981) 14(1) *Comparative and International Law Journal of Southern Africa* 1.
2 C Tapper *Cross and Tapper on Evidence* 8 ed (1995) at 29.
3 Zeffertt and Paizes 2 ed (2009) at 457.
4 1933 AD 56 at 68–71.
5 1996 (1) SACR 267 (A) at 294e.

CHAPTER 23 *RES GESTAE* | 251

were relevant to the events of that specific day were part of the *res gestae* and they were admitted at trial.

Generally, an evidentiary fact is considered to be relevant to a transaction because it forms part of the transaction or because it is closely connected in time and place to the transaction. However, an evidentiary fact, which is not strictly speaking relevant to a transaction, may also be part of the *res gestae*, and thus admissible, where it serves to explain or give a complete picture of the transaction. For example, in *Palmer v Minister of Safety and Security*,[6] the prior events leading up to a disputed police raid were held to be admissible *res gestae* because they served to give a complete picture of the reasons leading to the raid. Similarly, in *S v Van Vuuren*,[7] where the accused was charged with the unlawful shooting of an elephant, evidence of the tracking and pursuit of the animal was held to be admissible because it accompanied and explained the main fact in issue. In *R v De Beer*,[8] it was discovered during the course of giving evidence that the accused, charged with assaulting the victim with his fists and a piece of iron, had prior to this assault also stabbed the victim. The evidence of the prior stabbing was admissible as part of the *res gestae* because it explained the circumstances in which the assault with the piece of iron was committed.

23.2   Kinds of evidence forming part of the *res gestae*

The doctrine of *res gestae* embraces several different kinds of evidence and includes physical acts and reported statements. Reported verbal or written statements forming part of the *res gestae* are received at trial as original evidence.[9] The most important kinds of reported statements forming part of the *res gestae* are:
* statements that accompany and explain a relevant act
* spontaneous statements made during an emergency of some kind
* statements which prove state of mind
* statements which prove physical sensations.

23.2.1   Statements that accompany and explain a relevant act

A statement which accompanies and explains an act that is relevant to a fact in issue may be admitted as part of the *res gestae*:

> ... when there is an act accompanied by a statement which is so mixed up with it as to become part of the *res gestae*, evidence of such a statement may be given ...[10]

Often, people who are not called as witnesses make these statements which are thus technically hearsay. For example, in *Lenssen v R*,[11] the accused was charged with running a gambling house. The Court allowed the prosecution to admit as part of the *res gestae* testimony by police witnesses, who had maintained surveillance over the house, about what people had said as they entered or left the gambling house. The comments by these people

---

6 2002 (1) SA 110 (W) at 115D. Where the history of prior conduct by the police has a direct bearing on the issues to be proved or better explains such issues, such evidence will be relevant as forming part of the *res gestae*.

7 1983 (2) SA 34 (SWA).

8 1949 (3) SA 740 (A) at 746.

9 Prior to 1988, they were admitted as exceptions to the common law hearsay rule. After 1988, such statements will amount to hearsay if the maker is not called to testify and will, therefore, only be admissible if they satisfy the requirements of s 3(1) of the Law of Evidence Amendment Act 45 of 1988.

10 *Howe v Malkin* (1878) 40 LT 196.

11 1906 TS 154.

252 | THE LAW OF EVIDENCE IN SOUTH AFRICA

were relevant to whether or not the house was being used as a place of gambling. In *R v Kukubula*,[12] the accused pleaded guilty to making an imputation of witchcraft against Manjini. As a result of the imputation, Manjini had committed suicide. At the sentencing stage of the trial, the prosecution attempted to admit a letter by Manjini in which he wrote that he had committed suicide as a result of the imputation of witchcraft. The Court held that the letter was relevant in assessing the gravity of sentence. It admitted the letter, first, as a written statement which accompanies and explains a relevant act, namely, the reason why Manjini had killed himself and, second, to determine the deceased's state of mind at the time.[13]

To be admissible in terms of the common law exception to the hearsay rule, statements that accompany and explain a relevant act must conform to three conditions:

- The statement has to be relevant to the act it accompanied and can only be used to explain the act, not to prove it.
- The statement must be that of the actor – the person whose act the statement explains must make the statement.
- The person must have made the statement contemporaneously with the act to which it is relevant.

This third condition is a matter of degree and requires that the statement be sufficiently connected with the act to throw light on it and cannot merely amount to a subsequent reconstructed narration.[14] The element of contemporaneity has always been considered as one of the essential requirements for the application of the *res gestae* doctrine. For a court to admit a hearsay statement under the common law rules, the statement should be contemporaneous with the act or event and clearly associated with it in time, place and circumstance so that it becomes part of the thing being done. Where there is an interval between the act or event and the statement, which allows time for reflection, the statement will not be admitted because it is not part of the event itself but simply a reconstruction of a past event.[15] The testimony of the police witnesses in *Lenssen v R* and the written letter in *R v Kukubula* also amount to hearsay in terms of the statutory definition of hearsay. They would thus only be admissible if the requirements of section 3(1) of the Law of Evidence Amendment Act 45 of 1988 are satisfied.[16] The three conditions mentioned above may act as guidelines in this regard.

23.2.2 Spontaneous statements

In terms of the common law a human utterance or exclamation is a form of communication in the sense that a human act is sometimes so interwoven with words that the significance of the act cannot be understood without the correlative words.[17] For example, in *R v Taylor*,[18] the accused was charged with murdering his wife. Neighbours overheard the wife's voice exclaiming, 'John, please don't hit me any more, you will kill me.' The deceased wife's spontaneous exclamation, despite being hearsay, was admitted as part of the *res gestae* to

---

12 1958 (3) SA 698 (SR).
13 See 23.2.3 on statements that prove state of mind.
14 *Basson v Attorneys Notaries and Conveyancers' Fidelity Guarantee Fund Board of Control* 1957 (3) SA 490 (C).
15 *Teper v R* [1952] 2 All ER 447 (PC) at 449.
16 *S v Ramavhale* 1996 (1) SACR 639 (A) at 647d–e and *Van Willing and Another v S* (109/2014) [2015] ZASCA 52 (27 March 2015) at 22.
17 *Pincus v Solomon* (1) 1942 WLD 237 at 240–241.
18 1961 (3) SA 616 (N) at 618–619.

CHAPTER 23 *RES GESTAE* | 253

show that the accused was, in fact, beating his wife. A spontaneous statement made under the stress of nervous excitement, which is the result of an instinctive response, is likely to be truthful and not an invention or distortion. Similarly, in *S v Tuge*,[19] a victim of a robbery hastily scribbled on his hand the registration number of the robbers' getaway car as it sped from the scene. The victim subsequently wrote the number down on a piece of paper. During the trial, the victim who had written down the number could not be traced and the prosecution attempted to admit the piece of paper by calling another witness. On appeal, the Court held that the piece of paper was admissible, despite it amounting to hearsay, because 'the act of writing down the number was, in the circumstances, part of the *res gestae* accompanying the events constituting the robbery'.[20]

For a spontaneous statement to be admissible:

- the maker who uttered or wrote down the statement might not ordinarily be available as a witness
- there must have been an occurrence that resulted in stress or nervous excitement
- the maker must have made the statement while subject to stress or nervous excitement
- the maker must have made the statement spontaneously and it must not amount to a deliberate reconstruction of a past event.

The court has discretion in determining the degree of spontaneity required in a particular circumstance as long as the spontaneous statement is made up of words that are a consequence of or spring out of the relevant act.[21] A spontaneous statement is considered trustworthy and admissible because it is a sincere response to a circumstance of physical shock or nervous excitement and stress. It is the degree of spontaneity of the utterance in such a circumstance that gives an assurance of reliability.

However, it has also been argued that in a circumstance of nervous anxiety, where the mind's reflective power is absent, such a statement is more likely to be unreliable. Error is likely because nervous excitement does not improve a person's powers of observation or perception. For this reason, the courts have been reluctant to admit spontaneous statements concerning issues of identification.[22] The spontaneous statements in *R v Taylor* and *S v Tuge*, discussed above, amount to statutory hearsay. They would only be admissible if the requirements of section 3(1) of the Law of Evidence Amendment Act, 1988 are satisfied – the four conditions mentioned above may act as guidelines in this regard.

23.2.3 Statements that prove state of mind

In terms of the common law, a statement that demonstrates the state of mind of a person is admissible as part of the *res gestae* where the person's state of mind is relevant to an issue before the court. Such a declaration is admissible because it is often the best and the only evidence of a person's state of mind. The ways in which this type of statement may be admitted are discussed below:

- *Through direct evidence:* Where the person testifies as a witness in court as to his or her state of mind during the occurrence of the act or event.
- *Through statements of others:* Where a person's state of mind may be inferred from the statement of a third party who may have influenced the person. For example, in *R v Lalla*,[23]

---

19 1966 (4) SA 565 (A).
20 At 573.
21 *S v Tuge* 1966 (4) SA 565 (A) at 573G.
22 *R v John* 1929 WLD 50; *S v Mpofu* 1993 (3) SA 864 (N) at 874A.
23 1945 EDL 156.

the accused was charged with receiving stolen property. On appeal, it was held that the accused should have been permitted to admit evidence that a commercial traveller, from whom he had bought the goods, had told him that the goods were legitimate. This evidence was relevant to whether the accused knew that the goods had been stolen. Here, a degree of contemporaneity is required and a third party's statement is only admissible to prove a person's state of mind if it could have influenced the person at the time in issue.

- *Through simultaneous conduct:* Where the state of mind of a person at a particular time is at issue, then a person's statement at that time is admissible to prove such a state of mind. For example, in *Estate de Wet v De Wet*,[24] an insolvent's statement, in which he told a third party of the state of his assets and liabilities, was admitted for the purpose of establishing his state of mind, that is, knowledge of his poor financial position, at the time of the transaction in issue. Admissibility is therefore dependent on the degree of contemporaneity between the making of the statement and the time when the maker's state of mind is in issue.
- *Through a statement of intention:* A person's state of mind may be proved by his or her express and intentional assertion at the time. For example, a person's statement of intention to remain permanently in a particular country may be admitted because it is relevant to the issue of whether or not a person has acquired a domicile of choice.[25] These statements may also be admitted to show a person's state of mind about political or religious opinions, marital feelings or fear of a particular individual.

In criminal matters, to ensure reliability and to prevent the manufacture of evidence, a statement of intent is only admissible if it is adverse to the interest of the person making it. Selfserving statements of intent are not admissible.[26] For example, in *R v Mpanza*,[27] the accused's statement that he intended to rob and kill Indian shopkeepers was admitted against him. In *S v Holshausen*,[28] a transcript of a tape recording in which the appellant, convicted of the murder, was heard to say that he intended to 'get rid of her and himself' was admitted. In civil proceedings, statements of intent have been received at trial in England and the United States of America. In South Africa, there is little case law in this area although, in *Gleneagles Farm Dairy v Schoombee*,[29] the plaintiff's statement of intention was admitted to corroborate other evidence.

23.2.4 Statements of physical sensations

A person's express statement and involuntary gesture or reaction is admissible to prove a state of physical sensation or bodily feeling. For example, the following are admissible as evidence of physical sensations: the statement 'I have a headache', the statement 'my stomach hurts', a groan or doubling up in pain. The reason for the admissibility of such evidence is its reliability as it is often the best and only evidentiary source of a person's bodily sensations. The statement or reaction must have been made contemporaneously with the bodily sensation to which it refers. It is admissible to prove the existence of the physical sensation or symptom but not the cause that produced the sensation. In respect of the

---

24 1924 CPD 341 at 342.
25 *Senior and Another v CIR* 1960 (1) SA 709 (A) at 719.
26 Selfserving statements or statements of excuse are inadmissible because they infringe the rule against the use of prior consistent statements for the purpose of selfcorroboration.
27 1915 AD 348.
28 1984 (4) SA 852 (A).
29 1947 (4) SA 66 (E). See also *Albrecht v Newberry* 1974 (4) SA 314 (E).

statement 'My head hurts because X hit me with a cricket bat', only the first part – 'my head hurts' – would be admissible.[30]

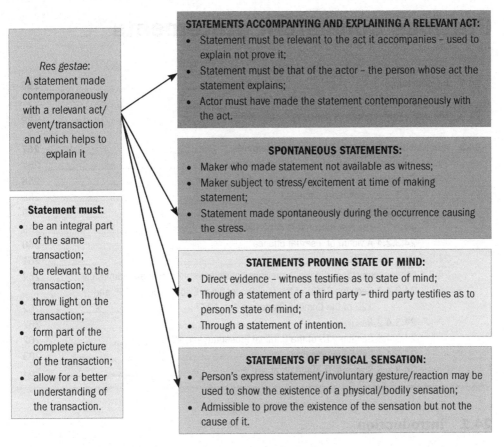

Figure 23.1 Res gestae

THIS CHAPTER IN ESSENCE

1. Evidentiary facts forming part of the *res gestae* are admissible for any of the following reasons:
   1.1 They form an integral part of the same continuous transaction.
   1.2 They are relevant to a transaction.
   1.3 They shed some light on the transaction due to their proximity in time, place or circumstance.
   1.4 They form part of the complete picture which allows for a better understanding of the transaction.
2. The doctrine of *res gestae* applies to several different kinds of evidence and includes physical acts and reported statements. The most important kinds of reported statements forming part of the *res gestae* are:
   2.1 statements that accompany and explain a relevant act
   2.2 spontaneous statements made during an emergency of some kind
   2.3 statements which prove state of mind
   2.4 statements which prove physical sensations.

---

30 *R v Kaiser* 1927 WLD 278.

Chapter 24

Previous consistent statements

24.1	**Introduction**	**256**
24.2	**The rule against previous consistent statements**	**256**
24.3	**Admissibility of previous consistent statements**	**257**
	24.3.1 To rebut a suggestion of recent fabrication	257
	24.3.2 Complaints in sexual cases where there is a victim	258
	24.3.2.1 A voluntary complaint	258
	24.3.2.2 The victim must testify	259
	24.3.2.3 The first reasonable opportunity	259
	24.3.2.4 A victim of a sexual offence	260
	24.3.3 Prior identification	261
	24.3.4 Other circumstances in which previous consistent statements are admissible	262
	24.3.4.1 Sections 34(2) of the Civil Proceedings Evidence Act, 1965 and 222 of the Criminal Procedure Act, 1977	262
	24.3.4.2 *Res gestae*	262
	24.3.4.3 Section 213 of the Criminal Procedure Act, 1977	262
	24.3.4.4 Refreshing memory	263
	24.3.4.5 Statements made on arrest	263

24.1 Introduction

A previous consistent statement is an oral or written statement made by a witness on a previous occasion that is substantially the same as the witness's testimonial statements made before a court.[1] In terms of the common law, a previous consistent statement is irrelevant and, therefore, inadmissible.[2] At trial, counsel may not ask a witness during examination-in-chief or re-examination whether he or she has previously made a statement which is similar to his or her testimony before the court. However, a previous inconsistent statement is relevant and admissible because it goes to the credibility of the witness. During cross-examination, counsel may ask a witness about previous statements that are inconsistent and differ substantially from the witness's testimony before the court.

24.2 The rule against previous consistent statements

The inadmissibility of previous consistent statements is principally based on the rule against self-serving statements and the rule against self-corroboration. Simply repeating the same

---

1 See further DT Zeffertt and AP Paizes *The South African Law of Evidence* 2 ed (2009) at 445–456; PJ Schwikkard and SE van der Merwe *Principles of Evidence* 3 ed (2009) at 104–120.

2 *S v Bergh* 1976 (4) SA 857 (A) at 865G; *S v Moolman* 1996 (1) SACR 267 (A) at 300C; *S v Scott-Crossley* 2008 (1) SACR 223 (SCA) at para 17.

CHAPTER 24   PREVIOUS CONSISTENT STATEMENTS | 257

statement several times does not make the statement any more truthful in the retelling.[3] Corroboration of a statement should come from an independent source and a witness cannot corroborate him- or herself by pointing out that he or she has said the same thing before.[4] A previous consistent statement is irrelevant for the following reasons:

- It has insufficient probative force.[5]
- It is easily fabricated.
- It is, in most cases, superfluous as it is expected of a witness to be consistent about what he or she has said on previous occasions on a particular topic.
- Admitting previous consistent statements may result in numerous collateral issues, which may be time-consuming and costly.

The relevance of a previous consistent statement is limited to rebutting an attack on the credibility of a witness. In such a case, its purpose is simply to show that the witness has always been consistent and has not made up his or her testimony at trial. It cannot be used as evidence of the truth of what the witness has said and cannot serve as corroboration of the witness's testimony.

24.3   Admissibility of previous consistent statements

However, a previous consistent statement will be relevant and admissible when it falls into three recognised exceptions.[6] These are:
- to rebut a suggestion of recent fabrication
- complaints in sexual cases where there is a victim
- dock identification.

24.3.1   To rebut a suggestion of recent fabrication

If it is suggested at trial that a witness has recently fabricated his or her evidence, the witness may rebut the suggestion of fabrication by introducing a written or oral statement made earlier which is consistent with his or her evidence, as illustrated in the case below.[7] The suggestion of recent fabrication may be direct, indirect or made by implication. In other words, it must directly or indirectly contain the implication that the witness invented the story, for example, 'When did you first invent this story?' The implication may suggest a deliberate, imagined or honestly mistaken invention. A suggestion made during cross-examination that a witness is lying or is merely unreliable does not amount to a suggestion of fabrication and does not open the window for the admission of a previous consistent statement.[8]

---

3   *R v Roberts* (1942) 28 Cr App R 102. The accused, charged with murder, testified that the death of the victim was an accident. The court refused to allow the accused also to testify that two days after the killing he had told his father that it was an accident. The testimony is inadmissible because it is self-serving and self-corroborative.

4   Neither may the witness call someone else to prove that the witness has said the same thing before.

5   *S v Scott-Crossley* 2008 (1) SACR 223 (SCA) at para 17; *S v Mkohle* 1990 (1) SACR 95 (A) at 99D.

6   In *Holtzhauzen v Roodt* 1997 (4) SA 766 (W) at 774A, it was held that there was no *numerus clausus* and that all relevant prior consistent statements are admissible. However, Zeffertt and Paizes 2 ed (2009) at 447–456 argue that there are only the three exceptions as they existed when English law was frozen on 30 May 1961.

7   *S v Bergh* 1976 (4) SA 857 (A) at 868.

8   *S v Bergh* 1976 (4) SA 857 (A).

Pincus v Solomon (1)

In *Pincus v Solomon (1)*,[9] a plaintiff testified that just before a road accident he had seen a lorry coming towards him. At cross-examination it was suggested that he had fabricated the sighting of the lorry as he had not mentioned the lorry when making his statement to the police. The Court allowed the plaintiff to admit evidence in rebuttal that he had mentioned the lorry to another witness shortly after the accident.

24.3.2 Complaints in sexual cases where there is a victim

In terms of the common law, in cases of a sexual nature, evidence of a voluntary complaint made by the victim may be admissible as a previous consistent statement if the complaint is made within a reasonable time (at first reasonable opportunity) after the commission of the alleged sexual offence. This common law rule has its origin in the medieval principle in English law that it was essential for a female rape victim to raise a hue and cry, that is, to raise a voluble and credible outcry, as soon as possible after the rape to succeed on a rape charge.[10] Although this rule no longer applies, the notion that if the victim did indeed raise a hue and cry that this should then be admissible has become part of the common law.

Unfortunately, the rule has had the effect of allowing the defence to argue that if the victim did not make a complaint at the first opportunity, a negative inference could be drawn about the credibility of the victim. The common law rule has thus been criticised for the following reasons:

- It does not have a rational basis.
- It is sometimes potentially prejudicial to both the victim and the accused.
- Silence on the part of the victim is often a legitimate psychological response to the post-traumatic stress caused by the violent sexual nature of the crime.
- In particular, the common law requirement that the victim must make a complaint at the first reasonable opportunity is unrealistic because it does not take into account the psychological damage caused to the victim by this type of crime.

For these reasons, the common law rule has been abolished by statute in Canada[11] and substantially modified by statute in Namibia.[12] In South Africa, sections 58 and 59 of the Criminal Law (Sexual Offences and Related Matters) Amendment Act 32 of 2007 attempt to address the above-mentioned problem and other sexual myths surrounding a complaint of sexual misconduct[13] by stating that no inference can be drawn from the absence of any previous consistent statement made by the complainant.

In terms of the common law, a previous consistent statement will be admissible where certain requirements have been met. These will be discussed below.

24.3.2.1 A voluntary complaint

The victim must have made the complaint voluntarily and not as a result of leading, suggestive or intimidating questions.[14] Any threat of violence, such as 'I will hit you unless you tell me what happened', or leading questions, such as 'Did X touch you on your private

---

9 1942 WLD 237 at 243.
10 Zeffertt and Paizes 2 ed (2009) at 447.
11 Section 275 of the Criminal Code.
12 Sections 6 and 7 of the Combating of Rape Act 8 of 2000.
13 Schwikkard and Van der Merwe 3 ed (2009) at 117–119.
14 *S v T* 1963 (1) SA 484 (A); *R v C* 1955 (4) SA 40 (N) at 40G–H.

CHAPTER 24   PREVIOUS CONSISTENT STATEMENTS | 259

parts?' or 'Did X assault you?', will render the answer inadmissible. However, the answer to a question, 'Why are you crying?' is considered voluntary and admissible.[15]

24.3.2.2   The victim must testify

If the victim does not testify, both the fact that a complaint was made and the contents of the complaint will be inadmissible. The principal reason for this is that the complainant must appear at trial and repeat the complaint to show consistency. Furthermore, the complaint would simply amount to a hearsay statement if the maker of the complaint, namely the victim, is not called to the witness box, as illustrated in the case below.

> **S v R**
>
> In S v R,[16] the complainant, an alcoholic, alleged that she had been raped in an ambulance by an assistant who claimed consent. At the hospital, she repeatedly alleged rape and was overheard by a nurse. At trial, the complainant, suffering from alcoholic amnesia, could not remember her repeated statements. The Court admitted her statement and condition to show her state of mind at the time of the rape.

24.3.2.3   The first reasonable opportunity

What amounts to a first reasonable opportunity largely depends on the circumstances of each individual case. In essence, it means that 'the complaint must be made ... at the earliest opportunity which, under all the circumstances, could reasonably be expected, and also it must be made to the first person to whom the complainant could reasonably be expected to make it'.[17]

The interpretation of a first reasonable opportunity is at the court's discretion and will depend on three factors:

- First, it hinges on the presence or absence of a person to whom the victim could reasonably be expected to make the first complaint.
- Second, it depends on whether or not the victim was old enough at the time of the sexual act to understand the immoral or illegal nature of the act.
- Third, it depends on whether the complainant, as a result of a certain lapse of time, could possibly be making a false complaint.[18]

The application of these principles can be seen in S v S and S v Cornick discussed below.

> **S v S**
>
> In S v S,[19] the accused, a schoolteacher, was charged with the rape of an 11-year-old girl at school while she was in his care. After the rape, the girl did not immediately report the act to the school because she wanted to tell her mother first. This was held by the judge to be a natural reaction of a young girl who had been through a traumatic experience.
>
> When the girl arrived home, she merely told her mother that the teacher had touched her private parts. The judge held this erratic behaviour to be natural for a sexually innocent 11-year-old girl. At the time when the girl had formed the intention to tell her mother about her ordeal she had been bleeding from her vagina, but when she reached home the bleeding had stopped. She was also

---

15   *R v Osborne* [1905] 1 KB 551 at 556.
16   1965 (2) SA 463 (W).
17   *S v Banana* 2000 (3) SA 885 (ZS) at 895F–G.
18   *S v V* 1961 (4) SA 201 (O).
19   1995 (1) SACR 50 (ZS) at 56D–H.

260 | THE LAW OF EVIDENCE IN SOUTH AFRICA

unaware that what the accused had done was unlawful. The complainant had a history of misbehaviour and was frequently detained at school as punishment and she did not want to trouble her mother with an explanation of what she assumed to be merely another form of punishment.

S v Cornick and Another

In S v Cornick and Another,[20] the complainant, 14 years old at the time of the rape, had waited over 19 years before making a complaint. She had psychologically buried the traumatic memory of the rape for over two decades. A chance meeting with one of her rapists revived her buried memory and she laid a charge of rape against the three accused.

The Court held that there were plausible explanations for her lengthy silence. She had been brought up by elderly and conservative grandparents who had never discussed matters of an intimate nature with her. She had only a distant relationship with her mother who had also never discussed sex or physiology with her and she had never had a boyfriend. In these circumstances, she did not realise what was happening to her when the three accused took turns raping her despite her protests. She knew she was being hurt but did not appreciate that she was being raped.

The Court held that it was not improbable that a young woman who had buried the memory of the traumatic event for many years would not appreciate, until her mid-twenties, the full extent of what had happened to her when the chance meeting with one of the accused triggered the memory.

24.3.2.4 A victim of a sexual offence

The offence must be of a sexual nature and the complainant must have been the victim of a sexual crime. Where the victim is an adult, the sexual act must have consisted of a degree of violence or, at a minimum, some degree of physical contact by the perpetrator with the victim.[21] The definition of victim includes children and the mentally disabled who may voluntarily participate in the sexual act but are incapable in law of giving consent.

(a) Limited evidential value

In terms of the common law, the evidentiary value of the complaint is usually limited to proving consistency on the part of the victim or complainant and it cannot be used to establish a lack of consent or for the purpose of corroboration.[22] The evidential value of a previous consistent statement may be summarised as follows:

> The fact that a witness telling a particular story at the trial told exactly the same story to the police soon after the alleged offence cannot supply corroboration although it may well strengthen the evidence and rebut any suggestion of subsequent fabrication. Repetition of a story does not corroborate it: and this is a corollary of the general proposition that the confirmatory evidence must come from an independent source.[23]

However, there is one exception:

> But this general proposition does not apply in one carefully circumscribed set of circumstances, where self-corroboration is possible – by means of the victim's distressed condition after the alleged incident.[24]

---

20 2007 (2) SACR 115 (SCA) at 32.
21 R v Burgess 1927 TPD 14. The common law rule narrowly applies to either female or male rape, indecent assault and similar offences.
22 S v Hammond 2004 (2) SACR 303 (SCA); S v Gentle 2005 (1) SACR 420 (SCA).
23 A Ashworth 'Corroboration and Self-corroboration' (1978) Justice of the Peace at 266–267.
24 Ibid.

CHAPTER 24   PREVIOUS CONSISTENT STATEMENTS   261

In *S v S*,[25] the Court considered the extremely shocked condition of the complainant when she reported the rape to be strong corroboration of her testimony that she had been raped. Two qualifications must be placed on this type of corroboration:
- First, the distressed condition must be carefully considered to ensure that it is not being faked.
- Second, if it is genuine, then the court must ensure that it is not attributable to something other than the alleged incident.[26]

(b) Statutory reform: sections 58 and 59 of the Criminal Law (Sexual Offences and Related Matters) Amendment Act, 2007

Sections 58 and 59 are meant to be remedial and to replace the common law exception and its requirements for the admissibility of a sexual complaint.[27] Section 58 reads:

> **Evidence relating to previous consistent statements by a complainant shall be admissible in criminal proceedings involving the alleged commission of a sexual offence: Provided that the court may not draw any inference only from the absence of such previous consistent statements.**

This means that the court may not draw an adverse inference against a complainant only because the victim has not made a previous consistent statement. A proper adverse inference affecting a complainant's credibility may be made in the appropriate circumstance taking into account various factors such as the nature of the complaint, the nature of the facts, time and place, inconsistencies in the various statements made, or a failure to say anything.

Section 59 reads:

> **In criminal proceedings involving the alleged commission of a sexual offence, the court may not draw any inference only from the length of any delay between the alleged commission of such an offence and the reporting thereof.**

This means that a court may not improperly infer that a mere delay in making a complaint has any significance. The court cannot rely only on the factor of delay but must take into account all the other factors that may be relevant in the circumstances of each case. Therefore sections 58 and 59 prevent a court from drawing an adverse inference against the complainant only from the 'absence' or 'lateness' of a sexual complaint without examining other relevant factors.

24.3.3   Prior identification

Identification in court is invariably undertaken by asking the witness to point out the accused in the dock. Admitting evidence of a previous identification is done to show that a witness who identified an accused at trial has also identified the accused on a previous occasion. Dock identification by itself has little probative value and serves only to confirm identification.[28] According to *Rasool v R*,[29] the evidence of a previous identification has probative value and should be regarded as relevant for the purpose of showing, from the very start, that the witness who is identifying the accused in the dock is not identifying the

---

25   1990 (1) SACR 5 (A) at 11C.
26   *S v Hammond* 2004 (2) SACR 303 (SCA) at paras 21–23.
27   Zeffertt and Paizes 2 ed (2009) at 450.
28   *R v M* 1959 (1) SA 434 (A). The identification goes only to consistency of identification; it does not serve to prove the accuracy of the description.
29   1932 NPD 112 at 118.

262 THE LAW OF EVIDENCE IN SOUTH AFRICA

said accused for the first time, but has identified the accused on some previous occasion in circumstances that give real weight to the identification. Prior identification by a witness carries more weight than dock identification. However, when the physical identification is supported or accompanied by identifying words, these identifying words are admissible.[30]

24.3.4 Other circumstances in which previous consistent statements are admissible

There are a number of statutory and other circumstances that allow for the admission of prior consistent statements.[31]

24.3.4.1 Sections 34(2) of the Civil Proceedings Evidence Act, 1965 and 222 of the Criminal Procedure Act, 1977

Section 34(2) of the Civil Proceedings Evidence Act, 1965[32] and section 222[33] of the Criminal Procedure Act, 1977 permit a presiding officer to allow a witness who is also giving oral evidence at trial (and in exceptional circumstances, even one who is not), in certain circumstances, to hand in a signed statement made after the incident under investigation. The previous written statement cannot serve as corroboration of the witness's oral evidence at trial, but serves only to establish consistency.

24.3.4.2 *Res gestae*

A previous consistent statement may also be admissible at trial if it forms part of the *res gestae*. However, it merely serves to establish consistency and cannot amount to corroboration of the witness who made the statement.

24.3.4.3 Section 213 of the Criminal Procedure Act, 1977

In terms of section 213 of the Criminal Procedure Act, 1977, a witness statement may be proved by consent between the prosecution and the accused without calling the witness

---

30 Zefferrt and Paizes 2 ed (2009) at 456.

31 Zeffertt and Paizes 2 ed (2009) at 456; Schwikkard and Van der Merwe 3 ed (2009) at 119–120.

32 S 34 Admissibility of documentary evidence as to facts in issue
   (1) In any civil proceedings where direct oral evidence of a fact would be admissible, any statement made by a person in a document and tending to establish that fact shall on production of the original document be admissible as evidence of that fact, provided –
   (a) the person who made the statement either –
       (i) had personal knowledge of the matters dealt with in the statement; or
       (ii) where the document in question is or forms part of a record purporting to be a continuous record, made the statement (in so far as the matters dealt with therein are not within his personal knowledge) in the performance of a duty to record information supplied to him by a person who had or might reasonably have been supposed to have personal knowledge of those matters; and
   (b) the person who made the statement is called as a witness in the proceedings unless he is dead or unfit by reason of his bodily or mental condition to attend as a witness or is outside the Republic, and it is not reasonably practicable to secure his attendance or all reasonable efforts to find him have been made without success.
   (2) The person presiding at the proceedings may, if having regard to all the circumstances of the case he is satisfied that undue delay or expense would otherwise be caused, admit such a statement as is referred to in subsection (1) as evidence in those proceedings –
   (a) notwithstanding that the person who made the statement is available but is not called as a witness;
   (b) notwithstanding that the original document is not produced, if in lieu thereof there is produced a copy of the original document or of the material part thereof proved to be a true copy.

33 S 222 Application to criminal proceedings of certain provisions of Civil Proceedings Evidence Act, 1965, relating to documentary evidence
   The provisions of sections 33 to 38 inclusive, of the Civil Proceedings Evidence Act, 1965 (Act 25 of 1965), shall *mutatis mutandis* apply with reference to criminal proceedings.

CHAPTER 24   PREVIOUS CONSISTENT STATEMENTS | 263

to testify. Where the witness in any event does testify at trial, his or her previous statement proved by consent serves only to show consistency and does not corroborate the witness.

24.3.4.4   Refreshing memory

In practice, a witness is allowed to refresh his or her memory in the witness box from an earlier written statement. The earlier statement used to refresh the memory has no independent probative value and may be handed in simply as a convenient record of the witness's testimony.[34]

24.3.4.5   Statements made on arrest

Statements made to the police at the moment of arrest are relevant and admissible to show the reaction of the accused to the arrest. An explanation given by an accused when found in possession of stolen property is relevant and admissible to establish consistency should the accused make the same explanation at trial.

THIS CHAPTER IN ESSENCE

1   Previous consistent statements are irrelevant and inadmissible for the following reasons:
  1.1   They have insufficient probative force.
  1.2   They are easily fabricated.
  1.3   They are, in most cases, superfluous.
  1.4   They may result in numerous collateral issues which, in turn, may be time-consuming and costly.
2   However, a previous consistent statement may be admissible in the following cases:
  2.1   where it is used to rebut a suggestion of recent fabrication
  2.2   where the case involves complaints in sexual cases involving a victim
  2.3   where it is used to show that a witness who identifies an accused at trial has also identified the accused on a previous occasion
  2.4   where a witness is giving oral evidence at trial and wishes to hand in a signed statement made after the incident under investigation
  2.5   where it forms part of the *res gestae*
  2.6   where, in terms of section 213 of the Criminal Procedure Act, 1977, a witness statement is proved by consent between the prosecution and the accused without calling the witness to testify
  2.7   where a witness wishes to refresh his or her memory in the witness box
  2.8   where the accused made a statement to the police at the moment of arrest.

---

34   *S v Bergh* 1976 (4) SA 857 (A) at 857.

Chapter 25

Hearsay evidence

25.1	**Introduction**	**265**
25.2	**The general rule**	**265**
	25.2.1 On oath	265
	25.2.2 Cross-examination	265
	25.2.3 Demeanour and credibility	266
25.3	**Statutory definition of hearsay**	**266**
	25.3.1 Section 3 of the Law of Evidence Amendment Act, 1988	267
	25.3.2 Constitutionality of section 3	268
25.4	**Admissibility of hearsay**	**268**
	25.4.1 By agreement: section 3(1)(*a*)	269
	25.4.2 Where the person testifies: sections 3(1)(*b*) and 3(3)	270
	25.4.3 In the interests of justice: section 3(1)(*c*)	270
	25.4.3.1 The nature of the proceedings	270
	25.4.3.2 The nature of evidence	270
	25.4.3.3 The purpose for which the evidence is tendered	271
	25.4.3.4 The probative value of the evidence	271
	25.4.3.5 The reason why the evidence is not given by the person on whose credibility the probative value depends	272
	25.4.3.6 Prejudice to opponents	272
	25.4.3.7 Any other factor which in the opinion of the court should be taken into account	273
25.5	**Other statutory exceptions**	**273**
	25.5.1 The Criminal Procedure Act, 1977	273
	25.5.1.1 Affidavits	274
	25.5.1.2 Written statements	274
	25.5.1.3 Preparatory examinations	274
	25.5.1.4 Former trials	274
	25.5.1.5 Business records	274
	25.5.1.6 Judicial proceedings	275
	25.5.1.7 Bankers' books	275
	25.5.2 The Civil Proceedings Evidence Act, 1965	275
	25.5.2.1 Affidavits	275
	25.5.2.2 Sunrise and sunset	275
	25.5.2.3 Bankers' books	275
	25.5.2.4 Documentary evidence	275
	25.5.3 Other examples	275
	25.5.3.1 Electronic evidence	275

CHAPTER 25   HEARSAY EVIDENCE   265

25.5.3.2 Companies' books 276
25.5.3.3 Age 276
25.5.3.4 Public documents 276

25.6   The South African Law Reform Commission (SALRC) Project 126 *Review of the Law of Evidence* Discussion Paper 113 *Hearsay and Relevance* 276

25.1   Introduction

In its essence, hearsay is merely a witness testifying about what he or she 'heard' another person 'say', hence the term 'hearsay'. It is a basic rule of procedure that for the oral or written testimony of a person to be admitted as evidence at trial, the person who made the oral or written statement must be called to appear before the court as a witness. Therefore, the oral or written statement of a non-witness is usually inadmissible at trial. Although this is a simplified description, inadmissible evidence of this type is called hearsay. For example, if witness B tells witness A, 'I saw the accused kill the deceased,' then only B actually saw the crime. If the prosecution only calls witness A to testify about what B told him or her, such evidence will be hearsay.

25.2   The general rule

The common law definition of hearsay, which focuses on the purpose for which the **hearsay evidence** is being tendered, has been replaced by a statutory definition in section 3(4) of the Law of Evidence Amendment Act 45 of 1988. Hearsay evidence is now defined as 'evidence, whether oral or in writing, the probative value of which depends upon the credibility of any person other than the person giving such evidence'.[1]

By applying this definition to the example above, we can see that the probative value of A's evidence actually depends on B's credibility, not A's credibility, because it was B who actually saw the crime, not A. This is the reason why the prosecution must call witness B to the witness stand to admit as evidence the statement, 'I saw the accused kill the deceased.'

Hearsay has always been defined as an exclusionary rule. This means that hearsay evidence is generally inadmissible. There are several reasons for this, all of which have their basis in the unreliability of hearsay evidence and in the potential prejudice that it can cause. These reasons will be discussed below.

25.2.1   On oath

For evidence to be admissible, witnesses have to testify under oath. With hearsay evidence, the statement that was made by the person who is not in court is not made under oath.[2]

25.2.2   Cross-examination

The moment a witness gives evidence, the opposing party acquires the right to cross-examine that witness. The person who made the statement on which the hearsay evidence is based

---

1   Also referred to as a declarant-orientated definition.
2   If the person is subsequently called to testify under oath, his or her hearsay evidence will be provisionally admissible in terms of s 3(3) of the Law of Evidence Amendment Act, 1988.

THE LAW OF EVIDENCE IN SOUTH AFRICA

266

is not called to the witness box and therefore cannot be tested in court through cross-examination. Furthermore, the statement that the person made cannot be challenged to assess the strength or weakness of the statement.[3] This right to cross-examine is now also a constitutional right.[4]

25.2.3 Demeanour and credibility

A court will observe every witness who gives evidence to examine their demeanour and assess their credibility as this will have an impact on how much weight the court attaches to the witness's evidence. Because the person who made the statement is not in court, the court is denied this opportunity and is therefore unable to evaluate the evidence properly.

Hearsay evidence is therefore unreliable, prejudicial to the party against whom it is admitted and may render a trial unfair. Historically, this has always been recognised and the exclusionary hearsay rule was developed in English common law to meet the needs of a trial by jury and to guard against a jury's probable inability to evaluate such evidence fairly.

DISCUSSION 25.1 **Should the rule against hearsay be abolished?**

South Africa has abolished the jury system and it has been suggested that there may, therefore, no longer be a justification for the continued existence of a hearsay rule. It is reasonable to argue that hearsay should be admissible at trial and that a judge should be allowed to assess its probative value and weight when making a judgment at the end of the trial. Alternatively, it may also be argued that hearsay should be allowed but that it should be subject to the cautionary rule that some form of safeguard be sought due to its inherent unreliability. What is your view?

The statutory definition of hearsay replaced the common law definition because the common law rule was somewhat vague in meaning and had developed into an inflexible rule of exclusion.[5] As a result, courts did not have the discretionary power to admit hearsay evidence, despite its relevance, if it fell outside the parameters of the recognised common law exceptions. Neither did courts have the discretionary power to create new exceptions. There was therefore a need to develop a new, flexible hearsay rule that allowed for the admission of hearsay where it was relevant, procedurally fair and in the interests of justice to do so.[6]

25.3 Statutory definition of hearsay

The following section will examine the statutory definition of hearsay, as outlined in section 3 of the Law of Evidence Amendment Act, 1988,[7] and will also discuss the constitutionality and procedural fairness of section 3.

---

3 The four dangers of hearsay are faulty perception, erroneous memory, insincerity and ambiguity in narration.
4 Section 35(3)(*i*) of the Constitution.
5 *Estate de Wet v De Wet* 1924 CPD 341 at 343: 'Evidence of statements made by persons not called as witnesses which are tendered for the purpose of proving the truth of what is contained in the statement'. The common law definition is an assertion-orientated definition.
6 DT Zeffertt and AP Paizes *The South African Law of Evidence* 2 ed (2009) at 385–388.
7 Sometimes also referred to as the Hearsay Amendment Act.

CHAPTER 25 HEARSAY EVIDENCE | 267

25.3.1 Section 3 of the Law of Evidence Amendment Act, 1988

Section 3 of the Law of Evidence Amendment Act, 1988 reads as follows:

3. Hearsay evidence

(1) Subject to the provisions of any other law, hearsay evidence shall not be admitted as evidence in criminal or civil proceedings, unless –

(a) each party against whom the evidence is to be adduced *agrees* to the admission thereof as evidence at such proceedings;

(b) the person upon whose credibility the probative value of such evidence depends, himself *testifies* at such proceedings; or

(c) the court, having regard to –

(i) the *nature* of the proceedings;

(ii) the *nature* of the evidence;

(iii) the *purpose* for which the evidence is tendered;

(iv) the *probative value* of the evidence;

(v) the *reason* why the evidence is not given by the person upon whose credibility the probative value of such evidence depends;

(vi) any *prejudice* to a party which the admission of such evidence might entail; and

(vii) any *other factor* which should in the opinion of the court be taken into account,

is of the opinion that such evidence should be admitted in the interests of justice. [Our emphasis]

(2) The provisions of subsection (1) shall not render admissible any evidence which is inadmissible on any ground other than that such evidence is hearsay evidence.

(3) Hearsay evidence may be provisionally admitted in terms of subsection (1)(b) if the court is informed that the person upon whose credibility the probative value of such evidence depends will himself testify in such proceedings. Provided that if such a person does not later testify in such proceedings, the hearsay evidence shall be left out of account, unless the hearsay evidence is admitted in terms of paragraph (a) of subsection (1) or is admitted by the court in terms of paragraph (c) of that subsection.

(4) For the purposes of this section –

'hearsay evidence' means evidence, whether oral or in writing, the probative value of which depends upon the credibility of any person other than the person giving such evidence;

'party' means the accused or party against whom hearsay evidence is to be adduced, including the prosecution.

The statutory definition of hearsay is still exclusionary in purpose but it is more flexible than the rigid rule-and-exception approach of the common law. The statutory definition gives the courts the power to admit hearsay in circumstances where the dangers attached to hearsay can be minimised or are insignificant.

The crucial question in applying the statutory definition of hearsay is to ask whether the probative value of the evidence sought to be admitted 'depends' on the credibility of a non-witness. Accordingly, evidence would be hearsay as defined in section 3(4) if its

268 | THE LAW OF EVIDENCE IN SOUTH AFRICA

probative value sufficiently depends on – that is, is controlled by or governed by – the credibility of a non-witness. Realistically, the probative value of evidence will never solely depend on a non-witness, hence the use of the term 'sufficiently depends on'. This is assessed by examining all the circumstances of the case including the testimony of other witnesses.[8]

25.3.2 Constitutionality of section 3

The constitutional validity of section 3(1)–(4) was put to the test in *S v Ndhlovu and Others*[9] where it was argued that the admission of hearsay constitutionally infringed the right to challenge evidence as defined in section 35(3)(*i*) of the Constitution. It was argued that hearsay was procedurally and substantially unfair as, first, hearsay could not be subject to cross-examination. Second, its admission was unfair in that the opposing party could not effectively counter the inferences that could be drawn from admissible hearsay.

The Supreme Court of Appeal reasoned that hearsay as an exclusionary rule, together with the 'interests of justice test' set out in section 3(1), did not unreasonably infringe the Constitution.[10] The Supreme Court of Appeal noted that the Constitution does not guarantee an entitlement to subject all evidence to cross-examination. What it does guarantee is the right to challenge evidence. The statutory hearsay rule in section 3 allows a party to challenge its admission and to scrutinise its probative value and its reliability. The Court held section 3 to be constitutionally sound because hearsay could not be admitted unless there were compelling reasons to do so. In addition, there were an adequate number of procedural duties on a judge to ensure fairness to the opposing party after the admission of hearsay.[11]

These procedural duties on a judge to ensure fairness include:
- guarding against the unreasonable admission of hearsay
- adequately explaining the evidentiary consequences of admitting hearsay to an unrepresented opposing party
- the judge's ability to protect an opposing party from the late or unheralded admission of hearsay.

Note that in terms of section 3(1)(*c*), hearsay cannot be admitted late in the proceedings to ambush an opposing party, but in section 3(1)(*b*) hearsay may be provisionally admitted at an early stage as long as the person testifies later in the proceedings. To ensure procedural fairness to the opposing party, the admission of hearsay must be dealt with clearly and timeously by the court. The opposing party should not be ambushed by the late admission of hearsay.[12]

25.4 Admissibility of hearsay

The Supreme Court of Appeal in *McDonald's Corporation v Joburgers Drive-Inn Restaurant (Pty) Ltd and Another*[13] stated that the decision by a trial court to admit hearsay evidence in terms of section 3 was not an exercise of judicial discretion but a decision of law. A court of

---

8 Zeffertt and Paizes 2 ed (2009) at 390–391.
9 2002 (2) SACR 325 (SCA).
10 At para 24.
11 See also *S v Molimi* 2008 (3) SA 608 (CC).
12 *S v Ndhlovu and Others* 2002 (2) SACR 325 (SCA) at para 17. In *S v Molimi* 2008 (3) SA 608 (CC) it was noted that a ruling on the admissibility of hearsay should be given prior to the accused testifying.
13 1997 (1) SA 1 (A) at 27D–E where the Court stated that 'a decision on the admissibility of evidence is, in general, one of law, not discretion and this Court is fully entitled to overrule such a decision by a lower court'. See also Zeffertt and Paizes 2 ed (2009) at 393.

appeal is entitled to overrule the decision of a lower court if its application of section 3 is found to be wrong.

Section 3(1)(*a*), (*b*) and (*c*) creates three exceptions of wide scope and admissibility.[14] These three exceptions allow hearsay to be admitted:
- by agreement in terms of section 3(1)(*a*)
- where the person, on whose credibility the evidence depends, testifies in terms of sections 3(1)(*b*) and 3(3)
- in the interests of justice in terms of section 3(1)(*c*).

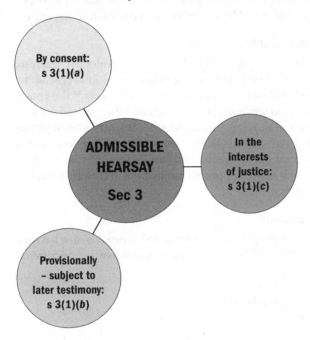

Figure 25.1 Admissible hearsay (section 3)

25.4.1 By agreement: section 3(1)(*a*)

Hearsay evidence may be admitted by an informed agreement or consent between the parties to trial proceedings. Consent must be based on a full understanding and appreciation of the potential prejudicial consequences of admitting hearsay evidence. Consent may be express, but a failure to object to its admission at trial may in certain circumstances be regarded as agreement. Tacit consent may also be inferred from a failure to object to hearsay evidence given under cross-examination.[15] In criminal proceedings, a judge must properly explain to an unrepresented accused the prejudicial consequences of consenting to the admission of hearsay.[16]

---

14 The old common law exceptions have been abolished although the court may take them into account when making a decision in terms of the interests of justice factors set out in s 3(1)(*c*).
15 *Mahomed v Attorney-General of Natal and Others* 1996 (1) SACR 139 (N).
16 *S v Ngwani* 1990 (1) SACR 449 (N). In *S v M M* 2012 (2) SACR 18 (SCA) the Supreme Court of Appeal observed the negative effect of an increasing trend that doctors' reports are simply handed in by consent, without the doctor being called to give evidence in terms of section 3(1)(*a*). The Court observed that this practice deprived the court of hearing the nuances of the doctor's oral evidence. See Bellengère A 'We'll Teach You a Lesson': The Role of the SCA as Educator and Disciplinarian – A Note on *S v Mashinini* 2012 1 SACR 604 (SCA) and *S v M M* 2012 2 SACR 18 (SCA) with reference to *S v Kolea* 2013 1 SACR 409 (SCA)' *Speculum Juris* 30 Part 2 2016.

25.4.2 Where the person testifies: sections 3(1)(b) and 3(3)

If the person on whose credibility the probative value of evidence depends testifies at a later stage of the proceedings, the hearsay evidence becomes admissible (section 3(1)(b)). A court may provisionally allow hearsay evidence on the understanding that the person will testify at some future time in the proceedings (section 3(3)). These provisions allow a party to admit evidence in a coherent manner, that is, without rendering the delivery of evidence fragmentary,[17] and without having to call the person as a witness at an early stage of the trial where this may be undesirable. If the person does not testify or repudiates the evidence, the hearsay evidence will not be taken into account unless it is admitted by agreement or in the interests of justice.

25.4.3 In the interests of justice: section 3(1)(c)

Hearsay evidence may be admitted in terms of the multiple factors listed under the 'interests of justice' provision. This provision is the most far-reaching of the exceptions created by section 3. According to the Supreme Court of Appeal in *S v Shaik and Others*,[18] the courts should not hesitate in admitting hearsay in terms of this provision and they should not lose sight of the true test for the admission of hearsay, that is, whether the interests of justice demands its reception. The court must assess all the factors according to the circumstances of a particular case. It is the combined assessment of all the factors, not an isolated assessment of individual factors, that will result in a proper application of the provision.[19] A discussion of these factors follows below.

25.4.3.1 The nature of the proceedings

It is easier to admit hearsay in civil proceedings where the standard of proof is on a balance of probabilities than in criminal proceedings.[20] The reluctance to admit hearsay in criminal trials is based on:
- the presumption of innocence
- the objection to the admission of unreliable, untested evidence
- the right of an accused to confront an accuser.[21]

Hearsay evidence may be admitted at bail applications,[22] inquest proceedings, in the Small Claims Court,[23] the Land Claims Court,[24] the Admiralty Court[25] and the Competition Tribunal, but not in interlocutory motion proceedings in the absence of urgency.[26]

25.4.3.2 The nature of evidence

When assessing the nature of hearsay evidence, that is, its reliability or unreliability, the courts will take into consideration a number of additional issues, such as the following:

---

17 *S v Ndhlovu and Others* 2002 (2) SACR 325 (SCA) at para 28.
18 2007 (1) SA 240 (SCA) at paras 170–171.
19 *S v Shaik and Others* 2007 (1) SA 240 (SCA) at paras 170–171. Where these factors overlap, it is more important to give effect to their combined weight than to regard each as a separate factor of admissibility.
20 Although s 2(2) of the Prevention of Organised Crime Act 121 of 1998 permits the admission of hearsay evidence in racketeering offences. The constitutionality of this section was upheld in *Savoi and Others v NDPP and Another* 2014 (1) SACR 545 (CC). Courts will, however, more readily admit hearsay evidence in criminal proceedings when the purpose of admitting the evidence is exculpatory. See *S v Rautenbach* 2014 (1) SACR 1 (GSJ).
21 *Metedad v National Employers' General Insurance Co Ltd* 1992 (1) SA 494 (W) at 499.
22 *S v Yanta* 2000 (1) SACR 237 (Tk).
23 S 26 of the Small Claims Courts Act 61 of 1984.
24 S 30(2)(a) of the Restitution of Land Rights Act 22 of 1994.
25 S 6(3) and (4) of the Admiralty Jurisdiction Regulation Act 105 of 1983.
26 *Swissborough Diamond Mines (Pty) Ltd and Others v Government of RSA and Others* 1999 (2) SA 279 (T) at 336.

- Was the person making the hearsay statement telling the truth? For example: Was the statement made voluntarily and spontaneously? Is it against the interests of the person? Does it pre-date the subject matter of the litigation? Did the person have a motive to lie? Does the person have a reputation for honesty?
- Did the person accurately remember and describe the events making up the statement? For example: What period of time has elapsed since the making of the statement? Are the events described by the person making the statement first-hand or second-hand, spontaneous, vivid, dramatic, simple or complex, unusual and unlikely to be forgotten? Do the events concern the person's own affairs or those of another?
- Did the person properly see or hear the events making up the statement? For example: Was there an opportunity for a clear and accurate observation of the events making up the statement? Does the person have poor eyesight or hearing? Is the court in a position to assess the person's perceptive powers accurately? Is there corroborating evidence supporting the accuracy of the statement?
- Was the person lucid and coherent when making the statement? For example: Is the statement oral or written? Is the statement vague and susceptible to inaccurate transmission or explanation?

25.4.3.3 The purpose for which the evidence is tendered

Hearsay evidence is more likely to be admitted when it is tendered to prove a subsidiary issue rather than a fundamental issue (although some cases hold the opposite).[27] It will be admitted for a compelling reason and not for a doubtful reason or illegitimate purpose, or for a purpose other than proving the truth of what the statement asserts.[28]

25.4.3.4 The probative value of the evidence

In determining whether hearsay evidence is sufficiently relevant to a fact in issue, the courts must assess the dual aspects of relevance, namely, assessing the probative weight of the evidence against the potential prejudice of its reception to an opposing party. In other words, what is the evidentiary weight of the hearsay evidence in relation to a fact in issue and does it reliably prove the fact in issue?[29]

The case that is relevant to this aspect is the case of *S v Rathumbu*,[30] which involved an appeal against the appellant's conviction for murdering his wife. The issue before the Court was to determine whether the trial court had properly admitted evidence which was a written, sworn statement by the appellant's sister. This evidence was that she had stated that she had seen the appellant stab the deceased with a knife. The State had conceded that without the statement, which was, in essence, hearsay evidence, the appeal should succeed.

The Court in this case stated that the probative value of the statement depended on the credibility of the witness at the time of making the statement. The central question was whether the interests of justice required that the prior statement be admitted despite the witness's later disavowal of it. The Court, having regard to the substantial corroboration for the truthfulness of the statement found in other evidence tendered by the State, held that it was correctly admitted by the trial court.[31]

---

27 *Hlongwane and Others v Rector, St Francis College and Others* 1989 (3) SA 318 (D); *S v Ramavhale* 1996 (1) SACR 639 (A) at 649D–E.
28 *Metedad v National Employers' General Insurance Co Ltd* 1992 (1) SA 494 (W).
29 *S v Ndhlovu and Others* 2002 (2) SACR 325 (SCA) at para 45.
30 2012 (2) SACR 219 (SCA).
31 *S v Rathumbu* 2012 (2) SACR 219 (SCA) at paras 222J and 223E.

272 | THE LAW OF EVIDENCE IN SOUTH AFRICA

25.4.3.5 The reason why the evidence is not given by the person on whose credibility the probative value depends

As explained above, the admissibility of hearsay evidence depends on minimising the degree of untrustworthiness, unreliability and prejudice to an opposing party. It will also depend on whether there are acceptable reasons for the failure of the person making the statement to testify. Acceptable reasons for a failure to testify include:

- the death of the person making the statement
- the ill health or mental instability of the person
- the absence of the person from the country during a trial
- the existence of legislation prohibiting a person from testifying[32]
- the fear of violent reprisals[33]
- an inability to trace the person[34]
- a reluctant person who is likely to lie about the correctness of an earlier out-of-court statement.

25.4.3.6 Prejudice to opponents

It has been argued that the admission of hearsay would place the opposing party at a procedurally unfair disadvantage. The admission of hearsay would:

- place an unfair burden of rebuttal on the opposing party
- prevent the opposing party from effectively countering inferences drawn from hearsay
- unfairly lengthen trial proceedings
- mean that the opposing party would be unable to cross-examine the person who made the hearsay statement since hearsay is not subject to the usual reliability checks which apply to first-hand testimony.

In *S v Ndhlovu and Others*, the Supreme Court of Appeal held that the use of hearsay by the prosecution did not amount to a procedural prejudice:[35]

> ... where the interests of justice require the admission of hearsay, the resulting strengthening of the opposing case cannot count as prejudice ... since in weighing the interests of justice the court must already have concluded that the reliability of the evidence is such that its admission is necessary and justified.

The Court concluded that the admission of hearsay did not unreasonably infringe the constitutional right to challenge evidence and that s 3(1)(c) constituted a justified limitation on the right to a fair trial set out in s 35(3)(i) of the Constitution:[36]

> [T]he Bill of Rights does not guarantee an entitlement to subject all evidence to cross-examination. What it contains is the right ... to 'challenge evidence'. Where that evidence is hearsay, the right entails that the accused is entitled to resist its

---

32 *Welz and Another v Hall and Others* 1996 (4) SA 1073 (C).

33 *Hlongwane and Others v Rector, St Francis College and Others* 1989 (3) SA 318 (D) at 325I; *S v Staggie and Another* 2003 (1) SACR 232 (C).

34 *Makhathini v Road Accident Fund* 2002 (1) SA 511 (SCA) at 524B.

35 2002 (2) SACR 325 (SCA) at para 50. However, with regard to extra curial admissions, the Constitutional Court in *Mhlongo v S; Nkosi v S* 2015 (2) SACR 323 (CC) overturned this decision, holding that s 3(1)(c) cannot be relied on to admit extra-curial admissions of an accused against a co accused. See also *S v Khanye and Another* 2017(2) SACR 630(CC) where the court restored the common law position that extra curial confessions or admissions of an accused are inadmissible against a co-accused.

36 At para 24.

CHAPTER 25   HEARSAY EVIDENCE   273

> admission and to scrutinise its probative value, including its reliability ... But where the interests of justice, constitutionally measured, require that hearsay evidence be admitted, no constitutional right is infringed.

The degree of prejudice caused by the admission of hearsay may be lessened if a court takes into account the following:

- Was the hearsay statement made under oath?
- Did the opposing party have any opportunity to question the person making the statement?
- Was the opposing party given a reasonable opportunity to analyse the statement and to prepare evidence in rebuttal?
- Would cross-examination have produced a positive or negative result for the opposing party?

25.4.3.7   Any other factor which in the opinion of the court should be taken into account

A court may take into account any other factor, depending on the circumstances of a case, as there is no fixed or closed list of such factors.[37] Although section 3 has abolished the common law exceptions to the hearsay rule, courts still refer to them as additional factors and may take them into account when exercising their discretion to admit hearsay in the interests of justice.

The more important common law exceptions are explained in the discussion on *res gestae* and include spontaneous statements, composite acts, declarations of state of mind and declarations of physical sensations.

Another old common law exception that has survived as a factor that the courts may refer to is that of dying declarations. These are statements made by a person, who has since died, in circumstances where the person was under a hopeless expectation of death. The person must have been a **competent witness** at the time of making the statement and the statement must be relevant to the person's death. These are admissible only in cases of murder or culpable homicide. The lack of a rational basis for this exception has seen it become increasingly less used and in some jurisdictions (England) it has been removed by legislation.[38]

25.5   Other statutory exceptions

Section 3 abolishes the common law exceptions but not the pre-1988 statutory exceptions. Section 3 also states that its provisions are 'subject to the provisions of any other law'. Therefore, a court may admit hearsay in terms of the broad exceptions set out in section 3(1)(c) or it may elect to receive hearsay in terms of a specific provision contained in another statute. Some of the most important statues that allow for the admission of hearsay evidence are the Criminal Procedure Act 51 of 1977 and the Civil Proceedings Evidence Act 25 of 1965.

25.5.1   The Criminal Procedure Act, 1977

The Criminal Procedure Act, 1977 allows for the admission of hearsay evidence in certain circumstances, outlined below.

---

37 Other factors which have been taken into account are consistency with the proved facts and the accused's participation in the events written into the hearsay document. See *Skilya Property Investments (Pty) Ltd v Lloyds of London Underwriting* 2002 (3) SA 765 (T).

38 In South Africa, see *R v Baloi* 1949 (1) SA 491 (T); *R v Dinehine* 1910 CPD 371. In England s 118(2) of the Criminal Justice Act, 2003 has abolished most of the common law exceptions to the hearsay rule, including a dying declaration.

25.5.1.1 Affidavits

To avoid the procedural inconvenience of admitting oral testimony, certain facts, as described in section 212 of the Criminal Procedure Act, 1977, may be admitted in the form of an affidavit which will constitute *prima facie* evidence of the facts contained therein. These are described below:[39]

- *Section 212(1):* Whether an act, transaction or occurrence did or did not take place in a state department, provincial administration, court of law or bank may be proved by way of affidavit. In terms of section 212A, an act, transaction or occurrence which takes place in a foreign state department, court or bank may also be proved by way of affidavit.
- *Section 212(2):* The fact that a person did not supply an official with information relevant to an issue in criminal proceedings may be explained by the official by way of an affidavit.
- *Section 212(3):* The registration and recording of official acts or matters required by law and the proof of such registration or recording may be proved by way of affidavit.
- *Section 212(4):* An examination or process and the test results thereof requiring skill in science, medicine, mathematics, computers, ballistics and so on, and relevant to an issue in criminal proceedings may be set out in the form of an affidavit. In examinations requiring skill in chemistry, anatomy or pathology, a certificate instead of an affidavit may be issued.
- *Section 212(5):* The existence and nature of precious metals and stones.
- *Section 212(7):* The condition and identity of a dead body.
- *Section 212(8):* The chain of custody, that is, the receipt, packing, marking and delivery, of an object.

25.5.1.2 Written statements

Section 213 allows a written witness statement, except that of an accused, to be admitted at trial in the place of oral evidence, but only with the consent of all the parties.

25.5.1.3 Preparatory examinations

Section 214 allows evidence by a witness recorded at a preparatory examination to be admitted at trial where the witness is dead, ill or incapable of attending the trial.

25.5.1.4 Former trials

Section 215 allows the recorded evidence of a witness at a prior trial to be admitted by way of affidavit at a later trial. Section 60(11B)(*c*) allows the record of bail proceedings to be admitted at trial.

25.5.1.5 Business records

Section 221 allows certain trade or business records compiled from information supplied by a person having personal knowledge of such trade or business to be admitted where the person is dead, physically or mentally ill and thus unfit to attend as a witness, out of the country, or cannot be found or identified.

---

39 In *S v Van der Sandt* 1997 (2) SACR 116 (W) at 132E, the Court stated that the evidence allowed by s 212 is usually peripheral to the real issues and often essential to the proper administration of justice. It does not unreasonably infringe the Constitution.

25.5.1.6 Judicial proceedings

Section 235 allows an original record of a judicial proceeding to be proved by way of a certified copy.

25.5.1.7 Bankers' books

In terms of section 236, bankers' books, that is, entries in ledgers, cashbooks, account books and so on, are admissible if proof is given, by way of an accompanying affidavit by an official in the service of the bank, that such entries have been made in the ordinary course of business and that the books are in the control and custody of the bank.

25.5.2 The Civil Proceedings Evidence Act, 1965

The Civil Proceedings Evidence Act, 1965 allows for the admission of hearsay evidence in certain circumstances, outlined below.

25.5.2.1 Affidavits

Section 22(1) allows any examination or process requiring skill in bacteriology, biology, chemistry, physics, pathology, and so on and which is relevant to an issue in civil proceedings to be admitted by way of an affidavit. This section is similar to section 212(4) of the Criminal Procedure Act, 1977.

25.5.2.2 Sunrise and sunset

Section 26 allows the admission of tables of sunset and sunrise times prepared by any official observatory and published in the ***Government Gazette***.

25.5.2.3 Bankers' books

In terms of section 28, bankers' books, that is, entries in ledgers, cashbooks, account books and so on, are admissible if proof is given by way of an accompanying affidavit by an official in the service of the bank that such entries have been made in the ordinary course of business and that the books are in the control and custody of the bank. This section is also similar to the corresponding section 236 of the Criminal Procedure Act, 1977.

25.5.2.4 Documentary evidence

Part VI (sections 33–38) of the Civil Proceedings Evidence Act, 1965 allows for the admission of documentary evidence of a fact in issue. In particular, section 34 permits the admission of an original document containing a statement made by a person about a fact in issue, provided that:
- the person who made the document must either have had personal knowledge of the facts contained in the document or, where the document forms part of a continuous record, they must have done so under a duty to record the statement
- the person must be called to testify unless the person is dead, unfit to attend, out of the country or cannot be found. The court has a discretion to admit such a document where undue expense or delay would result if it did not.

25.5.3 Other examples

25.5.3.1 Electronic evidence

Computer-generated evidence (that is, data messages) described in sections 12–15 of the Electronic Communications and Transactions Act 25 of 2002 may be admitted as hearsay

276 THE LAW OF EVIDENCE IN SOUTH AFRICA

evidence in terms of section 3(1) of the Law of Evidence Amendment Act, 1988 or section 221 of the Criminal Procedure Act, 1977.

25.5.3.2 Companies' books

The Companies Act 71 of 2008 in sections 50(4) and 51(1)(c) states that the securities register of a company shall constitute *prima facie* proof of the matters contained therein.

25.5.3.3 Age

A person's age may be proved by furnishing a birth certificate or the court may, in terms of section 337 of the Criminal Procedure Act, 1977, estimate a person's age.

25.5.3.4 Public documents

A document made by a public official in the execution of a public duty, intended for public use and to which there is public access, may be admitted as an exception to the hearsay rule. Although this is a common law hearsay exception, which has been abolished, the courts continue to be influenced by it.[40]

25.6 The South African Law Reform Commission (SALRC) Project 126 *Review of the Law of Evidence* Discussion Paper 113 *Hearsay and Relevance*

This discussion paper deals with an investigation that arose out of a previous study conducted in 2002. The findings of this study identified areas of the law of evidence that needed reform were identified and suggested the possibility of conducting such reform. The committee, which was tasked with finding the problem areas of the law of evidence, identified the topics of relevance and hearsay as the two topics for investigation.

The preliminary investigations pointed out the need to take into account the structural features of the courts, which include the limited role of lay assessors as well as the adversarial nature of the court proceedings.

This paper looks at the implications of the structural features for the law of evidence reform and reiterates the policy considerations identified in the preliminary survey. It also examines the hearsay evidence and relevance areas.

The recommendations put forward by this discussion paper[41] are summarised below:

1. *Retain the status quo (with or without the introduction of a notice requirement):* This option involves the giving of a notice by a party of his or her intention to rely on hearsay evidence and should be a factor taken into account when the court is determining a prejudicial effect of the hearsay evidence. The notice would remove the element of surprise and would count as a factor that favours hearsay evidence.[42]
2. *Free admission:* This option means that the hearsay rules in their entirety would be considered obsolete and hearsay would be freely admitted unless excluded on some other ground, for example relevance.[43]
3. *Free admission coupled with decision rules pertaining to weight:* This option means that if free admission is coupled with decision rules pertaining to weight it would eliminate

---

40 Zeffertt and Paizes 2 ed (2009) at 439–441.
41 SALRC Project 126 *Review of the Law of Evidence* Discussion Paper 113 *Hearsay and Relevance* (2008) at 49–57.
42 Ibid. at 49–52.
43 Ibid. at 52.

inefficiencies which arise from determining the admissibility of hearsay (as well as doubt in respect of admissibility) but would require presiding officers to articulate the basis on which they have afforded a particular weight to an item of hearsay evidence. This would then serve as a safeguard against a potential misuse of the hearsay evidence.[44]

4. *Apply different rules in civil and criminal trials:* This means that the approach to hearsay in civil trials should be an inclusionary one, which will be subject to safeguards. The admission in criminal trials should then be subject to the provisions that are similar substantially to the provisions of section 3 of the Law of Evidence Amendment Act, 1988.[45]

The current status of the discussion paper is that the closing date for commentary was 30 June 2008. However, there have not been any follow-up reports conducted nor has there been progress made on this discussion paper.

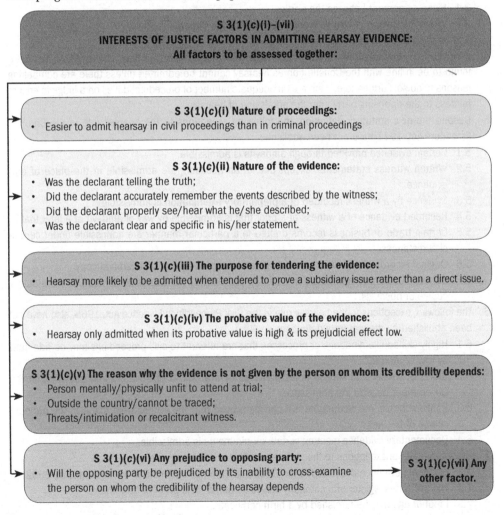

Figure 25.2 Hearsay: Interests of justice test

---

44 Ibid. at 52–53.
45 Ibid. at 53–57.

278 | THE LAW OF EVIDENCE IN SOUTH AFRICA

THIS CHAPTER IN ESSENCE

1   The common law definition of hearsay has been replaced with a statutory definition describing hearsay as 'evidence, whether oral or in writing, the probative value of which depends upon the credibility of any person other than the person giving such evidence'.

2   Generally, hearsay evidence is inadmissible for the following reasons:
   2.1   The witness who made the statement is not in court and under oath.
   2.2   The witness cannot be tested through cross-examination.
   2.3   The court is not able to observe the demeanour and evaluate the credibility of the witness who made the statement.

3   The statutory definition of hearsay has the effect of granting the courts the power to admit hearsay in the following cases:
   3.1   by an agreement between the parties
   3.2   where the person on whose credibility the evidence depends testifies
   3.3   in the interests of justice.

4   Although the constitutionality of the statutory definition of hearsay has been challenged, it has been found to be in line with the Constitution as hearsay cannot be admitted unless there are compelling reasons to do so. Furthermore, there are an adequate number of procedural duties on a judge to ensure fairness to the opposing party after the admission of hearsay.

5   Despite the new statutory definition, the following exceptions to the hearsay rule in the Criminal Procedure Act, 1977 have not been abolished:
   5.1   Certain evidence provided through affidavits is admissible.
   5.2   Written witness statements, except that of an accused, are admissible in the place of oral evidence.
   5.3   Evidence by a witness recorded at a preparatory examination is admissible.
   5.4   Recorded evidence of a witness at a prior trial is admissible by way of affidavit at a later trial.
   5.5   Certain trade or business records drafted in a particular manner are admissible under certain circumstances.
   5.6   Original records of a judicial proceeding can be proved by way of a certified copy.
   5.7   Bankers' books are admissible if it can be proved that the entries were made in the ordinary course of business.

6   The following exceptions to the hearsay rule in the Civil Proceedings Evidence Act, 1965, also have not been abolished by the statutory definition:
   6.1   Highly skilled examinations or processes that are relevant to civil proceedings may be admitted by way of affidavit.
   6.2   Tables of sunset and sunrise times prepared by any official observatory and published in the *Government Gazette* are admissible.
   6.3   Bankers' books are admissible if it can be proved that the entries were made in the ordinary course of business.
   6.4   Documentary evidence meeting certain requirements is admissible.

7   Other examples of exceptions to the statutory definition of hearsay include:
   7.1   Electronic evidence described in the Electronic Communications and Transactions Act, 2002.
   7.2   The securities register of a company serves as prima facie proof of its content.
   7.3   Proof of age may be furnished by a birth certificate.
   7.4   Public documents drafted by certain persons and meeting certain requirements are admissible.

8   The SALRC Project 126 *The Review of the Law of Evidence* Discussion Paper 113 *Hearsay and Relevance* identified a need to reform certain areas of the law of evidence. The following recommendations are put forward in this Discussion Paper:

8.1   The *status quo* should be retained with or without the requirement that a party intending to rely on hearsay evidence should give notice thereof.

8.2   The hearsay rules in their entirety should be considered obsolete and hearsay freely admitted unless excluded on some other ground.

8.3   If hearsay evidence was freely admitted, a safeguard could be built in by coupling the free admission with decision rules pertaining to the weight to be attached thereto.

8.4   Different rules should be applied in civil and criminal trials. Civil trials should follow an inclusionary approach, subject to safeguards, while the admission of hearsay in criminal trials should be subject to the provisions similar to the statutory definition of hearsay.

Chapter 26

Privilege

26.1	Definition of privilege	280
26.2	Private privilege	281
	26.2.1 Legal professional privilege	281
	26.2.1.1 The legal professional must act in a professional capacity	282
	26.2.1.2 The client must intend that the communication be made to a legal professional in confidence	282
	26.2.1.3 For the purpose of obtaining legal advice	283
	26.2.1.4 In respect of a pending or contemplated litigation	283
	26.2.1.5 The client must claim the privilege	283
	26.2.1.6 Legal professional privilege as a limited fundamental right	284
	26.2.1.7 Litigation privilege as opposed to legal professional privilege	285
	26.2.2 Witness's privilege against self-incrimination	285
	26.2.2.1 Legal basis of a witness's privilege against self-incrimination	285
	26.2.2.2 Rationales for a witness's privilege against self-incrimination	286
	26.2.2.3 Application of a witness's privilege against self-incrimination	286
	26.2.3 Accused's right to silence	288
	26.2.3.1 Common law right to silence	289
	26.2.3.2 Constitutional right to silence	290
	26.2.4 Other private privileges	293
	26.2.4.1 Professional privileges	293
	26.2.4.2 Marital privilege	294
	26.2.4.3 Statements made without prejudice	294
26.3	State privilege	294
	26.3.1 The common law development of state privilege	295
	26.3.2 Post-constitutional state privilege	296
	26.3.3 The Promotion of Access to Information Act, 2000 (PAIA)	298
	26.3.4 Police docket privilege	299
	26.3.4.1 Police docket	299
	26.3.4.2 Consultations with state witnesses	301
	26.3.5 Crime detection privileges	301
	26.3.6 Other state privileges	303
	26.3.6.1 Judicial proceedings	304
	26.3.6.2 Statutory privileges	304

26.1 Definition of privilege

Privilege is an essential evidentiary rule because it is considered to be in the interests of society that, in certain circumstances, an individual or the State may lawfully refuse to disclose relevant evidence at trial even if the privileged evidence is the only evidence

CHAPTER 26 PRIVILEGE | 281

available to a court. In addition, a court may not draw any adverse inference against an individual or a state organ claiming privilege. In essence, privilege protects the interests of the individual (private privilege) or the State (state or executive privilege) at the expense of abstract notions of justice.[1]

Privilege must be distinguished from other rules of evidence for two reasons:

- First, the exclusionary rules of evidence render certain types of evidence, such as similar fact, character, hearsay and opinion evidence, inadmissible due to the inherent unreliability of such evidence, their lack of probative value and the potential prejudicial effect that these types of evidence may have on the fairness of a trial. However, a claim of privilege serves to exclude admissible relevant evidence, which has none of the disadvantages of the above types of evidence, on the basis that it is justified by public policy.
- Second, privilege must be distinguished from the evidentiary rules concerning the competence and compellability of a witness to testify at trial. An incompetent witness lacks the capacity to testify and a non-compellable witness has the right to refuse to testify at trial altogether.

Generally, a witness who wants to invoke a privilege must take to the witness box and then raise the privilege on a question-by-question basis.

26.2 Private privilege

An individual who intends to claim a particular **private privilege** cannot refuse to attend court. The holder of a private privilege must claim, or waive, such privilege personally. A court cannot claim, or waive, a private privilege on behalf of the accused or any other witness. An individual must be fully aware at all times of the right to claim a particular privilege. It is the court's duty to inform an unrepresented accused or witness of the privilege available to them. To circumvent a private privilege, it is possible to admit secondary or circumstantial evidence to prove relevant facts in issue protected by privilege.

Private privilege is aimed at preventing the admission of relevant evidence at trial and is therefore limited to the following categories:

- legal professional privilege or attorney–client privilege, which may be claimed in civil and criminal proceedings
- a privilege against self-incrimination, which may be claimed by a witness or an accused who chooses to testify when there is a reasonable risk of a criminal prosecution
- an accused's pre-trial and trial right to silence
- other privileges, including marital privilege, parent–child privilege and statements made without prejudice.

26.2.1 Legal professional privilege

It is in the public interest to ensure the efficient and proper functioning of civil and criminal proceedings. In *S v Safatsa and Others*,[2] the Court held that the interests of the administration

---

1 DT Zeffertt and AP Paizes *South African Law of Evidence* 2 ed (2009) at 573–708; PJ Schwikkard and SE van der Merwe *Principles of Evidence* 3 ed (2009) at 123–55.
2 1988 (1) SA 868 (A) at 885–6. See also *South African Airways Soc v BDFM Publishers (Pty) Ltd and Others* 2016 (2) SA 561 (GJ) where the court held that legal advice privilege is not an absolute right in South African law.

282 | THE LAW OF EVIDENCE IN SOUTH AFRICA

of justice also require full, confidential, honest and frank communications between a client and an attorney. The privilege applies to all communications made for the purpose of giving or receiving legal advice. It is a fundamental rule necessary for the proper functioning of the legal system and not merely an evidentiary rule assisting in the proper functioning of any particular litigation. Legal professional privilege is more than a mere evidentiary rule and amounts to a fundamental right or substantive rule of law designed to reinforce the procedural rights set out in section 35 of the Constitution and to ensure a fair trial process, as illustrated in the case below.

Minister of Safety and Others and Security v Bennett and Others

In *Minister of Safety and Security and Others v Bennett and Others*,[3] the Court held that the privilege as a fundamental right is important because it is central to ensuring the constitutional imperative of a fair trial and reinforcing the constitutionally enshrined right to legal representation during legal proceedings. The privilege guarantees the right of every person to access legal representation and to consult with a legal advisor privately and confidentially.

Legal professional privilege may be claimed for any confidential communication or confidential document made by a client to a legal professional acting in a professional capacity for the purpose of pending litigation or merely for the purpose of obtaining legal advice. The requirements for legal professional privilege are set out below.

26.2.1.1 The legal professional must act in a professional capacity

A payment of a fee to an attorney or advocate in private practice is a good indication that this requirement has been met although a salaried, in-house legal advisor may also act in a professional capacity when giving legal advice to an employer.[4] Certain other factors are also good indicators such as whether the legal professional was acting professionally,[5] whether the legal professional was best suited to give advice and to consult with the client on the matter, and the place where the consultation was held.

26.2.1.2 The client must intend that the communication be made to a legal professional in confidence

The nature of the communication is important in determining whether the client intended it to be confidential. If the client intended the communication to be passed on to other parties or other independent parties are present during the making of the communication, then the client did not make the communication in confidence. Usually, a client intends a communication to be confidential when he or she makes it in a private place such as a legal professional's office. It is not usually interpreted to be confidential when made in a public place where it can easily be overheard.[6]

---

3 2009 (2) SACR 17 (SCA). See also *Euroshipping Corporation of Monrovia v Minister of Agricultural Economics and Marketing and Others* 1979 (1) SA 637 (C) at 643 where the Court held that the privilege is a fundamental right of a client.
4 *Mohamed v President of RSA and Others* 2001 (2) SA 1145 (C) at 1154.
5 *Van der Heever v Die Meester en 'Andere* 1997 (3) SA 93 (T).
6 *Giovagnoli v Di Meo* 1960 (3) SA 393 (N).

26.2.1.3 For the purpose of obtaining legal advice

The client must be seeking legal guidance and not some other form of advice.[7] The privilege cannot be claimed where the client seeks legal advice to plan or further a criminal or fraudulent activity.[8]

26.2.1.4 In respect of a pending or contemplated litigation

A communication made directly between attorney and client for the purpose of legal advice need not be connected to pending or actual litigation for the privilege to apply. However, statements from or communications to agents and other third parties will only be considered to be privileged when made after litigation is contemplated.[9]

26.2.1.5 The client must claim the privilege

The privilege attaches to the client and a court will not uphold the privilege unless the client claims it.[10] A legal professional claims the privilege on behalf of a client. Whether or not the requirements of legal professional privilege have been met are often questions of fact which are determined by the circumstances of each case.

Where a client waives the privilege, a legal professional is bound by such a waiver.[11] The client's waiver may be done directly or expressly, it may be implied or imputed, but at all times it must be made intelligently, knowingly and voluntarily.[12] An implied waiver requires an element of publication or disclosure of the communication, document or part of it by the client from whose behaviour the court can objectively conclude that the privilege was intentionally abandoned. An imputed waiver occurs where, regardless of the client's intention, fairness requires that the court conclude that the privilege was abandoned.

The privilege applies not only to communications between a client and a legal professional. Its scope extends to all employees of the law firm including professional assistants, candidate attorneys, associates, secretaries, interpreters, cleaners, drivers, and so on.

The privilege does not extend to independent third parties. When such a person acquires knowledge of the communication in the form of secondary evidence by, for example, inadvertently overhearing, intercepting or making copies of the communication, the independent party cannot be prevented from disclosing it. Where the communication comes into the possession of a third party through an unlawful act, a court may refuse to admit it on the basis of its discretion to exclude **unfairly obtained evidence**.

---

7   *S v Kearney* 1964 (2) SA 495 (A). In particular, s 201 of the Criminal Procedure Act 51 of 1977 requires the communication to be made after the legal advisor has been professionally employed to conduct the client's defence. See also *A Company and Others v Commissioner South African Revenue Services* 2014 (4) SA 549 (WCC) where it was held that attorneys' fee notes are not a privileged category of document. Privilege extends only to those parts of fee notes which disclose contents of privileged communications between attorney and client or from which such content may be inferred. See also *Competition Commission v ArcelorMittal SA Ltd and Others* 2013 (5) SA 538 (SCA) where the court held that a reference to part of a privileged document made during the course of pleading is sufficient to constitute waiver thereby destroying the privilege attached to the entire document and not just the part referred to.

8   *Harksen v Attorney-General, Cape and Others* 1999 (1) SA 718 (C).

9   *General Accident Fire and Life Assurance Corporation Ltd v Goldberg* 1912 TPD 494.

10 *Bogoshi v Van Vuuren NO and Others; Bogoshi and Another v Director, Office for Serious Economic Offences and Others* 1996 (1) SA 785 (A). Before legal professional privilege can be claimed the communication in question must have been made to a legal adviser acting in a professional capacity, in confidence, and for the purpose of pending litigation, or for the purpose of obtaining professional advice. See *Competition Commission v ArcelorMittal South Africa Ltd and Others* 2013 (5) SA 538 (SCA).

11 *S v Nkata and Others* 1990 (4) SA 250 (A).

12 *S v Tandwa and Others* 2008 (1) SACR 613 (SCA) at para 18.

284 | THE LAW OF EVIDENCE IN SOUTH AFRICA

Since legal professional privilege is a fundamental right, it may be claimed to prevent the seizure of confidential documents in terms of a valid police search and seizure warrant.[13] However, a court has an inherent power, especially during the process of civil discovery, to examine any document for which a claim of privilege has been made. A court's discretion to examine any document to determine whether a claim of privilege is valid should be used sparingly and only in special circumstances. These circumstances include where it is necessary and desirable for a just decision to be made or some reason exists which casts doubt on a claim of privilege.[14] A court also has the power to cut out portions from a privileged document not covered by the privilege.[15]

26.2.1.6 Legal professional privilege as a limited fundamental right

Where legal professional privilege, as a fundamental right, is in conflict with other constitutional rights, a court must seek to resolve the conflict by establishing a reasonable balance between the conflicting rights. For example, in certain circumstances the privilege may clash with a person's right to access information in terms of section 32 of the Constitution, as illustrated in the examples below.

Jeeva and Others v Receiver of Revenue, Port Elizabeth and Others
In *Jeeva and Others v Receiver of Revenue, Port Elizabeth and Others*,[16] the Court held that in certain circumstances the privilege constituted a reasonable and justified limitation on a person's constitutional right of access to information. The bias in favour of the privilege was due to its unique importance to the entire administration of justice.[17] The Court also noted that there could be circumstances where the privilege should not take precedence over the constitutional right of access to information.[18]

Thint (Pty) Ltd v National Director of Public Prosecutions and Others; Zuma v National Director of Public Prosecutions and Others
A similar balance was achieved in *Thint (Pty) Ltd v National Director of Public Prosecutions and Others; Zuma v National Director of Public Prosecutions and Others*[19] where the Court examined the relationship between the privilege, the Constitution and sections 28 and 29 of the National Prosecuting Authority Act 32 of 1998. These sections permit the search of premises under investigation, the seizure of objects or the examination and the making of copies of documents found on the premises.

South African Airways Society v BDFM Publishers Pty Ltd and others
In *South African Airways Society v BDFM Publishers Pty Ltd and others*[20] The court examined, *inter alia*, two aspects of legal professional privilege. First it held that the privilege is a negative right allowing the holder to elect to refuse to disclose information protected by the privilege, but that it was not a positive right allowing the holder to prevent or suppress a third party which had come to be in possession of the information from publishing it. Second it held that, when considering

---

13 *Bogoshi v Van Vuuren NO and Others; Bogoshi and Another v Director, Office for Serious Economic Offences and Others* 1996 (1) SA 785 (A).
14 *South African Rugby Football Union and Others v President of the RSA and Others* 1998 (4) SA 296 (T) at 302.
15 *Mohamed v President of RSA and Others* 2001 (2) SA 1145 (C) at 11591.
16 1995 (2) SA 433 (SE).
17 At 456.
18 At 456. See also *Van Niekerk v Pretoria City Council* 1997 (3) SA 839 (T) at 849; *Le Roux v Direkteur-Generaal van Handel en Nywerheid* 1997 (4) SA 174 (T).
19 2008 (2) SACR 421 (CC).
20 2016 (2) SA 561 (GJ).

CHAPTER 26 PRIVILEGE | 285

the suppression of information (the court referred to section 16 of the Constitution), circumstances may arise in respect of matters about which 'every citizen has a tangible interest to be informed' (para 65) and that in the circumstances of this case (which dealt with the publication of privileged information about SAA) 'public interest in being informed outweighs the right the right of SAA to confidentiality in the contents of the document' (para 65). The court thereby established that legal professional privilege is not an absolute right and is subject to a public interest over-ride.

26.2.1.7 Litigation privilege as opposed to legal professional privilege

A litigation privilege is distinct from that of legal professional privilege. However, it is often misinterpreted as an extension of legal professional privilege. A litigation privilege applies to contracted third parties or agents, such as private detectives, assessors and accountants, who are employed to generate information for the purpose of litigation. However, this only applies when:

- first, the communication between the client, the legal professional and the agent was made after the contemplation of litigation
- second, the communication was intended to be submitted to the legal professional.[21]

The litigation privilege is of fairly recent origin and initially applied only to criminal proceedings for reasons described in *R v Steyn* below. However, in *Phato v Attorney-General Eastern Cape and Another; Commissioner of SAPS v Attorney-General Eastern Cape and Others*,[22] it was artificially extended to cover civil proceedings as well.

> **R v Steyn**
> In *R v Steyn*,[23] the Court held that the litigation privilege is necessary to:
> - prevent unnecessary delays and postponements in the trial
> - prevent the trial being submerged in an irrelevant enquiry as to what has or has not been said by a witness
> - prevent an opponent from manufacturing evidence to contradict the revealed communication.

26.2.2 Witness's privilege against self-incrimination

26.2.2.1 Legal basis of a witness's privilege against self-incrimination

According to the Court in *R v Camane and Others*,[24] 'no one may be compelled to give evidence incriminating him- or herself ..., either before a trial or during a trial'. Therefore, the witness's privilege against self-incrimination, and the accused's right to silence, are premised on the central notion that an individual is entitled to a fair trial.[25] The witness's privilege against self-incrimination allows a witness, while in the witness box, to refuse to answer any questions which will incriminate him- or herself. This privilege is set out in

---

21 *General Accident Fire and Life Assurance Corporation Ltd v Goldberg* 1912 TPD 494.
22 1994 (2) SACR 734 (E).
23 1954 (1) SA 324 (A).
24 1925 AD 570 at 575. See also C Theophilopoulos 'The historical antecedents of the right to silence and the evolution of the adversarial trial system' (2003) 14(2) *Stellenbosch Law Review* 161.
25 There is a close constitutional relationship between professional legal privilege, the privilege against self-incrimination, the right to silence and the right to legal representation. These rights are necessary to ensure fairness during criminal and civil proceedings and are directly or by inference set out in s 35 of the Constitution.

286 | THE LAW OF EVIDENCE IN SOUTH AFRICA

the common law[26] and statutory law,[27] and is also defined in section 35(1)(*a*), (*b*) and (*c*) of the Constitution.

26.2.2.2 Rationales for a witness's privilege against self-incrimination

The justifications for the existence of a privilege against self-incrimination are based on the following rationales:

- A witness has a natural privilege against self-incrimination and an accused has a natural right to silence due to the presumption of innocence. This places the burden of proving the accused's guilt beyond a reasonable doubt on the shoulders of the prosecution.
- It is necessary to ensure that witnesses will come forward and testify freely with the knowledge that they will not be forced to incriminate themselves.
- All persons subjected to legal proceedings have a constitutional right to privacy and dignity.
- The public has an aversion to the inherent cruelty of compelling witnesses to incriminate themselves while in the witness box and thereby exposing themselves to a risk of criminal punishment.
- It is necessary to prevent an improper investigation by law enforcement officials, which may result in unreliable evidence.
- It is necessary to guarantee the truth-seeking function of a court.

26.2.2.3 Application of a witness's privilege against self-incrimination

In terms of section 203 of the Criminal Procedure Act, 1977, a witness in criminal proceedings may refuse to answer a question if the answer would expose the witness to a risk of possible future criminal prosecution. The privilege against self-incrimination may be invoked during a criminal or civil trial whenever there is a reasonable risk of a possible future criminal prosecution.[28] The privilege applies to any person regardless of whether he or she is a suspect, accused, witness, citizen, legal or illegal resident.

Section 35(3)(*j*) of the Constitution refers to the accused's right 'not to be compelled to give self-incriminatory evidence'. However, the wording of section 35(3) awards this right against self-incrimination only to the arrested or detained accused and specifically excludes the non-party witness. As a result of the narrow focus of section 35(3), the non-party witness privilege continues to be governed by common and statutory law. The witness or the witness's nominated legal representative must expressly invoke the non-party privilege. The witness is still required to testify and must claim the privilege on a question-by-question basis.[29] The witness must make the invocation timeously at the point when the incriminating question is asked. The non-party witness privilege may not be invoked by a witness who has already been convicted of the offence in question, or where the crime has prescribed, or where the witness no longer runs the risk of prosecution. The privilege against self-incrimination may only be claimed by the witness and does not extend to a spouse, relative or a third party. The court is obliged to warn the witness of the privilege and a failure to do

---

26 *S v Lwane* 1966 (2) SA 433 (A).

27 S 203 of the Criminal Procedure Act, 1977. 'No witness in criminal proceedings shall, except as provided by this Act or any other law, be compelled to answer any question ... by reason that the answer may expose him [or her] to a criminal charge.' See also ss 200, 204–5, 217 (admission of a voluntary confession), s 219A (admission of a voluntary admission) and s 14 of the Civil Proceedings Evidence Act 25 of 1965.

28 See *Waddell Eyles NO and Welsh NO* 1939 TPD 198; *S v Ramaligela en 'n Ander* 1983 (2) SA 424 (V); *R v Diedericks* 1957 (3) SA 661 (E). See also s 200 of the Criminal Procedure Act, 1977 read with ss 14 and 42 of the Civil Proceedings Evidence Act, 1965.

29 See *R v Kuyper* 1915 TPD 308 at 316; *R v Ntshangela en Andere* 1961 (4) SA 592 (A).

CHAPTER 26 PRIVILEGE | 287

so may render the incriminating testimony inadmissible in any future prosecution.[30] The privilege is said to flow naturally from an accusatorial type criminal justice system and is an important instrumental element of the fair trial principle.[31] It is also said to protect the witness's dignity,[32] privacy and personal autonomy[33] during the criminal process. The risk of self-incrimination must be real and appreciable and may not amount to a mere remote and naked possibility of legal peril.[34] The determination of risk is a matter of judicial discretion and the court may test the validity and substance of the witness's claim. The privilege not only applies to answers which may directly incriminate the witness but also to answers, though innocent in themselves, which may indirectly form a material link in the chain of causal proof, thereby ultimately leading to incriminating evidence and the risk of a criminal charge.[35]

The effect of the privilege against self-incrimination is ameliorated by section 204 of the Criminal Procedure Act, 1977.[36] This section targets **minor** co-offenders and is designed to elicit damaging testimony from these minor offenders to be used against **major** co-perpetrators in return for an indemnity against prosecution. In terms of section 204, the privilege falls away once a competent[37] and properly sworn witness is warned by the court[38] that there is an obligation to give self-incriminatory answers with regard to the offence specified by the prosecution.[39] The witness may be discharged from prosecution on the specified offence or any competent offence[40] if, in the opinion of the court, he or she has answered all questions in a frank and honest manner.[41] Once warned, the witness acquires a right or at least a legitimate expectation to a discharge.

The constitutional right against self-incrimination is recognised as a protection against unfair trial practices. If the right to a fair trial is not threatened, then the right against self-incrimination, entrenched in section 35(3)(j) of the Constitution, cannot be invoked. The individual appearing before a non-criminal investigatory enquiry or tribunal does not have a right against self-incrimination. The right against self-incrimination is only triggered once the suspect is arrested, charged or detained. In *Ferreira v Levin NO and Others; Vryenhoek and Others v Powell NO and Others*,[42] the Court held that an examinee before a liquidation enquiry[43] may be compelled to produce direct self-incriminatory evidence. However, this evidence may not be used in a subsequent criminal trial. The use-immunity set out in in this case is specifically limited to evidence directly obtained from the

---

30 It is established practice to warn the accused of the privilege. A failure to do so may render the testimony inadmissible at a future criminal trial. See *S v Lwane* 1966 (2) SA 433 (A) at 444B; *Magmoed v Janse van Rensburg and Others* 1993 (1) SA 777 (A) at 820.

31 S 35(3) of the Constitution – everyone has the right to a fair trial.

32 S 10 of the Constitution.

33 S 14 of the Constitution.

34 *S v Carneson* 1962 (3) SA 437 (T) at 439H. The risk must amount to the possibility, going beyond a mere fanciful possibility, of a criminal prosecution. The risk must be reasonable and not impossible or incredible.

35 *S v Heyman and Another* 1966 (4) SA 598 (A) at 608C; *Rademeyer v Attorney-General and Another* 1955 (1) SA 444 (T).

36 S 204 read with s 205. See also C Theophilopoulos 'The parameters of witness indemnity: A review of s 204 of the CPA' (2003) 120 *South African Law Journal* 373.

37 *S v Hendrix and Others* 1979 (3) SA 816 (D) at 818A.

38 *R v Qongwana* 1959 (2) SA 227 (A) at 230D–E; *S v Ncube and Another* 1976 (1) SA 798 (RA); *S v Dlamini* 1978 (4) SA 917 (N) at 919H.

39 *S v Waite* 1978 (3) SA 896 (O) at 898–899; *S v Bosman and Another* 1978 (3) SA 903 (O) at 905B–C.

40 S 204(1)(a)(iii) of the Criminal Procedure Act, 1977 or with regard to any offence in respect of which a verdict of guilty would be competent.

41 S 204(1)(a)(iv) of the Criminal Procedure Act, 1977. See *Mahomed v Attorney-General of Natal and Others* 1998 (1) SACR 73 (N).

42 1996 (1) SA 984 (CC) at para 159.

43 S 417(2)(b) of the Companies Act, 1973 (now repealed).

288 THE LAW OF EVIDENCE IN SOUTH AFRICA

examinee. Whether the prosecution may make indirect or derivative evidentiary use of facts sifted from the compelled testimony is a question to be decided on the merits of each individual circumstance and examined against the standard of a constitutional commitment to a fair trial.[44]

In terms of sections 14 and 42 of the Civil Proceedings Evidence Act, 1965, a witness in civil proceedings may invoke the privilege by refusing to answer questions which may expose the witness not only to a risk of a criminal charge but also to the risk of a penalty, usually an administrative penalty, or a forfeiture. The privilege which is defined in section 14 of the Civil Proceedings Evidence Act, 1965 is therefore much wider than the privilege defined in section 203 of the Criminal Procedure Act, 1977. A witness may also claim the privilege at inquest proceedings.[45]

DISCUSSION
26.1

Can juristic persons claim privilege?

An issue that has not been properly settled is whether a juristic person, that is, a company or corporation, may properly invoke the privilege with respect to incriminating testimony. This testimony is usually in the form of documentary evidence or some form of electronic communication which may expose the company to a probable future criminal prosecution.[46] The statutory definition of the privilege, section 203 of the Criminal Procedure Act, 1977, is similar to the English Criminal Procedure Act. The English Act allows for a claim of privilege by a juristic person and therefore a strong common law argument may be made for the retention of an English-style corporate privilege based on the *ratio decidendi* in *Triplex Safety Glass Co Ltd v Lancegaye Safety Glass (1934) Ltd*[47] and *Rio Tinto Zinc Corporation v Westinghouse Electric Corporation.*[48]

26.2.3 Accused's right to silence

The right to silence is a fundamental component of the accused's right to be presumed innocent until proven guilty.[49] The right to silence cannot be properly exercised unless the accused has a right to legal representation.[50] In the absence of a legal representative, the accused must be warned of the right to silence.[51] The accused's right to silence and the right not to be compelled to give incriminating evidence apply at the pre-trial as well as the trial stage.[52] The examples below illustrate how the courts have interpreted and applied the accused's right to silence.

---

44 *Ferreira v Levin NO and Others; Vryenhoek and Others v Powell NO and Others* 1996 (1) SA 984 (CC) at para 153. See also *Parbhoo and Others v Getz NO and Another* 1997 (4) SA 1095 (CC).

45 *Masokanye v Additional Magistrate Stellenbosch and Others* 1994 (1) SACR 21 (C); *S v Van Schoor* 1993 (1) SACR 202 (E).

46 C Theophilopoulos 'The corporation and the privilege against self-incrimination' (2004) 16(1) *South African Mercantile Law Journal* 17.

47 [1939] 2 KB 395, 408–9 (Eng CA 1938).

48 [1978] AC 547, 549, 563–66 (HL). Since *Triplex Safety Glass Co Ltd v Lancegaye Safety Glass (1934) Ltd*, the privilege has been available to corporations without any comment or analysis by the English courts. See *Rank Film Distributors Ltd v Video Information Centre* [1982] AC 380, 441–448 (HL).

49 C Theophilopoulos 'The evidentiary value of adverse inferences from the accused's right to silence' (2002) 15(3) *South African Journal of Criminal Justice* 321.

50 *S v Melani and Others* 1996 (1) SACR 335 (E) at 348; *S v Mathebula and Another* 1997 (1) SACR 10 (W) at 19.

51 *S v Mcasa and Another* 2005 (1) SACR 388 (SCA) at para 15.

52 See also *Thatcher v Minister of Justice and Constitutional Development and Others* 2005 (1) SACR 238 (C) at para 85.

CHAPTER 26   PRIVILEGE | 289

S v Sebejan and Others, S v Langa and Others and S v Mthethwa

In *S v Sebejan and Others*,[53] the Court held that a right to silence may also be claimed by a suspect during police interrogation. However, in *S v Langa and Others*[54] and *S v Mthethwa*,[55] the Court held that a right to silence did not apply to a suspect but only to an arrested, detained and accused person.

R v Camane and Others and S v Thebus and Another

In *R v Camane and Others*,[56] the Court held that the right to silence applies during and before trial. In *S v Thebus and Another*,[57] the Court held that the right to silence before and during trial is an important right aimed at protecting the right to freedom and dignity of an accused.

26.2.3.1   Common law right to silence

In terms of the common law, pre-trial silence by a suspect during the police interrogation stage has no evidentiary probative value[58] except in a number of limited circumstances:

- When the suspect is unable to explain a suspicious circumstance[59]
- When the suspect answers questions in a selective and evasive manner
- When the suspect is unable to explain away the possession of stolen goods[60]
- A failure by a suspect to reveal an alibi defence during a police interrogation (this may also give rise to an adverse inference which strengthens the prosecution's *prima facie* case at trial).[61]

However, once the suspect has been arrested and cautioned, a failure to deny a charge or to indicate a defence cannot amount to admissible evidence and no adverse inference may be drawn from such a failure at trial.[62]

At trial, the accused's failure to testify cannot be used to draw a direct inference of guilt. To do so would result in the accused being compelled to give evidence. The accused's right to silence at trial may be summarised as follows:

- The accused's silence at the pre-trial or the trial stage cannot justify the drawing of a direct inference at trial or amount to an admission of guilt.
- It is difficult to draw an adverse inference from the suspect's pre-trial silence and is much easier to do so from the accused's silence at trial. At the police station, the suspect is in a vulnerable position and in a hostile environment. There may be any number of reasons why the suspect refuses to cooperate with the police. However, at trial, the accused is represented by counsel and is therefore no longer vulnerable.
- The evidentiary value of silence at trial depends on whether the defendant has been cautioned by the police at the interrogation stage, by a magistrate at the preliminary hearing, by the judge at the trial stage or whether the defendant has voluntarily waived the right to silence.

---

53   1997 (1) SACR 626 (W) at 632.
54   1998 (1) SACR 21 (T).
55   2004 (1) SACR 449 (E) at 453.
56   1925 AD 570 at 575.
57   2003 (2) SACR 319 (CC) at para 54.
58   See *S v Maritz* 1974 (1) SA 266 (NC); *R v Patel* 1946 AD 903.
59   See *R v Barlin* 1926 AD 459 at 461–462.
60   See *S v Parrow* 1973 (1) SA 603 (A).
61   See *R v Mashelele and Another* 1944 AD 571 at 585 and *S v Zwayi* 1997 (2) SACR 772 (Ck). However, see *S v Thebus and Another* 2003 (2) SACR 319 (CC) where the Constitutional Court was divided on this issue.
62   See *R v Innes Grant* 1949 (1) SA 753 (A) at 764 where the Court held that during a preparatory examination the accused need not reveal a defence and no adverse inference may be drawn from a failure to do so.

THE LAW OF EVIDENCE IN SOUTH AFRICA

- Silence has only a limited evidentiary value and is dependent on whether the State has established a case that requires an answer. The accused's silence only becomes a relevant evidentiary factor once the prosecution has established a *prima facie* case built on extrinsic sources of evidence. The accused's failure to testify or to rebut the prosecution case may strengthen the prosecution case by leaving it uncontested with respect to vital facts in issue, but silence alone cannot be used to remedy a deficiency in the prosecution.[63]

26.2.3.2 Constitutional right to silence

The accused's common law right to silence must be contrasted with the accused's constitutional right to silence. Section 35(3)(*h*) of the Constitution prohibits the drawing of adverse inferences from the accused's failure to testify during the trial.[64] The fundamental core concept of the constitutional right is that the court cannot draw such an adverse inference from the accused's failure to testify. The accused's right to remain silent and not to testify, contained in section 35(3)(*h*), read with section 35(3)(*j*), are integral elements of a right to a fair trial. Silence at trial has no evidentiary value and cannot be directly or indirectly indicative of guilt.[65] The only permissible and narrow inference to be drawn is one based on the prosecution's *prima facie* case. The prosecution's *prima facie* case may well ripen into conclusive proof if it remains uncontested by the defence. Silence is merely a reasonable observation that the accused has failed to rebut a *prima facie* state case, which, by remaining uncontroverted, may eventually at the end of a trial harden into conclusive proof beyond a reasonable doubt.[66]

The accused's constitutional right to silence may be summarised as follows:
- All testimony gathered by the State in violation of the defendant's constitutional rights in terms of section 35 is automatically inadmissible unless the State can justify the infringement in terms of the limitation clause section 36.
- The common law warning, 'You have the right to remain silent but a failure to give evidence is a factor which may be taken into account and used against you', is unconstitutional in two respects. First, it gives silence an evidentiary value no longer permitted by section 35. Second, it indirectly compels the accused to take the stand and testify contrary to section 35(3)(*h*).[67] The preferred constitutional warning should read, '[You] have a constitutional right to silence and no adverse inference can be drawn from the fact that [you] have opted for silence.'[68]
- At the pre-trial and the trial stage, no adverse inferences may be drawn against the accused merely because he or she exercises his or her constitutional right to silence or refuses to testify.

---

63 See *S v Theron* 1968 (4) SA 61 (T) at 63–64; *S v Letsoko and Others* 1964 (4) SA 768 (A) at 776A–F; *S v Nkombani and Another* 1963 (4) SA 877 (A) at 893F–G.

64 See *S v Brown en 'n Ander* 1996 (2) SACR 49 (NC) at 63C where the Court held that an adverse inference from silence cannot strengthen a *prima facie* case based on direct evidence nor may silence be interpreted as an evidentiary fact with its own probative value. Compare with *S v Lavhengwa* 1996 (2) SACR 453 (W).

65 Note the interpretation given to the Fifth Amendment in *Griffin v California*, 380 US 609 (1965) at 614 where the no comment, no inference rule reinforces the constitutional notion that the accused cannot be penalised for a refusal to testify.

66 See *Osman and Another v Attorney-General, Transvaal* 1998 (4) SA 1224 (CC) at para 20; *S v Boesak* 2001 (1) SA 912 (CC) at 923D–H.

67 See *S v Hlongwane* 1992 (2) SACR 484 (N) at 487H–I. The Court held that the way in which the common law warning is worded virtually compels the accused to enter the witness stand.

68 See *S v Brown en 'n Ander* 1996 (2) SACR 49 (NC) at 65F–G; *S v Makhubo* 1990 (2) SACR 320 (O) at 322G.

- The only permissible inference to be drawn from silence depends on the accused's tactical use of the procedural mechanisms of the adversarial trial system. The accused's failure to take up the evidentiary burden at trial and to rebut the prosecution's case may well result in the prosecution's provisional proof becoming conclusive proof at the end of the trial.[69] Note that a number of recent cases have indirectly supported the principle that, in certain circumstances, an adverse inference may be drawn from the accused's silence which becomes an additional item of circumstantial evidence. This, when added to all the other evidence in the prosecution's possession, may augment the State's case and raise it to the level of a *prima facie* case sufficient to prove the guilt of the accused as illustrated in the cases below. In such a circumstance when the accused is faced with a 'cogent set of inculpatory facts',[70] silence as an item of circumstantial evidence can be probative and form the basis for a reasonable and fair adverse inference which, when added to the other evidence available to the prosecution, does not infringe the constitutional rights of the accused.

S v Chabalala

In *S v Chabalala*,[71] the Court held that the totality of the evidence against the accused, taken in conjunction with his silence, establishes a *prima facie* case excluding any reasonable doubt about the accused's guilt.

S v Tandwa and Others

In *S v Tandwa and Others*,[72] although the State's case against the accused consisted entirely of circumstantial evidence, the accused's silence and failure to testify to rebut the evidence strengthened the State's case because, in the absence of anything to gainsay it, the circumstantial web of evidence pointed overwhelmingly to the accused's guilt.

An important aspect of the right to silence is that it applies only to testimonial or communicative assertive types of evidence and not to non-testimonial physical evidence.[73] Section 37 of the Criminal Procedure Act[74] empowers police officers or any court before which criminal proceedings are pending[75] to take fingerprints or body-prints from an arrested or charged person[76] and also photographs.[77] A police official may also request a prison medical official, district surgeon, registered nurse or medical practitioner to take a blood sample or to examine the body of a concerned person for any distinguishing mark, characteristic, feature, condition or appearance.[78] Because section 37 allows for a serious

---

69 *S v Boesak* 2001 (1) SA 912 (CC) at para 24.
70 *R v Noble* (1997) 146 DLR (4th) 385 at para 15, per Lamar CJC dissenting.
71 2003 (1) SACR 134 (SCA) at paras 15, 20.
72 2008 (1) SACR 613 (SCA) at para 56.
73 C Theophilopoulos 'The privilege against self-incrimination and the distinction between testimonial and non-testimonial evidence' (2010) 127(1) *South African Law Journal* 107.
74 This section must be read together with s 225(1) 'admissibility of all relevant evidence of prints and bodily appearance'; s 225(2) 'evidence shall not be inadmissible even if the fingerprint, body-print, mark or characteristic and so on was not taken in accordance with s 37 or even if it was taken against the wish or will of the accused' and s 35(5) of the Constitution 'illegally and improperly obtained evidence is always inadmissible'. Section 37 seeks to ensure that the ascertainment of bodily features is carried out in a reasonable, orderly and decent manner, hence the condition that body searches of female suspects be undertaken by female officers, that blood samples be drawn by registered medical personnel and that fingerprints be taken without excessive publicity.
75 S 37(3).
76 S 37(1)(*a*).
77 S 37(1)(*d*).
78 S 37(1)(*c*) and (*d*).

THE LAW OF EVIDENCE IN SOUTH AFRICA

infringement of a person's bodily integrity, it must be interpreted within the terms of the constitutional right to human dignity (section 10 of the Constitution), the right not to be treated in a cruel, inhuman or degrading manner (section 12(1)(e)), the right to bodily integrity (section 12(2)) and, more importantly, the right to privacy (section 14).

In terms of the common law, the courts have always drawn a distinction between testimonial and non-testimonial evidence for the purposes of the application of the privilege as illustrated in the cases below.[79]

R v Camane and Others

In *R v Camane and Others*,[80] the Court approved of the distinction between testimonial and non-testimonial evidence. It noted that the privilege was based on the exclusion of all testimonial evidence obtained by state compulsion and that non-testimonial or passive physical evidence, such as bodily complexion, stature, marks or features, were excluded from the ambit of the privilege.

Seetal v Pravitha NO and Another

The Court in *Seetal v Pravitha NO and Another*[81] drew a firm line between communicative, self-incriminatory evidence covered by the privilege and non-communicative, self-incriminatory evidence which was not covered by the privilege.

However, the constitutionality of section 37 has been challenged. The vital question arising here is whether section 37 is also in conflict with section 35(1)(c) of the Constitution. This section states that 'everyone has the right not to make an admission that could be used in evidence against that person'. Section 35(3)(j) states that 'every accused person has the right not to be compelled to give self-incriminating evidence'. A series of post-Constitution cases, in particular *S v Huma and Another (2)*,[82] have clearly held that none of the constitutional rights to privacy, dignity, bodily integrity or the right not to give self-incriminatory evidence are violated by the taking of non-communicative and passive body samples. In essence, section 37 does not unreasonably violate the constitutional rights of a person, especially when these personal rights are balanced against the State's duty to ensure the effective administration of the justice system. Examples of other post-Constitution cases are given below.

Minister of Safety and Security and Another v Gaqa

In *Minister of Safety and Security and Another v Gaqa*,[83] the forcible surgery on the accused to remove a bullet from his leg was held not to be an unconstitutional violation of his right not to incriminate him- or herself and the right to privacy and bodily integrity.

Minister of Safety and Security and Another v Xaba

However, in *Minister of Safety and Security and Another v Xaba*,[84] the Court held a similar request for forcible surgery to remove a bullet to be an unconstitutional violation of the accused's rights.

---

79 See also *Ex parte Minister of Justice: In re R v Matemba* 1941 AD 75 at 82–83; *Nkosi v Barlow NO en Andere* 1984 (3) SA 148 (T) at 154F–H; *S v Duna and Others* 1984 (2) SA 591 (CkS) at 595G–H.
80 1925 AD 570.
81 1983 (3) SA 827 (D) at 830H, 846H–847C and followed in *S v Monyane and Others* 2001 (1) SACR 115 (T) at 130.
82 1995 (2) SACR 411 (W) at paras 419C, 416B–H per Claassen J. See also *S v Maphumulo* 1996 (2) SACR 84 (N) at 90C–D per Combrink J; *S v Langa and Others* 1998 (1) SACR 21 (T) at 27C–D; *S v Orrie and Another* 2004 (1) SACR 162 (C).
83 2002 (1) SACR 654 (C).
84 2004 (1) SACR 149 (D).

The accused may invoke the privilege against self-incrimination during a bail application prior to trial, but if the accused chooses not to testify or answer incriminating questions, he or she may run the risk of having bail refused. In addition, section 60(11B)(*c*) of the Criminal Procedure Act, 1977 allows for the admission of the bail record at trial and all evidence given by the accused at the bail application. The accused must therefore make an informed decision during a bail application whether to speak or to remain silent, as illustrated below.

> **S v Dlamini; S v Dladla and Others; S v Joubert; S v Schietekat**
> In S v Dlamini; S v Dladla and Others; S v Joubert; S v Schietekat,[85] the Court held that the right to silence was not impaired if the accused, acting freely and in the exercise of an informed choice, chose to testify in support of a bail application. The right to silence and the right to fair trial was also not impaired if the testimony given at a bail application was used against the accused at trial.

26.2.4   Other private privileges

Other private privileges include professional privileges, **marital privilege** and statements made without prejudice.

26.2.4.1   Professional privileges

The existence of a privilege which protects the communications made between various categories of individuals can only be justified on the basis that certain relationships need to be protected and preserved in the interests of public policy. Therefore, the professional relationship which exists between attorney and client, and the personal marital relationship that exists between spouses, is protected. However, these types of privileges, including the privilege against self-incrimination, also serve to exclude relevant evidence from a court. It is for this reason that professional types of privilege are limited and do not extend to other professional relationships such as doctor–patient, banker–account holder, priest–penitent, accountant–client relationships, and so on.

Exceptions are bankers who possess a limited privilege and may refuse to disclose their books until ordered by a court to do so.[86] Also, section 29(3) of the Electronic Communications and Transactions Act 25 of 2002 provides a limited privilege for a cryptographer who is not required to disclose at trial any confidential information or trade secrets of a client. Cryptography is a service provided to a sender or recipient of a data message which stores and protects the integrity and authenticity of the data message.

In future, the number of professional privileges may well increase as it can be argued that the right to privacy in section 14(*d*) of the Constitution, which provides that everyone has the right not to have the privacy of their communications infringed, allows for the extension of professional privilege to other professions such as the doctor–patient relationship.[87] Similarly, no parent–child privilege exists and the courts can compel parents to testify against their children at trial.[88] However, it may be argued that as parents are

---

85   1999 (2) SACR 51 (CC) at para 17.
86   S 236(4) of the Criminal Procedure Act, 1977; s 31 of the Civil Proceedings Evidence Act, 1965.
87   A limited doctor-patient privilege is recognised in s 79(7) of the Criminal Procedure Act, 1977 which attaches a limited form of privilege to any statement made by an accused referred for mental observation.
88   S 192 of the Criminal Procedure Act, 1977.

entitled to assist their child once legal proceedings have been instituted against the child,[89] it is justifiable that parent–child communications made during legal proceedings should be afforded the same privilege as communications between attorney and client.

26.2.4.2   Marital privilege

In terms of section 198(1) of the Criminal Procedure Act, 1977 and section 10 of the Civil Proceedings Evidence Act, 1965, a **marital privilege** exists between spouses who may refuse to disclose any communication from the other spouse made during the course of a marriage.[90] In terms of section 198(2), the privilege exists in respect of all communications made during the course of a marriage and continues after divorce with regard to all communications made while the marriage was in existence. Even communications made between spouses during the course of a putative marriage are protected, but communications made between ex-spouses after a divorce are not. Also, a widow may not refuse to disclose a communication from a spouse made during the existence of the marriage.

Section 199 of the Criminal Procedure Act, 1977 and section 12 of the Civil Proceedings Evidence Act, 1965 permit a spouse to refuse to answer any question during legal proceedings if the other spouse is entitled to claim a privilege of any kind. Thus, a spouse may refuse to answer a question on the ground that it may incriminate the other spouse. This refusal is based on the other spouse's privilege against self-incrimination.

26.2.4.3   Statements made without prejudice

A statement made without prejudice, either expressly or implicitly, during the course of a *bona fide* negotiation for the settlement of a dispute may not be disclosed in evidence at trial without the consent of both parties. The reasons for the existence of this privilege are based on the express or tacit consent of the parties that they will respect the privilege as well as public policy considerations. Parties then have the freedom to settle disputes without the fear that what they have said during a negotiation may be held against them at trial.[91] The privilege applies, irrespective of whether the actual words 'without prejudice' are used, when:

- the statement forms part of a *bona fide* attempt to negotiate a settlement; and
- the statement is directly or indirectly connected to the dispute.

Statements which are irrelevant or entirely unconnected to the dispute are not protected. The privilege continues to exist until the dispute is finally settled. Once the dispute is concluded, the reasons for the privilege fall away and so does the privilege. A court may examine any document to determine whether this privilege attaches to it.

26.3   State privilege

The State may refuse to disclose relevant evidence, that is, communications between government officials, or between officials and other individuals, to a court when it would be

---

89   S 73(1) and (2) of the Criminal Procedure Act, 1977.

90   For the purpose of legal proceedings, a marriage includes customary and indigenous marriages, religious marriages and any civil union as defined in the Civil Union Act 17 of 2006.

91   *KLD Residential CC v Empire Earth Investments 17 (Pty) Ltd* 2017 (6) SA 55 (SCA). A communication made without undue prejudice may be adduced as evidence at trial for the limited purpose of interrupting the running of prescription. See also *ABSA Bank Ltd v Hammerle Group* 2015 (5) SA 215 (SCA) where a without prejudice admission of indebtedness made by a company which amounts to an admission of insolvency is admissible in liquidation proceedings.

CHAPTER 26 PRIVILEGE | 295

prejudicial to the public interest.[92] In certain circumstances, the disclosure of sensitive state information concerning state security, military secrets, high government policy, international diplomatic initiatives and the proper functioning of state organs would be harmful to the national security interests of the country. Therefore, the need to preserve state secrecy by withholding evidence will take precedence over the fair administration of justice.

The residuary clauses of section 202 of the Criminal Procedure Act, 1977 and section 42 of the Civil Proceedings Evidence Act, 1965 apply the English law of evidence about state privilege to South Africa. These provisions also allow state privilege to be claimed in respect of police crime prevention strategies, police investigatory methods and the identity of police informers. In addition, any state claim of privilege will be influenced by the Bill of Rights, provisions of the Promotion of Access to Information Act 2 of 2000 and the Protection of Information Act 84 of 1982, which will be replaced by the Protection of Information Bill 6 of 2010 when it is eventually promulgated.

Although state and private privilege are similar in principle, there are several procedural differences between them:[93]

- First, with private privilege, the privileged fact may be proved by other evidence, secondary or circumstantial, but this cannot be done with state privilege.
- Second, private privilege must be claimed by the holder of the privilege – a court cannot claim the privilege on behalf of the holder. State privilege, however, may be claimed by a court *mero motu*.
- Finally, private privilege may be voluntarily waived by the holder, but state privilege must be waived on the express authority of the relevant minister.

26.3.1 The common law development of state privilege

State or executive privilege has its origin in the English common law.[94] The most significant developments in the rules governing state privilege occurred after the Second World War. In *Duncan v Cammell Laird and Co Ltd*,[95] a 1942 House of Lords case, a plaintiff was unsuccessful in obtaining the design blueprints and all contracts for a submarine from the Admiralty, the state organ which owned the submarine. The House of Lords held that disclosure of the sensitive documentation was prejudicial to public policy because it would cause serious harm to national security as Britain was at the time engaged in the Second World War. The litigant's right to disclosure was thus outweighed by the public interest in preserving national security. It is important to note that there was heavy criticism of an aspect of the judgment, namely, that a court could not question the State's claim to privilege, thereby doing away with a court's power to evaluate and review a claim of state privilege.

---

92 The controversial Protection of Information Bill 6 of 2010 may render many aspects of the current law of state privilege obsolete. At the time of writing general opinion is that there are still several clauses that need to be addressed before the Bill should be signed into law. One such clause is the classification clause which permits the Minister of State Security to classify information if good cause is shown and if Parliament agrees. Another cause for concern is the definition of 'national security' contained in the Bill as the definition includes guarding against the 'exposure of economic, scientific or technological secrets vital to the Republic'. Other issues include the fact that simple possession and disclosure of classified information by any person is made a crime, the absence of a public interest defence, as well as concerns about the independence of the 'classification review panel'. See further C Theophilopoulos 'State privilege, protection of information and legal proceedings' (2012) 129(4) *South African Law Journal* 637 at 645–650.

93 Schwikkard and Van der Merwe 3 ed (2009) at 159–160.

94 The early position in English common law was that the State possessed the final say in all matters concerning the security of the State, including all non-security matters.

95 [1942] 1 All ER 587 (HL).

296 | THE LAW OF EVIDENCE IN SOUTH AFRICA

In *Van der Linde v Calitz*,[96] the South African Appellate Division refused to follow *Duncan v Cammell Laird and Co Ltd* despite being procedurally obliged to do so. Instead, it referred to a 1931 Privy Council decision in *Robinson v State of South Australia (No 2)*,[97] in which it was held that a court did possess a power of review over State claims of privilege. The Court in *Van der Linde v Calitz* held that a court retains a residual power to overturn a State objection if it is satisfied that the objection is unjustified or cannot be sustained on reasonable grounds and if the court is in a position to examine the relevant information and make an informed decision.[98] There were certain circumstances where public policy considerations required the disclosure of state information in the interests of the fair administration of justice.

In essence, the conflict between the individual's interest in, access to and disclosure of relevant information and the State's interest in preserving the secrecy of relevant information are really two different aspects of the same public policy considerations that must be weighed against each other to achieve a proper balance. This depends on the factual circumstance. Sometimes the individual's interest in disclosure trumps the State's interest in non-disclosure. In other circumstances, however, the State's interest in non-disclosure of relevant information outweighs the individual's interest even when it would be to the material disadvantage of the litigant at trial. An independent and objective court is the best forum in which to balance these conflicting interests to determine which interest is to triumph.

The *Van der Linde v Calitz* decision was subsequently ratified in 1968 by the House of Lords decision in *Conway v Rimmer and Another*.[99] This decision reversed the decision in *Duncan v Cammell Laird and Co Ltd* and reasserted judicial control and review over State claims of privilege. However, in 1982, section 66 of the Internal Security Act 74 of 1982 replaced the *Van der Linde v Calitz* decision. This section gave the State an absolute and unquestioned power to refuse to disclose any relevant information on matters affecting the security of the State (section 66(1)) although in non-security matters the court retained a residual power of review (section 66(2)).

26.3.2 Post-constitutional state privilege

The repeal of section 66 of the Internal Security Act[100] and the enactment of the Constitution have created two different approaches on how state privilege is defined:

- The common law approach explained above argues that the rules and procedures of the common law have been revived and can be developed to conform with the spirit, purport and objects of the Bill of Rights. The common law principles, based on the fundamental tenets of public policy set out in *Van der Linde v Calitz*,[101] may be moulded onto a constitutional procedural framework along selected guidelines suggested by Joffe J in *Swissborough Diamond Mines (Pty) Ltd and Others v Government of RSA and Others*.[102]
- The constitutional approach argues that the common law principles have been displaced by the Constitution. This approach relegates the common law concept of state privilege

---

96 1967 (2) SA 239 (A).
97 [1931] AC 704 (A).
98 1967 (2) SA 239 (A) at 260.
99 [1968] 1 All ER 874 (HL).
100 Repealed by s 1 of the Safety Matters Rationalisation Act 90 of 1996.
101 1967 (2) SA 239 (A).
102 1999 (2) SA 279 (T).

CHAPTER 26 PRIVILEGE | 297

to a historical footnote and allows the competing considerations of public policy that defined it to find a new home in constitutional jurisprudence.[103]

However, both approaches incorporate a balancing test that requires a weighing up of competing values to make an objective and balanced assessment based on proportionality.

The constitutional approach is set out succinctly by the Constitutional Court in *Independent Newspapers (Pty) Ltd v Minister for Intelligence Services: In re Masetlha v President of the RSA and Another.*[104] In this case the applicant had applied for the compelled public disclosure of restricted material contained in the records of certain court proceedings. The Minister for Intelligence Services objected to the disclosure of the restricted material on the ground of material security. The Court held that an objective and fair assessment required the striking of a 'harmonious balance between the two or more competing claims': on the one hand, the applicant's right to 'open justice' and, on the other, 'the constitutionally derived power and duty of the executive to make and implement national security policy'.[105]

The individual litigant's claim for 'open justice' was based on a bundle of constitutional rights including the right to freedom of expression (section 16(1)), the right of access to courts (section 34) and the right to a public trial before an ordinary court (section 35(3)(c)). These rights are relative and not absolute, and may be subject to reasonable and justifiable limitations when balanced against the State's duty to implement national security policy.[106]

In turn, the Constitution imposed on the government a bundle of duties including the duty to preserve peace and secure the well-being of the people (section 41(2)), to maintain national security (sections 44(2), 146(2) and 198), to defend and protect the Republic (section 200(2)), to establish and maintain intelligence services (section 209(1)) and to prevent, combat and investigate crime (section 205(3)).

To arrive at a harmonious balance between the litigant's right to open justice and the State's duty to impose national security policy, the Court had to weigh all the circumstances. These included relevant factors such as:

- the nature of the proceedings
- the extent and character of the information sought to be kept confidential
- the connection of the information to national security
- the grounds advanced for claiming disclosure of the information or for refusing it
- whether the information was already in the public domain
- the impact of the disclosure (or non-disclosure) on the ultimate fairness of the proceedings before the Court.[107]

Both the common law and the constitutional approaches require the same set of practical procedural guidelines to arrive at an objective and fair decision. The necessary procedural framework must be based on the broad characteristics of an open and accountable democratic order founded on fairness and equality. The procedural

---

103   Zeffertt and Paizes 2 ed (2009) at 782.
104   2008 (5) SA 31 (CC) per Moseneke DCJ.
105   At para 56.
106   At paras 39–40.
107   At para 55.

THE LAW OF EVIDENCE IN SOUTH AFRICA

framework may be formulated from some of the guidelines suggested by Joffe J in *Swissborough Diamond Mines (Pty) Ltd and Others v Government of RSA and Others*,[108] in the following manner:

- A court is not bound by the ***ipse dixit*** of a cabinet minister or state official, irrespective of whether the objection is made in regard to a class of documents or a specific document, and irrespective of whether it relates to matters of state security or any other matter affecting the public interest.
- A court is entitled to examine the evidence to determine the strength of the public interest affected and the extent to which the interests of the litigant and the interests of justice might be harmed by the non-disclosure of the evidence.
- A court has to balance the extent to which it is necessary to disclose the evidence for the purpose of doing justice against the public interest in its non-disclosure.
- Where necessary, a court may call a witness to give oral evidence *in camera* to arrive at the proper balance. It may permit cross-examination of any witness or probe the validity of the State's objection by itself.
- The primary onus of proof should rest on the State's shoulders to show why it is necessary for the information to remain secret. The burden on the State is a heavy one, requiring the State to show:
  - ◆ first, the likelihood, rather than a possibility, of a particular harm, rather than a generic harm, to the State's interest by the disclosure of the information
  - ◆ second, that the harm of disclosure is greater than that which would be caused to the interests of justice by non-disclosure.
- A court should also possess the procedural ability to inspect any sensitive document in private, called a judicial peep, and to allow a partial disclosure of the document in the interests of justice.[109]

26.3.3   The Promotion of Access to Information Act, 2000 (PAIA)

Section 32(1) of the Constitution awards everyone a right of access to:
- first, any information held by the State
- second, any information held by a private person that is required for the exercise or protection of any right.

The Promotion of Access to Information Act 2 of 2000 (PAIA) was enacted to give effect to section 32(1) of the Constitution. To access information in terms of the constitutional right, a party must institute legal proceedings by means of the enforcement mechanisms set out in the PAIA.[110]

The important provisions of the PAIA are:
- section 3, which states that the PAIA applies to public or private records containing any form of recorded information in the control or possession of a public or private body

---

108   1999 (2) SA 279 (T) at 343–344.

109   Zeffertt and Paizes 2 ed (2009) at 784–785. In *The President of the Republic of South Africa and Others v M & G Media Ltd* 2011 (2) SA 1 (SCA) at para 52, the Court (in denying a claim of state privilege in the 'Khampepe-Moseneke Report') stated that courts should be cautious in exercising their right to 'peek' because courts 'earn the trust of the public by conducting their business openly and with reasons for their decisions' and consequently, 'a court should be hesitant to become a party to secrecy with its potential to dissipate that accumulated store of trust'.

110   *Institute for Democracy in SA and Others v African National Congress and Others* 2005 (5) SA 39 (C) at para 17.

CHAPTER 26 PRIVILEGE | **299**

- section 5, which states that the PAIA applies to the exclusion of any other legislation that prohibits or restricts the disclosure of a public or private record, and that is materially inconsistent with the object or provisions of the PAIA
- section 11, which provides that a requester must be given access to the records of a public body if the requester has complied with all the procedural requirements set out in the PAIA, and access to that record does not fall within the parameters of any ground of refusal set out in Chapter 4 of the PAIA
- Chapter 4 of the PAIA, which sets out the circumstances and grounds on which access to certain types of records must be or may be refused, subject to the provisions of section 46. Section 46 states that, despite any other provisions to the contrary in Chapter 4, an information officer of a public body must give access to a public record where:
  - first, the disclosure of the record would reveal evidence of a substantial contravention of or failure to comply with the law, or the disclosure will reveal an imminent and serious public safety or environmental risk
  - second, the public interest in the disclosure of the record clearly outweighs the harm contemplated in the provision in question.

State privilege and the PAIA work well together and are usually not in conflict with each other because both function in different spheres. State privilege applies to intra-curial legal proceedings and is concerned with a state refusal to disclose relevant evidence at trial, whereas the PAIA is concerned with the extra-curial exercise of the right to access public and private records. Nevertheless, in the remote event of a conflict, section 5 states that the PAIA takes preference over state privilege as any conflict must be resolved in the PAIA's favour. PAIA, however, does not apply after the commencement of legal proceedings.[111]

26.3.4 Police docket privilege

Docket privilege is essentially a litigation type privilege and should properly be dealt with in the context of private privilege. However, it is deliberately incorporated in the section under state privilege as a matter of convenience and because it is coherently connected to the detection of crime privileges.

26.3.4.1 Police docket

A police docket is divided into three parts:
- Section A contains witness statements, documentary evidence and expert reports.
- Section B contains memoranda and other reports.
- Section C contains the investigation diary.

During the pre-constitutional period, the State had a blanket docket privilege. In terms of this privilege, witness statements obtained by a police investigation for the purpose of a criminal trial were privileged from disclosure to an accused.[112] The blanket privilege usually applied to section A but could be extended to the other sections in the docket.

---

111 *PFE International Inc (BVI) and Others v Industrial Development Corporation of South Africa Ltd* 2013 (1) SA 1 (CC).
112 *R v Steyn* 1954 (1) SA 324 (A).

The Court in *Shabalala and Others v Attorney-General Transvaal and Another* ('*Shabalala's* case'),[113] did away with the notion of a blanket privilege as it held it to be an unreasonable and unjustifiable infringement of an accused's constitutional right to a fair trial. The Court adopted a flexible discretionary approach whereby granting or denying access to the information contained in a docket is to be assessed on a case-by-case basis by balancing the interests of the accused to a fair trial against the State's interest in protecting the ends of justice.

The accused's interest in obtaining access to a docket may be based on the following considerations:

- To enable an accused to prepare a defence properly
- To challenge the State's evidence properly
- To identify defence witnesses able to contradict state witnesses
- To prepare properly for cross-examination of state witnesses
- To identity weaknesses and contradictions in the State's evidence.

The State's interest in denying access to a docket may be based on a risk that a disclosure of witness statements would reasonably result in the intimidation of witnesses, the disclosure of state secrets, the disclosure of the identity of informers, impede the proper ends of justice, and so on. The State bears the onus of objectively satisfying a court that there is a reasonable risk that access would impair the interests of justice.

The principles set out in *Shabalala's* case are as follows:

- An accused should be entitled to access documents in a docket that are exculpatory or that are *prima facie* likely to be helpful to the defence unless the State can, in the circumstances, justify a refusal of such access on the grounds that it is not justified for the purpose of a fair trial.
- An accused's right to a fair trial includes access to witness statements (section A of the docket) and any contents of a docket (sections B and C) as are relevant to enable an accused to exercise that right properly unless the prosecution can justify a denial of access on the ground that it is not justified for the purpose of a fair trial.
- The State is entitled to refuse access to any particular document in a docket on the grounds that:
  - it is not justified for the purpose of a fair trial, or
  - there is a reasonable risk that access to the document would disclose the identity of an informer or state secrets, or lead to the intimidation of witnesses, or otherwise prejudice the proper ends of justice.
- Even where the State has satisfied the court that the denial of access to information in a docket is justifiable, the court retains a discretion to grant access. It must balance the degree of risk involved in attracting the potential prejudicial consequences the prosecution seeks to avoid if such access is permitted against the degree of the risk that a fair trial may not ensue for the accused if such access is denied.

---

113   1995 (2) SACR 761 (CC) at 790–791.

The following principles further define the scope and procedural application of docket privilege:

- When the State refuses or fails to produce documents, a court may review such failure or refusal and order a new trial where there is a reasonable possibility that the fairness of the trial has been compromised by the failure or refusal.
- The request for documents to be produced is made through a discovery procedure. This requires no more than a straightforward letter to the prosecution asking for copies of the relevant documents.
- The producing of documents by the prosecution does not amount to the furnishing of further particulars. The prosecution is not bound by the contents of the documents and the contents of the documents cannot be incorporated into the charge.
- The prosecution cannot keep documents away from the accused by deliberately leaving them out of the docket or by falsely claiming that another organ of State is in possession of the documents.
- The producing of documents must be made before the commencement of a trial.
- The presiding judicial officer has a duty to inform an accused, especially an unrepresented accused, of the rights set out in *Shabalala*'s case, including the right to access witness statements in the docket.
- In terms of section 60(14) of the Criminal Procedure Act, 1977, an accused does not have access to the docket during a bail application unless the prosecutor otherwise directs. However, in terms of section 60(11)(*a*), an accused must be awarded a reasonable opportunity in which to show that exceptional circumstances exist for the granting of bail. This can only be done by granting the accused reasonable access to the police docket.

26.3.4.2 Consultations with state witnesses

The Court in *Shabalala*'s case also allowed and set out the circumstances for an accused to consult with a state witness. These are as follows:

- An accused has the right to consult a state witness without prior permission of the prosecuting authority where the right to a fair trial will be impaired.
- The accused, or his or her legal representative, should approach the prosecuting services for consent to hold such a consultation. If consent is granted, a prosecution official is entitled to be present and to record the consultation. If consent is refused, an accused is entitled to approach a court for permission to consult.
- An accused cannot compel a consultation with a state witness if the witness declines to be consulted or there is a reasonable risk that such a consultation might lead to the intimidation of a witness, the tampering with a witness's evidence, the disclosure of state secrets, the disclosure of the identity of an informer or might otherwise prejudice the proper ends of justice.

26.3.5 Crime detection privileges

The purpose of this type of public privilege is to protect police investigating techniques, procedures and the methodology of crime detection. This privilege has evolved to prevent the disclosure at trial of:

- communications between police officials that relate to the methods used in a criminal investigation[114]

---

114 *R v Abelson* 1933 TPD 227; *S v Peake* 1962 (4) SA 288 (C).

- communications made between informers and their police handlers to prevent the public exposure of the informer's identity.

These privileges are controlled by section 205 of the Criminal Procedure Act, 1977 and are intimately connected to docket privilege as set out in *Shabalala and Others v Attorney-General Transvaal and Another*, above, and *Els v Minister of Safety and Security*.[115] Accordingly, when a court assesses the crime detection privileges it must do so by balancing the accused's need for a fair trial against the legitimate interests of the State in enhancing and protecting the ends of justice.[116]

The crime detection privileges must also be read with section 39 of the PAIA, which concerns the extra-curial access to state information. Section 39(1), subject to the provisions of section 46, states that an information officer of a public body may refuse access to a record if such access is prohibited by section 60(14) of the Criminal Procedure Act, 1977 or contains information about police investigatory methodology or the prosecution of offenders. Refusal to disclose a record may reasonably be made where disclosure would impede a prosecution, reveal the identity of a confidential source, result in the intimidation of a witness or prejudice the fairness of a trial.

DISCUSSION	**A unified theory of state privilege**
26.2	Zeffertt and Paizes argue for the future development of a unified theory since there is a convergence of operating principles between the PAIA, the balancing exercise set out in *Shabalala v Attorney-General of the Transvaal* which applies to docket privilege, and the crime detection privileges. All these should logically be sheltered under a single umbrella.[117]

The definition of an informer who may claim the privilege has been succinctly described:

> Anyone who gives useful information about the commission of a crime, and needs protection against those who may suffer from his disclosure, should get that protection so as to encourage these disclosures.[118]

An informer is therefore someone who has relevant information concerning the commission of a crime. A person who has been interrogated by the police after the accused has already been arrested cannot be defined as an informer. A police officer is not an informer and needs no inducement to disclose information except where the police officer is undercover or in disguise. The reason for protecting communications between an informer and a police handler is to ensure that the identity of the informer is not made public and also to encourage members of the public to report information about crimes to the police. Therefore, a police witness at trial may refuse to answer a question or to provide a document that would tend to reveal the identity of an informer or the contents of the information supplied by the informer. There is also a corresponding duty on the court to ensure that the privilege is upheld irrespective of whether or not the parties at trial have claimed the privilege. The

---

115 1998 (2) SACR 93 (N) at 98.
116 *Shabalala and Others v Attorney-General Transvaal and Another* 1995 (2) SACR 761 (CC) at 790.
117 Zeffertt and Paizes 2 ed (2009) at 792.
118 *R v Van Schalkwyk* 1938 AD 543 at 548.

CHAPTER 26 PRIVILEGE | 303

privilege may be claimed in circumstances where public policy demands confidentiality. These are:

- when the name of the informer must be kept secret to protect the confidential relationship between the informer and the police handler
- when sources of police information must be confidential to encourage informers to come forward and provide information, and to ensure the truthfulness and completeness of the informer's information.[119]

Alternatively, the privilege may be relaxed in the following circumstances:

- Where it is in the interests of justice to do so
- Where it is necessary to prove an accused's innocence
- When the reason for confidentiality no longer exists (the informer's identity has already been revealed and is public knowledge).

To claim the privilege, the claimant must meet the following conditions:

- The communication between informer and handler must arise from the expectation that it will remain confidential and will not be publicly disclosed.
- The element of confidentiality must be an integral part of the maintenance of the relationship between the informer and the handler.
- The relationship must be one that, in the opinion of the community, ought to be maintained.
- The disclosure of the communication will cause greater harm than the benefit that will be gained from the correct disposal of the litigation.[120]

The privilege may be waived as discussed in the following cases. In *R v Van Schalkwyk*,[121] the Court held that it is difficult to see how public policy can be served by prohibiting an informer from disclosing his or her identity. If the identity of the informer is known, there is no reason for concealment and the privilege would be merely an artificial obstacle to proof. However, where the State can show that public policy demands the maintenance of the privilege, a court is bound to refuse disclosure even where the informer was willing to waive the privilege.

Similarly, the Court in *Swanepoel v Minister van Veiligheid en Sekuriteit*[122] held that an informer privilege is based on a substantive right – the right to privacy – and is not a mere evidentiary rule. Therefore, it has to be assessed in terms of the fair trial constitutional rights and the common law rules when not in conflict with the constitutional rights. Reference would also have to be made to the relevant provisions of the PAIA.

26.3.6 Other state privileges

A brief discussion of other state privileges follows.

---

119 *Ex parte Minister of Justice: In re R v Pillay and Others* 1945 AD 653 at 658.
120 *Suliman v Hansa* 1971 (4) SA 69 (D). The analysis of the scope of the informer's privilege in this case is similar to that set out in *Shabalala and Others v Attorney-General Transvaal and Another* and the provisions of s 46(*b*) of the PAIA.
121 1938 AD 543 at 553.
122 1999 (2) SACR 284 (T).

26.3.6.1 Judicial proceedings

Judges, as a rule of practice, cannot be compelled to give evidence of a matter over which they have presided. Judges do remain **compellable witnesses** in law and may be subpoenaed to appear in civil proceedings but only with the leave of a court. Magistrates can be called to give evidence about proceedings before them. However, although compellable, it is undesirable for attorneys and advocates to give evidence about proceedings in which they are or were engaged, especially when such evidence can be provided by other witnesses.

26.3.6.2 Statutory privileges

Section 67(1) read with section 68(1)(*b*) and (4) of the Tax Administration Act 28 of 2011 prevents the disclosure of the private financial affairs of a taxpayer by Inland Revenue officials. Leave of a court must always be obtained to produce these financial documents at trial.

Section 38(3) of the Financial Intelligence Centre Act 38 of 2001 (FICA) protects the identity of persons at trial whose duty it is to report suspicious banking transactions and suspicious electronic transfers of money to or from the Republic.

PRIVILEGE AGAINST SELF-INCRIMINATION	RIGHT TO SILENCE
PROCEDURAL RIGHT CL STATUTORY (S 203 CPA), CONSTITUTION 35(1)(a)(b)(c)	PROCEDURAL RIGHT CL ENTRENCHED CONSTITUTIONAL RIGHT IN S 35(1)(3)
Applies to oral testimony at the trial stage	Applies to oral testimony at the pre-trial and trial stage
Applies to any witness or accused	Applies only to the arrested or detained accused
Witness must take to the witness box and testify	Accused may refuse to take to the witness box and testify
Privilege claimed on a question by question basis	Accused has a blanket right and may refuse to a answer any questions
May be claimed only for questions which pose a real/ appreciable risk of incrimination	May be claimed for all questions
No adverse inference may be drawn from claim	No adverse inference may be drawn from claim
Court must warn witness of privilege – although state may grant immunity from prosecution (s 204)	Court must warn accused of right – may be voluntarily waived
To protect the witness's dignity, privacy and personal autonomy	Right flows form the presumption of innocence and right to legal representation

Figure 26.1 *Privilege against self-incrimination and the right to silence*

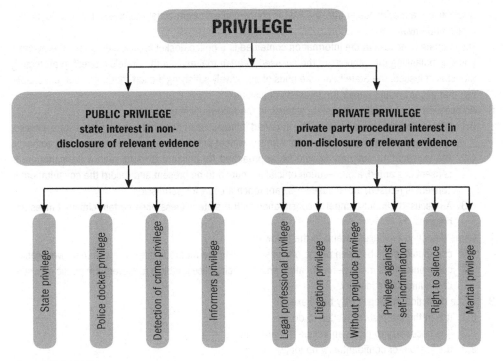

Figure 26.2 Privilege

THIS CHAPTER IN ESSENCE

1. Private privilege is aimed at preventing the admission of relevant evidence at trial and is, therefore, limited to the following:
    1.1 legal professional privilege or attorney–client privilege
    1.2 a witness's privilege against self-incrimination
    1.3 an accused's pre-trial and trial right to silence
    1.4 other privileges such as marital privilege, parent–child privilege and statements made without prejudice.
2. The State may refuse to disclose relevant evidence if it were to be prejudicial to the public interest. State privilege differs from private privilege in the following regard:
    2.1 The privilege fact may not be proved by other evidence.
    2.2 State privilege may be claimed by a court *mero motu*.
    2.3 State privilege must be waived on the express authority of the relevant minister.
3. Since the repeal of section 66 of the Internal Security Act, 1982 and the enactment of the Constitution, there are two approaches on how to define state privilege. In terms of the common law approach, the rules and procedures of the common law have been revived and can be developed to conform with the spirit, purport and objects of the Bill of Rights. The constitutional approach argues that the common law principles have been displaced by the Constitution. Both approaches incorporate a balancing test that requires weighing up competing values to make an objective and balanced assessment based on proportionality.
4. State privilege and the PAIA do not conflict with each other because they operate in different spheres. While state privilege applies to intra-curial legal proceedings and is concerned with a state refusal to

disclose relevant evidence at trial, the PAIA is concerned with extra-curial exercise of the right to access public and private records.

5 The granting of access to the information contained in a police docket is assessed on a case-by-case basis by balancing the interests of the accused to a fair trial against the State's interest in protecting the ends of justice. The State bears the onus of objectively satisfying a court that there is a reasonable risk that access would impair the interests of justice.

6 An accused may consult with a state witness in the following circumstances:

6.1 Where the right to a fair trial will be impaired if the accused does not consult with a state witness, an accused can consult with a state witness without prior consent from the prosecuting authority.

6.2 The prosecuting authority should be approached for consent to hold such a consultation. If consent is granted, a prosecution official is entitled to be present and record the consultation. If consent is refused, the accused may approach a court for permission.

6.3 An accused cannot compel a consultation with a state witness once certain circumstances are present.

7 Crime detection privileges extend to the following:

7.1 communications between police officials regarding the methods used in a criminal investigation

7.2 communications made between informers and their police handlers to prevent the public exposure of the informer's identity.

8 Crime detection privileges may be relaxed if:

8.1 it is in the interests of justice to do so

8.2 it is necessary to prove an accused's innocence

8.3 the reason for confidentiality no longer exists.

9 Judges cannot be compelled to give evidence of a matter over which they have presided. The same rule does not apply to magistrates. It is also undesirable for attorneys and advocates to give evidence about proceedings with which they were involved.

10 Inland Revenue officials may only disclose the private financial affairs of a taxpayer with leave of a court.

11 In terms of the FICA, the identity of persons responsible for reporting suspicious banking transactions and suspicious electronic transfers of money to or from the Republic may not be disclosed during trial.

PART FIVE

THE RULES OF TRIAL

CHAPTER 27	Witnesses: competence and compellability	308
CHAPTER 28	Opening statements	319
CHAPTER 29	Evidence-in-chief	325
CHAPTER 30	Cross-examination	335
CHAPTER 31	Re-examination	346
CHAPTER 32	Closing address	350
CHAPTER 33	Objections	357
CHAPTER 34	Refreshing memory	360
CHAPTER 35	Previous inconsistent statements	365
CHAPTER 36	Hostile witnesses	368

Chapter 27

Witnesses: competence and compellability

27.1	**Introduction**	**309**
27.2	**Competence**	**309**
27.3	**Compellability**	**309**
27.4	**Legal rules applicable**	**309**
	27.4.1 Civil law	309
	27.4.2 Criminal law	309
	27.4.3 General rules	310
27.5	**Exclusions**	**310**
	27.5.1 Mentally incompetent and intoxicated witnesses	310
	27.5.2 Evidence of the accused	311
	27.5.3 Evidence of the co-accused	311
	27.5.4 Husband and wife	312
	27.5.4.1 Communications between husband and wife	312
	27.5.4.2 Questions that a spouse may refuse to answer	312
	27.5.4.3 Accused's spouse as a witness for the defence	312
	27.5.4.4 Accused's spouse as a witness for the prosecution	313
	27.5.4.5 Spouses as co-accused	313
	27.5.5 Child witnesses	314
	27.5.6 Hearing and speech impaired persons as witnesses	314
	27.5.7 Foreign language speakers as witnesses	314
	27.5.8 Judicial officers as witnesses	314
	27.5.9 Officers of the court as witnesses	315
	27.5.10 Members of Parliament as witnesses	315
	27.5.11 Foreign heads of state and diplomats as witnesses	315
	27.5.12 The President as a witness	315
27.6	**Procedural aspects of competence and compellability**	**315**
	27.6.1 Objections	315
	27.6.2 Recalcitrant witnesses	315
	27.6.3 Section 205: means of compelling witnesses to testify	316
	27.6.4 Deciding on competence and compellability of witnesses	317

CHAPTER 27   WITNESSES: COMPETENCE AND COMPELLABILITY | 309

27.1   Introduction

The most common way to place evidence before a court or tribunal is for a party to a dispute to call and lead the evidence of witnesses. As the law of evidence has developed, so rules have been introduced to ensure the **reliability** of witnesses. Other rules have been developed based on public policy considerations to exclude certain classes of witnesses from giving evidence at all. These rules relate to the competence and compellability of witnesses.

27.2   Competence

A witness is **competent** (qualified and able) to give evidence if he or she can do so lawfully.[1] With a few exceptions, all persons are considered to be competent to give evidence.

27.3   Compellability

A witness is **compellable** if he or she may lawfully be obliged to give evidence. Most witnesses who are competent can be compelled to give evidence.[2]

27.4   Legal rules applicable

We will discuss the legal rules applicable to witness competence and compellability below.

27.4.1   Civil law

Section 8 of the Civil Proceedings Evidence Act 25 of 1965 states that 'every person shall be competent and compellable to give evidence in any civil proceedings' unless excluded from doing so by the Act itself or by any other law. This includes any English rule inherited by virtue of the 30 May 1961 rule.[3] These exclusions are considered in section 27.5 below.

27.4.2   Criminal law

Section 192 of the Criminal Procedure Act 51 of 1977 states that every person is both competent and compellable to give evidence in criminal proceedings unless expressly excluded by the Act or by virtue of section 206.[4] The effect of this section is that it makes the English common law regarding competence applicable as it was on 30 May 1961 and as amended by statute.

Section 206 reads as follows:

> The law as to the competency, compellability or privilege of witnesses, which was in force in respect of criminal proceedings on the thirtieth day of May 1961, shall apply in any case not expressly provided for by this Act or any other law this Act or any other law.

---

1   Z Cowen and PB Carter *Essays on the Law of Evidence* (1956) at 220. 'A competent witness is a person whom the law allows a party to ask, but not compel, to give evidence.'
2   Cowen and Carter (1956) at 220. 'A compellable witness is a person whom the law allows a party to compel to give evidence.'
3   S 42 of the Civil Proceedings Evidence Act, 1965.
4   S 192 of the Criminal Procedure Act, 1977. 'Every person not expressly excluded by [the Criminal Procedure Act] from giving evidence shall, subject to the provisions of section 206, be competent and compellable to give evidence in criminal proceedings.'

310 THE LAW OF EVIDENCE IN SOUTH AFRICA

27.4.3 General rules

The effect of the statutory sections is identical although they are differently phrased. All witnesses are thus presumed competent and compellable in both criminal and civil matters.[5] This also means that if a witness is not competent by virtue of any rule or law, the parties themselves cannot agree to the admission of evidence by that witness.[6]

27.5 Exclusions

However, instances do arise where, by virtue of the common law or by virtue of statutory provisions, the court may regard certain witnesses as incompetent and they are thus not allowed to testify. Alternatively, the court may regard certain witnesses as competent but not compellable and thus cannot be forced to testify. We will deal with the most important instances below.

27.5.1 Mentally incompetent and intoxicated witnesses

In both civil and criminal proceedings, witnesses who are impaired by some mental disability or **intoxication** are not competent to give evidence. The statutory provisions relating to respective proceedings differ slightly from one another.

Section 9 of the Civil Proceedings Evidence Act, 1965 states:

> No person appearing or proved to be afflicted with idiocy, lunacy or insanity, or to be labouring under any imbecility of mind arising from intoxication or otherwise, whereby he is deprived of the proper use of reason, shall be competent to give evidence while so afflicted or disabled.

In contrast, section 194 of the Criminal Procedure Act, 1977 describes the exclusion as follows:

> No person appearing or proved to be afflicted with mental illness or to be labouring under any imbecility of mind due to intoxication or drugs or the like, and who is thereby deprived of the proper use of his reason, shall be competent to give evidence while so afflicted or disabled.

The main differences between the two sections are that section 194 uses the all-encompassing term 'mental illness' in place of 'idiocy, lunacy and insanity' used in section 9 and section 194 makes specific reference to drugs.

The way in which section 194 of the Criminal Procedure Act, 1977 is to be applied was set out in *S v Katoo*,[7] in which the Court emphasised the two-stage nature of the test. This requires not only that evidence of incompetence be presented, but also that a trial court investigate whether a witness is deprived of the proper use of his or her reason as a result of the incompetence. The Court set out this test as follows:

> Two requirements must collectively be satisfied before a witness can be disqualified from testifying on the basis of incompetence:

---

5 PJ Schwikkard and SE van der Merwe *Principles of Evidence* 3 ed (2009) at 422.
6 *S v Thurston en 'n Ander* 1968 (3) SA 284 (A) at 291.
7 2005 (1) SACR 522 (SCA) at paras 10–11. The trial court prevented the State from calling a girl who was mentally challenged to give evidence on a rape charge. On appeal, the Court held that, in spite of medical evidence that the girl was an 'imbecile' with the mental age of a four-year-old child, the trial court should properly have investigated whether she was deprived of the proper use of her reason.

CHAPTER 27 WITNESSES: COMPETENCE AND COMPELLABILITY | 311

It must appear to the trial court or be proved that the witness suffers from

(a) a mental illness or

(b) that he or she labours under imbecility of mind due to intoxication or drugs or the like; and

It must also be established that as a direct result of such mental illness or imbecility, the witness is deprived of the proper use of his or her reason.

27.5.2 Evidence of the accused

The accused and his or her spouse are competent witnesses for the defence. However, an accused can only be called as a witness on his or her own application, that is, if he or she elects to testify. This means that the accused cannot be forced to testify.[8] Section 35(3)(j) of the Constitution also provides that a person has the right not to be compelled to give self-incriminatory evidence.

27.5.3 Evidence of the co-accused

A co-accused may, and often does, testify against the accused while testifying in his or her own defence.[9] However, because a co-accused is also an accused in his or her own right in criminal proceedings, all the protection and rights available to an accused also apply to all co-accused. A co-accused is a competent witness, but he or she cannot be forced to testify. In other words, he or she is not compellable.[10] This is also a constitutionally protected right.[11] The State may, however, call a co-accused as a state witness if he or she is no longer a co-accused. This may occur if:[12]

- there is a separation of trials
- the charge is withdrawn against the co-accused (Where the charge is withdrawn, the co-accused is usually dealt with in terms of section 204 of the Criminal Procedure Act, 1977. This provides that a witness who may incriminate him- or herself is obliged to give evidence and to do so frankly and honestly in exchange for being discharged and indemnified from prosecution for the offence specified by the prosecutor.)[13]
- the Deputy Public Prosecutor stops prosecution against the co-accused
- the co-accused has already been acquitted, or convicted and sentenced[14] (It would be undesirable to let the former co-accused testify before being sentenced because of the risk of the evidence being falsified in the hope of passing the greater portion of the blame to the remaining accused or of receiving a lighter **sentence**).[15]

The rule stating that a co-accused cannot be compelled to testify also applies to the situation where an accused wishes to call a co-accused as a witness for the defence. If the co-accused elects to remain silent, he or she cannot be compelled to give evidence for the accused. To do so would result in an infringement of this right as the co-accused may give

---

8 S 196(1)(a) of the Criminal Procedure Act, 1977.

9 In such a situation, the cautionary rule dealing with the evidence of co-accused and accomplices applies. See ch 41 The cautionary rule.

10 S 196(1)(a) of the Criminal Procedure Act, 1977.

11 S 35(3)(j) of the Constitution provides that a person has the right not to be compelled to give self-incriminatory evidence.

12 For an alternative description of these categories, see DT Zeffertt and AP Paizes *The South African Law of Evidence* 2 ed (2009) at 820–823.

13 This is the provision that provides for the often referred to 'turning state's witness' procedure.

14 For example, one of the co-accused pleads guilty. Usually, the trials will be separated.

15 *Ex parte Minister of Justice: In re R v Demingo and others* 1951 (1) SA 36 (A)

312 | THE LAW OF EVIDENCE IN SOUTH AFRICA

self-incriminating evidence. As stated in *S v Lungile and Another*,[16] 'the right of an accused to *subpoena* a co-accused as witness cannot override the right of the latter not to incriminate himself or to remain silent at his trial'.[17]

27.5.4 Husband and wife

A husband may call his wife as a witness in support of his case and vice versa. There are, however, various rules that govern the extent to which one spouse can be compelled to give evidence against the other.

27.5.4.1 Communications between husband and wife

In civil proceedings, a spouse can be compelled to give evidence for his or her spouse and can even be compelled to give evidence against his or her spouse. However, this does not mean that a spouse is completely unprotected in civil cases. Although a spouse may be compelled to take the witness stand, he or she can refuse to disclose any communication made between them during the course of a marriage.[18] This is effectively the exercise of **marital privilege**.[19] This applies even if the marriage was dissolved or annulled after the communication took place.[20]

For the purpose of the law of evidence, a marriage includes customary marriages or unions under local indigenous law and marriages under any system of religious law.[21] The same applies for a solemnised same-sex union.[22]

In criminal proceedings, section 198 of the Criminal Procedure Act, 1977 provides that no spouse can be 'compelled to disclose any communication which [the other spouse] made to him [or her] during the marriage'. This is an expression of the rule relating to marital privilege and should not be confused with compellability.[23]

27.5.4.2 Questions that a spouse may refuse to answer

In both civil and criminal proceedings, a spouse cannot be compelled to answer a question that his or her wife or husband cannot be compelled to answer.[24]

27.5.4.3 Accused's spouse as a witness for the defence

The husband or wife of an accused is both competent and compellable to give evidence on behalf of his or her spouse.[25] If a co-accused wishes to call the spouse of another co-accused, he or she may do so, but the husband or wife of an accused is not a compellable witness for a co-accused.[26]

---

16 1999 (2) SACR 597 (SCA) at 605D.
17 In this case, the Court did not even allow the first accused to separate his trial from that of his co-accused in order to be able to call the co-accused as a witness.
18 S 10(1) of the Civil Proceedings Evidence Act, 1965.
19 For a full discussion on marital privilege, see ch 26 Privilege.
20 S 10(2) of the Civil Proceedings Evidence Act, 1965.
21 S 10A of the Civil Proceedings Evidence Act, 1965.
22 S 13 of the Civil Union Act 17 of 2006.
23 For more on this see Part Four and Zeffertt and Paizes 2 ed (2009) at 705–707.
24 S 12 of the Civil Proceedings Evidence Act, 1965 and s 198(1) of the Criminal Procedure Act, 1977.
25 S 196(1) of the Criminal Procedure Act, 1977.
26 S 196(1)(*b*) of the Criminal Procedure Act, 1977.

27.5.4.4 Accused's spouse as a witness for the prosecution

The husband or wife of an accused is competent[27] to give evidence against the accused in a criminal trial but is not compellable to do so unless the accused is charged with:[28]

(a) any offence committed against the person of either of them or of a child of either of them;

(b) any offence under Chapter 8 of the Child Care Act, 1983 ..., committed in respect of any child of either of them;

(c) any contravention of any provision of section 31(1) of the Maintenance Act, 1998;

(d) bigamy;

(e) incest;

(f) abduction;

(g) any contravention of any provision of sections 2, 8, 10, 12, 12A, 17 or 20 of the Sexual Offences Act, 1957;

(gA) any contravention of any provision of section 17 or 23 of the Criminal Law (Sexual Offences and Related Matters) Amendment Act, 2007;

(h) perjury committed in connection with ... any judicial proceedings instituted ... by the one of them against the other, or in connection with ... criminal proceedings in respect of any offence included in this subsection; or

(i) the statutory offence of making a false statement in any affidavit or any affirmed, solemn or attested declaration [associated with such criminal proceedings].

27.5.4.5 Spouses as co-accused

If a husband and wife are charged jointly and either or both of them testify in their own defence, the evidence given is admissible against the other spouse in spite of the fact that the person testifying would not have been a competent witness for the prosecution.[29]

DISCUSSION	Are sections 196(2) and 195(1) of the Criminal Procedure Act, 1977
27.1	**materially incompatible?**

Due to the complicated way the law of evidence has developed, common law developments and statutory developments are sometimes not always completely synchronised. This has resulted in areas where there are slight disjunctures. In terms of the common law, a spouse was previously not competent to testify for the prosecution. This was changed by statute (section 195(1) of the Criminal Procedure Act, 1977) so a spouse is now competent to testify, but not compellable. Section 196(2) of the Criminal Procedure Act, 1977 was enacted when a spouse was considered incompetent. As this is no longer the case, this section is arguably no longer required.[30]

---

27 In *S v Mgcwabe* (2015) (2) SACR 517 (ECG) the court held that the evidence of a spouse, voluntarily given for the State against her husband, was wrongly admitted as she had not been advised that she was not obliged to testify. This, notwithstanding that she had deliberately handed over real evidence to the police before her husband had even been charged.

28 S 195(1)(*a–i*) of the Criminal Procedure Act, 1977.

29 S 196(2) of the Criminal Procedure Act, 1977.

30 Schwikkard and Van der Merwe 3 ed (2009) at 429.

27.5.5 Child witnesses

Children are not prevented from giving evidence merely because of their age. A child is deemed competent to testify if the presiding officer is satisfied that a child witness in a particular case:

- has sufficient intelligence
- can communicate effectively
- is capable of understanding what it means to tell the truth, to distinguish it from what is false and comprehends that it is wrong to lie.

However, the evidence given by children is often regarded with caution.[31] Children are both competent and compellable to testify against their parents, but it is undesirable that they should be compelled to do so. For the court to be satisfied that a child is sufficiently intelligent to understand what it is to tell the truth, that is, to distinguish the truth from a lie, the court itself may question the child or the legal representative or prosecutor may do so. If the court considers the child to be competent, the child must give evidence on oath[32] or after making an affirmation.[33] Failure to do so constitutes a fatal irregularity.[34]

27.5.6 Hearing and speech impaired persons as witnesses

A witness is not incompetent merely on the grounds of being hearing or speech impaired.[35] The usual practice is to use the services of a qualified interpreter who is able to convey the information expressed by the witness in sign language.

27.5.7 Foreign language speakers as witnesses

As long as there is a competent sworn translator available to translate the testimony of a foreign language speaker into one of the official languages, such a witness is competent. Although there is no specific **cautionary rule** in this regard, common sense dictates that much may, literally, be lost in translation.

27.5.8 Judicial officers as witnesses

A judge or magistrate may not give evidence in the case that he or she is hearing.[36] However, it is permissible for a magistrate, to whom an extracurricular confession has been made, to be called to testify in a **trial-within-a-trial** if the accused challenges the voluntariness of the confession. A presiding officer may also testify on a matter of which he or she bears knowledge in another court. Although judges are competent witnesses, in civil cases they

---

31 See the discussion on the cautionary rule in ch 41.
32 S 162(1) of the Criminal Procedure Act, 1977 and s 39 of the Civil Proceedings Evidence Act, 1965.
33 S 163 of the Criminal Procedure Act, 1977 and s 40 of the Civil Proceedings Evidence Act, 1965.
34 In *S v Raghubar* (148/12) [2012] ZASCA 188 (30 November 2012), the Supreme Court of Appeal set aside a man's conviction and sentence for indecently assaulting a six-year-old boy because the magistrate did not follow the correct procedure in taking the boy's evidence. After asking a few perfunctory questions, the magistrate asked the appellant's legal representative if he was prepared to accept that the witness, who was 14 years old at the time of the trial, was competent to give evidence. The magistrate then went on to ask the witness if he believed that God would punish him if he lied. The Supreme Court of Appeal held that the enquiry undertaken by the magistrate fell far short of meeting that suggested by the Constitutional Court in *Director of Public Prosecutions, Transvaal v Minister of Justice and Constitutional Development and Others* 2009 (2) SACR 130 (CC). In this case, Ngcobo J held that s 164 of the Criminal Procedure Act, 1977 did not require that a child understand the abstract concepts of truth and falsehood, but that he or she understands what it means to relate only what happened and nothing else.
35 Previously referred to as deaf and dumb witnesses.
36 *R v Sonyangwe* 1908 22 EDC 394. If presiding officers are in such a position, they should recuse themselves whereafter they will be able to give evidence.

CHAPTER 27 WITNESSES: COMPETENCE AND COMPELLABILITY | 315

may not be subpoenaed to appear as witnesses without permission from the court in which they are due to appear. In addition, suitable dates must be arranged in consultation with the Judge President of the division in which they are employed.[37]

27.5.9 Officers of the court as witnesses

Attorneys, advocates and prosecutors are competent and compellable witnesses. However, for the sake of the dignity of the profession, it is undesirable for them to testify in cases in which they are professionally involved. Lawyers enjoy a privilege in respect of communications made to them by clients for the purposes of obtaining legal advice (which does not further the commission of a crime). Therefore, although they may be compelled to give evidence in general, on the basis of the legal professional privilege, they cannot be compelled to testify on these communications.

27.5.10 Members of Parliament as witnesses

Members of Parliament cannot be compelled to give evidence 'as a witness or defendant in civil proceedings or as a witness in criminal proceedings, pending completion of his or her business in Parliament' unless the court is situated at the seat of Parliament.[38]

27.5.11 Foreign heads of state and diplomats as witnesses

Foreign heads of state and diplomatic staff are not compellable as witnesses.[39]

27.5.12 The President as a witness

The State President is both competent and compellable as a witness. However, for policy reasons, the decision to compel him or her to give evidence should not be taken lightly.[40]

27.6 Procedural aspects of competence and compellability

For procedural purposes, it is necessary to distinguish between the concepts of compellability and privilege. Compellability relates to whether a party to litigation can force a witness to give evidence. Privilege relates to whether a witness, who has been called and is in the process of testifying, can be forced to answer a particular question.[41]

27.6.1 Objections

If a compellable witness believes he or she may refuse to answer a question on the grounds of privilege, for example an attorney in respect of communications with a client, the witness must be sworn in before raising an objection to a particular question that is put to him or her.

27.6.2 Recalcitrant witnesses

A compellable witness may not refuse to attend court. If this witness does so, he or she may be arrested and brought to the court where he or she is due to testify.[42] A compellable witness

---

37 S 47 of the Superior Courts Act 10 of 2013.
38 S 9 of the Powers, Privileges and Immunities of Parliament and Provincial Legislatures Act 4 of 2004. The witness's absence must be supported by a certificate issued by the Speaker of the National Assembly or Chairperson of the Provincial Council as the case may be. Note that this section does not apply to the accused in criminal proceedings.
39 S 3 of the Diplomatic Immunities and Privileges Act 37 of 2001.
40 *President of the Republic of SA and Others v SA Rugby Football Union and Others* 2000 (1) SA 1 (CC).
41 Privilege is dealt with in ch 26.
42 Ss 170(2) and 188 of the Criminal Procedure Act, 1977, s 36 of the Superior Courts Act 10 of 2013, High Court Rule 38, s 51 of the Magistrates' Courts Act 32 of 1944 and Magistrates' Courts Rule 26,

THE LAW OF EVIDENCE IN SOUTH AFRICA

may not refuse to take the oath or affirmation, or refuse to give evidence or answer questions, without a valid claim of privilege in respect of civil proceedings or without just excuse in criminal proceedings.

The penalty for refusing in the case of civil proceedings is committal to prison for **contempt of court**. In the case of criminal proceedings, the penalty is a sentence of imprisonment for a period not exceeding two years. If the question relates to an offence listed in Part III of Schedule 2 (all serious offences), the court may impose a sentence not exceeding five years.[43] Part III Schedule 2 offences include:
- sedition
- public violence
- arson
- murder
- kidnapping
- child stealing
- robbery
- housebreaking, whether under the common law or a statutory provision, with intent to commit an offence
- contravention of the provisions of sections 1 and 1A of the Intimidation Act 72 of 1982
- any conspiracy, incitement or attempt to commit any of the abovementioned offences
- treason.

The procedure applicable is for the court to enquire in a summary manner into the refusal and to determine whether the witness has a just excuse. This is a question of fact rather than law and will depend on the circumstances of each case.[44] The courts have interpreted the term 'just excuse' to be wider than a lawful excuse.[45] In *Attorney-General, Transvaal v Kader*,[46] the State had called the respondent to testify in a prosecution against seven accused persons. The respondent claimed that it would have been humanly intolerable for him to have to testify as the stress caused in part by a fear of being ostracised by the community for doing so would aggravate his mental health problems. In dealing with the issue of a just excuse, the Court made the following important points:
- There is an onus on a balance of probabilities on the witness who refuses to testify to show just excuse.
- A legal representative may assist the witness during the enquiry.
- The rules relating to compellability are not absolute and bend to policy considerations.
- The Court must weigh the potential benefit of the evidence against the degree of suffering or inconvenience that giving the evidence would cause the witness.
- Just excuse is not necessarily restricted to circumstances where it would be humanly intolerable to force the witness to testify.

27.6.3 Section 205: means of compelling witnesses to testify

A prosecutor may approach a court in terms of section 205 of the Criminal Procedure Act, 1977 to request it to require that a witness appears before a judicial officer to produce evidence that is material or relevant to an alleged offence. A failure to provide the information

---

43 S 189 of the Criminal Procedure Act, 1977.
44 *Attorney-General, Transvaal v Kader* 1991 (4) SA 727 (A).
45 Ibid.
46 1991 (4) SA 727 (A).

CHAPTER 27 WITNESSES: COMPETENCE AND COMPELLABILITY | **317**

required may lead to a sentence of imprisonment unless the provision of such information is not necessary for the administration of justice or the maintenance of law and order.

In *S v Cornelissen; Cornelissen v Zeelie NO en Andere*,[47] the police had opened a case on the basis of a report by a journalist and then sought to compel the journalist to give evidence. The police had, however, failed to interview other traceable witnesses and could thus have obtained the evidence elsewhere.

In assessing whether the evidence that the prosecutor requires is necessary for the administration of justice and the maintenance of law and order, the Court held that it was necessary to strike a balance between three factors:

- The freedom of the individual
- The need for the effective prosecution of crime
- The need for the press to be able to report freely and fairly.

The constitutionality of section 205 was unsuccessfully challenged in *Nel v Le Roux NO and Others*.[48] In this case, the Constitutional Court found that section 205 of the Criminal Procedure Act, 1977 was not inconsistent with the Constitution as section 189(1) of the Criminal Procedure Act, 1977, which is linked to section 205, provides adequate protection by permitting a refusal to testify if the witness has a just excuse.

27.6.4 Deciding on competence and compellability of witnesses

In terms of section 193 of the Criminal Procedure Act, 1977, the court in which the criminal proceedings are conducted must decide questions of competence and compellability. The court does this by holding a trial-within-a-trial at which evidence may be led. In some circumstances, the court will itself ask questions to enable it to arrive at a decision without holding a trial-within-a-trial. The court and the parties may call and question other witnesses.

THIS CHAPTER IN ESSENCE

1 A competent witness is one who may give evidence lawfully.
2 All persons are considered to be competent witnesses and most competent witnesses are also compellable witnesses. The following exceptions apply:
   2.1 Mentally incompetent and intoxicated witnesses are not competent to give evidence in both civil and criminal proceedings.
   2.2 An accused is a competent but not a compellable witness for the defence.
   2.3 A co-accused is a competent witness but cannot be compelled to testify. The State may, however, call a co-accused as a state witness if he or she is no longer a co-accused.
   2.4 Spouses are competent and compellable witnesses for each other. Spouses can, however, rely on marital privilege regarding communication made between them during the course of a marriage. Spouses also cannot be compelled to answer a question which the other one cannot be compelled to answer. In criminal proceedings, spouses can be compelled to testify against each other only when charged with a specific crime.

---

47   1994 (2) SACR 41 (W).
48   1996 (3) SA 562 (CC).

2.5 Any evidence given by a spouse as a co-accused is admissible against the other spouse despite the fact that the first-mentioned spouse would not have been a competent witness for the prosecution.

2.6 Children are deemed competent to testify if it is clear that they have sufficient intelligence, can communicate effectively and are capable of understanding the difference between right and wrong.

2.7 Hearing and speech impaired persons are competent to testify through the use of a qualified interpreter.

2.8 Foreign language speaking witnesses are competent to testify through the use of a competent sworn translator.

2.9 Judicial officers are not competent witnesses in cases pending before them, but may testify in a trial-within-a-trial or in cases pending before other courts.

2.10 Officers of the courts are competent and compellable witnesses although it is undesirable for them to testify in cases in which they are professionally involved.

2.11 Members of Parliament can be compelled to testify but only when Parliament is not in session or if the court is situated at the seat of Parliament.

2.12 Foreign heads of state and diplomatic staff cannot be compelled to testify.

2.13 The State President is both a competent and compellable witness.

3 A compellable witness who refuses to attend court, take the oath or affirmation or refuses to give evidence or answer questions without a valid claim of privilege (civil matters) or just excuse (criminal proceedings) could be held in contempt of court and sentenced to imprisonment for two to five years (criminal proceedings).

4 A witness may be compelled to testify or produce evidence on behalf of the State through a request made in terms of section 205 of the Criminal Procedure Act, 1977.

5 In criminal proceedings, the court in which the proceedings are conducted must decide questions of competence and compellability by means of a trial-within-a-trial.

Chapter 28

Opening statements

28.1 Introduction: the sequence of the trial 319

28.2 Legal basis for the opening statement 319

28.3 Content of the opening statement 320

28.4 Procedure for opening statements 320

28.5 Practical aspects of opening statements 321

28.6 Practical examples of opening statements 322
28.6.1 Civil trial in High Court: opening address by counsel for plaintiff
in motor accident case 322
28.6.2 Criminal trial in High Court: opening address by prosecutor in fraud case 322

28.1 Introduction: the sequence of the trial

In essence, the fact-finding procedures of all adversarial trials and hearings are substantially the same:

- They start with a brief introduction called the **opening statement**.
- This is followed by the examination-in-chief. Here, counsel calls in sequence the witnesses supporting the complainant's case, that is, the plaintiff in civil cases and the prosecution in criminal cases.
- The defence then cross-examines the witnesses.
- The complainant re-examines the witnesses.
- When all the complainant's witnesses have been called, its case is closed.
- The defendant, or accused in criminal matters, opens its case. The defendant repeats the same sequence and closes its case.
- The **closing argument**, or **closing address**, commences.
- Finally, the court gives its decision or judgment.[1]

28.2 Legal basis for the opening statement

An opening statement or opening address is a feature of civil and criminal trials. It occurs when the court gives a litigant or party the opportunity to explain what their case is about and what evidence they intend to lead to support their contentions. In other words, it is the opportunity to outline what the party hopes to prove.

---

1   See Annexure A Civil trial process and Annexure B Criminal trial process.

320 | THE LAW OF EVIDENCE IN SOUTH AFRICA

For civil trials, the Rules of Court for the High Courts and Magistrates' Courts make provision for opening statements.[2] Although Rule 29(3) of the Magistrates' Courts Rules does not clearly indicate that this provision covers an opening address, it seems clear that this is what was intended.[3] The Criminal Procedure Act 51 of 1977 governs opening statements in criminal trials.[4] In civil trials in the High Court and in all criminal trials, an opening statement is optional, not compulsory.[5] However, in civil trials in the Magistrates' Courts, a magistrate may compel a party to outline their case.[6] Because the rules do not specifically refer to the right to make an opening address, the question has arisen as to whether a party has the right to make such an address if the magistrate has not compelled them to do so. Case law makes it clear, however, that a party does have such a right. Price J in *Weintraub v Oxford Brick Works (Pty) Ltd*[7] commented that it seems self-evident that a party should be entitled to explain the case they intend to present.

28.3 Content of the opening statement

The opening statement is not an occasion for comment on the strength or otherwise of a party's case, the opponent's case or the qualities of the proposed witnesses. Sections 150 and 151 of the Criminal Procedure Act, 1977 specifically provide that the opening statement shall be 'without comment'. They should also be short and succinct as the respective rules of court also emphasise the aspect of brevity.

In criminal trials, the prosecutor should not refer in the opening statement to incriminating statements made by the accused which he or she intends to prove during the trial. This is because the admissibility of such statements is often disputed and requires a ruling by the court after a trial-within-a-trial. Therefore, the accused could be prejudiced if the prosecutor discloses the contents of such a statement before the court has decided on its admissibility. However, if it is clear that there will be no **objection** to the admissibility of such a statement, there can be no objection to the prosecutor disclosing the contents during the opening address.[8]

28.4 Procedure for opening statements

The prosecutor in a criminal trial and the party presenting their case first in a civil trial, usually the plaintiff, deliver their opening addresses at the outset of the trial before leading any evidence. The defence in a criminal trial and the opposing party, usually the defendant, in a High Court civil trial are required to deliver their opening addresses, if any, after the prosecution and plaintiff have closed their cases and the court has not granted a discharge in terms of section 174 of the Criminal Procedure Act, 1977 in criminal trials or absolution from the instance in civil trials.[9]

---

2 High Court Rule 39(5); Magistrates' Courts Rule 29(3).
3 LTC Harms *Civil Procedure in Magistrates' Courts* (1997) B29.3.
4 Ss 150 and 151.
5 This is clear from the use of the word 'may' in the respective rules.
6 'The court may, before proceeding to hear evidence, require the parties to state shortly the issues of fact or questions of law which are in dispute and may record the issues so stated.'
7 1948 (1) SA 1090 (T).
8 *R v Kritzinger* 1953 (1) SA 438 (W).
9 See s 151 of the Criminal Procedure Act, 1977 and Rule 39(7) of the High Court Rules. Rule 29(3) of the Magistrates' Courts Rules seems to require that if the magistrate calls on a party to outline its case, the party should do this at the beginning of the trial and not necessarily at the commencement of that party's case.

CHAPTER 28 OPENING STATEMENTS | **321**

Therefore, in criminal trials and High Court civil trials, the accused or defendant does not have the right to make an opening address at the outset of the trial before the prosecution or plaintiff has commenced presenting their case. However, in a criminal trial the accused can present something similar to an opening statement at the outset of the trial before the prosecutor leads any evidence under the guise of making a plea explanation under section 115 of the Criminal Procedure Act, 1977. Strictly speaking, a plea explanation under section 115 would be made together with a plea which is made before any opening address by the prosecutor.

Price J was probably correct when he said of Rule 29(3) of the Magistrates' Courts Rules:

> It is indeed astonishing that it could have been thought necessary to provide in a Rule of Court that the magistrate can ask or require the parties to state the issues and that he can then write down what the parties say the issues are. One would have thought that such a detail could well be left to the common sense of the magistrate and the parties. ... It only shows the danger of over-legislating.[10]

28.5 Practical aspects of opening statements

As we have already indicated, the opening address is generally not compulsory. It is, however, a good idea in any complex case to deliver an opening address.[11]

If handled correctly, the opening address is an opportunity to clarify a party's case. An attorney or counsel delivering an opening address should realise that while he or she has been preparing the case for days, weeks or even months, and is thoroughly versed in the facts and law, the bench will have little, if any, idea of what the trial will be about. We can compare the opening address to a précis of an article or chapter in a book. It should be brief but informative, remembering always that the hearer, like the reader, does not have any detailed knowledge of what is to follow. Sequence and clarity are thus essential. The delivery of a good opening address requires practice. It may happen that in an opening address counsel indicates that a witness will give certain evidence, whereas the actual testimony eventually given by the witness may differ. It may also happen that counsel states that the plaintiff will rely on certain limited legal points, but that later in the trial the plaintiff wishes to rely on additional legal points. It seems that, generally, a party is not bound by what counsel states in the opening address.[12]

However, if a party through their counsel deliberately sets out in the opening address to confine the issues for adjudication, the court may well hold that the party may not cover other issues during the trial.[13] Even though the opening address is not binding on a party, it may still afford material for cross-examination if a witness states something in evidence which differs from what was foreshadowed in the opening address.

Despite what we have said about the non-binding effect of an opening address, it is good practice to choose words carefully when preparing and presenting an opening address. In particular, be wary of quoting the *ipsissima verba* of what a witness will say. People who repeat something they have already recounted rarely use identical words each time. To

---

10 *Weintraub v Oxford Brick Works (Pty) Ltd* 1948 (1) SA 1090 (T) at 1091.
11 E Morris *Technique in Litigation* 6 ed (2010) at 198–205. The author (at 198) goes so far as to say that every civil case, at least, should have an opening address.
12 See *S v V* 1995 (1) SACR 173 (T) and *S v Mbata en andere* 1977 (1) SA 379 (O) for criminal cases, and *Standard Bank of SA Ltd v Minister of Bantu Education* 1966 (1) SA 229 (N) at 242–243 for civil cases.
13 *S v Davidson* 1964 (1) SA 192 (T) at 194G.

322 | THE LAW OF EVIDENCE IN SOUTH AFRICA

protect a witness against awkward cross-examination, it is usually a good idea to confine any comments about the proposed evidence to generalities and to avoid direct quotation.

28.6 Practical examples of opening statements

28.6.1 Civil trial in High Court: opening address by counsel for plaintiff in motor accident case

Judge. This is an action for damages arising from a motor collision in which a vehicle belonging to the plaintiff was written off in a collision with a vehicle being driven by the defendant. The extent of the damages is R150 000. The defendant has admitted, in the pleadings, to being the driver of the vehicle which collided with the plaintiff's vehicle and that the extent of the damages is R150 000. He has, however, placed in dispute that he in any way negligently caused those damages.

The plaintiff will endeavour to prove that the defendant was in fact negligent, and that his negligence caused the damages suffered by the plaintiff. The plaintiff alleges that the defendant was negligent in one or more of the following ways:
- He failed to keep a proper lookout.
- He drove in an excessive speed in the circumstances.
- He failed to apply his brakes timeously or at all.

Three witnesses will be called on behalf of the plaintiff. The plaintiff herself will testify that she was driving her Toyota Corolla in High Street, Mkhizeville, at 10 a.m. on the day in question (a Monday). She intended turning right into West Street so she put on her indicator, moved to the right of her lane and slowed down. At this point, the defendant, who was driving behind her, slammed his car into the back of the plaintiff's car, causing the alleged damages. Mrs Dhlamini will also testify for the plaintiff. She was a passenger in the plaintiff's car and will confirm the evidence of the plaintiff. The third witness is Mr Jackson, a bystander on the pavement on the corner of High and West Streets. He will testify that the plaintiff had her indicator on to turn right, that she slowed down and moved to the right of her lane. At this point, the defendant's car slammed into the back of the plaintiff's car. After the collision he asked the defendant what had happened. The defendant replied to the effect that he was unsure as he was busy inserting a CD into the CD player at the time of the collision.

Note the simplicity of the outline of proposed evidence. Even if the judge has not had any opportunity to prepare for the trial, he or she should have no difficulty in understanding what the trial is about after listening to the opening address. The exact detail of what will be stated in evidence is not set out so the plaintiff and her witnesses are unlikely to be embarrassed in cross-examination by challenges that their evidence does not exactly match what was said during the opening address. In particular, the account of what the defendant told Mr Jackson does not purport to quote exact words.

28.6.2 Criminal trial in High Court: opening address by prosecutor in fraud case

Judge and learned assessors. The accused is charged with the crime of fraud. It is alleged that he sold a close corporation, Goldtouch CC, to the complainant, Mr Singh, as a going concern, claiming that it was a highly profitable concern operating a supermarket, and that it had assets worth R2 million more than its liabilities. In fact, the close corporation had been running at a loss for the last five years and was insolvent. The State alleges that the accused placed an advertisement in the press, offering the CC for sale at the price of R2,2 million, and claiming that it operated a 'highly profitable supermarket'. The complainant, who was interested in acquiring a supermarket business, made enquiries after seeing the advertisement. When he visited the accused in response to the advertisement, the accused presented him with balance sheets for the last five years that showed that the CC was doing very well and that its assets exceeded its liabilities by R2 million. The State alleges that these balance sheets did not reflect the true state of affairs and that they had been fraudulently drawn up at the instance of the accused.

In support of its case the State will call five witnesses. The complainant, Mr Singh, will testify that he was seeking a supermarket business and that he responded to an advertisement offering for sale a CC that operated a supermarket. He telephoned the number appearing in the advertisement and spoke to someone who, it emerged later, was the accused. He then arranged to visit the accused. At the meeting between the accused and the complainant, the accused assured him that the business was highly profitable and showed him balance sheets for the past five years that confirmed the profitability of the CC. The accused claimed that he was only selling because he intended emigrating. Mr Singh was impressed by the balance sheets and made an offer to buy the CC for R2,1 million. The accused accepted the offer and Mr Singh paid the agreed price. After taking over the CC he soon realised that the business was in fact not profitable and indeed was insolvent. Further enquiries revealed that the balance sheets shown to him were false. Attempts to cancel the sale and recover his money proved fruitless. Had he known the true state of affairs, he would never have purchased the business.

The State will also call two employees of the supermarket who will testify about the true state of affairs.

The fourth witness will be the auditor of the CC who will testify that the balance sheets presented to the complainant by the accused had been falsified. The actual correct balance sheets show that the CC had been trading at a loss for five years and was insolvent. The auditor is widely experienced, having testified in over 20 criminal trials in the past.

[Note that this last sentence is impermissible. Section 150(1) of the Criminal Procedure Act, 1977 specifically states that the opening address should be 'without comment'.]

The fifth witness will be a friend of the accused to whom the accused made a verbal statement about the true state of affairs of the business. In view of the fact that the accused may challenge the admissibility of this statement, the contents of this statement will not be disclosed at this stage.

[Note how the prosecutor carefully avoids going into the contents of the incriminating statement as there could be an argument about the admissibility of the statement. If the statement is ruled inadmissible, there can be no suggestion that the prosecutor improperly informed the court about the contents and thereby prejudiced the accused.]

In addition to the oral evidence, there will be a number of items of documentary evidence such as the advertisement to which the complainant responded, the false

324 | THE LAW OF EVIDENCE IN SOUTH AFRICA

balance sheets as well as the true balance sheets, other business records of the CC and the cheque made out by the complainant as payment for the CC.

THIS CHAPTER IN ESSENCE

1   Parties in both civil and criminal proceedings are permitted to deliver an opening statement explaining to the court what their case is about and what evidence they intend to lead in support of their contentions.

2   In civil trials in the High Courts and in all criminal trials, an opening statement is optional, not compulsory.

3   In civil trials in the Magistrates' Courts, a magistrate may compel a party to provide an opening statement.

4   Opening statements must be short and succinct and may not contain any incriminating statements or comments on the strength of the parties' cases or the qualities of the proposed witnesses.

5   Opening statements are led at the outset of the trial by the prosecutor in criminal matters or the plaintiff in civil matters. The accused in criminal matters and the defendant in civil matters deliver their opening statements after the prosecutor and plaintiff have closed their cases and no discharge or absolution from the instance has been granted.

6   Although an opening statement is not compulsory, it is advisable in complex cases.

7   Generally, parties are not bound by what has been said in the opening statement.

Chapter 29

Evidence-in-chief

29.1	Introduction	325
29.2	Legal basis for evidence-in-chief	325
29.3	Prohibition on leading questions during evidence-in-chief	326
29.4	Exceptions to the rule against leading questions	327
29.5	Procedure for evidence-in-chief	327
29.6	Practical aspects of evidence-in-chief	328
29.7	Practical examples of evidence-in-chief	330
	29.7.1 Civil trial in High Court: evidence-in-chief of plaintiff in motor accident case	330
	29.7.2 Criminal trial in High Court: evidence-in-chief of complainant in fraud case	331

29.1 Introduction

Evidence-in-chief or examination-in-chief is the usual name given to the evidence that a party presents in support of their case. 'The purpose of examination-in-chief is to present evidence favourable to the version of the party calling the witness. The method most frequently adopted is the question and answer technique.'[1] Evidence-in-chief is the first stage in the process of putting evidence on the record. The next two stages are cross-examination and re-examination. Evidence-in-chief is referred to as the first stage because it precedes the other two stages in sequence at a trial. We could also call it the constructive part of presenting evidence in that the party leading evidence-in-chief is attempting to use the evidence to build their case.

29.2 Legal basis for evidence-in-chief

The basic system of adjudicating legal disputes through our courts in South Africa is called the adversarial system. It is also known as the Anglo-American, strict or common law system. The adversarial system leaves the gathering and presentation of evidence to the parties[2] and relies on challenge by cross-examination to test the soundness of evidence. The party

---

1 PJ Schwikkard and SE van der Merwe *Principles of Evidence* 3 ed (2009) at 364.
2 This is known as the system of party control in that the parties themselves control the evidence that they wish to disclose to the court. The court will thus only hear evidence that the parties have presented and not any other, possibly valuable and useful, evidence.

326 | THE LAW OF EVIDENCE IN SOUTH AFRICA

presenting evidence presents their evidence by way of evidence-in-chief and waits for challenge by way of cross-examination.[3]

Although evidence-in-chief is indirectly referred to in legislative provisions,[4] its common law origins are clear. These legislative provisions do not explain or define evidence-in-chief, but assume that its meaning and function are already part of our law.

29.3 Prohibition on leading questions during evidence-in-chief

Th basic rule of evidence-in-chief is that the witnesses are generally required to give their account in their own words in response to specific questions from the party calling them. This rule is usually expressed in the form that a party may not ask leading questions of their witnesses.[5] This means that the party leading their evidence-in-chief may not put words in the mouth of their witnesses by indicating which answer is required. Another way of stating this requirement is that a party is generally required to ask open-ended questions which do not suggest a particular answer. For example, 'Where were you at 11 a.m. on 27 April 1994?' is a legitimate, non-leading question during evidence-in-chief, whereas 'Were you queuing up to vote at the Smalltown voting station at 11 a.m. on 27 April 1994?' is a leading question.

The questioning may also not assume the existence of a fact that still requires proof.[6] For example, it would not be permissible to ask, 'Where were you standing when the victim was shot?' if the witness has not yet stated that he or she saw the victim being shot.

The essence of the objection to a leading question is that the nature of the question asked reduces the weight of the answer given. For example, the question to a witness, 'You saw the accused stab the deceased in the left arm and right side of his neck, correct?', can only elicit the answer 'yes' or 'no', both of which have very little weight. The witness is merely confirming or denying the questioner's statement. This question would not be permitted in examination-in-chief because it is clearly a leading question.

However, leading questions can take many different forms. What the court will consider is whether the weight of the answer is reduced by the nature of the question. Thus, even if the question had been phrased, 'Did you see the accused stab the deceased in the left arm or the neck?', it would still be disqualified as a leading question. The reason is that the witness has been 'led' to choose one of only two options – the left arm or the neck – and has not been given a free choice of response.[7]

There are further reasons for the rule against leading questions. First, it guards against prejudice to the other party as asking leading questions may encourage a witness to state something that he or she does not have actual knowledge of simply to please the party calling him or her.[8] Asking leading questions, if unchecked, can constitute a serious irregularity and

---

3   For a discussion of the adversarial system, see Schwikkard and van der Merwe 3 ed (2009) at 6–13.

4   For criminal cases, see s 150(2)(*a*) and s 151(2)(*a*) of the Criminal Procedure Act 51 of 1977, which state that the party '... may examine the witnesses' without explaining what 'examine' means. High Court Rules 39(5) and 39(7) for civil cases simply state that the party '... may proceed to the proof ...', whereas Magistrates' Courts Rule 29(7) uses the expression 'adduce ... evidence'.

5   See also C Tapper Cross and Tapper on Evidence 12 ed (2010) at 295.

6   High Court Rules 39(5) and 39(7) for civil cases simply state that the party '... may proceed to the proof ...', whereas Magistrates' Courts Rule 29(7) uses the expression 'adduce ... evidence'.

7   See R Palmer and D McQuoid-Mason Basic Trial Advocacy Skills (2000) at 57–58.

8   'Counsel is prohibited from putting leading questions to his own witness because of the risk that the witness may perhaps think that such questions are an invitation, suggestion or even instruction to him to answer them, not unbiasedly or truthfully, but in a way that favours the party calling him.' See *S v Rall* 1982 (1) SA 828 (A) at 831D–E per Trollip AJA.

CHAPTER 29   EVIDENCE-IN-CHIEF | **327**

lead to the setting aside of a verdict on appeal.[9] The second, and related, reason is that value is added to an answer that is not given in response to undue prompting.

29.4   Exceptions to the rule against leading questions

The general rule is that leading questions are impermissible in evidence-in-chief. However, in the interests of expedition, the rule is relaxed in the case of non-contentious issues such as the witness's name, address and occupation, or other matters which are no longer in dispute. Often, an opposing party will indicate that they do not mind if a witness is led on a particular aspect. Sometimes a leading question is permissible simply because there is no other convenient way of getting the witness to cover a specific aspect.[10] For example, a previous witness may have said that this witness did something and this witness is then required to comment on that statement. It would be difficult to elicit a response without putting the matter directly, such as: 'Witness X has said that you were in the company of Y on that afternoon. Were you in Y's company?' In general, the judicial officer will exercise discretion to ensure that progress is made without prejudicing a party.

29.5   Procedure for evidence-in-chief

During evidence-in-chief a witness responds to a series of questions from counsel for the party calling the witness (the 'examiner'). This is to ensure that the witness focuses on what is relevant and does not venture into inadmissible areas such as hearsay.[11] If a witness is accustomed to giving evidence, he or she can usually be trusted to give evidence with a minimum amount of questioning.[12]

The general practice is that witnesses for a party do not sit in court prior to being called to give evidence. This is to ensure that witnesses give evidence without any possibility that they may have consciously or unconsciously tailored their evidence to fit in with what they heard a previous witness say.[13]

In criminal trials, the position is different because the accused is required and entitled to be present throughout the trial, barring some isolated exceptions.[14] This means that an accused who testifies after other witnesses could consciously or unconsciously adapt his or her evidence to fit in with what has gone before. Therefore, the Criminal Procedure Act, 1977 specifically provides that the accused shall testify before other defence witnesses unless the court allows otherwise.[15] This tends to limit the accused's opportunities for adapting evidence, at least as far as defence witnesses are concerned.

It sometimes happens that an accused initially chooses not to testify, but then changes his or her mind at a later stage after other witnesses have testified. The accused will still be allowed to testify, but the court is entitled to draw any appropriate inference as the fact that the accused was in court during earlier testimony may well detract from the value of his or

---

9   *S v B* 1996 (2) SACR 543 (C) and cases there cited.
10   Zeffertt and Paizes 2 ed (2009) at 895.
11   Schwikkard and Van der Merwe 3 ed (2009) at 364.
12   Ibid.
13   *S v Moletsane* 1962 (2) SA 182 (E) at 182 and *S v Mpofu* 1993 (3) SA 864 (N) at 867H–J. See also E Morris *Technique in Litigation* 6 ed (2010) at 180 and 184.
14   See ss 158 and 159 of the Criminal Procedure Act, 1977.
15   S 151(1)(*b*)(i) of the Criminal Procedure Act, 1977.

THE LAW OF EVIDENCE IN SOUTH AFRICA

her evidence. In criminal trials, the requirements of fairness in having the accused present throughout the trial trump the lesser issue of possible adaptation of evidence.

The general practice for witnesses not to be in court prior to giving evidence is usually relaxed when dealing with expert witnesses. In this case, it is customary to permit expert witnesses to be in court to listen to evidence on which they may be required to comment or where their expertise is needed to understand it. The basis for this exception is that they are less likely to temper their evidence to fit in with what has gone before. Also, they would be unable to comment usefully on other evidence if they have not heard it themselves.

Expert witnesses are often required to be in court when the opposing party's expert witness testifies so that they can listen to the evidence, assess it and provide guidance and assistance to their client and counsel. In some circumstances, an expert sits in court to hear certain evidence only, while in other circumstances an expert may be required to hear all the other evidence to make informed comment. An example of the latter type of situation is when a psychiatrist is required to give an opinion on whether the accused in a criminal trial was mentally competent at the time he or she committed the alleged offence.

29.6 Practical aspects of evidence-in-chief

The party presenting its case is known as the *dominus litis*. This literally means 'master of the case'. The term is usually applied to the prosecution, but could be applied to any party presenting its case. What it means in practice is that the party presenting the case chooses which witnesses to call, the sequence of the witnesses subject to section 151 of the Criminal Procedure Act, 1977 and what questions to ask of each of their witnesses.

This flows naturally from the adversarial nature of our system. The system permits a party to present its case in the most favourable light by calling only those witnesses that will best advance their case and leading their evidence to make it appear as advantageous as possible.[16] This is subject to the duty not to present a dishonest case by leaving out portions of possible evidence so as to give a skewed picture.[17]

The style of leading individual witnesses can vary greatly. For instance, different techniques are required for a witness who is not accustomed to giving evidence especially if nervous, an over-talkative witness, an uneducated witness and a stubborn witness. Experienced witnesses, such as some police witnesses and expert witnesses, require little steering, whereas others may need to be kept on a tight rein. The type of language used for questioning each witness (what linguists call a 'register') should be appropriate to that witness. For example, when dealing with an unsophisticated witness, counsel should avoid complicated language and complex, hypothetical questions. When questioning a witness through an interpreter, short, simple questions work best. It is always a good idea to ensure that only one thing is asked in each question as this avoids ambiguity in the answer.

It is important to interview a witness in advance, not only to be sure of what he or she will say, but also to form an idea of how best to lead his or her evidence. It can be helpful to explain the nature and purpose of giving evidence to the potential witness. Rehearsing a witness too closely can be counterproductive as the witness may then come across in an artificial way, detracting from the spontaneity and value of his or her evidence.

The sequence of questioning is usually important. Sometimes a chronological sequence works best, especially if the event is vivid and unusual for the witness. For example, a victim

---

16 See *S v Van der Westhuizen* 2011 (2) SACR 26 (SCA) at paras 3–14.
17 For instance, by leaving out part of what someone said to the witness in a way that misrepresents what was actually said.

of a robbery will usually be able to give a coherent, chronological account of the incident without much guidance. However, this style does not work as well for certain types of witnesses. A witness who is required to testify about some routine event that took place long ago and had no particular significance for him or her, even at the time, will find it difficult to get to the point if led in a purely chronological way. For example, imagine a bank teller to whom a particular cheque was presented for cashing on a particular day three years ago. It may perhaps be better to break the chronological sequence in such a case as illustrated in the example below.

Q: Ms Naidoo, do you work as a teller at the Downtown branch of Multibank?
A: Yes.
Q: Please look at Exhibit G: what is it?
A: It is a cheque made out to cash for the amount of R10 000, drawn on our branch and dated 4 June 2007.
Q: Have you ever seen that document before?
A: Yes.
Q: Please describe the circumstances in which you first saw that document.
A: It was presented to me for payment at the bank on the same day, 4 June 2007. I was working as teller number four on that day. I can identify the cheque because I placed my date stamp and initials on it. A man came into the bank and presented the cheque to me for encashing.
Q: What did you do when the cheque was presented to you?
A: I asked the man who presented it how he wanted the money and gave him the cash.
Q: Are you able to identify that person today?
A: No, it was too long ago. I do hundreds of such transactions each week.
Q: Why did you cash the cheque?
A: Because I thought the man was entitled to it.
Q: What would you have done had you known that the man presenting it had stolen it from the rightful owner?
A: I would definitely not have cashed it. I would have given him some pretext for waiting while I got clearance and then gone to my supervisor to report the matter.

Sometimes a witness will omit something during the course of evidence-in-chief. Counsel then has to decide quickly whether to interrupt the witness's account to elicit the omitted material, perhaps running the risk of disturbing the flow of the narrative. Alternatively, counsel may decide to wait until the end of the witness's evidence to return to the point, perhaps running the risk of having difficulty in getting the witness back to the exact stage of the omitted material. Experience will assist counsel in making the right decision.

It is not just the sequence of questioning for each witness that is important. It can be even more important to choose the optimum sequence for calling the witnesses. In a complicated trial, especially, much thought should go into the planning of a coherent sequence of witnesses. If there are multiple issues, it is usually helpful to call all the witnesses on one issue before moving on to a different issue. It is usually a good idea to commence and conclude evidence-in-chief with a good witness as far as counsel can anticipate that they will be good witnesses. This will create a favourable impression with the court in the beginning and also at the end. Counsel can then call witnesses that are anticipated to be less effective between the good witnesses.

THE LAW OF EVIDENCE IN SOUTH AFRICA

Witnesses often require much support. For example, the complainant in a rape case will usually be subjected to persistent attacks on his or her credibility and may be vulnerable. If he or she is called as the opening witness, the attack may leave permanent damage to the case as well as the complainant's psyche. However, if there are several items of corroborating evidence, it may be better to lead this evidence first to give the complainant a firm footing when he or she is eventually called to testify.

Documents can be a useful means of supporting a witness. Many shaky witnesses have been saved because of one or more documents that support their version.[18]

It takes experience to decide when enough evidence has been led. For example, if there are 50 witnesses to a particular incident, it usually is not necessary to call all 50 as three, four or five may be sufficient. If this is the case, counsel needs to make a reasoned decision about which ones to call. Interviews with potential witnesses will assist with this decision.

There has been some misunderstanding in the past about the particular duty of a prosecutor in a criminal trial to present the case fairly as a 'minister of the truth'. From time to time the argument is heard, usually by counsel for the accused when challenging a conviction on appeal, that the prosecutor is under a duty to lead all available evidence. There is no such duty on a prosecutor. The prosecutor, under our system, can pick and choose from available evidence to present the strongest possible case. However, there is a duty to make available to the defence all witnesses known to but not called by the prosecution.[19] There is also a duty on the prosecution to divulge any information favourable to the accused that the defence may not be aware of.[20]

Furthermore, there is no duty to lead a witness on everything that the witness may possibly say on a given topic. For example, if there have been several witnesses that have already covered a particular issue, a further witness may be called merely to cover a particular aspect for which support for the other witnesses is desirable, not to state everything about the entire event.

29.7 Practical examples of evidence-in-chief

29.7.1 Civil trial in High Court: evidence-in-chief of plaintiff in motor accident case

Q: Ms Nkomo, are you the plaintiff in this matter?

A: Yes.

Q: Are you a single woman, aged 32, working as a journalist for the *Daily Bugle*?

A: Yes.

Q: On 13 April 2011 were you the owner of a 2009 model Toyota Corolla with registration number QQQ 456 GP?

A: Yes.

Q: What was the value of that car at that time?

A: R150 000.

Q: On that day, 13 April 2011, at 10 a.m. were you travelling in High Street, Mkhizeville, in an easterly direction?

A: Yes. I was at work on my way to an assignment for the newspaper.

---

18 See ch 11 for a discussion of the principles relating to the proof and use of documents in evidence.

19 *S v Van der Westhuizen* 2011 (2) SACR 26 (SCA) at paras 3–14 and cases there cited. See also *R v Heilbron* 1922 TPD 99.

20 *S v Van Rensburg* 1963 (2) SA 343 (N).

CHAPTER 29 EVIDENCE-IN-CHIEF | 331

[Note that the questions thus far are mainly leading questions, but they are unobjectionable because they are non-contentious. Also, if counsel does not lead the plaintiff on these issues, time would be wasted unnecessarily. The subsequent questioning below is not leading.]

Q: Were you alone in the car?

A: No, I had with me as a passenger, Mrs Nonka Dhlamini, a fellow journalist who was working with me on the assignment.

Q: Will you please tell the court what happened?

A: I was driving down High Street and I wanted to turn right into West Street. West Street runs into High Street and there is a stop street for traffic in West Street where it joins High Street. I was doing about 50 kilometres per hour. About 50 metres before the intersection I put my indicator on to turn right, slowed down and made sure I was at the right-hand side of my lane. I checked my rear-view mirror and it appeared as if traffic behind me was aware of my intentions. There was no traffic coming from the front in High Street and I prepared to turn right by engaging second gear. Just as I was about to turn, I felt and heard a huge bang from the rear. My car then went out of control and crashed into a lamppost on the right-hand side of High Street. Fortunately, Mrs Dhlamini and I were not injured. I got out of my car and saw that another car had crashed into it from the rear.

Q: Who was the driver of that other car?

A: It was the defendant, Mr Smith. He was still in the driver's seat of his car when I got out of my car.

Q: What vehicle was he driving?

A: It was a large car, a Mercedes I think. I am not sure of the registration number.

Q: Did Mr Smith say anything in your presence about why he drove into your car?

A: Not really. He merely accused me of slowing unexpectedly.

Q: What happened next?

A: I called the police and informed them about the accident. The police then arrived on the scene after a little while and took measurements.

Q: What damage did your car suffer?

A: It was damaged in front where it hit the lamppost. It was also extensively damaged at the back where the other car collided with it.

Q: What happened to your car after the collision?

A: It was towed away to a garage. The garage subsequently informed me that the car could not be repaired and that it was thus a write-off.

Q: Were you insured against the damage?

A: No.

Q: So how much loss did you suffer?

A: Well, the entire value of the car was R150 000. The car was sold as scrap, but the scrap value just covered the towing fee and assessment by the garage.

Q: Thank you, that is all.

29.7.2 Criminal trial in High Court: evidence-in-chief of complainant in fraud case

Q: Mr Singh, are you the complainant in this case?

A: Yes, that's right.

Q: Did you ever have business dealings with the accused?

THE LAW OF EVIDENCE IN SOUTH AFRICA

A: Yes, I bought a supermarket business from him.

Q: Please tell the court how this came about.

A: I had inherited some money from my late father and I was keen to acquire a business. I saw an advert in the press that was offering a supermarket for sale as a going concern. It said that the supermarket was highly profitable and the asking price was R2,2 million.

Q: Please look at the newspaper cutting I am showing you. Is that the advertisement you saw?

A: Yes. It was in the *Daily Mail* of 6 May 2010.

Q: May that be Exhibit A, My Lady?

Judge: Yes.

Q: What happened next?

A: I phoned the number appearing in the advert, Exhibit A, and spoke to someone who said he was Mr Smit, the owner of the business. I made an appointment to see him and went round to the supermarket on 8 May.

Q: Where was the supermarket situated?

A: In Leopard Street, Brownsville, here in Mpumalanga.

Q: What happened when you went there?

A: Mr Smit introduced himself as the owner of the business, saying he was emigrating and thus wanted to sell the supermarket.

Q: Is Mr Smit here in court today?

A: Yes, sitting over there in the dock. He is the accused.

Q: Please carry on.

A: Mr Smit showed me balance sheets for the past five years and from them it was clear that the business was very profitable. The assets exceeded the liabilities by some R2 million.

Q: Are these the balance sheets you were shown, for 2005, 2006, 2007, 2008 and 2009?

A: Yes.

Q: My Lady, may these be Exhibits B, C, D, E and F respectively?

Judge: Yes.

Q: Please carry on, Mr Singh.

A: Mr Smit explained that the business was in the name of a close corporation, Goldtouch CC. It looked to me as if this was just the sort of business I was after and I was very impressed. He said the price was R2,2 million. After some haggling, we agreed on a price of R2,1 million. I later signed a written agreement to buy the CC for that price.

Q: Please look at the document I am now showing you. Is that the original agreement signed by you and the accused?

A: Yes it is.

Q: My Lady, may that be Exhibit G?

Judge: Yes.

Q: What happened next?

A: I paid the price by way of electronic transfer and took over the supermarket on 1 July 2010, the date agreed in Exhibit B.

Q: What happened after that?

A: Not long after taking over, I discovered that things were not at all well. Business was slow and overheads were high. I discussed the matter with some of the

CHAPTER 29 EVIDENCE-IN-CHIEF | **333**

older members of the staff who had been working there for years. They told me that the business had been struggling for years. When I showed them the balance sheets, Exhibits B, C, D, E and F, they said something must be wrong and suggested that I speak to Mr Jones, the auditor. I then went to see Mr Jones who said that these balance sheets were not correct. He then showed me copies of the correct ones. From the correct balance sheets it was clear that the CC was in fact insolvent.

Q:	Are these the balance sheets Mr Jones showed you?

A:	Indeed.

Q:	May they be Exhibits H, I, J, K and L, My Lady?

Judge:	Yes.

Q:	Carry on, please, Mr Singh.

A:	Creditors started demanding to be paid and there wasn't sufficient money coming in to pay them. Eventually, they put the business into liquidation. I got nothing out.

Q:	Did you ever see or hear of the accused again?

A:	I tried to trace him and eventually found that he was working in a bar in a small town in the Karoo. When I phoned him and asked him about the balance sheets he had shown me and all the rosy stuff he had said about the business, he was very evasive. Further enquiries indicated to me that he had a gambling problem, that he had no assets and that it would be pointless to sue him.

Q:	So, Mr Singh, how much money did you lose?

A:	The entire R2,1 million I paid for the business, as well as an additional R50 000 of my own money that I used to pay the wages of the staff when the bank would not advance any more money.

Q:	Would you have bought the CC had you known that, in fact, it had been running at a loss for years and was insolvent?

A:	Most certainly not.

Q:	No further questions.

Note that in both cases, the evidence-in-chief covers what the plaintiff and prosecutor, respectively, set out to prove through these witnesses. The questions were short and to the point, and easy for the witnesses to understand.

As we have pointed out, leading questions are impermissible except where they deal with non-contentious issues. What is the effect if a leading question is nevertheless asked on a contentious issue?[21] Is the resulting answer inadmissible evidence? Some cases appear to give this impression.[22] The better view, however, is that the answer is not inadmissible *per se*, but that it carries little if any weight.[23]

THIS CHAPTER IN ESSENCE

1	Examination-in-chief takes place before cross-examination and re-examination. The purpose of examination-in-chief is to enable the party who has called a witness to put his or her evidence before the court.

21	This problem would usually arise if a trial court has wrongly allowed a leading question and there is a challenge on appeal.

22	See, for instance, the *obiter dictum* in S v *Maradu* 1994 (2) SACR 410 (W) at 413J–414A.

23	S v *Bailey* 2007 (2) SACR 1 (C) at 10A–B and see Palmer and McQuoid-Mason (2000) at 57.

2   No leading questions may be put to a witness during examination-in-chief. However, this rule is relaxed in the case of non-contentious issues such as a witness's name, address and occupation. Furthermore, counsel may not ask a witness a question which assumes the existence of a fact which still has to be proved.

3   Generally, witnesses do not sit in court prior to testifying to eliminate the possibility of them adapting their testimony. This general rule is, however, relaxed in the case of expert witnesses. Also, in criminal trials, the accused is required to be present throughout the entire trial and thus usually testifies before other defence witnesses.

4   The party presenting its case (*dominus litis*) has freedom in respect of the witnesses he or she wants to call, the sequence of the witnesses and the questions that counsel will ask each witness.

5   It is important to interview witnesses in advance to gain clarity on what they will say and to make a decision on how best to lead their evidence.

6   Prosecutors are not obliged to lead all available evidence, but are obliged to make available to the defence all witnesses known to but not called by the prosecution.

7   There is no duty to lead a witness on everything that he or she might possibly say on a particular topic.

Chapter 30

Cross-examination

30.1	**Introduction**	**335**
30.2	**Legal basis for cross-examination**	**336**
30.3	**Procedure for cross-examination**	**336**
30.4	**Practical examples of cross-examination**	**337**
	30.4.1 Civil trial in High Court: cross-examination of defendant in motor accident case	337
	30.4.2 Criminal trial in High Court: cross-examination of complainant in fraud case	340

30.1 Introduction

Cross-examination is a fundamental feature of our system of evidence gathering. Wigmore, the great authority on the law of evidence, called it '... beyond any doubt the greatest legal engine ever invented for the discovery of the truth'.[1] Cross-examination takes place after a witness has given evidence-in-chief for the party calling that witness and is the exchange between that witness and counsel for the opposing party. We sometimes refer to cross-examination as the questioning of the witness by the opposing party,[2] but this is not strictly correct. If there are many parties, each party other than the party calling the witness has the opportunity of cross-examining the witness even if that witness has not given any adverse evidence at all against the party in question.[3]

The purpose of cross-examination is to:

- test the accuracy and veracity of a witness's evidence
- demolish, water it down or qualify it wherever possible
- elicit favourable evidence for the cross-examining party
- put your client's version to the witness to allow the witness to respond.[4]

Cross-examination has long fascinated the public at large as it can provide considerable drama as well as entertainment. Many films and TV shows, many works of fiction and many accounts of the life and work of famous lawyers draw attention to the dramatic power of cross-examination. However, despite its potential for drama, there is no guarantee that cross-examination will always be dramatic or entertaining. The lengthy cross-examination

---

1 JH Wigmore *Wigmore on Evidence* 3 ed, Vol. 5 (1940) at para 1367, p. 29.
2 See for instance PJ Schwikkard and SE van der Merwe *Principles of Evidence* 3 ed (2009) at 366.
3 E du Toit et al *Commentary on the Criminal Procedure Act* (1987) at 22–79 (Revision service 59, 2017) defines it simply as '... the name given to the questioning of the witnesses by the party (or parties) who did not call the witness'.
4 See Du Toit commentary on s 166 of the CPA (1987) (Revision Service 59, 2017) at 22–78. This is especially prevalent in criminal matters where the defence relies on an alibi. See also *Mohammed v State* (605/10) [2011] ZASCA 98 (31 May 2011).

336 | THE LAW OF EVIDENCE IN SOUTH AFRICA

of an auditor, for example, on highly technical evidence about business records and accounting principles is unlikely to yield much fascination for the average spectator.

Cross-examination has been the subject of extensive legal writing by authors throughout those parts of the globe that follow the adversarial system. The range of writing on the subject is too wide for coverage in a single chapter.[5] In addition, all the main works on the law of evidence devote considerable space to the topic.[6]

30.2 Legal basis for cross-examination

The Criminal Procedure Act 51 of 1977 spells out the right of the prosecution to cross-examine the accused and other defence witnesses. The accused also has the right to cross-examine prosecution witnesses as well as co-accused and any witnesses called by a co-accused.[7] In addition, the prosecution and the accused may cross-examine witnesses called by the court, but only with **leave of the court**.[8]

The High Court Rules have little to say on the subject of cross-examination. They clearly assume that the nature of cross-examination as well as rules for cross-examination form part of the common law.[9] The Magistrates' Courts Rules do not even mention cross-examination. In *S v Msimango and Another*[10] the Court held that the right of an accused to challenge evidence in section 35(3)(i) of the Constitution undoubtedly included the right to cross-examination.

30.3 Procedure for cross-examination

There are a number of rules, statutory as well as common law, on the subject of cross-examination. The following is a list of the more significant rules:

- Cross-examination is a right and the denial or improper restriction of the right usually constitutes a serious irregularity.[11] This right comes into existence the moment a witness is sworn in. Thus it exists even if for some or other reason a witness after being sworn in does not give any evidence-in-chief.[12]
- Ordinarily, only one legal representative on behalf of each party may cross-examine.[13] If a party chooses to be legally represented, the legal representative and not the client may cross-examine.[14]

---

5 The main authorities on the subject in South Africa are G Colman *Cross-examination: A Practical Handbook* (1970); JP Pretorius *Cross-examination in South African Law* (1997); E Morris *Technique in Litigation* 6 ed (2010) and R Palmer and D McQuoid-Mason *Basic Trial Advocacy Skills* (2000) ch 7.

6 See, for example, DT Zeffertt and AP Paizes *The South African Law of Evidence* 2 ed (2009) at 906–920; Schwikkard and Van der Merwe 3 ed (2009) at 365–375.

7 S 166(1) of the Criminal Procedure Act, 1977.

8 S 166(2) of the Criminal Procedure Act, 1977. Ordinarily, the court will allow all parties to cross-examine such witnesses, but if a witness is being recalled by the court after a party has already called the witness, it would not be fair to allow the party who originally called the witness to cross-examine the witness. See *R v Kumalo* 1952 (3) SA 223 (T) at 226A–D.

9 See High Court Rule 39(8).

10 2010 (1) SACR 544 (GSJ) at para 27.

11 *S v Le Grange and Others* 2009 (1) SACR 125 (SCA).

12 For example, if a party calls a witness, who is then sworn in, and the party then decides not to ask any questions of the witness.

13 High Court Rule 39(8) for civil trials. The Criminal Procedure Act, 1977 is silent on this point, but it is a well-established rule of practice that only one person may cross-examine for each party: *S v Basson* 2001 (2) SACR 537 (T) and *S v Yanta* 2000 (1) SACR 237 (Tk). In *S v Basson*, the Court exceptionally allowed cross-examination of the accused by more than one member of the prosecuting team because the trial was long and involved, and members of the prosecuting team had specialised in different aspects of the case. The Court imposed strict limitations on this indulgence to prevent abuse of the process.

14 *R v Baartman* 1960 (3) SA 535 (A) at 538A.

CHAPTER 30   CROSS-EXAMINATION   **337**

- A court may restrict cross-examination if the process is being abused or becomes unduly protracted.[15]
- Cross-examination is not restricted to matters that have been covered during evidence-in-chief. A cross-examiner is allowed a wide latitude, especially regarding matters of credibility. Answers on matters that focus solely on credibility are final.[16]
- Cross-examination can be vigorous, but must stay within the bounds of fairness and courtesy.[17] It follows that misleading cross-examination is impermissible, for example suggesting something as a proved fact when it is not a proved fact.[18]
- A cross-examining party must challenge in cross-examination any part of a witness's evidence that they do not agree with. Failure to do so can lead to an adverse credibility finding against them if they attempt to argue that their version should be accepted in preference to that of the witness.[19]

30.4   Practical examples of cross-examination

30.4.1   Civil trial in High Court: cross-examination of defendant in motor accident case

Q: Mr Jones, where were you going when the collision occurred?

A: I was on my way to see a customer.

Q: Why?

A: This customer had complained about the quality of the work our workmen had carried out at her shop and my boss sent me to sort out the problem.

Q: Had you dealt with this customer before?

A: Yes.

Q: Was she, what is known as, a difficult customer?

A: I would say fairly difficult. When our firm did a job for her before, she had complaints about the way the work was done. I had to calm her down, it took some doing.

Q: Was she an important customer?

A: All our customers are important.

Q: Was she one of the bigger customers your firm has?

A: Yes, I would say so.

Q: So losing her custom would be a setback for your firm?

A: You could put it that way.

Q: And were you thinking about how to deal with her as you were travelling that day?

A: I was still concentrating on my driving as I was heading for her place of business.

Q: Please answer the question: were you thinking about how to pacify her as you were heading towards her premises?

A: To some extent, yes.

---

15 See s 166(3)(*a*) of the Criminal Procedure Act, 1977 for the general position in criminal trials. See also s 227(2) to 227(7) of the Criminal Procedure Act, 1977 for special powers of restriction of cross-examination of victims in sexual cases. Furthermore, the Supreme Court of Appeal made an adverse costs awards against a party that cross-examined for too long. See *Africa Solar (Pty) Ltd v Divwatt (Pty) Ltd* 2002 (4) SA 681 (SCA).

16 *S v Zwane and Others* 1993 (3) SA 393 (W).

17 *S v Nkibane* 1989 (2) SA 421 (NC).

18 Colman *Cross-examination: A Practical Handbook* (1970) at 18–23.

19 See *S v Boesak* 2000 (1) SACR 633 (SCA) at paras 43–47 and *S v Boesak* 2001 (1) SACR 1 (CC) at paras 17–28.

338 | THE LAW OF EVIDENCE IN SOUTH AFRICA

Q: Mr Jones, you stated in your evidence-in-chief that you could not avoid the collision. Correct?

A: Yes, that is so.

Q: How long have you been driving a car?

A: About 10 years.

Q: From what I can gather, you use your car in the course of business?

A: That is so.

Q: So you do much of your driving during business hours in town?

A: I would agree with that.

Q: So you would consider yourself an experienced driver?

A: I would say so.

Q: At what speed were you travelling just before the accident?

A: At around 50 kilometres per hour.

Q: Did you consider that to be a safe speed in the circumstances?

A: Well, I thought it was.

Q: How far behind the plaintiff were you driving just before she braked suddenly?

A: I am not sure, it varied.

Q: What was the closest that you got to her car before, as you say, it suddenly braked?

A: I am not sure of the distance.

Q: If you are not able to estimate it in metres, could you point it out here in court?

A: I would say it was about from where I am now to that table over there.

Q: I estimate that to be about five metres, My Lord.

Judge: Yes, that seems to be correct.

Q: Was this distance that you have pointed out more or less constant?

A: I would say so, but it probably varied slightly.

Q: So we can assume that your car and the plaintiff's car must have been travelling at about the same speed?

A: I suppose so.

Q: This was a fairly busy part of town, not so?

A: Yes, I would say so.

Q: And there were numerous pedestrians on either side of the road?

A: Yes, I agree.

Q: As well as numerous other cars travelling in the vicinity?

A: Well, quite a few other cars.

Q: In a situation with numerous other cars, as well as many pedestrians, emergencies can arise, not so? With cars having to stop suddenly?

A: Sometimes they do. I don't recall one happening on that day, though.

Q: But I assume you had in mind that an emergency of that nature was always a possibility in that situation?

A: I suppose so.

Q: With the speed you were travelling at and the distance you were maintaining behind the plaintiff's car, could you have stopped in time if the plaintiff needed to stop suddenly?

A: I think so.

Q: How would you rate your reaction time?

A: I would say about average, it certainly isn't problematic.

Q: Well, it might interest you to know that at 50 kilometres per hour, the speed you claim you were doing, a car covers 13,8 metres per second. Do you want me to go through the calculations with you?

CHAPTER 30   CROSS-EXAMINATION   339

A: No, I accept what you say.

Q: So, if you were about five metres behind the plaintiff that would give you less than half a second to react if she had to stop suddenly?

A: Yes, I see your point.

Q: Do you still insist that you were travelling a safe distance behind the plaintiff for the speed you were doing?

A: I would say so.

Q: If that is so, why did you collide with the rear of the plaintiff's car?

A: Because she stopped so suddenly.

Q: Did you notice her brake lights going on before the accident?

A: I don't recall noticing them.

Q: Did you notice her indicator light showing that she was turning right?

A: Definitely not.

Q: Does that mean that that they were not on or merely that you did not notice them?

A: I would say that the indicator was not on.

Q: How can you be sure the indicator light was not on if you aren't sure that you noticed the brake lights come on?

A: Because I am sure that if I had seen them indicating, I would have been alerted to the possibility of a turn and would have slowed down earlier.

Q: You stated earlier that you were thinking about how to handle the irate customer you were on your way to. Does that not perhaps explain why your full attention was not on the traffic ahead of you?

A: No, I don't think so.

Q: You don't think so. Does that mean that you are not sure?

A: No, I am actually sure that I was concentrating.

Q: But if so, why were you not able to stop in time, even though you were travelling, what you considered to be, a safe distance behind the plaintiff?

A: Well, I jammed on the brakes as soon as I saw the car in front braking, but I still crashed into that car.

Q: How could that have happened if you were maintaining a safe following distance?

A: I think there must have been something slippery on the road, such as oil or gravel.

Q: Do you mean that your car skidded just prior to impact?

A: Yes.

Q: That is very interesting. In your counsel's cross-examination of the plaintiff nothing was said about a skid.

A: Well, I did tell my lawyer about it. He must have forgotten to mention it.

Q: Nor did you mention a skid in your evidence-in-chief.

A: No.

Q: Are you going to blame your lawyer for that as well?

A: I don't know about that.

Q: I put it to you that you were in fact travelling too fast in the circumstances, travelling too close to the rear of the plaintiff's vehicle, and that you did not keep a proper lookout on the road ahead. What do you say to that?

A: No, I disagree with you on all those points.

Q: No further questions, My Lord.

There is not much material in this example for the cross-examiner to work with. Cross-examining counsel nevertheless succeeds in making inroads into the defendant's evidence

THE LAW OF EVIDENCE IN SOUTH AFRICA

by chipping away at his version. Counsel starts, seemingly innocuously, by asking about where the defendant was going and why. In the course of answering this line of questioning, the defendant gives counsel something to work with – the possibility that the defendant was not driving with due attention on account of his preoccupation with the tricky encounter he was about to have with a difficult customer.

Counsel then switches attack to the adequacy of the defendant's following distance. Counsel starts by getting the defendant to admit that he is an experienced driver and that he is used to driving in town conditions. This limits the defendant's ability to be evasive when further questioning takes him closer to the events on the day. The questioning then covers the adequacy or inadequacy of the following distance he was maintaining. It goes on to explore whether he noticed indicator or brake lights. In the process, this causes the witness to become unsure of himself and thus slightly nervous. This type of pressure can sometimes cause a witness to feel the need to come up with something to deflect the pressure. It works in this instance as the witness is tempted to be creative by blaming the slipperiness of the road surface for his inability to brake in time. This excuse is an improvisation. Improvisations often assist the astute cross-examiner as is the case here. In seeking to deflect pressure, the witness gets into more trouble by raising something that would, if true, have been raised at an earlier stage.

30.4.2 Criminal trial in High Court: cross-examination of complainant in fraud case

Q: Mr Singh, you made a bad bargain when you bought this business, did you not?

A: Yes, it turned out very badly.

Q: Running a business is a complex matter. Would you agree?

A: Well, I am not sure about that. The accused made it seem very simple when he told me how well the supermarket was doing.

Q: You must know that numerous factors can cause a business to fail: general economic conditions in the country, local economic conditions and matters such as population movement away from certain areas?

A: Well, I suppose so.

Q: How well a business is being run is a crucial factor, is it not?

A: I would agree. But the accused assured me that this supermarket was a top-quality business with a strong customer support base.

Q: Mr Singh, how old are you?

A: Forty-three, My Lady.

Q: What did you do for a living before you bought the CC from the accused?

A: I started out as a bank clerk for a few years. After that I worked as a salesman for a spare-part business in the motor industry. Then I ran a dry-cleaning business on behalf of an uncle for about five years.

Q: So it seems you have had quite a lot of exposure to the business world?

A: Well, I have never owned my own business before.

Q: That is not what I asked. Please stick to the question.

A: Just repeat the question, please.

Q: It's a simple question, Mr Singh. You have had quite a lot of exposure to the business world?

A: I suppose so, but never before have I been involved with a supermarket.

Q: All businesses rely on profitability to survive, not so?

A: I am not sure, I have no wide experience of many different types of businesses.

Q: Surely, Mr Singh, businesses do not survive if they are not profitable?

A: I cannot say for sure.

Q: People do not run businesses in order to lose money, surely?

A: Well, if you put it that way.

Q: Is there any other way of putting it?

A: [No answer]

Q: It was very important to you that this business you were interested in acquiring was profitable?

A: Yes.

Q: In your evidence-in-chief you drew attention to this when you described the advert, Exhibit A, and when you told the court what the accused said to you when you went to see him. Correct?

A: Yes.

Q: People selling things, whether it's clothing, cars, food or whatever, are keen to make their wares seem attractive. Do you agree?

A: I do.

Q: The same would go for a business that is being sold, not so?

A: I suppose so.

Q: Any sensible person would want to make sure, before buying, that the product is as good as the seller claims?

A: Well, maybe not quite as good as the claim, but at least to the point that the buyer thought he was getting value.

Q: Exactly. Any sensible buyer wants to be sure he or she is getting value before concluding a sale?

A: If you put it like that.

Q: When you went into this deal, you were investing a large sum of money?

A: Yes, it was over R2 million.

Q: So it follows, surely, that you, as a sensible buyer, would want to make sure that you were getting good value?

A: But I was told by the accused, Mr Smit, that the business was a good proposition.

Q: Did you take any steps, apart from listening to Mr Smit and looking at the balance sheets he showed you, to verify the profitability of the business?

A: I am not sure what you are getting at.

Q: Mr Singh, please answer the question. It is not a difficult one. Did you take any other steps, other than listening to what Mr Smit said and looking at the balance sheets you say he showed you, to check whether the supermarket was profitable?

A: Well, I thought about the deal quite a lot before deciding to go ahead.

Q: But did you take any steps to check the information Mr Smit gave you?

A: Not really.

Q: Why not?

A: Because I did not know what other steps to take.

Q: Come, come, Mr Singh. You have worked in a bank and in a motor spare business, and you have run a dry-cleaning business. Are you seriously suggesting to the court that you did not know that there are ways and means of checking on the profitability of a business?

A: Such as what?

Q: It is for me to ask the questions and you to answer them. I am asking you whether you want the court to believe that you did not know you could get expert advice from, for example, independent accountants, about the profitability of the business.

A: I did not think of that.

Q: Did you think of checking with Mr Jones, the auditor, that the information you had been given was correct?

A: No, I did not.

Q: Why not?

A: Because I did not have time to do that.

Q: Why the rush?

A: Because I was keen to take over the business without delay so that I could start earning profits.

Q: But, Mr Singh, you are now putting the cart before the horse. Whether you will make any profits at all will depend on the profitability of the business. It makes no sense to rush into things if you are not sure that they are going to work out?

A: Well, I did not think of this at the time.

Q: Are you now suggesting that the reason for your failure to verify the information was that you did not think of doing so?

A: Yes, that's right.

Q: A moment ago you said that the reason was that you did not have time, correct?

A: I did say that.

Q: Well, what is the reason: that you did not have time to verify or that you did not think of verifying?

A: Both, really.

Q: You see, Mr Singh, I want to suggest to you that you have not been honest with the court. The real reason for your apparent lack of interest in verifying the information was something quite different. What do you say to that?

A: No, I disagree.

Q: I want to move to the issue of the source of the money that you used to purchase the business. You said in evidence-in-chief that you had inherited the money from your late father?

A: Yes.

Q: When you say inherited, do you mean in the ordinary course, via a will, leaving a sum of money to you, which was properly processed through the Master's office?

A: Yes, I think so.

Q: Why are you uncertain, Mr Singh?

A: Well, because I don't understand all of those legal processes.

Q: Who was the executor in the estate of your late father?

A: It was Mr Chetty, the attorney.

Q: That's right. Would you please look at the document I am now showing you. Is that the final distribution account in your father's estate?

A: Yes, it is.

q: May that be Exhibit M, My Lady?

Judge: Yes.

Q: Do you see that the sum of money that you received from the estate, according to Exhibit M, is R40 000?

A: Yes.

CHAPTER 30   CROSS-EXAMINATION   343

Q: So you inherited the sum of R40 000 from your father?
A: Yes.
Q: In evidence-in-chief you gave the clear impression that the money you used to buy the business came from your father's estate?
A: Well, some of it.
Q: It now turns out that the most you could have used from your father's estate was the sum of R40 000. That is a small proportion of the sum you paid for the business, not so?
A: Yes.
Q: Where did the rest of the money come from?
A: From my savings.
Q: How did you acquire these savings?
A: From my salary.
Q: Where did you keep these savings?
A: In a cupboard at home.
Q: Are you suggesting that you kept the amount of over R2 million in cash at home?
A: Yes.
Q: Why keep such a large amount in cash? You get no interest on the money and run the risk of loss through theft or fire?
A: Because I don't trust banks.
Q: Yet you worked in a bank for a number of years?
A: Yes, but I still don't trust them.
Q: When you started running the supermarket, after the purchase of the business, the supermarket operated a bank account, I assume?
A: Yes.
Q: What about your lack of faith in banks?
A: Well, you can't operate a business today without having a bank account so I had no choice, really.
Q: And when you ran your uncle's dry-cleaning business, I assume that business made use of a bank account?
A: Yes. Once again, I had no choice about that.
Q: Getting back to the purchase price, are you suggesting that you paid Mr Smit in cash, banknotes, for the business?
A: Not all of it, the R40 000 from my father's estate was paid by electronic transfer from my bank account.
Q: So you do have some faith in banks after all?
A: Not much.
Q: Mr Singh, if I understand you correctly, you paid for the business by way of electronic transfer in the sum of R40 000 from your bank account and the rest, some R2 060 000, in cash, banknotes?
A: Your arithmetic seems correct.
Q: In your evidence-in-chief, Mr Singh, you stated that you paid the purchase price by way of electronic transfer. Correct?
A: Yes.
Q: But we have now seen that that evidence was untrue.
A: It was partially true, I did pay R40 000 by way of electronic transfer.
Q: Why did you not tell the court that the vast bulk of the price was paid in cash, banknotes?

A: I don't really know.

Q: Are you trying to hide anything from the court, Mr Singh?

A: No.

Q: Mr Singh, why did you not tell the court that the great bulk of the purchase price came from your savings in cash?

A: No reason, really.

Q: Why did you mention that you had inherited money from your father if you did not intend to convey the impression that that was the source of money for the purchase of the business?

A: I have no answer.

Q: Mr Singh, I am going to suggest to you what actually happened with your purchase of the supermarket. Listen carefully to what I say and then respond. It is correct that most of the cash price was paid by banknotes. You told Mr Smit that you had 'hot money' in cash that you were seeking to launder through some transaction that had the appearance of legitimacy. You asked Mr Smit to come up with balance sheets that made the transaction seem attractive to a purchaser so that no suspicion would attach to your purchase. He then produced the balance sheets (Exhibits H, I, J, K and L) to accommodate you. What do you say to that?

A: I deny it.

Q: Well, that is what Mr Smit, the accused, will say when he gives evidence.

A: It is not true at all.

Q: And I put it to you further that this explains why you bought the business for cash, but chose not to tell the court the true source of your money.

A: No, that is not so.

Q: And why you gave the court the clear impression that you bought the business with money you had inherited from your father.

A: No.

Q: And it explains why you made no apparent attempt to verify the profitability of the business from independent sources.

A: That is not so.

Q: And it was only when the auditor, Mr Jones, found out about your attempt to launder money through the purchase of the business that you claimed that Mr Smit, the accused, had misled you into the deal.

A: I deny that.

Q: No further questions, My Lady.

The cross-examination does not extract an admission from the witness that he has been untruthful. Cross-examination rarely results in such outright concessions. It seeks to build steadily on a number of improbabilities and inconsistencies until the time is ripe to put the accused's version to the witness. The cross-examination does not succeed in totally demolishing the case for the prosecution, but it does succeed in showing the witness to be far less convincing than he would have appeared after giving evidence-in-chief. It thus gives the accused a stronger chance to have his version of events accepted, at least, as being reasonably possibly true.

The style of questioning is fairly concise and avoids long, cumbersome questions. Most of the questions are not open-ended as they invite a 'yes' or 'no' answer. Sometimes, however, the cross-examiner does ask open-ended questions, where he or she feels no harm will come of it or where he or she is not sure what the answer will be.

It is frequently stated that a cross-examiner should only ask questions to which he or she already knows the answer.[20] This is an over-statement of the position. In several places in this cross-examination counsel does not know exactly what the answer will be but knows that the question will expose a shaky area of the witness's testimony. Counsel then relies on his or her skill and experience to exploit the answers to difficult questions. For example, just about any answer a person gives to a question about why he or she keeps a sum of R2 million in banknotes at home will give the cross-examiner further material to exploit. Similarly, whatever answer the witness gives to explain why he took no steps to verify the profitability of the business independently is likely to prove feeble, at best, for the witness, and probably quite damaging to his credibility. The proposition mentioned in the first sentence of this paragraph should thus be re-stated – a cross-examiner should only ask questions which he or she is reasonably sure will lead to answers that will suit him or her (either through what the witness says directly or through the opportunity of exploitation) or at least will do the cross-examining party no harm.

THIS CHAPTER IN ESSENCE

1   Cross-examination occurs after a witness has given evidence-in-chief. The aim of cross-examination is to test the accuracy and veracity of a witness's evidence or the witness's reliability and credibility.
2   The Criminal Procedure Act, 1977 specifically provides for the right of the prosecution to cross-examine the accused and other defence witnesses, as well as the accused's right to cross-examine prosecution witnesses.
3   The accused and the prosecution may cross-examine witnesses called by the court, but only with leave of the court.
4   The most significant rules applicable to cross-examination are as follows:
   4.1   Cross-examination is a right and any denial or improper restriction thereof will constitute a serious irregularity.
   4.2   Only one legal representative on behalf of each party may cross-examine.
   4.3   Cross-examination may be restricted by a court if the process is being abused or unduly protracted.
   4.4   Cross-examination may extend beyond matters covered during evidence-in-chief.
   4.5   Cross-examination must always stay within the bounds of fairness and courtesy.
   4.6   The party conducting the cross-examination must challenge any part of a witness's evidence which they do not agree with to prevent an adverse credibility finding against them if they then argue that their version should be accepted in preference to that of the witness.
5   There are various practical aspects to cross-examination which a practitioner should practise on a regular basis to master.

---

20   See Morris 6 ed (2010) at 237.

Chapter 31

Re-examination

31.1	Introduction	346
31.2	Legal basis for re-examination	346
31.3	Procedure for re-examination	347
31.4	Practical aspects of re-examination	347
31.5	Practical examples of re-examination	347
	31.5.1 Civil trial in High Court: re-examination of plaintiff in motor accident case	347
	31.5.2 Criminal trial in High Court: re-examination of complainant in fraud case	348

31.1 Introduction

Re-examination occurs when the party who presented evidence-in-chief has the opportunity to question their witness again after the opposing party has cross-examined that witness. The main purposes of re-examination are to:
- clarify evidence that has been extracted in cross-examination[1]
- clarify any misconceptions and misunderstandings that may have arisen
- repair any damage that may have been done to the witness's credibility during cross-examination.

31.2 Legal basis for re-examination

Re-examination is part of our common law system of evidence gathering.[2] The Criminal Procedure Act 51 of 1977 specifically mentions re-examination as a right although the Act does not fully explain what it is.[3] The High Court Rules also refer to re-examination in passing, but without any explanation of what it means.[4] The Magistrates' Courts Rules do not mention it all.[5] However, failure to allow re-examination is a serious irregularity.[6]

---

1   See *S v Ramalope* 1995 (1) SACR 616 (A) at 616–618 for the purpose and origin of re-examination.
2   *S v Ramalope* 1995 (1) SACR 616 (A).
3   S 166(1). The section states that re-examination may cover '... any matter raised during the cross-examination of that witness'.
4   High Court Rule 39(8).
5   Rule 29, dealing with the course of a trial, is totally silent on the subject of re-examination.
6   *S v Ramalope* 1995 (1) SACR 616 (A).

31.3 Procedure for re-examination

Re-examination is not confined to material raised for the first time in cross-examination. Thus, a party has the right to re-examine on any matter raised during cross-examination even if it was also raised during evidence-in-chief.[7] Generally, no new evidence may be raised during re-examination. However, if a party wishes to raise new material for the first time during re-examination, they must obtain the permission of the court to do so.[8] The opposing party will then be entitled to cross-examine the witness on that new evidence.

As with evidence-in-chief, leading questions are not permitted during re-examination.[9]

31.4 Practical aspects of re-examination

Re-examination is a right, not a duty, and it should be exercised judiciously. One of the problems with re-examining a witness is that counsel has little idea of what the witness might say. Many witnesses in re-examination will simply compound any confusion that arose during their cross-examination. If a witness's evidence has been harmed during cross-examination, it is usually difficult to repair the damage during re-examination. The soundest approach is probably to avoid re-examination unless counsel is fairly sure that it will improve matters.[10] When in doubt, it is best not to re-examine. If counsel does re-examine, it is usually a good idea to refer the witness to a particular passage of the cross-examination in which an ambiguity arose so that the witness knows what aspect is being covered in re-examination.

31.5 Practical examples of re-examination

31.5.1 Civil trial in High Court: re-examination of plaintiff in motor accident case

Q: Ms Nkomo, during cross-examination you were asked how long you had been in possession of a driving licence and you answered 'Six months'.

[This is a leading question because it invites a particular answer. It is not objectionable, however, because it is non-contentious and it would be time-consuming to come to this point by asking only open-ended questions.]

A: Yes, that is correct.
Q: What did you understand by the term 'driving licence' in the question you were answering?
A: I thought it meant an ordinary driving licence, the type you get from the municipal traffic department after you pass your test.
Q: How long have you actually been driving a vehicle?
A: For over 10 years.
Q: Did you have any form of authority to drive a vehicle before you acquired what you have called an 'ordinary driving licence'?

---

7   *S v Ramalope* 1995 (1) SACR 616 (A).
8   DT Zeffertt and AP Paizes *The South African Law of Evidence* 2 ed (2009) at 921.
9   PJ Schwikkard and SE van der Merwe *Principles of Evidence* 3 ed (2009) 3 ed at 374.
10 E Morris *Technique in Litigation* 6 ed (2010) 284–6. Also see R Palmer and D McQuoid-Mason *Basic Trial Advocacy Skills* (2000) at 87–88.

348 | THE LAW OF EVIDENCE IN SOUTH AFRICA

> A: Yes, I was employed in the Defence Force for 10 years, and soon after joining I acquired a special military licence to drive military vehicles on all roads in South Africa.
> Q: What do you have to do to get a special military licence?
> A: You receive intensive training for three months, then you undergo a rigorous test – more difficult than the test you take for an ordinary driving licence. I got my military licence at the first attempt.
> Q: How often did you drive vehicles when in the Defence Force?
> A: Daily, in the course of my duties as a press liaison officer.

The witness had given an answer in cross-examination that gave the impression that she was an inexperienced driver. This could have led to an argument that her driving at the time of the collision did not meet the standard of a reasonable driver. Re-examination has clarified the matter satisfactorily and has enhanced the case of the plaintiff. Counsel conducting the re-examination obviously knew that the plaintiff had been driving for many years with a military licence and it was thus safe to embark on re-examination to highlight this fact.

31.5.2 Criminal trial in High Court: re-examination of complainant in fraud case

> Q: Mr Singh, during cross-examination you were questioned about your failure to get an expert accountant to evaluate the close corporation before you decided to buy. You answered that you do not trust accountants.

[This is a leading question but unobjectionable for the reasons given in the previous example.]

> A: Yes, that is what I said.
> Q: Why did you give that answer?
> A: Because I do not trust accountants.
> Q: Why do you not trust accountants?
> A: Because once before, when I was running a dry-cleaning business, I had my accountant report me to the tax people for failing to submit VAT statements and payments.

This example illustrates the danger of using re-examination as a form of damage control. Mr Singh's original answer during cross-examination may not have been favourable, but it was by no means as damaging as the further explanation elicited during re-examination. Apart from demonstrating that the complainant had previous business experience and thus ought to have been wary of the dangers of buying a business without a thorough check, re-examination brought out the damaging piece of information that he has dishonest tendencies.

THIS CHAPTER IN ESSENCE

1   A witness is re-examined after the opposing party's cross-examination. Re-examination is done to:
    1.1   clarify evidence extracted in cross-examination
    1.2   clarify any misconceptions and misunderstandings that may have arisen
    1.3   repair damage to the witness's credibility.

CHAPTER 31 RE-EXAMINATION | **349**

2 Although re-examination has its origins in the common law, it is also mentioned as a right in the Criminal Procedure Act, 1977 and the High Court Rules, albeit with no explanation as to its meaning. No mention of re-examination is made in the Magistrates' Courts Rules.

3 Re-examination is a right that should be exercised judiciously.

4 It is usually best to avoid re-examination as it could possibly compound the confusion. If, however, re-examination is essential, it is best to keep the scope of the questions as narrow and specific as possible to focus the witness's attention.

Chapter 32

Closing address

32.1 Introduction	**350**
32.2 Legal basis for the closing address	**350**
32.3 Practical aspects of the closing address	**351**
32.4 Practical example of a closing address	**353**
32.4.1 Civil trial in High Court: closing address for the plaintiff in motor accident case	353

32.1 Introduction

A closing address or closing argument is the argument that each party delivers at the end of the trial after the conclusion of all the evidence. The usual sequence is:
- first, a closing address by the first party, that is, the prosecutor or plaintiff
- then a closing address by the second party, that is, the accused or defendant
- finally, a reply by the first party.

The closing address can embrace the evidence (facts) and legal issues (substantive and procedural) of the case. This chapter will confine itself to argument on evidence.

32.2 Legal basis for the closing address

Parties have a right to address the court at the end of the trial. Failure to permit this usually constitutes a serious irregularity.[1] Both the High Court Rules and the Magistrates' Courts Rules for civil cases provide for this right,[2] as does the Criminal Procedure Act 51 of 1977 for criminal trials.[3] However, there are some restrictions contained in the statutory provisions governing closing addresses. High Court Rule 39(10) states that more than one counsel for a party may take part in the closing address, but restricts the reply to one counsel only. Section 175(2) of the Criminal Procedure Act, 1977 limits the prosecutor's right of reply to issues of law only unless the court gives leave to reply on fact.

The court usually decides on issues of admissibility of evidence when the evidence in question is tendered. Any party who objects to its admissibility usually makes their challenge at this point. However, there is no rule stating that a court cannot later make a ruling on admissibility if there was no challenge at the time.[4] Therefore, a party can still use their

---

1 *Transvaal Industrial Foods Ltd v BMM Process (Pty) Ltd* 1973 (1) SA 627 (A). See also *R v Cooper* 1926 AD 54.
2 High Court Rule 39(10) and Magistrates' Courts Rule 29(14).
3 S 175 of the Criminal Procedure Act, 1977.
4 *Langham and Another NNO v Milne NO and Others* 1961 (1) SA 811 (N) at 817A–C.

CHAPTER 32   CLOSING ADDRESS   **351**

closing address to object to the admissibility of evidence. The court's ruling to admit evidence made during a trial is provisional and can be reversed if new facts subsequently emerge.[5]

Sometimes, counsel makes concessions during argument, either of their own accord or in response to a difficult line of questioning from the bench. Ordinarily, such concessions do not bind a client unless they are meant to be formal admissions.[6] On the one hand, it is not a good idea to make admissions too readily as they may have a negative impact. On the other hand, stubborn persistence with an indefensible attitude towards a particular point or witness can also be counterproductive.[7]

32.3   Practical aspects of the closing address

The main purpose of a closing address is to sum up the evidence and argue on matters of evaluation and weight. In addition, a closing address should also deal with any issues of admissibility that still require consideration. Detailed principles relating to evaluation and weight are dealt with in Part Six. In particular, attention should be paid to issues such as:

- the need for all the evidence to be assessed holistically, not piecemeal
- the consideration of probabilities and improbabilities
- the reliability or unreliability of witnesses and opportunities for observation
- the absence or presence of interest or bias
- the intrinsic merits or demerits of the testimony itself
- the witnesses' demeanour
- any inconsistencies and contradictions in the evidence or the absence thereof
- any corroboration of evidence presented
- the application of the cautionary rule
- the failure of a party to cross-examine a witness on a particular point
- the failure to testify or to call a particular witness
- the treatment of an alibi defence
- credibility
- the principles applicable to circumstantial evidence.

Sometimes the court will call for written heads of argument. On other occasions, if time allows, the submission of written heads of argument can be useful even when not required by the court, especially in long or complicated cases. Heads of argument give counsel the opportunity to arrange the argument in a logical manner and to ease the task of the bench. Judicial officials are only human and a well laid out argument will stand a greater chance of success than one that is haphazard.

Whether arguing with or without heads of argument, it is important to have a clear structure to the argument, so give some time to the development of the structure. The structure for arguing on the evidence is particularly important as evidence given during a trial, especially a long one, can be confusing. A frequent mistake made by counsel, and sometimes by the bench, is a purely chronological approach to the evidence, as illustrated in the example below.

---

5   *R v Solomons* 1959 (2) SA 352 (A) at 362E–F. See also PJ Schwikkard and SE van der Merwe *Principles of Evidence* 3 ed (2009) at 48.

6   *Saayman v Road Accident Fund* 2011 (1) SA 106 (SCA); *S v Gouws* 1968 (4) SA 354 (GW).

7   E Morris *Technique in Litigation* 6 ed (2010) at 296.

THE LAW OF EVIDENCE IN SOUTH AFRICA

> The first witness said A, B and C in evidence-in-chief. During cross-examination it was put to her that she was wrong about B and C, but she steadfastly maintained her viewpoints.
>
> She did concede, however, that she might have been wrong about A. The second witness supported the first witness about B, and added D and E. In cross-examination ....

This can be extremely tiresome to follow and is usually not particularly helpful. Argument will be of much greater assistance to the court if it gathers the evidence and rearranges it in some organised form.

Whether presented with or without the aid of heads, argument will benefit from some form of numbering or labelling system. This makes the sequence and interrelationship of the parts much easier to follow and thus, in all likelihood, more compelling. If counsel starts by informing the bench that the argument will be presented in five sections, namely A, B, C, D and E and gives the headings of the five sections, the court will have a much better idea of the argument.

There is often a written transcript of the evidence available. This is usually called a running transcript because it is produced in daily volumes as the case runs. The argument should contain references to exact passages in the transcript. Such references are far more useful than generalised remarks such as, 'The complainant stated in evidence that he would not have bought the CC but for the misleading balance sheets the accused showed him.'

To simplify the task of preparing final argument in a long case, counsel should regularly, preferably at the end of each court day, make a summary of the effect of the evidence given on that day. Counsel should do this whether there is a running transcript or not. Although this may seem like a lot of work, especially when one is tired at the end of a full day in court, it will pay dividends when the time comes to prepare final argument.

A useful way of organising a closing argument for the first party (plaintiff or prosecutor) in a case involving disputed evidence is the following:

A. State the overall legal issues (what needs to be established).
B. Establish where the onus lies.
C. What legal aspects are common cause and what are still in dispute?
D. What primary facts are common cause and what are still in dispute?
E. Credibility of main witnesses, for example the plaintiff and defendant, or complainant and accused. Counsel will usually defend the one and attack the other. This part of the argument requires much thought and some ingenuity. Sometimes the strengths and weaknesses of various witnesses will be obvious, but often a telling argument on credibility only comes to light after much thought. In addition, counsel should mention supporting witnesses here, showing how they contribute to the credibility of the main witness or witnesses. Also include legal principles relating to the assessment of credibility according to requirements of the case.
F. After deciding on the credibility of the witnesses, what does their evidence actually show? In other words, how does it prove the primary facts and how does it therefore satisfy the legal issues?
G. What should the court find based on the above?[8]

---

8 Morris 6 ed (2010) at 292–293 sets out a slightly different format, also under seven headings.

In a complex case, this list can be expanded to cater for the many sub-issues that will require attention.

The opposing party's task is usually more destructive than constructive. It seeks not so much to establish things positively as to undermine the case constructed by the first party. The format given above can be adapted for the second party's argument.

32.4 Practical example of a closing address

32.4.1 Civil trial in High Court: closing address for the plaintiff in motor accident case

Counsel will present the argument for the plaintiff under various headings, labelled A to H. These are:

A. Overall legal issues

B. Onus

C. Legal aspects that are common cause and those still in dispute

D. Facts that are common cause

E. Facts still in dispute[9]

F. Evaluation of evidence

G. What primary facts the evidence establishes

H. Conclusion.

A. Overall legal issues

As this is a claim for damages, the plaintiff has to show that the defendant negligently caused the damage to the plaintiff's car as claimed by her in the pleadings. This involves decisions on causation, damages, wrongfulness and negligence.

B. Onus

There are no special defences here and thus the onus rests on the plaintiff to establish her case on a balance of probabilities.

C. Legal aspects that are common cause and those still in dispute

The defendant has admitted in the pleadings that his car collided with the plaintiff's car, thus causing the damage, and that the extent of the loss is indeed R150 000. What is still in dispute is the issue of negligence. As set out in the leading case of *Kruger v Coetzee*,[10] on the issue of negligence, the plaintiff must show that:

- the reasonable person in the position of the defendant would have foreseen the possibility of harm and patrimonial loss
- the reasonable person would have taken reasonable measures to prevent that possible outcome and
- the defendant did not take such measures.

The issue for decision, therefore, is whether the defendant's conduct amounted to negligence in terms of these legal principles.

---

9   For an example of a closing address in a criminal trial, see R Palmer and D McQuoid-Mason *Basic Trial Advocacy Skills* (2000) at 89–94.

10   1966 (2) SA 428 (A) at 430E–F.

354 | THE LAW OF EVIDENCE IN SOUTH AFRICA

D. Facts that are common cause
1. The plaintiff and her passenger, Mrs Dhlamini, were travelling in the plaintiff's car on the day and at the place in question.
2. The plaintiff intended turning right from High Street into West Street.
3. As she was about to turn, the defendant's car crashed into the back of her car, causing her car to collide with a lamppost on the corner of High and West Streets.
4. The plaintiff's car was a write-off and the loss suffered was R150 000.
5. The defendant did not brake or swerve prior to the collision.
6. The witness, Mr Jackson, called by the plaintiff, was standing on the corner of High and West Streets at the time of the collision and witnessed it happening. He conducted a conversation with the defendant after the collision.

E. Facts still in dispute
1. Whether the plaintiff indicated, by means of her car's indicator lights, her intention to turn right at the intersection
2. Whether the plaintiff slowed gradually or whether she suddenly stopped without warning
3. Whether the defendant told the witness Mr Jackson after the collision that he was inserting a CD into his car's CD player just prior to the collision and that he was thus unsure how it came about that his car collided with the rear of the plaintiff's car.

[Note that the outline of the argument is clear and the argument is systematic, simply laid out and easy to follow.]

F. Evaluation of evidence
The plaintiff was a good witness. Her evidence was clear and she was not shaken in cross-examination. It is common cause that she did intend turning into West Street from High Street and her account of events fits in with the probabilities of how a driver in those circumstances would behave.

Her account was supported by the evidence of Mrs Dhlamini, her passenger. Mrs Dhlamini was a colleague and friend of the plaintiff, and it is, therefore, open to argument that she was biased in favour of the plaintiff. Against that, however, it must be noted that she did not go out of her way to support the plaintiff's evidence in every possible way. She stated that they were on their way to West Street, and that the car slowed down gradually and moved to the right before the turn and immediately before the collision. However, it is significant that she stated during evidence-in-chief that she cannot say whether the indicator was on or not. On that issue, she stated that the car radio was on, which would have masked the clicking sound of an indicator. She also stated that she was not looking at the dashboard at the time and thus did not see if the little light showing the functioning of the indicator was blinking. A witness who was biased would have been inclined to state, definitely, that she had noticed that the indicator was on. Mrs Dhlamini was emphatic that the car slowed down gradually and she was unshakeable during cross-examination.

Mr Jackson, the bystander, was an impressive witness. He was completely independent, knowing neither of the parties, and he gave the strong impression that he was objective and careful. He noticed that the plaintiff's car slowed down gradually and that the indicator was on to show an intention to turn right. This evidence is in complete harmony with the plaintiff's evidence. It is common cause that he spoke to the defendant after the collision although the content of that conversation is disputed. He claims that the defendant admitted to him that he had been inserting a CD into his car's CD player just before the accident and that he did not know how the accident occurred. Despite rigorous cross-examination, he kept to his account of the conversation.

The accused was a poor witness. He claimed that the plaintiff stopped suddenly, without any indication or warning, and that he could not prevent his car from colliding with hers. He contradicted himself on whether he had noticed the brake lights on her car, and if so, at what exact stage he first noticed the brake lights. His version implies that the plaintiff drove her car in a reckless manner, yet he cannot account for the fact that the independent witness, Mr Jackson, described the plaintiff's driving as careful. In particular, the defendant's evidence was unsatisfactory on the question of what he said to Mr Jackson after the accident. Mr Jackson stated that he had expressly asked the defendant: 'What happened?' Mr Jackson stated that the defendant then told him that he did not know and that he was busy inserting a CD at the time. The defendant's version of the conversation was that the witness asked him: 'What happened to you?' He thought this was an enquiry about whether he was injured in the collision. He then replied that he did not know. This explanation does not hold water. If the witness had wanted to enquire about possible injuries, he would surely have been more explicit. If the witness had made such an enquiry, it is highly unlikely that the defendant would have answered that he did not know if he was injured. He would have been more likely to say something such as 'No, not as far as I know.' The defendant could give no explanation as to why Mr Jackson would lie that he (the defendant) had mentioned inserting a CD into the CD player. Nor could he account for the coincidence that, after the accident, there was indeed a CD in the CD player and that the CD cover was open on the passenger seat of the car. Th evidence of the defendant, therefore, stands to be rejected.

G. What primary facts the evidence establishes

Therefore, it is submitted that the evidence plainly shows that the plaintiff did slow down and indicate her intention of turning right, that the defendant did not brake at all, and that just before the accident, his attention was focused on inserting a CD into the player, not on the road ahead.

H. Conclusion

Driving without concentrating on traffic ahead, especially in a busy urban environment, clearly constitutes negligence. Therefore it is submitted that judgment should be given for the plaintiff.

THIS CHAPTER IN ESSENCE

1   At the end of a trial, first the prosecutor in criminal matters or counsel for the plaintiff in civil matters delivers a closing address. Then counsel for the accused in criminal matters or the defendant in civil matters delivers their closing address. The first-mentioned party has the opportunity to reply to last-mentioned's closing address.

2   Counsel uses a closing address to:

   2.1   sum up evidence

356 THE LAW OF EVIDENCE IN SOUTH AFRICA

2.2 argue matters of evaluation and weight

2.3 deal with any issues of admissibility.

3 Concessions made by a party's legal representative during argument ordinarily do not bind the client unless they are meant to be formal admissions. Legal representatives should, however, refrain from making such concessions as they could have a negative impact.

4 Prosecutors may only reply on issues of the law and not on fact unless the court permits otherwise.

5 Counsel can present closing addresses with or without the use of heads of argument.

Chapter 33

Objections

33.1	Introduction	357
33.2	Legal aspects of objections	357
33.3	Practical aspects of objections	358
33.4	Practical example of objections	358
	33.4.1 Civil trial in High Court: objections during evidence-in-chief in motor accident case	358

33.1 Introduction

Raising an **objection** is the legal term for the process whereby a party, during litigation, argues that an opponent is about to take or has taken an impermissible procedural or evidential step. If the court upholds an objection, the opponent is not allowed to begin or continue with that step. If the court overrules the objection, then the opponent is allowed to continue.

A party can object to a wide range of steps taken by the other party. However, this chapter will focus on objections about evidential steps. Objections can concern the calling of a particular witness, a line of questioning involving a particular witness or an attempt to admit certain real or documentary evidence. They can involve virtually the whole range of the rules of evidence. Objections are part of the cut and thrust of litigation and often arise without prior warning. No party is obliged to raise an objection but, as we will note in due course, not objecting at the appropriate time can have adverse consequences for the party failing to make an objection. This is one of the reasons why it is vital that legal practitioners conducting litigation have a thorough grasp of the rules of evidence.

33.2 Legal aspects of objections

Objections are mainly a question of practice. There is little case law and virtually no statute law on the subject. The main legal issue is that a party wishing to object to evidence should do so timeously, that is, when the opposing party presents the contentious evidence or asks the disputed question. Failure to object in time can result in a party losing the right to object to such evidence at a later stage.[1] However, in criminal trials, courts tend to be less harsh on an accused who fails to object in time.[2]

---

1 *Transnet Ltd v Newlyn Investments (Pty) Ltd* 2011 (5) SA 543 (SCA) at paras 17–19. Also see R Palmer and D McQuoid-Mason *Basic Trial Advocacy Skills* (2000) at 68.
2 *S v Sinkankanka and Another* 1963 (2) SA 531 (A) at 538E.

358 | THE LAW OF EVIDENCE IN SOUTH AFRICA

Courts almost invariably rule on an objection before proceeding with the rest of the trial. This is to enable parties to decide how to proceed with their cases.

33.3 Practical aspects of objections

Counsel usually makes objections as the opposing party starts presenting the contentious evidence or asking the contentious question. The court, unless it considers the objection to be so lacking in merit as not to require any response, gives the opposing party an opportunity to indicate whether they wish to persist with the line of evidence objected to. If the opposing party retreats, the objection has succeeded and the trial resumes. If the opposing party indicates that they are contesting the objection, the objecting party proceeds to present argument by elaborating on their objection. Thereafter, the opposing party responds. If the point is an involved one, then the court may grant the parties time to research and prepare argument. The court can either give a ruling immediately after the conclusion of argument or it may take time to consider and deliver judgment.

It is sometimes undesirable that the witness remains in court while the objection is being argued as the witness may then hear the very material that the objection is designed to prevent from coming to the witness's attention. In such a situation, the presiding officer will ask the witness to wait outside while the parties present their objections and the court makes a ruling.

In some instances, the damage will already have been done by the time the objection is made, for example if a party puts a leading question to a witness during evidence-in-chief. In such a case, counsel has to try to rescue the situation as best as possible, for example by arguing at the end of the trial that the answer the witness gave should not count for much because it was given in answer to a leading question.

If it is necessary for the court to determine certain factual issues to decide on the merit or otherwise of the objection, it will proceed with a trial-within-a-trial. This is the standard way for courts to decide on disputed facts relating to the admissibility of evidence. For example, if a prosecutor wishes to present evidence of an admission by the accused and the defence contests the admissibility thereof on the grounds that the statement was not made voluntarily, the court will decide the factual issue of voluntariness in a trial-within-a-trial. All the evidence led during a trial-within-a-trial is not evidence in the trial itself. If a party wishes to place evidence led during the trial-within-a-trial before court for the purpose of the main trial, it should lead that evidence again during the main trial.

33.4 Practical example of objections

33.4.1 Civil trial in High Court: objections during evidence-in-chief in motor accident case

The following example takes place during evidence-in-chief of a witness for the plaintiff.

MS JACOBS (PLAINTIFF'S COUNSEL):	Ms Soga, do you know how much the repairs to the plaintiff's car cost the plaintiff?
WITNESS:	Yes.
MS JACOBS:	How do you know the amount?

WITNESS:	The man at the repair shop told me.
MS JACOBS:	Would you please tell the court what the amount WAS?
MR VOSLOO (DEFENDANT'S COUNSEL):	Objection, My Lord. This is hearsay evidence.
JUDGE:	What do you say to that, Ms Jacobs?
MS JACOBS:	I submit that, even though this is hearsay evidence, the court should admit it provisionally under section 3(1)(*b*) of the Law of Evidence Amendment Act 45 of 1988, as the man from the repair shop will be called to testify later. If Your Lordship requires, I can produce further authority dealing with this issue.
JUDGE:	Well, let's first hear what Mr Vosloo has to say on this matter.
MR VOSLOO:	I submit that this is not a proper case for relying on section 3(1)(*b*).
JUDGE:	In that case, Ms Jacobs, please present your argument.

At this point, counsel for the plaintiff presents her argument followed by counsel for the defendant.

THIS CHAPTER IN ESSENCE

1 During litigation parties can object to impermissible procedures or evidentiary steps.
2 Although there is no duty to object, failure to do so timeously could have adverse consequences.
3 Ultimately, the court can accept or reject an objection and can even adjourn the matter to give the parties time to research and prepare arguments. Afterwards, the court can grant a ruling immediately or take time to consider and deliver judgment.

Chapter 34

Refreshing memory

34.1	Introduction	360
34.2	Consequences of refreshing memory	361
34.3	Refreshing memory before giving evidence	361
34.4	Adjourning to refresh memory	362
34.5	Refreshing memory while under oath	362

34.1 Introduction

The adversarial system places a great deal of emphasis on the value of oral testimony. People believe that the oral evidence that a witness gives in court is more reliable than other secondary sources of evidence because it is tested by cross-examination. Unfortunately, this is not always the case for several reasons. There are other, often more reliable, primary sources of evidence available, for example photographs or video footage, or even documentary records. Human observation has been clinically proven to be unreliable. Also, significantly, the delay between the event and the actual hearing in court when the evidence is presented may be several years. This means that a witness's memory, or lack thereof, is an additional factor contributing to the unreliability of the evidence presented.

Nevertheless, our courts persist with a reliance on oral testimony and witnesses are generally not allowed to refer to written statements or documents when testifying. This has been partially modified by statute,[1] which allows documents to be used to supplement a witness's evidence if the witness cannot remember the events in question.[2]

Therefore, to reduce the number of factors undermining reliability, several conventions have developed that allow witnesses to refresh their memory, while at the same time try to prevent new and more convenient memories being artificially created.

Refreshing a witness's **memory** can occur at any or all of three distinct stages:
- Before the witness testifies, that is, in preparation for testifying
- During an adjournment granted to allow the witness to refresh his or her memory
- While the witness is in the witness box during his or her testimony.

The rules regulating each stage and the effect thereof will be discussed below.

---

1 Part IV of the Civil Proceedings Evidence Act 25 of 1965 (which is also applicable to criminal proceedings due to s 222 of the Criminal Procedure Act 51 of 1977).
2 However, documents cannot be used to corroborate a witness's oral testimony. S 35(2) of the Civil Proceedings Evidence Act, 1965.

34.2 Consequences of refreshing memory

If a witness cannot recall an incident clearly or at all, it is imperative that the party calling the witness attempt to jog the witness's memory. Counsel usually does this by presenting the witness with an earlier statement made by the witness, perhaps closer to the time of the incident, for example a police accident report, a statement made to an insurance assessor or a note in a police officer's incident book. If the witness, on reading the statement, is reminded of the incident, the witness can then go on to relate the incident in his or her own words. The statement has refreshed the witness's memory. In this way, the court will receive oral evidence and has no need of the earlier consistent statement.

DISCUSSION	A reason to remember
34.1	In a High Court trial involving a motor vehicle accident in which several people were killed, the attending police officer was unable to recall the specific accident as it had occurred five years earlier and on a stretch of road where he had attended numerous similar accidents over the years. In one brief glance at the statement he had made at the time he saw the word KFC and immediately said, 'I remember this accident clearly. We all called it the KFC accident because the driver had been eating from a bucket of KFC and there was chicken all over the road among the bodies.' This is a clear example of the police officer's present recollection of the accident being revived by a glance at the statement.

However, it may occur that the earlier statement does not jog the witness's memory. The witness may recognise the statement as being his or her own, but may be unable to recollect the details of the incident. In such circumstances, the witness can merely stand by his or her earlier statement, claiming that if that is what was recorded at the time, then that must be what he or she witnessed. The witness cannot, therefore, present oral evidence that is of any use to the court. In such a case, the court would be more concerned with the witness's earlier statement, which is then usually presented to the court in the form of documentary evidence.[3]

34.3 Refreshing memory before giving evidence

Proper trial preparation is a vitally important aspect of any process of litigation. This includes locating witnesses and then preparing them for trial. Preparation involves:
- obtaining the witnesses' version of events
- comparing this to any other version available, for example earlier recorded statements they made, photographs, statements by other witnesses and real evidence
- refreshing the witnesses' memory in case they have forgotten or become confused about what they witnessed
- going through what they will say in court to hear if they will give their evidence in an ordered, concise manner.

Obviously, this preparation must not involve coaching witnesses in what to say. If a witness is unsatisfactory, it is better not to call the person. It is unethical and punishable to school witnesses in the evidence counsel wants them to give.

---

3 *S v Bergh* 1976 (4) SA 857 (A) at 865C–D

362 | THE LAW OF EVIDENCE IN SOUTH AFRICA

Refreshing a witness's memory at this stage is perfectly acceptable. In fact, being allowed to prepare properly for trial is an important procedural right and refreshing a witness's memory is a vital part of this preparation.[4] Practically speaking, there is no way to prevent or monitor this sort of refreshing of memory. In fact, it would be undesirable to do so as the ensuing trial would then become a test of memory instead of an enquiry into the facts.

If counsel uses a document to refresh a witness's memory at this stage, that document does not need to be presented to the court. If it is a privileged document, it remains privileged. Any evidence that the witness subsequently gives in court will be considered to be proper oral evidence.

34.4 Adjourning to refresh memory

Adjournments often occur while a witness is testifying, for example for lunch. A witness who the court has sworn in and not yet released, remains under oath during such an adjournment. Thus, it is not permitted for either of the parties to the dispute, any legal representatives or any other witnesses to communicate with this witness during such an adjournment. It is considered highly unethical to do so and will undoubtedly be brought to the court's attention should it occur.

However, it is possible to ask the court to grant a short adjournment specifically to allow a witness to refresh his or her memory.[5] This will usually occur if there was no time to prepare properly with the witness, for example if the witness arrived during the course of the trial or if his or her earlier statement was only made available during the trial. Before a court will grant such an adjournment, it must be satisfied with regard to the following:
- The witness indicates he or she cannot recall the events about which he or she is required to testify due to the lapse of time.
- The witness made an earlier statement that contains his or her recollection of the event.
- The witness did not have an opportunity to read his or her statement before entering court to testify.
- The witness wishes to have the opportunity to read it before continuing.

In such a case, the objective is to approximate the pre-trial opportunity a witness would have had to refresh his or her memory and the consequences would be the same. If the witness is then able to recall the incident, he or she can then present oral testimony and the document need not be produced. If not, the document should be produced as it is the contents thereof that constitute the evidence the court wishes to hear or see.

34.5 Refreshing memory while under oath

Irrespective of how much preparation may have occurred, a witness may forget all or part of their oral testimony. This may occur for a variety of reasons such as the witness being nervous, the witness having witnessed many similar events in similar situations, for instance a police officer who has attended numerous accident scenes at the same location, or simply a long lapse of time.

---

4 PJ Schwikkard and SE van der Merwe *Principles of Evidence* 3 ed (2009) at 442 where the authors state, 'It is possible to argue that pre-trial refreshment of memory is a procedural right based on the fundamental rule that a party should be given an adequate opportunity to prepare for the trial.'
5 *R v Da Silva* [1990] 1 All ER 29.

CHAPTER 34 REFRESHING MEMORY | 363

If it is apparent that a witness cannot remember, then it is possible according to the common law to ask the court to grant the witness an opportunity to refresh his or her memory from an earlier statement while remaining in the witness box. To do this, the applicant must do the following:

- The applicant must prove that the witness has personal knowledge of the event about which he or she is testifying. This is important because it is a means of sifting out hearsay evidence and so the court must actually find this to be the case.
- The applicant must prove to the court's satisfaction that the witness genuinely cannot recollect the event in question. If this were not the case, it would be a circumvention of the rule against previous consistent statements.
- The applicant must establish the authenticity of the document that he or she intends to use. This is usually done by the witness showing that he or she made the statement, or caused it to be made on their instructions,[6] or read and verified it (perhaps by signing off on it), or heard it read back to them and verified it.[7]
- The applicant must prove that the events were fresh in the witness's memory when the statement was made or when the witness caused the statement to be made on his or her behalf. The statement need not be contemporaneous[8] with the incident but the events must have been fresh in the witness's memory when the statement was written, recorded or read, and then verified.
- The applicant must use the original document. This is not always possible, for example the original may have been destroyed. In addition, this may not be required. For example, the opponent may not object to using a copy, the witness may be able to establish the accuracy of the copy or the witness may even be able to testify from his or her refreshed memory. However, if the witness has no independent recollection, even after trying to refresh his or her memory, then the applicant must use the original document.
- The applicant must produce the document. If possible, the applicant must hand the original to the court and to the opponent. The document may be privileged, but if a party seeks to rely on it to refresh a witness's memory, this privilege will have to be waived. However, an opponent may waive his or her right to the document, or the court may restrict cross-examination to the parts of the document that were used.[9]

THIS CHAPTER IN ESSENCE

1   Witnesses are allowed to refresh their memory with an earlier statement made by them. If a witness's memory is refreshed, the court will accept the witness's oral evidence instead of the earlier consistent statement. If, however, the witness's memory is not refreshed, the court would rather stand by the witness's earlier statement and not accept any oral evidence by the witness.

2   It is vital to refresh a witness's memory before trial and any documents used to refresh the witness's memory need not be presented to the court.

---

6   The person who made it should be called to testify to the authenticity of the document. See *R v O'Linn* 1960 (1) SA 545 (N).
7   *R v Kelsey* (1982) 74 Cr App R 213 at 217.
8   Some early English decisions indicate that the statement must have been contemporaneous. *Doe d Church and Phillips v Perkins* (1790) 3 Term Rep 749 753, 100 ER 838.
9   *R v Scoble* 1958 (3) SA 667 (N) at 670D.

364 THE LAW OF EVIDENCE IN SOUTH AFRICA

3 Adjournments for the purpose of refreshing a witness's memory are permissible if the court is satisfied that the witness:

3.1 cannot recall the events he or she is required to testify on

3.2 made an earlier statement containing his or her recollection of the event

3.3 did not have an opportunity to read his or her statement before testifying and

3.4 wishes to read his or her statement before continuing.

4 Witnesses can be given the opportunity to refresh their memory while under oath if:

4.1 it is shown that the witness has personal knowledge of the event he or she is testifying on

4.2 it can be shown that the witness genuinely cannot recollect the event

4.3 the authenticity of the document is established

4.4 it is proved that the events were fresh in the witness's memory when the statement was made and

4.5 the original document is used and produced to the court.

Chapter 35

Previous inconsistent statements

35.1	Introduction	365
35.2	Procedure for dealing with previous inconsistent statements	365
35.3	Evidentiary consequences of previous inconsistent statements	366

35.1 Introduction

One of the most important purposes of cross-examination is to undermine the credibility of the witness who is being cross-examined. This does not necessarily mean that a party needs to show that the witness is deliberately being untruthful. The witness's credibility can also be undermined if it can be shown that he or she is forgetful, uncertain or was just unobservant. One of the best ways to do this is to show the court that the witness has not been consistent in his or her evidence over time.

Thus, if a party is in possession of a statement made by a witness prior to the trial and the witness then deviates from this statement when testifying, then bringing the statement and the differences to the court's attention may have a profound effect on the way the court views the witness's evidence. We refer to such a statement as a **previous inconsistent statement**.

It is permitted to cross-examine a witness on the basis of a previous inconsistent statement that he or she made. However, this is only permissible if the statement relates to the issues and is in no way collateral. If not, it is of no relevance whether it is consistent or not.

35.2 Procedure for dealing with previous inconsistent statements

Through the residuary clauses,[1] the law that regulates the procedure to be adopted when cross-examining on a previous inconsistent statement is section 4 of the English Criminal Procedure Act of 1865. It sets out the steps for this procedure as follows:

- *Step 1:* Ask the witness if he or she has made a statement on a previous occasion that is inconsistent with the evidence that he or she has just given in court.
- *Step 2:* Give the witness enough detail about the statement that you are hoping to use to enable him or her to identify the occasion.[2] Failure to do this undermines the effectiveness of producing it.

---

1 S 190 of the Criminal Procedure Act 51 of 1977 and s 42 of the Civil Proceedings Evidence Act 25 of 1965.
2 '... the circumstances of the supposed statement, sufficient to designate the particular occasion, must be mentioned to the witness ...' S 4 of the English Criminal Procedure Act of 1865.

366 | THE LAW OF EVIDENCE IN SOUTH AFRICA

- *Step 3:* If the witness admits having made such a statement, then give him or her an opportunity to explain the inconsistency.
- *Step 4:* If the witness denies having made such a statement, then you must prove the statement[3] by following the correct procedures to establish originality and authenticity[4] as with any documentary evidence.

We need not show the witness the statement before cross-examining him or her, but if we intend to contradict the witness's evidence by referring to what he or she said in the earlier statement, then we must provide the witness with a copy and the opportunity to explain the discrepancy.[5]

35.3 Evidentiary consequences of previous inconsistent statements

The contents of the earlier statement are not themselves considered to be evidence about the event in respect of which the statement was made.[6] The real value of the statement is that it shows inconsistency on the part of the witness, thereby undermining the witness's credibility. However, recent developments in the common law would seem to suggest that our courts are prepared to consider the contents of a previous inconsistent statement to be admissible not only to attack the credibility of a witness but also as evidence of their contents. In *S v Mathonsi*,[7] the Court stated that:

> **The time has come for the rule limiting the use of prior inconsistent statements to impeaching the credibility of the witness to be replaced by a new rule recognising the changed means and methods of proof in modern society.**

The Court then went on to state that the court *a quo* 'was entitled to make substantive use of the previous inconsistent statement ... and to give the statement, as evidence, the appropriate weight after taking into account all the circumstances.'[8]

This indicates quite clearly a new approach to the use of previous inconsistent statements.[9] The Court also set out certain guidelines to be followed when seeking to rely on such statements for their probative value.[10] Whether or not these will be adopted remains to be seen.

---

3   'If a witness ... does not distinctly admit that he has made such a statement, proof may be given that he did in fact make it ...' S 4 of the English Criminal Procedure Act, 1865.

4   *S v Govender and Others* 2006 (1) SACR 322 (E) at 327B–F provides an accurate and clear summary of the procedures to follow to ensure that the earlier statement was deposed to properly.

5   S 5 of the English Criminal Procedure Act, 1865 specifically provides, 'A witness may be cross-examined ... without such writing being shown to him, but if it is intended to contradict such witness by the writing, his attention must ... be called to those parts of the writing which are to be used for the purpose of so contradicting him ...'

6   *Hoskisson v R* 1906 TS 502; *R v Beukman* 1950 (4) SA 261(O).

7   2012 (1) SACR 335 (KZP) at para 33.

8   *S v Mathonsi* 2012 (1) SACR 335 (KZP) at para 52.

9   See A Bellengère and S Walker 'When The Truth Lies Elsewhere: A comment on the admissibility of prior inconsistent statements in light of *S v Mathonsi* 2012 (1) SACR 335 (KZP) and *S v Rathumbu* 2012 (2) SACR 219 (SCA)' *SACJ* 2013 26(2) 175–185.

10   The Court adopted the test set out in the Canadian case of *R v B (KG)* [1993] 1 SCR 740 which is as follows:
     1. Would the evidence have been admissible if given in court? 2. Was the statement voluntary? 3. Was it made under oath or in circumstances wherein the person making it understood the importance of speaking the truth? 4. Is the statement reliable? 5. Was it made in circumstances in which the person making it would be liable to prosecution if it was deliberately false?

CHAPTER 35   PREVIOUS INCONSISTENT STATEMENTS   **367**

Nonetheless, proving that a witness has been inconsistent will have an impact on the witness's credibility, the level of which will depend on the circumstances of each case. The following factors will affect the impact that it has:

- The degree of inconsistency
- Whether it was about material or unimportant facts
- The possibility of the inconsistency being due to error.[11]

The witness should not be asked to choose between the statements, but should instead be asked to tell the truth.

THIS CHAPTER IN ESSENCE

1   It is permissible to cross-examine witnesses on a previous inconsistent statement made by them. The procedure is briefly as follows:

   1.1   Ask the witness whether he or she has made a previous inconsistent statement.

   1.2   Provide the witness with enough detail about the statement referred to to enable him or her to identify it.

   1.3   If the witness admits making a previous inconsistent statement, give him or her the opportunity to explain the inconsistency.

   1.4   If the witness denies making a previous inconsistent statement, the originality and authenticity of the statement must be proved.

2   The content of a previous inconsistent statement is admissible as a method for attacking the credibility of the witness. In fact, in light of recent judicial developments, it seems as though previous inconsistent statements will soon also be considered as evidence of the facts stated therein.

---

11   The Court in *S v Mafaladiso en Andere* 2003 (1) SACR 583 (SCA) at 593E–594H sets out several principles that should be considered when assessing the impact of such contradictions.

Chapter 36

Hostile witnesses

36.1	Introduction	368
36.2	Calling other witnesses to counter unfavourable evidence	368
36.3	Proving a previous inconsistent statement against our own witness	369
36.4	Declaration of hostility: cross-examining our own witness	370

36.1 Introduction

The **principle of party control**, an intrinsic part of the adversarial system, means that parties to litigation choose which witnesses they wish to call, which ones to omit and what evidence they wish to present. For this reason, parties are expected to stand by their witnesses. Only in extreme circumstances are parties permitted to impeach their own witnesses, for example by being permitted to cross-examine them.

The circumstances of a case dictate who will be potential witnesses. The consequence of this is that many witnesses are reluctant, nervous, resentful, uninformed or uneducated and blatantly untruthful. Even enthusiastic and helpful witnesses may have ulterior motives for testifying. Thus, witnesses often deviate from the evidence they were expected to give, sometimes dramatically. The end result is that, from time to time, it may be necessary to impeach our own witnesses, for example by showing that our own witness is being deliberately untruthful and trying to undermine our case.

There are a number of methods that we may use to attempt to counter a witness whose evidence is detrimental to our case, including:

- calling other witnesses to contradict the evidence of the recalcitrant witness
- using a previous inconsistent statement against our own witness
- applying to declare our witness a **hostile witness**, thereby permitting us to cross-examine our own witness.

36.2 Calling other witnesses to counter unfavourable evidence

If our own witness gives unfavourable evidence, the simplest method to counter this is to call other or further witnesses who will give evidence that contradicts the account given by this particular witness. We can highlight the differences in closing argument. The court will then be in a position to draw its own conclusions about the reliability of the witness who was contradicted by several other witnesses called by the same party.

CHAPTER 36   HOSTILE WITNESSES | 369

36.3   Proving a previous inconsistent statement against our own witness

We can use a previous inconsistent statement not only in cross-examination of an opponent's witness, but also to impeach the credibility of our own witness. When searching for and selecting witnesses we often read statements made by potential witnesses. We keep these statements on file for use when preparing the witness for trial. If a witness then unexpectedly deviates from such a statement when testifying, we have the earlier contradictory statement at hand which we can use to impeach the witness's credibility.

The common law did not allow this in an unlimited way, but statute now specifically makes provision for it.[1] We are thus entitled to prove a previous inconsistent statement. However, this does not entitle us to cross-examine our own witness so proving a previous inconsistent statement will usually take place during examination-in-chief or re-examination. The procedure[2] to adopt is similar to the one used when cross-examining a witness for the opponent using such a statement[3] and is as follows:

- Ask the witness if he or she has made a statement on a previous occasion that is inconsistent with the evidence he or she has just given in court.
- Give the witness enough detail about the statement that we are hoping to use to enable him or her to identify the occasion. Failure to do this undermines the effectiveness of producing the previous inconsistent statement.
- If the witness admits having made such a statement, then give him or her an opportunity to explain the inconsistency.
- If the witness denies having made such a statement, then we must prove the statement, that is, follow the correct procedures to establish originality and authenticity as we would with any documentary evidence.

Again, the consequences that follow are similar to the consequences that flow from proving such a statement against an opponent's witness. The contents of the earlier statement are not themselves considered to be evidence about the event in respect of which the witness made the statement.[4] However, recent judicial developments seem to indicate that the position is in the process of changing to allow the contents of the earlier statement to be considered as evidence of the facts stated therein.[5] Nonetheless, the real value of the statement is that it shows inconsistency on the part of the witness, thereby undermining the witness's credibility.

Proving that the witness has been inconsistent will have an impact on the witness's credibility, the level of which will depend on the circumstances of each case. The degree of inconsistency, whether it was about material or unimportant facts, and the possibility of it being due to error will all affect the impact that it has.[6]

We cannot assume that either one of the two statements is correct. We should therefore not ask the witness to choose between the statements. Instead, give the witness the opportunity to tell the truth. However, following the case of *S v Mathonsi*, it seems that the court is entitled, on weighing up all the evidence as a whole, to rely on the contents of the

---

1   S 190(2) of the Criminal Procedure Act 51 of 1977; s 7 of the Civil Proceedings Evidence Act 25 of 1965.
2   Extrapolated from s 7 of the Civil Proceedings Evidence Act, 1965.
3   See ch 35 Previous inconsistent statements.
4   *Hoskisson v R* 1906 TS 502; *R v Beukman* 1950 (4) SA 261 (O).
5   See *S v Mathonsi* 2012 (1) SACR 335 (KZP) and the discussion in ch 35.
6   The Court in *S v Mafaladiso en Andere* 2003 (1) SACR 583 (SCA) at 593E–594H sets out several principles that should be considered when assessing the impact of such contradictions.

370 | THE LAW OF EVIDENCE IN SOUTH AFRICA

earlier statement as being a correct reflection of the facts, provided it is satisfied that the evidence supports this conclusion.[7]

36.4 Declaration of hostility: cross-examining our own witness

Sometimes, the testimony of our witness goes beyond being merely inconsistent with an earlier statement and appears to be deliberately damaging to our own case. In such a circumstance, it is possible to apply to the court to have the witness declared hostile in order to be granted permission to cross-examine him or her.[8] We usually make such an application during the witness's evidence-in-chief or re-examination. If the application is successful, we are entitled to cross-examine our own witness.[9]

It is not enough to show that the witness is merely 'unfavourable'.[10] To persuade the court[11] that a witness is hostile, we need to establish that the witness does not actually want to tell the truth 'at the instance of the party calling him'.[12] We refer to the witness as having an **antagonistic *animus***.[13] The test is a subjective one and is not easy to satisfy given that we have not yet been allowed to cross-examine the witness. The court will consider several factors in deciding whether to grant such an application and, thus, allow cross-examination. These factors include, among other things:[14]

- the fact that a previous inconsistent statement was proved (this is just one factor, but can be very influential)[15]
- the nature of the inconsistencies which can be very influential[16]
- the witness's demeanour which may also indicate that he or she is hostile[17]
- the relationship between the witness and the parties to the case[18]
- the fact that a state witness in a criminal trial may receive section 204 indemnity[19] (such a witness may have a strong motive to be hostile)
- if a party was deceived into calling the person as witness.[20]

---

7 2012 (1) SACR 335 (KZP) at para 52 where the court stated that a court is 'entitled to make substantive use of the previous inconsistent statement ... and to give the statement, as evidence, the appropriate weight after taking into account all the circumstances'. See A Bellengère and S Walker 'When The Truth Lies Elsewhere: A comment on the admissibility of prior inconsistent statements in light of *S v Mathonsi* 2012 (1) SACR 335 (KZP) and *S v Rathumbu* 2012 (2) SACR 219 (SCA)' *SACJ* 2013 26(2) 175–185.

8 Constitutional implications for the rule against cross-examination: s 35(3)(i) of the Constitution refers to the 'right to adduce and challenge evidence' but does not limit this right to cross-examination of the opponent's witness only. Therefore, it is arguable that a party has a right to challenge all the evidence presented, irrespective of which party called the witness. In the United States of America, *Chambers v Mississippi* 410 US 284 (1973) allowed the accused to cross-examine a witness he had called.

9 This will entitle the cross-examiner to use all the tools at his or her disposal, including a previous inconsistent statement, as was the case in *S v Mathonsi* 2012 (1) SACR 335 (KZP).

10 *S v Steyn en Andere* 1987 (1) SA 353 (W) at 355F.

11 The onus of doing so rests on the party making the application. *S v Steyn en Andere* 1987 (1) SA 353 (W) at 358G–H.

12 *S v Steyn en Andere* 1987 (1) SA 353 (W) at 357H quoting JF Stephen *Digest of the Law of Evidence* 12 ed (1914) Article 147.

13 For more on this topic, see CN Scoble *The Law of Evidence in South Africa* 3 ed (1952) at 352.

14 See *City Panel Beaters v Bhana and Sons* 1985 (2) SA 155 (D) at 160H–J where the Court stated that it was 'undesirable to lay down any rigid formula'.

15 *City Panel Beaters v Bhana and Sons* 1985 (2) SA 155 (D) at 160C–D.

16 *S v Steyn en Andere* 1987 (1) SA 353 (W) at 357C–D.

17 *S v Steyn en Andere* 1987 (1) SA 353 (W) at 357A–B.

18 *Jabaar v South African Railways and Harbours* 1982 (4) SA 552 (C) at 555d.

19 *S v Steyn en Andere* 1987 (1) SA 353 (W) at 357F.

20 *R v Wellers* 1918 TPD 234.

CHAPTER 36   HOSTILE WITNESSES | **371**

> **DISCUSSION 36.1**
>
> **Declaring a witness hostile: refresh; confront; declare hostile**
>
> When a witness you have called suddenly starts giving evidence against you, you should not automatically assume that the witness is hostile. It is possible that the witness has made a mistake. Therefore, the first step is to ask the witness if he or she wishes to refresh his or her memory from an earlier statement if one was made. If the answer is 'no', this is probably confirmation of hostility.
>
> If the answer is 'yes', allow the witness to refresh his or her memory.[21] Then lead the witness afresh on the point he or she testified against you. If the witness now testifies in accordance with his or her statement, the problem is solved. If not, then prove the inconsistent statement.[22] If the witness, on being confronted with the contradiction, refuses to confirm it or does do so but gives a far-fetched explanation, you may then apply to the court to have the witness declared a hostile witness. You may now cross-examine the witness on his or her contradictory evidence.

Thus:

- refresh the witness's memory
- confront the witness with his or her previous inconsistent statement
- apply to the court to have the witness declared a hostile witness.

THIS CHAPTER IN ESSENCE

1   We can contradict unfavourable evidence given by our own witness through the testimony of other or further witnesses.

2   Alternatively, we can impeach the credibility of a witness through the use of a previous inconsistent statement. The procedure to prove the existence of a previous inconsistent statement is briefly as follows:

2.1   Ask the witness whether he or she has made a previous inconsistent statement.

2.2   Provide the witness with enough detail on the statement referred to to enable him or her to identify it.

2.3   If the witness admits making a previous inconsistent statement, give him or her the opportunity to explain the inconsistency.

2.4   If the witness denies making a previous inconsistent statement, we must prove the originality and authenticity of the statement.

3   The content of a previous inconsistent statement is therefore admissible as a method for attacking the credibility of the witness. In fact, in light of recent judicial developments, it appears that previous inconsistent statements will soon also be considered as evidence of the facts stated therein.

4   We can apply to the court to have a witness declared hostile if his or her testimony goes beyond being merely inconsistent and appears to be deliberately damaging the case of the party on whose behalf the witness is testifying. If successful, we are entitled to cross-examine our own witness. A subjective test is used to determine whether a witness has the necessary 'antagonistic *animus*' and the court takes several factors into account before reaching a decision on the matter.

---

21   Following the procedure set out in ch 34 Refreshing memory.
22   Following the procedure set out above in section 36.3.

PART SIX

Evaluation of evidence

CHAPTER 37	Evaluation of evidence	374
CHAPTER 38	Creditworthiness: credibility and reliability	382
CHAPTER 39	Inherent probabilities	388
CHAPTER 40	Contradictions and discrepancies	391
CHAPTER 41	The cautionary rule	394
CHAPTER 42	Corroboration	404
CHAPTER 43	Identification: visual and voice	408
CHAPTER 44	Circumstantial evidence	412
CHAPTER 45	Demeanour	416
CHAPTER 46	Assessment of mendacity	419
CHAPTER 47	Failure to testify	422
CHAPTER 48	Judicial notice	426
CHAPTER 49	Presumptions	433
CHAPTER 50	Admissions, pointings out and confessions	440

Chapter 37

Evaluation of evidence

37.1	**Introduction**	**374**
37.2	**The process of evaluation**	**374**
	37.2.1 Factual basis	374
	37.2.2 A dispute of fact	375
	37.2.3 Resolving a dispute of fact	375
37.3	**General principles for the evaluation of evidence**	**376**
	37.3.1 Credibility	376
	37.3.2 Credibility and probabilities	376
	37.3.3 Piecemeal reasoning	377
	37.3.4 Further evaluation principles	379
	37.3.5 A practical example of the principles of evaluation	379

37.1 Introduction

The **evaluation of evidence** refers to the process of examining and assessing the evidence presented to determine:
- exactly what facts have been proved by the evidence
- alleged facts that are not supported by the evidence
- how the facts fit together to form a complete picture from which the court can draw conclusions.

Evaluation of the evidence is thus the process that the court follows when assessing and assigning weight to it. This task is the court's role or prerogative and no exhaustive analysis of the process of evaluation exists. However, several guidelines have developed over time. We will discuss the process that the courts follow in evaluating evidence and the principles that guide them in doing so in some detail in the chapters that follow but this chapter will provide a brief overall view of the process and principles.

37.2 The process of evaluation

37.2.1 Factual basis

An important part of the evaluation of evidence involves first establishing the factual basis of the case as this is necessary to decide the legal issues in the case. We collect the facts of the case from:
- admitted or agreed facts, also called common cause facts
- facts found proved in accordance with the relevant standard of proof where there is a dispute of fact
- inferences that we can draw from common cause and proved facts.

CHAPTER 37   EVALUATION OF EVIDENCE | 375

37.2.2   A dispute of fact

A dispute of fact is a disagreement between the parties regarding a material allegation, or set of allegations, that makes up an essential element on which they rely in support of their claim or defence. At the trial, the parties try to prove the allegations and responses that are in dispute by means of evidence and other probative material.[1] Evidence in support of an allegation is not yet proof. 'Proof of a fact' means that the court has received evidence with regard to a factual allegation and has accepted such allegation to be true. In other words, the evidence has proved the alleged fact.

37.2.3   Resolving a dispute of fact

In *Stellenbosch Farmers' Winery Group Ltd and Another v Martell et Cie and Others*,[2] the Supreme Court of Appeal explained how a court should resolve factual disputes and ascertain, as far as possible, where the truth lies between conflicting factual assertions:

> To come to a conclusion on the disputed issues a court must make findings on (a) the credibility of the various factual witnesses; (b) their reliability; and (c) ... the probability or improbability of each party's version on each of the disputed issues. In light of the assessment of (a), (b) and (c), the court will then, as a final step, determine whether the party burdened with the onus of proof has succeeded in discharging it. The hard case, which will doubtless be a rare one, occurs when a court's credibility findings compel it in one direction and its evaluation of the general probabilities in another. The more convincing the former, the less convincing will be the latter. But when all factors are equipoised probabilities prevail.

Where a court fails to analyse the evidence as set out above, it effectively fails to resolve the dispute and thereby denies the parties a fair hearing.[3]

We can describe the overall process in general in the following way. The court isolates and states the different questions of law and fact that need to be determined. During the course of the judgment these findings should progress from one issue to the next although they may flow into each other and overlap. The court then evaluates the evidence and other probative material submitted to determine whether it is sufficiently credible and reliable in its essential features, and together, sufficient to prove or disprove the propositions of fact. The court then weighs up the totality of proved facts supporting each material allegation to determine whether they are sufficient to prove the material allegation, and whether these together are sufficient to discharge the onus of proof on a claim, charge or defence.

Thus, ultimately, the court evaluates the evidence presented to determine whether the evidence and other probative material support the plaintiff's or the State's version in its essential features.[4] Also, if the defendant's or accused's version is so supported, the court determines whether the plaintiff's or State's version is sufficiently more probable. In both criminal and civil cases, the assessment is of the probabilities. In a criminal case, the court

---

1   This includes oral, documentary and/or real evidence, formal admissions and evidentiary presumptions or inferences that can be drawn from proved or common cause facts.

2   2003 (1) SA 11 (SCA) at para 5.

3   *Sasol Mining (Pty) Ltd v Commissioner Nggeleni and Others* [2011] 4 BLLR 404 (LC).

4   Substantive law determines the material facts or elements of claim, charge or defence that need to be pleaded and proved. For instance, in a claim for damages under s 68 of the Labour Relations Act 66 of 1995, the applicant must plead and prove that its employees engaged in an unprotected strike, conduct by the respondent/s in contemplation or in furtherance of the strike and loss attributable to this conduct. Similarly, if an accused is charged with, for instance, theft, the State must allege and prove all the elements that make up the offence of theft.

THE LAW OF EVIDENCE IN SOUTH AFRICA

must decide whether, on *all* the evidence and other probative material presented by both parties, the probabilities favour the State to such an extent that there can be *no reasonable doubt* of the accused's guilt. The accused can secure an acquittal even on an improbable version provided that the version is not so improbable that it cannot reasonably possibly be true. In a civil case, the court must decide whether, on *all* the evidence, the plaintiff's version is *more probable* compared to the defendant's version.

37.3 General principles for the evaluation of evidence

37.3.1 Credibility

The court should not assess the credibility of a witness in terms of only one factor, or even a select few factors, and especially not only by the personal impression made by a witness's demeanour and confident performance in the witness box.[5] In addition, the court should not regard the credibility of witnesses and the probability or improbability of what they say as separate enquiries to be considered piecemeal. All the assessment factors are part of a single investigation and are measured and weighed against each other. These factors include:

- questions of demeanour and impression
- the prospects of any partiality, prejudice or self-interest
- the importance of any **discrepancies** or contradictions
- the testing of a particular story against facts that cannot be disputed and against the **inherent probabilities**.

An adverse credibility finding against the witnesses of one party does not warrant excluding the party's evidence from serious consideration. By doing so, a judge effectively denies the party a fair hearing.[6] The court's rejection of the testimony of a witness does not necessarily establish the truth of the contrary. The disbelief of the statement of a witness merely removes an obstacle to the acceptance of evidence tending to prove the contrary.[7]

The credibility of a witness and the cogency of a version built on the evidence of such a witness may not necessarily overlap. A bad witness can testify to something that is highly probable without affecting the probabilities. An honest and reliable witness may give a very improbable account which may be exposed as fallacious for reasons independent of the witness's credibility, including his or her honesty, memory and accuracy of exposition.[8]

37.3.2 Credibility and probabilities

Sometimes, the credibility of a witness may be in conflict with the probabilities of the case. Deciding which to prefer, if either, and why, is the task of the court. The Supreme Court of Appeal in *Santam Bpk v Biddulph*[9] held that, as a general rule, it is undesirable to rely on a credibility finding as a sole basis for assessing the probative value of evidence. Of course, there are occasions when on the face of the record of a witness's evidence, the witness's testimony is so riddled with patent inconsistencies and contradictions that their credibility and the unreliability of that testimony is glaringly obvious. Ordinarily, though, findings of

---

5   *S v Kelly* 1980 (3) SA 301 (A) at 308B–D: 'Demeanour is, at best, a tricky horse to ride.'
6   *Network Field Marketing (Pty) Ltd v Mngezana NO and Others* (2011) 32 ILJ 1705 (LC).
7   *R v Weinberg* 1939 AD 71; *S v M* 2006 (1) SACR 135 (SCA).
8   F Snyckers 'The Law of Evidence' *Annual Survey of South African Law* (2003) 869 at 874.
9   2004 (5) SA 586 (SCA) at 589 para 5.

CHAPTER 37 EVALUATION OF EVIDENCE | **377**

credibility cannot be judged in isolation, but should be considered in light of the proved facts and the probabilities of the matter under consideration.

As stated in *Mabona and Another v Minister of Law and Order and Others*,[10] the credibility of witnesses and the probability or improbability of what they say are part of a single investigation into the acceptability or otherwise of a version. In this single investigation, questions of impression are measured against the content of a witness's evidence, the importance of any discrepancies or contradictions are assessed and a particular story is tested against facts which cannot be disputed and against the inherent probabilities.

In the case of *Network Field Marketing (Pty) Ltd v Mngezana NO and Others*,[11] the Court found that an analysis of the conflicting evidence using a balance of probabilities, rather than resorting to credibility findings, would have produced a more accurate factual finding.

In *Minister of Safety and Security and Others v Craig and Others NNO*,[12] the Supreme Court of Appeal held that although courts of appeal are slow to disturb findings of credibility, they generally have liberty to do so where a finding of fact does not primarily depend on the personal impression made by a witness's demeanour, but rather on inferences and other proved facts and on probabilities. The Supreme Court of Appeal found that the witness's version, which the trial court had preferred, was contrived and inconsistent with the overall probabilities of the case.

37.3.3 Piecemeal reasoning

The court must avoid a piecemeal process of reasoning and may not decide a matter based on inferences that arise only from selected facts considered in isolation, and not together with all proved facts.[13] It must ask what inferences can be drawn from the sum of all the evidence considered together. It must evaluate the evidence of each witness in the context of the evidence in the case as a whole.

It is wrong to separate the evidence into compartments, to examine each party's case in isolation and thereby to hold that it is internally consistent and probable. Concluding which party wins depends on the totality of the evidence and this conclusion must account for all of it. However, the credibility and cogency of portions of the evidence can, and often should, be assessed individually at interim stages of the matter. Some items are inherently suspect or cogent while others are suspect or cogent when viewed in light of other evidence led in the case. However, when we have to answer the question of whether the required burden of proof has been discharged, it is better to look at everything together to the extent that this is possible. In other words, there is nothing wrong with first ascribing cogency or weight to various pieces of evidence, either viewed jointly or severally, and then considering whether these products, together, yield a particular result. What tends to lead to error is when the assessment of the evidence is compartmentalised in the final analysis.[14]

We must be careful of the weight and significance awarded to mutually destructive and conflicting versions. The question at the end of the trial in criminal cases always is: 'Did the State, on all the evidence led, prove the guilt of the accused beyond reasonable doubt?' In civil cases, the question is, 'Did the party with the onus, on all the evidence led, prove its version to be more probable?'

---

10 1988 (2) SA 654 (SE) at 662.
11 (2011) 32 ILJ 1705 (LC) at para 17 referring to *Santam Bpk v Biddulph* 2004 (5) SA 586 (SCA) at 589 para 5.
12 2011 (1) SACR 469 (SCA).
13 *R v Sacco* 1958 (2) SA 349 (N) at 353.
14 Snyckers *Annual Survey* (2003) at 874.

In a criminal case, a bad version put forward by the accused, which is not reasonably possibly true, need not even be relevant to the question of whether his or her innocence is reasonably possible. It is often highly prejudicial to an accused to focus on whether his or her story is reasonably possible rather than on whether the State managed, on all the evidence before the court, to exclude all doubt about his or her guilt.[15] The Supreme Court of Appeal has stated the approach that 'the accused's version' must be measured against the State's version. Its corollary, that the accused's version must be held to be reasonably possibly true for an acquittal, irrespective of the cogency of the State's version, tends to lead to error. The evidence must be evaluated in its entirety.[16]

In *S v Cornick and Another*,[17] the Supreme Court of Appeal concluded that proof beyond reasonable doubt had been established on the basis that the State's evidence, viewed together, was convincing even though the appellant's version might suggest the contrary when 'viewed in isolation'. In *S v Ngcina*,[18] the Supreme Court of Appeal held that it was incorrect for a court to treat 'an alibi defence as a separate issue to … identification'. Having considered the accused's alibi in the totality of the evidence, the Court concluded that the complainant's identification evidence, although honestly given, was not reliable and could not be used to exclude the possibility that the accused was elsewhere at the time of the robbery.

The Supreme Court of Appeal in *S v Chabalala*[19] held that a strong challenge to the cogency of a central piece of the evidence did not necessarily preclude a finding beyond reasonable doubt based on the total view of the evidence. Where there were deficiencies in an identification parade and where such a parade was undoubtedly central to the question of proper identification of the accused, it was wrong in totality to think that the evidence was to be approached as if the State had to stand or fall by the integrity of the parade. A court should avoid the temptation to latch onto one apparently obvious aspect without assessing it in the context of all the evidence and the full picture presented in evidence.

In *S v Ramabokela and Another*,[20] the Court stated that because an identification parade was flawed, it had low probative value. However, the court *a quo* had correctly accepted the identification evidence when viewed in its totality, including the fact that it had been corroborated in material respects, as credible and reliable. This is not consistent with the earlier approach in *S v Mia and Another*.[21] Here, the Supreme Court of Appeal held that should the trial court find that a particular witness is unreliable and reject his or her evidence for that reason, then that evidence plays no further part in the determination of the guilt or innocence of the accused in the absence of satisfactory corroboration.

In *S v Janse van Rensburg and Another*,[22] the Court was faced with two conflicting versions and an absence of objective facts to support either version. It found that while the accused's version was highly suspect, it could not be said to be not reasonably possibly true beyond reasonable doubt based on the 'totality of the evidence and the probabilities'.

---

15 Ibid.
16 *S v Trainor* 2003 (1) SACR 35 (SCA).
17 2007 (2) SACR 115 (SCA).
18 2007 (1) SACR 19 (SCA) at para 18.
19 2003 (1) SACR 134 (SCA) at para 15.
20 2011 (1) SACR 122 (GNP).
21 2009 (1) SACR 330 (SCA).
22 2009 (2) SACR 216 (C).

37.3.4 Further evaluation principles

The court can only make inferences from primary facts that have been proved according to the relevant standard of proof.

The court must deal with the evidence of both parties comparatively to point out why it prefers a party's version on a contested point and to give reasons for preferring one version to the other.[23]

The court must also consider the defects in a party's case in light of all the evidence in the case. In *S v Jochems*,[24] the Supreme Court of Appeal found the defects in the appellant's evidence did not materially assist the State in discharging the onus because the evidence of the state witnesses, on which the State relied, was open to serious criticism.

The weight the court assigns to particular items of evidence is also important. The court may find that certain evidence, while constituting proof, does not carry much weight or that certain evidence, considering its nature, may bear more strongly on the balance of probabilities. Weight refers to how much effect or impact, if any, the different items of evidence have on proving or disproving a fact in dispute or the parties' respective cases. In *S v Jochems*,[25] the Court found that the evidence showed that there was a possible motive for the state witnesses to lie and implicate the accused falsely. The trial court was aware of this but did not give it sufficient weight in evaluating the credibility and reliability of the witnesses.

The court may not draw adverse inferences against a witness for reasons not put to the witness in cross-examination, for example contradictions. The court must give the parties the opportunity to be heard in respect of every piece of evidence that a court intends to regard.[26]

The court may take into account that a party, for no good reason, did not call an available, material-supporting witness.

37.3.5 A practical example of the principles of evaluation

The case of *Mabona and Another v Minister of Law and Order and Others*,[27] discussed above, illustrates well the principles of evaluation as set out in this chapter. The first plaintiff had claimed that the fourth defendant, a policeman, had assaulted her while in his custody by suffocating her and boxing her ears with his fists. The Court found that while the plaintiff created a favourable impression from the point of view of demeanour, her evidence regarding the suffocation claim was inconsistent and improbable. The Court, however, despite these criticisms of the plaintiff, accepted her second claim. The judge evaluated the evidence as follows:[28]

> But there is one feature in the evidence which corroborates her story in one particular respect and which bears strongly upon the balance of probabilities. Within a few days of her release from police custody she was examined by a doctor and found to have a perforation of the left eardrum. The probabilities are overwhelming that this injury was sustained whilst [she] was in police custody. There is no suggestion anywhere that [she] was injured prior to arrest. The second defendant noticed no signs of injury or discomfort in his dealings with her. Although the *onus* of proof remains on the first plaintiff an inference of a police assault will readily be drawn if she was uninjured before her arrest, and found to have an injury of this

---

23 *S v Mocke* 2008 (2) SACR 674 (SCA); *S v Guess* 1976 (4) SA 715 (A) at 718–719.
24 1991 (1) SACR 208 (A).
25 1991 (1) SACR 208 (A).
26 *Dairybelle (Pty) Ltd v FAWU and Others* [2001] 6 BLLR 595 (LC). See also the discussion on cross-examination in ch 30.
27 1988 (2) SA 654 (SE).
28 At paras 663–664.

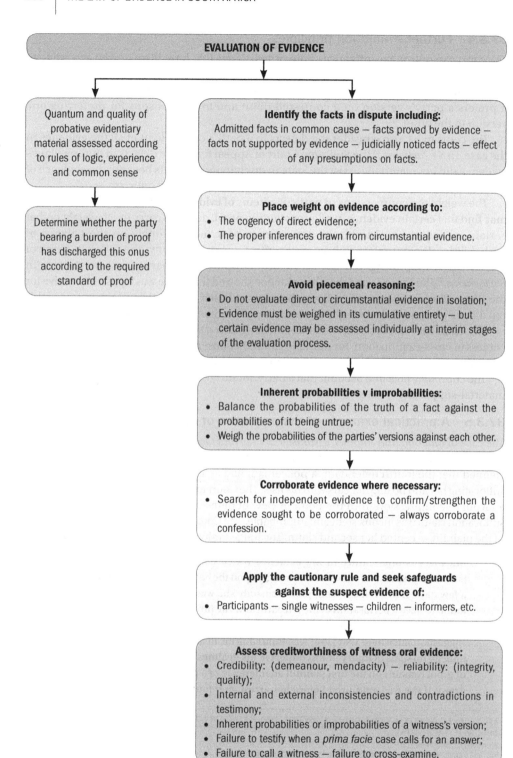

Figure 37.1 Evaluation of evidence

CHAPTER 37 EVALUATION OF EVIDENCE 381

nature immediately thereafter, unless there is some innocent explanation for the injury. There is no innocent explanation. The second defendant testified that the first plaintiff became hysterical during the course of her interrogation and fell to the ground as if suffering from epilepsy. This she denies. She also denies being epileptic. While it does not appear probable that the innocuous interrogation deposed to by the second defendant would give rise to an hysterical fainting fit, I cannot dismiss this evidence as utterly fanciful ... . But I cannot accept the suggestion that the first plaintiff might have perforated her eardrum in the course of the fall. ... I understood [the medical witness who first examined the plaintiff] to regard this [suggestion] as ... highly unlikely, if not impossible, in the case of this perforation. This is because of the mechanism of the injury ... The first plaintiff's account of how the fourth defendant boxed both her ears with both fists, and how she immediately experienced a thundering in the ears seems to me to conform more closely to medical description of how the injury occurred, than the possibility of a fall. The fourth defendant had the opportunity to assault the first plaintiff prior to the first plaintiff's interrogation. She was in his charge during the second plaintiff's interrogation. The fourth defendant was not shown to be an unsatisfactory witness, and his demeanour was good. But when I weigh his denial against the first plaintiff's accusations and her description of how he assaulted her, I find that her evidence, supported by the medical evidence, is the more probable, credible and acceptable evidence, even despite the criticisms of it to which I have already referred.

THIS CHAPTER IN ESSENCE

1   In any type of proceedings, we should first determine the factual basis of a case as it provides the foundation for determining the legal issues in the case.
2   A dispute of fact arises where parties disagree on a material allegation, or set of allegations, which forms an essential element of their claim or defence. Once the court has received evidence pertaining to a factual allegation and has accepted such an allegation as the truth, the evidence is considered to be proof of a fact.
3   Ultimately, a court will resolve a dispute of fact by evaluating the evidence presented to determine whether the evidence and other probative material supports the plaintiff's version in a civil matter or the State's version in a criminal matter.
4   A court should not determine the credibility of a witness in isolation but in light of factors pertaining to the witness's demeanour, proved facts as well as the probabilities of the matter under consideration.
5   When evaluating evidence, the court should adhere to the following principles:
    5.1 The court should evaluate evidence in light of all the proven facts.
    5.2 The court must draw inferences from the sum of all the evidence considered together.
    5.3 The court can draw inferences only from primary facts proved according to the relevant standard of proof.
    5.4 The court must compare parties' evidence to show why it prefers one party's version to that of the other party.
    5.5 The court must consider any defects in a party's case in light of all the evidence in the case.
    5.6 The court must take into account the weight assigned to particular items of evidence.
    5.7 The court must give parties the opportunity to be heard in respect of every piece of evidence it intends to consider.
    5.8 The court should consider that an available, material-supporting witness was not called.

Chapter 38

Creditworthiness: credibility and reliability

38.1 Introduction	382
38.2 The credibility of witnesses	382
38.3 Mendacity: assessing the evidence of the lying witness	384
38.4 Reliability of witnesses	385

38.1 Introduction

Creditworthiness refers to an overall assessment of a witness's evidence, taking into account the witness's credibility and the reliability of the evidence given by the witness. Creditworthiness is sometimes abbreviated as the witness's **credit**. Once the court has made a creditworthiness assessment of the witness's evidence, it will decide what weight to attach to the witness's evidence.

38.2 The credibility of witnesses

Credibility concerns an evaluation of a witness's truthfulness (veracity) only. We infer the veracity of a witness from specific conduct of the witness which tends to show that he or she is or is not truthful of disposition, in other words, not honest, and is thus not a believable witness.[1] Note that the witness may be truthful but mistaken. This would render the witness an unreliable witness, but not necessarily an untruthful witness.

The Supreme Court of Appeal[2] has held that the court's finding on the credibility of a particular witness will depend on its impression about the veracity of the witness. The veracity of the witness will in turn depend on a variety of subsidiary factors such as:

- the witness's candour and demeanour in the witness box
- his or her bias, latent and blatant
- internal contradictions in his or her evidence
- external contradictions with what was pleaded or put on his or her behalf
- the probability or improbability of particular aspects of his or her version
- the calibre and cogency of his or her performance compared to that of other witnesses testifying about the same incident or events.

---

1 Because the veracity and reliability of a witness depend on that witness's conduct, cross-examination is allowed on a much wider range of things than merely the facts of the case. Things that have little to do with the case may still show that the witness is a liar or unreliable. This is why cross-examination aimed at attacking the credibility of a witness may go beyond questions relating directly to the merits of the case.

2 *Stellenbosch Farmers' Winery Group Ltd and Another v Martell et Cie and Others* 2003 (1) SA 11 (SCA).

The court may evaluate the veracity of the witness by considering the following factors, the weight and relevance of which depends on the circumstances:[3]

- Is the witness a truthful or untruthful person: has he or she been convicted of perjury or other offences involving dishonesty or has he or she made false statements previously?[4]
- Is the witness, although an untruthful person, telling the truth on this issue?
- Is the witness, although a truthful person, telling something less than the truth on this issue?
- Was it demonstrated that the witness deliberately misstated something contrary to his or her own knowledge and belief, in other words, that he or she was consciously being untruthful on a contested point. Alternatively, was it a case of making a false statement in the firm belief that he or she was telling the truth?
- Is the witness's account altered (exaggerated, diminished or fabricated) by unconscious bias or a motive to lie?
- With regard to the personal impression made by the witness's demeanour and the calibre and cogency of his or her performance compared to that of other witnesses testifying about the same incident or events, did the witness give his or her evidence confidently and without hesitation? Was the witness evasive or unresponsive? In other words, did the witness answer the questions put to him or her, give long explanations not asked for or take a long time to answer to play for time while thinking of an answer? Alternatively, was the questioning just confusing?
- Does the witness's account conflict with:
  - his or her conduct
  - his or her own prior statements made in or out of court (does the witness's evidence in court differ from what he or she said on a previous occasion in respect of the same issue?)
  - known, admitted or incontrovertible facts
  - contemporaneous notes or statements of the issue in question made by him- or herself or others[5]
  - what was pleaded or put on behalf of the party he or she is testifying for and/or with the evidence of other witnesses, especially those found to be good witnesses?
  - If so, are there reasonable explanations for these contradictions?

- Is the witness's version inherently probable? In other words, does it accord with the way we expect things to happen or ordinary people to behave under the circumstances prevailing at the time of the incident in question based on common sense, common experience and the ordinary course of nature?
- Is the witness's evidence generally consistent with the overall probabilities of the case and the overall theory of the case put forward by the party he or she is testifying for?
- Is the witness's evidence corroborated by other accepted evidence from a different source? The absence of corroboration, of course, is not a ground for rejecting the

---

3   See the Supreme Court of Appeal judgment in *Stellenbosch Farmers' Winery Group Ltd and Another v Martell et Cie and Others* 2003 (1) SA 11 (SCA); *Hees HC v Nel JT* 1994 (1) PH F11 (TPD) at 31; *Onassis v Vergottis* [1968] 2 Lloyd's Rep 403 431 and the article by HC Nicholas 'The credibility of witnesses' (1985) 102 *South African Law Journal* at 32.

4   An alternative view is that the fact that a witness's evidence was disbelieved or rejected in some other proceedings is not relevant to his or her credibility in the present proceedings because his or her evidence could have been rejected for a variety of reasons irrelevant to his or her credibility in the case before the court. The conclusion of the court in the other proceedings is irrelevant opinion evidence. See DT Zeffertt and AP Paizes *The South African Law of Evidence* 2 ed (2009) at 914–917.

5   Lord Pearce in *Onassis v Vergottis* [1968] 2 Lloyd's Rep 403 431 stated that it is a truism that with every day that passes, the memory becomes fainter and the imagination becomes more active. For this reason, a witness, however honest, rarely persuades a judge that his or her present recollection is preferable to that which was taken down in writing immediately after the incident in issue.

384 | THE LAW OF EVIDENCE IN SOUTH AFRICA

evidence of a good witness. Corroborating evidence merely adds weight to the evidence of a witness.

It is often suggested during cross-examination that a witness's failure to explain why another witness would commit perjury adversely affects his or her credibility. However, the court should not take this factor into consideration when assessing the credibility of a witness. In *S v Lotter*,[6] the Court found that the accused's failure to provide a cogent explanation as to why the complainant would lay a false rape charge against him was central to the trial court's rejection of his version. The Court held that the trial magistrate had misdirected herself in drawing an adverse inference from the accused's inability to explain the complainant's motive to implicate him falsely. An accused should not be expected to provide an explanation as to why a complainant may lay a charge. This view is consistent with the burden of proof and the presumption of innocence.[7]

38.3 Mendacity: assessing the evidence of the lying witness

We usually refer to assessing the evidence of a lying witness as an assessment of the witness's **mendacity**.[8]

> 'The fact that a witness has lied in one respect shows that he [or she] is capable of lying in other respects ... A lie requires proof of conscious falsehood, [in other words], proof that the witness has deliberately misstated something contrary to his [or her] own knowledge or belief. The question then is what is the effect of proof of a witness's mendacity on one ... or on more than one occasion?' ... "It is not correct that a person who tells a single lie is therefore necessarily lying throughout his [or her] testimony nor that there is any probability that he [or she] is so lying. The probability is to the contrary".[9]

There is no rule that the mere fact that a witness is found to be untruthful in one respect means that the witness's evidence as a whole automatically stands to be rejected. The maxims *semei mentitus semper mentitur*, once untruthful, always untruthful, and *falsum in uno, falsum in omnibus*, false in one thing, false in all, do not apply in our law of evidence.[10] In *S v Oosthuizen*,[11] the Court said:

> ... where a witness has been shown to be deliberately lying on one point, the trier-of-fact may (not must) conclude that his evidence on another point cannot safely be relied upon ... The circumstances may be such that there is no room for honest mistake in regard to a particular piece of evidence: either it is true or it has been deliberately fabricated. In such a case the fact that the witness has been guilty of deliberate falsehood in other parts of his evidence is relevant to show that he may have fabricated the piece of evidence in question. But in this context the fact that he has been honestly mistaken in other parts of his evidence is irrelevant, because the fact that his evidence in regard to one point is honestly mistaken cannot support an inference that his evidence on another point is a deliberate fabrication.

---

6 2008 (2) SACR 595 (C).
7 PJ Schwikkard *Annual Survey of South African Law* (2008) 855 at 872.
8 See ch 46 Assessment of mendacity.
9 Nicholas 'The credibility of witnesses' at 32-33 referring to *Wigmore on Evidence*.
10 PJ Schwikkard and SE van der Merwe *Principles of Evidence* 3 ed (2009) at 536; *R v Gumede* 1949 (3) SA 749 (A).
11 1982 (3) SA 571 (T) at 577B.

CHAPTER 38   CREDITWORTHINESS: CREDIBILITY AND RELIABILITY   385

Ultimately, 'the question is not whether a witness is wholly truthful in all that he [or she] says, but whether the court can be satisfied beyond reasonable doubt in a criminal case, or on a balance of probabilities in a civil [case], that the story which the witness tells is a true one in its essential features'.[12] In *S v Burger and Others*,[13] the Supreme Court of Appeal stated that courts should avoid a situation where an accused person is convicted 'merely as punishment for untruthful evidence'. The focus should be on whether the State has managed, on all the evidence, to exclude all doubt about his or her guilt. This means the evidence can include the fact that the accused gave false evidence but the court cannot primarily focus on this fact.[14]

According to *R v Abdoorham*,[15] the Court may be satisfied that a witness is speaking the truth notwithstanding that he or she is in some respects an unsatisfactory witness. The Court may accept such evidence for the following reasons:
- There is no indication that the witness was biased or deliberately lying.
- Corroboration exists for a certain aspect of the evidence.
- There is some plausible reason for the unsatisfactory aspect of the evidence.
- The evidence is generally consistent with the overall probabilities of the case.
- From a quantitative point of view, the satisfactory aspects of the evidence outweigh the unsatisfactory aspects. In this regard, the nature, extent and materiality of the lies will be relevant.

38.4   Reliability of witnesses

Obviously, the evidence of a lying witness, in other words a witness with no credibility, is usually not reliable. However, it is not necessary to find that a witness is dishonest to find that his or her evidence is unreliable. We may also infer the reliability of a witness from specific conduct and testimony of the witness, namely his or her powers of perception, memory and accuracy of narration.

The Supreme Court of Appeal has held[16] that a witness's reliability will depend on:
- his or her bias, latent and blatant
- external contradictions with what was pleaded or put on his or her behalf
- the probability or improbability of particular aspects of his or her version
- the opportunities he or she had to experience or observe the event in question
- the quality, integrity and independence of his or her recall thereof.

When assessing the reliability of the evidence, the court must take into account whether the following was shown from surrounding circumstances or other facts:
- The witness had a good opportunity to observe what he or she had seen or experienced. In other words, the conditions under which the witness saw, heard or experienced what he or she has recounted to the court were conducive to an accurate observation and perception of the events.
- The witness's memory is accurate.
- The witness has reconstructed the events correctly.

---

12   Nicholas 'The credibility of witnesses' at 35.
13   2010 (2) SACR 1 (SCA).
14   See also *S v MG* 2010 (2) SACR 66 (ECG).
15   1954 (3) SA 163 (N).
16   *Stellenbosch Farmers' Winery Group Ltd and Another v Martell et Cie and Others* 2003 (1) SA 11 (SCA).

386 | THE LAW OF EVIDENCE IN SOUTH AFRICA

- The witness has the ability to recount dispassionately. In other words, the witness has no association with the party he or she is testifying for and has no interest in the case. The witness will thus not tend to alter his or her version or his or her interpretation of events deliberately or subconsciously.
- The witness's recollection was not tampered with by someone suggesting facts to him or her or discussing the matter with other witnesses. The witness is thus recounting his or her version of the events.
- The witness's version is not inherently improbable.
- The witness's recollection of events was aided by notes or statements he or she made at the time of the event or close to the time of the event when the event was still fresh in his or her mind.
- The witness had reason to take notice of and remember the event he or she is testifying to.
- The witness gave a clear and understandable picture of the scene or event. The Supreme Court of Appeal in *S v Jochems*[17] noted that the trial court was given a confused picture of the scene and thus no foundation was laid for the court to test objectively whether reliable identification was feasible.
- The witness's account is probable.[18]
- The witness's version was given in response to questions that did not suggest the answer on important disputed facts.

DISCUSSION	Mendacity, mistaken assumptions and reliability
38.1	Abel was prosecuted for allegedly driving negligently or recklessly through a red traffic light and colliding with Ben's car in the intersection of Clark and Manning Roads in Durban. The eyewitness for the prosecution, Mrs Armstrong-Jones, a 77-year-old widow, made a statement to the police shortly after the collision. She stated, *inter alia*, that she was walking her dog up the hill in Moore Road immediately prior to the collision and that she saw Abel's car driving through the red traffic light at the intersection and colliding with Ben's car inside the intersection.
	Abel's version was that the traffic light had been green for him and that it was Ben who had entered the intersection against the red traffic light. As this was a criminal case, the defence merely had to raise a reasonable doubt on the State's version and did not have to show that Abel's version was the more probable one.
	It was the defence's theory that Mrs Armstrong-Jones had not actually seen Abel's car enter the intersection but that the sound of the collision had attracted her attention. When she looked up, the traffic light facing her was red so she had assumed that Abel had gone through a red traffic light. Based on this theory, Mrs Armstrong-Jones was telling the truth as she saw it and was not being dishonest.
	In her evidence-in-chief, Mrs Armstrong-Jones confirmed the version in her statement. However, when it was put to her under cross-examination that she must

---

17 1991 (1) SACR 208 (A).

18 In *S v Jochems*, the Supreme Court of Appeal pointed out that had the accused in fact looked up at the State witnesses so that the witnesses had had a good view of the accused, one would have expected them, or at least one of them, to have volunteered this as an important part of their identification. That they did not may be an indication that a glance in the direction of the observers on a third-story landing at night with lightning coming from above and some distance away would not necessarily reveal the faces of the men below.

have had a big fright when she heard the sound of the cars colliding, she answered, 'I almost fell on my back.'

On the basis of this response, it was clear that Mrs Armstrong-Jones had only looked at the intersection for the first time after the collision had occurred, at which stage the traffic lights facing her were red. The court could therefore not discount the reasonable possibility that the traffic lights were in fact green at the time that Abel entered the intersection. This established a reasonable doubt in Abel's favour. Note that the prosecution was so confident in their single state witness that they failed to call corroborating technical evidence about the time intervals taken for the traffic lights to change from green to amber to red. Abel was thus acquitted on the charge of negligent or reckless driving. Mrs Armstrong-Jones had not been deliberately untruthful, but her evidence was nevertheless unreliable as it could not establish the crucial issue of the colour of the traffic lights at the time that Abel entered the intersection.

THIS CHAPTER IN ESSENCE

1 The credit given to evidence depends largely on the:
   1.1 credibility of the witnesses
   1.2 reliability of their evidence
   1.3 weight to be attached to the evidence.
2 The veracity and reliability of a witness determines his or her credibility. Both these factors are inferred from the specific conduct of the witness and through a consideration of various factors.
3 There is no rule in the South African law of evidence that if a witness is untruthful in one respect, his or her evidence as a whole should be rejected. The ultimate rule is whether a court can be satisfied beyond reasonable doubt in a criminal case, or on a balance of probabilities in a civil case, that the witness's story is essentially true.
4 The reliability of a witness depends on:
   4.1 whether he or she has shown bias (latent or blatant)
   4.2 whether he or she has exhibited any external contradictions with what was pleaded or put on his or her behalf
   4.3 the probability or improbability of his or her version
   4.4 the opportunities he or she had to experience or observe the event in question
   4.5 the quality, integrity and independence of his or her recall of the event in question.

Chapter 39

Inherent probabilities

39.1 Introduction 388

39.2 Probabilities 388

39.1 Introduction

Inherent probabilities concern the weight the court gives to a witness's version on a contested point by reason of its intrinsic logic or lack of logic. They relate to the court's evaluation of the likelihood of an event having occurred as the witness says it did given:
- the context made available to and accepted by the presiding officer[1]
- the general probabilities of the case
- assumptions about human behaviour and the ordinary course of nature that the presiding officer adopts for the purposes of evaluation.

39.2 Probabilities

When we speak of something as being inherently probable, we think that the chances of it having happened are better than even. It accords with the general probabilities of the case and with the way we expect things to happen or ordinary people to behave under the circumstances prevailing at the time of the incident based on common sense, common experience and the ordinary course of nature. Improbable means the opposite. We describe the evidence of a witness which stands in contrast to what we may reasonably expect to happen in a given context as improbable. The court will probably reject or view such evidence with circumspection.

The court need only make estimates of probability where there is uncertainty about a fact. Once the court is certain that a particular event or behaviour did occur, it need not then ask whether it considers it probable or improbable. The court should also measure or balance the probabilities of the truth of a particular averment against the probabilities of it being untrue.

The case of *S v Jochems*[2] illustrates what might be considered improbable in the circumstances of a particular case. The state witnesses who identified the accused were on a balcony three floors above the accused some distance away. It was at night and there was lightning. However, none of the state witnesses testified that the accused had looked up at them, affording them a good look at the accused. The Court pointed out that it would have expected them or at least one of them to have volunteered this information. The Court then

---

1 Probabilities are assessed in light of proved facts.
2 1991 (1) SACR 208 (A).

CHAPTER 39 INHERENT PROBABILITIES | 389

said that the fact that they had not done so may indicate that such an upward glance by the accused would not necessarily have revealed the face of the accused.

The court cannot, on the mere *a priori* improbability of an event alleged by a witness, find that the witness is less credible. A bad witness can testify to something that is very probable and not affect the degree to which the version is probable. An honest and reliable witness may give an account that is very improbable and which may be exposed as fallacious for reasons independent of the credibility of the witness.[3]

Inherent improbability, on its own, is not sufficient to discredit the assertion. The court must also assess the probability against the credibility of the witness and other witnesses whose testimony bears on the evaluation of probability and whose evidence in turn is subject to a similar assessment. When deciding between two conflicting versions on a matter, the court will not only consider the inherent probabilities of the details asserted by either witness, but also any indication that it can glean by watching and listening to the witnesses as to their veracity and the objective reliability of their evidence. The probability the court attaches to the assertions of the one witness may affect the probability the court attaches to the assertion of the other witness and vice versa.

The court can accept direct credible evidence even if that evidence conflicts with probabilities arising from human experience or expert opinion. In *Mapota v Santam Versekeringsmaatskappy Bpk*,[4] the appellant had claimed damages from the respondent as a result of injuries he had allegedly sustained when a bus had knocked him over and driven over his left foot. There were two witnesses to the accident. However, the appellant gave the only direct evidence on how the injury occurred. The respondent's medical witness opined that it was improbable that the appellant had sustained the injuries in the manner described by the appellant, but that he could not exclude the reasonable possibility that they were caused in that way. The magistrate had dismissed the appellant's claim on the ground that, in light of the medical evidence, the appellant had not proved on a preponderance of probabilities that his injuries had been caused by the bus. The Supreme Court of Appeal disagreed. The Court held that the appellant's version was the only one which rested on direct evidence and his evidence, apart from the scientific medical evidence, was not inherently improbable. Moreover, the evidence was satisfactory in other respects, was partially supported by two witnesses and the scientific medical evidence did not exclude the reasonable possibility that his injury had been sustained as he claimed.[5]

The court must base an assessment of probabilities on a sound premise. In *S v Mafiri*,[6] the appellant had been charged with possession of a firearm found under a pillow in a bedroom of his house. The appellant testified that he was unaware of the firearm and that the room was, at the time, occupied by a third party. The trial court had regarded it as inherently improbable that a third person would leave his room unlocked with a firearm under the pillow.

The Supreme Court of Appeal pointed out that this finding rested on the premise that the room had an external door. This was based on the evidence of one state witness, which was, however, contradicted by the evidence of the other state witness. Here it did not matter which state witness was telling the truth – the version presented by the appellant could not

---

3 F Snyckers *Annual Survey of South African Law* (2003) 869 at 874.
4 1977 (4) SA 515 (A).
5 *Mapota v Santam Versekeringsmaatskappy Bpk* 1977 (4) SA 515 (A): headnote.
6 2003 (2) SACR 121 (SCA).

be held to be inherently improbable based on an assumption or premise that required one of the state witnesses to be preferred above the other.[7]

There are limitations on the extent to which a presiding officer can resort to personal experience of human behaviour and social interaction to provide guidance on the question of fact. The presiding officer should limit his or her assumptions about these things to facts that are generally known and should not draw conclusions as to probability in areas where his or her knowledge and experience are doubtful. In certain situations, assumptions about human behaviour should be informed by expert knowledge provided to and accepted by the court.

In *S v M*,[8] Cameron JA held that, in the context of the phenomenon of domestic sexual predation which includes characteristics of complicity and fear, it was not improbable that a young girl who claimed to have been subjected to sex against her will would have continued to associate with the man concerned. This case also illustrates that the context in which the act that is being evaluated took place is important. Fact-finding should also not be based on racial and gender stereotyping since it may result in unwarranted generalisations being made.[9]

Although it may be difficult to describe theoretically, it is not difficult to recognise in reality an improbability or probability. For instance:

- It is improbable that it would not have occurred to an identifying witness to tell the investigating officer that the person he allegedly saw committing the offence in question stared menacingly at him before fleeing and that this provided a good opportunity to see the face of the alleged perpetrator.
- It is improbable that a person with an innocent state of mind will try to cover his tracks, flee the scene of a crime or accident, or remove fingerprints from an object he has handled.
- It is probable that if something on a highway runs down a man it will be a motor vehicle and not some other form of traffic.

THIS CHAPTER IN ESSENCE

1   If a witness's evidence is contrary to what may reasonably be expected to happen in a given context, the court will consider it to be improbable and reject it or, at the very least, view it with caution.

2   It is only when there is uncertainty about a fact that a court should estimate the probability of certain events happening.

3   A court should not base a finding regarding a witness's credibility on the *a priori* improbability of an event alleged by such witness.

4   Inherent improbability on its own is not sufficient to discredit an assertion, but should also be assessed against the credibility of the witnesses whose testimony bears on the evaluation of probability.

5   Direct credible evidence can be accepted even if that evidence conflicts with probabilities arising from human experience or expert opinion.

6   Any assessment of probabilities must be based on a sound premise.

7   There are limitations on the extent to which a presiding officer can resort to personal experience of human behaviour and social interaction to provide guidance on the question of fact.

---

7   See also *S v Jochems* 1991 (1) SACR 208 (A) for an insightful assessment of inherent improbabilities.

8   2006 (1) SACR 135 (SCA).

9   In *S v Scott-Crossley* 2008 (1) SACR 223 (SCA) at 237C, the Supreme Court of Appeal rejected the trial court's stereotyping of relationships between farm workers and their employers. The trial court effectively assumed that, in general, the nature of the relationship between farm workers and their employers is characterised by docile submissiveness.

Chapter 40

Contradictions and discrepancies

40.1 Introduction	391
40.2 Contradictions	391

40.1 Introduction

An **internal inconsistency or self-contradiction** arises when there is a **contradiction** between versions given by the same witness. An example of this type of contradiction is when there is a difference between the witness's *viva voce* evidence (what he or she said in court) and a previous statement (what the same person said in a prior statement or correspondence).

An **external inconsistency** arises when one witness contradicts another witness on the same side. It could also arise when a version given is inconsistent with documents produced, including contemporaneous notes or statements on the issue in question made by others, with known or proved facts, and/or with what was pleaded or put on behalf of the party for whom the witness is testifying.

A more subtle inconsistency arises when the evidence of a witness conflicts with the inherent probabilities. The question that the court asks of every version given by every witness is whether or not the version given by the witness is in accordance with the general probabilities of the case. The court will assess whether the witness behaved in the way we would expect ordinary people to behave under the circumstances prevailing at the time of the relevant incident. If the witness did not do so, the evidence of this witness may clash with the inherent probabilities of the case.[1]

40.2 Contradictions

A common but not infallible indication that a witness is untruthful or unreliable is that the witness contradicts him or herself, or contradicts another witness. The theory is that a witness who is telling the truth will be consistent in the version he or she gives. An untruthful witness has to make up a story, remember it and repeat it accurately. If a witness, or two or more witnesses, gives consistent evidence, this may be a strong indication that his or her story is a credible one.

The converse is, however, not true. Discrepancies between witnesses may arise, not necessarily because the witness has deliberately misstated something contrary to his or her knowledge and belief, but because people perceive events differently and from different vantage points. They remember things differently, have different views on what is important

---

1 CG Marnewick *Litigation Skills for South African Lawyers* Rev ed (2003) at 283.

392 | THE LAW OF EVIDENCE IN SOUTH AFRICA

and have varying skills in communicating what they have witnessed.[2] It follows that an argument based purely on a list of contradictions between witnesses leads nowhere as far as veracity is concerned. The argument must go further and show that one of the witnesses is lying. Lack of consistency between witnesses does not afford any basis for an adverse finding on their credibility. Where different witnesses make contradictory statements, it is true that at least one of them is erroneous. However, the court cannot, merely from the fact of the contradiction, say which one.[3]

Minor contradictions between two witnesses testifying for the same party or giving contradictory evidence on a single detail which does not go to the heart of the matter in dispute is not a basis for making an adverse credibility finding and rejecting the entirety of a witness's evidence, even if the contradiction could be construed as an anomaly.[4]

S v Jochems,[5] discussed above, provides a good guideline on how contradictions should be assessed. The Supreme Court of Appeal held that the mere fact that there were contradictions between the evidence of the accused and his witness on a contested factual issue is not, of itself, a sufficient ground for rejecting the evidence of the accused. There was no doubt that there were differences in matters of detail. A trial court needs to consider the significance or otherwise of such differences and evaluate the whole of the evidence of each of the witnesses. Thus, if a good witness is contradicted by an indifferent witness, this is no reason for rejecting the evidence of the good witness. In this case, no adverse findings of demeanour were made against the accused. Also, it was not suggested that there was any inherent improbability in his version of what had occurred on the night in question. Moreover, there were possible explanations for the differences which the trial court had not considered.

The Supreme Court of Appeal came to the opposite conclusion in respect of contradictions between the versions of the state witnesses. The Court found that there were serious inconsistencies on material points. These inconsistencies could not be explained away on the basis that they were the sort of peripheral differences of detail one would expect from witnesses testifying to events that had happened a long time ago. The inconsistencies related directly to the probabilities and to what the witnesses were able to see and did see at a crucial stage. They became more significant when considered in light of the fact that the witnesses, on their own versions, had observed the events from exactly the same point of observation throughout the relevant period. In addition, the rest of their evidence was marred by inherent improbabilities and a possible motive to implicate the appellant.

It is sometimes suggested that selfcontradiction is more serious since it renders both versions of the witness suspect while in the case of contradictions between witnesses, it may still be possible to accept one of the versions as being correct. The Supreme Court of Appeal in *S v Scott-Crossley*[6] held that while minor contradictions between the versions of several witnesses should not on their own lead to the rejection of a witness's testimony, the same reasoning could not apply where the witness's own testimony contained material contradictions. The focus, however, should rather be on the nature and effect of the

---

2 Ibid. at 368.

3 HC Nicholas 'The credibility of witnesses' (1985) 102(1) *South African Law Journal* 32 at 36.

4 *Network Field Marketing (Pty) Ltd v Mngezana NO and Others* (2011) 32 ILJ 1705 (LC) at para 21 referring to *President of the Republic of SA and Others v SA Rugby Football Union and Others* 2000 (1) SA 1 (CC).

5 1991 (1) SACR 208 (A).

6 2008 (1) SACR 223 (SCA).

CHAPTER 40   CONTRADICTIONS AND DISCREPANCIES | **393**

contradiction.[7] This is illustrated in *S v Mafiri*,[8] where two state witnesses had contradicted each other on a point. This meant that the accused's version was no longer inherently improbable due to the contradiction.

The Supreme Court of Appeal in *S v Scott-Crossley* noted the well-accepted general rule that previous consistent statements have no probative value.[9] It ruled that the court *a quo* had incorrectly taken into account a witness's consistency with his prior statement to the police in determining credibility.

THIS CHAPTER IN ESSENCE

1   A witness is deemed untruthful or unreliable if he or she contradicts him- or herself (internal inconsistency or self-contradiction) or contradicts another witness (external inconsistency).

2   Minor contradictions between two witnesses testifying for the same party and/or giving contradictory evidence on a single detail which does not go to the heart of the matter in dispute does not constitute sufficient ground for making an adverse credibility finding and rejecting the entirety of the witness's evidence.

3   Self-contradiction renders both versions of a witness suspect, while in the case of contradictions between witnesses, one of the versions may be accepted as correct.

---

7   See, for example, *Dreyer and Another NNO v AXZS Industries (Pty) Ltd* 2006 (5) SA 548 (SCA); *Louwrens v Oldwage* 2006 (2) SA 161 (SCA).

8   2003 (2) SACR 121 (SCA). See also the discussion of *S v Mafiri* in ch 39.

9   2008 (1) SACR 223 (SCA).

Chapter 41

The cautionary rule

41.1 Introduction **394**

41.2 Status of the cautionary rule **395**

41.3 Definition of the cautionary rule **395**

41.4 Purpose of the cautionary rule **395**

41.5 Compliance with the cautionary rule **395**

41.6 Specific applications of the cautionary rule **396**
    41.6.1 The risk of deliberate false evidence 396
        41.6.1.1 Participants (including accomplices) 396
        41.6.1.2 Other examples 398
    41.6.2 The cautionary rule applied to the single witness's evidence 398
    41.6.3 The cautionary rule applied to children's evidence 399
    41.6.4 The cautionary rule applied to evidence of identification 400
    41.6.5 *S v Jackson*: abolition of the cautionary rule in sexual offences 400

41.7 Conclusion **401**

41.1 Introduction

A court should not base its findings on unreliable evidence or evidence that is not trustworthy. As a result, if the court is faced with evidence that appears suspect, it should satisfy itself that such evidence is supported or confirmed in some way to ensure that it can safely rely on the evidence. This principle is generally referred to as the **cautionary rule.**[1]

It is worth noting that there are really two aspects to the rule:

- First, the court should be cautious when relying on evidence that it suspects may be unreliable.
- Second, the court should seek some safeguard when doing so.

Keep in mind that this rule only provides guidance to the court and does not constitute a mechanical test.

---

1 This is sometimes referred to in the plural as the cautionary rules. However, we have used the term 'cautionary rule' throughout this chapter as it is, strictly speaking, a single cautionary rule comprising two parts with a number of applications.

The concept of the cautionary rule is closely related to the concept of corroboration, which we discuss in chapter 42. We have dealt with these concepts in this order because, first, both concepts relate to the weight or probative value of evidence. Second, in practice, corroborating evidence is frequently used to satisfy or comply with the second part of the cautionary rule.

41.2 Status of the cautionary rule

The cautionary rule is a rule of practice. This means that the rule is not contained in legislation but has been developed through case law. This does not, however, mean that the cautionary rule is not of a binding nature. The rule has been 'hardened' by precedent into a legal rule. Where a specific type of evidence clearly attracts the application of the cautionary rule, the court is under an obligation to follow this rule. Failure to apply the rule will result in a conviction being set aside on appeal. In the treatment of such evidence, the presiding officer is also expected to indicate that he or she did, in fact, approach the evidence with caution. This was confirmed in the case of *S v Mgengwana*[2] where the Court found that the trial court magistrate had merely paid lip service to the cautionary rule without actually adopting a cautionary approach to the evidence of accomplices. Accomplices are a category of witnesses that requires a cautionary approach.

41.3 Definition of the cautionary rule

The first part of the cautionary rule is that the court is required to follow a cautionary approach when evaluating certain categories of evidence which experience has shown to be unreliable. Although our courts are under an obligation to do this, our courts have also pointed out that a cautionary approach should not replace the exercise of common sense.[3]

The second aspect of the cautionary rule requires that the court must find some safeguard to reduce the danger of a wrong finding based on the evidence to which the cautionary rule applies. This safeguard may take a variety of forms, one of which is corroboration. The court may apply any one of a number of factors to satisfy the cautionary rule, for example through the application of human experience or logic.

41.4 Purpose of the cautionary rule

The purpose of the cautionary rule is self-evident. It is designed to ensure that the courts do not make a finding in a particular matter based on evidence which judicial experience has shown tends to be unreliable. By requiring the courts to seek some sort of safeguard, the rule ensures that the court applies its mind to the unreliability of the evidence, considers the pitfalls that such evidence creates, and carefully and deliberately finds some reassurance that the evidence can be relied on.

41.5 Compliance with the cautionary rule

As indicated above, the second part of the cautionary rule may be satisfied by means of a variety of factors that can provide the safeguard that the court needs. These factors do not

---

2 1964 (2) SA 149 (C).
3 *S v Snyman* 1968 (2) SA 582 (A) at 585.

THE LAW OF EVIDENCE IN SOUTH AFRICA

form a closed list. Corroboration of the potentially unreliable evidence may be a sufficient safeguard to indicate that the court can rely on the evidence in question, but there may also be other indicators to the trustworthiness of the evidence. The court does not necessarily have to find evidence that agrees with the potentially unreliable evidence as evidence that supports another aspect of the case may suffice. Even false evidence given by an opposing witness may satisfy the court that the initial evidence is reliable.

Two of the factors that can provide the safeguard that the court needs – namely, where the accused has lied to the court and where the accused fails to testify – are specifically discussed below.[4] Another factor is where the potentially unreliable witness has implicated someone near and dear to him or her. For example, in *R v Gumede*,[5] an accomplice incriminated a close relative against whom he had no apparent grudge. The Court regarded this as an indication that he had no ulterior motive and that his evidence was therefore reliable.

41.6 Specific applications of the cautionary rule

The cautionary rule requires a court to be suspicious or wary of certain categories of evidence either because of the type of witness who is the source of the evidence, such as accomplices, co-accused, single witnesses or children, or because of the subject, such as identification evidence or evidence in sexual offences.[6] Quite often a witness may fall into more than one of the applicable categories.

41.6.1 The risk of deliberate false evidence

A discussion of the categories of witnesses who may be likely to give deliberate false evidence follows below.

41.6.1.1 Participants (including accomplices)

The cautionary rule applies to persons who, as a result of their alleged involvement in a specific crime currently being tried, may have a motive to incriminate falsely other persons. The rule applies to anyone who has committed an offence in connection with the same criminal transaction that forms the subject matter of the charge. This category of witnesses includes co-accused and accomplices. Accomplices are persons who were present at the crime and participated in some way, but who did not perpetrate the crime themselves. Accomplices are liable to be prosecuted either for the same offence with which the accused is charged or as an accessory before or after the fact.

DISCUSSION	Perpetrator or accessory after the fact?
41.1	An accessory after the fact is a person who is not him- or herself a perpetrator of the principal crime but who helps or encourages the principal perpetrator in some way after the commission of the offence. An accessory may provide financial assistance, conceal the crime, prevent the perpetrator from being apprehended or fail to report the crime. Some recent examples where people were convicted of being an accessory after the fact include assisting a co-accused to drag the deceased's body away from the scene

---

4 See ch 46 Assessment of mendacity and ch 47 Failure to testify.

5 1949 (3) SA 749 (A).

6 *S v Jackson* 1998 (1) SACR 470 (SCA), codified by legislation, s 60 of the Criminal Law (Sexual Offences and Related Matters) Amendment Act 32 of 2007, provides that no automatic cautionary rule applies in sexual assault cases.

> of a shooting (*S v Terblanche*[7]) and a police officer found guilty of concealing a murder involving a colleague who later committed suicide (*S v Pillay*[8]).

Our courts do not require a specific degree of participation for the cautionary rule to apply. The rule will apply in all cases where the participant, first, has a possible motive to incriminate another person falsely and, second, has the ability to do so as a result of his or her participation in the specific crime.

With regard to the first requirement, this is especially prevalent when the prospect of indemnity in terms of section 204 of the Criminal Procedure Act 51 of 1977 may provide the witness with an incentive to lie.[9] The court should also be vigilant with the evidence of a single witness who seeks indemnity.[10]

With regard to the second requirement, remember that an accomplice has an intimate knowledge of the circumstances under which the crime was committed. The accomplice's intimate knowledge of these details may enable him or her to 'colour in' his or her testimony to make it look as though he or she is a satisfactory witness whose evidence should carry much weight. This person may be in a position to paint a favourable picture of him- or herself while also falsely incriminating the accused in an attempt to persuade the court that the accused was the actual culprit. In so doing, the accomplice may hope to be acquitted or to receive a more lenient sentence. The reasons for applying the cautionary rule in the case of an accomplice are clearly set out in *S v Hlapezulu*.[11]

In such cases, the cautionary rule requires that the court only relies on the testimony of this type of witness if there is corroborating evidence connecting the accused to the crime. Alternatively, in the absence of such corroborating evidence, there must be an indication of another nature that the evidence of the accomplice is reliable to the extent that the risk of a wrong conviction has been excluded.

The Court in *S v Masuku*[12] summarised the principles relating to the cautionary rule in cases involving accomplices thus:

1. Caution is imperative.
2. An accomplice has a motive to lie.
3. Corroboration merely of the details of the crime, not the implicating of the accused, does not indicate that the accomplice is truthful.
4. Corroboration must directly implicate the accused.
5. An accomplice may provide corroborating evidence provided he or she is a reliable witness.
6. If there is no such corroboration, there must be some other indication that the accomplice is a reliable witness.
7. This indication may be the fact that the accused is an unreliable witness or did not testify.
8. The risk of false incrimination is reduced if the accomplice is a friend of the accused.

---

7   2011 (1) SACR 77 (ECG).
8   [2011] ZAWCHC 106.
9   In *S v Ndawonde* 2013 (2) SACR 192 (KZN) the Court considered the evidence of an accomplice who had already received indemnity and concluded that they were in a different position to a witness who has not yet been granted indemnity.
10   *Naude and Another v S* [2011] 2 All SA 517 (SCA) at para 34.
11   1965 (4) SA 439 (A).
12   1969 (2) SA 375 (N) at 375–377.

398 | THE LAW OF EVIDENCE IN SOUTH AFRICA

9. If none of the above factors is satisfied, the court may only convict on the basis of accomplice evidence if it is mindful of the risks.
10. The same principles apply where accomplice evidence is used to corroborate another accomplice's evidence.

41.6.1.2 Other examples

The evidence of a number of other categories of witnesses, who tend to give false evidence deliberately, may also attract the application of the cautionary rule. These include, among others:

- co-accused[13]
- police traps[14]
- the plaintiff in paternity and seduction cases[15]
- private detectives[16]
- handwriting experts[17]
- persons who claim against the estates of deceased persons.[18]

41.6.2 The cautionary rule applied to the single witness's evidence

It is often said that the evidence of a single witness must be approached with caution. However, this is a simplification of the actual position.[19] The Criminal Procedure Act 51 of 1977 actually refers to the 'single evidence'[20] of a witness. This has given rise to some confusion. The cautionary rule does not apply to single evidence but only to evidence given by a single witness. The following example illustrates the difference.

> An accused is charged with theft. The State calls two witnesses. Witness A testifies that he saw the accused pick up and conceal a watch on his person. Witness B testifies that the accused offered him a watch for sale. Neither A nor B is a single witness as each gives evidence that supports the other. However, A is the only witness who gives evidence about the taking of the watch and B is the only witness who gives evidence about the fact that the accused offered to sell him the watch. Therefore, on a technical reading of the Act, both A and B give 'single evidence'.
>
> However, neither A nor B is a single witness and the cautionary rule is therefore not applicable. In fact, B's evidence about the identity of the accused and the particulars of the watch corresponds with A's evidence on these points. Although B does not testify to the actual act of theft, B's evidence provides support for part of A's evidence. This reassures the court that it can safely rely on A's evidence.

Section 208 of the Criminal Procedure Act, 1977 provides that an accused may be convicted of any offence on the single evidence of any competent witness. Section 16 of the Civil Proceedings Evidence Act 25 of 1965 contains a similar provision in the context

---

13 *S v Dladla* 1980 (1) SA 526 (A); *S v Johannes* 1980 (1) SA 531 (A).
14 *S v Mabaso* 1978 (3) SA 5 (O); *S v Ramroop* 1991 (1) SACR 555 (N).
15 *Mayer v Williams* 1981 (3) SA 348 (A).
16 *Preen v Preen and Another* 1935 NPD 138.
17 *S v Van Dyk* 1998 (2) SACR 363 (W) at 375g–h; *Annama v Chetty and Others* 1946 AD 142 at 154.
18 *Borcherds v Estate Naidoo* 1955 (3) SA 78 (A).
19 The court in *S v Sauls and Others* 1981 (3) SA 172 (A) at para 180E cautioned that there are 'indefinite degrees in this character we call credibility'. This was endorsed in *Modiga v The State* [2015] ZASCA 94 at para 32.
20 S 208 of the Criminal Procedure Act, 1977.

CHAPTER 41   THE CAUTIONARY RULE | 399

of civil proceedings. This seems to be at odds with the cautionary rule but our courts have balanced the need to be cautious with the statutory scope afforded for reliance on a single witness. For example, in *S v Mahlangu and another*[21] the court reiterated the need for the evidence of a single witness to be substantially satisfactory in every material respect or to be corroborated in order for a court to base a finding on it, but went on to say that such corroboration could be found in the improbability of the other party's version.

> **DISCUSSION**
> **41.2**
>
> **The meaning of 'clear and satisfactory in every material respect'**
>
> According to *R v Mokoena*,[22] an accused should not be convicted on the evidence of a single witness unless it appears that his testimony is 'clear and satisfactory in every material respect'. This dictum has given rise to some confusion about what exactly is required when a court is faced with the cautionary rule in the case of single evidence. Does this mean that an accused cannot be convicted if there are shortcomings in the witness's evidence? The Courts in *S v Sauls*[23] and *S v Webber*,[24] as well as academic authors,[25] seem to indicate, convincingly, that an accused may be convicted even though there are shortcomings in the single witness's testimony. The court should consider the merits and demerits of the witness's single evidence. The court must then decide whether he or she is trustworthy and whether, despite the shortcomings, defects or contradictions, it is nevertheless satisfied that the witness has told the truth. The evidence must be satisfactory, not perfect.[26] Ultimately, the test remains whether the standard of proof, the guilt of the accused beyond reasonable doubt, has been satisfied.

41.6.3   The cautionary rule applied to children's evidence

The cautionary rule also used to apply to evidence given by children[27] because they were regarded as being imaginative and it was believed that they were susceptible to suggestion and manipulation.[28] The automatic application of the cautionary rule in the case of children has been criticised and the South African Law Commission has recommended its abolition.[29] There are also numerous recent judgments that have criticised the automatic assumption that children are unreliable witnesses.[30] The exact scope of the cautionary rule has therefore become unclear. What is, however, clear is that certain important points should be considered when assessing the evidence of child witnesses. These are given below:

*   *Age of child:* It is not possible to determine that the evidence of children below a specific age must attract the cautionary rule. This is because the development of one individual

---

21 2011 (2) SACR 164 (SCA).
22 1932 OPD 79.
23 1981 (3) SA 172 (A).
24 1971 (3) SA 754 (A).
25 DT Zeffertt and AP Paizes *The South African Law of Evidence* 2 ed (2009) at 962–965.
23 1981 (3) SA 172 (A).
27 See also ch 27 Witnesses: competence and compellability and ch 58 Children's evidence.
28 *R v Manda* 1951 (3) SA 158 (A) at 163 and *S v Hanekom* 2011 (1) SACR 430 (WCC) at para 15.
29 SALC Project 107 Discussion Paper 102 *Sexual Offences: Process and Procedure* (2002) at 31.3.4.7.
30 *Director of Public Prosecutions v S* 2000 (2) SA 711 (T) and *S v Vumazonke* 2000 (1) SACR 619 (C).

400 THE LAW OF EVIDENCE IN SOUTH AFRICA

child may happen at a different pace to another. However, the age of a specific child is an important consideration. Where the witness is a very young child, the court will require substantial confirmation of the child's evidence.

- *Oath or affirmation:* Whether the child took the oath or was affirmed as a witness can also not be used to determine if the cautionary rule applies because a child who has not been sworn in as a result of his or her youthfulness may still be intelligent, observant and honest enough to give reliable testimony.

41.6.4 The cautionary rule applied to evidence of identification

The correct identification of the accused as the perpetrator of the crime is a vital element of the prosecution's case.[31] It is, however, easy to make a mistake when identifying a specific person as the perpetrator. Even an honest and credible witness can make a mistake when identifying someone, as summed up by the Court in *S v Mthetwa*:[32]

> Because of the fallibility of human observation, evidence of identification is approached by the courts with some caution. It is not enough for the identifying witness to be honest. The reliability of its observation must also be tested.

The importance of ensuring the reliability of single evidence was also recently emphasised in *S v Nyabo*.[33]

Identification of an accused can take place in a number of ways and under very different circumstances. For example, a witness may identify the accused in court. As the accused is usually in the dock and all attention is already focused on him or her, identifying him or her under these circumstances is of little probative value.[34]

An identification made at a formal identification parade is of greater probative value. However, it is important that the parade was conducted properly[35] if the evidence is to have its greatest effect. An improperly conducted identification parade may not always render the evidence inadmissible, but will have a negative impact on its weight.[36]

41.6.5 *S v Jackson*: abolition of the cautionary rule in sexual offences

For many years, the cautionary rule was also applicable to evidence given by complainants in sexual offences cases. However, it has been argued that the cautionary rule is irrational and based on the outdated assumption that complainants in sexual cases, mostly women, were particularly unreliable witnesses. It therefore hampered rather than enhanced decision making.

In 1998, the Supreme Court of Appeal held in *S v Jackson*[37] that the rule was inapplicable. The Court held that the rule was based on 'an irrational and outdated perception' which 'unjustly stereotypes complainants in sexual cases (overwhelmingly women) as particularly unreliable'.[38] The legislature dealt the rule a final blow in section 60 of the Criminal Law

---

31 See ch 43 Identification: visual and voice.
32 1972 (3) SA 766 (A) at 768A–B.
33 [2009] 2 All SA 271 (SCA). See also *S v Mulula* [2014] ZASCA 103 at para 4 and *S v Sithole* [2013] ZASCA 55.
34 PJ Schwikkard and SE van der Merwe *Principles of Evidence* 3 ed (2009) at 548 note 140.
35 *S v Daba* 1996 (1) SACR 243 (E).
36 *R v Kola* 1949 (1) PH H100 (AD).
37 1998 (1) SACR 470 (SCA).
38 1998 (1) SACR 470 (SCA) at 476e–f.

(Sexual Offences and Related Matters) Amendment Act 32 of 2007. This section states that a court may not treat the evidence of complainants in sexual offences cases with caution because of the sexual nature of the offence.[39]

DISCUSSION 41.3

Have *S v Jackson* and section 60 of Act 32 of 2007 changed anything?

It is arguable that, despite the decision in *S v Jackson*[40] and section 60 of the Criminal Law (Sexual Offences and Related Matters) Amendment Act, 2007, the courts in general will continue to treat the uncorroborated testimony of sexual complainants with caution. This is not necessarily because it is a sexual case, but because they would exercise caution in dealing with any uncorroborated evidence where the case is based on one person's word against another. In addition, in serious cases such as rape and murder, the courts may well be motivated to apply caution because of the severe consequences of wrongful convictions. In any event, we should be careful not to elevate the section 60 amendment to a general rule of law, establishing a presumption of credibility in favour of sexual complainants.

Consider whether you agree with the above-mentioned opinions.[41]

41.7 Conclusion

An important aspect of the cautionary rule arises in situations where there are multiple reasons to apply the rule. Examples of such situations are where a child who is a single witness gives evidence of identity or where a child is also an accomplice in a crime. Is it possible to have a situation where a double or triple cautionary rule applies? On the one hand, we must accept that there may be degrees of application of the cautionary rule otherwise the concept of the cautionary rule would be nonsensical. We should also keep in mind that each aspect of the cautionary rule has its own reasons for existence and scope. The cautionary rule may also be satisfied in different ways. In the case of single evidence, the cautionary rule applies because the evidence is not supported. Where an accomplice testifies, his or her evidence must be regarded with caution because he or she has intimate knowledge of the facts of the alleged crime and he or she may have expectations of being given more favourable treatment. The court will, accordingly, have to apply its mind separately to each instance in which the cautionary rule may apply.

---

39   You can also find a more comprehensive discussion of the rule in ch 20 where we examine various categories of evidence specifically applicable in sexual offences cases.
40   1998 (1) SACR 470 (SCA).
41   See too ch 20: Evidence in sexual offences cases.

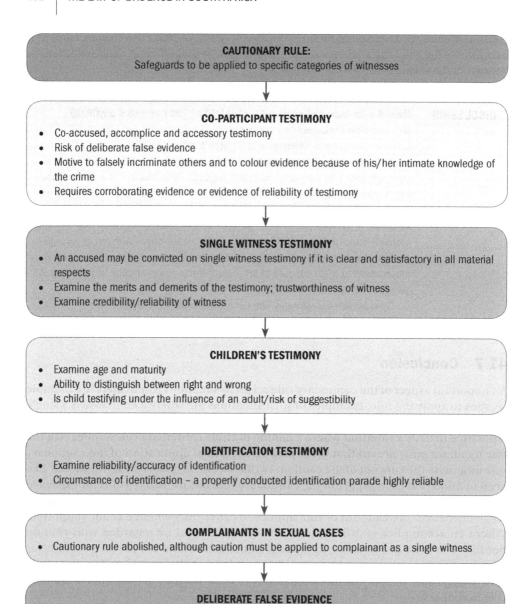

Figure 41.1 The cautionary rule

THIS CHAPTER IN ESSENCE

1 The cautionary rule is a rule of practice which developed through case law and which a court is obliged to follow.
2 The cautionary rule entails that the courts:
   2.1 should follow a cautionary approach when evaluating unreliable evidence
   2.2 should find some safeguard when doing so.

CHAPTER 41 THE CAUTIONARY RULE | **403**

3 The cautionary rule finds specific application in respect of evidence from witnesses who tend to be unreliable.

4 Such witnesses include accomplices, co-accused, single witnesses, children, police traps, the plaintiff in paternity and seduction cases, private detectives, handwriting experts and persons who claim against the estates of deceased persons.

5 The cautionary rule also requires a court to be suspicious or wary of certain categories of evidence either because of the type of witness who is the source of the evidence, such as accomplices, co-accused, single witnesses or children, or because of the subject matter of such evidence, such as identification evidence.

6 In *S v Jackson*,[42] the Court held the cautionary rule to be inapplicable in sexual offences cases because it was based on an irrational and outdated perception which stereotypes complainants in sexual offences cases (mostly women) as particularly unreliable. The rule was eventually abolished by section 60 of the Criminal Law (Sexual Offences and Related Matters) Amendment Act, 2007. This section prohibits a court from treating the evidence of complainants in sexual offences cases with caution due to the sexual nature of the offence.

---

42 1998 (1) SACR 470 (SCA).

Chapter 42

Corroboration

42.1	**Introduction**	**404**
42.2	**Meaning of corroboration**	**405**
42.3	**Process of corroboration**	**405**
42.4	**Characteristics of corroborating evidence**	**405**
	42.4.1 Admissibility	405
	42.4.2 Independent source	405
42.5	**Corroboration and the cautionary rule**	**406**
42.6	**Corroboration of confessions**	**406**
42.7	**Conclusion**	**407**

42.1   Introduction

This chapter examines the definition and process of corroboration, as well as the characteristics that evidence should have to serve as corroboration. It also examines the relationship between corroboration and other evidentiary concepts, such as the cautionary rule and consistency, and concludes with a brief examination of the statutory requirement of corroboration contained in section 209 of the Criminal Procedure Act 51 of 1977.

Corroboration and the cautionary rule are two separate concepts. The cautionary rule requires the court to seek some form of safeguard to reassure itself that the evidence it is relying on is trustworthy. In practice, corroborating evidence is frequently used to satisfy this aspect of the cautionary rule by providing this safeguard. However, they are related in the sense that both concepts have a bearing on the weight or probative value of evidence and both serve as an aid in the fact-finding process. This means that they are generally only applicable when the court is considering evidence that has already been admitted to determine how much weight or value it should be given.[1]

---

1   It may be necessary to return to the discussion of the difference between admissibility and weight of evidence in ch 6.

CHAPTER 42   CORROBORATION   **405**

42.2   Meaning of corroboration

DPP v Kilbourne[2] provided a clear and useful description of what exactly the term 'corroboration' means:

> Corroboration is therefore nothing other than evidence which 'confirms' or 'supports' or 'strengthens' other evidence ... It is, in short, evidence which renders other evidence more probable. If so, there is no essential difference between, on the one hand, corroboration and, on the other, 'supporting evidence'.

In the case of *R v W*[3] in 1949, the Appellate Division set out the nature of corroboration as follows:

> [I]t must be emphasised immediately that by corroboration is meant other evidence which supports the evidence of the complainant, and which renders the evidence of the accused less probable on the issues in dispute.

From the above, it is possible to identify the essential elements of the process of corroboration. Corroboration is a process through which evidence is strengthened or supported by other independent evidence.[4]

42.3   Process of corroboration

Corroboration is a simple process. First, identify the evidence that requires corroboration. Second, identify other sources that may support it. Finally, present the corroborative evidence to the court in the appropriate format. Oral evidence of a witness can be corroborated by oral testimony from another witness, or by handing into court an item of real evidence or even a document that links up with the evidence requiring corroboration. For example, the evidence of a witness who saw a car accident may corroborate the evidence of one of the drivers or it may show that the driver's evidence is unreliable. A signed invoice may corroborate oral evidence about delivery in terms of a contract. The list of possible examples is endless.

42.4   Characteristics of corroborating evidence

The following sections describe the characteristics of corroborating evidence.

42.4.1   Admissibility

To support evidence already admitted, corroboration evidence must itself be admissible. If for any reason the corroboration evidence is inadmissible, for example it is hearsay, evidence about a prior consistent statement or an inadmissible admission, then it may not be used as corroboration.

42.4.2   Independent source

Corroborating evidence must be from an independent source. This means that the corroborating evidence must not be from the same source as the initial evidence. In other words, it has to be independent from the evidence that needs corroborating. This rule is known as the *rule against self-corroboration*. The rationale behind this rule is that evidence

---

2   [1973] 1 All ER 440 at 463A–B.

3   1949 (3) SA 772 (A) at 778–779. Quoted with approval in *S v Gentle* 2005 (1) SACR 420 (SCA) at 430J to 431C and also in *Fletcher and Another v S* [2010] 2 All SA 205 (SCA).

4   See *S v B* 1976 (2) SA 54 (C).

406 THE LAW OF EVIDENCE IN SOUTH AFRICA

from the same source, or which is not independent, is merely a restatement or repetition of the evidence that needs corroborating. It therefore does not provide the court with any information which it does not already know.[5] However, there is a limitation on this rule against self-corroboration – it only applies to oral evidence. Thus a witness is entitled to corroborate his or her oral testimony with real, or even documentary, evidence. For example, a witness who testifies that he or she was assaulted is permitted to produce photographs of the injury he or she suffered, or to show the court the scars of the injury (real evidence).

42.5 Corroboration and the cautionary rule

The cautionary rule is closely related to the process of corroboration because corroborative evidence usually provides the safeguard required by the cautionary rule. However, the terms 'corroboration' and 'the cautionary rule' are not synonymous because there are also significant differences between them. The cautionary rule specifically does not refer to the need to seek corroboration but instead refers to the need to seek 'some form of safeguard'. The notion of a safeguard is a much broader concept than the concept of corroboration. Corroboration is a narrow specific concept that will always provide a safeguard. A safeguard is a much less specific or exacting concept. It can include any form of reassurance that the court chooses, even if such safeguard would never qualify as corroboration in the legal sense.

42.6 Corroboration of confessions

If the State is seeking the conviction of an accused on the sole basis of a confession that the accused has made,[6] then section 209 of the Criminal Procedure Act, 1977 requires that the confession be corroborated in a material respect before the court can convict the accused. In all other cases, corroborating evidence may be useful to strengthen other evidence but it is not a statutory requirement. Section 209 is thus the only instance where corroboration is required by the Criminal Procedure Act, 1977. The purpose of this provision is to provide a safeguard against conviction of an accused based on a false confession. Although false confessions do not occur often, it is nevertheless dangerous to rely on a confession as the only evidence indicating that the accused committed the crime. Such a confession may have been made by mistake, out of ignorance or possibly to protect someone else.

Section 209 provides that an accused may be convicted on the basis of his or her confession. However, it sets out two additional requirements, either of which the State must meet, before the accused can be found guilty. The first alternative is that the confession must be confirmed in a material respect. This focuses on the confession itself and requires that an important aspect of the confession be corroborated. The second alternative requires proof by means of evidence *aliunde* the confession, in other words evidence outside the confession, that the offence in question was indeed committed. This focuses on the offence and requires that the existence of the offence be corroborated.

The first alternative in section 209 requires merely that the confession be 'confirmed in a material respect'. Thus, this requirement may be satisfied by using any form of evidentiary material. This means that admissions, presumptions and judicial notice may also serve as corroborating evidence for this purpose.

---

5 This rule is discussed comprehensively in ch 24 in the context of the rule regarding previous consistent statements.

6 Presuming, of course, that it was made in compliance with all the requirements to render it a valid confession – see ch 50 Admissions, confessions and pointings out.

CHAPTER 42 CORROBORATION | **407**

R v Blyth[7] provides an excellent example of this first alternative. The accused's confession that she had murdered her husband by poisoning him was confirmed in a material respect by the results of an autopsy which showed that he had died of arsenic poisoning. The confirmation need not itself show the commission of the crime, or that the accused is guilty, but it must confirm a material aspect of the confession.

In *S v Mjoli and Another*,[8] the Court held that the contents of the accused's own section 115 not guilty plea statement, as well as his or her answers to questions put to him during section 115 proceedings, may serve as 'confirmation in a material respect' of that same accused's confession.[9] The second alternative in section 209, however, requires proof by means of other evidence. Therefore only evidence, and not the wider category of evidentiary material,[10] will suffice. Any type of evidence, such as oral evidence or circumstantial evidence, may provide such proof.

Even in cases where the court finds that a confession has been confirmed in a material respect, or the court finds the crime to have actually been committed, a conviction will only follow if the court is satisfied that, on the basis of all the evidence, the State has proved its case beyond a reasonable doubt.[11]

42.7 Conclusion

It is important to keep in mind that evidence in a criminal case must be considered in its totality, as emphasised in the recent case of *S v Mia and Another*.[12] Therefore, as is the case with the application of the cautionary rule, corroboration will not alter the standard of proof. However, corroboration may give more weight to the evidence presented by a specific party.

THIS CHAPTER IN ESSENCE

1 Corroboration refers to the process through which the evidence of a witness is confirmed, supported or strengthened by other evidence.
2 Corroborative evidence can take the form of oral evidence, real evidence or documentary evidence.
3 Corroborative evidence must be admissible and come from an independent source before it can support evidence already admitted.
4 Although corroboration and the cautionary rule are two separate concepts, they are related in the sense that they both have a bearing on the weight or probative value of evidence and both serve as an aid in the fact-finding process. Furthermore, corroboration usually provides the solution to the cautionary rule. However, the two concepts are not synonyms as the cautionary rule refers to the need to seek some form of a safeguard, which is a broad concept, while corroboration is a narrow, specific concept that will always provide a safeguard.
5 A confession made by an accused must be corroborated in a material respect before a conviction ensues. In all other cases, corroborating evidence may be useful to strengthen other evidence but it is not a statutory requirement.

---

7 1940 AD 355.
8 1981 (3) SA 1233 (A).
9 This wide interpretation of s 209's 'confirmation in a material respect' requirement has been subject to trenchant academic criticism as it arguably violates the right against self-incrimination – see A Kruger *Hiemstra's Criminal Procedure* (2008) at 24-10(1)–24-11 and PJ Schwikkard and SE van der Merwe *Principles of Evidence* 3 ed (2009) at 532.
10 Evidentiary material is an umbrella term which refers to judicial notice, presumptions, admissions and evidence. Evidence, however, is the term used to describe a narrower concept which includes oral, documentary and real evidence as well as evidence generated by electronic devices as discussed in Part Three.
11 *S v Mbambo* 1975 (2) SA 549 (A) at 554B–C.
12 2009 (1) SACR 330 (SCA); [2009] 1 All SA 447 (SCA).

Chapter 43

Identification: visual and voice

43.1	**Introduction**	**408**
43.2	**Visual identification**	**408**
43.3	**Voice evidence**	**408**
43.4	**Legal rules applicable**	**408**
	43.4.1 Visual identification	409
	43.4.1.1 Reliability of observation	409
	43.4.1.2 Recollection	409
	43.4.1.3 Narration	409
	43.4.2 Identification parades	410
	43.4.3 Dock identification	410
	43.4.4 Photographic identification	410
	43.4.5 Voice identification	410

43.1 Introduction

In both civil and criminal proceedings the alleged wrongdoer may be a person who was previously unknown to the plaintiff or complainant respectively. It then becomes necessary to lead evidence that links the alleged wrongdoer to the wrongdoing. This chapter will examine two means of identifying a wrongdoer.

43.2 Visual identification

Visual identification is the witness's direct evidence that the person against whom the claim is made or who is charged criminally is the same person that the witness saw commit the delict or crime to which the case relates.

43.3 Voice evidence

Voice evidence is direct evidence that identifies the alleged wrongdoer on the basis of the sound of his or her voice as recollected by the witness or as recorded mechanically or electronically.

43.4 Legal rules applicable

In the following sections we will discuss the various legal rules applicable to the types of identification.

43.4.1 Visual identification

Human observation and recollection is fallible. A witness's evidence of a person's appearance must therefore be approached with 'some caution'.[1] It is not sufficient that the witness honestly believes that he or she has identified the right person. We must also test the reliability of the observation. There are a number of factors[2] that must be weighed, one against the other, in light of the totality of the evidence and the probabilities. We will give a description of these factors below.[3]

43.4.1.1 Reliability of observation

The following factors influence the reliability of the witness's observation:
- *The strength of the witness's eyesight and whether he or she wears prescription glasses:* If so, we must establish whether the witness was wearing them at the time.
- *The circumstances in which the observation occurred:* These include the state of the light; the witness's distance from the alleged wrongdoer; the witness's vantage point, for example out in the open, behind a bush, out of the window of a moving bus, from behind or the side, and also whether the person was running, moving or part of a crowd; and the length of time of the observation.
- *Any preconceptions that the witness may have:* There is a danger that a witness's impression may be distorted by his or her prejudices and preconceptions. The witness may, for instance, believe that persons who belong to a certain class have specific characteristics.
- *The witness's state of mind:* This includes considerations such as whether the witness had particular reason to notice or whether his or her attention was focused elsewhere. Shock may also distort recollection.
- *The distinctiveness of the person's appearance:* This includes, in particular, any distinguishing features such as identifying marks, facial features, clothing and deformities.

43.4.1.2 Recollection

Recollection is influenced by factors such as:
- the age of the witness
- whether the person identified had striking features
- the length of the time since the observation
- whether the witness was shown photographs of the suspect or saw them in a newspaper that may have influenced him or her.

43.4.1.3 Narration

Narration refers to whether the witness can give a clear and honest account of what he or she saw.

---

1 *S v Mthetwa* 1972 (3) SA 766 (A) at 768A. 'Because of the fallibility of human observation, evidence of identification is approached by the courts with some caution'.
2 For another comprehensive listing of the factors that the court takes into account, see *S v Mthetwa* 1972 (3) SA 766 (A) at 768.
3 *R v Mputing* 1960 (1) SA 785 (T).

43.4.2 Identification parades

We must also treat identification parades with caution because of the high risk of suggestibility and rigging.[4] Section 35(5) of the Constitution requires that evidence must be excluded if it violates any rights in the Bill of Rights to the extent that it renders the trial unfair or it is otherwise detrimental to the administration of justice. Even irregularities that fall short of justifying exclusion of the evidence under this section may lead to the lessening of the weight of the evidence.[5] Take care to ensure that the persons on parade are of a similar height, build, age and appearance, including clothing, and that the witness does not see the participants before the parade. Where there are many suspects, several parades should be held. As an additional precaution, the witness should be told to identify the suspect 'if such a person is on parade'.

43.4.3 Dock identification

The identification of a wrongdoer in court carries little weight unless it confirms an independent prior identification. This is because the isolation of the accused in the dock in court directs and focuses the attention of any witness and is tantamount to pointing out the accused for identification. However, it is not inadmissible.[6]

43.4.4 Photographic identification

Photographs may be used to identify a possible suspect or to confirm the identity of a suspect. However, this may reduce the value of a subsequent identification of a suspect on an identity parade as it is possible that the witness will make this identification on the basis of the photographs and not on his or her recollection of the scene.

43.4.5 Voice identification

Voice identification can be made in two ways. Qualified experts can make voice identification based on a comparison of voice recordings. Alternatively, voice identification can be made by voice identification parades where a witness is asked to identify the suspect from a number of persons based on the sound of the suspect's voice. These parades have been described as 'silly' because the suspect can easily disguise his or her voice.[7] We should thus approach such evidence with caution.[8]

THIS CHAPTER IN ESSENCE

1 Visual identification refers to the direct evidence of a witness who saw the person against whom the delictual claim is made or who is charged criminally with committing the crime.
2 Before admitting visual identification evidence, we must show that:
  2.1 the witness's observation is reliable
  2.2 the witness's recollection was not influenced by other factors
  2.3 the witness can give a clear and honest account of what he or she saw.

---

4 *R v Kola* 1949 (1) PH H100 (A).
5 *S v Bailey* 2007 (2) SACR 1 (C) at para 44.
6 For more, see PJ Schwikkard and SE van der Merwe *Principles of Evidence* 3 ed (2009) at 119 and 548.
7 *S v M* 1963 (3) SA 183 (T).
8 *S v M* 1972 (4) SA 361 (T).

CHAPTER 43   IDENTIFICATION: VISUAL AND VOICE | **411**

3   Evidence collected during an identification parade must be excluded if it violates any rights in the Bill of Rights to the extent that it renders the trial unfair or is otherwise detrimental to the administration of justice.
4   The identification of a wrongdoer in court carries little weight unless it confirms an independent prior identification.
5   Photographs may be used to identify a possible suspect or to confirm the identity of a suspect.
6   Voice evidence refers to the identification of an alleged wrongdoer on the basis of the sound of his or her voice. We should approach this evidence with caution due to the inherent danger of the suspect disguising his or her voice.

Chapter 44

Circumstantial evidence

44.1	Introduction	412
44.2	Circumstantial evidence in criminal proceedings	412
44.3	Circumstantial evidence in civil proceedings	414

44.1 Introduction

We may prove facts in issue either by direct evidence or by indirect evidence. We also refer to indirect evidence as circumstantial evidence. Circumstantial evidence is not provided by the direct testimony of eyewitnesses, but from associated facts from which we may infer the facts in issue. Circumstantial evidence is therefore often described as evidence that requires a court to draw inferences or conclusions.[1]

An example of direct evidence would be where a witness testifies that he was present in a room where he saw the accused point a gun at and shoot the deceased. If the witness instead testifies that he was standing outside the room where the body of the deceased was subsequently found when he heard a shot and saw the accused emerge with a gun in his hand, this would be circumstantial evidence linking the accused to the killing of the deceased.

Although it may seem as though circumstantial evidence is weaker than direct evidence, this is not always the case.[2] Sometimes the silent evidence speaks the loudest. For example, in a bank robbery, the fingerprint lifted from a deposit slip that the robber was seen handling before the robbery may be regarded as stronger evidence of his presence at the robbery than the direct identification evidence of the bank teller. There will, however, also be cases in which the inference will be less compelling and direct evidence more trustworthy.[3]

44.2 Circumstantial evidence in criminal proceedings

The danger with circumstantial evidence is that there may be other inferences that can be drawn from the facts. In the murder example above, there could have been another possible explanation for the accused emerging from the room, where the deceased was found, with a smoking gun in his hand. He could perhaps have witnessed the deceased commit suicide by shooting himself and may then have picked up the gun, for example, to ensure that it was not stolen while on his way to call an ambulance.

---

1 PJ Schwikkard and SE van der Merwe *Principles of Evidence* 3 ed (2009) at 21.
2 *S v Reddy and Others* 1996 (2) SACR 1 (A) at 8I quoting *Best on Evidence* 10 ed para 297: 'Even two articles of circumstantial evidence, though each taken by itself weigh but as a feather, join them together, you will find them pressing on a delinquent with the weight of a mill-stone ...'. See also *S v Shabalala* 1966 (2) SA 297 (A) at 299.
3 *S v Mcasa and Another* 2005 (1) SACR 388 (SCA) at para 8.

CHAPTER 44   CIRCUMSTANTIAL EVIDENCE | **413**

To reduce the likelihood of an error, certain rules have been developed for the evaluation of circumstantial evidence. In the case of *R v Blom*,[4] the Court laid down two 'cardinal rules of logic':

1.   **The inference sought to be drawn must be consistent with all the proved facts. If it is not, then the inference cannot be drawn.**
2.   **The proved facts should be such that they exclude every reasonable inference from them save the one sought to be drawn. If they do not exclude [all] other reasonable inferences, then there must be a doubt whether the inference sought to be drawn is correct.[5]**

The reason why the proved facts must exclude other reasonable inferences in the second rule is that in criminal cases the required level of proof is beyond a reasonable doubt. This does not mean that if the second rule is satisfied, the accused will necessarily be convicted although this will usually be the case. Even where the court may draw a reasonable inference to the exclusion of all other reasonable inferences, it must nevertheless assess that inference to be persuasive beyond a reasonable doubt before it can rely on the inference to sustain a criminal conviction. The case below provides an example of where these rules were applied to two separate charges, theft of a motor vehicle and theft of copper cable, with a different outcome.

Godla v S

In *Godla v S*[6] the complainant's truck and some copper cable in a storeroom were stolen from his farm. The following day he found the truck near a neighbouring farm with the appellant and two others cleaning the copper cable nearby. All three ran away when they saw the complainant. There was no direct evidence linking the appellant to either theft.

The Court found that the circumstantial evidence did not conclusively point to the appellant's guilt beyond reasonable doubt in respect of the theft of the truck. There was a possibility that another person, including the owner of the neighbouring farm, those who had fled or others not found at the scene could have stolen the truck and abandoned it for unknown reasons.

In respect of the copper wire, the appellant claimed he was doing nothing wrong but was just waiting for the farm owner to return. The Court found the appellant guilty on this charge based on the circumstantial evidence.

The value of circumstantial evidence does not lie in each individual piece, as each on its own might be easily explained away, but in the combination of all the separate pieces viewed together. In *Godla v S*,[7] the Court described this process as follows:

> **In principle the court, which has to deal with circumstantial evidence, must not only look at the evidence of the State or of the accused in isolation but it must consider the cumulative effect of the circumstantial evidence in the case.**

Therefore, when weighing up circumstantial evidence, it is important that all the pieces of evidence are taken into account together as even one piece that does not fit with a possible

---

4   1939 AD 188.
5   *R v Blom* 1939 AD 188 at 202–203.
6   (A98/2009) [2011] ZAFSHC 46.
7   (A98/2009) [2011] ZAFSHC 46 (3 March 2011) at para 9. See also *Nxumalo v S* [2010] 1 ALL SA 325 (SCA).

414 THE LAW OF EVIDENCE IN SOUTH AFRICA

inference will render that inference inapplicable. In *S v Reddy and Others*,[8] the Court emphasised the importance of assessing the evidence as a whole by stating that:

> In assessing circumstantial evidence one needs to be careful not to approach such evidence upon a piece-meal basis and to subject each individual piece of [such] evidence to a consideration of whether it excluded the reasonable possibility that the explanation given by the accused is true. The evidence needs to be considered in its totality.

There are many circumstances that may create inferences of an accused's guilt, including:
- the accused fleeing from the scene as in the above example
- the accused's resistance to arrest
- the accused's presence at the time and place of the crime
- the general conduct of the accused.

Much scientific evidence is circumstantial because it calls for the court to draw an inference from it. This is also true of fingerprints, which are usually used to tie the accused to some object or to the scene of the crime.

44.3 Circumstantial evidence in civil proceedings

The onus of proof in civil proceedings is on a balance of probabilities. This is a lower standard of proof than that applied in criminal proceedings. The second rule in *R v Blom* is therefore not applicable as the court need only choose the *most reasonable* inference that corresponds with the proved facts and not the *only reasonable* inference. As a result, the rule for civil cases is that:

> The proved facts should be such as to render the inference sought to be drawn more probable than any other reasonable inference. If they allow for another more or equally probable inference, the inference sought to be drawn cannot prevail.[9]

CIRCUMSTANTIAL EVIDENCE		
Indirect evidence	The court must draw an inference from the circumstantial evidence about the facts in issue – based on a number of rules of logic set out in *R v Blom*	
CRIMINAL PROCEEDINGS		**CIVIL PROCEEDINGS**
Two cardinal rules of logic: 1) The inference sought to be drawn about the fact in issue must be consistent with all the proved facts; 2) The inference drawn must be the only inference that can be drawn from the proved facts. (i.e. the proved facts must be such that they exclude every reasonable inference from them save the one sought to be drawn) ▪ establishes proof beyond a reasonable doubt		1) The inference sought to be drawn must be consistent with all the proved facts; but 2) It is sufficient if it is the most probable inference from amongst several inferences. ▪ establishes proof on a balance of probabilities

Figure 44.1   Circumstantial evidence

---

8   1996 (2) SACR 1 (A) at 8C–G.
9   *Macleod v Rens* 1997 (3) SA 1039 (E) at 1049B–C.

THIS CHAPTER IN ESSENCE

1 Circumstantial evidence refers to indirect or associated facts from which the court must draw inferences or conclusions.
2 When evaluating circumstantial evidence in criminal proceedings, the following rules should be observed:
   2.1 Any inferences must be consistent with the proved facts. If not, the inference cannot be drawn.
   2.2 The proved facts must exclude every reasonable inference except the one sought to be drawn.
   2.3 The pieces of evidence should not be viewed in isolation but taken into account together.
3 The rule for evaluating circumstantial evidence in civil proceedings is that the proved facts must render the inference sought to be drawn more probable than any other reasonable inference. If there is another more or equally probable inference, the inference sought to be drawn cannot prevail.

Chapter 45

Demeanour

45.1	**Introduction**	**416**
	45.1.1 Appearance	416
	45.1.2 Manner of testifying	416
	45.1.3 Other factors	416
45.2	**Legal rules applicable**	**417**
	45.2.1 Fallibility of demeanour	417
	45.2.2 Trial court's observations	417

45.1　Introduction

One of the things that the court can take into account to assist in determining the credibility of a witness is the demeanour of the witness. The demeanour of a witness is how the witness behaves in the witness box. Demeanour comprises a number of different factors including, but not limited to, those discussed below.

45.1.1　Appearance

In considering the witness's appearance, the court will look at how the witness appears in the witness box in respect of the image he or she projects and the behaviour the witness exhibits.

45.1.2　Manner of testifying

In assessing the witness's manner of testifying, the court may consider a few questions. Was the witness confident? Did he or she speak clearly and without hesitation? Was the witness evasive? How did the witness react to awkward questions? Did the witness fidget nervously? Did the witness have a nervous facial tic? Did the witness stammer? Did the witness make ready concessions or was he or she evasive or sarcastic?

45.1.3　Other factors

A court will also consider the witness's character, personality, the overall impression he or she creates and 'a thousand other considerations' that 'cumulatively contribute to shaping demeanour'.[1]

1　*Cloete NO and Others v Birch R and Another* 1993 (2) PH F17 (ECD) at 51 quoted in *S v Shaw* [2011] ZAKZPHC 32: AR 342/10 (1 August 2011) at para 78.

45.2 Legal rules applicable

The legal rules applicable to demeanour are discussed below.

45.2.1 Fallibility of demeanour

The usefulness of demeanour as an aid to determining the truthfulness of a witness has limitations. Judicial officers are not necessarily trained experts and it is dangerous to assume that all triers of fact have the ability to interpret correctly the behaviour of witnesses.[2] It is possible that a crafty witness may simulate an honest demeanour while an honest witness may be shy or nervous, thus giving the impression of dishonesty.

Where different cultures are involved or where the evidence is interpreted from one language to another, the court must take particular care. To someone from one culture a witness who speaks in a low voice and avoids looking directly at the questioner may be seen as being shifty and dishonest. However, to someone from another culture this behaviour may be considered to be a sign of deference and respect.

The court should not rely on demeanour alone but should see it as merely a factor in determining credibility. The court should consider demeanour along with other relevant factors, including the probability of the witness's story, the reasonableness of his or her conduct, the witness's memory, the consistency of the witness's version and his or her interest in the matter. It is an irregularity for a court to base a decision on demeanour alone without considering the probabilities.[3]

45.2.2 Trial court's observations

An appeal court will generally be reluctant to interfere with the observations of a trial court regarding demeanour because, as the Constitutional Court pointed out in *President of RSA and Others v Sarfu and Others*:

> The trial court sees and hears the witness testifying and is thus able to evaluate how a witness responds to questions and produces answers. This immediate relationship between witness and trier of fact enables the latter to assess the evidence in the light of the behaviour and conduct of the witness while testifying, whereas the court of appeal is restricted to the written record of the witness's oral testimony.[4]

However, the Court cautioned that the advantages the trial court enjoys should not be overemphasised 'lest the appellant's right of appeal becomes illusory'.[5] The Court applied the dictum from *R v Dhlumayo and Another*[6] to the effect that where there is a misdirection on fact by the trial judge, the appellate court is then able to disregard his or her findings on fact (even though based on credibility, in whole or in part) and come to its own conclusion.

In *S v Robiyana and Others*,[7] the High Court pointed out that a court is not obliged to accept the evidence of a witness purely because the court was unable to make an adverse demeanour finding in respect of the witness or even if the demeanour of the witness was good. It concluded that references to demeanour should only back up conclusions reached by an objective assessment of the facts.

---

2 *President of RSA and Others v Sarfu and Others* 2000 (1) SA 1 (CC) at 79.
3 *Medscheme Holdings (Pty) Ltd and Another v Bhamjee* 2005 (5) SA 339 (SCA) at para 14.
4 *President of RSA and Others v SA Rugby Football Union and Others* 2000 (1) SA 1 (CC) at 79.
5 Ibid. at 77.
6 1948 (2) SA 677 (A).
7 2009 (1) SACR 104 (Ck).

418 THE LAW OF EVIDENCE IN SOUTH AFRICA

The trial magistrate or judge should also properly motivate his or her credibility findings in favour of or against the witnesses.[8]

THIS CHAPTER IN ESSENCE

1   When determining the credibility of a witness, the court will consider the demeanour of the witness.
2   When evaluating a witness's demeanour, the court will pay attention to the following:
　2.1   the appearance of the witness in the witness box
　2.2   the manner in which he or she testifies
　2.3   various other factors such as the witness's character and personality.
3   If the court bases a decision on demeanour alone without considering these factors, it is considered to be an irregularity.
4   Generally, appeal courts are reluctant to interfere with a trial court's observations on a witness's demeanour. However, appeal courts can deviate from this approach where there was a misdirection on fact by the trial judge or where the trial court was unable to make an adverse demeanour finding in respect of the witness.

---

8   *S v J* 1998 (2) SA 984 (SCA) at 1006.

Chapter 46

Assessment of mendacity

46.1 Introduction	419
46.2 Means of assessing mendacity	419
46.3 Legal rules applicable	420

46.1 Introduction

Mendacity is, quite simply, the tendency to be untruthful or to lie. One of the aims of the law of evidence is to present the truth and to ensure that witnesses tell the truth to the presiding officer to enable him or her to arrive at a just decision. An element of the process in doing so is to eliminate whatever is not the truth. Thus, establishing whether a witness is lying and, if so, what effect this is going to have on the evidence presented is an important aspect of the presentation of evidence.

46.2 Means of assessing mendacity

There are scientific means available, such as polygraph testing and functional magnetic resolution, for establishing whether someone might be lying.[1] **Polygraph** testing is based on the recording of physiological functions while functional magnetic resolution records brain activity.[2] These scientific means are not relied on in courts where the primary tool for establishing whether a witness is lying is cross-examination. As Wigmore remarked:

> Cross-examination is the greatest legal engine ever invented for the discovery of truth .... 'You can do anything,' said Wendell Phillips, 'with a bayonet – except sit upon it.' A lawyer can do anything with cross-examination – if he is skillful enough not to impale his own cause upon it.[3]

Wigmore's enthusiasm for cross-examination as a tool for uncovering the truth is perhaps misplaced. Cross-examination[4] aims to test the reliability, credibility, powers of observation and recall of a witness. We can also use it to explore the inherent probabilities or

---

1 See ch 53 on polygraphs where it is pointed out that polygraphs merely establish whether the respondent has provided an abnormal response (in comparison to the respondent's other responses) to a question which might possibly, among other possible interpretations, be interpreted to argue that the respondent was not truthful in her or his response.
2 See ch 53 Polygraphs and voice-stress analysers.
3 JH Wigmore *Wigmore on Evidence* 3 ed, Vol. 5 (1940) at para 1367, p. 29.
4 See ch 30 Cross-examination.

420 | THE LAW OF EVIDENCE IN SOUTH AFRICA

improbabilities of a version.[5] There are many other means of establishing whether a witness is mendacious.[6]

46.3 Legal rules applicable

A court should not be too quick to assume that someone is lying because of apparent contradictions in their evidence:

> It is not the case that lack of consistency between witnesses affords any basis for an adverse finding on their credibility. Where contradictory statements are made by different witnesses, obviously at least one of them is erroneous, but one cannot, merely from the fact of the contradiction, say which one. It follows that an argument based only on a list of contradictions between witnesses leads nowhere so far as veracity is concerned. The argument must go further, and show that one of the witnesses is lying. It may be that the court is unable to say where the truth lies as between the contradictory statements, and that may affect the question of whether the onus of proof has been discharged: but that has nothing to do with the veracity of the witnesses.[7]

Contradictions can relate to other proved facts, the evidence of other witnesses and the witness's own earlier evidence or statements. Where there is a contradiction, we can only say that one statement is erroneous but we may not be able to identify which one. An error in itself does not establish a lie. As the witness is human, he or she may merely be making a mistake. The circumstances for mendacity must be such that there is no possibility of an honest mistake. Even where the witness has been shown to be deliberately lying on one point, this does not lead to the conclusion that his or her evidence on another point cannot safely be relied on.[8] Not every error made by a witness will affect his or her credibility. In each case the court has to make an evaluation, taking into consideration the nature of the contradictions, their number and importance, and their bearing on other parts of the witness's evidence.[9]

Where the statement made by one witness contradicts that made by another witness, this goes to show only that one of the statements is erroneous. We cannot draw a conclusion as to the credibility of either of the witnesses. It is necessary to show which witness is lying.

Where a witness contradicts his or her own earlier statement, the court must consider the following factors:
- the manner in which the earlier statement was taken down
- whether there were language and cultural differences between the witness and the person taking the statement down
- the quality of any translation
- whether the witness was given the opportunity to explain the discrepancies.[10]

---

5 See ch 39 Inherent probabilities.
6 For some of the other devices and methods used, see ch 38 Creditworthiness: credibility and reliability, ch 39 Inherent probabilities, ch 40 Contradictions and discrepancies, and ch 55 Demeanour.
7 HC Nicholas 'The credibility of witnesses' (1985) 102(1) *South African Law Journal* 32 at 35–36.
8 *S v Oosthuizen* 1982 (3) SA 571 (T) at 577B–D.
9 *S v Oosthuizen* 1982 (3) SA 571 (T) at 576G–H.
10 *S v Govender and Others* 2006 (1) SACR 322 (E).

CHAPTER 46   ASSESSMENT OF MENDACITY | **421**

Where an accused is proved to be lying, this in itself does not mean that the accused necessarily committed the offence. In *S v Burger and Others*,[11] the Court stated that untruthful evidence did not fill the gaps in the State's case and thereby lead to a finding of guilt. The State is required to provide evidence linking the accused to the crime. In the past, prosecutors often used the case of *R v Mlambo*[12] to support the proposition that if an accused chose to lie, he or she could not receive the benefit of other possible explanations. As was pointed out in *S v Campos*[13] the dicta relied on from *R v Mlambo* was actually the minority judgment. The courts now are more inclined to guard against the idea that a party should lose his or her case as a penalty for perjury or mendacity.

The Court in *S v Mtsweni*[14] set out the approach to be taken in respect of a lying witness in the following way. While lying is a factor that a court may take into consideration in drawing inferences of guilt, the court should not place too much weight on it. It is necessary to take into account, *inter alia*:

- the nature, extent and materiality of the lies and whether they necessarily indicate an awareness of guilt
- the witness's age, development level, cultural and social position insofar as they provide an explanation for the lies
- possible reasons why people lie, for example to provide a more plausible story than what actually happened
- the possibility that the truth was denied out of fear of being linked to the crime in any way at all, however trivial.[15]

It is a common fallacy that because one party to a dispute is found to be lying, the other party is presumed to be telling the truth. However, 'the rejection of the testimony of a witness does not necessarily establish the truth of the contrary.'[16]

THIS CHAPTER IN ESSENCE

1   Although cross-examination is the primary tool for establishing a witness's mendacity or tendency to be untruthful, there are also many other means of establishing whether a witness is mendacious.
2   Contradictions in a witness's evidence are not necessarily an indication of the witness's mendacity as contradictions can also relate to other proved facts, the evidence of other witnesses and the witness's own earlier evidence or statements.
3   Where the statements of different witnesses contradict each other, no conclusion can be drawn as to the credibility of either of them as this merely shows that one of the statements is erroneous.
4   When considering lying as a factor in drawing inferences of guilt, the court should also consider the following:
    4.1   the nature, extent and materiality of the lies and whether they indicate an awareness of guilt
    4.2   personal characteristics of the accused
    4.3   the reasons for the lies
    4.4   the possibility that the witness lied out of fear of being linked to the crime.

---

11   2010 (2) SACR 1 (SCA).
12   1957 (4) SA 727 (A) at 738B–E.
13   2002 (1) SACR 233 (SCA).
14   1985 (1) SA 590 (A).
15   *S v Mtsweni* 1985 (1) SA 590 (A) at 593I–594D.
16   PJ Schwikkard and SE van der Merwe *Principles of Evidence* 3 ed (2009) at 536. See also *R v Weinberg* 1939 AD 71 at 80 and *S v M* 2006 (1) SACR 135 (SCA) at para 281.

Chapter 47

Failure to testify

47.1 Introduction 422

47.2 Legal rules applicable 422
    47.2.1 Criminal proceedings 422
    47.2.2 Civil proceedings 424

47.1 Introduction

In a case where a party or the State has placed evidence before the court and that evidence is sufficient to provide a *prima facie* case, there is usually an evidentiary burden to provide rebutting evidence to avoid the preliminary conclusion of liability or guilt from becoming final. We use the term 'failure to testify' to describe the decision and subsequent conduct of a party or accused not to testify in support of their own case or defence. The word 'failure' itself suggests that a negative inference can be attached to the fact that a party or the accused does not testify. However, this is not necessarily the case.

47.2 Legal rules applicable

A discussion of the legal rules applicable to both criminal and civil proceedings will follow below.

47.2.1 Criminal proceedings

The right to silence is firmly rooted in both the common law and statute.[1] In terms of section 35(1)(*a*) of the Constitution, a person has the right to remain silent when arrested. When it comes to giving evidence, sections 35(3)(*h*) and 35(3)(*j*) add the rights to be presumed innocent, to remain silent and not to testify during the proceedings. There may, however, still be consequences that flow from the accused's failure to testify. If there is evidence of such a nature that it would result in a conviction if left unchallenged, the failure to testify may lead to the conclusion that there is sufficient evidence to convict the accused. The Supreme Court of Appeal in *S v Mdlongwa*[2] explained this as follows:

> Where there is direct evidence implicating an accused in the commission of an offence, the prosecution case is *ipso facto* strengthened where such evidence is uncontroverted due to the failure of the accused to testify.

---

1   *Osman and Another v Attorney-General, Transvaal* 1998 (4) SA 1224 (CC).
2   2010 (2) SACR 419 (SCA) at para 25.

CHAPTER 47 FAILURE TO TESTIFY | 423

The right not to testify was also considered by the Constitutional Court in *S v Boesak*[3] where it concluded that:

> If there is evidence calling for an answer, and an accused person chooses to remain silent in the face of such evidence, a court may well be entitled to conclude that the evidence is sufficient in the absence of an explanation to prove the guilt of the accused. Whether such a conclusion is justified will depend on the weight of the evidence.

Note, however, that an accused's decision to remain silent is not necessarily a factor that the court will take into account when making a decision regarding the guilt of the accused. However, in certain circumstances, it may appear as though the court has considered it as a factor. This certainly seemed to be the case in the past where Holmes JA, in *S v Mthetwa*,[4] stated:

> Where, however, there is direct *prima facie evidence* implicating the accused in the commission of the offence, his failure to give evidence, *whatever his reason may be* for such failure, in general *ipso facto* tends to strengthen the State case, because there is nothing to gainsay it and therefore less reason for doubting its credibility or reliability ...[5]

The constitutional right not to be compelled to testify would be infringed if an adverse inference[6] could be drawn against an accused who chooses to remain silent. This is because the threat of an adverse inference would place indirect pressure on an accused to testify. This was comprehensively addressed in *S v Brown en 'n Ander*,[7] in which the Court set out the following five principles relating to this issue:

1. No adverse inference can be drawn because of the refusal, itself, to testify.[8]
2. If there is an uncontroverted *prima facie* case against the accused, the accused's silence is not a 'fact' and has no probative value.[9]
3. The court must decide only on whether the *prima facie* case alone should harden into proof beyond reasonable doubt.[10]
4. An accused's silence cannot prevent logical inferences being drawn from an uncontradicted State case.[11]
5. An accused's silence is thus not a factor or a piece of evidence itself and therefore no indirect compulsion to testify exists.[12]

---

3   2001 (1) SA 912 (CC) at para 24.
4   1972 (3) SA 766 (A) at 769A-E.
5   This was interpreted to mean that an accused's silence in such circumstances was a factor that could strengthen the State's case. However, see the comments in *S v Brown en 'n Ander* 1996 (2) SACR 49 (NC) at 63B-C where Buys J stated that he believes that Holmes JA merely meant, 'niks meer sê nie, as dat die direkte getuienes van die Staat onweerspraak staan en dat daar gevolglik minder rede is om daardie getuienes te betwyfel.'
6   An 'adverse inference' in this context refers to cases where the court makes a negative finding against the accused solely on the basis of his or her failure to testify, irrespective of the effect this failure to testify has on the strength of the State's case. In other words, the court is in effect saying: 'You refused to testify - therefore you must have something to hide and are probably guilty.'
7   1996 (2) SACR 49 (NC).
8   *S v Brown en 'n Ander* 1996 (2) SACR 49 (NC) at 60F-G.
9   *S v Brown en 'n Ander* 1996 (2) SACR 49 (NC) at 63H-I and see also R v Sole 2004 (2) SACR 599 (LesHC) at 684F-G.
10 *S v Brown en 'n Ander* 1996 (2) SACR 49 (NC) at 61H-I.
11 *S v Brown en 'n Ander* 1996 (2) SACR 49 (NC) at 61I-63C.
12 *S v Brown en 'n Ander* 1996 (2) SACR 49 (NC) at 64I-65G. See also *Osman and Another v Attorney-General, Transvaal* 1998 (4) SA 1224 (CC) at 22.

424 | THE LAW OF EVIDENCE IN SOUTH AFRICA

These five principles are not independent selfstanding rules as a court will *always* consider the *effect* on the State's case of the absence of any contradictory evidence due to the accused's failure to testify. For example, if the accused fails to testify, it may be that the State's case is so weak that a conviction cannot be justified. In other cases, however, crucial evidence by State witnesses may stand unchallenged and may therefore be relied on by the court to support a conviction.[13]

The court in *S v Tandwa and Others*[14] provides a fitting summary of the legal position applicable to a failure to testify in criminal proceedings:

> An accused has the constitutional right to remain silent but this choice must be exercised decisively as 'the choice to remain silent in the face of evidence suggestive of complicity must, in an appropriate case, lead to an inference of guilt'.

47.2.2 Civil proceedings

Although the onus in a civil claim is different from that in a criminal case, the effect of a defendant failing to testify is similar to that of an accused failing to do so. The court may find against the defendant on the basis of the evidence led.

An example can be found in the much-followed case of *Galante v Dickinson*.[15] This case involved a civil claim for damages arising from a motor vehicle accident in which the defendant failed to testify. Schreiner JA stated that an inference is to be drawn if a party himself fails to give evidence:

> In the case of the party himself who is available, as was the defendant here, it seems to me that the inference is, at least, obvious and strong that the party and his legal advisers are satisfied that, although he was obviously able to give very material evidence as to the cause of the accident, he could not benefit and might well, because of the facts known to himself, damage his case by giving evidence and subjecting himself to cross-examination.[16]

According to Schreiner JA, if the defendant fails to testify, the Court is entitled to choose the explanation that favours the plaintiff in the case where there are two more or less equally plausible explanations on the evidence.

However, the defendant's failure to testify will only count against him and in favour of the plaintiff where the evidence led by the plaintiff is sufficient to lead to the conclusion that the plaintiff's version is, on a balance of probabilities, the 'more natural, or plausible, conclusion from amongst several conceivable ones, even though that conclusion may not be the only reasonable one'.[17]

The effect of failing to testify will depend on the individual circumstances of every case.[18] The importance of testifying was stressed in *Klaasen v Commission for Conciliation,*

---

13 See *S v Boesak* 2001 (1) SA 912 (CC).

14 2008 (1) SACR 613 (SCA) at 615 I–J.

15 1950 (2) SA 460 (A).

16 *Galante v Dickinson* 1950 (2) SA 460 (A) at 465. The principle is, in fact, often referred to as the Galante rule. '[W]here the defendant was himself the driver of the vehicle the driving of which the plaintiff alleges was negligent and caused the accident, the court is entitled, in the absence of evidence from the defendant, to select out of two alternative explanations of the cause of the accident which are more or less equally open on the evidence, that one which favours the plaintiff as opposed to the defendant.'

17 *Jordaan v Bloemfontein Transitional Local Authority and Another* 2004 (3) SA 371 (SCA) at para 20.

18 See *Olivier v Minister of Safety and Security and Another* 2008 (2) SACR 387 (W) at 393E–F, where the Court held that in the circumstances of the case no adverse inference could be drawn from the failure of a party to give evidence.

Mediation and Arbitration and Others.[19] The Labour Court decided that it was an irregularity for the commissioner not to have warned the applicant of the danger associated with a failure to testify.

In *Beukes v Mutual and Federal Insurance Co Ltd,*[20] a witness was not called to testify even though he had been in Court throughout the trial and was able to testify, and no reason had been put forward for his failure to give evidence. The Court held that his failure to testify led to the inescapable inference that his evidence would have prejudiced the defendant's case.

A legal representative may be reluctant to call his or her client to testify out of a fear that the client may inadvertently make admissions and concessions that fill the gap in the case of another party (or the State), or that the client will create a poor impression in the mind of the court. It is clear that this is a risky tactic and the legal representative would be wise to discuss the possible consequences of such a move with the client.

THIS CHAPTER IN ESSENCE

1   Although an accused has the right to be presumed innocent, to remain silent and not to testify during criminal proceedings, a failure to testify may lead to the conclusion that there is sufficient evidence to secure a conviction. However, an accused's decision to remain silent is not necessarily a factor which the court will take into account when making a decision regarding the guilt of the accused. In fact, the constitutional right not to be compelled to testify can be infringed if an adverse inference is drawn against an accused who remains silent as it places indirect pressure on an accused to testify. Therefore, no adverse inference can be drawn from an accused's failure to testify and his or her silence is not a factor or piece of evidence with probative value.

2   However, an accused's failure to testify cannot prevent a court from concluding that the evidence, in the absence of an explanation by the accused, is sufficient to prove the accused's guilt.

3   The failure to testify in civil proceedings will count against one party in favour of the other party if there is sufficient evidence for the conclusion that the latter party's version is, on a balance of probabilities, the more plausible conclusion from among several conceivable ones. However, the effect of a failure to testify will depend on the individual circumstances of every case.

---

19   [2005] 10 BLLR 964 (LC).
20   1990 NR 105 (HC).

Chapter 48

Judicial notice

48.1 Introduction **426**

48.2 Categories of judicial notice **427**
48.2.1 Notorious facts of general knowledge 427
48.2.2 Facts of local notoriety 428
48.2.3 Facts easily ascertainable 428

48.3 Examples of instances where courts may take judicial notice **428**
48.3.1 The nature of animals 428
48.3.2 Political matters 428
48.3.3 Maps and historical facts 429
48.3.4 Words 429
48.3.5 Scientific instruments 429

48.4 South African law **430**
48.4.1 Common law, legislation and customary international law 430
48.4.2 Foreign law 430
48.4.3 Customs and indigenous law 430
48.4.4 Judicial notice by the Constitutional Court 431

48.5 Legal rules applicable to judicial notice **432**

48.1 Introduction

The parties to a dispute must adduce relevant evidence in respect of any facts required to prove their respective cases at trial. However, there are some facts that it may not be necessary for the parties to prove by way of admitting evidence. Judicial notice is a legal doctrine that allows a fact to be accepted by a judicial officer without proof where it is so notorious or well known that it cannot reasonably be doubted. A judicially noticed fact may be either a fact in issue or an evidentiary fact adduced to show the existence of a fact in issue. These facts may be judicially noticed at trial in order to save time and trial costs, as well to prevent the admission of unnecessary and superfluous evidence.

According to *R v Tager*,[1] it is necessary to distinguish between notorious facts (i.e. facts which are so well known as to be incapable of dispute between reasonably informed persons), of which a court may take judicial notice, and facts which a judge knows simply

---

1 *R v Tager* 1944 AD 339 at 344.

CHAPTER 48   JUDICIAL NOTICE   **427**

through personal observation, on which a court cannot rely. These two parameters are flexible – providing a judge with a wide discretion – and therefore it is impossible to set out a complete list of notorious facts.[2] Also, notorious facts change over time with the advent of new technologies and new social or cultural behaviours. Therefore, no closed list of facts of which a court may take judicial notice can be developed.

It must also be noted that once a court has taken judicial notice of a fact it has the following evidentiary effect at trial:[3]

1. The judicially noticed fact need not be proved and is no longer in issue.
2. For the purpose of ensuring uniformity of decision-making, once a judicially noticed fact is admitted at trial it establishes a binding precedent for all courts.
3. The judicially noticed fact cannot be rebutted but any inferences drawn from the judicially noticed fact may be rebutted during the ordinary course of a trial.

R v Tager held further that judicial notice should be applied with caution by a judicial officer as its application at trial deprives the parties of the opportunity to cross-examine on the judicially noticed fact. The one exception to this rule is that where a judicially noticed fact is drawn from an authorised source the validity, reputation or accreditation of the source material may be critically questioned by a party.

48.2   Categories of judicial notice

Judicial notice may be taken of notorious facts which fall into a number of broad categories.[4] These are (i) facts of general notoriety or well-known facts based on general knowledge, (ii) facts of local notoriety or local facts well-known to reasonably informed persons within the local area or jurisdiction of a particular court, and (iii) facts which may be easily ascertained by reference to authorised sources. In addition judicial notice may be taken of the Law (i.e. established legal principles) as a matter of convenience.

48.2.1   Notorious facts of general knowledge

An example of a notorious fact of general knowledge is the fact that there are 12 months in a year and seven days in a week. Other examples of general notorious facts include the fact that alcohol is an intoxicating substance;[5] South Africa possesses a national and public road network;[6] no two fingerprints are exactly the same;[7] and a court may take judicial notice of the fact that when a set of traffic lights facing in one direction at a right-angled intersection is green the other set of traffic lights is probably red.[8] Another example, which demonstrates the flexible approach of the courts, is that with the advent of democracy and the Constitution, South African citizens feel strongly about politicians appointed to public office.[9]

---

2   *S v Mthimkulu* 1975 (4) SA 759 (A) at 'no hard and fast rule can or should be laid down [as] much will depend upon the facts and circumstances of each individual matter'.
3   DT Zeffertt and AP Paizes *The South African Law of Evidence* 2 ed (2009) at 866–867.
4   Zeffertt and Paizes (2009) at 865; PJ Schwikkard and SE van der Merwe *Principles of Evidence* 3 ed (2009) at 481–482.
5   *R v Masapha* 1958 (3) SA 480 (O).
6   *R v Bikitsha* 1960 (4) SA 181 (E).
7   *R v Morela* 1947 (3) SA 147 (A).
8   *Gomes v Visser* 1971 (1) SA 276 (T); *S v De Lange* 1972 (1) SA 139 (C); *S v Lund* 1987 (4) SA 548 (N).
9   *The Citizen v McBride* 2010 (4) SA 148 (SCA).

48.2.2 Facts of local notoriety

Facts of local notoriety include facts that are notorious among all reasonably well-informed people in the local area or jurisdiction where the court sits. Examples include the fact that a local road passing next to the court is a public road;[10] the location of rivers in a particular place; and that a particular crime is prevalent within the court's jurisdiction. This latter fact may be used for the purposes of sentencing.

48.2.3 Facts easily ascertainable

Facts easily ascertainable are facts that, although not within the general knowledge of reasonably well informed persons, may be readily established through reference to reliable resources such as almanacs, maps, dictionaries and textbooks, etc. Examples include the exact times of sunrise and sunset,[11] the phases of the moon during a month; the times of the tides in a particular area; on which day of the week a particular date falls and facts that are beyond reasonable dispute that may be established from official maps.

48.3 Examples of instances where courts may take judicial notice

It is impossible to set out a defined list of notorious facts which fall into the above three broad categories. Judicial notice may be taken from a wide ambit of well-known facts ranging from notorious facts about crime and social conditions (i.e. that South Africa is a country with high levels of illiteracy, poverty, **corruption** and violent crime) through to notorious facts about financial matters and trade practices (i.e. that inflation causes a depreciation in the value of money; that public companies are incorporated for the purpose of making a profit and that banks charge interest on overdrawn accounts). Listed here are some of the most common examples of notorious and easily ascertainable facts.

48.3.1 The nature of animals

Judicial notice may be taken of the instinctive behaviour of domesticated animals;[12] and that wild animals remain potentially dangerous even when semi-tamed;[13] that scabs is a well-known sheep disease;[14] and that brand marks on cattle do not fade completely.[15] However, a court may not take judicial notice of the fact that ordinary fowls are home-loving birds that do not wander off like other livestock,[16] nor may a judge use his or her personal knowledge to determine the age of an animal.

48.3.2 Political matters

A court may take judicial notice of the existence of a state of war between countries, the type of political system in a specific country; the extent of territorial waters and the constitutional developments that led to the promulgation of an Act. However, where there is any doubt about a political matter such as the relationship between South Africa and another state,

---

10 *R v Adkins* 1955 (4) SA 242 (GW).
11 S 229 of the Criminal Procedure Act 51 of 1977 and s 26 of the Civil Proceedings Evidence Act 25 of 1965 provide that times published in the *Government Gazette* are to be regarded as proof of the exact times of sunrise and sunset.
12 *Parker v Reed* 1904 21 SC 496.
13 *Bristow v Lycett* 1971 (4) SA 223 (RA).
14 *R v Bunana* 1958 (1) SA 573 (E).
15 *R v Maduna* 1946 EDL 334.
16 *S v Soko and Another* 1963 (2) SA 248 (T).

CHAPTER 48 JUDICIAL NOTICE | 429

such as an extradition treaty, the courts will refuse to take judicial notice and require a certificate of explanation from the relevant minister.

48.3.3 Maps and historical facts

A court may take judicial notice of any historical or sociological fact on the bases that these facts are reliably ascertainable from a relevant reference textbook etc. A court may also take judicial notice of information contained in maps and other pictorial images which are easily ascertainable or are of sufficient notoriety. In *Consolidated Diamond Mines of South West Africa Ltd v Administrator, South West Africa*,[17] the Court took judicial notice of various administrative acts made by the German colonial government during its occupation of South-West Africa, now known as Namibia.

48.3.4 Words

The meanings of words used in legislation may be established by reference to authoritative dictionaries.

48.3.5 Scientific instruments

Where a scientific instrument is in common use and its technology has become well known to an ordinary person such a scientific instrument may be judicially noticed on the basis of its general notoriety. Scientific and other instruments such as watches, calculators, photography, X-rays, thermometers, etc. that are in everyday use and which are considered to be reliable and trustworthy by the ordinary person on the street are usually judicially noticed.[18] However, the functioning of complex scientific instruments may only be judicially noticed, according to *S v Mthimkulu*,[19] after examining (i) the nature of the process and instrument involved in a particular case, (ii) the extent to which the evidence of the functioning of such an instrument is challenged, and (iii) the nature of the enquiry and the *facta probanda* in the case. This means that expert testimony must be adduced in order to determine the trustworthiness of the functioning of a complex instrument and the accuracy of its measurements. It is only in exceptional circumstances that the functioning of an instrument will be judicially noticed without the need for expert testimony.

According to *R v Harvey*,[20] judicial notice of evidence of a recording from a scientific instrument depends on whether the instrument is sufficiently well known for its trustworthiness and reliability, and in *S v Fuhri*[21] the court held that the science behind the functioning of a speed trap camera had advanced to such a level of general acceptance that a court could take judicial notice of the photographs and other measurements recorded by it. However, in *S v Bester*[22] it was held that judicial notice could not be taken of a new type of blood-alcohol testing device labelled the Drager Alcotest breath analyser and that the new technology on which this device was based had to be proved by way of expert evidence. The court applied the test set out in *S v Mthimkulu* in reaching its decision.

---

17 1958 (4) SA 572 (A).
18 *S v Strydom* 1978 (4) SA 748 (E).
19 1975 (4) SA 759 (A).
20 1969 (2) SA 193 (RA).
21 1994 (2) SACR 829 (A).
22 2004 (2) SACR 59 (C); *S v Jones* 2004 (2) SACR 59 (C). In *S v Helm* 2015 (1) SACR 550 (WCC), the court found that gas chromatography–mass spectrometry (GC-MS) could not be judicially noticed and the requisite expert testimony had to be called for.

430 | THE LAW OF EVIDENCE IN SOUTH AFRICA

48.4 South African law

Generally, a court may take judicial notice of the common law and indigenous law, including Acts of Parliament, proclamations, regulations and other matters published in the *Government Gazette* as a matter of convenience. A South African court may also take judicial notice of foreign law including customary international law.

48.4.1 Common law, legislation and customary international law

A court may take judicial notice of common law as it would be absurd to call an expert witness to prove the law to a judicial officer. This means that a party's legal representative may only bring a relevant legal point to the notice of the court by way of argument and may not lead evidence in this regard. Similarly, a judicial officer may consult an authoritative legal text on his or her own initiative to understand and interpret a legal point in question. Section 224 of the Criminal Procedure Act read with section 5 of the Civil Proceedings Evidence Act states that judicial notice may be taken of any law or any matter published in the *Government Gazette* or a provincial Official Gazette. Judicial notice can therefore be taken of all Acts of Parliament, provincial parliaments, legislation by municipal and other legislative structures.

Previously, in *Nduli and another v Minister of Justice and others*,[23] it was said that international law was part of South African law but only when the origins of such law could be found in Roman-Dutch law. Section 232 read with section 39(1)(*b*) of the Constitution now states that customary international law is a part of South African law to the extent that it does not conflict with the Constitution, an Act of Parliament or the common law. Similarly, section 233 states that every court must prefer any reasonable interpretation that is consistent with international law. Therefore, judicial notice may be taken of international law as a notorious fact except where it is unclear or in conflict with established South African law.[24]

48.4.2 Foreign law

When the law of a foreign state is necessary for the purpose of comparison with South African law or is relevant to a fact in issue before a South African court, judicial notice may be taken of that foreign law. An obvious example would be the Law of England which forms a significant portion of the common law of evidence as it was frozen on 30 May 1961. Section 39(1)(*c*) of the Constitution states that when interpreting the Bill of Rights a court may have regard to comparable foreign law. When the law of a foreign state is itself in issue a court may in terms of section 1(1) of the Law of Evidence Amendment Act 45 of 1988 take judicial notice thereof to the extent that the foreign law can be readily ascertained and with sufficient certainty. However, where the foreign law is not easily ascertainable or is unclear, expert evidence may be called for, and where reliance is placed on foreign statutory law the relevant foreign statute must be produced for inspection before the court.

48.4.3 Customs and indigenous law

In terms of section 1 of the Law of Evidence Amendment Act a court may take judicial notice of indigenous law as long as it can be readily established with sufficient certainty and

---

23 1978 (1) SA 893 (A).
24 *AZAPO and Others v President of the Republic of South Africa and Others* 1996 (4) SA 671 (CC). See also *S v Petane* 1988 (3) SA 51 (C).

provided that it is not in conflict with public policy or natural justice. Furthermore, section 1(1) makes specific provision for judicial notice to be taken of lobola/bogadi or similar customs.

48.4.4 Judicial notice by the Constitutional Court

In *S v Lawrence; S v Negal; S v Solberg*[25] the Constitutional Court drew a distinction between adjudicative and legislative facts. Judicial notice of legislative facts may be required where a court is faced with questions concerning the constitutional validity of a statute or common law rule based on grounds of public policy which depend on an analysis of social, economic, political or scientific facts. In this regard Rule 31 of the Constitutional Court Rules may be used as a justification for taking judicial notice of these legislative facts.

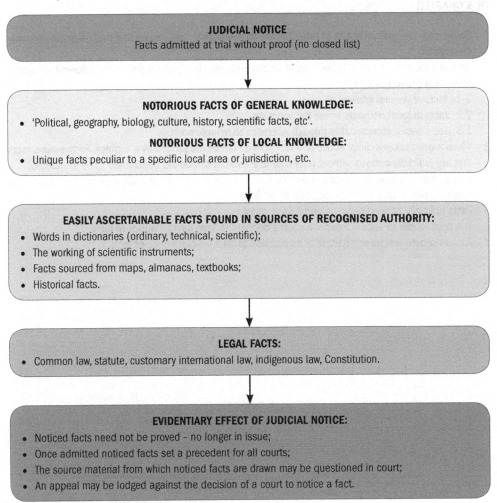

Figure 48.1 Judicial notice

---

25 1997 (4) SA 1176 (CC).

432 | THE LAW OF EVIDENCE IN SOUTH AFRICA

48.5 Legal rules applicable to judicial notice

Facts and materials introduced under judicial notice need not be formally introduced by a witness. Where facts may be judicially noticed without undertaking an inquiry or referring to a reliable source, these are considered to be irrefutable. It is not permissible for a party to lead evidence to disprove these facts. However, where it is necessary to ascertain the facts from a source, evidence may be led disputing the reliability of the source. These facts are considered only to be *prima facie* proof. A party may appeal against a court's decision to take judicial notice of a fact. When deciding to take judicial notice of a fact, the court should first inform the parties of its intention to do so.[26]

THIS CHAPTER IN ESSENCE

1 Courts can take judicial notice of facts that are so notorious or well known that they cannot reasonably be doubted.
2 Although there is no closed list of facts of which courts may take judicial notice, the following categories serve as a broad guideline:
   2.1 facts of general knowledge
   2.2 facts of local notoriety where the court sits
   2.3 facts easily ascertainable through reference to reliable sources.
3 When a court takes judicial notice of a fact, it need not be introduced by a witness. Furthermore, facts that are judicially noticed without reference to a reliable source are considered to be irrefutable.
4 Parties may not lead evidence to disprove facts judicially noticed although a party may dispute the reliability of a source used to ascertain these facts.
5 Facts judicially noticed serve as *prima facie* proof.
6 It is permissible to appeal against a court's decision to take judicial notice of facts.
7 A court should first inform parties of its decision to take judicial notice of facts.

---

26 *S v Heilig* 1999 (1) SACR 379 (W).

Chapter 49

Presumptions

49.1	Introduction	433
49.2	Irrebuttable presumptions of law	434
49.3	Rebuttable presumptions of law	434
49.4	Rebuttable presumptions of fact	435
49.5	Reverse onus statutory presumptions and the Constitution	436
49.6	Examples of presumptions	438
	49.6.1 Rebuttable presumptions of law	438
	49.6.2 Rebuttable presumptions of fact	438
	49.6.3 Other examples of presumptions	438
	49.6.4 Documents	438

49.1 Introduction

Judicial notice is one of the ways evidence may be taken into consideration without anyone testifying about it. Presumptions, by allowing for the admissibility of information without testing it, are another way in which a court accepts facts without the need for parties to lead evidence to prove these facts. This effectively means that the court proceeds directly to an evaluation of the information without first assessing its admissibility. A presumption thus entitles the court to infer, assume or accept that a fact, set of circumstances or state of affairs exists, usually until the contrary is proved. For example, everyone is presumed to be sane unless they are proved to be otherwise. Presumptions, like judicial notice, exist to save time and money, but also reflect policy considerations, as embodied by the presumption of innocence.

Many presumptions exist in common law and many have also been created by statute. Presumptions are traditionally classified into irrebuttable presumptions of law, rebuttable presumptions of law and presumptions of fact.[1] Of these three types, only the rebuttable presumption of law may be regarded as a genuine presumption.

---

1   *Tregea and Another v Godart and Another* 1939 AD 16 at 28 refers to three kinds of presumptions: (i) presumptiones juris et de jure, (ii) presumptiones juris and (iii) presumptiones hominis.

49.2   Irrebuttable presumptions of law

This is a contradiction in terms as irrebuttable presumptions of law are really rules of substantive law formulated to look like rules of evidence.[2] An example of a so-called irrebuttable presumption is that children of seven or younger are presumed to be *doli* and *culpa incapax*, in other words, that they lack the capacity to form the intention to commit a crime. This is really a rule of substantive law which furnishes conclusive proof of the fact presumed and cannot be rebutted.[3]

49.3   Rebuttable presumptions of law

Rebuttable presumptions of law are rules of law that compel the provisional assumption of a fact. They come into operation once some basic fact is proved and stand until contradicting evidence destroys them. According to Wigmore, a rebuttable presumption of law is a genuine rule of law which requires a court to reach a conclusion in the absence of evidence to the contrary.[4] Such a presumption may take the form of a rule of general application, for example the presumption of innocence, or it may compel the provisional assumption of a fact which will stand unless destroyed by countervailing evidence, for example the presumption of law in respect of bigamy created by the language of section 237 of the Criminal Procedure Act 51 of 1977.

Rebuttable presumptions of law have the following effect on the burden of proof:[5]

- First, a rebuttable presumption of law may create a *permissible inference*. In respect of this type of presumption, a court is not compelled to draw such an inference. However, if it chooses to do so, it places a *tactical burden* on the accused who may call for evidence in rebuttal, but is not obliged to do so.
- Second, a rebuttable presumption of law may create a *mandatory conclusion*. Where a court draws a mandatory conclusion, it casts an *evidentiary burden* on the accused who is obliged to call for evidence in rebuttal.
- Third, the drawing of a mandatory conclusion may also have the effect of casting the *primary burden of proof* on the accused in the form of a *reverse onus*.

Whether a rebuttable presumption of law places an evidentiary burden or a legal burden in the form of a reverse onus on the person against whom the presumption operates depends on the language contained in the presumption. For example, in a statutorily defined rebuttable presumption of law, the use of the words 'evidence of a fact shall be *prima facie* proof of' or the words 'in the absence of evidence to the contrary' creates an evidentiary burden. However, when a provision states that 'X has happened unless the contrary has been proved', then a primary burden of proof in the form of a reverse onus rests on the person who is faced with rebutting the presumption.[6]

---

2   *Scagell and Others v Attorney-General, Western Cape and Others* 1997 (2) SA 368 (CC) at para 30.

3   For more on irrebuttable presumptions of law, see Part Two: Basic concepts. The age below which children are presumed *doli incapax* in respect of criminal matters has now been increased to 10 by s 7(1) of the Child Justice Act 75 of 2008.

4   JH Wigmore *Wigmore on Evidence* 3 ed (1940) at s 2491.

5   DT Zeffertt and AP Paizes *The South African Law of Evidence* 2 ed (2009) at 186–187; PJ Schwikkard and SE van der Merwe *Principles of Evidence* 3 ed (2009) at 501–502. See *R v Downey* (1992) (13) Cr 4th 129 (SCC); *S v Zuma and Others* 1995 (2) SA 642 (CC) at para 24.

6   See ch 5 for an analysis of the effect the Constitution has had on reverse onus clauses.

49.4 Rebuttable presumptions of fact

Rebuttable presumptions of fact are inferences that may be drawn from particular factual circumstances. A presumption of fact differs from a presumption of law. First, a presumption of fact, although labelled a presumption, is not a rule of law. It is merely an inference of probability that a court may draw from the available factual evidence before it. In essence, presumptions of fact are merely frequently occurring examples of circumstantial evidence. According to *Arthur v Bezuidenhout and Mieny*:[7]

> There is in truth but one kind of presumption [i.e. a rebuttable presumption of law], and the term presumption of fact should be discarded as useless and confusing.

Second, a presumption of fact has no effect on the primary burden of proof in its true sense. However, it may impose a tactical burden or an evidentiary burden on the person against whom it operates. An example of this type of presumption is a *res ipsa loquitur* situation, meaning the matter, or thing, speaks for itself. According to this presumption of fact, where an accident occurs in a way that does not usually happen unless there is negligence, the court may from the facts draw the inference that there was negligence.[8]

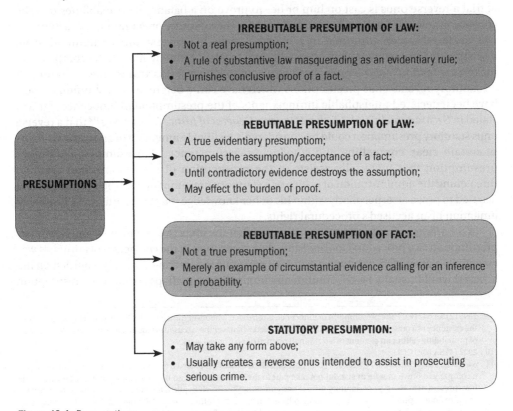

Figure 49.1 Presumptions

---

7   1962 (2) SA 566 (A) at 574 per Ogilvie Thompson JA.
8   *Arthur v Bezuidenhout and Mieny* 1962 (2) SA 566 (A). In *Buthelezi v Ndaba* 2013 (5) SA 437 (SCA) it was noted that the maxim *res ipsa loquitur* seldom applies in determining medical negligence as the complexities of surgery mean that the fact that something went wrong during an operation cannot automatically lead to an inference of negligence.

49.5 Reverse onus statutory presumptions and the Constitution

It is a fundamental principle of criminal proceedings that the presumption of innocence and the right to silence as set out in section 35(3)(*h*) of the Constitution place the primary burden to prove an accused's guilt squarely on the prosecution. This means that the prosecution must prove all the elements of a crime beyond a reasonable doubt before an accused may be convicted. The prosecution is said to carry a fixed primary burden of proof. According to *S v Zuma*[9] and *S v Singo*,[10] to take this burden away from the prosecution and place it on the accused (to prove his or her innocence) would amount to an unjustifiable infringement of the presumption of innocence. It would also infringe on the accused's right to remain silent and the right not to testify at proceedings. It would create the possibility that the accused could be convicted despite the existence of reasonable doubt. In a number of cases the Constitutional Court has had to strike down presumptions set out in various statutes which place a burden of proof on the accused – the so-called reverse onus. For example, section 217(1)(*b*)(ii) of the Criminal Procedure Act states that an informal confession made to a peace officer and reduced to writing before a magistrate is presumed to have been freely and voluntarily made by the accused. Should the accused want to retract the written confession at trial a reverse onus is cast on him or her to prove on a balance of probabilities that the confession was not freely and voluntarily made. The statutory presumption in section 217 was declared unconstitutional in *S v Zuma* as such a reverse onus amounted to an unjustifiable infringement of an accused's right to silence, the right not to be compelled to make a confession and the right not to be a compellable witness against oneself. Although all statutory reverse onus presumptions which have come before the Constitutional Court have been declared unjustifiable infringements of the presumption of innocence,[11] it was stated in *S v Manamela and Another (Director General of Justice Intervening)*[12] that a reverse onus statutory presumption could be considered a justifiable limitation of an accused's rights in certain clear, compelling and convincing circumstances. For example, a statutory presumption that materially assists in the prosecution of serious criminal conduct threatening the administration of justice or a statutory presumption placing a burden on the accused to prove facts peculiarly within his or her knowledge may be regarded as a justifiable limitation of an accused's procedural rights.

In *S v Mbatha; S v Prinsloo*,[13] it was argued that the objective of a reverse onus statutory presumption as a procedural tool assisting the prosecution in the conviction of criminals was essentially a good idea. Although a statutory presumption creating a true legal burden on the accused would usually be constitutionally unjustifiable, perhaps a statutory presumption

---

9   1995 (2) SA 642 (CC) 'the presumption of innocence is infringed whenever the accused is liable to be convicted despite the existence of a reasonable doubt', and it is also infringed whenever the 'accused is required to establish ... on a balance of probabilities either an element of a [criminal] offence or an excuse' at 25.

10   2002 (4) SA 858 (CC).

11   *S v Coetzee and Others* 1997 (3) SA 527 (CC). Section 332(5) of the CPA placed a reverse onus on a director or servant of a company to prove that he or she did not take part in the commission of an offence by the company and could not have prevented it. This type of statutory reverse onus presumption which required the director or servant of the company to prove an exception or defence was found to be an unjustifiable infringement of the presumption of innocence for the same constitutional reasons set out in *S v Zuma* and *S v Singo*. See also *S v Bhulwana; S v Gwadiso* 1996 (1) SA 388 (CC); *S v Mello and Another* 1999 (2) SACR 255 (CC) where various provisions creating reverse onuses in the Drugs and Drug Trafficking Act 140 of 1992 were found to infringe the accused's constitutional rights.

12   2000 (3) SA 1 (CC) 'a reverse onus in the true sense would only be justifiable if the risk and consequences of a wrongful conviction was outweighed by the risk and consequences of guilty persons escaping conviction simply because of a rigid adherence to an absolute watertight presumption of innocence' at 28.

13   1996 (2) SA 464 (CC), s 40(1) of the repealed Arms and Ammunition Act 75 of 1969 where a person in control of premises in which unlicensed guns had been found was required to prove that the guns did not belong to him/ or her was found to be an unconstitutional reverse onus unjustifiably infringing the person's presumption of innocence.

merely placing a reverse onus in the form of an evidentiary burden on the accused could well pass constitutional muster. In *Scagell and Others v Attorney-General, Western Cape and Others*,[14] the court considered section 6(3) of the Gambling Act,[15] a provision which placed a reverse onus in the form of an evidentiary burden on a person in charge of premises in which gambling equipment was found to rebut a case of '*prima facie* evidence' that the premises were being used for the purpose of illegal gambling. Although the court found that section 6(3) merely imposed an evidentiary burden on the accused and not a burden in the true sense, it was nevertheless unconstitutional as it would have led to the conviction of an innocent person against whom there was insufficient relevant evidence to secure a conviction beyond a reasonable doubt. Here the Constitutional Court is referring to an evidentiary burden in the form of a mandatory conclusion rather than in the form of a permissive inference (see above). It has also been argued that a statutory presumption which places a reverse onus in the form of a permissive inference on the shoulders of an accused may well be considered constitutionally justifiable as it merely places a tactical burden on an accused to adduce evidence in rebuttal but who could also choose not to do so.[16]

The presumption of innocence does not apply in civil proceedings and therefore statutory presumptions placing a reverse onus on a defendant in civil claims for delictual damages are constitutionally justifiable as long as there is a rational connection between the purpose for which these presumptions were created and the actual use of the presumption. For example, in *Prinsloo v Van der Linde and Another*[17] and *Gouda Broedery Bpk v Transnet*,[18] the courts considered various statutory presumptions which placed a reverse onus on a defendant landowner to show that he or she was not negligent when a veld fire starts and spreads from his or her land to other property, causing damage. These statutory presumptions of negligence were held to be constitutionally justifiable as long as they were given a restrictive rather than a liberal interpretation.

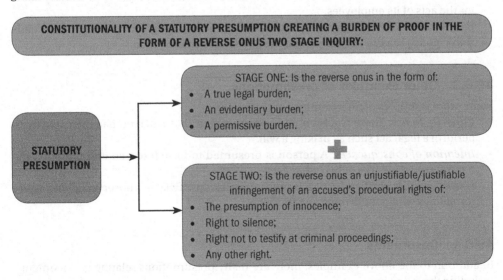

Figure 49.2 Statutory presumption

---

14 1997 (2) SA 368 (CC).
15 Gambling Act 51 of 1965.
16 Zeffertt and Paizes (2009) at 193.
17 1997 (3) SA 1012 (CC) concerning s 84 of the Forest Act 122 of 1984.
18 2005 (5) SA 490 (SCA) concerning s 34 of the National Veld and Forest Fire Act 101 of 1998.

49.6 Examples of presumptions

49.6.1 Rebuttable presumptions of law

Some examples of rebuttable presumptions of law are as follows:

- *Marriage:* At common law, the validity of a marriage is rebuttably presumed once evidence is produced showing that a marriage ceremony was performed.
- *Death:* Section 1 of the Dissolution of Marriages on Presumption of Death Act 23 of 1979 allows for the dissolution of a marriage on application to the High Court by the spouse of a missing person presumed to be dead. See also section 2 of the Inquests Act 58 of 1959.
- *Paternity of a child born out of wedlock:* Section 36 of the Children's Act 38 of 2005 states that if a person had sex with the mother of a child during the conception period, that person is presumed to be the biological father of the child.
- *Sanity:* At common law, every accused person is rebuttably presumed to be sane.
- *Bigamy:* Section 237 of the Criminal Procedure Act, 1977 states that when it can be proved that a marriage ceremony between the accused and another person took place within South Africa, other than the ceremony relating to the bigamous marriage, it is presumed that the South African marriage is lawful and binding.

49.6.2 Rebuttable presumptions of fact

Some examples of rebuttable presumptions of fact are as follows:

- *Latent defects:* The seller's liability for latent defects may be presumed if it can be shown that the latent defects existed at the time of the sale.
- **Vicarious liability:** It is presumed that an employee driving a motor vehicle does so with the authorisation of the employer. It is presumed that an employer is vicariously liable for the acts of its employees.
- *Possession of stolen property:* It is presumed that a person caught in possession of recently stolen goods is a thief or knows that the goods have been stolen.

49.6.3 Other examples of presumptions

Some other examples of presumptions are as follows:

- *Capacity to act:* There is a rebuttable presumption that a person has the capacity to perform a legal act such as making a will.
- *Intention of consequences:* A person is presumed to have foreseen and intended the natural consequences of his or her acts.
- *Formal validity of official acts:* It is presumed that an official has observed all necessary formalities when performing an official act.

49.6.4 Documents

In addition to the above examples, there are many presumptions relating to documents, including the following:

- Alterations made to a will are presumed to have been made after it was executed.
- Birth, death and marriage certificates are *prima facie* proof of what they relate to if issued by the requisite authority.
- A lost document is presumed to have been properly stamped.
- A person is presumed to have known the contents of a document that he or she signed.

THIS CHAPTER IN ESSENCE

1 Presumptions permit a court to accept a fact without hearing evidence on that fact.
2 Irrebuttable presumptions of law are rules of substantive law which furnish conclusive proof of the facts presumed and cannot be rebutted.
3 Rebuttable presumptions of law are rules of law that compel the provisional assumption of a fact until contradicting evidence is tendered.
4 If a rebuttable presumption of law creates a permissible inference, a court is not compelled to draw such an inference. However, if the court chooses to do so, the accused may decide to present evidence in rebuttal, but is not obliged to do so.
5 If a rebuttable presumption of law creates a mandatory conclusion 'in the absence of evidence to the contrary', a court must draw such a conclusion and the accused bears an evidentiary burden to present evidence in rebuttal.
6 If a rebuttable presumption of law creates a mandatory conclusion 'unless the contrary is proved', a court must draw such a conclusion and a primary burden of proof is placed on the accused in the form of a reverse onus to prove it does not apply.
7 Rebuttable presumptions of fact are inferences that may be drawn from particular factual circumstances. These differ from a presumption of law in two ways:
   7.1 First, presumptions of fact are not rules of law.
   7.2 Second, a presumption of fact does not affect the primary burden of proof. It may, however, impose a tactical burden or an evidentiary burden on the person against whom it operates.
8 A presumption contained in a statute which places a reverse onus either in its true sense or in the form of a mandatory evidentiary burden on an accused is considered to be constitutionally invalid because it results in an unjustifiable infringement on an accused's presumption of innocence and an unjustifiable infringement of the procedural right to silence and the right not to testify during criminal proceedings.

Chapter 50

Admissions, pointings out and confessions

50.1	**Introduction**	**441**
50.2	**A brief history of developments on admissions, pointings out and confessions in criminal proceedings**	**442**
50.3	**Formal admissions in criminal proceedings**	**442**
50.4	**Informal admissions in criminal proceedings**	**444**
	50.4.1 Definition of an informal admission	444
	50.4.2 The admissibility of informal admissions	445
	50.4.3 Vicarious admissions: co-perpetrators and authorisation	446
50.5	**Pointings out**	**449**
	50.5.1 Defining a pointing out	449
	50.5.2 The admissibility of pointings out	450
	50.5.3 The *Samhando* exception	450
50.6	**Confessions**	**451**
	50.6.1 Defining a confession	451
	50.6.2 The intention to make a confession	451
	50.6.3 Determining whether a statement contains a confession or an admission	452
	50.6.4 The admissibility of confessions	452
	50.6.4.1 The general test of admissibility of confessions	453
	50.6.4.2 Technical prerequisites in terms of section 217 of the Criminal Procedure Act, 1977	455
	50.6.4.3 Confessions: the State's burden of proof	456
	50.6.4.4 Confessions to lesser or related offences	456
	50.6.4.5 Confirmation of confessions: section 209 of the Criminal Procedure Act, 1977	456
50.7	**Formal admissions in civil matters**	**459**
	50.7.1 Introduction	459
	50.7.2 Intention to make a formal admission	460
	50.7.3 Withdrawal of a formal admission	460

CHAPTER 50 ADMISSIONS, POINTINGS OUT AND CONFESSIONS | 441

50.1 Introduction

This chapter gives a general overview of formal and informal **admissions**, pointings out and confessions in criminal proceedings and their respective admissibility requirements, and also provides a brief overview of formal admissions in civil proceedings.[1]

In criminal proceedings admissions (formal and informal), pointings out and confessions constitute what is referred to as detrimental testimonial evidence. An admission is an acceptance of a prejudicial fact(s) by the accused person, which in its totality may not constitute all the elements of an offence. An admission is something less than a confession. It constitutes an acceptance of only one or more (but not all) of the elements of the offence and does not amount to an unequivocal acknowledgement of guilt, which may be tantamount to a plea of guilty. In the case of an admission a defence of some sort is still available to, and can be raised by, the accused. However, an accused may be convicted on the basis of admissions if such admissions end up constituting all the elements of an offence that need to be proved, even though she or he has pleaded not guilty.[2] A confession, on the other hand, is a voluntary and unequivocal admission of guilt to all the elements of an offence. This admission of guilt must have no excuse nor defence. It could be an admission of guilt to an offence for which the accused is charged or a related or lesser offence. A pointing out constitutes the physical act of pointing out a scene or location, a person or something (real evidence) related to the offence, by the accused.

For all this testimonial evidence to be admitted, certain rules, principles and procedures must be adhered to as provided for by statutory and common law. They must also take into consideration the provisions of section 35 of the Constitution, which details the rights of accused, arrested and detained persons, the Bill of Rights and the exclusionary rule in section 35(5). One of the key rules is that they must have been made freely and voluntarily for them to be admissible as evidence. If they are not made freely and voluntarily, then they must be excluded as they may constitute unlawfully or unconstitutionally obtained evidence, which the courts are obliged to exclude under section 35(5) of the Constitution, particularly if such evidence is collected through rights violations and its admission would lead to an unfair trial or be detrimental to the administration of justice.[3] The main issue with regards to pointings out, admissions and confessions, when not obtained freely and voluntarily, is that they offend against free trial rights such as the right to remain silent and the right or privilege against self-incrimination, which are covered in section 35(3) of the Constitution. It is considered unfair for the accused to self-convict through compulsion as this flies in the face of natural justice and fair play – it is the State that bears the onus of proof beyond a reasonable doubt in criminal matters.[4]

Testimonial evidence or evidence that is collected or obtained through the involvement of an accused person is therefore treated with some level of circumspection by our courts. Where the accused challenges the manner in which that evidence was acquired, the courts are obliged to initiate processes to verify the validity of those challenges. So too with real evidence that derives from such testimonial evidence, for example, where an accused claims to have been tortured or coerced into making a confession or a pointing out. Below we

---

1 The detailed and specific steps to follow in dealing with formal and informal admissions in criminal proceedings is covered in specialised textbooks on criminal procedure. Likewise, admissions made in civil proceedings are covered in specialised civil procedure textbooks. See, for example, S Peté, D Hulme, M du Plessis, R Palmer, O Sibanda and T Palmer *Civil Procedure: A Practical Guide* 2 ed (2011).

2 *S v Ncube; S v Mphateng en 'n Ander* 1981 (3) SA 511 (T).

3 See ch 16 Unconstitutionally obtained evidence in criminal cases: section 35(5) of the Constitution.

4 Wells (2013) at 13.

discuss different types of admissions (formal and informal), pointings out and confessions and the rules that apply to their admission as evidence.

In a civil matter, a formal admission is a statement made by a party or his or her representative either orally in court or in writing in the pleadings. In a formal admission, the party admits a fact in issue. The court considers and accepts a formal admission to be conclusive proof of an issue. We discuss, below, the statutory position with regard to formal admissions in civil matters, the requirement of an intention to make an admission, how such an admission can be withdrawn, and the effects both of making an admission and withdrawing it.

50.2 A brief history of developments on admissions, pointings out and confessions in criminal proceedings

Confessions, pointings out and admissions are evidence of actions or statements made by an accused or their co-accused, outside court, which may implicate them in the commission of an offence. The rules regulating the admissibility of these statements in South African law emanate from English common law which was incorporated into the British colonies of South Africa in mid to late 1800s.[5] South African case law prior to independence from Britain on 31 May 1961 is still applicable and binding on our courts, provided that it passes constitutional muster.[6] Prior to 1918, South African law did not distinguish between admissions and confessions.[7] The distinction was introduced when the Criminal Procedure Code Act, Act 31 of 1917 became effective in 1918. This Act introduced the term 'confession', to refer to an admission of guilt on every element of the crime.[8] Other statements which did not conform to this, although prejudicial to the accused, became admissions. These differences were made clearer when the 1917 Act was repealed and replaced by the Criminal Procedure Act, Act 56 of 1955.[9] The latter Act was replaced by the Criminal Procedure Act, 1977 which introduced sections 217, 218, 219 and 220 which regulate the making and admissibility of confessions, pointings out, informal admissions and formal admissions.

50.3 Formal admissions in criminal proceedings

There are two forms of **formal admissions**. The first is made by the accused in terms of section 115(2)(*b*) of the Criminal Procedure Act, 1977 when an accused enters and explains his or her plea of not guilty. If the accused admits to some prejudicial facts, the presiding officer is obliged to seek consent from the accused to note and record such admissions as formal admissions.[10] When an accused makes an admission during his or her plea explanation[11] and consents to its recording by the presiding officer, it is then deemed to be a formal admission in terms of section 220 of the Criminal Procedure Act, 1977.[12] However,

---

5   S Lutchman 'S v Litako 2014 SACR 431 (SCA): A clarification on extra curial statements and hearsay' PER/PELJ 2015 (18)2 430 at 431.
6   At 432.
7   See Mhlongo v S; Nkosi v S (CCT 148/14; CCT 149/14) [2015] ZACC 19; 2015(2) SACR 323 (CC); 2015(8) BCLR 887 (CC) (25 June 2015).
8   See [2015] ZACC 19.
9   See [2015] ZACC 19.
10   See section 115 of the Criminal Procedure Act, 1997.
11   An explanation of plea basically outlines the basis of the accused's defence.
12   See section 115(2)(*b*).

CHAPTER 50 ADMISSIONS, POINTINGS OUT AND CONFESSIONS | 443

where the accused does not consent to the noting of the admission in terms of section 115(2)(*b*), it could nonetheless be noted as an informal admission by the court. It is important to highlight that the accused may decide not to explain his or her plea or to answer any questions during the arraignment proceedings – where the accused pleads and may elect to exercise his right to remain silent and put the State to the proof of all elements of the offence. Another important factor is that when the accused explains the plea, she or he is not under oath and is not subject to cross-examination, and the submissions made do not amount to evidence in favour of or against the accused.[13]

In instances where he or she decides to explain his plea, the presiding officer has to warn the accused, especially an unrepresented accused, that she or he is not obliged to answer questions or explain his or her defence and that he or she has a right to remain silent. The presiding officer is also obliged to explain the implications of admissions made by the accused during the amplification of his or her plea of not guilty. While a formal admission under section 115(2)(*b*) is made during the arraignment phase of the trial, section 220 admissions can be made at any stage during the trial when an issue in dispute becomes common cause. Section 220 of the Criminal Procedure Act, 1977, which primarily governs formal admissions in criminal proceedings, reads as follows:

> **An accused or his or her legal adviser or the prosecutor may in criminal proceedings admit any fact placed in issue at such proceedings and any such admission shall be sufficient proof of such fact.**

Note that as per this section both the accused and the State may now make formal admissions. A formal admission must be made with the intention that the statement operates as an admission.[14] The presiding officer should record precisely which facts are being admitted. If a legal representative makes a formal admission on behalf of an accused, the accused must confirm that he or she instructed that the facts be admitted and that the content of such admission is correct.[15]

In effect, a formal admission renders the admissions made to be *common cause* between the State and the defence. A formal admission is therefore automatically admissible. There has been considerable judicial debate about whether a formal admission constitutes *sufficient* proof or *conclusive* proof of a fact. In *S v Seleke*[16] and *S v Sesetse en Andere*[17] the Courts seemed to imply that an accused could retract a formal admission by leading evidence that contradicts it. Thus, at the end of the case, when a court is weighing up all the evidence, if the formal admission remains uncontradicted, it stands and if the evidence as a whole contradicts it, it fails. In other words, an uncontradicted formal admission becomes conclusive proof of the fact so admitted.

More recent cases have made it clear that a formally admitted fact is proved beyond contention and is regarded as though the prosecution has proven that fact beyond a reasonable doubt. In other words, if an accused admits a fact, the consequence is, firstly, that the prosecution does not have to lead evidence in respect of that fact, and

---

13 *R v Valachia & another* 1945 826 (AD), cited in *DPP v Heunis* (196/2017) [2017] ZASCA 136 (29 September 2017) at 15.

14 *R v Barlin* 1926 AD 459; *S v Grove-Mitchell* 1975 (3) SA 417 (A); *S v Eiseb and Another* 1991 (1) SACR 650 (Nm); *S v Groenewald* 2005 (2) SACR 597 (SCA).

15 See also the provision of section 115(3) of Criminal Procedure Act, 1977 which requires that where the legal representative replies on behalf of an accused person in the explanation of plea, the accused is required by the court to declare whether she or he confirms the replies of the legal representatives or not.

16 1980 (3) SA 745 (A).

17 1981 (3) SA 353 (A).

444 | THE LAW OF EVIDENCE IN SOUTH AFRICA

secondly, the accused can no longer challenge or dispute that fact in his or her evidence or closing argument.[18]

It is possible,[19] although uncommon, to withdraw a formal admission once it has been made in court. To do so, the accused needs the court's permission because withdrawing an admission is potentially prejudicial to the State's case.[20]

50.4 Informal admissions in criminal proceedings

50.4.1 Definition of an informal admission

An **informal admission** is a statement adverse or detrimental to the interests of its maker. While formal admissions are made in court to the presiding officer, informal admissions could be made to anyone, even outside court (extra-judicially). In a criminal context, an accused could make an informal admission about a fact or facts relating to the offence in question. For example, an accused in a rape trial may admit that he had sexual intercourse with the complainant or that he was at the scene of the incident.

The rationale for using an informal admission as an item of evidence is that whatever an accused says to his or her detriment is likely to be the truth. If the admission is ruled admissible,[21] the entire statement containing the admission, whether the statement is oral or in writing, is rendered admissible. This includes both the incriminatory and the exculpatory (intended as an excuse) parts of the statement.

For example, an accused's legal representative may inform the court that the accused admits being at the house on the night of the rape – this is the informal admission. However, the accused denies having forceful sexual intercourse with the complainant – this is the exculpatory part of the sentence that does not contain an admission. As a result, an accused may enjoy the benefit of having a self-serving statement admitted, which is usually not allowed. However, the self-serving part of the statement is generally not given as much weight as the adverse part, as illustrated in the case below. In *S v Nduli and Others*,[22] the Court said that:

> A statement made by a man against his own interest generally speaking has the intrinsic ring of truth, but his exculpatory explanation and excuses may well strike a false note and should be treated with a measure of distrust as being unsworn, unconfirmed, untested and self-serving.

Exculpatory statements cannot be blindly ignored by the courts. In *S v December*, the Court said that exculpatory statements which were not supported by credible evidence cannot be taken to be truthful but 'may serve to alert a court to a possibility of events or circumstances not otherwise revealed by the evidence' and must be given due regard.[23]

Informal admissions consist of statements made by the accused but not noted or confirmed by the court as formal admissions during the explanation of plea. When an accused testifies during the trial, she or he may also make statements which amount to

---

18 See *S v Groenewald* 2005 (2) SACR 597 (SCA) at para 33 and *S v Van der Westhuizen* 2011 (2) SACR 26 (SCA) at para 34.

19 For an alternative argument, see *S v Malebo en Andere* 1979 (2) SA 636 (B).

20 *S v Seleke en 'n Ander* 1980 (3) SA 745 (A) and *S v Sesetse en 'n Ander* 1981 (3) SA 353 (A).

21 See ch 55 The trial-within-a-trial.

22 1993 (2) SACR 501 (A) at 505G–506A. See also *R v Valachia and Another* 1945 AD 826 at 835.

23 See *S v December* 1995 (1) SACR 438 (A) at 444B–E.

CHAPTER 50   ADMISSIONS, POINTINGS OUT AND CONFESSIONS | **445**

informal admissions. These could also be made when the defence cross-examines witnesses during the trial where the legal representatives of an accused put up an alternative averment or the version of the accused to the witness. Informal admission could also be made by conduct, for instance, where an accused fails to dispute allegations made by witnesses during their testimony.[24] While failure to dispute may not necessarily amount to proof, especially where an accused elects to remain silent, a court may draw adverse inferences from the absence of a rebuttal.[25] When an accused changes a guilty plea into a not guilty plea, the replies made by the accused when questioned under section 112(1) become informal admissions.[26] A pointing out of a place, person or something that is linked to evidence of a commission of an offence by an accused is also an informal admission.[27]

Note the following aspects of informal admissions:

- An informal admission can be oral or written and may be made before or during the trial.
- It can be made by conduct (failure to rebut adverse evidence).[28]
- The maker of an informal admission need not have known that what he or she said was adverse to their interest or was intended to be adverse to their interest.[29]
- An informal admission could be made by an accused to anyone voluntarily outside court and could be admissible when that person testifies as a witness (not co-accused)[30] that it was made by an accused voluntarily to him or her and there is no dispute to its voluntariness.
- An informal admission may be express or implied.
- Formal court documents, such as not guilty plea statements in terms of section 115 of the Criminal Procedure Act, 1977, may also contain informal admissions.
- The mere fact that an informal admission has been made is not an indicator of the weight the court will attach to such admission. At the end of the trial, the court will consider the evidential value of the informal admission in light of all the evidence as a whole.

50.4.2   The admissibility of informal admissions

Section 219A of the Criminal Procedure Act, 1977 governs the admissibility of an informal admission. In terms of section 219A, the accused must have made an informal admission *voluntarily* and the State must prove voluntariness beyond a reasonable doubt.[31] In *S v Yolelo*,[32] the Court commented that section 219A merely codified the common law voluntariness test for admissibility as no new definition was included when section 219A was inserted into the Criminal Procedure Act, 1977 in 1979.[33]

The common law test for the voluntariness of an informal admission is derived from the case of *R v Barlin*.[34] The Court held that an informal admission is voluntarily made if it was not '... induced by any promise or threat proceeding from a person in authority.'[35]

---

24 See *S v Boesak* 2000 (1) SACR 633 (SCA).
25 At paras 46–47.
26 See sections 112(1) and 113 of the Criminal Procedure Act, 1977.
27 See section 218 of the Criminal Procedure Act, 1977 and the discussion on pointings out below.
28 *S v Boesak* 2000 (1) SACR 633 (SCA).
29 *R v Barlin* 1926 AD 459; *S v Nombewu* 1996 (2) SACR 396 (E); *S v Langa and Others* 1998 (1) SACR 21 (T).
30 *S v Ndhlovu and Others* 2001 (1) SACR 85 (W).
31 *S v Mpetha and Others* (2)1983 (1) SA 576 (C); *S v Schultz and Another* 1989 (1) SA 465 (T); *S v Yolelo* 1981 (1) SA 1002 (A).
32 1981 (1) SA 1002 (A).
33 By the Criminal Procedure Amendment Act 56 of 1979.
34 1926 AD 459 at 462.
35 There are numerous cases interpreting the meanings of these terms: see *R v Magoetie* 1959 (2) SA 322 (A); *S v Radebe and Another* 1968 (4) SA 410 (A); *S v Segone* 1981 (1) SA 410 (T); *S v Robertson en Andere* 1981 (1) SA 460 (C); *S v Schultz and Another* 1989 (1) SA 465 (T); *S v Peters* 1992 (1) SACR 292 (E).

446 | THE LAW OF EVIDENCE IN SOUTH AFRICA

Therefore, the court will apply the following test to decide whether an admission is admissible or not:

- The court will first decide on the evidence as to which part of an oral or written statement contains an informal admission or whether certain conduct amounts to an informal admission or not.
- The court will then apply the test in *R v Barlin*, asking first whether the informal admission was made to a person in authority over the accused,[36] or whether that person in authority made an illegal or improper threat[37] or promise[38] to the accused.
- The court will decide if any threat or promise was, in fact, improper or illegal, and whether the accused made the informal admission as a result of the improper threat or promise, that is, the admission was *induced* by the improper threat or promise.

If the voluntariness of the informal admission is disputed, its admissibility will be determined in a trial-within-a-trial.[39]

50.4.3 Vicarious admissions: co-perpetrators and authorisation

A vicarious or extra-curial admission is a statement made by a third person that becomes admissible against the accused even though the accused did not personally make it. The general rule is that admissions are not vicariously admissible as they are usually only admissible against their makers. There are, however, two exceptions to this rule. [40]

The first exception is where a co-perpetrator makes an executive statement in furtherance of a **common purpose** to commit a crime and this statement becomes admissible against all who were party to that joint criminal venture.

The second exception is where the accused expressly or implicitly authorises the maker of the statement to make it on his or her behalf. A party may make an admission on another party's behalf. To do so, they must have the authority to make the statement on the other party's behalf. This authority can stem from the relationship between the two parties, such as principal and agent, employer and employee, master and servant, partners or, most importantly, from the attorney–client relationship.

The question of admissibility of extra-curial admissions has recently become a subject of debate in our courts following the reasoning of the Supreme Court of Appeal in *Ndhlovu and Others v S*,[41] discussed below, which was not followed by the same court in *S v Litako*.[42] This issue has however been put to rest through the Constitutional Court's intervention in *Mhlongo v S; Nkosi v S*.[43]

Relying on section 3(1)(c) of the Law of Evidence Amendment Act, 1988, the SCA in *Ndhlovu and Others v S*[44] held that extra-curial statements (informal admissions or hearsay evidence) made by a co-accused against an accused were, in the interest of justice,

---

36 This term has been fairly widely interpreted to include even the employer of an accused person. *R v Michael and Another* 1962 (3) SA 355 (SR).

37 A threat would obviously include an actual assault on the accused as the implied threat is that the assault will continue unless the accused cooperates.

38 Robust interrogation is permissible provided it does not amount to illegal or improper promises. *S v Khan* 2010 (2) SACR 476 (KZP).

39 See ch 55 The trial-within-a-trial.

40 *Mhlongo v S; Nkosi v S* [2015] ZACC 19 at 39.

41 [2002] 3 All SA 760 (SCA).

42 *S v Litako* 2014 (2) SACR 431 (SCA).

43 [2015] ZACC 19 at 39.

44 [2002] 3 All SA 760 (SCA).

admissible. In *S v Litako*,[45] the court discussed the development of the English common law rule and jurisprudence decided before 31 May 1961, when South Africa became independent from Britain, which is binding on South African courts.[46] The common law rule is that out of court (extra-curial) admissions made by an accused against a co-accused are not admissible against a co-accused but only against their maker. The *R v Moore* dicta cited in *S v Litako*[47] better captures this common law rule:

> [T]he fact that he has pleaded Guilty is no evidence against his co-prisoner ... the accepted principle being that a man's confession is evidence only against himself and not against his accomplices. If a prisoner pleads Guilty, it does not affect his co-prisoner.

The Court in *Litako*[48] noted that the law in South Africa developed along this common law principle as captured in sections 219 and 219A of the Criminal Procedure Act, 1977, which respectively regulate the admission confessions and informal admissions. These sections in the CPA, the Court observed, do not envisage a situation where extra-curial confessions and admissions are tendered as evidence against anyone else but the maker.[49]

In *Mhlongo v S; Nkosi v S*,[50] the Constitutional Court concurred with the reasoning in *Litako* and ruled unanimously that extra-curial admissions of an accused were inadmissible against a co-accused, unless the two common law exceptions, outlined earlier above, are met. In *Mhlongo v S; Nkosi v S* two accused (accused 2 and 4) appealed against the decisions of the High Court and the SCA, where their convictions and sentences based on the extra-curial admissions of their co-accused (accused 1, 3, 6 and 7) had been upheld.[51]

DISCUSSION	**The trouble with one's accomplices and their admissions**
50.1	In the Constitutional Court, the appellants argued that the admission of the extra-curial admissions of their co-accused against them violated their rights to equality before the law and to a fair trial. The Court did not decide the fair trial aspects of the case but decided the case on the right to equality before the law submission. The appellants had argued that informal admissions and confessions, which are both extra-curial statements, were treated differently by case law.[52] In this regard they cited the *Ndhlovu* judgement, which allowed extra-curial admissions to be admitted in the interest of justice, relying on the Law of Evidence Amendment Act, 1988.
	The Constitutional Court critiqued the *Ndhlovu* judgement on several different grounds. It said that in Ndhlovu, the common law rule that an extra-curial statement

---

45 2014 (2) SACR 431. See also a discussion of this case in S Lutchman '*S v Litako* 2014 SACR 431 (SCA): A clarification on extra curial statements and hearsay' (2015) 18(2) *PER* at 429-(i).

46 Lutchman (2015) at 431–432.

47 2014 (2) SACR 431 at 33.

48 At 38.

49 At 38

50 [2015] ZACC 19.

51 One interesting fact of this appeal is that the appellants had been incarcerated for over a decade and had to apply for condonation for late filing of their appeal to the Constitutional Court as a result of insufficient resources as they had sought assistance from the Legal Aid South Africa without success. They were eventually assisted by a fellow inmate who was a law student in drafting their appeal to the Constitutional Court. See [2015] ZACC 19 at 13–15.

52 See [2015] ZACC 19 at 14.

by an accused is inadmissible against a co-accused was relaxed, noting that the SCA had found that extra-curial admissions, but not confessions, were admissible against a co-accused if the requirements of section 3 of the Law of Evidence Amendment Act, 1988 which deals with the admission of hearsay evidence are met, no constitutional principles are offended, and it was in the interest of justice to admit such evidence.[53] It said that the SCA omitted to: first, deal with the common law rule against allowing admissions to be tendered against a co-accused,[54] second, deal adequately with provisions of section 3(2) of the Law of Evidence Amendment Act, 1988 which provided for additional grounds, beyond that of hearsay evidence, for non-admissibility;[55] third, give regard to the provisions of section 219A of the Criminal Procedure Act which expressly allow admissions to be admitted only against their maker, citing *Litako and Others v S* approvingly; and fourth, give regard to whether the Law of Evidence Amendment Act, 1988 altered the position at common law that extra-curial admissions are inadmissible against co-accused subject to the two common law exceptions.[56] It concluded in respect to the latter point that:

A statute must be interpreted in a manner that makes the least inroads into the common law. Together with section 3(2), another indicator that the Evidence Amendment Act did not alter the common law is to be found in section 3(1) which provides that '*subject to the provisions of any other law* hearsay shall not be admitted as evidence' unless certain stipulated requirements are met. The Evidence Amendment Act altered the common law in relation to hearsay evidence but it did not alter or intend to alter the common law in relation to the admissibility of extra-curial statements made by an accused against co-accused.[57]

The *Ndhlovu* judgment, as observed by Lutchman, is still relevant when it comes to the analysis of the Law of Evidence Amendment Act, 1988 in relation to hearsay evidence.[58] The Court in *Mhlongo v S; Nkosi v S*, therefore, clarified the law with regards to extra-curial admissions, reverting to the common law position prior to the *Ndhlovu* judgment. At paragraphs 35, 37 and 38 the Court said that:

It is difficult to conceive of any rational reason why an admission ought to be admissible against a co-accused but not a confession. The State offered no reason for this differentiation. The rationale for precluding the admissibility of a confession – the inherent dangers in using statements by co-accused – which is expressly guaranteed in section 219 of the CPA, apply equally to admissions ... The differentiation between accused implicated by confessions versus admissions cannot be lawfully sustained ... The pre-*Ndhlovu* common law position that extra-curial confessions and admissions by an accused are inadmissible against co-accused must be restored.[59]

---

53   At 26.
54   At 27.
55   At 28–29.
56   At 31.
57   At 31, emphasis in the original. Footnotes omitted.
58   Lutchman (2015) at 433.
59   *Mhlongo v S; Nkosi v S* [2015] ZACC 19.

CHAPTER 50 ADMISSIONS, POINTINGS OUT AND CONFESSIONS

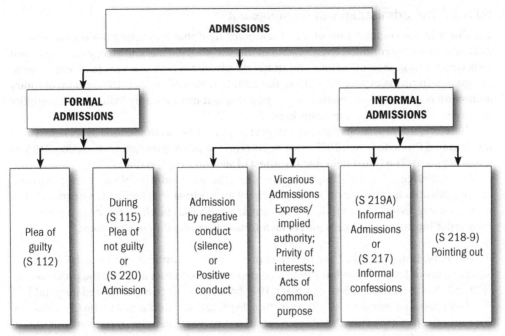

Figure 50.1 *Admissions*

50.5 Pointings out

50.5.1 Defining a pointing out

In South African law, a **pointing out** is 'an overt act whereby the accused indicates physically to the inquisitor the presence or location of some thing or place actually visible to the inquisitor.'[60] In short, therefore, the pointing out is the *overt physical indication*. A pointing out can, therefore, never contain words, either as an oral or written component.

For example, if an accused points to a stolen television set with his right index finger and says, 'This is the television set I stole from the house,' the physical action of pointing using his finger amounts to the pointing out. The oral statement that the accused made at the same time as the pointing out must be separately assessed to determine whether it contains any informal admissions or amounts to a confession.

Furthermore, using the mechanism of a pointing out in an attempt to circumvent the rules relating to the admissibility of a confession or an admission is prohibited. In *S v Witbooi and others*[61] the court held that a pointing out in circumstances that would not have aided the investigation of the crime, other than to obtain self-incriminating evidence, is tantamount to a confession in the guise of a pointing out. Thus evidence obtained as a result of such a pointing out must comply with the law relating to the admissibility of confessions, as set out in section 217 of the Criminal Procedure Act, 1977, if it is to be deemed admissible.

---

60   *S v Nkwanyana* 1978 (3) SA 404 (N) at 405H.
61   2018 (1) SACR 670 (ECG).

450 THE LAW OF EVIDENCE IN SOUTH AFRICA

50.5.2 The admissibility of pointings out

The Court in the seminal case of *S v Sheehama*[62] held that a pointing out is essentially a communication by conduct. It is a statement that the accused has knowledge of the relevant facts which *prima facie* operates to his or her disadvantage and amounts to an extra-curial admission. In terms of section 219A of the Criminal Procedure Act, 1977, no involuntary admission is admissible in court. Thus, a pointing out must comply with the admissibility requirement of informal admissions in section 219A.[63]

Therefore, the provisions that used to govern pointings out in sections 218(1) and (2) of the Criminal Procedure Act, 1977 must be interpreted in conjunction with section 219A as a starting point. The Court held that the effect of section 218(2) is that:

- the evidence of a pointing out which is *otherwise admissible* does not become inadmissible merely because it forms part of an inadmissible confession or statement
- conversely, evidence of a pointing out which is *otherwise inadmissible* does not become admissible because it forms part of an admissible confession or statement.[64]

In summary, it appears that, for practical purposes, all pointings out must be tested for admissibility in terms of section 219A as admissions by conduct and that the provisions of section 218 of the Criminal Procedure Act, 1977 have been effectively rendered inoperable.[65]

They must also comply with all the section 35 protections contained in the Constitution. For example, *in S v Mabaso*[66] where the accused was not given the opportunity to obtain legal advice before making a pointing out and an incriminating statement, the court held that the right to a fair trial required the exclusion of both the pointing out and the incriminating statement. The right to a fair trial must be protected and observed at all stages of the proceedings.

50.5.3 The *Samhando* exception

The *Sheehama* decision did not authoritatively decide the continued application in our law of the *Samhando* exception. In *R v Samhando*,[67] the Court held that if something is discovered as a result of an inadmissible confession and the object so discovered has substantial apparent weight, the evidence of the discovered object would be admissible *even if* the police were led to the object by information obtained through an inadmissible confession or admission. This is called the *theory of confirmation by subsequently discovered facts*.

In *Samhando*'s case, police investigators badly assaulted the accused. Samhando then took the investigators to a tree and pointed out the bloodstained clothing of the deceased whom he had killed with an axe. He thereafter also pointed out the axe itself which was lying some distance away from the tree. The trial court admitted the evidence of *what* was found, that is, the bloodied clothing and the axe, but excluded the evidence of statements containing admissions by the accused. The rationale for this approach was that a statement that was

---

62 1991 (2) SA 860 (A).

63 Section 219A was enacted in 1979, two years after the coming into force of the Criminal Procedure Act, 1977. It therefore impliedly overrules any conflicting provision contained in the Criminal Procedure Act, 1977, including section 218(1) and (2), the provision that used to govern the admissibility of admissions.

64 At 881. The *Sheehama* decision was confirmed in *S v January: Prokureur-Generaal, Natal v Khumalo* 1994 (2) SACR 801 (A) and *S v Abbott* 1999 (1) SACR 489 (SCA). Also see SS Terblanche, DP van der Merwe, BC Naude and K Moodley *The Law of Evidence: Cases and Statutes* 4 ed (2009) at 119.

65 See, in general, DT Zeffertt and AP Paizes *The South African Law of Evidence* 2 ed (2009) at 554–559.

66 2016 (1) SACR 617 (SCA). See also *S v Magwaza* 2016 (1) SACR 53 (SCA).

67 1943 AD 608.

CHAPTER 50 ADMISSIONS, POINTINGS OUT AND CONFESSIONS | 451

otherwise inadmissible can become admissible if it is confirmed in material respects by facts that are subsequently discovered.

Samhando's case was not followed in *S v Khumalo*,[68] but appeared thereafter to be overruled in *S v Jordaan*.[69] In this case evidence about weapons discovered following a pointing out was held to be admissible. However, it appears that this debate has now been laid to rest by the *S v January*[70] decision where the Supreme Court of Appeal held that the provisions of section 219A(1) precluded any reliance on the *Samhando* exception. The reasoning behind this is that the language of section 219A clearly and unambiguously allows no exception to the requirement of voluntariness.[71]

50.6 Confessions

50.6.1 Defining a confession

The generally recognised definition of a confession is that it is an extra-curial statement of the accused that is an unequivocal admission of guilt to all the elements of the crime.[72]

However, in practical terms, a confession is merely a series of informal admissions that cover all the elements of the crime. Note that there is no independent entity called a 'confession' – a confession must be contained in a written or oral statement. For this reason, a pointing out on its own, being an informal admission by conduct, can never amount to a confession as the *mens rea* element cannot be satisfied by the evidence of a pointing out only.

Similarly, with regard to crimes that require *mens rea*, an admission of the *actus reus* will not normally amount to a confession, no matter how prejudicial such an admission appears to be.[73] This is because intention is an essential element of a confession and the lack of intention, or insanity, mistake, compulsion, self-defence or automatism, may still be raised by the accused as a defence. It is irrelevant that the possibility of the accused being able to raise the defence is remote or that such a defence would be hopeless in light of the circumstances. However, a court can look at the surrounding circumstances to determine whether the statement does exclude any possible defence.

50.6.2 The intention to make a confession

A further issue that the court must examine is whether the accused had the intention, known as *animus confitendi*, to make a confession. Often, statements that are detrimental to the accused were intended by the accused to be exculpatory. The courts have adopted an objective approach to this issue, as illustrated in the case below, and the accused's intention is generally not considered relevant.

S v Yende

In *S v Yende*,[74] the Court said the test is whether the accused intends to admit facts which make him or her guilty, whether he or she realises it or not. The test is not whether the accused intends

---

68 1992 (2) SACR 411 (N).
69 1992 (2) SACR 498 (A).
70 1994 (2) SACR 801 (A).
71 Also see *S v Sheehama* 1991 (2) SA 860 (A) and *S v Mokahtsa* 1993 (1) SACR 408 (C).
72 *R v Becker* 1929 AD 167.
73 *S v Mofokeng* 1982 (4) SA 147 (T) at 149.
74 1987 (3) SA 367 (A).

THE LAW OF EVIDENCE IN SOUTH AFRICA

to admit that he or she is guilty. To decide whether a statement amounts to a confession, the statement must be considered as a whole. Regard must be had not only to what appears in the statement, but also to what is necessarily implied from it. If the content of the statement does not expressly admit all the elements of the offence or exclude all grounds of defence, but does so by necessary implication, the statement amounts to a confession.

If all the elements of the offence are admitted, then the presence of an exculpatory intention will not prevent the statement from being a confession. If the statement falls short of admitting any element, then it is not a confession, even when it has a prejudicial effect. However, in crimes where *mens rea* in the form of intention is required, the element of intention will not be admitted where the accused makes a statement with exculpatory intent.[75]

50.6.3 Determining whether a statement contains a confession or an admission

Establishing whether a statement amounts to a confession, or merely an admission, or perhaps neither, depends on several factors. Obviously, the words used and the content of what was said are an important starting point. To be classified as a confession, the accused must have admitted to every element of the crime in question and this should be tantamount to a plea of guilty.

For example, the statement 'I raped her' will constitute a confession while the statement 'I had sex with her' will not. This is because the word 'rape' has a specific legal meaning which includes all the elements, namely intention and penetration without consent. The second statement, however, amounts only to an admission of intercourse and does not indicate that there was a lack of consent. Thus, it is still open to the accused to raise a defence about such consent. Things are seldom so clear-cut and a court has to be mindful of factors such as illiteracy, racial and cultural differences, the language spoken and the translation thereof in assessing the statement.

Therefore, in deciding whether a statement amounts to a confession or merely an admission, the context in which the statement is made is crucial. This was emphasised by Schreiner JA in *R v Duetsimi*:[76]

> In all cases where the crown seeks to prove a statement made by an accused person in order to establish his guilt, it is essential to examine the circumstances in which the statement was made and everything that was said by the accused on the occasion in question and on occasions associated with the occasion in question, in order to ascertain whether the statement was or was not a confession, and in either event, whether the conditions required for admissibility were present. Unless the trial judge is satisfied that the necessary foundations for the admission of the statement ... have been proved, the statement must be excluded.

50.6.4 The admissibility of confessions

Section 217 of the Criminal Procedure Act, 1977 governs the admissibility of statements containing confessions in trial proceedings.

---

75 *R v Hanger* 1928 AD 459 at 463.
76 1950 (3) SA 674 (A) at 678–679.

50.6.4.1 The general test of admissibility of confessions

Section 217(1) of the Criminal Procedure Act, 1977 states the general test of admissibility for confessions:

> Evidence of any confession made by any person in relation to the commission of any offence shall, if such confession is proved to have been freely and voluntarily made by such person in his sound and sober senses and without having been unduly influenced thereto, be admissible in evidence against such person at such criminal proceedings relating to such offence ...

According to section 217(1), it therefore seems that confessions must satisfy three requirements to be admissible. They must be proved to:
- have been made freely and voluntarily
- while the person making it is in his or her sound and sober senses
- without having been unduly influenced to make the statement.

The traditional view is that 'freely and voluntarily' and 'without undue influence' are separate requirements, each having a distinct meaning.[77] Schwikkard and Van der Merwe recognise that 'in practice the inquiry as to whether the statement was made voluntarily is ... subsumed in the inquiry as to whether the statement was made without undue influence'.

However, in practice, the State only actually has to prove two requirements: the 'sound and sober senses' and the 'undue influence' requirements.[78] Once the State has proved that the accused made the confession without undue influence and while he or she was in his or her sound and sober senses, the conclusion is automatically reached that it was made 'freely and voluntarily'.[79] Thus, although the freely and voluntarily requirement is stated in the general test for admissibility in section 217(1) of the Criminal Procedure Act, 1977, it is not a separate requirement but merely a conclusion reached after the other two requirements have been proved. In a nutshell, therefore, the test is: freely and voluntarily = no undue influence + accused in his or her sound and sober senses.

The accused must have confessed in the absence of any undue influence. Undue influence means deceit, promises, the threat of violence or actual violence by any other person who is not necessarily in a position of authority. Threatened violence or violence by a person in authority would affect the 'undue influence' requirement, thereby leading to the conclusion that the confession was not 'freely and voluntarily' obtained.

This definition of undue influence is sufficiently wide to apply to influence exerted both by people in authority and people not in authority. Determining whether undue influence has been brought to bear on the accused to confess is also a question of fact as is the case for the other requirements for an admissible confession.

Determining whether undue influence exists depends on the surrounding circumstances of the case. The fact that there is a lengthy interrogation is not enough to have the confession excluded unless the accused's freedom of choice is affected. Some of the factors that can exert an undue influence are confrontation, fatigue, detention, solitary confinement, youthfulness, psychological torments, violence or threats of violence. Some examples of claims of undue influence, both successful and unsuccessful, are given in the cases below.

---

77 PJ Schwikkard and SE van der Merwe *Principles of Evidence* 3 ed (2009) at 338. Zeffertt and Paizes 2 ed (2009) at 530–531.

78 Schwikkard and Van der Merwe 3 ed (2009) at 338. See also Zeffertt and Paizes 2 ed (2009) at 531–538.

79 Thus, the phrase 'freely and voluntarily' is a tautology as it merely means that the confession must have been made *voluntarily*, that is, of the maker's own free will. The extra word 'freely' is therefore redundant.

R v Michael and Another

In *R v Michael and Another*,[80] the Court said that there was undue influence where the declarant was given the impression that he would not be prosecuted if he were to make a confession or that his family would be cared for if he were to be found guilty, and that afterwards he would be reinstated in his job.

R v Afrika

In *R v Afrika*,[81] the Court held that it is not undue influence if the declarant was merely admonished or encouraged to speak the truth.

S v Kearney

In *S v Kearney*,[82] the Court held that it is not undue influence if the declarant was promised that the statement would be kept secret.

S v Sampson and Another

In *S v Sampson and Another*,[83] the Court held that confronting a suspect with another suspect's statement to induce or trick him or her into making a confession may amount to undue influence.

S v Williams

In *S v Williams*,[84] the Court held that it is not undue influence to allow one accused to hear what another accused is telling the police.

S v Ndika and Others

In *S v Ndika and Others*,[85] the Court held that a self-induced expectation of a benefit does not constitute undue influence.

S v Bakane and Bakane v The State

In *S v Bakane*[86] the court *a quo* found that slapping and rough-handling amounting to an assault but not torture does not automatically exclude a confession, but that a causal connection (which was not shown) was needed between the rough-handling and the confession. The court admitted the confession as, in its opinion, it had not rendered the trial unfair and it was not in the interests of justice to exclude it. However, on appeal, the SCA overturned this decision holding that the onus rested on the state to prove the confession was admissible, which they were unable to do. The state was, in fact unable to show that the accused had even seen the confession he was purported to have signed after being assaulted.

S v Gcam-gcam

In *S v Gcam-gcam*[87] the court noted that courts need to be vigilant over confessions made by suspects in police custody and also that courts need to be sceptical when a suspect repudiates a confession at the first opportunity.

The requirement that the accused must have been in his or her sound and sober senses when he or she confessed means that the accused must have been *compos mentis*, that is, of sound mind. Therefore, the accused must not have been mentally compromised and must have

---

80   1962 (3) SA 355 (SR).
81   1949 (3) SA 627 (O).
82   1964 (2) SA 495 (A) at 500F.
83   1989 (3) SA 239 (A).
84   1991 (1) SACR 1 (C).
85   2002 (1) SACR 250 (SCA).
86   2017 (1) SACR 576 (GP) and (1180/2016) [2017] ZASCA 182 (5 December 2017) respectively.
87   2015 (2) SACR 501 (SCA).

CHAPTER 50 ADMISSIONS, POINTINGS OUT AND CONFESSIONS | 455

understood what he or she was saying. This is also a question of fact decided by the court, as illustrated in the case below.

R v Blyth

In *R v Blyth*,[88] Mrs Blyth was charged with murdering her husband. After his death, she had a quarrel with her boyfriend. To take revenge on him, she wrote a letter to the police saying that she had killed her husband. The defence argued that she was not in her sound and sober senses when she wrote the letter. The Court held that the provision did not require that the State had to negate all mental excitement on the part of the declarant and the fact that she was in emotional turmoil did not mean that she was not in her sound and sober senses.

It is, therefore, important that the magistrate or justice of the peace recording the confession observe the accused so that they can ascertain that he or she was of sound mind when making it. The fact that the accused was intoxicated does not necessarily mean he or she was not in his sound and sober senses. The test is whether the accused was too drunk to appreciate what he or she was saying. If so, then the accused may not have been in his or her sound and sober senses. The same test is applied to confessions made while suffering under the effects of mental stress or drugs.

50.6.4.2 Technical prerequisites in terms of section 217 of the Criminal Procedure Act, 1977

Section 217(1)(*a*) contains a technical safeguarding provision to protect arrested persons against abusive police behaviour and to try to minimise the incidence of falsely induced confessions. In essence, the provision requires any oral statement containing a confession made to a peace officer[89] to be reduced to writing and confirmed before a magistrate or a justice,[90] and any written statement made to a peace officer to be confirmed in writing before a magistrate or a justice.

A magistrate as defined in section 1 of the Criminal Procedure Act, 1977 excludes regional magistrates, who are therefore *not permitted* to confirm confessions. Also in terms of section 1, a justice is a justice of the peace as provided for in the Justices of the Peace and Commissioner of Oaths Act 16 of 1963. In terms of the schedule attached to this Act, commissioned police officers are also justices of the peace. (A proposed amendment to preclude commissioned police officers from confirming confessions has not yet been implemented.)

If these provisions are not complied with, the entire statement containing the confessions, whether oral or written, will not be admissible in court.[91] Remember, however, that a confession can be made to *any* person: the only test of admissibility is whether the confession was freely and voluntarily made as discussed in 50.6.4.1 above. It is only when the statement is made to a peace officer[92] that it has to be confirmed before a magistrate or a justice.

---

88   1940 AD 355.
89   As defined in s 1 of the Criminal Procedure Act, 1977.
90   As defined in s 1 of the Criminal Procedure Act, 1977.
91   In *S v Mashengoane* 2014 (2) SACR 623 (GP) the court imposed a duty on the prosecutor to bring to the court's attention any shortcomings in any confession reduced to writing before a magistrate.
92   As defined in s 1 of the Criminal Procedure Act, 1977, including police officials and other categories of officials defined in s 1 of the Criminal Procedure Act, 1977.

456 THE LAW OF EVIDENCE IN SOUTH AFRICA

50.6.4.3 Confessions: the State's burden of proof

If the admissibility of a confession is disputed by the defence, this dispute will be resolved in a trial-within-a-trial.[93]

The State must prove beyond a reasonable doubt that the confession is admissible. The State can prove through direct or circumstantial evidence that the accused made the confession. This requirement seems simple, but it has not been without controversy.

Section 217(1)(b)(ii) previously presumed that a confession was admissible unless the accused proved it was not. In *S v Zuma and Others*,[94] the Court held that such a clause, which stated that in the absence of proof to the contrary the confession was presumed to be voluntary, had the effect of placing an onus on the accused to prove his or her innocence and thus was unconstitutional. Section 217(1)(b)(ii) of the Criminal Procedure Act, 1977 has therefore been rendered *pro non scripto* by this case.

50.6.4.4 Confessions to lesser or related offences

To distinguish between a confession and an admission, we must establish whether all the elements have been admitted to or whether only certain limited aspects have been conceded. This requires a comprehensive knowledge of the elements that constitute each and every crime. This includes the ability to differentiate between common law and statutory crimes, to distinguish between **dolus** crimes, **culpa** crimes and strict liability offences, and to understand the concepts of **vicarious** and strict **liability**. This is important because it is possible that a confession may not include an admission of every element of the crime concerned and it will, therefore, be classified as an admission and not a confession. However, it may constitute a confession to a lesser offence which is a competent verdict,[95] for example one with fewer or different elements.

Our law was developed to recognise that statements containing confessions to crimes relate to the crime actually charged on the charge sheet for the purposes of relying on the section 217 protection. The reason for this is that in the course of the police investigations, the nature and type of crimes being investigated may change as new evidence emerges during the investigation. Thus, for example, on his or her arrest, the accused may be informed he or she is being arrested on charges of murder and robbery. Later, the accused may be informed that he or she has been charged with murder and theft. When the charge sheet is finally drafted on completion of the investigation, the accused may be charged with culpable homicide and fraud. In such circumstances, it is obviously artificial and procedurally unfair to suggest that the accused could rely on section 217 protection based on confessions to only the last two crimes.

50.6.4.5 Confirmation of confessions: section 209 of the Criminal Procedure Act, 1977

The question that arises once a confession is admitted into court, having complied with all the section 217 admissibility requirements, is whether that confession constitutes sufficient evidence on which to convict an accused. Section 209 of the Criminal Procedure Act, 1977 entitles the court to convict on the single evidence of a confession of the accused. However, the confession has to be confirmed in a material respect. Alternatively, there must be

---

93 See ch 55 The trial-within-a-trial.
94 1995 (1) SACR 568 (CC). See also ch 5 Impact of the Constitution on the law of evidence.
95 In *S v Gcaba* 1965 (4) SA 325 (N), the Court said that confessing to a lesser offence would amount to a confession, of which the accused could properly be convicted.

evidence *aliunde* the confession that the offence has actually been committed. This means that there must be independent evidence other than the confession that shows that the offence was committed. The former requirement is obviously more reliable in that it seeks a direct link between the confession and the crime, as illustrated in the case below.[96] The latter is less reliable as it requires evidence only that the crime took place and nothing necessarily linking the confessor to it. It therefore does not significantly reduce the risk of a wrongful conviction based solely on a confession.

R v Blyth
The direct link between the confession and the crime need not prove every element of the crime. It need merely confirm a material aspect of the confession. Thus, in *R v Blyth*,[97] the accused confessed to the murder of her husband by poisoning him with arsenic. The Court considered traces of arsenic in the deceased's body to be confirmation of the confession even though they did not prove the murder itself, for example the deceased could have committed suicide.

Sometimes the courts have controversially relied on what appears to be fairly insubstantial evidence to provide section 209 confirmation. For example in *S v Mjoli and Another*,[98] the Court found the requisite 'confirmation in a material respect' in the contents of the accused's own section 115 not guilty plea statement. This decision has come in for much criticism over the years as many commentators consider it to be a violation of the rule against self-corroboration.

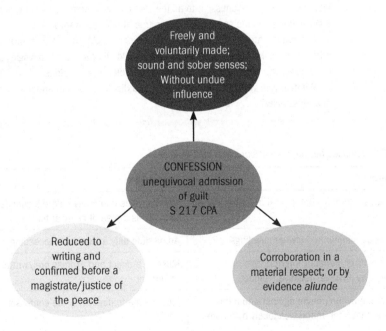

Figure 50.2 Confessions

---

96 *R v Blyth* 1940 AD 355.
97 1940 AD 355. See ch 42 Corroboration.
98 1981 (3) SA 1233 (A).

458 | THE LAW OF EVIDENCE IN SOUTH AFRICA

DISCUSSION 50.2

Should the legal test for admissions, pointings out and confessions be the same?

As the law stands, informal admissions are admissible if the admission was not induced by a threat or promise by a person in authority over the accused (section 219A of the Criminal Procedure Act, 1977). However, a much wider general test applies to the admissibility of confessions, namely, that the accused must have made the confession while he or she was in his or her sound and sober senses and, in addition, must not have been made due to improper ('undue') influence (section 217(1) of the Criminal Procedure Act, 1977).

Since the decision in *S v Sheehama*,[99] pointings out should effectively be treated as informal admissions by conduct and are therefore subject to the same admissions test as informal admissions.

The Court suggested in *S v Agnew and Another*[100] that perhaps the time had come to abolish what the Court called the 'artificial' distinction between admissions and confessions, and to apply the same general test contained in section 217(1) of the Criminal Procedure Act, 1977 to both, namely, whether the statement was made 'freely and voluntarily', in other words without undue influence, and while the accused was in his or her sound and sober senses. The Court noted that in many cases, admissions could be as damaging to the accused as confessions and that both violated the right against self-incrimination. The Court noted, however, that historically the more lenient admissibility test for admissions was justified on the basis that informal admissions were not as prejudicial to the accused's case as confessions. Admitting a confession into court, being an admission to all the elements of a crime, almost invariably led to a conviction while the same was seldom true of informal admissions.

The South African Law Reform Commission (SALRC)[101] has proposed that admissions, pointings out and confessions should all be subject to a single general rule of admissibility, namely, the current test applicable to confessions.

What, in your view, are the advantages and disadvantages of adopting a single rule of admissibility?

Table 50.1 *Differences between admissions and confessions*

Admissions	Confessions
May be made informally before trial or formally at trial	May be made informally before a criminal trial or formally as a plea of guilty at trial
Admissible at criminal and civil proceedings	Admissible only at criminal proceedings
May be directly or indirectly inferred from oral testimony or by positive/negative conduct	Must be a direct and express oral/written statement
Must be made by the person against whom it is tendered except when made vicariously by a third party	Must be made directly by the confessor

---

99 1991 (2) SA 860 (A).
100 1996 (2) SACR 535 (C).
101 SALC Project 73 *Simplification of Criminal Procedure: A more inquisitorial approach to criminal procedure – police questioning, defence disclosure, the role of judicial officers and judicial management of trials* (2002).

Admissions	Confessions
Adverse to its maker's interests and admissible as an exception to the hearsay rule as it is highly trustworthy and reliable	Adverse to its maker's interests and admissible as an exception to the hearsay rule as it is highly trustworthy and reliable
Admits to one or more but not all the essential elements of a crime or a civil dispute	An admission to all the essential elements of a specific crime
Prejudicial but does not in itself directly result in a conviction	Highly prejudicial, amounts to an unequivocal acknowledgment of guilt and leads directly to a conviction
S 219A requirements: • voluntarily made • not induced by any promise or threat from a person in authority • statutory requirements for admissibility are less strict	S 217 requirements: • freely and voluntarily made • in one's sound and sober senses without undue influence • if made to a peace officer must be reduced to writing before a magistrate or justice of the peace Statutory requirements for admissibility are strict
S 219A(1) creates a presumption and reverse onus on a person to prove that an admission reduced to writing was not voluntarily made Not yet declared unconstitutional	S 217(1)(*b*)(ii) created a presumption and reverse onus on the accused to prove that a confession reduced to writing was not freely and voluntarily made Declared unconstitutional
No need to corroborate an admission	S 209: must corroborate a confession

Pointings out (s 218)
- The physical act of pointing out is essentially a communication by conduct and amounts to an informal admission or confession.
- To be admissible it must meet the requirements set out in s 219A or s 217 of the CPA.
- Real evidence discovered as a result of an inadmissible pointing out may never-the-less be admitted where it meets the fair trial and administration of justice legs of s 35(5) of the Constitution.

50.7 Formal admissions in civil matters

50.7.1 Introduction

In terms of section 15 of the Civil Proceedings Evidence Act 25 of 1965, once a party makes a formal admission, it is neither necessary for a party to prove, nor competent to disprove, a fact admitted on the record.[102] A fact is admitted on the record when it is clearly and unequivocally admitted, expressly or by necessary implication, in the pleadings or orally at the trial, and the presiding officer records the fact.[103] In the case of pleadings, as discussed above, the rules of court require the defendant to 'admit or deny or confess and avoid all material facts alleged'[104] when drafting their plea to the plaintiff's particulars of claim. The rules go on to provide that if a party does not respond to every allegation in their plea, then

---

102 '... it shall not be necessary for any party in any civil proceedings to prove, nor shall it be competent for any such party to disprove any fact admitted on the record of such proceedings.' S 15 of the Civil Proceedings Evidence Act, 1965.
103 DT Zeffertt and AP Paizes *Essential Evidence* (2010) at 303 and footnote 149.
104 High Court Rule 22(2).

460 | THE LAW OF EVIDENCE IN SOUTH AFRICA

this lack of response will be considered to be an admission.[105] The consequence of this is that the plaintiff does not need to lead evidence to prove that fact.

50.7.2 Intention to make a formal admission

It is essential that a party has the intention to make the formal admission.[106] If it does not appear that the party had the intention to make the admission, then the court cannot accept it as a formal admission. The intention to make the admission can be elicited from a clear, unambiguous admission recorded in the pleading.

Let us consider an example. A plaintiff may make the following allegations in his or her particulars:

> The defendant was under the influence of alcohol and proceeded to cause a fight with my husband by slapping him across his face.

The defendant may respond in his plea:

> I admit that I was under the influence of alcohol when I slapped him across the face.

The defendant has clearly and unequivocally admitted that he was under the influence of alcohol and also, by necessary implication, that he slapped the husband across the face.

Intention can also be elicited from a failure to deny an allegation by the other side. For example, in response to the same allegation the defendant may plead:

> I did not cause the fight as I did not strike the first blow. The plaintiff's husband swore at me and punched me, to which I responded by slapping him across the face.

The defendant clearly admits to slapping the husband across the face and, by omission, also admits that he was under the influence of alcohol. The only part of the allegation that is denied is that he caused the fight.

50.7.3 Withdrawal of a formal admission

Once a party has admitted a fact, usually in the pleadings, the party may change their mind and wish to withdraw their admission. Although a party is entitled to do so,[107] this may cause difficulties as the other party may have started trial preparation on the basis of the admission and will now have to start afresh or seek further witnesses.[108] A party therefore cannot withdraw a formal admission unless it meets two requirements:

- First, the party must show that it made a **bona fide** mistake in making the admission.
- Second, the party must show that the ensuing amendment to the pleadings, in other words the withdrawal, will not cause prejudice to the opposing party which cannot be cured by an appropriate order for costs.

A *bona fide* mistake could be based on an error of judgment, a misunderstanding between lawyer and client, or an error in the drafting of the plea. An error is more likely to occur when

---

105 '... every allegation of fact in the combined summons or declaration which is not stated in the plea to be denied or to be admitted, shall be deemed to be admitted.' High Court Rule 22(3).

106 *AA Mutual Insurance Association Ltd v Biddulph and Another* 1976 (1) SA 725 (A) at 735.

107 *Whittaker v Roos and Another* 1911 TPD 1092; *Morant v Roos and Another* 1911 TPD 1092 at 1102–1103. The Court held that it would be reluctant to deny a party the opportunity to amend its pleadings, by which is meant to withdraw an admission. See also *S v Daniels en 'n Ander* 1983 (3) SA 275 (A).

108 *President Versekeringsmaatskappy Bpk v Moodley* 1964 (4) SA 109 (T) at 110–111.

CHAPTER 50 ADMISSIONS, POINTINGS OUT AND CONFESSIONS | 461

the admission is one by omission, for example where a poorly drafted plea, in error, fails to respond to an allegation, thereby admitting it.[109]

The second part of the test requires that no prejudice must occur which cannot be cured by a costs award. It is not considered prejudice to the opponent if the effect of the withdrawal of the admission is that the opponent loses their case. Prejudice in the legal sense, and in this instance, would occur if the effect of the withdrawal had a negative impact on the way the opponent conducts their case. For example, they may have disposed of crucial evidence, believing it was not needed as the other party had already given an admission. The second aspect of this part of the test acknowledges that there will always be a measure of prejudice as the opponent will now have to prove the previously admitted fact and this will cost time and money to do so. An adverse costs award simply means that the party withdrawing an admission will have to bear any costs their opponent incurs in dealing with the consequences.

Formal admissions are withdrawn by way of amendments to the pleadings. The party wishing to withdraw the admission must apply to the court and must satisfy the court that it has met the two requirements. The party can show this by way of affidavit or through oral evidence. Once the party has withdrawn the admission, it cannot be relied on. However, the fact that it was made, and was then withdrawn, is itself a piece of evidence that can be used.[110]

THIS CHAPTER IN ESSENCE

1   In criminal proceedings an accused may admit any fact placed in issue at such proceedings and any such admission shall be sufficient proof of the fact. Once an accused has made a formal admission, it is automatically admissible. A formal admission can only be withdrawn with the court's permission.

2   Informal admissions can be oral, written, express or implied and can be made before or during trial.

3   Informal admissions can also be contained in formal court documents.

4   The maker of an informal admission need not have known that his or her admission was adverse to his or her interest, or was intended to be adverse to his or her interest.

5   A court will determine the evidential value of an informal admission in light of the informal evidence as a whole at the end of a trial.

6   An accused must make an informal admission voluntarily. The onus rests on the State to prove such voluntariness beyond reasonable doubt.

7   The test to determine the admissibility of an informal admission is as follows:

   7.1   A court will decide which part of an oral or written statement contains an informal admission or whether certain conduct amounts to an informal admission.

   7.2   The court will then determine whether the informal admission was made by a person in authority over the accused or whether the accused was threatened or coerced into making the informal admission.

   7.3   If so, a court will determine whether the accused made the informal admission as a result of the improper threat or promise.

8   A vicarious admission is a statement made by a third person that becomes admissible against the accused even though the accused personally did not actually make it. Generally, vicarious admissions are inadmissible, save for the following two exceptions:

   8.1   where a co-perpetrator makes an executive statement in furtherance of a common purpose to commit a crime and this statement becomes admissible against all who were party to that joint criminal venture

   8.2   where the maker of the statement was authorised expressly or implicitly by the accused to make it on his or her behalf.

---

109   *Absa Bank Ltd v Blumberg and Wilkinson* 1995 (4) SA 403 (W).
110   *S v Mbothoma en 'n Ander* 1970 (2) SA 530 (O).

9 A pointing out refers to an overt physical indication and can, therefore, never contain words, whether written or oral.

10 All pointings out must be tested for admissibility in terms of section 219A of the Criminal Procedure Act, 1977 as admissions by conduct.

11 A confession refers to a series of informal admissions that cover all the elements of a crime and must be contained in a written or oral statement.

12 An essential element of a confession is the accused's intention to make a confession. Lack of intention can be raised by the accused as a defence.

13 When determining whether a statement amounts to a confession, an admission or neither, the following factors should be considered:

   13.1 the words used in the statement

   13.2 the content and context of the statement

   13.3 whether the accused admitted to every element of the crime in question.

14 For a confession to be admissible, it must be clear that:

   14.1 the accused made the confession freely and voluntarily

   14.2 the accused was in his or her sound and sober senses when he or she made the confession

   14.3 the accused was not unduly influenced to make the confession

   14.4 an oral or written statement containing a confession made to a peace officer was put in writing and confirmed before a magistrate or a justice.

15 Disputes regarding the admissibility of a confession will be resolved in a trial-within-a-trial.

16 The State has the burden of proving that the confession is admissible beyond reasonable doubt.

17 A confession that does not include an admission of every element of the crime concerned may constitute a confession to a lesser offence.

18 A court can convict an accused on the single evidence of his or her confession. The confession must, however, be confirmed in a material respect or there must be evidence other than the confession that shows that the offence was committed.

19 In civil proceedings a party can admit a fact in issue by means of a formal admission. The party can do this either orally in court or in writing in the pleadings. A formal admission is considered to be conclusive proof of an issue. It is therefore neither necessary to prove, nor competent to disprove, the particular fact admitted.

20 A party must, however, have the intention of making a formal admission otherwise it will not be accepted by the court.

21 A party can only withdraw a formal admission if:

   21.1 it has made a *bona fide* mistake when making the admission

   21.2 the ensuing amendment will not prejudice the opposing party.

22 Formal admissions are withdrawn by way of amendments to the pleadings.

PART SEVEN

Scientific forensic evidence

CHAPTER 51	Fingerprints and body-prints	464
CHAPTER 52	Blood typing and DNA testing	468
CHAPTER 53	Polygraphs and voice-stress analysers	474
CHAPTER 54	Neurotechnology and neurological evidence	480

Chapter 51

Fingerprints and body-prints

51.1   Introduction 464

51.2   Fingerprints and body-prints 465

51.3   Footprints 466

51.1   Introduction

Fingerprint and body-print evidence is admissible and, in the right circumstances, can be of considerable probative value, particularly in criminal matters. Note that the term 'body-print' is now used to refer to palmprint, footprint and other similar evidence. The Criminal Procedure Act 51 of 1977 refers to a body-print, and no longer to a palmprint or footprint.[1] 'Body-print' is defined to mean 'prints other than fingerprints, taken from a person and which are related to a crime scene, but excludes prints of the genitalia, buttocks or breasts of a person'.[2]

Fingerprint and palmprint evidence is based on the premise that no two humans have identical fingerprints or palmprints. In other words, every person's prints are unique. Therefore, the essential characteristic of fingerprint, palmprint and even footprint evidence is that it is comparative in nature. It requires a print, usually obtained from a crime scene, to be compared to those on a database or that of an accused to establish whether there is a similarity between the two sets of prints or for exclusionary purposes.

Two important implications arise from this. The first implication is that a comparative analysis between two sets of prints must be made. Such analysis and the evidence arising therefrom will generally require expert testimony.[3] However, in terms of section 212 of the Criminal Procedure Act, 1977, such evidence may be presented by way of an affidavit.[4] The second implication is that at least one set of the prints must be taken from the accused or a suspect to conduct an analysis. Sections 37 and 225 of the Criminal Procedure Act, 1977 provide that such forms of evidence may be obtained from an accused, even without the accused's consent, and still be admissible.

---

1   The Criminal Law (Forensic Procedures) Amendment Act 6 of 2010, which came into force in January 2013, substitutes body-print for palmprint and footprint throughout the Criminal Procedure Act.

2   Section 36A of the Criminal Procedure Act. Sections 36A and 36B contain detailed provisions dealing with the taking and handling of finger and body-prints.

3   Once an expert provides evidence that is accepted as credible, it constitutes *prima facie* proof and an onus rests on the accused to rebut the proof. See *Seyisi v S* (117/12) [2012] ZASCA 144 (28 September 2012) at para 12.

4   Section 212(4)(*a*) reads as follows: 'Whenever any fact established by any examination or process requiring any skill ... (vi) in ballistics, in the identification of finger prints or body-prints ... is or may become relevant to an issue at criminal proceedings, a document purporting to be an affidavit made by a person ... that he or she has established such a fact ... shall, upon its mere production ... be prima facie proof of such fact ...'.

CHAPTER 51   FINGERPRINTS AND BODY-PRINTS | **465**

These provisions have been challenged, albeit unsuccessfully, on several grounds:

- First, they have been challenged at common law on the basis that they violate the rule against self-incrimination.[5]
- Second, they have been challenged on constitutional grounds in that they violate the constitutional rights not to be compelled to make a confession against oneself (section $(35)(1)(c)$), to remain silent (section $35(3)(h)$) and not to be compelled to give self-incriminating evidence (section $35(3)(j)$). They also constitute an infringement of a person's right to privacy and dignity (sections $14(a)$ and 10 respectively)).[6]

51.2   Fingerprints and body-prints

Fingerprint evidence is perhaps the best known and most widespread of the forms of scientific evidence commonly used. Usually, the police lift fingerprints found, for example, at the crime scene and send them to police fingerprint experts for analysis. These experts then compare the prints to those on a database[7] to identify the person. Alternatively, where fingerprints from a suspect have been taken and sent for analysis, the two sets of fingerprints can be compared.

If there are sufficient points of similarity – the accepted norm is that seven points are sufficient[8] – the prints are regarded as being those of the individual concerned and will carry whatever evidentiary implication the circumstances in which they were found would indicate. For example, they may indicate the presence of an accused at a crime scene or the identity of a body.

Evidence of points of similarity is usually presented by way of an affidavit[9] although it may be done orally. Sometimes, evidence is presented with a comparison chart describing the way the comparison was made, commenting on the points of significance, providing an opinion and providing reasons for the opinion expressed by the expert. Once admitted, fingerprint evidence carries significant probative value.

DISCUSSION	**Fingerprint analyses: how many comparison points are enough?**
51.1	Twelve concordant characteristics are used in fingerprint identification. The South African courts of law are prepared to accept seven concordant characteristics as being 'beyond reasonable doubt' in the case of finger-, hand- and footprints.[10]
	'...the SAPS Criminal Record Centre stipulates that two prints are regarded as corresponding and from the same origin if at least seven ridge characteristics can be

---

5 See *Ex parte Minister of Justice: In re R v Matemba* 1941 AD 75.

6 *S v Huma and Another* (2) 1995 (2) SACR 411 (W). It is arguable that s 39 of the Constitution does not preclude the admissibility of evidence of other body parts such as lip-print comparisons. Indeed, the Criminal Law (Forensic Procedures) Amendment Act, 2010 now specifically refers to body-prints.

7 South African Police Service Act, 1995 with the insertion of s 15A. This section provides for the establishment of a database on which fingerprints, body-prints and photographic images must be stored and made readily available in computerised or other forms. In addition, the South African Police Service Act, 1995 now provides, in s 15B, that when searching the database for the detection of crime, the investigation of an offence, the identification of missing persons, the identification of unidentified human remains and the conducting of a prosecution, recourse may be had to other state databases, including those of the Departments of Home Affairs and Transport.

8 *S v Kimimbi* 1963 (3) SA 250 (C) and *S v Nala* 1965 (4) SA 360 (A).

9 S 212 of the Criminal Procedure Act, 1977 as amended by the Criminal Law (Forensic Procedures) Amendment Act, 2010.

10 VM Phillips and CF Scheepers 'Comparison between fingerprint and dental concordant characteristics' (1990) 8(1) *Journal of Forensic Odontostomatology* 17, 19.

identified on both prints that correspond in respect of type, size, direction, position and relation to each other and further, where no unexplainable differences exist between the two prints'.[11]

Most of the South African cases dealing with fingerprint analysis have accepted that seven points of similarity are sufficient for purposes of identification.[12] At the other extreme, the United Kingdom requires, as the norm, 16 points of similarity. This standard is controversial and can be criticised for being too high a standard.

This raises the question: how many points of comparison should be required to infer proof beyond a reasonable doubt?

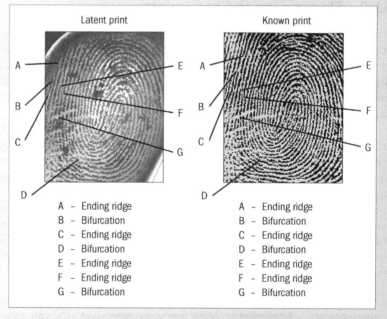

Figure 51.1 Fingerprint comparison with seven points of similarity

51.3 Footprints

Unlike fingerprints, footprints do not necessarily require expert evidence. Such evidence is admissible subject to the standard requirement of all opinion evidence, namely, that it is of appreciable assistance to the court. The circumstances under which such evidence will be of assistance to the court vary. For example, the footprints may be either shod (for example, an imprint left by shoes, rather than a naked human foot)[13] or unshod. Plaster casts or photographs of footprints are readily examinable by the court itself without the need for opinion evidence.[14] However, a bare footprint may be treated like a fingerprint or palmprint and will thus require opinion evidence.[15]

---

11 L Meintjes-Van der walt 'Fingerprint evidence: Probing myth and reality' 152 at 156 note 26. http://www.academia.edu/931537/Fingerprint_evidence_probing_myth_or_reality_fingerprint_evidence, referring to C Lansdown, W Hoal and A Lansdown *South African Criminal Law and Procedure* 6 ed (1957) at 625-626.
12 Cases such as *S v Blom* 1992 (1) SACR 649 (E) and *S v Nyathe* 1988 (2) SA 211 (O).
13 *S v Mkhabela* 1984 (1) SA 556 (A); *Mtoto v S* (A488/14) [2015] ZAWCHC 45 (22 April 2015).
14 *R v Makeip* 1948 (1) SA 947 (A).
15 *S v Limekayo* 1969 (1) SA 540 (E).

DISCUSSION	The murder of Inge Lotz[16]
51.2	A young university student, Inge Lotz, was found murdered in her apartment and fingerprint evidence allegedly taken from a DVD case placed the accused at the scene at the relevant time. However, an international fingerprint expert discredited the prints, arguing that they were not taken from a flat surface like a DVD case, but had been taken from a curved one i.e. a glass. The fingerprints thus did not necessarily place the accused at the apartment at the relevant time.
	In addition, evidence of a bloody footprint found at the murder scene was also tendered. It was alleged that the print matched a shoe of the accused. This too was discredited by an international expert witness. It was argued by the defence that the police had deliberately misrepresented the origin of the fingerprints and also withheld important information about the footprint, thus undermining any probative value they may have had.

THIS CHAPTER IN ESSENCE

1 Fingerprint and body-print evidence is admissible because of its high probative value. To be admissible, the following requirements must be met:

   1.1 An expert must do a comparative analysis between two sets of prints.

   1.2 At least one set of the prints must be taken from the accused or a suspect.

2 These forms of evidence will remain admissible even if they were obtained from the accused without his or her consent.

3 Footprint evidence does not necessarily require expert evidence and will be admissible if it assists the court.

---

16 *S v Van der Vyver* 2008 (1) SA 556 (C).

Chapter 52

Blood typing and DNA testing

52.1	**Blood tests**	**468**
	52.1.1 Criminal cases	468
	52.1.2 Civil cases	469
52.2	**DNA testing**	**470**
	52.2.1 How DNA testing works	470
	52.2.2 Process of DNA testing	470
	52.2.3 Probative value of DNA testing	471
	52.2.4 Procedure for admitting DNA evidence	471
	52.2.5 Chain of custody of DNA evidence	472
	52.2.6 Pre-trial disclosure of DNA evidence	472

52.1 Blood tests

The results of blood tests are admissible in both criminal and civil matters and are used in a number of cases. The most common are criminal charges of driving under the influence of alcohol and civil proof of paternity cases. However, the usefulness of blood tests is by no means limited to these types of cases.

52.1.1 Criminal cases

In criminal cases that involve establishing blood alcohol levels, blood tests are of significant probative value. For a blood sample to be admissible, it must be taken from a suspect in the manner prescribed by section 37 of the Criminal Procedure Act 51 of 1977. While certain bodily samples may be drawn by police for forensic DNA analysis,[1] the police themselves are not allowed to take a blood sample, although a sample may be taken at their insistence. A prescribed person, usually a district surgeon, a registered medical practitioner or a nurse, must take the blood sample.[2]

Section 37 makes it clear that an individual may not refuse to provide a blood sample, but this has been challenged. The courts, although there is some inconsistency in their approach, have adopted the attitude that although the taking of an involuntary sample may infringe constitutional rights to privacy and bodily integrity, this infringement is justifiable and it does not constitute an infringement of the right against self-incrimination.[3]

When the prosecution wishes to lead such evidence, the sample taking must comply with the prescribed process and a clear, unbroken *chain of custody* must be established. This is

---

1   Chapter 5B of the South African Police Service Act 68 of 1995 regulates police powers in taking some bodily samples, including buccal samples.

2   Section 37(2)(*a*).

3   *S v Orrie and Another* 2004 (1) SACR 162 (C).

CHAPTER 52 BLOOD TYPING AND DNA TESTING | 469

required to ensure that the integrity of the evidence is not compromised. This means that every step of the process must be documented in terms of section 212(8) of the Criminal Procedure Act, 1977 including:

- the point where the sample was taken
- the equipment used to draw the sample
- the receptacle in which it was stored
- custody of the sample before and while in transit
- delivery
- analysis.

Such evidence is usually given by way of affidavit and the information relating thereto forms part of the information contained in the police docket to which the defence is entitled.[4]

52.1.2 Civil cases

When *red blood cell tests* are conducted to analyse the blood itself to determine, for example, paternity, then the results are of less probative value than the results of tests that ascertain whether there are traces of other elements in the blood sample such as alcohol or other drugs. Red blood cell tests are valuable only as an exclusionary tool. They are not accurate enough or, more correctly, red blood cell analysis is not individually unique enough, to be an identification mechanism. Such tests are merely capable of proving a negative, for example that a particular individual could not be the father of a particular child.

HLA tissue typing[5] is based on white blood cell testing. It is a more advanced and much more accurate method of testing and is regarded by our courts as being accurate to 99,85 per cent.[6] This is, of course, an oversimplification of the complexities involved in HLA analysis. In tests to exclude paternity, the lack of identical HLA antigens between child and alleged father will automatically exclude paternity. In cases where some HLA match occurs, the probabilities, provided the HLA analysis is done in sufficient depth, are arguably in the region of a 99 per cent exclusion.[7]

There is no civil statutory provision or an equivalent of section 37 of the Criminal Procedure Act, 1977 that provides statutory authority for blood tests in civil matters. Instead, courts rely on their **inherent jurisdiction** to order such tests in circumstances when they deem it necessary to do so. This is often the case in paternity cases.[8]

However, the approach of the courts in this regard is not uniform throughout the country. Furthermore, there is the argument, not yet tested in court, that such an order may be an unconstitutional invasion of privacy of the person being tested. This argument is unlikely to be upheld given the provisions of section 28(2) of the Constitution which provides, 'A child's best interests are of paramount importance in every matter concerning the child'. Of course,

---

4 *Shabalala and Others v Attorney-General of Transvaal and Another* 1995 (2) SACR 761 (CC).
5 HLA means human leucocyte antigen. It refers to the major histocompatibility complex (MHC). This is a gene cluster situated on chromosome 6 which is used in assessing compatibility for organ transplant cases. HLA types are inherited and thus HLA tissue typing is very accurate in determining matches in paternity cases.
6 *Van der Harst v Viljoen* 1977 (1) SA 795 (C).
7 U Shankarkumar 'The Human Leukocyte Antigen (HLA) System' (2004) 4(2) *International Journal of Human Genetics* 91 at 101.
8 *Seetal v Pravitha NO and Another* 1983 (3) SA 827 (D) and *M v R* 1989 (1) SA 416 (O), referred to subsequently in *Botha v Dreyer (now Moller)* (4421/08) [2008] ZAGPHC 395 (19 November 2008), in which the High Court laments the unsatisfactory state of the law. On appeal to the Supreme Court of Appeal, it was held that scientific tests on a child to determine paternity should not be ordered where paternity has been shown on a balance of probabilities (*YM v LB* (465/09) [2010] ZASCA 106 (17 September 2010)).

470 | THE LAW OF EVIDENCE IN SOUTH AFRICA

this provision cannot be invoked if the paternity dispute is in respect of a person who is over the age of 18.

Section 36 of the Children's Act 38 of 2005 provides for a presumption that unless evidence to the contrary is led, a person who is proved to have 'had sexual intercourse with the mother of the child at any time when that child could have been conceived' is presumed to be the biological father of that child. This places a burden on the alleged father to lead evidence to create a reasonable doubt which is usually done by submitting to a blood test. The refusal to do this no longer gives rise to the presumption that the refusal is intended to conceal the truth concerning the paternity of the child, but does require the person so refusing to be warned of the impact that such refusal may have on his credibility.[9]

52.2 DNA testing

Research and development in the field of DNA analysis is intensely scientific. The **forensic** evidentiary value of DNA analysis is therefore secondary to the development of DNA research for other primary reasons. Setting aside these primary scientific research objectives and focusing on the implications for evidence, we find that **DNA testing** is incredibly accurate. Every person's DNA is unique to that individual unless that person is one of a set of identical twins. DNA analysis can thus be of extraordinary probative value. The Supreme Court of Appeal in *S v SB*[10] sets out information about both the theory and practice of DNA testing.

52.2.1 How DNA testing works

The human body comprises cells and each cell contains a nucleus. There are 46 chromosomes divided into 23 pairs in each nucleus. Each chromosome comprises between 20 000 and 25 000 genes. These genes are arranged in pairs in a thread-like line with a slight spiral twist – the famous double helix pattern – and comprise deoxyribonucleic acid or DNA.

Every person's DNA is different. However, because 23 chromosomes are inherited from a person's father and a matching pair of 23 chromosomes are inherited from a person's mother, making up the 23 pairs and totalling 46 chromosomes, each person's DNA has certain characteristics in common with each parent's DNA. This, of course, also applies to any offspring that that person may have. Thus, the evidentiary value of DNA evidence goes well beyond paternity cases and can be used for individual identification, even of deceased persons. Furthermore, for purposes of analysis, DNA can be extracted from almost any human cell, thus providing a wide range of sources. The most common sources are semen, blood, hair follicles, skin and bone.

52.2.2 Process of DNA testing

The two parallel, linked strands of genetic material are linked at base points called nucleotides. There are about 3 billion nucleotides in each nucleus. The order of these nucleotides is different in every human. Short sections of non-gene type DNA[11] are examined and a band reflecting the DNA structure is printed out. These bands can then be compared

---

9 Section 37 of the Children's Act, 2005.
10 2014 (1) SACR 66 (SCA).
11 Using non-gene type DNA sidesteps genetically determined characteristics, thus avoiding prejudice or victimisation based on characteristics such as race, for example.

to check for matches. Such a comparison may be made with other samples taken, for example, from a crime scene or a DNA database.[12]

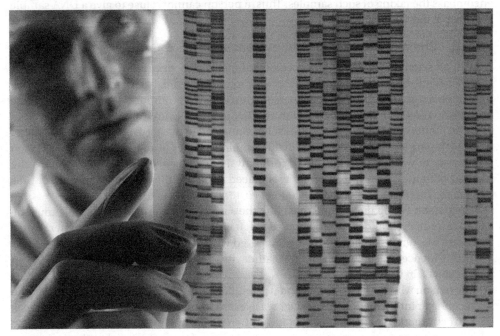

Figure 52.1 DNA analysis printout

52.2.3 Probative value of DNA testing

DNA evidence is extremely accurate. For example, in paternity cases it has been held that DNA provides an accuracy level of 99,94 per cent or, phrased as an exclusionary test, it reduces the odds that a person is not the father to 0,06 per cent.

52.2.4 Procedure for admitting DNA evidence

With DNA evidence, the evidentiary chain commences well before trial. With the possibility of litigation in mind, it starts with the taking of the initial sample. In criminal cases, detectives or, more commonly, forensic field workers from criminal record centres take the initial sample from the scene of a crime. Medical and health care practitioners may also take a DNA sample in a hospital.[13] Taking DNA samples from individuals, however, is now regulated by sections 36A and 36D of the Criminal Procedure Act, 1977 which allow the police[14] to take

---

12 South Africa has a National DNA Criminal Intelligence Database (NCIC), but it is at present very limited. Legislation has been passed, the Criminal Law (Forensic Procedures) Amendment Act 37 of 2013, which amends *inter alia* the South African Police Service Act and expands and regulates the DNA database.
13 As L Meintjes-Van der Walt *DNA in the Courtroom: Principles and Practice* (2010) at 63–73 points out, there are a number of potentially fatal problems that can arise at this stage. The person taking the sample may not be sufficiently trained or may lack experience, the quality of the sample may be poor, police crime kits are often incomplete and there may be delays in delivery of the sample to the laboratory.
14 Section 36A(1)(*b*) '"authorized person" means-... (ii) with reference to buccal samples, any police official or member of the Independent Police Investigative Directorate, referred to in the Independent Police Investigative Directorate Act, who is not the crime scene examiner of the particular case, but has successfully undergone the training prescribed by the Minister of Health under the National Health Act, in respect of the taking of a buccal sample'.

THE LAW OF EVIDENCE IN SOUTH AFRICA

non-intimate and buccal[15] DNA samples.[16] Although section 37 of the Criminal Procedure Act, 1977 does not specifically refer to the taking of DNA samples, it is sufficiently broad to encompass the taking of such samples. Thus, a person cannot refuse to give a DNA sample as with a blood sample.[17]

52.2.5 Chain of custody of DNA evidence

As with all scientific evidence, the accuracy of measurement is immaterial if the forensic evidence is not directly linked to the accused or relevant person. In civil matters, for example, the sample must have come from the person from whom it is purported to have come. There must be no risk that it was confused with another person's sample or was tampered with. In criminal matters, the DNA evidence must be connected to the accused, in other words, that it is what it purports to be. Each stage of the sample's journey from the moment it was taken all the way to when it was submitted for analysis must be accounted for, as well as the method of transport, in whose care it was placed and even the receptacle in which it was contained. This is referred to as the chain of custody.

The person taking the sample must link the sample to the crime. The sample must be linked to its analysis and it must be proved that it was properly safeguarded, in other words, that there was no possibility of it being tampered with.

This evidence is usually presented by affidavits from each of the following people who were involved in the process:

- The person who took the sample and who confirms its source, how it was taken, that the receptacle into which it was placed was sealed immediately prior to use, that it was correctly marked or identified, that it was then sealed and to whom it was given
- The person or persons receiving it into their custody, confirming that the seals were untampered with and confirming delivery
- The laboratory, confirming receipt from whom and that the receptacle was sealed on receipt thereof.[18]

52.2.6 Pre-trial disclosure of DNA evidence

Due to the complexity of DNA evidence, it is imperative that sufficient pre-trial disclosure of DNA evidence takes place to allow the opposing party in civil matters or the accused in criminal matters to prepare adequately for the trial and to challenge the evidence presented. This is regulated by the standard rules governing pre-trial disclosure or discovery in civil matters, and by the common law in criminal matters, as expounded in *Shabalala and Others v Attorney-General of Transvaal and Another*[19] and developed in *S v Crossberg*.[20] It is arguable that this duty encompasses the need to make available the evidence, notes and basis on which any statistical analysis was made.[21]

---

15 Section 36A(1) (cB) 'buccal sample' means a sample of cellular material taken from the inside of a person's mouth.

16 In *S v Carolus* 2008 (2) SACR 207 (SCA) and *Mugwedi v The State* (694/13) [2014] ZASCA 23 (27 March 2014) para 2 the issue of crime kits not being available at the hospital to enable doctors to take a sample for DNA analysis was raised by the courts which reiterated that it is imperative in sexual assault cases, especially those involving children, that DNA tests be conducted.

17 If the sample is a blood sample, or an intimate sample, then it must be taken by a medical practitioner or a nurse.

18 For a more detailed description, see Meintjes-Van der Walt (2010) at 14 and 15.

19 1995 (2) SACR 761 (CC).

20 2008 (2) SACR 317 (SCA) at paras 75–80.

21 Meintjes-Van der Walt (2010) at 27.

CHAPTER 52   BLOOD TYPING AND DNA TESTING   473

THIS CHAPTER IN ESSENCE

1   Blood tests are admissible in both criminal and civil matters and are used in a number of cases because of their high probative value.

2   In criminal cases that involve establishing blood alcohol levels, the blood sample must be taken by the person prescribed in section 37 of the Criminal Procedure Act, 1977, namely a district surgeon, registered medical practitioner or nurse, to be admissible. Also, before this evidence can be led, a clear and unbroken chain of custody must be established.

3   In terms of section 37 of the Criminal Procedure Act, 1977, an individual may not refuse to provide a blood sample. Although this has been challenged on constitutional grounds, it has been found to be justifiable and does not infringe the right against self-incrimination.

4   In the absence of any civil statutory provision providing statutory authority for blood tests in civil matters, courts rely on their inherent jurisdiction to order such tests if deemed necessary.

5   In civil cases, red blood cell tests are of less probative value as they are not accurate enough to serve as an identification mechanism. Our courts regard HLA tissue typing as being more accurate than red blood cell tests.

6   Due to the accuracy of DNA testing and the fact that no two individuals have the same DNA, this type of analysis carries a high probative value as evidence.

7   DNA evidence must be linked to the crime. The sample must be linked to its analysis and it must be proved that it was properly safeguarded.

8   DNA evidence is presented by means of affidavits from each of the following people involved in the process:

8.1   The person responsible for taking the sample

8.2   The person(s) receiving it into their custody

8.3   The laboratory.

9   The opposing party in civil matters or the accused in criminal matters must receive sufficient pre-trial disclosure of the intention to use DNA evidence during trial so as to enable them to prepare adequately for the trial and challenge the evidence.

Chapter 53

Polygraphs and voice-stress analysers

53.1 Polygraphs (lie-detectors)	**474**
53.1.1 Scientific reliability of polygraph tests	474
53.1.2 Admissibility of polygraph tests	475
53.1.3 Unresolved issues in South Africa and the approach in the United States of America	476
53.1.4 Arguments against admissibility of polygraph tests	476
53.1.4.1 Collateral issues	477
53.1.4.2 Unreliability	477
53.1.4.3 Weight of opinion evidence	477
53.1.4.4 Probative value versus practicality	477
53.1.4.5 Probative value versus prejudice	477
53.1.4.6 Admissibility of opinion evidence	478
53.2 Voice-stress analysers	**478**

53.1 Polygraphs (lie-detectors)

A **polygraph** is a device that measures and records momentary physiological changes in respiration, blood pressure, heart rate, pulse and skin current associated with the sweating of the palms which take place in response to questions put to an examinee. Generally, an examiner asks the examinee questions, some of which are directly relevant to a specific matter under investigation while others are unconnected to the matter. Although commonly referred to as a **lie-detector**, a polygraph does not measure lying or deception – it merely records physiological activity in the examinee.

An examiner then purports to infer from the recorded physiological results that an examinee was deceptive in answering questions relating to a factual issue. The theoretical assumption underlying the use of polygraph testing is that a fear of detection will produce a measurable physiological reaction in a person who knows that he or she is lying. Accordingly, the polygraph purportedly measures the fear of deception rather than deception itself.

53.1.1 Scientific reliability of polygraph tests

Researchers are divided on the scientific reliability and accuracy of polygraph tests. In *Fawu obo Kapesi and Others v Premier Foods Ltd t/a Blue Ribbon Salt River*, two expert witnesses could not agree on this after days of testimony on polygraph tests.[1] The controversy lies in

---

1   [2010] 9 BLLR 903 (LC).

the interpretation of and the inferences drawn from the physiological responses to the questions.

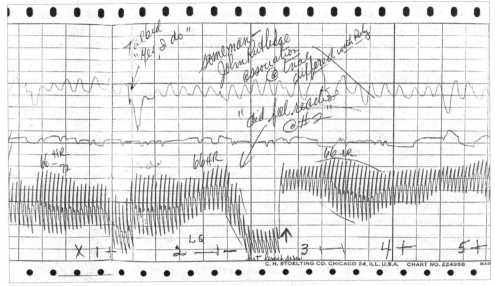

Figure 53.1 Polygraph test and printout

Critics of the test submit that there is no unique pattern of bodily responses that manifest when a person lies or fears detection. Polygraph tests merely indicate that a subject was in a heightened state of general emotional arousal and not that this was necessarily occasioned by a deceptive frame of mind. Polygraph tests cannot distinguish anxiety, stress, tension or indignation from deception. There is also a hypothesis that people, including different ethnic groups, react differently to stress. A range of variables may have an impact on the accuracy of the test, including the competence and experience of the examiner in formulating appropriate questions, conducting the test and in drawing the relevant inferences from the results.

Most polygraphers are not qualified psychologists so their level of expertise often does not allow them to discount the fact that other psychological states may produce the same bodily responses as the ones that they interpret as deception. While the evidence they provide about the physiological responses they record may be accurate, it is ultimately on a psychological question that they tender evidence, namely the presence or absence of a deceptive mindset. Neither the science nor their own area of expertise permits them to draw the deductions that they often do.

53.1.2 Admissibility of polygraph tests

After considering extensive expert evidence on the subject, the Court in *Fawu obo Kapesi and Others v Premier Foods Ltd t/a Blue Ribbon Salt River*[2] held that polygraph testing can do no more than show the existence or non-existence of deception and found that, even on this score, scientists are divided. In the context of a disciplinary process in an employment or labour dispute, the polygraph can be a useful tool in the investigation process but cannot

---

2 [2010] 9 BLLR 903 (LC).

476 | THE LAW OF EVIDENCE IN SOUTH AFRICA

on its own be used to determine the guilt of an employee. The Court held that the results of a polygraph may be taken into account in assessing the credibility of a witness and in assessing the probabilities where other supporting evidence is available. This is provided that there is clear evidence on the qualifications of the polygrapher and that it is clear from the evidence that the test was done according to acceptable and recognised standards.[3]

This has been the general recent approach in labour arbitrations as well. In most matters the issue was whether or not the applicant employee had committed misconduct. In the face of circumstantial evidence against the employee or the presence of other grounds for believing that the employee was dishonest in his or her version, the arbitrators received the results of a polygraph test to strengthen the weight of the evidence against the employee.[4]

53.1.3 Unresolved issues in South Africa and the approach in the United States of America

It is, however, difficult to discern from the above rulings the basis on which the scientific arguments that questioned the way polygraph examiners draw conclusions from the recorded physiological responses were overcome. A further problem is that the courts did not determine what constitutes acceptable and recognised polygraph test standards and the qualifications of polygraphers. There is no regulatory framework in South Africa on these issues.

In the United States of America, the concerns regarding the scientific validity of polygraphs led the US Federal Government to pass the Employee Polygraph Protection Act of 1994. This requires polygraph tests to be administered in terms of specified standards and by operators who possess specified minimum qualifications. The employee may secure in advance a copy of the questions and has the right to counsel before each phase of the test.

An American court[5] suggested a three-step enquiry into the admissibility of polygraph test results:

- Whether the evidence is relevant and reliable
- Whether the evidence assists the court in determining the facts in issue
- Whether the evidence has an unfairly prejudicial effect, because if it does, this would substantially outweigh its probative value.

Evidence of the fact that an examinee's body betrayed signs of deception (if not deception alone) when they answered a question that is material to the issue before a court would seem to be logically relevant. This evidence would be of reasonable assistance to a court in the exercise of its fact-finding duty and could possibly lead to a more reliable assessment by the court of the examinee's credibility.

53.1.4 Arguments against admissibility of polygraph tests

However, there are a number of arguments against the admissibility of polygraphs in a South African context and these will be discussed below.

---

3 *Fawu obo Kapesi and Others v Premier Foods Ltd t/a Blue Ribbon Salt River* [2010] 9 BLLR 903 (LC); *Truworths Ltd v CCMA and Others* [2008] JOL 22565 (LC); *SATAWU and Others v Protea Security Services* (unreported case number JS754/2001: 24 November 2004).

4 *SACCAWU obo Dolo v Somerset Wines International (Pty) Ltd* [2009] 10 BALR 1069 (CCMA); *FN Mzimela and United National Breweries (SA) (Pty) Ltd* (2005) 14 CCMA 8.23.11 and *DHL Supply Chain (Pty) Ltd v De Beer NO and Others* (DA4/2013) [2014] ZALAC 15; [2014] 9 BLLR 860 (LAC); (2014) 35 ILJ 2379 (LAC) (13 May 2014) at para 9. For a contrary view, see *Steen and Wetherleys (Pty) Ltd* (2005) 15 CCMA 7.1.6; *Sosibo and Others v Ceramic Tile Market* (2001) 22 ILJ 811 (CCMA).

5 *United States v Posado* 57 F 3rd 428 (5th Cir) (1995).

53.1.4.1 Collateral issues

There is no consensus in the scientific community that polygraph evidence is reliable. There is also no regulatory framework in South Africa on what constitutes acceptable and recognised polygraph test standards and qualifications for polygraphers. The enquiry into admissibility would therefore probably result in a proliferation of collateral factual and legal disputes. The examinee, who is a party to the proceedings, may be procedurally disadvantaged or otherwise exposed to a lengthy trial involving issues that, although logically relevant, are legally too remote to assist the court in its ultimate decision on the merits of the case. In *Gemalto South Africa (Pty) Ltd v Ceppwawu obo Louw and Others*,[6] 23 out of 189 employees who signed a petition refusing to subject themselves to a polygraph test were charged and dismissed. The Labour Appeal Court held that the reasons for which the employees were dismissed did not serve the real purpose of the polygraph test and there was no rational link between the dismissal and the alleged misconduct. The dismissal was therefore held to be substantively unfair.

53.1.4.2 Unreliability

In terms of the theoretical framework on which polygraphy rests, test results may be significantly influenced by examiner behaviour. Aside from satisfactory compliance with pre-test procedures and disclosure of questions, nothing short of replaying the entire videotaped encounter between examiner and examinee in a subsequent tribunal would suffice to establish the reliability of the test result.[7]

53.1.4.3 Weight of opinion evidence

Moreover, there is the risk that this time-consuming and expensive enquiry would not justify the final result which is merely the opinion of someone else that the witness concerned is truthful or untruthful according to a questionable test.[8]

53.1.4.4 Probative value versus practicality

The probative value of polygraph evidence is already theoretically slim. When this is considered against the practical disadvantages of receiving such evidence, it does not seem worthwhile.

53.1.4.5 Probative value versus prejudice

Even if polygraph evidence could be expeditiously received, there is the question of whether it should be. In answering this, note that it is not sufficient that evidence is relevant for it to be admissible. In addition, evidence must not unfairly prejudice the party against whom it is being adduced and the use of that evidence may not be against public policy.

It may be argued that polygraph evidence, which purports to show deception on the part of a witness, so prejudices the mind of a trier of fact against the witness that its production may only be fair if the probative value of this evidence is extremely high. However, this is not the case. Even in those cases where labour tribunals have allowed it, the evidence was only received as secondary corroborative evidence.

---

6 *Gemalto South Africa (Pty) Ltd v Ceppwawu obo Louw and Others* (2015) 36 ILJ 3002 (LAC).

7 According to PJ Schwikkard and SE van der Merwe *Principles of Evidence* 3 ed (2009) at 49, 'A proliferation of side-issues can, for example, arise where a court decides to admit evidence of the results of a polygraph test'.... Was the polygraphist competent? Was he [or she] an expert in this fairly novel 'technique' of determining credibility? 'Were appropriate questions asked during the session? Did the machine function properly? How reliable is the final result?'

8 Schwikkard and Van der Merwe 3 ed (2009) at 48–49.

478 | THE LAW OF EVIDENCE IN SOUTH AFRICA

The only way the probative value of polygraph evidence, *as expert evidence*, could be increased is if its generation takes place under national, legally regulated, uniform and independent standards. These do not exist in South Africa and it would be against public policy to allow the admission of expert evidence gathered under unregulated circumstances when it is so prejudicial and so light in inherent weight.

53.1.4.6 Admissibility of opinion evidence

Polygraph evidence is also arguably irrelevant opinion evidence because it is the duty of the court to make findings of credibility wherever necessary and it begs the very question the court is qualified to decide without assistance, namely, whether a witness's account of facts is dishonest or evasive.[9] In *Holtzhauzen v Roodt*,[10] the defendant attempted to admit the evidence of a hypnotherapist as an expert witness to testify that, in his opinion based on hypnotherapy sessions, the defendant was telling the truth about a rape incident. The Court excluded the evidence as irrelevant and, therefore, inadmissible on the basis that the proposed evidence of the hypnotherapist would displace the value judgment of the Court and shift the fact-finding responsibility of the Court to the witness. The Court itself had to and could decide matters of credibility without the opinion of the hypnotherapist. The Supreme Court of Canada has similarly found the results of polygraphs to be inadmissible as evidence of credibility.[11] In *DHL Supply Chain (Pty) Ltd v De Beer NO and Others*,[12] the Labour Appeal Court held that, despite the absence of expert evidence to establish the cogency of the concept of polygraphs and their efficacy in the evidence led in the case, the evidence of the polygraph test was taken at face value, an approach apparently based on a willingness by the Labour Court in the past to attribute a degree of respectability to such a process.

53.2 Voice-stress analysers

A **voice-stress analyser** is a monograph, not a polygraph, because only one physiological response is focused on – the voice. The Labour Court in *Mahlangu v CIM Deltak, Gallant v CIM Deltak*[13] refused to admit the results of a voice-stress analyser on the basis that voice patterns differ greatly between cultural groups and that there is no universal system of voice patterns reflecting emotions as there is, for example, in the case of fingerprints. The Court found it unacceptable for the respondent employer in this case to use an American voice analysis test to examine black South Africans for the purpose of determining whether they were telling the truth.

THIS CHAPTER IN ESSENCE

1   The result of a polygraph may be taken into account in internal disciplinary hearings in assessing a witness's credibility and in assessing probabilities. However, the results are not admissible in court.

2   There is no regulatory framework in South Africa on polygraph test standards and the qualifications of polygraphers.

---

9   T Cohen, A Rycroft and B Whitcher *Trade Unions and the Law in South Africa* (2009) at 106. See also Schwikkard and Van der Merwe 3 ed (2009) at 49.
10   1997 (4) SA 766 (W).
11   *R v Beland* [1987] 2 SCR 398. See also *United States v Scheffer* 523 US 303 (1998).
12   *DHL Supply Chain (Pty) Ltd v De Beer NO and Others* (2014) 35 ILJ 2379 (LAC).
13   (1986) 7 ILJ 346 (IC).

3 According to the American three-step enquiry into the admissibility of polygraph test results, before admitting the evidence a court needs to consider whether this type of evidence:
  3.1 is relevant and reliable
  3.2 assists the court in determining the facts in issue
  3.3 has an unfairly prejudicial effect.
4 The admissibility of polygraphs in South Africa is contested on the following grounds:
  4.1 The enquiry into admissibility would probably result in a proliferation of collateral factual and legal disputes.
  4.2 Test results may be significantly influenced by examiner behaviour.
  4.3 The time-consuming and expensive enquiry would not justify the final result.
  4.4 The probative value of the evidence does not outweigh the practical disadvantages of receiving such evidence.
  4.5 The probative value of the evidence does not outweigh the prejudice in the mind of the trier of fact against the witness.
  4.6 Polygraph evidence is considered to be irrelevant opinion evidence.
5 Voice-stress analysis evidence is not admissible due to the fact that there is no universal system of voice patterns reflecting emotions.

Chapter 54

Neurotechnology and neurological evidence

54.1 Introduction 480

54.2 How forensic brain scan analysis (FBSA) works 481

54.3 Testing methodology 482

54.4 The use of forensic brain scan analysis (FBSA) in criminal cases 483

54.5 Future application of forensic brain scan analysis (FBSA) 485

54.6 How functional magnetic resonance imaging (fMRI) works 485

54.7 The use of fMRI in court cases 485

54.8 Future application of fMRI 486

54.1 Introduction

Neuroscientific evidence is a relatively new forensic science that attempts to provide neurological evidence of a person's knowledge or ignorance of a fact by scanning or analysing that person's brain. Two examples of neurotechnology being developed for potential use in court are forensic brain scan analysis (FBSA) and functional magnetic resonance imaging (fMRI). Forensic brain scan analysis, also called brain fingerprinting, is a procedure that has the objective of establishing if a person has *knowledge* of given information or not.[1] This knowledge is detected by using an EEG[2] to measure certain brainwave responses of the person being tested. The person sits in front of a computer and clicks on various preloaded images, sentences and phrases in a controlled environment. It can be used as a pre-trial investigative tool to eliminate people as possible suspects and possibly could even be used during trial proceedings to settle disputes that may arise in the course of the trial.[3]

FBSA cannot indicate or prove that the person being tested, called the **subject**, is being untruthful or not. It merely attempts to establish whether or not the subject has *knowledge*

---

1   Dr Lawrence Farwell, a **cognitive** psychophysiologist with expertise in electroencephalography (EEG), invented the brain fingerprinting test and pioneered its use.

2   Electroencephalography.

3   The use during trial of FBSA is purely speculative at this stage as legislative amendments would be required to make its use possible.

of certain information. It is, therefore, not a lie-detector or polygraph,[4] but a knowledge-detector. Also, as the FBSA test relies solely on brainwave responses, brain fingerprinting is not influenced by the emotional state of the subject.

Functional magnetic resonance imaging (fMRI) is an extension of standard magnetic resonance imaging (MRI), (which is in widespread and common use in mapping brain anatomy), to mapping and measuring brain function. FMRI 'provides a three-dimensional image of both cortical and sub-cortical activity of the brain' and as such 'it has greater descriptive potential' than forensic brain scan analysis.[5]

54.2 How forensic brain scan analysis (FBSA) works

The FBSA technique initially relied on detecting and interpreting the behaviour of only the electrical brainwave known as P300. The P300 brainwave is emitted from the brain as soon as the brain detects information of particular significance. For example, in crime investigations, there is certain information only the perpetrator would have stored in his or her brain such as the number and description of items of jewellery stolen, the facial features of a victim or the identity of the members of a syndicate. The P300 brainwave is effectively the key indicator of unique knowledge – things only the guilty or involved person would know.

In simple terms, the subject is tested on three kinds of information contained in a series of questions in which the three kinds of information are randomly distributed. The three kinds of information are:

- irrelevant information the subject does not know
- relevant information the subject does know
- relevant information *only* the perpetrator would know.

If there is a correlation between the brainwave responses to questions containing information as per the first and third points above, this result would be a strong indicator that the subject has no knowledge of the alleged crime or other wrongdoing in issue and can be discarded as a suspect. However, if there is a correlation between the brainwave responses to questions containing information as per the second and third points, this result would be a strong indicator that the subject does have knowledge of the alleged crime or other wrongdoing in issue and can be detained as a suspect.

The technique relies solely on the detection and interpretation of EEG signals and no oral or written responses are required from the subject. The responses, therefore, are completely outside the subject's control and cannot be manipulated by him or her.

Dr Farwell and his associates later further developed and refined the initial P300 test into the so-called MERMER test (memory and encoding related multifaceted electroencephalographic response), in which additional features were added to the P300 test resulting in a very high level of reported accuracy. In essence, in addition to measuring the immediate brain response to a stimulus (300 milliseconds after the stimulus in the P300 test), the extended test also includes testing the MERMER, which are the secondary brainwave responses (up to 1 400 milliseconds after the stimulus).[6]

---

4 See ch 53 Polygraphs and voice-stress analysers.
5 CJ Kraft CJ and J Giordano J (2017) 'Integrating Brain Science and Law: Neuroscientific Evidence and Legal Perspectives on Protecting Individual Liberties' *Frontiers in Neuroscience* 11: 621.
6 See LA Farwell and SS Smith 'Using brain MERMER testing to detect knowledge despite efforts to conceal' (2001) 46(1) *Journal of Forensic Sciences* at 135.

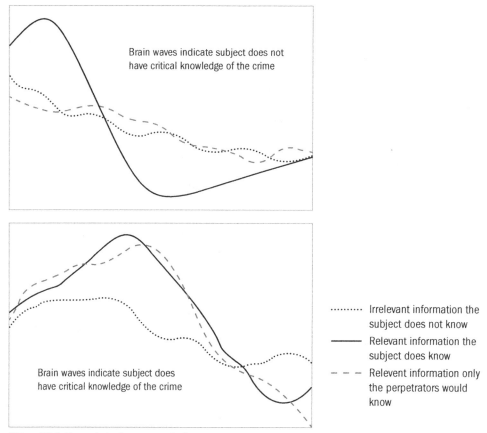

Figure 54.1 Forensic brain scan analysis

54.3 Testing methodology

The subject is fitted with a headband containing electronic sensors that detect brainwaves and is seated before a computer monitor. Various stimuli are then shown on the screen, which could include words, phrases, diagrams, pictures or photographs. Typically, a sequence of 30 to 50 stimuli is presented in a single testing within which three types of stimulus are randomly distributed. These are outlined below:

- *Irrelevant stimuli:* These are words, phrases, diagrams, pictures or photographs that are not relevant to the case being investigated and of which the subject has no prior knowledge.
- *Target stimuli:* These are words, phrases, diagrams, pictures or photographs that are relevant to the case being investigated and are known to the subject.
- *Probe stimuli:* These are words, phrases, diagrams, pictures or photographs that are relevant to the case being investigated that only the perpetrator would know. The probe stimuli (probes) are carefully selected items of information known only to the investigators and perpetrators of the crime or incident. This information would not be known to persons not involved in the crime or incident.

Before the test is administered, various safeguarding steps are taken, including an explanation of the test methodology and questions aimed at ensuring the subject has no

CHAPTER 54   NEUROTECHNOLOGY AND NEUROLOGICAL EVIDENCE   **483**

innocent knowledge of the probes. The test is then administered and the P300 brainwaves and MERMERs are subsequently analysed to determine one of the following:

- the finding of 'information present', in other words, the test indicates that the subject does have knowledge of the probes
- a finding of 'information absent' in other words, the subject does not have knowledge of the probes. See also Figure 54.1.

It is important to emphasise that the purpose of FBSA is to detect *knowledge*, not *guilt*. For example, even if the P300 and MERMER tests show that the subject indeed has knowledge of the probes, there may be some explanation for that knowledge which is not necessarily indicative of the subject's guilt.

54.4   The use of forensic brain scan analysis (FBSA) in criminal cases

In the United States of America, brain scan analysis has been referred to in order to help determine guilt or lack of guilt in a selection of criminal court cases including the cases of Grinder, Slaughter and Harrington. Dr Farwell applied his P300/MERMER test in these three cases, as discussed below.

Grinder was a serial killer who was charged with the murder of Julie Helton in 1984. Initially, there was insufficient evidence to prosecute him. However, in 1999, the P300/ MERMER test detected that knowledge about vital circumstances and information concerning the murder of the victim was stored in Grinder's brain. This helped persuade Grinder to plead guilty to the charges facing him. He was found guilty of her rape and murder, and was sentenced to life imprisonment without parole.[7]

In *Slaughter v State*,[8] Slaughter was sentenced to death for the murder of his ex-girlfriend and their 11-month-old daughter. He tried to have his conviction overturned by submitting to a brain fingerprinting test, the results of which showed that he had no knowledge of the crime scene. This information was used as evidence in his appeals.

However, the Oklahoma Court of Appeals rejected brain fingerprinting evidence as unreliable.

The Court stated that it was not presented evidence showing:

- extensive testing of brain fingerprint testing
- a low error rate among tests performed
- objective standards to control its operation
- that the test was generally accepted within the 'relevant scientific community'.

The failure to provide such evidence to support the claims raised led the Court to conclude that the evidence did not exist. Slaughter's appeal was unsuccessful and he was executed in 2005 despite exculpatory evidence from a brain fingerprinting test supported by exculpatory DNA evidence. The court, in a reliance on a technicality, opined that the brain fingerprinting evidence was of no evidentiary value.

---

7   Unreported. For an overview, see AJ Roberts 'Everything new is old again: Brain fingerprinting and evidentiary analogy' (2007) 9(1) *Yale Journal of Law and Technology* 234 at 257–264
8   108 P 3d 1052, 2005 OK CR 6.

484 | THE LAW OF EVIDENCE IN SOUTH AFRICA

In *Harrington v State of Ohio*,[9] brain fingerprinting in general, and Dr Farwell's P300/MERMER test in particular, was fully discussed in 2001. In a landmark decision, the Court admitted the brain fingerprinting evidence of Harrington under the *Daubert* Rule,[10] but ultimately did not decide the matter on this evidence. Harrington was acquitted on other grounds. The real importance of the case is that it provides a detailed explanation and overview of the P300/MERMER test and sets a precedent for its admissibility in other court cases.

In 1977, Harrington was accused of the murder of a security guard. At his trial he testified that he had not been present at the crime scene and presented alibi evidence. Several witnesses placed him at a concert many miles from the crime scene. However, a jury convicted him of murder and sentenced him to serve a life sentence without the possibility of parole. Harrington filed a petition, the US equivalent of review proceedings, asking the Court to set aside his conviction on three grounds and grant him a new trial. The three grounds were:

1. newly discovered evidence that some of the state's trial witnesses had recanted their trial testimony
2. evidence that police or prosecutors failed to disclose to the defendant prior to trial certain police reports which pointed to possible alternative suspects in the case
3. newly discovered evidence in the form of new brain fingerprinting technology which purported to show that he was not at the scene of the crime and was, instead, at the scene of his alibi.

The expert called in support of the third ground above was Dr Farwell, who tested Harrington with his P300 test using the protocols and safeguards developed by him to ensure the integrity of the procedure.

In summary, the Appeal Court's findings on Dr Farwell's evidence are described below with extracts from the court record:

- *The significance of brain fingerprinting/P300 to the Harrington case:* 'Brain fingerprinting: it is an EEG test of a subject's "guilty knowledge" related to a specific remembered event or circumstance such as a crime scene. It can also probe for exonerating knowledge, for example, details relating to an alibi;'[11]
- *The accuracy of the brain fingerprinting test:* Dr. Farwell had conducted tests on 170 test subjects in both lab-simulated and real-life circumstances. In 163 of these tests an accurate result was produced and the other 7 were 'indeterminate', in other words, no

---

9   659 N.W. 2d 509 (IOWA 2003).
10   Before *Daubert et ux., individually and as guardians ad litem for Daubert, et al. v. Merrell Dow Pharmaceuticals, Inc.* 509 U.S. 579 (1993), the test for admitting scientific expert evidence was based on the principle of 'general acceptance' formulated in *Frye v United States*, 293 F. 1013 (D.C. Cir. 1923). This meant that scientific expert evidence would only be admissible if the principle on which it was based was 'sufficiently established to have gained general acceptance in the particular field in which it belongs'. However, the Federal Rules of Evidence (Rule 702) state with regard to testimony by expert witnesses:

> **A witness who is qualified as an expert by knowledge, skill, experience, training, or education may testify in the form of an opinion or otherwise if:**
> **(a) the expert's scientific, technical, or other specialized knowledge will help the trier of fact to understand the evidence or to determine a fact in issue;**
> **(b) the testimony is based on sufficient facts or data;**
> **(c) the testimony is the product of reliable principles and methods; and**
> **(d) the expert has reliably applied the principles and methods to the facts of the case.**

In the *Daubert* case, the US Supreme Court held that Frye's 'general acceptance' test was superseded by the adoption of Federal Rule 702. The Court held that 'general acceptance' is not a necessary precondition to the admissibility of scientific evidence under the Federal Rules of Evidence, but the Federal Rules of Evidence do assign to the trial judge the task of ensuring that an expert's testimony both rests on a reliable foundation and is relevant to the task at hand.

11   *Harrington v State of Ohio* 659 N.W. 2d 509 (2003) at 760.

CHAPTER 54 NEUROTECHNOLOGY AND NEUROLOGICAL EVIDENCE | **485**

result was offered. The test conducted on Harrington yielded *determinate* results, confirming that he knew nothing about the crime and that he did not participate in the commission of the crime. The statistical confidence level was 99 per cent.[12]

The Court found Dr Farwell's P300 test to be reliable and accurate.

However, these findings of the Court were *obiter* as the Court did not have to rely on them to find in Harrington's favour. He was set free in 2003 after 25 years in prison after the Ohio Supreme Court found that the prosecutors had committed an irregularity which resulted in a failure of justice by concealing reports about another man seen near the scene with a shotgun.

54.5   Future application of forensic brain scan analysis (FBSA)

To date, the admissibility of brain fingerprinting has not been tested in a South African court. Dr Farwell's P300/MERMER test has, however, been extensively tested and reviewed by both the Federal Bureau of Investigation (FBI) and Central Intelligence Agency (CIA) in the United States of America and has proved to be extremely accurate and reliable.

There have also been a number of critics of brain fingerprinting, especially Rosenfeld who has produced results that are far less impressive than Farwell's. Farwell has countered Rosenfeld's figures in detail, pointing out that Rosenfeld's methods differed markedly from the strict methodology of his P300/MERMER tests.[13]

Despite the decision in *Harrington v State of Ohio*, it appears that the science and practice of brain fingerprinting faces the same long hard road to scientific and legal acceptance travelled by the proponents of DNA testing before the latter became generally accepted as conclusively reliable.

54.6   How functional magnetic resonance imaging (fMRI) works

Functional magnetic resonance imaging (fMRI) measures brain activity by detecting changes associated with blood flow.[14] Blood flow to an area of the brain increases when that area is in use and so, by measuring the blood-oxygen-level dependent contrast, neural activity in a particular area of the brain can be mapped. 'Studies of deception detection ... rely on subtle changes in the blood-oxygenation level of specific areas in the brain, generally, the fronto-parietal lobes and loci and networks of the limbic system.'[15] These studies can claim 90 per cent or higher accuracy rates.[16]

54.7   The use of fMRI in court cases

At least two companies – Cephos, LLC and No Lie MRI, Inc. – offer fMRI services as a means of lie detection. However, as Kraft and Giordano point out, '[a]ctual conditions in the context

---

12   Ibid. at 761–765.

13   LA Farwell 'Brain fingerprinting: Comprehensive corrections to Rosenfeld' (2011) 8(2) *Scientific Review of Mental Health Practice 56*. Available online at: http://www.larryfarwell.com/pdf/Scientific-Review-of-Mental-Health-Practice-Farwell-Brain-Fingerprinting-Comprehensive-Corrections-to-Rosenfeld-dr-larry-farwell-dr-lawrence-farwell.pdf

14   SA Huettel, AW Song and G McCarthy *Functional Magnetic Resonance Imaging* 2 ed (2008).

15   JG Hakun et al. 'Towards clinical trials of lie detection with fMRI' *Social Neuroscience* (2009) 4(6) at 518–527; E Rusconi and T Mitchener-Nissen, 2013 'Prospects of functional magnetic resonance imaging as lie detector' *Frontiers in Human Neuroscience* 7:594 in CJ Kraft and J Giordano (2017) 'Integrating Brain Science and Law: Neuroscientific Evidence and Legal Perspectives on Protecting Individual Liberties' *Frontiers in Neuroscience* 11:621.

16   Rusconi and Mitchener-Nissen op cit at note 15 supra.

486 | THE LAW OF EVIDENCE IN SOUTH AFRICA

of a criminal investigation are likely to vary widely from those of the laboratory setting'[17] and 'fMRI deception detection can be intentionally countered by "experienced" individuals with intent to deceive.'[18]

Functional MRI has therefore been used far less than FBSA in court. In *United States v Semrau*[19] the defendant attempted to admit fMRI evidence (a lie detection report) that would show that he was telling the truth when he denied the allegations against him. The trial court disallowed the evidence[20] and the decision was upheld on appeal,[21] the court holding that the evidence 'failed to meet the standards of general acceptance and known error rates outlined by Daubert'.[22] Other attempts to have fMRI evidence admitted, even in states which do not apply the *Daubert* test, have also been unsuccessful, with the court, for example, in *Wilson v Corestaff Services*[23] stating '... even a cursory review of the scientific literature demonstrates that the plaintiff is unable to establish that the use of the fMRI test to determine truthfulness or deceit is accepted as reliable in the relevant scientific community'.[24]

54.8 Future application of fMRI

FMRI is beset by many obstacles, both practical and legal, that undermine its immediate value and, thus use, in court. Rusconi and Mitchener-Nissen summarise the position as follows: '... in nearly every article published by independent researchers in peer reviewed journals, the respective authors acknowledge that fMRI research, processes, and technology are insufficiently developed and understood for gatekeepers to even consider introducing these neuroimaging measures into criminal courts as they stand today for the purpose of determining the veracity of statements made. Regardless of how favourable their analyses of fMRI or its future potential, they all acknowledge the presence of *issues yet to be resolved*'.[25]

THIS CHAPTER IN ESSENCE

1 A forensic brain scan analysis (FBSA) cannot determine whether the subject is being untruthful or not, but merely attempts to establish whether or not the subject has knowledge of certain information.

2 The FBSA technique relies on detecting and interpreting the behaviour of the P300 electrical brainwave. This brainwave is emitted from a person's brain immediately after the brain detects information of particular significance. The subject is tested on the following three kinds of information in a series of questions:

---

17 CJ Kraft and J Giordano J (2017) op cit at note 15 supra.
18 G Ganis, JP Rosenfeld, J Meixner, RA Kievit and HE Schendan 'Lying in the scanner: covert countermeasures disrupt deception detection by functional magnetic resonance imaging' *Neuroimage* (2011) 55(1) at 312–319.
19 *United States v Semrau* (2012). 2nd Circuit Court of Appeals of the United States. No. 11-5396, 6.
20 The evidence had already been disallowed at a pre-trial hearing. See G Miller 'fMRI Lie Detection Fails a Legal Test' *Science* 11 Jun 2010 328(5984) at 1336–1337.
21 *United States v Semrau* 693 F.3d 510 (6th Cir. 2012) at 516.
22 CJ Kraft and J Giordano J (2017) op cit at n 15 supra. The court in *Daubert v Merrell Dow Pharmaceuticals, Inc.* (1993) 509 U.S. 579 set out guidelines for admitting scientific expert testimony.
23 *Wilson v Corestaff Services. L.P.* 2010 NY Slip Op 20176 [28 Misc 3d 425].
24 In the state of New York the test for the admissibility of expert evidence is set out in *Frye v United States* (293 F 1013 [DC Cir 1923]). The judge in *Wilson v Corestaff Services. L.P.* 2010 NY Slip Op 20176 [28 Misc 3d 425] provides a succinct summary of this test as follows: 'New York courts permit expert testimony if it is based on scientific principles, procedures or theory only after the principles, procedures or theories have gained general acceptance in the relevant scientific field, proffered by a qualified expert and on a topic beyond the ken of the average juror.'
25 Rusconi and Mitchener-Nissen op cit at note 15 supra.

CHAPTER 54   NEUROTECHNOLOGY AND NEUROLOGICAL EVIDENCE | **487**

2.1 irrelevant information the subject does not know

2.2 relevant information the subject does know

2.3 relevant information only the perpetrator would know.

3   A strong correlation between the brainwave responses to questions containing the information in the first and third points above is a strong indicator that the subject has no knowledge of the alleged crime.

4   A strong correlation between the brainwave responses to questions containing the information in the second and third points above is a strong indicator that the subject has knowledge of the alleged crime.

5   FBSA relies solely on the detection and interpretation of EEG signals and not on oral or written responses by the subject. A subject's responses to the questions are, therefore, completely beyond his or her control and cannot be manipulated by him or her.

6   Brain fingerprinting has been referred to in a number of criminal cases in the United States of America.

7   The admissibility of FBSA has yet to be tested in a South African court.

8   Functional magnetic resonance imaging (fMRI) measures brain activity by detecting changes associated with blood flow.

9   fMRI is offered as a means of lie detection.

10 fMRI evidence has been disallowed in the United States of America.

11 The admissibility of fMRI has yet to be tested in a South African court.

PART EIGHT

Special evidentiary procedures

CHAPTER 55 The trial-within-a-trial 490

CHAPTER 56 Estoppel 498

CHAPTER 57 The parol evidence rule 504

CHAPTER 58 Children's evidence 508

CHAPTER 59 Evidence in labour matters 514

CHAPTER 60 Evidence obtained by means of entrapment 533

CHAPTER 61 Evidentiary problems with the Prevention of Organised Crime Act, 1998 (POCA) 538

Chapter 55

The trial-within-a-trial

55.1	**Introduction**	**490**
55.2	**Principles of a trial-within-a-trial**	**491**
55.3	**Procedure in a trial-within-a-trial**	**492**
	55.3.1 When is a trial-within-a-trial held?	492
	55.3.2 Procedure	492
	55.3.3 Ruling	494
55.4	**Burden of proof in a trial-within-a-trial**	**495**
55.5	**Appeal against the ruling in a trial-within-a-trial**	**495**

55.1 Introduction

The trial-within-a-trial procedure evolved in criminal jury trials in England.[1] The procedure was used as a means of dealing with the admissibility of disputed evidence without the jury's presence so that the jury would not be influenced by the contentious evidence. It was believed that any adverse evidence or matters of witness credibility would possibly influence the jury against the accused.

A trial-within-a-trial deals with admissibility of evidence and is only held during the State's case. The procedure is usually used when the admissibility of evidence is disputed, mostly on the basis that it was obtained unlawfully, unfairly or unconstitutionally from the accused. The disputed evidence may be in the form of an oral or written statement or conduct by the accused. It may include extra-curial admissions, confessions, pointings out, identification parades, privileged documentation or any evidence obtained as a result of unauthorised or unlawful searches, seizures or **entrapment**.[2] The procedure can also be used to determine the competency of a particular witness to testify, for example a child.[3] A failure to hold a trial-within-a-trial where the admissibility of a statement is in issue constitutes a material irregularity on the part of the trial court.

The advantage of using the trial-within-a-trial procedure is that it enables the accused to ensure that contested evidence is kept out of the record of the trial testimony. Furthermore,

---

1 In England, a trial-within-a-trial is sometimes referred to as *voir dire*.
2 E du Toit, FJ de Jager, A Paizes, A St Q Skeen and S van der Merwe S *Commentary on the Criminal Procedure Act* (1987) [Service Issue 52, 2014] 24-98N-22.
3 Where the competency of the accused is in issue the special dispensation set out in ss 77 and 79 of the Criminal Procedure Act 51 of 1977 becomes applicable.

CHAPTER 55   THE TRIAL-WITHIN-A-TRIAL | **491**

it ensures that the admissibility of the contested evidence is decided at the point when the State attempts to introduce it before the start of the accused's own case. This ensures that the accused knows at the end of the State's case what evidence stands against him or her. The accused can then make an informed decision on whether to testify or not.

What an accused says in the trial-within-a-trial cannot be used against him or her in the trial itself. An accused may elect to give evidence under oath to give a full picture to the court during this separate enquiry of admissibility. This evidence cannot be used later in the actual trial because the accused is still entitled to exercise his or her right to remain silent in the trial itself.

This rule goes further. If the accused elects to testify in the actual trial, he or she is entitled to give a completely different account to the account given during the trial-within-a-trial. The court must then assess the accused's credibility as if he or she had told only one story. The prosecution is not allowed to put to the accused person the differences between his or her versions in the trial-within-a-trial and the main trial.

There is no trial-within-a-trial procedure in civil matters. In a civil trial the court listens to all the evidence. In arriving at a decision, the court will then exclude unfairly obtained evidence or other inadmissible evidence if the court is of the view that such evidence should not be taken into account.[4]

55.2   Principles of a trial-within-a-trial

A trial-within-a-trial is a separate enquiry on the admissibility or non-admissibility of evidence. This evidence is usually in the form of an extra-judicial statement that the State seeks to tender in its bid to prove its case against the accused. The extra-judicial statement must be relevant to the case. If it is not, the normal rules of admissibility will ensure that it is not admitted. The crux of a trial-within-a-trial is whether the evidence the State seeks to tender complies with the requirements of admissibility in terms of the Constitution, the Criminal Procedure Act 51 of 1977, other applicable statutory law or the common law.

The issues in a trial-within-a-trial are largely dependent on the facts of each particular case, the surrounding circumstances and the nature of the evidence that is being disputed. The issues that the accused person puts in dispute determine the ambit of each particular trial-within-a-trial.

In terms of section 145(4) of the Criminal Procedure Act, 1977, a judicial officer may sit with or without assessors in a trial-within-a-trial. The assessors may be excluded from a trial-within-a-trial where the judicial officer is of the opinion that it is in the interests of justice that they do not participate, especially where they are inexperienced. In such a case, the judicial officer will decide the issue of admissibility alone. Once the trial-within-a-trial has been completed, the assessors will resume with the trial on the merits. The presiding officer decides issues of pure law, although issues of law and fact are often linked. The role of the assessors is to assist the presiding officer in deciding whether the state's version or that of the accused should prevail.

However, the trial-within-a-trial is not completely separated from the main trial. Sometimes evidence led during the trial can be referred to in the-trial-within-a-trial. At other times evidence canvassed during the trial-within-a-trial may be referred to during the main trial. The common law regulating this has developed through a number of

---

4   *Shell SA (Edms) Bpk en Andere v Voorsitter, Dorperaad van die Oranje-Vrystaat en Andere* 1992 (1) SA 906 (O); *Lenco Holdings Ltd and Others v Eckstein and Others* 1996 (2) SA 693 (N) at 701H–704D.

492 | THE LAW OF EVIDENCE IN SOUTH AFRICA

decisions. In *S v Muchindu*,[5] the Court held that the trial court engaged in the trial-within-a-trial should have the main trial fully in prospect. This effectively means that evidence already led in the main trial can be referred to in the trial-within-a-trial to put everything in context. Thereafter, however, the trial-within-a-trial cannot be referred to when the main trial resumes.

In *S v Nglengethwa*,[6] the Court held that those parts of the prosecution's evidence relevant to the accused's guilt adduced in the trial-within-a-trial will be taken into account in determining his guilt in the main trial. The Court said it was nonsensical and a waste of costs, time and energy to repeat in the main trial the evidence of state witnesses already presented during the trial-within-a-trial. However, the evidence of the accused in the trial-within-a-trial cannot be used in the main trial against him or her.

The effect of these two judgments is that evidence adduced in the proper trial or the trial on the merits may be put to the witnesses and the accused in the trial-within-a-trial. Evidence of state witnesses adduced in a trial-within-a-trial may also be put to the accused in the proper trial. However, evidence of the accused in the trial-within-a-trial may not be used to determine his or her guilt in the main trial.

55.3 Procedure in a trial-within-a-trial

55.3.1 When is a trial-within-a-trial held?

A trial-within-a-trial is always held during the State's case and can be held at any time during their case. This means that the State may even begin its case by entering directly into a trial-within-a-trial. A trial-within-a-trial is unlikely during the defence's case unless the State challenges the competency of a defence witness. There can never be a trial-within-a-trial on a criminal appeal or review.

55.3.2 Procedure

Once the admissibility of a statement or piece of evidence is placed in dispute during the State's case, a trial-within-a-trial must be held. The court will declare that the admissibility of the statement is in dispute and will then formally declare that it is entering into a trial-within-a-trial. This is for record purposes.

If the prosecutor is in doubt as to whether the disputed statement is an admission or confession,[7] he or she must warn the presiding officer of this doubt so that the presiding officer can investigate whether it is a confession or not.[8] This is important because a confession has stringent prerequisites for admissibility, unlike an admission. There is therefore a complete preliminary enquiry whether a disputed statement is an admission or confession in a trial-within-a-trial.

The defence may indicate to the court the grounds of inadmissibility it intends disputing or leave the State to prove all the requirements of admissibility. By indicating the grounds of inadmissibility, the defence helps the court to narrow down the scope of issues to be canvassed during the trial-within-a-trial.

As the State bears the onus of proof in a trial-within-a-trial, it has the duty to begin leading evidence in support of its case for admissibility. It must establish a *prima facie* case

---

5   2000 (2) SACR 313 (W).
6   1996 (1) SACR 737 (A).
7   *S v Bontsi* 1985 (4) SA 544 (BG) at 547.
8   *S v K and Another* 1999 (2) SACR 388 (C).

CHAPTER 55   THE TRIAL-WITHIN-A-TRIAL | **493**

of admissibility by the close of its case. If the prosecutor refers a state witness to the disputed statement, the actual contents of the statement must be concealed, especially those copies handed to the bench.

Some parts of the disputed statement may have to be unsealed. This is usually the preliminary part as it often indicates whether the formal prerequisites for admissibility have been satisfied by whoever was recording the statement. The preliminary part of the statement will have:

- the name of the accused
- the name and official capacity of the person recording the statement
- the place, time and date of the recording of the statement
- warnings and appraisals of the accused on his or her constitutional and other rights, if any
- observations on his or her state of mind or sobriety
- observations on his or her bodily appearance such as scars and injuries
- explanations recorded for scars or injuries
- whether the accused has been assaulted, threatened, coerced or influenced by anyone to make the disputed statement.
- whether the accused claimed or waived his or her right to silence and/or his or her right to legal representation or consultation before making the disputed statement
- the duration of the recording of the disputed statement
- the medium of language used in the communication and recording of the disputed statement
- whether an interpreter was used
- usually also the signatures of all who were party to the making of the disputed statement, including the interpreter's certificate.

If a verbal statement is in dispute, the witness to whom it was made cannot state what was said until the court rules on the statement's admissibility. The state witness who testified to the circumstances surrounding the making of the disputed statement can be cross-examined by the defence. During cross-examination, the defence is entitled to put its own factual version surrounding the making of the disputed statement to the witness. Thereafter the State can re-examine its witness. This procedure will be followed until the State exhausts its list of witnesses and closes its case in the trial-within-a-trial.

Once the State has closed its case in the trial-within-a-trial, the defence has two options. It can either close its case or lead evidence in rebuttal. The accused may testify and will then be subjected to cross-examination and may be re-examined. He or she may elect not to testify but may still call other defence witnesses to testify.

If the accused does testify, it is preferable that he or she do so first. If the accused calls other witnesses, they can only testify about facts that are within their personal knowledge. A practical example would be a fellow prisoner who was detained with the accused and who actually saw the battered accused when he was brought back to the police cell by the investigating officer. Another defence witness may be the district surgeon who examined the accused and found bruises and contusions consistent with application of force or a blunt object.

In a trial-within-a-trial the accused is a competent but not a compellable witness. The accused can thus exercise his or her right to silence and close his or her case without giving evidence in rebuttal. However, where the State has made out a *prima facie* case on admissibility, it may be prudent for the accused to testify to raise a reasonable doubt about

THE LAW OF EVIDENCE IN SOUTH AFRICA

the State's contention of admissibility. If the accused elects to give evidence, for example on the admissibility of a statement, he or she cannot be cross-examined on his or her guilt, but can be cross-examined on the making of the statement in dispute and on his or her credibility on the evidence in question, as illustrated in the case below.[9] However, the accused cannot be attacked on the truthfulness of the statement since the court has not yet ruled on its admissibility. The contents of a statement are not relevant to its admissibility and looking at the contents at this stage would be prejudging the issue of admissibility.

S v Gxokwe and Others

In *S v Gxokwe and Others*,[10] the Court said an accused may be cross-examined on the question of voluntariness and his or her credibility on voluntariness. The cross-examination is not usually on whether the statement is true. The contents of the statement and the truthfulness of the statement are ordinarily not considered to be relevant to the issue of its admissibility. The finding in the trial-within-a-trial that the statement is the accused's own and is true may pre-empt the decision to be made by the Court at the conclusion of the trial.

Where the accused alleges that the contents of the statement originated from the investigating officer, then the prosecution, with the leave of the court, may cross-examine the accused on the contents of the statement even though the court has not ruled on the admissibility of that statement. The reason for allowing cross-examination in these circumstances is to show that the accused is the true author of the statement.

Once the defence has closed its case, the State will present its argument as to why the statement should be admissible. Thereafter, the defence will present its argument and the State will be allowed to reply on matters of law.

55.3.3 Ruling

At the conclusion of a trial-within-a-trial, the court has to rule on whether the evidence is admissible or not. It may give its ruling immediately or it may reserve its ruling and adjourn to deliberate on the issues raised. The main trial cannot resume until the court has given its ruling on the dispute in the trial-within-a-trial. When giving its ruling, the court may provide reasons or it may give a ruling only and reserve its reasons. It may then give its reasons during the delivery of the judgment at the conclusion of the whole case. Sometimes it is preferable that the court does not give reasons at the end of the trial-within-a-trial stage as the trial is not yet over and especially if the court has made credibility findings on the state witnesses and the accused.

Where the court rules the statement to be admissible and the main trial recommences, the whole document has to be unsealed. The person who recorded the statement is called as a witness to read the statement into the record of the main trial. This witness can be cross-examined by the defence. The focus will now shift from the admissibility to the contents of the statement.

If the court rules the statement to be inadmissible, the document is then handed back to the prosecutor with the sealed parts intact. Thereafter, the main trial will resume, without that document.

---

9   *S v Gxokwe and Others* 1992 (2) SACR 355 (C).

10   1992 (2) SACR 355 (C).

CHAPTER 55   THE TRIAL-WITHIN-A-TRIAL | 495

55.4   Burden of proof in a trial-within-a-trial

In a trial-within-a-trial, the prosecution has to prove beyond a reasonable doubt that a statement is admissible.[11] It is the admissibility of the statement, not its contents, that is proved in a trial-within-a-trial. The contents of the statement are proved in the main trial. Proof of admissibility of the statement may be by direct evidence or from the surrounding circumstances of the case, which may or may not include documentary and real evidence. The proof must be proof of compliance with the admissibility requirements for that type of evidence beyond a reasonable doubt.

This means that where the court finds that there is a reasonable possibility that the statement does not meet with any of the requirements of admissibility, it will rule that the statement is inadmissible. Conversely, if there is no reasonable doubt as to compliance with all admissibility requirements, the court will rule that the statement is admissible.

Sometimes an accused may elect not to testify. This may be risky, but there is no compulsion on an accused to testify and his or her failure to do so is not a factor that the court is entitled to take into account.[12]

55.5   Appeal against the ruling in a trial-within-a-trial

The decision of a court in a trial-within-a-trial is interlocutory. It is not a final decision and a court may reconsider and overrule its ruling to admit a statement. If new facts bearing on its admissibility come to light, it is the court's duty to reconsider the issue immediately so that the situation does not arise where an accused is cross-examined on an otherwise inadmissible statement. This may be prejudicial to the accused and it may not be possible to excise the inadmissible evidence from the record. A ruling of admissibility may even prompt the accused to testify when he or she would otherwise have decided not to. Therefore, a ruling that the statement is admissible is only provisional as it can still be overturned before the completion of the main trial.

If the ruling of the court is that a statement is inadmissible, this cannot be overturned even if new evidence emerges later justifying its admissibility, the reason for which is illustrated in the case below.

S v Molimi

In *S v Molimi*,[13] Nkabinde J said:

> ... when a ruling on admissibility is made at the end of the case, the accused will be left in a state of uncertainty as to the case he is expected to meet and may be placed in a precarious situation of having to choose whether to adduce or challenge evidence.

The State bears the burden of proof and, therefore, if it fails to persuade the court of a statement's admissibility when it has an opportunity to do so, the evidence thereafter remains inadmissible. If the evidence were suddenly declared admissible, the prejudice to

---

11 The onus is on the State to prove that the accused's fundamental rights were not infringed in the procurement of the evidence, not on the accused to prove the breach of his or her fundamental rights. See E du Toit, FJ de Jager, A Paizes, A St Q Skeen and S van der Merwe *Commentary on the Criminal Procedure Act* (1987) [Service Issue 55, 2015] 24–56J. However, in terms of s 252A(6) of the Criminal Procedure Act, 1977, the State only has to prove the admissibility of entrapment evidence on a balance of probabilities.

12 *S v Hlongwa* 2002 (2) SACR 37 (T) at 51B–55E.

13 2008 (3) SA 608 (CC) at para 42.

THE LAW OF EVIDENCE IN SOUTH AFRICA

the accused, who has conducted a defence based on the inadmissibility of a piece of evidence, would be so significant as to render the trial unfair.

As the whole trial is not yet over, no appeal can lie against the ruling of the court at the trial-within-a-trial stage. An appeal can only be entertained after the whole case, including sentencing, has been completed and disposed of. The appeal on the ruling in a trial-within-a-trial will be based squarely on the record of the trial court.

DISCUSSION	**Trial-within-a-trial: two views on reform**
55.1	The trial-within-a-trial procedure has been severely criticised. Hugo and Nugent[14] argue that this procedure has too much artificial formalism. This results in manifestly unjust outcomes that are at variance with the expectations of the public at large. It dictates a rigorous application of rules of evidence invented and developed in other places and for other societies to prevent lay juries from drawing inferences from or finding proof in evidence that does not justify it. Applying such a procedure may result in outcomes that defy logic and raise the ire of the community because of perceived easy acquittals due to legal technicalities. The procedure militates against a fair conviction and frequently allows guilty persons to go free. Both believe that the rules of the trial-within-a-trial stifle the search for truth.

In South Africa, there are no juries. Thus, trained judicial officers make and give judgments that are open to analysis by lawyer and layman alike and particularly by an appeal court.

A trained judicial officer is capable of separating the wheat from the chaff and if he or she is unable to do so, then an appeal court should be able to do so.

Both judges contend that the trial-within-a-trial procedure should be abolished. They also argue that the admissibility of confessions, admissions, pointings out and identification parades should be dealt with as with any other issue in a criminal trial without entering into a separate and insulated enquiry.

If the trial-within-a-trial procedure is abolished, the State would be able to introduce evidence of an extra-curial confession by leading the evidence of the person to whom it was made. After the State has closed its case and has *prima facie* established, *inter alia*, the admissibility of the confession, the accused will face the choice of whether or not to rebut the *prima facie* evidence. At present, witnesses who give evidence in a trial-within-a-trial and on other issues are called twice, are cross-examined twice and findings on their credibility are made twice. If the same procedure is adopted, no witness need be called twice.

An alternative solution is to deal with the trial-within-a-trial in another courtroom before a different judge. Thus, the trial proceedings are temporarily stopped and the matter is then adjourned to another court to hear the trial-within-a-trial. At the conclusion of the trial-within-a-trial, only the other court's decision is given to the trial judge and the trial then continues. This would minimise the contamination of the court's mind, for example by preventing premature adverse credibility impressions, and help to maintain the fairness of the trial.

---

14   JH Hugo 'A tale of two cases' (1999) 12(2) *South African Journal of Criminal Justice* 204; RW Nugent 'Self-incrimination in perspective' (1999) 116(3) *South African Law Journal* 501.

> In *S v Hena And Another* (2006) 2 SACR 33 (SE) at 39, the Court decided the issue of the admissibility of evidence without holding a trial within a trial. This procedure was permitted for two reasons: firstly, it had been agreed between the parties to deal with the issue of admissibility in argument once all the evidence had been heard, and secondly, the facts relevant to the issue of admissibility were common cause.

THIS CHAPTER IN ESSENCE

1   A trial-within-a-trial deals with the admissibility of evidence which is disputed, usually on the basis that it was obtained unlawfully, unfairly or unconstitutionally from the accused.
2   A trial-within-a-trial has the following advantages:
   2.1   It ensures that contested evidence is kept out of the record of the trial.
   2.2   It ensures that the admissibility of the contested evidence is decided before the accused leads his or her case.
3   Nothing an accused says during a trial-within-a-trial can be used against him or her in the trial itself.
4   There is no trial-within-a-trial in civil matters.
5   The issues in a trial-within-a-trial depend largely on the facts of the case, the surrounding circumstances and the nature of the evidence disputed.
6   A judicial officer can preside over a trial-within-a-trial with or without the assistance of assessors.
7   Although a trial-within-a-trial is a separate enquiry into the admissibility or non-admissibility of evidence, it is not completely separated from the main trial as evidence led during the trial can be referred to in the trial-within-a-trial and vice versa.
8   A trial-within-a-trial is always held during the State's case and can be held at any time during their case.
9   A trial-within-a-trial is to be conducted according to a specific procedure.
10   A court may give its ruling immediately at the conclusion of a trial-within-a-trial or it may reserve its ruling and adjourn to deliberate on the issues raised.
11   The ruling of the court is, to a certain extent, interlocutory in that a court is entitled to overrule itself later by declaring a statement, which it had previously found to be admissible, to be inadmissible if new evidence emerges during the trial that casts doubt on its admissibility.
12   There can be no appeal against the ruling of the court at the trial-within-a-trial because the whole trial has not yet been concluded. However, the ruling in a trial-within-a-trial can be appealed against as part of an appeal in the main trial.
13   The burden of proof in a trial-within-a-trial rests on the State which has to prove beyond reasonable doubt that a particular statement is admissible.
14   An accused is not compelled to testify during a trial-within-a-trial, but failure to do so may be risky.

Chapter 56

Estoppel

56.1	**Introduction**	**498**
56.2	**Essential elements of estoppel**	**498**
	56.2.1 A representation of a factual position	499
	56.2.2 The party must have relied on the representation	499
	56.2.3 The representation must have induced a reasonable belief on the part of the party relying on estoppel	499
	56.2.4 The party acted or failed to act to his or her detriment	500
	56.2.5 The representation must have been the cause of the party's detrimental action	500
	56.2.6 Can a representation be made negligently?	501
56.3	**Legal rules applicable to estoppel**	**501**
	56.3.1 Defence of claim	501
	56.3.2 In replication	501
56.4	**Estoppel by judgment**	**502**
	56.4.1 Civil proceedings	502
	56.4.2 Criminal proceedings	502

56.1 Introduction

Estoppel does not actually relate to placing evidence before a court.[1] On the contrary, it is an equitable doctrine adopted from English law[2] that prevents a party in a dispute from denying the truth of something alleged. It does this by denying them the opportunity of leading contrary evidence or by preventing the denial in some other way.

Estoppel has therefore been defined as a rule that prevents a party from denying the truth of a representation made to another party if the latter, believing the representation to be true, acted on the strength of it to his or her detriment or prejudice.

It is thus a rule of substantive law, although English in origin, but is frequently discussed in the law of evidence because of its evidentiary impact.

56.2 Essential elements of estoppel

The above definition encapsulates all the essential elements of estoppel, which are discussed in detail below.

---

1 *Aris Enterprises (Finance) (Pty) Ltd v Protea Assurance Co Ltd* 1981 (3) SA 274 (A) at 291D–E.
2 The South African doctrine differs slightly in application to the English one and thus English precedent is not useful. See *Trust Bank van Afrika Bpk v Eksteen* 1964 (3) SA 402 (A). See also DT Zeffertt and AP Paizes *The South African Law of Evidence* 2 ed (2009) at 3.

CHAPTER 56 ESTOPPEL | 499

56.2.1 A representation of a factual position

For estoppel to be applied, there must have been a representation made orally, in writing or by some act or conduct including silence or inaction. Silence or inaction only amounts to a representation where there is a duty to speak to prevent the party to whom the representation is made from acting to his detriment.[3] The representation must have been clear and unequivocal[4] and it must have been unambiguous.[5]

56.2.2 The party must have relied on the representation

In accordance with this principle, if a party acts to his or her detriment as a result of factors other than the representation, even though a representation was made, estoppel will not operate.[6]

56.2.3 The representation must have induced a reasonable belief on the part of the party relying on estoppel

There are two important things to consider here:
- First, the representation must have induced a belief in the mind of the party relying on estoppel about the other party. This is a question of fact to be inferred from the circumstances. This element of causation is discussed below.
- Second, it must have been a reasonable belief. The question of what constitutes a reasonable belief has been the subject of judicial scrutiny.

DISCUSSION 56.1

A reasonable belief?

In *Lourens en 'n Ander v Genis*,[7] a party was induced to bore for water, unsuccessfully, on the basis of a representation by a person that his child had X-ray vision and had seen water below the surface. The Court held that a reasonable person would not have been misled by this misrepresentation. Thus believing this representation was not considered to be a reasonable belief.

This precedent has since been overturned and in *Orville Investments (Pty) Ltd v Sandfontein Motors*,[8] the Court held that the test was whether or not the person actually believed the misrepresentation. Thus, the reasonableness of the person's belief is relevant only to establishing whether it induced the action.

In *Tactical Reaction Services CC v Beverley Estate II Homeowners' Association*,[9] the plaintiff's offer to contract was communicated by the plaintiff to the defendant. The defendant, through a representative, communicated the defendant's acceptance of the offer by means of an email to the plaintiff. The plaintiff averred that the defendant through its conduct had induced the plaintiff into the reasonable belief that the defendant was accepting the offer.

---

3 *Saridakis t/a Auto Nest v Lamont* 1993 (2) SA 164 (C); *Road Accident Fund v Mothupi* 2000 (4) SA 38 (SCA).
4 *B and B Hardware Distributors (Pty) Ltd v Administrator, Cape and Another* 1989 (1) SA 957 (A).
5 *Southern Life Association Ltd v Beyleveld NO* 1989 (1) SA 496 (A).
6 *Standard Bank of SA Ltd v Stama (Pty) Ltd* 1975 (1) SA 730 (A) at 743.
7 1962 (1) SA 431 (T).
8 2000 (2) SA 886 (T).
9 (2007/16441) [2010] ZAGPJHC 102 (5 November 2010).

The Court held that:

> In order for a court to find that a contract has come into existence under the doctrine of quasi-mutual assent or estoppel, as in this case, there must be a representation which, through conduct, induces a reasonable belief on the part of the other party, that the former was accepting the offer thereby precluding such former party from denying the existence of such contract ... The question that has to be asked, is whether or not the party who is trying to resile from the contract is to blame in the sense that by his conduct he has led the other party, as a reasonable man, to believe that he was binding himself.[10]

Any pre-knowledge as to the real or factual legal position applicable to the circumstances will tend to minimise the chances that the representee will be considered to have been misled by the representation.

56.2.4 The party acted or failed to act to his or her detriment

Again, two important aspects are included in this element:
- First, there must have been an act (or a failure to act) which, also, is determined on the facts.
- Second, the act must have been to the representee's detriment.

In *De Klerk v Absa Bank Ltd and Others*,[11] the trial court had found that the plaintiff had produced insufficient evidence to prove that he had suffered a loss as a result of making an investment on the strength of promises of growth contained in a brochure. The court had found that as he could not prove that he would have invested his money more profitably elsewhere, accordingly he had not acted to his detriment. The Supreme Court of Appeal overturned this decision, saying that it was not necessary for the plaintiff to have proved the exact quantum of his loss to show he had acted to his detriment.

56.2.5 The representation must have been the cause of the party's detrimental action

The element of causation requires that the representation must have induced the belief. If a party is induced to act by something other than the representation, then estoppel will not operate. In *Stellenbosch Farmers' Winery Ltd v Vlachos t/a The Liquor Den*,[12] the appellant had supplied goods on credit to the respondent, the owner of a bottle store. The respondent sold the bottle store to a third party without telling the appellant. The appellant continued to sell on credit to the new owner who absconded without settling the debt. The appellant sought to hold the respondent liable for its loss, alleging that the respondent by failing to inform it of the sale had made a representation on which the appellant had relied to its detriment.

The Supreme Court of Appeal found that although the respondent had been under a duty to disclose that the business had been sold, the appellant was induced to continue to extend credit by the third party's deception and its own negligence rather than by the respondent's silence.[13]

---

10 At para 24.
11 2003 (4) SA 315 (SCA).
12 2001 (3) SA 597 (SCA).
13 The Constitutional Court recently set out the essential elements of estoppel in the field of agency in the case of *Makate v Vodacom Ltd* 2016 (4) SA 121 (CC) (26 April 2016) (a case better known as the 'Please Call Me' case) at para 48.

CHAPTER 56 ESTOPPEL | 501

56.2.6 Can a representation be made negligently?

This is not one of the standard requirements for estoppel to operate. A negligent act will usually only be regarded as sufficient conduct to constitute a representation in certain situations, for example where a person is silent or inactive when there is a duty on them to speak or act, as illustrated in the case below. The representation in such a case is the negligent silence of the person who owes the other a duty to speak.

> **Government v National Bank of SA Ltd**
>
> In *Government v National Bank of SA Ltd*,[14] a postmaster failed to lock up his office stamp as he was required to do by law. A friend of his used the stamp to complete stolen postal orders without his knowledge. The postal orders were cashed at the bank and the Post Office sued the bank for the amount paid. The bank's defence was that the Post Office was estopped from relying on the forgery because it had occurred through the negligence of the postmaster. The Appellate Division held that the postmaster did not owe a duty to the bank.

56.3 Legal rules applicable to estoppel

The legal rules applicable to estoppel can be summarised by saying that estoppel is a shield of defence and not a sword of attack. In other words, estoppel cannot be used in the offensive or as a cause of action but only to defend a claim or in replication to a defence raised.[15] This will be explained below by using two practical examples.

56.3.1 Defence of claim

A tenant of premises pays the monthly rental to a person other than the person nominated in a rental agreement (to the landlord instead of the letting agent) for a number of years without the landlord objecting. If the landlord decides to evict the tenant citing a breach of contract (payment not in accordance with the agreement), the tenant can raise the defence that the landlord, as a result of his conduct, is estopped from averring that the tenant is in breach.

56.3.2 In replication

A person takes out a car insurance policy but habitually pays the monthly premium later than the period allowed in the policy. The insurance company always accepts late payment without objection and at no time warns the person that his or her policy will lapse for late payment or informs the person that his or her policy has lapsed.

The insured person's car is involved in an accident and he or she claims from the insurance company. The insurance company repudiates the claim on the basis that at the time of the accident the insured was behind on his or her payments and the policy had lapsed accordingly. The insured can replicate against this defence by claiming that the insurance company is estopped from averring that the policy had lapsed because its conduct led him or her to believe that it would not enforce the clause allowing it to cancel the policy for late payment.

It is clear, from the case law, academic opinion and the examples cited above, that estoppel is a rule of substantive law and is not actually an evidentiary rule.

---

14 1921 AD 121.
15 *Oriental Products (Pty) Ltd v Pegma 178 Investments Trading CC and Others* 2011 (2) SA 508 (SCA).

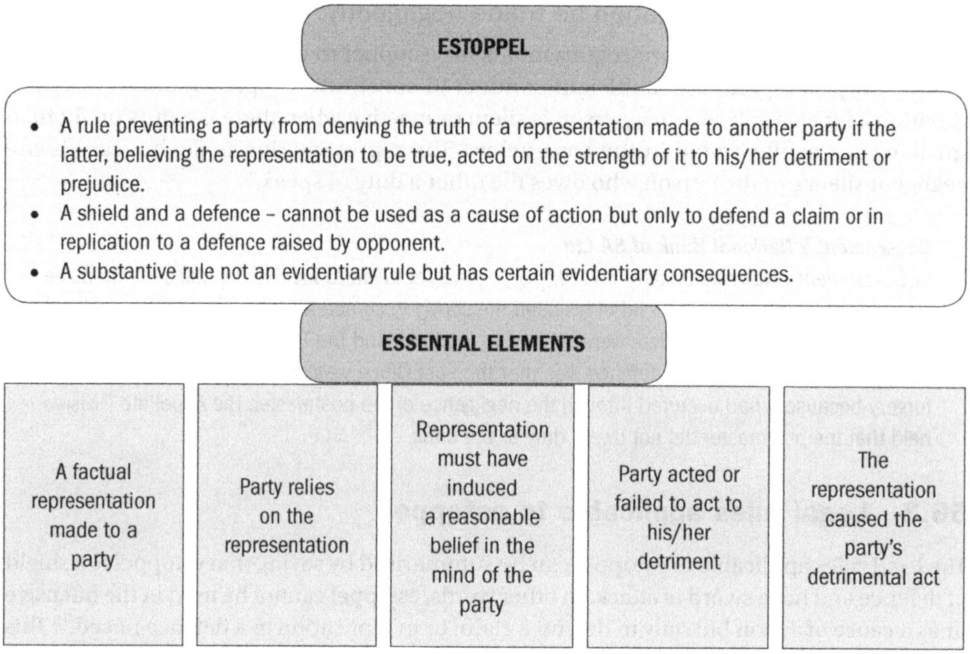

THE LAW OF EVIDENCE IN SOUTH AFRICA

ESTOPPEL

- A rule preventing a party from denying the truth of a representation made to another party if the latter, believing the representation to be true, acted on the strength of it to his/her detriment or prejudice.
- A shield and a defence – cannot be used as a cause of action but only to defend a claim or in replication to a defence raised by opponent.
- A substantive rule not an evidentiary rule but has certain evidentiary consequences.

ESSENTIAL ELEMENTS

A factual representation made to a party	Party relies on the representation	Representation must have induced a reasonable belief in the mind of the party	Party acted or failed to act to his/her detriment	The representation caused the party's detrimental act

Figure 56.1 Estoppel

56.4 Estoppel by judgment

This is a form of estoppel in which a party to a legal proceeding alleges that the proceeding should not be allowed to continue as it has already been dealt with on a previous occasion by a competent court.[16]

56.4.1 Civil proceedings

In South Africa, the term '*res judicata*' is used to describe a situation in which a matter comes before a court but the matter has already been heard by that court or another court. The principle enables a party to raise an exception to the continuance of the proceedings. The exception is referred to as the *exceptio rei judicatae* and is available to a party if the matter has already been adjudicated on and has reached final judgment.[17] To succeed, the party raising the exception, usually the defendant, must show the following:

- The new matter is based on the same subject matter. In other words, it must be the same cause of action or arise from the same facts.
- The new matter must seek the same relief.
- The new matter must be between the same parties.

56.4.2 Criminal proceedings

The South African term, adopted from English law, that describes the plea that an accused can raise if he or she has either been previously convicted or acquitted of a crime and has

---

16 Obviously, this principle is not applicable to appeals and reviews, which are technically continuations of the same legal proceeding, not duplications thereof.

17 See *Man Truck and Bus (SA) (Pty) Ltd v Dusbus Leasing CC and Others* 2004 (1) SA 454 (W).

subsequently been charged again with the same offence is ***autrefois convict*** when previously convicted or ***autrefois acquit*** when previously acquitted. The well-known American term 'double jeopardy' is often used. To succeed, the accused must show the following:

- The two matters relate to the same or substantially the same offence.
- The previous judgment was by a competent court.

THIS CHAPTER IN ESSENCE

1 The defence of estoppel prevents a party from denying the truth of a representation made to another party if the latter, believing the representation to be true, acted on the strength of it to his or her detriment or prejudice.

2 To succeed with the defence of estoppel, the following requirements must be met:

2.1 There must have been a representation made orally, in writing or by some act or conduct.

2.2 The party must have relied on the representation.

2.3 The representation must have induced a reasonable belief on the part of the party relying on estoppel.

2.4 The party must have acted (or failed to act) and the act (or failure to act) must have been to the representee's detriment.

2.5 The representation must have been the cause of the party's detrimental action.

3 Estoppel can only be raised in respect of negligent behaviour if a person has a duty to speak or act but remains silent or inactive.

4 In civil proceedings, a party can raise the exception of res judicata if a matter comes before a court but the matter has already been heard by that court or another court. To succeed, the party raising the exception must show that the new matter:

4.1 is based on the same subject matter

4.2 seeks the same relief

4.3 is between the same parties.

5 If an accused in criminal proceedings has either been previously convicted or acquitted of a crime and subsequently been charged with the same offence, he or she can raise the plea of autrefois convict when previously convicted or autrefois acquit when previously acquitted. To succeed, the accused must show that:

5.1 the two matters relate to the same or substantially the same offence

5.2 the previous judgment was by a competent court.

Chapter 57

The parol evidence rule

57.1	**Introduction**	**504**
57.2	**Requirements for the parol evidence rule**	**504**
	57.2.1 Single memorial	504
	57.2.2 Intention of the parties	505
57.3	**Exceptions to the parol evidence rule**	**505**
	57.3.1 Statutory restrictions	505
	57.3.2 Rectification	505
	57.3.3 Validity	505
	57.3.4 Partial record	506

57.1   Introduction

A written contract is regarded as being the complete record of what was agreed between the parties in the interests of certainty and finality. This is known as the *parol evidence rule* although it is sometimes referred to as the *extrinsic evidence rule*. The general rule is that a document, usually a contract, that records a juristic or legal act, or a transaction, is regarded as being conclusive of the terms of the agreement. Generally, no extrinsic or outside evidence, whether oral or written, may be led to contradict or add to the terms of the agreement.

For example, when you take out a contract at a health club, the salesperson may tell you that you can cancel the contract at any time without incurring penalties. However, when you later cancel the contract, you are told that it contains a term stating that cancellation penalties are due. In terms of the parol evidence rule, you would not be permitted to lead evidence of what the salesperson told you in an attempt to claim that it is a term of the agreement.

However, there are exceptions to this approach which we will consider below.

57.2   Requirements for the parol evidence rule

The rule is not automatically applicable to all contracts or legal transactions and several requirements need to be satisfied for it to come into effect.

57.2.1   Single memorial

The parol evidence rule applies to written documents such as agreements, negotiable instruments and wills but generally not to receipts and memoranda. The rule, formulated

CHAPTER 57   THE PAROL EVIDENCE RULE | **505**

by Wigmore[1] and approved by the Appellate Division in *National Board (Pretoria) (Pty) Ltd and Another v Estate Swanepoel*,[2] is as follows:

> **When a jural act is embodied in a single memorial, all other utterances of the parties on that topic are legally immaterial for the purpose of determining what are the terms of their act.**

57.2.2   Intention of the parties

For the rule to apply, it is necessary that the parties deliberately intended to embody or record their agreement in writing and for this to be the sole record of the terms of the agreement. This intention need not be expressed but can be inferred objectively from the document and the circumstances.

57.3   Exceptions to the parol evidence rule

There are a number of exceptions to the parol evidence rule, some of the most important of which are considered below.

57.3.1   Statutory restrictions

Ever-increasing areas of the law are being regulated by statute. Section 93 of the National Credit Act 34 of 2005 provides that credit agreements must be in writing. Section 50(1) of the Consumer Protection Act 68 of 2008 allows the minister to prescribe categories of consumer agreements that must be in writing. The effect of reducing such agreements to writing is similar to the parol evidence rule as external evidence is excluded. However, both these Acts imply that external evidence is permissible. Section 90(2)(*h*) and (*i*) of the National Credit Act, 2005 makes it unlawful for an agreement to include an acknowledgement that, before the agreement was made, no representations or warranties were given. The equivalent provision of the Consumer Protection Act, 2008 is section 51(1)(*g*). Both these sections imply that evidence may be led as to a prior representation having been made.

57.3.2   Rectification

If the agreement incorrectly reflects the terms agreed on by the parties, they can apply to court to have the agreement rectified to reflect their true intention. Extrinsic evidence may be led to prove their true intention.[3]

57.3.3   Validity

Extrinsic evidence may be led to challenge the validity of the underlying **jural** act of which the document is proof.[4] An example of where this might happen is where a party claims the agreement was induced by fraud or was due to mistake. Likewise, evidence is permissible to prove a signature.[5]

---

1   JH Wigmore *Wigmore on Evidence* 3 ed, Vol. 9 (1940) at para 2425, p. 76.
2   1975 (3) SA 16 (A) at para 26.
3   *ABSA Technology Finance Solutions Pty (Ltd) v Michael's Bid A House CC and Another* 2013 (3) SA 426 (SCA) where the court held that parol evidence was not admissible to alter the terms of the written agreement in the absence of a plea of rectification, fraud or simulation.
4   *Kok v Osborne and Another* 1993 (4) SA 788 (SE).
5   *SAI Investments v Van der Schyff NO and Others* 1999 (3) SA 340 (N).

57.3.4 Partial record

Where the parties did not intend the whole of the agreement to be recorded, it is permissible for them to provide evidence regarding aspects that were not included.[6] It may be necessary for a court to attempt to reconcile any contradictions that may exist between the recorded aspect of the agreement and the other evidence. Therefore, if there is a term in a contract in which the parties agree that the contract constitutes the entire agreement and that no other representations are binding on the parties, this would provide the evidence necessary to prove that the parties intended that the whole of the agreement be recorded. Conversely, the absence of such a term allows a party to argue that the parties did not intend the written contract to reflect the whole agreement and that extrinsic evidence should be permissible. This exception is really a restatement of the requirement that the parties intended the rule to apply.

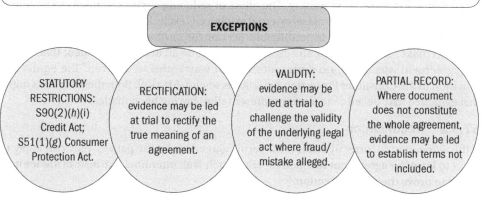

Figure 57.1 The parol evidence rule

THIS CHAPTER IN ESSENCE

1. The parol evidence rule holds that no extrinsic oral or written evidence may be led to contradict or add to the terms of an agreement.
2. For the parol evidence rule to be applicable to contracts or legal transactions, the following requirements must be met:
    2.1 The written document must not be a receipt or memoranda.
    2.2 The parties must have the deliberate intention to embody or record their agreement in writing and for such document to be the sole record of the terms of the agreement.

---

6 *Johnston v Leal* 1980 (3) SA 927 (A).

CHAPTER 57 THE PAROL EVIDENCE RULE | 507

3 The following exceptions apply to the parol evidence rule:

   3.1 Section 93 of the National Credit Act, 2005 provides that credit agreements must be in writing.

   3.2 Section 50(1) of the Consumer Protection Act, 2008 allows the minister to prescribe categories of consumer agreements that must be in writing.

   3.3 Section 51(1)(*g*) of the Consumer Protection Act, 2008 and section 90(2)(*h*) and (*i*) of the National Credit Act, 2005 imply that evidence may be led as to a prior representation having been made.

   3.4 An agreement that incorrectly reflects the terms agreed on by the parties can on application to court be rectified to reflect their true intention.

   3.5 Extrinsic evidence may be led to challenge the validity of the underlying jural act of which the document is proof.

   3.6 Where the parties did not intend the whole of the agreement to be recorded, they are permitted to provide evidence regarding aspects that were not included.

Chapter 58

Children's evidence

58.1 Introduction **508**

58.2 Children and the oath **509**

58.3 Evaluating the testimony of children **510**
    58.3.1 Evidence of previous consistent statements 511
    58.3.2 Evidence of delay in reporting 511
    58.3.3 Evidence of character and previous sexual history 511
    58.3.4 Children's evidence and the cautionary rule 512

58.1 Introduction

Child witnesses are often called by the prosecutor, either as the complainant or as an eyewitness to the crime, to testify against an alleged offender. A large percentage of children who testify are victims of crimes of a sexual nature.[1] In such an instance, it can be extremely difficult for the child to testify in court. The reasons relate, *inter alia* to the child's lack of maturity and developmental shortcomings.[2] Being a victim of abuse adds even more complexities such as the inability to function as an individual and to cope with the process of testifying.[3] The Constitutional Court has recognised that testifying about intimate details in front of the perpetrator and being exposed to hostile cross-examination both cause secondary trauma.[4]

Various sections in the Criminal Procedure Act 51 of 1977 deal with accommodating child witnesses when they have to testify in criminal trials. These provisions relate to *in camera* proceedings,[5] the appointment of intermediaries[6] and the use of electronic equipment.[7]

---

1 G Jonker and R Swanzen 'Intermediary services for child witnesses testifying in South African criminal courts' (2007) 4(6) *SUR Revista Internacional de Direitos Humanos [International Journal on Human Rights]* 95 present a study that shows that over a period of 41 months from a total of 1 496 cases involving children that occurred in three courts in Gauteng, 64,52 per cent were victims of rape and 27,57 per cent were victims of indecent assault.

2 K Müller and A van der Merwe 'Judicial management in child abuse cases: Empowering judicial officers to be the "boss of the court"' (2005) 18(1) *South African Journal of Criminal Justice* 41 at 42–43.

3 Ibid. at 43.

4 *Director of Public Prosecutions, Transvaal v Minister of Justice and Constitutional Development and Others* 2009 (2) SACR 130 (CC) at para 108.

5 S 153 of the Criminal Procedure Act, 1977. Note further that in terms of s 154(3) there is also a prohibition on the identification of a child witness under the age of 18 years old but the prohibition does not extend into the child's majority. See *Centre for Child Law and others v Media24 Ltd and others* 2017 (2) SACR 416 (GP).

6 S 170A of the Criminal Procedure Act, 1977.

7 S 158 of the Criminal Procedure Act, 1977.

CHAPTER 58   CHILDREN'S EVIDENCE | **509**

A child may further experience feelings of fear and anxiety directly related to a lack of knowledge and understanding of what a court looks like, what the legal process entails, who the role players involved are and of his or her own role within the process. Proper court preparation of a general nature should therefore receive attention in all instances where a child witness is involved and serves an important role in reducing the child's fear and anxiety. The ultimate purpose of such preparation is to empower the child with knowledge and understanding so that he or she can testify more effectively and accurately.[8] However, before a child is allowed to testify, the court must be satisfied that he or she understands the importance of telling the truth.

58.2   Children and the oath

Section 164(1) of the Criminal Procedure Act, 1977 authorises a court to allow a child who does not understand the nature or the importance of an oath[9] or a solemn affirmation[10] to give evidence without taking an oath or making an affirmation. In such a case, the presiding officer is required to admonish (warn) the child to speak the truth. Thus, notwithstanding the child's lack of understanding the oath, he or she can still be a competent witness. There is no minimum age for a competent witness and, therefore, whether the child witness is indeed competent must be decided in each case. A finding that a child is or is not competent to testify may be based on any relevant grounds such as ignorance flowing from youthfulness, poor education or any other cause.[11]

However, the court is required to satisfy itself that the child understands what it means to tell the truth before admonishing it. If the court finds that a child witness does not have the ability to make the distinction between truth and lies, such a child will not be considered competent and will, therefore, not be allowed to testify in court. The Constitutional Court reiterated that understanding what it means to tell the truth gives the assurance that the child's evidence can be relied on.[12] The evidence of a child who does not understand what it means to tell the truth is not reliable and it would undermine the accused's right to a fair trial if such evidence were to be admitted. Section 164 of the Criminal Procedure Act, 1977 thus eliminates the risk of a conviction based on unreliable evidence.

Although desirable, a formal enquiry into whether a child understands the oath or affirmation is not a prerequisite before a decision can be made merely to warn the witness to tell the truth.[13] In *S v B*,[14] the Supreme Court of Appeal criticised the court *a quo*'s narrow interpretation of section 164 in requiring a formal enquiry. The importance of truthfulness should generally be covered by an enquiry satisfying the court that the witness understands that an adverse sanction will generally follow the telling of a lie. When a direct question does not elicit a clear response, the court can further question the child in this regard.[15]

---

8 K Müller *Preparing Children for Court: A Handbook for Practitioners* (2004) at 8.
9 S 162 of the Criminal Procedure Act, 1977.
10 S 163 of the Criminal Procedure Act, 1977.
11 This approach in *S v B* 2003 (1) SA 552 (SCA) at para 15 was confirmed in *Director of Public Prosecutions, KwaZulu-Natal v Mekka* 2003 (4) SA 275 (SCA) at para 11 as the correct approach.
12 *Director of Public Prosecutions, Transvaal v Minister of Justice and Constitutional Development and Others* 2009 (2) SACR 130 (CC) at para 166.
13 *S v B* 2003 (1) SA 552 (SCA) at para 15.
14 2003 (1) SA 552 (SCA) at para 15.
15 In *Director of Public Prosecutions, Transvaal v Minister of Justice and Constitutional Development and Others* 2009 (2) SACR 130 (CC) at paras 167–168, the Court highlighted that courts require special skills for the successful questioning of children and in its absence they must rely on the intermediary's assistance in this regard. See also *S v Raghubar* 2013 (1) SACR 398 (SCA).

510 | THE LAW OF EVIDENCE IN SOUTH AFRICA

The case of *S v QN*[16] provides a good example of how to question a six-year-old witness:

> 'Do your parents ever give you a hiding?' to which N replied: 'Yes. My mother [hits] me if ever I am naughty at home.' The magistrate continued: '... What do you mean naughty?' to which N replied, 'My mother gives me a hiding when I am telling lies.' This was followed by the question, 'So is it a good or a bad thing to tell lies?' to which the reply was given, 'It's a bad thing, Your Worship' ... 'The court is satisfied that the witness, due to her age, will not understand the nature and import of the oath. However, the court is satisfied that she is a competent witness'.

On appeal, it was found that there was no basis for requiring a judicial officer to go any further than the above in arriving at the conclusion that a witness is competent. The Court pointed out that there are many cases where the courts have stopped far short of a formal enquiry.[17]

In *Director of Public Prosecutions, KwaZulu-Natal v Mekka*,[18] the magistrate made a finding that the complainant was a person who, from ignorance arising from her youthfulness, did not understand the nature and import of the oath. The SCA held that the magistrate saw and heard the complainant and the court of appeal was in no position to question the correctness of the finding. It is not necessary, before section 164 is invoked, that the witness must appreciate that a punishment similar to that for perjury will follow if they 'wilfully and falsely' state an untruth.[19]

58.3 Evaluating the testimony of children

Although a child's evidence forms simply one piece of the evidence at the end of a trial, it can be crucial to the outcome of the case since the child is often the only witness present during the abuse. Courts have often been criticised for excluding children's evidence for no good reason, as illustrated in the cases below.[20]

S v S

In *S v S*,[21] the Court cited several perceptions held by judicial officers that can largely be attributed to misunderstandings of children and which may lead to unjustified acquittals in sexual abuse matters:

- the risks involved in children's evidence and that their memories are unreliable
- that they are egocentric and highly suggestible
- that they have difficulty distinguishing fact from fantasy
- that they make false allegations, especially of a sexual nature
- that they have difficulty in understanding the truth.

---

16 2012 (1) SACR 380 (KZP) at paras 11 and 13.
17 Ibid.
18 2003 (4) SA 275 (SCA) at para 11.
19 Ibid. at para 11.
20 See K Müller 'The enigma of the child witness: A need for expert evidence' *Child Abuse Research in South Africa* (2003) 4(2) 2–9 who argues that to understand accurately the testimony of children, judicial officials need to improve their knowledge of children, for example matters of child development, child language and child behaviour, including perceptions, fears and beliefs.
21 1995 (1) SACR 50 (ZS) at 54H–I.

CHAPTER 58   CHILDREN'S EVIDENCE   **511**

S v Vilakazi
In *S v Vilakazi*,[22] the Court emphasised the necessity for the proper understanding of the child's evidence:

> From judicial officers who try such cases it calls for *accurate understanding and careful analysis of all the evidence*. For it is in the nature of such cases that the available evidence is often scant and many prosecutions fail for that reason alone. In those circumstances each detail can be vitally important.

The Criminal Law (Sexual Offences and Related Matters) Amendment Act 32 of 2007 (hereafter referred to as the Sexual Offences Act, 2007) enacted certain rules about how the court must deal with evidence of child complainants in sexual matters when evaluating it. These rules are briefly discussed below, as well as the cautionary rule applicable to children's testimony.

58.3.1   Evidence of previous consistent statements

The evidence that the complainant in a sexual crime case told someone about the sexual crime soon after the offence (the first report) has always been allowed. This rule is based on an old belief that if a complainant did not immediately after the rape urgently report the assault to someone, he or she was probably lying about whether the rape had taken place or whether it had been without his or her consent. This is known as the hue and cry rule[23] and is no longer applicable. Section 58 of the Sexual Offences Act, 2007 now provides that evidence of previous consistent statements by a complainant is admissible and that the court cannot assume that the complainant is lying if there is no such evidence.

58.3.2   Evidence of delay in reporting

Judicial officers were often sceptical about complaints of a sexual nature where the complainant did not report the crime as soon as possible after the sexual act had happened. Section 59 of the Sexual Offences Act, 2007 now provides that the court may not draw any negative conclusion from the length of any delay between the time when the crime was committed and when it was reported by the victim. Research has shown that children often delay disclosure of sexual abuse and that it is further a gradual process.[24]

Section 59 of the Sexual Offences Act, 2007 aims to rectify the erroneous assumption that when a child has been abused, the very first thing he or she will do is to disclose the abuse. A finding of untruthfulness about a child's allegation of sexual abuse must, therefore, not solely depend on the fact that a considerable time has elapsed since the abuse and the disclosure thereof. The court should always keep in mind that various factors may influence the disclosure process, for example the perpetrator's threats to silence the child or the child's shame. Also, in intrafamilial cases of abuse, the nonabusing parent may not want disclosure for various reasons such as economic or emotional dependency on the perpetrator.

58.3.3   Evidence of character and previous sexual history

Section 227 of the Criminal Procedure Act, 1977, as amended by the Sexual Offences Act, 2007, provides that no evidence of the previous sexual history of any complainant, including

---

22 2009 (1) SACR 552 (SCA) at para 21.
23 See chapter 20 for more detail on the 'hue and cry' rule.
24 T Sorensen and B Snow 'How children tell: The process of disclosure in child sexual abuse' (2000) 1(2) *Child Abuse Research in South Africa* 36 at 48.

512 | THE LAW OF EVIDENCE IN SOUTH AFRICA

children, may be presented as evidence in court. If an accused wants to introduce evidence about a child complainant's previous sexual experience, he or she must apply to court for permission to lead such evidence.[25] A court must not allow such evidence if it aims to support a suggestion that by reason of the sexual nature of the complainant's experience, he or she is more likely to have consented or is less worthy of belief.[26]

58.3.4 Children's evidence and the cautionary rule

Judicial officers have traditionally perceived children as being imaginative and suggestible, and thus unreliable, and insisted on a cautionary approach to the evaluation of their evidence. Despite research indicating that there is very little reason to assume that children are more unreliable or less accurate than adults,[27] the legislature has refused to abolish the cautionary rule.[28] However, the courts have held that the cautionary rule should not automatically be applied to children.[29] Common sense based on the facts of each case should dictate whether caution is to be applied and to what extent. Therefore, in some cases involving single child witnesses, as with adult witnesses, the court may rely solely on their evidence.[30] However, in other cases, caution and possible corroboration will be required.

Although a rational distinction should be made between the evidence of adults and children, it appears that the point of departure of judicial officers should be different. A child's testimony should generally be viewed as trustworthy unless there is some feature that signals danger and requires a cautionary approach. Factors that could alert the court relate to the character and intelligence of the child, the likelihood of false identification and the presence of a motive to conceal the truth.[31] Age *per se* should not be such a factor. The question to be answered in respect of a child witness is whether his or her evidence is clear and satisfactory in material respects.

THIS CHAPTER IN ESSENCE

1   A child who does not understand the nature or importance of an oath or a solemn affirmation can testify without giving such oath or solemn affirmation. The presiding officer must then simply admonish (warn) the child to speak the truth. However, before admonishing the child, the court must satisfy itself that he or she understands what it means to tell the truth.

2   The question of whether a child witness is competent must be decided on a witness-by-witness and case-by-case basis.

---

25   S 227(2)(*a*) and 227(4).

26   S 227(6). For a more detailed discussion, see ch 20 Evidence in sexual offences cases.

27   H Combrinck 'Monsters under the bed: Challenging existing views on the credibility of child witnesses in sexual offence cases' (1995) 8(3) *South African Journal of Criminal Justice* 326; P Zieff 'The child victim as witness in sexual abuse cases: A comparative analysis of the law of evidence and procedure' (1991) 4(1) *South African Journal of Criminal Justice* 21.

28   See s 20 of the draft Sexual Offences Bill SALC Discussion Paper 102 *Sexual offences: Process and procedure* (2002) at 852 and also s 60 of the Sexual Offences Act, 2007 that abolishes the cautionary rule with regard to all complainants of sexual offences.

29   *Director of Public Prosecutions v S* 2000 (2) SA 711 (T) following *S v J* 1998 (2) SA 984 (SCA); *S v Jackson* 1998 (1) SACR 470 (SCA) at 715 where the traditional cautionary rule applied to women in sexual offences was abolished.

30   See *S v QN* 2012 (1) SACR 380 (KZP) as an example where the child's evidence was accepted.

31   CWH Schmidt and DT Zeffertt (revised by DP van der Merwe) *Evidence* (1997) at 130 (by analogy of the traditional approach to look for truthfulness). In *Woji v Santam Insurance Co Ltd* 1981 (1) SA 1020 (A) at 1028A–E, the Court proposed the determination in each case of the individual child's capacity to observe, recollect and narrate the incident in question.

3 Evidence of a previous consistent statement made by a complainant in a sexual crime is admissible and the court cannot assume that a complainant is lying if there is no such evidence.
4 The court may not draw any negative conclusion from the delay between the commission of the crime and when it was first reported by the victim.
5 Evidence of the previous sexual history of any complainant, including children, may be presented as evidence in court.
6 The cautionary rule should not automatically be applied to children and any application thereof should be guided by common sense based on the facts of each case.

Chapter 59

Evidence in labour matters

59.1	**Introduction**	**515**
59.2	**The onus of proof in labour matters**	**515**
	59.2.1 The onus of proof in the Labour Relations Act, 1995	515
	59.2.2 The onus of proof in the Employment Equity Act, 1998	516
	59.2.3 The onus of proof in unfair labour practices	516
59.3	**The standard of proof in labour disputes**	**516**
59.4	**Shifting the evidentiary burden in labour matters**	**517**
	59.4.1 The evidentiary burden in labour matters	517
	59.4.2 The right to remain silent in labour hearings	517
59.5	**The conduct of arbitrations held in terms of the Labour Relations Act, 1995**	**518**
	59.5.1 Oral evidence in arbitration hearings	518
	59.5.2 Documentary evidence in arbitration hearings	518
	59.5.3 Real evidence in arbitration hearings	518
	59.5.4 Labour arbitration procedure	518
	59.5.5 Arbitrations as hearings *de novo*	520
	59.5.6 The duty to begin in arbitration hearings	520
59.6	**Admissibility of evidence in arbitrations**	**520**
	59.6.1 Discussions at conciliation proceedings	520
	59.6.2 Hearsay evidence in arbitrations	521
	59.6.3 Opinion evidence in arbitrations	523
	59.6.4 Illegally and improperly obtained evidence in labour matters	524
	59.6.4.1 Entrapment in labour matters	524
	59.6.4.2 Interception of communications in labour matters	524
	59.6.4.3 Admissibility of improperly obtained evidence in labour matters	525
	59.6.5 Monitoring and searches in labour matters	527
	59.6.6 Admissions and confessions in labour matters	527
	59.6.7 The parol evidence rule in labour matters	527
	59.6.8 Legal privilege in labour matters	528
	59.6.9 Evidence in earlier proceedings in labour matters	528
	59.6.10 Similar fact evidence in labour matters	528
59.7	**Proof without evidence in labour matters**	**528**
59.8	**Evaluation of evidence in arbitrations**	**529**
59.9	**Internal disciplinary hearings**	**530**
59.10	**The Labour Court**	**530**

CHAPTER 59   EVIDENCE IN LABOUR MATTERS   **515**

59.1   Introduction

Labour disputes arise from the relationship between employers and employees, or the termination thereof.[1] How evidence is presented and its admissibility depends on whether the proceedings are internal disciplinary proceedings, statutory arbitrations conducted by the Commission for Conciliation, Mediation and Arbitration (CCMA) or relevant bargaining council in terms of section 138 of the Labour Relations Act 66 of 1995, or Labour Court proceedings.

The CCMA and bargaining councils have jurisdiction to arbitrate, among others:
- disputes about unfair dismissals related to an employee's conduct or capacity
- constructive dismissals
- the non-renewal of fixed-term contracts
- unfair labour practices
- the interpretation and application of settlement and collective agreements.[2]

Provision is made in the CCMA rules for applications for **condonation** and the variation and rescission of awards.

The Labour Court has trial jurisdiction over, among others:
- automatically unfair dismissals
- strike dismissals
- retrenchments[3]
- damage claims arising from unprotected strike action[4]
- unfair discrimination claims[5]
- contractual disputes
- other claims under the Basic Conditions of Employment Act 75 of 1997.

The Labour Court also presides over applications in a host of matters, including urgent applications, strike interdicts and reviews of arbitration proceedings and awards. Parties may agree in writing that a dispute otherwise reserved for adjudication by the Labour Court be arbitrated by the CCMA or relevant bargaining council.

59.2   The onus of proof in labour matters

59.2.1   The onus of proof in the Labour Relations Act, 1995

Section 192 of the Labour Relations Act, 1995 places the onus of proving misconduct and the fairness of any dismissal on the employer. Where a dismissal is disputed, the onus rests on the employee to prove that a dismissal took place.

In an automatically unfair dismissal dispute, the employee has an evidentiary burden to produce evidence which shows a credible possibility that he or she was dismissed in one of the senses provided for in section 187 of the Labour Relations Act, 1995. If the employee does this, the onus is on the employer to prove that the dismissal was fair.

---

1   See T Cohen, A Rycroft and B Whitcher *Trade Unions and the Law in South Africa* (2009) at 99–113. See also J Grogan *Labour Litigation and Dispute Resolution* (2010) at 17.
2   Ss 191(5)(*a*) and 24 of the Labour Relations Act, 1995.
3   S 191(5)(*b*) of the Labour Relations Act, 1995.
4   S 68 of the Labour Relations Act, 1995.
5   S 10 of the Employment Equity Act 55 of 1998.

516 | THE LAW OF EVIDENCE IN SOUTH AFRICA

For example, in the case of a pregnant employee, if the employee is able to raise a believable possibility that her dismissal was due to her pregnancy, then the onus will shift to the employer to prove on a balance of probabilities that the employee was not dismissed because of her pregnancy in order to avoid the finding that the dismissal was automatically unfair. Alternatively, if the employer admits that the dismissal was based on the employee's pregnancy, the employer will have to prove that the dismissal constituted fair discrimination.[6]

59.2.2 The onus of proof in the Employment Equity Act, 1998

Where a complainant alleges unfair discrimination in terms of the Employment Equity Act 55 of 1998, he or she has an evidentiary burden to prove discrimination. In other words, the complainant must prove a link between the alleged differentiating conduct and a prohibited discriminatory ground listed in section 6(1) of the Employment Equity Act, 1998. If the complainant does this, unfairness will be presumed until the employer establishes that the discrimination is fair.

However, in a recent case, *Matjhabeng Municipality v Mothupi NO and Others*,[7] the employee claimed discrimination on the basis of lack of experience. Lack of experience is a listed ground because section 20(5) of the Employment Equity Act, 1998 states that an employer may not unfairly discriminate against a person solely on the grounds of that person's lack of experience. The Labour Court held that the employer's raising of the defence of an inherent requirement of the job is not elevated to the level of an onus to prove that such an inherent requirement is not unfair. The onus lies with the employee to prove that the said discrimination on the basis of lack of experience is unfair, not the other way around. If the alleged differentiation was on an unlisted ground, the complainant will have to establish unfairness.[8]

59.2.3 The onus of proof in unfair labour practices

In unfair labour practice disputes, the employee bears the onus of proving that the conduct or practice complained of falls within the statutory definition of an unfair labour practice and that the conduct of the employer was unfair.

59.3 The standard of proof in labour disputes

In labour disputes, the degree of proof required to discharge an onus is the balance of probabilities. For example, where an employee is accused of misconduct or the employer is accused of unfair dismissal, the employer, to discharge its onus, does not need to show that the facts are inconsistent with any possible or even reasonable inference except that the employee committed the specific misconduct in question and, in the latter case, that the dismissal was fair. Instead, the employer need only show that, on *all* the evidence presented by both parties, its version is more probable than the employee's version.

When the evidence permits more than one reasonable inference – one pointing to guilt and the other to innocence – the selected inference must, by the balancing of probabilities, be the more plausible of the possible inferences. For example, in *Potgietersrus Platinum Ltd v CCMA and Others*,[9] the Court held that an arbitrator incorrectly applied the required

---

6 See *Kroukam v SA Airlink (Pty) Ltd* (2005) 26 ILJ 2153 (LAC); *Janda v First National Bank* (2006) 27 ILJ 2627 (LC).
7 (2011) 32 ILJ 2154 (LC).
8 S 11 of the Employment Equity Act, 1998. See also *Chizuna v MTN (Pty) Ltd and Others* [2008] 10 BLLR 940 (LC).
9 (1999) 20 ILJ 2679 (LC). See also *Avril Elizabeth Home for the Mentally Handicapped v CCMA and Others* (2006) 27 ILJ 1644 (LC).

CHAPTER 59   EVIDENCE IN LABOUR MATTERS | **517**

standard of proof. It accepted the remote possibility that persons other than the accused employees had committed a theft, thus superseding the overwhelming and greater probability that the employees had committed the theft. Arbitrators, charged with the burden of deciding whether to confirm a dismissal, may nevertheless weigh the alternative inferences strictly and require clear and convincing evidence that the dismissal was justified.[10]

59.4   Shifting the evidentiary burden in labour matters

This section will explore the circumstances in which the evidentiary burden shifts and where the right to remain silent is applicable.

59.4.1   The evidentiary burden in labour matters

During an arbitration, while the overall onus never shifts, the need to present or counter evidence may rest on different parties. For example, in a misconduct case, once the employer has fleshed out its allegations with evidence to a degree that its version requires an answer or rebuttal lest it be believed, the evidentiary burden shifts onto the accused employee to prove otherwise.

In *Woolworths (Pty) Ltd v CCMA and Others*,[11] video footage capturing an employee concealing merchandise on her person while working in a retail store constitutes a *prima facie* case of dishonesty against the employee. This then shifts the evidentiary burden to the employee. In the absence of a credible and probable explanation from the employee, the inference that the arbitrator can most reasonably draw is that the employee acted dishonestly and that the employer has discharged its onus.

An employee is not entitled to the benefit of the doubt as to the convincing nature of his or her explanation. On raising a particular defence, an evidentiary burden falls on the employee to establish that his or her version is likely. It is not necessary for the employer to adduce evidence to disprove positively a defence, especially if the defence is within the unique knowledge of the employee.[12] An employer must prove its own case on a balance of probabilities. If it does so, it therefore flows that the employee's case is false.

During a trial, the court does not conduct a plurality of enquiries to make piecemeal evaluations of which party bears the evidentiary burden and whether they have satisfied this burden. At the end of the trial, when the court is evaluating the evidence, it will consider this issue. The effect of a party's failure to adduce evidence in rebuttal will depend on the reliability and weight of the evidence against him or her.

However, the nature of arbitrations is such that the parties are often unrepresented and unskilled in the art of evaluating their evidentiary burden. During a trial, arbitrators may then have to make such piecemeal evaluations in order to advise a party to produce a certain witness or document so that both parties are given a fair hearing.

59.4.2   The right to remain silent in labour hearings

Some disciplinary offences may be crimes as well. The employee faces a choice between possibly losing his or her case in a disciplinary hearing or arbitration through failing to reply to accusations or disclosing evidence that may lead to his or her conviction in a subsequent

---

10   'Room for doubt: The standard of proof in dismissal cases' *Employment Law Journal* (2000) Vol. 16 February 12.

11   (2011) 32 ILJ 2455 (LAC) at 34.

12   *Pillay v Krishna and Another* 1946 AD 946 at 951; *National Media Ltd and Others v Bogoshi* 1998 (4) SA 1196 (SCA) at 1218E–F.

518 THE LAW OF EVIDENCE IN SOUTH AFRICA

criminal trial. In this situation, an employee is not entitled to a stay of the disciplinary or arbitration proceedings until the completion of the criminal trial.

In addition, the employee is not immune from the evidentiary burden to rebut a case made against him or her on the basis of a right against self-incrimination and the right to remain silent. Section 35 of the Constitution pertains to criminal proceedings not labour proceedings.[13] Arguably, should an employee make incriminating statements during a labour case, he or she may apply in the criminal trial for the statements to be suppressed on the grounds that their use in that forum would constitute a violation of his or her right to remain silent.

59.5 The conduct of arbitrations held in terms of the Labour Relations Act, 1995

The arbitrator fulfils a role similar to that of a judge in that he or she receives oral evidence and argument, assesses the evidence and makes a decision called an award.

59.5.1 Oral evidence in arbitration hearings

Oral evidence includes a witness's oral statements about the facts of a case. The witness is present at the arbitration and can, therefore, be questioned about his or her evidence. Witnesses of the parties remain outside the hearing until called to give evidence. Where a witness listens to the testimony of earlier witnesses, the arbitrator cannot refuse to allow the witness to give evidence but should approach the witness's evidence with caution.[14]

59.5.2 Documentary evidence in arbitration hearings

Documentary evidence includes affidavits, written statements, written agreements, employment policies, minutes and transcripts of meetings and disciplinary hearings, medical certificates, letters, SMSs, computer printouts of emails, business records, photos, videos and surveillance camera evidence. Generally, the person who was the author, signatory, producer or had some other connection to a document sufficient to authenticate it and its contents must introduce the document into evidence. An exception is where the parties agree beforehand on the form of a document (what it purports to be) and its contents.

59.5.3 Real evidence in arbitration hearings

Real evidence includes physical items. Witnesses who can identify and explain the items usually introduce them into evidence.

59.5.4 Labour arbitration procedure

In terms of section 138 of the Labour Relations Act, 1995, the arbitrator may conduct the arbitration in a manner that he or she considers appropriate to determine the dispute fairly and quickly. The arbitrator must deal with the substantial merits of the dispute with the minimum of legal formalities. Subject to the discretion of the arbitrator as to the

---

13 *Davis v Tip NO and Others* 1996 (1) SA 1152 (W); *New Forest Farming CC v Cachalia and Others* (2003) 24 ILJ 1995 (LC); *NUMSA and Volkswagen of SA (Pty) Ltd* (2003) 12 Private 1.8.1; *SAMWU obo Abrahams and Others v City of Cape Town* (2008) 17 LC 4.2.1; *Mohlala v Citibank and Others* (2003) 24 ILJ 417 (LC); *Kayser and Department of Correctional Services* (1998) 7 CCMA 8.14.3.

14 *Natal Shoe Components CC v Ndawonde* (1998) 19 ILJ 1527 (LC).

CHAPTER 59 EVIDENCE IN LABOUR MATTERS | **519**

appropriate form of the proceedings, a party to the dispute may give evidence, call witnesses, question the witnesses of any other party and address concluding arguments to the arbitrator.

Some suggest that the fundamental rules of a fair hearing require that parties must be afforded the rights to call witnesses and to cross-examine witnesses of the other party unless they have agreed to waive these rights.[15] Others suggest that section 138 permits arbitrators to adopt either an adversarial procedure where the parties control the flow of evidence and question the witnesses or an inquisitorial approach where the arbitrator does most of the questioning and determines the flow of evidence. Wallis AJ in *Naraindath v CCMA and Others*[16] suggested that arbitrators should only adopt the traditional adversarial approach where the true issue depends on the resolution of a clear dispute of fact which can only be determined by listening to evidence and determining the credibility of witnesses.

Where an inquisitorial approach is used or the parties' right to call and cross-examine witnesses is restricted because of a procedure adopted by the arbitrator, this will not of itself give rise to grounds for review. However, there may be grounds for review where the restriction leads to an unfair outcome because the parties were not afforded a fair opportunity to present their respective cases and to challenge the evidence of the other party due to the manner in which the arbitrator conducted the questioning and controlled the flow of evidence.[17]

The inquisitorial approach would be warranted where the parties are unrepresented and unskilled in the art of presenting, eliciting and testing evidence. Arbitrators may not allow the ignorance of a lay litigant to favour the other party unfairly. They are required to take charge of the proceedings when the unaided parties do not realise what is expected of them. When appropriate, arbitrators should in an even-handed manner assist lay representatives to present and put their version to opposing witnesses. They should also warn them of the consequences of not leading evidence on particular issues or of not putting their version to the other parties' witness where the evidence of the witness contradicts, modifies or otherwise has an impact on their version.[18]

Where arbitrators have adopted the inquisitorial method, they must ensure that they are adequately briefed on the background of the case. They must peruse all relevant documents so that they deal with the real issues and avoid leading witnesses in the wrong direction.

Irrespective of the procedure used, arbitrators are obliged to ascertain and resolve the real dispute between the parties and to deal with the substantial merits of the dispute. They may thus require submissions on issues the parties did not raise and call for information beyond what the parties decide to present.[19]

---

15   See generally Grogan (2010) at 291 and the cases he refers to.

16   (2000) 21 ILJ 1151 (LC).

17   *Naraindath v CCMA and Others (2000)* 21 ILJ 1151 (LC); *Shoprite Checkers (Pty) Ltd v Ramdaw NO and Others* (2000) 21 ILJ 1232 (LC); *County Fair Foods (Pty) Ltd v Theron NO and Others* (2000) 21 ILJ 2649 (LC); *Mutual and Federal Insurance Co Ltd v CCMA and Others* [1997] 12 BLLR 1610 (LC).

18   *Dimbaza Foundries Ltd v CCMA and Others* (1999) 20 ILJ 1763 (LC); *Consolidated Wire Industries (Pty) Ltd v CCMA and Others* (1999) 20 ILJ 2602 (LC); *B and D Mines (Pty) Ltd v Sebotha NO and Another* [1998] 6 BLLR 573 (LC); *Leboho v CCMA and Others* (2005) 26 ILJ 883 (LC); *Scholtz v Commissioner Maseko NO and Others* (2000) 21 ILJ 1854 (LC); *Sikhula Sonke obo Pedro v CCMA and Others* (2007) 28 ILJ 1322 (LC); *Mutual and Federal Insurance Co Ltd v CCMA and Others* [1997] 12 BLLR 1610 (LC); *Char Technology (Pty) Ltd v Mnisi and Others* [2000] 7 BLLR 778 (LC).

19   *CUSA v Tao Ying Metal Industries and Others* [2009] 1 BLLR 1 (CC). See also *Leboho v CCMA and Others* (2005) 26 ILJ 883 (LC); *Armstrong v Tee and Others* (1999) 20 ILJ 2568 (LC); *Legal Aid Board v John NO and Another* (1998) 19 ILJ 851 (LC); *Karbochem Sasolburg (A Division of Sentrachem Ltd) v Kriel and Others* (1999) 20 ILJ 2889 (LC); *PPWAWU and Another v Commissioner CCMA (Port Elizabeth) and Another* [1998] 5 BLLR 499 (LC); *Natal Shoe Components CC v Ndawonde* (1998) 19 ILJ 1527 (LC).

520 | THE LAW OF EVIDENCE IN SOUTH AFRICA

59.5.5 Arbitrations as hearings *de novo*

Arbitrations are hearings *de novo*. The arbitrator must base his or her decision on the evidence led at the arbitration.

> The parties are not restricted to the evidence led at a disciplinary hearing and may lead further or new evidence. However, they may not lead evidence relating to events that transpired after the dismissal except when it comes to relief. The transcript of an internal disciplinary hearing may be used for testing the consistency of testimony given at the arbitration.
>
> Where the parties do not intend leading additional evidence and merely dispute the conclusion drawn from the evidence led at the disciplinary hearing and how the law ought to have been applied, they may agree that the arbitrator decide the matter on the existing record and only address the issue of the law.

59.5.6 The duty to begin in arbitration hearings

The party who bears the onus should begin leading evidence. However, when appropriate, the arbitrator may rule, on application or *mero motu*, that the other party begins. It is unreasonable, for example, to expect an employee challenging his or her suspension as an unfair labour practice to begin if the employer has given no reason for the suspension even though the employee still bears the onus of proving the suspension unfair.[20]

59.6 Admissibility of evidence in arbitrations

Admissibility refers to whether a party may introduce a particular item of evidence at the hearing and/or whether the arbitrator must take such evidence into account. Arbitrators are required to observe the most basic of the rules of evidence such as those relating to the onus of proof, standard of proof, relevance and privileged information. However, section 138 directs them to deal with the admissibility of evidence with a minimum of legal formalities.

Generally, if the evidence appears to be logically and legally relevant, arbitrators should admit it. There must be some advance indication that the evidence, if received, may assist the arbitrator in deciding the case. There should also be an indication that such evidence has the potential to shed light on what actually happened where there is a dispute of fact. The evidence should not lead to protracted investigations into collateral issues which, once determined, would be too remote and have little probative value with regard to the true issues. In some instances, the relevance of the evidence adduced will be immediately apparent, for example the testimony of an eyewitness to the disputed event. At other times, its potential will only emerge from a juxtaposition of the evidence in question and other pieces of known facts, for example hearsay evidence.

Explanations about and the admissibility of the different kinds of evidence are fully discussed in other chapters. The sections that follow therefore focus only on issues that commonly arise in arbitrations and disciplinary hearings.

59.6.1 Discussions at conciliation proceedings

Before a dispute is referred for statutory arbitration or for trial at the Labour Court, it must first be referred for conciliation to the CCMA or relevant bargaining council. Conciliation is

---

20 *Sajid v The Juma Masjid Trust* (1999) 20 ILJ 1975 (CCMA).

CHAPTER 59 EVIDENCE IN LABOUR MATTERS 521

aimed at settling the dispute. Therefore, any admissions made in the process are 'without prejudice communications' and no person may refer to anything said or not said at the conciliation during any subsequent proceedings.

59.6.2 Hearsay evidence in arbitrations

In terms of section 138 of the Labour Relations Act, 1995, the rule against the admission of hearsay evidence applies less strictly in arbitrations.[21] Hearsay evidence, as in all court cases, is not strictly relevant. For example, evidence that a witness saw the accused employee take the missing computer (eyewitness testimony) is highly relevant in any hearing but only if that witness comes to testify. If the witness does not testify, the evidence of this witness lacks probative value because he or she cannot be cross-examined to test the truth of his or her claims. The hearsay evidence only becomes relevant and admissible:

- if the party relying on it has a good reason for not bringing the original witness
- if the evidence fits in with or is offered up to confirm other admissible evidence
- if it is procedurally logical[22] to do so as described in the case below.

It is only when the hearsay evidence fits into the overall jigsaw of hard facts that have been presented that it may assume significant weight.

Naraindath v CCMA and Others

In *Naraindath v CCMA and Others*,[23] the employer relied on a transcript of testimony given at a disciplinary hearing without calling the witnesses. The employee did not challenge the evidence at the disciplinary hearing as he and his representative had withdrawn at the start of the hearing. Wallis AJ found that it was not irregular for the arbitrator to have continued the arbitration once this evidence had been placed before him by looking to the employee for an explanation of his stance regarding the charges. Depending on the explanation, the arbitrator would then be able to decide whether or not it was necessary for the witnesses to be called to the arbitration.

Employees often rely on medical certificates and reports as evidence at hearings. These should ordinarily be admissible where the employee (patient), as the recipient of the certificate, testifies to its authenticity and the correctness of the circumstances under which it was produced. However, where the employee wishes to rely on the disputed contents about which he or she has no specialised knowledge, the contents will be hearsay in the absence of the doctor's testimony. Generally, 'hearsay' certificates can be taken into account where they are offered to corroborate a version.[24]

Employers often rely on forensic or other business reports made up of documents created by more than one person. In *Foschini Group v Maidi and Others*,[25] the Labour Appeal Court held that, given section 138, an arbitrator had not acted in an irregular manner by admitting

---

21 *Foschini Group v Maidi and Others* (2010) 31 ILJ 1787 (LAC); *Le Monde Luggage CC t/a Pakwells Petje v Dunn and Others* [2007] 10 BLLR 909 (LAC); *Southern Sun Hotels (Pty) Ltd v SACCAWU and Another* (2000) 21 ILJ 1315 (LAC); *Naraindath v CCMA and Others* (2000) 21 ILJ 1151 (LC); *Fawu obo Kapesi and Others v Premier Foods Ltd t/a Blue Ribbon Salt River* [2010] 9 BLLR 903 (LC).

22 As happened in *Naraindath v CCMA and Others* (2000) 21 ILJ 1151 (LC).

23 (2000) 21 ILJ 1151 (LC).

24 *Le Monde Luggage CC t/a Pakwells Petje v Dunn and Others* [2007] 10 BLLR 909 (LAC). See, however, *Mgobhozi v Naidoo NO and Others* [2006] 3 BLLR 242 (LAC) where, in the context of a labour court application, the Court questionably held that a medical certificate annexed to a founding affidavit constituted inadmissible hearsay evidence in the absence of a supporting affidavit by the doctor.

25 (2010) 31 ILJ 1787 (LAC).

522 | THE LAW OF EVIDENCE IN SOUTH AFRICA

and treating a financial manager's testimony as reliable when part of the forensic report he had presented was hearsay. This was because the forensic report was derived from records maintained by the stock controllers who were not called as witnesses. Also, there was no plausible suggestion that the data recorded by the stock controllers was false or inaccurate.

In any event, the Criminal Procedure Act 51 of 1977 and the Civil Proceedings Evidence Act 25 of 1965 allow for the reception of hearsay evidence in documentary form, including business records and statements made in business records compiled in the ordinary course of business.[26] In the case of electronic evidence, section 15 of the Electronic Communications and Transactions Act 25 of 2002 provides that:

- computer printouts of business records made in the ordinary course of business are admissible against any person in civil, criminal and disciplinary enquiry proceedings under any law and administrative proceedings without the testimony of the person who made the entry
- they constitute rebuttable proof of the facts contained therein if accompanied by a certificate from a manager stating that the contents are correct and accurate.

This places a duty on the person challenging the form and content of such electronic business documents to provide forensic or other evidence that the record is false or otherwise unreliable as described in the case below.[27]

LA Consortium and Vending CC t/a LA Enterprises and Others v MTN Service Provider (Pty) Ltd and Others

In *LA Consortium and Vending CC t/a LA Enterprises and Others v MTN Service Provider (Pty) Ltd and Others*,[28] the Court held that decision makers may rely on the evidence of a witness who was not personally involved in making any of the inputs to an electronic business report he or she was presenting, but who could analyse, understand and draw conclusions from the data generated by the employer's systems. The margin of error in effecting electronic entries is minimal and will generally be made by employees acting within the scope of their employment. The fact that more than one person contributed to their existence does not constitute a valid objection to the admission of data messages into evidence and the court affording them 'due weight'.

It has been suggested that computer printouts of information created by a device (computer) without human intervention may be treated as real evidence. This would include, for example, cell phone records.

With hearsay evidence, the arbitrator should distinguish the objectively ascertainable aspects from those aspects of the evidence that may require direct testimony. The arbitrator can give considerable weight to those aspects that can be objectively ascertained and do not rely on perception or opinion. However, the arbitrator can give diminished weight or discard altogether those aspects of the evidence that may require direct testimony if there is no direct evidence or corroboration as it is evidence that needs to be tested by cross-examination, as illustrated in *Ismail v Nationwide Airlines* below. Also on this basis, in *Sigasa v Kemklean Hygiene Systems*,[29] an arbitrator allowed the evidence of a letter of complaint, made by a

---

26 See Part VI of the Civil Proceedings Evidence Act, 1965 and ss 221 and 222 of the Criminal Procedure Act, 1977.
27 *LA Consortium and Vending CC t/a LA Enterprises and Others v MTN Service Provider (Pty) Ltd and Others* Case No A5014/08, (19 August 2009) (SCHC).
28 Case No A5014/08 (19 August 2009) (SCHC).
29 [1997] 4 BLLR 494 (CCMA).

CHAPTER 59   EVIDENCE IN LABOUR MATTERS | 523

motorist against an employee for bad driving, to show that the employee was on an unauthorised route. However, the arbitrator disallowed the evidence where the employer sought to use it to show the employee's bad driving.

Ismail v Nationwide Airlines

In *Ismail v Nationwide Airlines*,[30] the employer dismissed an employee for making improper remarks to a passenger. The employee denied making any such remarks. As the passenger had returned overseas, the employer relied on an affidavit from the passenger which, although hearsay, the arbitrator admitted because the witness could not attend the hearing. However, he did not afford the contents of the affidavit much weight on the grounds that the contents were highly subjective and because they related to the principle facts in dispute. The contents, therefore, needed to be tested by cross-examination and/or be confirmed by other admissible evidence, which they were not.

59.6.3   Opinion evidence in arbitrations

Generally, witnesses may depose only to the facts that they have observed. The opinion of a witness is irrelevant and thus inadmissible evidence. An example is the testimony of a chairperson of an internal disciplinary hearing who states that in his or her view, the employee did commit the misconduct in issue. It is the job of the arbitrator to decide if the employee committed the misconduct by drawing inferences from proved facts presented by witnesses.

However, sometimes the arbitrator is not qualified to drawn inferences from certain facts and may rely on the opinion of an expert witness. The expert witness, because of his or her special knowledge and skills, is better able to draw such inferences.

It is difficult to draw a clear distinction between facts and inferences because most assertions made by people generally involve the expression of inferences. The arbitrator should, therefore, draw a line between those inferences that are considered objectionable and those that are not.

Lay or non-expert witnesses are permitted to give opinion evidence where they will not be able to express themselves meaningfully without doing so and where they are better placed than the arbitrator to make an inference. These witnesses may express an opinion based on general human experience and knowledge. This includes whether a person was intoxicated, the general condition of a thing, whether a vehicle was going fast or slow, the handwriting of someone he or she knows and the emotional state of a person, for example whether the person was angry or distressed.

In cases involving intoxication, the Court in *S v Edley*[31] stated:

> It seems to me that the more gross and manifest the physical manifestations of intoxication noted by credible and reliable laymen are, the more readily may medical evidence be dispensed with and that the more equivocal the physical manifestations or indications of intoxication may be, the greater would be the need for the State to lead medical evidence of the accused's condition at the relevant time.

Therefore, it is incorrect to say that only technical and medical evidence of intoxication is admissible, as described in the following case. The Court in *Exactics-Pet (Pty) Ltd v Patelia*

---

30   Unreported (KN 23530).
31   1970 (2) SA 223 (N) at 226.

524 | THE LAW OF EVIDENCE IN SOUTH AFRICA

NO and Others[32] held that an arbitrator was incorrect to hold that only technical and medical evidence of intoxication is admissible and that the results can only be admitted under strict conditions appropriate in a criminal trial. Where a lay witness testifies that the accused employee had slurred speech, smelt of alcohol, had an unsteady walk, red eyes, and so on, and the employee does not satisfactorily explain his behaviour, the employer has offered a more probable version.

The *Hollington* rule does not apply to arbitrations because such proceedings do not amount to civil proceedings in terms of section 42 of the Civil Proceedings Evidence Act, 1965. Accordingly, an arbitrator may take into consideration, as rebuttable *prima facie* evidence, the finding and observations of a court of law, such as a criminal court or Labour Court, on a relevant related matter.[33]

A controversial method of obtaining opinion evidence against employees is the use of polygraph tests, which is discussed in Part Seven.

59.6.4 Illegally and improperly obtained evidence in labour matters

59.6.4.1 Entrapment in labour matters

Entrapment takes place when the employer engages 'agents' to conclude 'deals' with employees involving illicit transactions. It entails cooperating with an employee in the commission of an offence. In *Cape Town City Council v SAMWU and Others*,[34] the Court found that the evidence obtained in the **trap** *in casu* (what the employees did and said during the trap and the information uncovered by the agent) was inadmissible because there was no proper pre-existing suspicion about the employees. In addition, the agent had exceeded the bounds set by section 252A of the Criminal Procedure Act, 1977 by actively encouraging and unduly inducing the employees to commit the offence. The onus rests on the employer to show that the trapping was fairly conducted.[35]

59.6.4.2 Interception of communications in labour matters

The Regulation of Interception of Communications and Provisions of Communication-related Information Act 70 of 2002 (RICA) prohibits, with exceptions, the intentional interception of direct or indirect communications. Direct communications include oral communications between two or more persons that occur in the immediate presence of all the participants, such as face-to-face conversations and meetings between two or more persons. Indirect communications refer to electronic and telecommunications such as faxes, phone conversations, phone records, emails and other forms of computer communications and usage, including text and visual images. Intercept includes:
- the monitoring of a direct and indirect communication by means of a monitoring device
- the viewing, examination or inspection of the contents of any indirect communication
- the diversion of any indirect communication from its intended destination to any other destination.

---

32 (2006) 27 ILJ 1126 (LC).

33 *Nel v Law Society; Cape of Good Hope* 2010 (6) SA 263 (ECG).

34 (2000) 21 ILJ 2409 (LC).

35 See also *Phadu and Others v Department of Health: Free State* [2004] 2 BALR 167 (PHWSBC); *Mbuli and Spartan Wiremakers CC* (2004) 25 ILJ 1128 (BCA); *NUMSA obo Abrahams v Guestro Wheels* [2004] 4 BALR 520 (CCMA); *Caji and African Personnel Services (Pty) Ltd* (2005) 26 ILJ 150 (CCMA); *NUMSA obo Nqukwe and Others v Louwveld Implement and Farm Equipment (Life)* [2003] 8 BALR 909 (CCMA).

The prohibition applies only to third party interception and not to participant interception. This is where one of the parties to the communication records and/or divulges it to a third party or records his or her own conversation.[36] A third party may intercept a communication with the consent of one of the parties to the communication or may access communications that are in the public domain, such as unrestricted access to Facebook.[37]

To fall foul of the Act, the prohibited interception must be intentional. An accidental or chance discovery of a message is not covered by the prohibition.[38] Section 6 of the Act contains a further exception to the prohibition that applies specifically to the workplace. The section permits employers to intercept the indirect communications of their employees without the employees' consent in the following circumstances:

- The communications must have been made via the electronic and telecommunications systems provided for use wholly or partly in connection with the employer's business.
- The employees must have been notified in advance that indirect communications made via the employer's electronic and telecommunication system may be intercepted.
- The employer may not intercept communications at random and without a proper reason.
- The consent of the systems controller must be obtained in each case. The systems controller is defined as a 'natural person' in the case of a private body or any partner in a partnership and the chief executive officer (or person duly authorised by him or her) in the case of a juristic person.

The purpose of the interception must be to 'establish the existence of facts' relevant to the business and/or to 'secure' the system.

59.6.4.3 Admissibility of improperly obtained evidence in labour matters

The question that arises is whether an employer, who acquires information about an employee by means that are not sanctioned by the law, may use this information against an employee in disciplinary and arbitration proceedings. The Court in *Lotter v Arlow and Another*[39] held that a tribunal in a civil case does have discretion to exclude improperly obtained evidence. In this regard, the court should examine all relevant considerations, including:

- whether the evidence could have been obtained lawfully
- whether justice could have been achieved by following ordinary procedures
- whether there was a deliberate violation of another's constitutional rights.

Arbitration and disciplinary proceedings are not civil court proceedings and section 138 of the Labour Relations Act, 1995 provides that admissibility rules must not be applied with the same strictness as they are applied in courts of law. The Industrial Court (which preceded the Labour Court) has suggested that in labour matters the adjudicator has no discretion to exclude illegally or improperly obtained evidence.[40] However, in later decisions, the Labour Court refused to admit evidence that was obtained in contravention of criminal legislation

---

36 *Dauth v Brown and Weirs Cash & Carry* [2002] 8 BALR 837 (CCMA); *Volkwyn v Truworths Ltd* [2002] 4 BALR 455 (CCMA).
37 *Sedick and Another v Krisray (Pty) Ltd* [2011] 8 BALR 879 (CCMA).
38 *Smuts v Backup Storage Facilities and Others* [2003] 2 BALR 219 (CCMA).
39 2002 (6) SA 60 (T).
40 *Goosen v Caroline's Frozen Yoghurt Parlour (Pty) Ltd and Another* (1995) 16 ILJ 396 (IC).

526 | THE LAW OF EVIDENCE IN SOUTH AFRICA

that regulates entrapment. The Court held that the onus is on the employer to prove its conduct was fair.[41]

Based on an employee's constitutional right to fair labour practices, it is suggested that an arbitrator does indeed have the discretion to exclude illegally and improperly obtained evidence. In this context, fairness may be defined in terms of balancing the employee's right to dignity and privacy, the employer's right to protect its business and the rule that an employer's decisions should be substantively and procedurally fair where the rights of employees are concerned.[42] Based on this and the fact that section 6 of the Labour Relations Act, 1995 already accommodates the balancing of rights and prejudice, the arbitrator should consider the following factors in determining whether to admit the evidence:

- whether the evidence could have been obtained lawfully
- whether the employer knowingly and deliberately contravened any law that regulates the gathering of the evidence, such as RICA
- whether there was a pre-existing suspicion that the employee was committing misconduct
- whether there were reasonable grounds for believing that evidence relating to that offence may be found in the communications of the employee.

Thus, for example, if an employee is charged with absenteeism, there is no reason to intercept his or her email because evidence from the employee's attendance record and eyewitness testimony can establish the existence of facts.

In *Moonsamy v The Mailhouse*,[43] the arbitrator stated that telephone conversations are a 'very private affair'. The employer must show that there are compelling reasons within the context of business that necessitate that the contents of those conversations are disclosed. He drew the line at continual tapping of an employee's business telephone and found that the employer could have and had, in fact, acquired evidence against Moonsamy by less intrusive means. In *Sugreen v Standard Bank of SA*,[44] the employer had obtained a tape recording of a conversation between one of its managers and a service provider, which revealed a bribe. The service provider made the tape recording and gave it to the employer. The arbitrator differentiated this case from *Moonsamy v The Mailhouse* on the basis that there were few other methods by which the evidence could have been acquired, that the recording was made during business hours and using the employer's telephone. In any event, it was a case of 'participant monitoring', which is permitted by RICA.

In another matter,[45] the employer monitored the telephone conversations of certain employees and used hidden video cameras to record their conversations. The arbitrator did not admit the evidence on the basis that the employer had no evidence to justify the monitoring and that no legal alternatives to the monitoring were considered.

The Court in *Protea Technology Ltd and Another v Wainer and Others*[46] pointed out that an employee may receive and make calls that have nothing to do with his or her employer's

---

41 *Cape Town City Council v SAMWU and Others* (2000) 21 ILJ 2409 (LC). The Court appears to have conflated the enquiry as to whether the evidence was improperly obtained with the admissibility enquiry.

42 The fact that s 6 permits interception only under certain conditions indicates that employees do have rights in these situations.

43 (1999) 20 ILJ 464 (CCMA).

44 (2002) 23 ILJ 1319 (CCMA).

45 See the unreported SAA arbitration award referred to by C Mischke in 'The monitoring and interception of electronic communications: Obtaining and using e-mail and other electronic evidence' (2001) 10 *Contemporary Labour Law* 91.

46 1997 (9) BCLR 1225 (W).

CHAPTER 59   EVIDENCE IN LABOUR MATTERS | **527**

business. The employee making such calls has a legitimate expectation of privacy and the employer cannot compel him or her to disclose the substance of such calls. However, the employer may have access to the content of conversations involving the employer's affairs.

In *Bamford and Others v Energiser (SA) Limited*,[47] the arbitrator sanctioned the collection and storage of email messages from employees' private mailboxes on the basis that the content of the messages (crude jokes and pornographic material) could not be construed as private. Moreover, when the company conducted an audit of its system when technical problems arose through overloading, it was seeking to establish the existence of facts indicating the root of the technical problem. It needed to secure the system's effective operation and, in the process, discovered improper use of the system, which amounted to misconduct.

The Court in *S v Dube*[48] held that a conversation between car thieves was not 'confidential' and hence was excluded from protection under the former Interception and Monitoring Prohibition Act 127 of 1992.

59.6.5   Monitoring and searches in labour matters

An employer is entitled to monitor its premises and the conduct of employees in operational areas, excluding change-rooms and toilets, through video and other camera surveillance for the purpose of protecting its business and property. Evidence obtained in these circumstances is admissible as there is no legitimate expectation of absolute privacy in these areas. Evidence obtained from searches of employees' workstations or body searches is admissible if the employer had good reason to suspect an offence. In the case of a body search, the employee must have contractually agreed to such searches, the search must have been conducted decently and it must be shown that other less drastic methods of detection were not available.

59.6.6   Admissions and confessions in labour matters

Admissions not formally agreed to may be denied or explained away during a hearing. However, the stricter criminal law rules on the admissibility of informal admissions should not be applied in arbitrations.

Where an employee voluntarily and in the absence of undue influence confesses to misconduct, the confession may be admitted and the employee may be found guilty of the misconduct if he or she has admitted all the elements of it. The employer does not have to confirm the confession in a material respect or adduce evidence other than the confession to prove the misconduct.[49]

Whether a confession was made voluntarily and in the absence of undue influence is an objective enquiry. For example, the confession is admissible where an employee confesses when given a choice between facing a disciplinary hearing or admitting the misconduct.

59.6.7   The parol evidence rule in labour matters

Parties to a written agreement, for example a collective agreement, are bound by what is written in the agreement. They may not seek to prove, contradict or change the written terms of the agreement through oral evidence unless the agreement itself is unclear and ambiguous on the matter.

---

47   [2001] 12 BALR 1251 (P).

48   2000 (2) SA 583 (N).

49   *OK Bazaars (a division of Shoprite Checkers) v CCMA and Others* (2000) 21 ILJ 1188 (LC).

528 | THE LAW OF EVIDENCE IN SOUTH AFRICA

However, where an employment relationship is disputed, arbitrators may permit extrinsic evidence and look behind an otherwise clear agreement to determine whether there is an employment relationship between the parties. The arbitrator may presume such a relationship exists where the employee proves certain facts listed in section 200A of the Labour Relations Act, 1995 unless the contrary is proved by the employer.

Witnesses may not be asked to interpret a contract or be asked about the meaning of certain words in a contract unless certain words have a peculiar institutional or industry meaning. Interpretation is a matter of law and not fact. Accordingly, the arbitrator must decide a matter after listening to argument from both representatives.[50]

59.6.8 Legal privilege in labour matters

Legal professional privileged communications include communications which were made between a party to a dispute and his or her union representative and which were made in the context of the party seeking legal advice and in preparation of litigation.

59.6.9 Evidence in earlier proceedings in labour matters

The testimony of a witness in earlier proceedings is admissible at a subsequent trial provided that:
- the proceedings are between the same parties
- the issues are substantially the same
- the witness cannot be called
- the opposing party had a full opportunity to cross-examine the witness.[51]

59.6.10 Similar fact evidence in labour matters

Similar fact evidence is a form of character evidence that apportions liability or guilt based on past misconduct of a similar nature. It is generally excluded because a person should be held liable based on reasons directly connected to the matter in dispute, and not what he or she did or may have done in the past. For example, the fact that the accused employee has a warning for assault cannot serve as evidence that he or she is guilty in a different case of assault before the arbitrator. A warning for assault, if current, will be relevant to the issue of sanction only.

However, similar fact evidence may be used to identify a culprit if the method and substance (*modus operandi*) in a number of his or her previous offences is strikingly similar to those alleged in the present case or if it tends to show a course of conduct. For example, proof of fraud may depend on evidence of a systematic course of action.

Fair notice of an intention to rely on similar fact evidence should, in fairness, be given to the other side so they are prepared to deal with it.

59.7 Proof without evidence in labour matters

The general rule is that a party must prove the facts of its case by leading evidence. However, evidence need not be adduced to prove facts that may be legally presumed from other proved facts or to prove facts formally admitted. For example, in terms of section 25 of the Prevention and Combating of Corruption and Corrupt Activities Act 12 of 2004, an arbitrator can presume that if an employee who ostensibly had the power to make a decision

---

50 *KPMG Chartered Accountants (SA) v Securefin Ltd and Another* 2009 (4) SA 399 (SCA).
51 S 34 of the Civil Proceedings Evidence Act, 1965 and s 215 of the Criminal Procedure Act, 1977.

CHAPTER 59 EVIDENCE IN LABOUR MATTERS | 529

beneficial to another party receives any unauthorised gratification from such a party, this gratification was offered and accepted with the intention for the parties to act corruptly. Should the accused employee provide a plausible explanation, this presumption will be rebutted.

Formal admissions are admissions that the parties, before the hearing, formally agree to in the process of admitting and denying allegations in statements of case, in a pre-arbitration minute or in the narrowing of issues by the arbitrator. The arbitrator may consider the agreed facts as proved and no evidence will be led to dispute such facts. Formal admissions may be withdrawn if it is shown that they were made in error or are ambiguous.

59.8 Evaluation of evidence in arbitrations

The fact that evidence is admitted does not mean that it is automatically true or even particularly persuasive. It is still open to the arbitrator to find that certain evidence, which he or she admitted, is untrue, unreliable or improbable and should be rejected. Alternatively, the arbitrator may find that certain admitted evidence, while constituting proof, does not carry much weight.

Once the evidence and concluding arguments have been presented, the arbitrator must evaluate all the evidence together to determine the facts of the case. In other words, the arbitrator must evaluate which relevant facts have been admitted or proved, and what inferences he or she can draw from these facts. In addition, the arbitrator must evaluate whether the party who bore the onus of proof has sufficiently proved all the elements of its case and has a more probable version than the other party. The Labour Court, in *Sasol Mining (Pty) Ltd v Ngzeleni NO and Others*,[52] pointed out that when resolving disputes of fact, the proper approach is to make findings based on:
- the credibility of witnesses
- the inherent probability or improbability of the version that is proffered by the witnesses
- the reliability of their evidence
- an assessment of the probabilities of the irreconcilable versions before the arbitrator.

Only then can the arbitrator make a finding on whether a party has discharged the onus of proof. If none of this is done, then the arbitrator has manifestly failed to resolve the dispute and has effectively denied the affected parties a fair hearing. In this case, the arbitrator had merely regurgitated the extensive testimony presented and made no proper attempt to analyse it. He had considered irregularly that the mere existence of conflicting versions between the employer and employee must lead inevitably to a finding that the onus of proving a fair dismissal had not been discharged by the employer. He also had disregarded material contradictions in the employee's evidence and had failed to notice that much of the company's evidence had gone unchallenged. In *Network Field Marketing (Pty) Ltd v Mngezana NO and Others*,[53] the arbitrator also barely

---

52 (2011) 32 ILJ 723 (LC); (Unreported JR 1595/08) [2010] ZALC 141, 1 October 2010. The Labour Court recommended the approach set out by the Supreme Court of Appeal in *Stellenbosch Farmers' Winery Group Ltd and Another v Martell et Cie and Others* 2003 (1) SA 11 (SCA). See also *Network Field Marketing (Pty) Ltd v Mngezana NO and Others* (2011) 32 ILJ 1705 (LC); *Southern Sun Hotel Interests (Pty) Ltd v CCMA and Others* (2010) 31 ILJ 452 (LC); *Lukhanji Municipality v Nonxuba NO and Others* [2007] 2 BLLR 130 (LC); *ABSA Investment Management Services (Pty) Ltd v Crowhurst* [2006] 2 BLLR 107 (LAC); *Absa Brokers (Pty) Ltd v Moshoana NO and Others* [2005] 10 BLLR 939 (LAC); *Blue Ribbon Bakeries v Naicker and Others* [2000] 12 BLLR 1411 (LC); *Marapula and Others v Consteen (Pty) Ltd* [1999] 8 BLLR 829 (LC); *Twine v Rubber Rollers (Pty) Ltd* [1999] 3 BLLR 285 (LC); *Early Bird Farms (Pty) Ltd v Mlambo* [1997] 5 BLLR 541 (LAC).

53 (2011) 32 ILJ 1705 (LC).

530 | THE LAW OF EVIDENCE IN SOUTH AFRICA

evaluated the evidence and did not explain why it was necessary to resort to and rely solely on credibility findings when the balance of probabilities so clearly favoured the employer. The arbitrator's bold conclusion that the company witnesses were unreliable was based on one minor contradiction between two witnesses. This was insufficient to impugn the reliability of their evidence *in toto* (completely). On review, the company only had to show that had the arbitrator reasoned correctly, he or she would have arrived at different conclusions.

Other examples of failing to evaluate the evidence properly include:
- arbitrators drawing adverse inferences against the employer for reasons not put to its witnesses in cross-examination
- failing to take into account that a party, for no good reason, had not called an available material supporting witness
- failing to rely on or evaluate properly circumstantial evidence
- incorrectly taking into account alleged inconsistencies between the evidence given by certain witnesses at the disciplinary hearing and that given at the arbitration in the absence of these inconsistencies being put to the witnesses. Parties must be given the opportunity to be heard in respect of every piece of evidence that an arbitrator intends to take into account.[54]

59.9 Internal disciplinary hearings

The principles relating to procedure, evidence and the assessment of evidence applicable to arbitrations generally apply in disciplinary hearings but with a greater measure of flexibility. The Labour Court has stated that an internal disciplinary hearing is not a quasi-criminal trial or a civil trial. The hearing is merely an opportunity afforded to the employee to state a case in response to the allegations levelled against him or her by the employer. It is an opportunity for dialogue and reflection before any decision is taken on whether the employee is guilty of misconduct or not. If the employee is found guilty, then it is an opportunity to agree the appropriate sanction in the circumstances. In internal disciplinary hearings there is no place for formal procedures that incorporate all the elements of a criminal trial, including the leading of witnesses, technical and complex charge sheets, requests for further particulars, the strict application of the rules of evidence, legal argument and the like.[55]

59.10 The Labour Court

The normal rules of evidence, as applied in civil proceedings, apply in trials and applications in the Labour Court. The Labour Court's status as a 'superior court' and the fact that it is a court of record means that when it comes to procedural matters like rules of evidence, it is obliged to follow the law as laid down by statute and decisions of the Supreme Court of Appeal and the High Court.[56]

---

54 See respectively *Dairybelle (Pty) Ltd v FAWU and Others* [2001] 6 BLLR 595 (LC); *Absa Investment Management Services (Pty) Ltd v Crowhurst* [2006] 2 BLLR 107 (LAC); *Standard Bank of SA Ltd v Mosime NO and Another* [2008] 10 BLLR 1010 (LC); *Portnet (a division of Transnet Ltd) v Finnemore and Others* [1999] 2 BLLR 151 (LC).

55 *Avril Elizabeth Home for the Mentally Handicapped v CCMA and Others* (2006) 27 ILJ 1644 (LC); *Fawu obo Kapesi and Others v Premier Foods Ltd t/a/ Blue Ribbon Salt River* [2010] 9 BLLR 903 (LC).

56 *Mqobhozi v Naidoo NO and Others* [2006] 3 BLLR 242 (LAC). Trials are referred to as 'referrals' in Rule 6 of the Rules for the Conduct of Proceedings in the Labour Court.

CHAPTER 59   EVIDENCE IN LABOUR MATTERS | 531

THIS CHAPTER IN ESSENCE

1   The Labour Relations Act, 1995 places the onus of proving misconduct and the fairness of any dismissal on the employer. If this is disputed, the employee has the onus of proving that a dismissal took place.

2   In cases of alleged unfair discrimination in terms of the Employment Equity Act, 1998, the complainant has the evidentiary burden to prove discrimination. If the complainant does this, unfairness will be presumed until the employer has established that the discrimination is fair.

3   In unfair labour practice disputes, the employee bears the onus of proving that the conduct or practice falls within the statutory definition of an unfair labour practice and that the conduct of the employer was unfair.

4   The degree of proof required to discharge an onus in all labour disputes is the balance of probabilities.

5   Although the overall onus never shifts, the need to present or counter evidence may rest on different parties during an arbitration.

6   The right to remain silent only pertains to criminal proceedings and not labour proceedings. However, should an employee make incriminating statements during a labour case, such statements can be suppressed on the grounds that their use in a subsequent criminal trial would violate the right to remain silent.

7   Oral, documentary and real evidence may be presented during arbitrations subject to certain rules similar to those applicable to criminal and civil proceedings.

8   An arbitration may be conducted in a manner that the arbitrator considers appropriate to determine the dispute fairly and quickly. The arbitrator must, however, deal with the substantial merits of the dispute with the minimum of legal formalities.

9   Arbitrations are hearings *de novo* and an arbitrator must base his or her decision on the evidence led at the arbitration.

10 The party who bears the onus of proof should start with leading evidence. However, the arbitrator may, on application or *mero motu*, rule that the other party begins.

11 The general rule is that evidence that appears to be logically and legally relevant should be admitted by arbitrators.

12 Labour disputes must first be referred for conciliation to the CCMA or relevant bargaining council before they proceed to statutory arbitration or trial at the Labour Court.

13 Hearsay evidence becomes relevant and admissible if:
    13.1 the party relying on it has a good reason for not bringing the original witness
    13.2 the evidence fits in with or is offered up to confirm other admissible evidence
    13.3 it is procedurally logical to do so.

14 An arbitrator should distinguish between objectively ascertainable aspects, which can be given considerable weight, and aspects of the evidence that require direct testimony, which can be given diminished weight or discarded altogether in the absence of direct evidence or corroboration as they need to be tested by cross-examination.

15 Opinion evidence is irrelevant and, therefore, inadmissible in labour disputes. However, opinion evidence against employees may be obtained through polygraph tests.

16 Evidence obtained as part of an entrapment deal is inadmissible in labour disputes.

17 Employers are permitted to intercept the indirect communications of their employees without the employees' consent in the following circumstances:
    17.1 The communications were made via the electronic and telecommunications systems provided in connection with the employer's business.
    17.2 The employees received notice in advance that indirect communications made via the employer's electronic and telecommunication system may be intercepted.

532 | THE LAW OF EVIDENCE IN SOUTH AFRICA

    17.3 The employer may not intercept communications at random and without a proper reason.

    17.4 The consent of the systems controller must be obtained in each case.

    17.5 The interception must be done with the aim of establishing the existence of facts relevant to the business and/or to secure the system.

18 Based on an employee's constitutional right to fair labour practices, an arbitrator seemingly has the discretion to exclude illegally and improperly obtained evidence. When exercising his or her discretion an arbitrator has to consider whether:

    18.1 the evidence could have been obtained lawfully

    18.2 the employer knowingly and deliberately contravened any law regulating the gathering of evidence

    18.3 there was a pre-existing suspicion that the employee was committing misconduct

    18.4 there were reasonable grounds for believing that evidence relating to that offence may be found in the employee's communications.

19 With regard to other forms of monitoring and searches, the following rules apply:

    19.1 Evidence obtained by an employer through video and other camera surveillance in the course of monitoring its premises and the conduct of employees in operation areas, excluding change-rooms and toilets, is admissible as there is no legitimate expectation of absolute privacy in these areas.

    19.2 Evidence obtained from searches of employees' workstations or body searches with consent is admissible if the employer had good reason to suspect an offence.

20 An employee who voluntarily and without undue influence confesses to misconduct may, if he or she admitted all the elements of the offence, be found guilty of the misconduct.

21 Where an employment relationship is in dispute, arbitrators may permit extrinsic evidence and look behind an otherwise clear agreement to determine whether there is an employment relationship between the parties.

22 Communications made between a party to a dispute and a union representative fall within the scope of legal professional privilege and the rules applicable thereto.

23 The testimony of a witness in earlier proceedings is admissible at a subsequent trial if:

    23.1 the proceedings are between the same parties

    23.2 the issues are substantially the same

    23.3 the witness cannot be called

    23.4 the opposing party had a full opportunity to cross-examine the witness.

24 Similar fact evidence may be used to identify a culprit if the method and substance in a number of his or her previous offences are strikingly similar to those alleged in the present case or if it tends to show a course of conduct.

25 There is no need to adduce evidence to prove facts that may be legally presumed from other proved facts or to prove facts formally admitted.

26 An arbitrator still has the ultimate duty of finding that certain admitted evidence is untrue, unreliable or improbable and, therefore, should be rejected.

27 The principles relating to the procedure, evidence and the assessment of evidence in arbitrations also apply to disciplinary hearings, albeit with a greater measure of flexibility.

28 When it comes to procedural matters like rules of evidence, the Labour Court is obliged to follow the law as laid down by statute and decisions of the Supreme Court of Appeal and the High Court.

Chapter 60

Evidence obtained by means of entrapment

60.1 Introduction 533

60.2 Cautionary approach to entrapment: section 252A of the Criminal
Procedure Act, 1997 533

60.3 Procedure for challenging entrapment evidence 537

60.1 Introduction

Entrapment is a controversial area of our law. A trap is a term used to describe a person who is used to entrap another in criminal behaviour. Historically,[1] the main purpose of using a trap was to entrap a known or suspected criminal to bring to an end to his or her criminal activities. The essential danger is that the law empowering the use of entrapment may be abused to entice normal members of society to commit crimes which they would not have committed but for the enticement. Crossing this fine line between providing the opportunity to commit a crime and inducing or enticing innocent people to commit crimes has been the subject of many of the decided cases dealing with entrapment in our law.[2] The ultimate purpose of the entrapment provisions is the combatting of crime – not the creation of crime.[3] Simply put then, a trap is a person who interacts with an accused in circumstances where the trap is used as bait to obtain the conviction of the accused.[4] In *S v Malinga and Others*,[5] Holmes JA described a trap thus:

> ... a person who, with a view to securing the conviction of another, proposes certain criminal conduct to him, and himself ostensibly takes part therein. In other words, he creates the occasion for someone else to commit the offence.

60.2 Cautionary approach to entrapment: section 252A of the Criminal Procedure Act, 1997

Because of the ever-present danger of enticing innocent people to commit crimes instead of providing the opportunity to suspected criminals to commit crimes, the courts have

---

1 For a historical overview of entrapment, see the SALC Project 84 Working Paper 52 *The Application of the Trapping System* (1994).
2 See *S v Spies and Another* 2000 (1) SACR 312 (SCA) and *Amod v S* [2001] 4 All SA 13 (E).
3 R Dworkin 'The serpent beguiled me and I did eat: Entrapment and the creation of crime' (1985) 4(1) *Law and Philosophy* 17 at 24–30.
4 See *S v Ohlenschlager* 1992 (1) SACR 695 (T) at 753G–H.
5 1963 (1) SA 692 (A) at 693F–G.

534 | THE LAW OF EVIDENCE IN SOUTH AFRICA

always approached evidence of entrapment with caution.[6] In 1996, the Criminal Procedure Act 51 of 1977 was amended by the insertion of section 252(A).[7] Section 252A(1) reads as follows:

> Any law enforcement officer, official of the State or any other person authorised thereto for such purposes ... may make use of a trap or engage in an undercover operation in order to detect, investigate or uncover the commission of an offence, or to prevent the commission of any office, and the evidence so obtained shall be admissible if that conduct does not go beyond providing an opportunity to commit an offence: Provided that where the conduct goes beyond providing an opportunity to commit an offence a court may admit evidence so obtained subject to subsection (3).[8]

Section 252A attempts to provide detailed safeguards to ensure the integrity of trapping procedures and to provide for the exclusion of evidence in certain circumstances.[9] Section 252A(1) provides the general authorisation for entrapment operations. It also specifically provides that evidence about the entrapment operations may be excluded by the court if the conduct of the officials involved in the trapping operation goes beyond only providing an opportunity to commit an offence.

It is significant that where the court finds that the people involved in entrapment operations in fact went beyond merely providing the opportunity to commit a crime and induced or enticed the subjects of the entrapment to commit a crime, the evidence concerned is not automatically excluded. The court still has a discretion in terms of section 252A(3) to admit this evidence.

Before making a decision on whether to admit or exclude the entrapment evidence by applying section 252A(3), the court must first make a determination whether the evidence concerned indicates conduct that goes beyond the mere opportunity to commit an offence. Section 252A(2) sets out a number of factors and sub-factors which the court is obliged to consider in deciding whether the conduct went beyond providing an opportunity to commit an offence, namely:

1. whether the approval of the relevant Provincial Director of Public Prosecutions (PDPP) or the National Director of Public Prosecutions (NDPP) had been obtained for the investigation methods used, and whether the DPP guidelines for entrapment operations were correctly followed[10]
2. the nature of the offence under investigation, including threats to the public or security of the State, the prevalence of the offence in the area and the seriousness of the offence

---

6 See generally about the cautionary approach to traps: *S v Chesane* 1975 (3) SA 172 (W) at 173G-H; *S v Ohlenschlager* 1992 (1) SACR 695 (T) at 725H-726B; *R v Zahlan and Another* 1951 PH H69 (AD) at 160; *S v Mabaso* 1978 (3) SA 5 (O) at 7; *R v Omar and Another* 1948 (1) SA 76 (T) at 79; *S v Snyman* 1968 (2) SA 582 (A) at 585 F-G.

7 S 1 of the Criminal Procedure Second Amendment Act 85 of 1996.

8 E du Toit, FJ de Jager, A Paizes, A St Q Skeen and S van der Merwe S *Commentary on the Criminal Procedure Act* (1987) 24-128 (Revision Service 45, 2010) are of the opinion that this section authorises the use of traps and undercover operations only in certain circumstances. However, Wallis AJA in *S v Kotzè* 2010 (1) SACR 100 (SCA) (as he then was) at para 21 is of the opinion that there is no such qualification. For current purposes, it is not necessary to give an opinion on the matter. S 252A(2)(*a*) lists as a factor in deciding whether conduct went beyond providing an opportunity to commit an offence, the question whether, prior to the setting of a trap or the use of an undercover operation, approval (if it was required) was obtained from the Director of Public Prosecutions to engage in such investigation methods and the extent to which the instructions or guidelines issued by the Director of Public Prosecutions were adhered to. It is therefore essential that authorisation be obtained before any trap is set up.

9 S 252A(1-7).

10 See para 3.3 (Content of Application to Set a Trap) of DPP General Guidelines of 4 June 2004.

CHAPTER 60 EVIDENCE OBTAINED BY MEANS OF ENTRAPMENT 535

3. the availability of other crime detection or prevention techniques
4. whether an average person in the position of the accused would have been induced to commit the crime by the conduct of the setters of the trap
5. the degree of persistence and number of attempts made by the official or his agents before the accused succumbed and committed the offence
6. the type of inducement used, including the degree of trickery, deceit, misrepresentation or reward[11]
7. the timing of the entrapment conduct, especially whether the trapping officials instigated the commission of the offence or became involved in existing unlawful activity
8. whether the conduct involved the exploitation of human characteristics or emotions, such as sympathy, friendship or economic circumstances, to increase the probability of the commission of the offence
9. whether a particular vulnerability of the accused, such as a mental handicap or substance addiction, was exploited
10. the proportionality of the extent of the involvement of the entrapment officials or their agents compared to the accused also taking into account the commission of any illegal acts by the officials or their agents
11. any implied or express threats by the officials or their agents against the accused
12. whether, prior to setting up the trap, a reasonable suspicion existed that the accused had previously committed the same or similar offence
13. whether the officials or their agents acted in good or bad faith
14. any other factor, which, in the opinion of the court, has a bearing on the question as to whether the officials or their agents went beyond merely providing an opportunity to commit an offence.

Section 252A(3)(*a*) provides that if, after considering the above factors, the court finds that the conduct concerned indeed goes further than merely providing an opportunity to commit an offence, the court may refuse to allow such evidence. This is provided the evidence was obtained in an improper or unfair manner and if admission of such evidence would render the trial unfair or would otherwise be detrimental to the administration of justice.

Section 252A(3)(*b*) provides specific guidelines on how the court should consider the admissibility criteria of 'rendering the trial unfair or being detrimental to the administration of justice'. This subsection provides that in this assessment the court shall weigh up the public interest against the personal interest of the accused, taking into account the following factors where applicable:

- the nature and seriousness of the offence, including:
  - ◆ whether security of the state or public order is affected
  - ◆ the difficulty of detecting or preventing the crime without the use of a trap
  - ◆ the frequency of commission of that type of offence
  - ◆ whether the offence was so indecent or serious that a trap was justified
- the effect of the entrapment operation on the interests of the accused, including:
  - ◆ the disregarding of the accused's rights or applicable legal requirements
  - ◆ the ease with which the applicable legal requirements could have been complied with

---

11 In terms of s 3 of the Finance and Financial Adjustments Acts Consolidation Act 11 of 1977, where the trap relates to the illegal trade in precious metals and stones, a trap may be paid up to one third of the amount paid by the entrapped purchaser in the affected transaction. This practice obviously creates extreme ethical dangers.

- prejudice to the accused resulting from improper or unfair conduct
- the nature of any infringement of any constitutional right
- whether the means used in setting up the entrapment operation were proportional to the seriousness of the offence
- any other factor which the court considers relevant.

Section 252A(3)(*b*) therefore provides a set of specific criteria for the assessment of the admissibility of entrapment evidence which goes beyond the mere opportunity to commit a crime. In contrast, the similar criteria in section 35(5) of the Constitution are open-ended and therefore much more flexible. A significant difference between the section 252A(3) admissibility test and that contained in section 35(5) of the Constitution is that in the former, the court retains a discretion to admit nevertheless the evidence even where the finding is made that the admission of the evidence concerned would render the trial unfair or would otherwise be detrimental to the administration of justice. Section 35(5) of the Constitution, however, obliges the court to exclude such evidence. It seems, with regard to the supremacy clause of the Constitution,[12] that once the court has made a determination applying section 252A(3) that the entrapment operation would render the trial unfair or be detrimental to the administration of justice, it will be obliged to exclude this evidence despite its apparent discretion[13] not to do so.

Section 252A, therefore, regulates the entrapment system with an exclusionary rule that is similar to the one contained in section 35(5) of the Constitution. The main difference is that the exclusionary rule in section 252A comes into operation when police conduct goes beyond providing an opportunity to commit an offence. The exclusionary rule in section 35(5) of the Constitution comes into operation when a right in the in the Bill of Rights has been infringed.

However, these two exclusionary rules function on the same basis. In terms of section 252A(3)(*a*), entrapment evidence obtained through conduct that went beyond providing an opportunity to commit an offence can only be excluded if certain requirements are met:
- First, the evidence must have been obtained in an improper or unfair manner. Taking into account the wide meaning of a right to a fair trial, this essentially means that it must infringe on the right to a fair trial.
- Second, the admission of the evidence must render the trial unfair or otherwise be detrimental to the administration of justice. These are exactly the same requirements that must be met for exclusion in terms of section 35(5) of the Constitution.

However, section 35(5) of the Constitution states that evidence obtained in violation of a right in the Bill of Rights *must* be excluded if the requirements are satisfied, whereas section 252A(3)(*a*) states that entrapment evidence *may* be excluded if the requirements of the section are met. This seems to imply that a court has a discretion to exclude such evidence. This is not, in fact, true and a court is obliged to exclude such evidence because, if it does not do so in terms of section 252(A), it is nonetheless bound to do so in terms of section 35 of the Constitution. Section 252(A) remains useful because it provides guidelines to which a court must refer when deciding whether entrapment evidence should be excluded.

---

12   S 2 of the Constitution which provides that in the case of a conflict between the Constitution and any other law, the Constitution will prevail.

13   S 252A(3)(*a*) reads that the court 'may' refuse to allow such evidence: in the circumstances, the word 'may' will have to be read as 'must' refuse to allow such evidence.

CHAPTER 60 EVIDENCE OBTAINED BY MEANS OF ENTRAPMENT | 537

60.3 Procedure for challenging entrapment evidence

If the defence challenges the admissibility of entrapment evidence, its admissibility will be considered in a trial-within-a-trial.[14] It is important that the accused provide the grounds on which the admissibility of the evidence is challenged.[15] However, the burden of proof to show that the evidence is admissible rests on the prosecution. Although section 252A(6) provides that the burden must be discharged on a balance of probabilities, in *S v Kotzè*[16] the Supreme Court of Appeal decided that the trial court must be satisfied that the basis for the admissibility of the evidence has been established beyond a reasonable doubt.

Some instances of entrapment are so morally reprehensible that instead of simply excluding individual items of otherwise admissible evidence, a court can stay the entire process against the accused.[17] This happens in circumstances where the entrapment proceedings are regarded as an abuse of process. In such cases, the accused can argue that he or she should not be tried at all.[18] If this is unsuccessful, then the accused can resort to arguing that the entrapment evidence should not be admitted in term of section 252(A)(3) of the Criminal Procedure Act, 1977, read with section 35(5) of the Constitution.[19]

THIS CHAPTER IN ESSENCE

1   Evidence of entrapment will be admissible if the conduct during the trap does not go beyond providing an opportunity to commit an offence. If it does, the evidence may be inadmissible if:
    1.1   it was obtained in an improper or unfair manner
    1.2   the admission thereof would render the trial unfair
    1.3   it would be detrimental to the administration of justice.
2   Although similar, the main difference between the exclusionary rule in section 252A of the Criminal Procedure Act, 1977 and the rule contained in section 35(5) of the Constitution is that the rule in section 252(A) applies to situations where police conduct goes beyond providing an opportunity to commit an offence, while the exclusionary rule in section 35(5) applies when a right in the Bill of Rights has been infringed.
3   Issues of exclusion in terms of section 252(A) are considered during a trial-within-a-trial. An accused must provide the grounds on which the admissibility of the evidence is challenged. The burden of proof to show that the evidence is admissible beyond reasonable doubt rests on the prosecution.
4   In circumstances where the entrapment proceedings are regarded as an abuse of process, a court can order a stay in the entire process against the accused.

---

14   See *Lachman v S* 2010 (2) SACR 52 (SCA) at para 26 where the Court referred to both s 252A(6) of the Criminal Procedure Act, 1977 and *S v Matsabu* 2009 (1) SACR 513 (SCA) at para 8 in describing the desirability of using the trial-within-a-trial process.
15   See s 252A(6) of the Criminal Procedure Act, 1977 and *S v Kotzè* 2010 (1) SACR 100 (SCA) at para 19.
16   2010 (1) SACR 100 (SCA).
17   See, for example, the facts in the cases of *S v Nortjé* 1996 (2) SACR 308 (C); *S v Hayes en 'n Ander* 1998 (1) SACR 625 (O); *Amod v S* [2001] 4 All SA 13 (E); *R v Mack* [1988] 2 SCR 903 and *United States v Lard* 734 F 2d 1290 (8th Cir)(1984).
18   RJC Munday *Evidence* 4 ed (2007) at 48 explains: 'Abuse of process arises where the circumstances in which the prosecution has come to be brought are such as to amount to what Lord Steyn in Latif [1996] 1 WLR 104 at 112 designated "an affront to the public conscience" or what Lord Bingham in *Nottingham City Council v Amin* [2000] 1 WLR 1071 at 1076 called matters "deeply offensive to ordinary notions of fairness".'
19   See *Singh and Others v S* 2016 (2) SACR 443 (SCA) where the Court was called upon to consider this.

Chapter 61

Evidentiary problems with the Prevention of Organised Crime Act, 1998 (POCA)

61.1 Introduction 538

61.2 Section 1(2) and (3) of the POCA: knowledge, intention and negligence 538

61.3 Section 2(2) of the POCA: expansion of common law of evidence
   in racketeering cases 539

61.1 Introduction

The Prevention of Organised Crime Act 121 of 1998 (POCA)[1] came into force in 1999 as the primary statutory tool to fight organised crime.[2] The POCA consolidated and expanded on previous legislation aimed at combatting organised crime.[3] It also introduced new types of criminal offences, including **racketeering**,[4] gang-related offences[5] and money laundering offences.[6]

A controversial, and as yet unresolved, issue that has arisen in the passing of the POCA is that a number of evidentiary statutory definitions have been included in the Act to make it easier for the State to prove these new offences. These definitions relate to both *mens rea* and to general common law concepts of evidence, and are contained in section 1(2) and (3) and section 2(2) of the POCA.

61.2 Section 1(2) and (3) of the POCA: knowledge, intention and negligence

The established common law *mens rea* concepts of intention (*dolus*) and negligence (*culpa*) have, for most purposes, been replaced in the POCA by a new concept of 'knowledge'. Section 1(2) of the POCA[7] defines knowledge as follows:

---

1 The POCA was modelled on the United States of America RICO (Racketeer-influenced and Criminal Organisations) law. See G Kemp, S Walker, R Palmer, D Baqwa, C Gevers, B Leslie and A Steynberg *Criminal Law in South Africa* 2 ed (2015) ch 45. Oxford University Press
2 The POCA is part of an array of statutes designed to counter organised and commercial crime, including the Financial Intelligence Centre Act 38 of 2001 (FICA), the Prevention and Combating of Corrupt Activities Act 12 of 2004, the Drugs and Drug Trafficking Act 140 of 1992 and the Protection of Constitutional Democracy Against Terrorist and Related Activities Act 33 of 2004.
3 Proceeds of Crime Act 76 of 1996.
4 S 2 of the POCA.
5 S 9 of the POCA.
6 Ss 4, 5 and 6 of the POCA.
7 Definitions and Interpretations.

CHAPTER 61 EVIDENTIARY PROBLEMS WITH THE PREVENTION OF ORGANISED CRIME ACT, ...

(2) For purposes of this Act a person has knowledge of a fact if:
    (a) the person has actual knowledge of that fact; or
    (b) the court is satisfied that:
        (i) the person believes that there is a reasonable possibility of the existence of that fact; and
        (ii) he or she fails to obtain information to confirm the existence of that fact.

This definition is further expanded and qualified by section 1(3):

(2) For the purposes of this Act a person ought reasonably to have known or suspected a fact if the conclusions that he or she ought to have reached are those which would have been reached by a reasonably diligent and vigilant person having both:
    (a) the general knowledge, skill, training and experience that may reasonably be expected of a person in his or her position; and
    (b) the general knowledge, skill, training and experience that he or she in fact has.

By using the term 'knowledge' instead of the recognised common law terms of *dolus* and *culpa*, the statute has expanded the definition of 'knowledge'. An accused person could be found guilty of the serious crimes contained in POCA[8] in circumstances where the State has merely to prove that an accused 'ought reasonably to have known or suspected a fact' because a reasonable person in the position of the accused would have formed such a suspicion.

The result is that the accused's *mens rea* is effectively proved at the very low level of imputed knowledge based on the suspicions of the so-called reasonable person. This expanded definition of knowledge may well be found to violate a person's right to a fair trial and, in particular, the presumption of innocence provisions in section 35(3) of the Constitution.[9]

In *Savoi and Others v National Director of Public Prosecutions and Another* the question arose regarding the constitutionality of a provision of POCA for criminalising conduct (in that case the crime of racketeering) where an accused 'ought reasonably' to have known that his conduct would constitute an offence of racketeering. While the High Court found that the statutory provision was overbroad and vague and declared it unconstitutional, in *Savoi* the Constitutional Court did not agree with the High Court.[10]

61.3 Section 2(2) of the POCA: expansion of common law of evidence in racketeering cases

In relation to racketeering offences as provided for in section 2 of the POCA, the common law rules of evidence are controversially qualified by section 2(2) which reads as follows:

(2) The court may hear evidence, including evidence with regard to hearsay, similar facts or previous convictions, relating to offences contemplated in subsection (1), notwithstanding that such evidence might otherwise be inadmissible, provided that such evidence would not render a trial unfair.

---

8 Racketeering, money laundering and criminal gang activities.
9 S 35(3)(*h*). See *S v Manamela and Another (Director-General of Justice Intervening)* 2000 (3) SA 1 (CC). Also, depending on the offence being challenged and the prevailing circumstances in society, an argument could, of course, be made to save this expanded definition by application of the limitations clause in s 36 of the Constitution.
10 *Savoi and Others v National Director of Public Prosecutions and Another* 2014 (1) SACR 545 (CC) and 2014 (5) SA 317 (CC).

THE LAW OF EVIDENCE IN SOUTH AFRICA

To date, there are no reported cases specifically interpreting this provision and the section itself appears, on the face of it, to be somewhat self-contradictory. We can envisage few circumstances where it would be justified to ignore the statutory prerequisites for the admission of hearsay evidence[11] without rendering the trial procedure unfair and thereby violating section 35(3) of the Constitution. Section 3 of the Law of Evidence Amendment Act, 1988 already provides the court with a discretion to admit hearsay evidence where it is in the interests of justice to do so, having regard to the various factors enumerated in that section.[12] Section 2(2) of the POCA may relieve the court of the necessity of strictly adhering to the provisions of section 3(1) of the Law of Evidence Amendment Act, 1988 and may justify a more lenient approach to the admission of such evidence. However, it seems that the factors that must be considered in section 3 of the Law of Evidence Amendment Act, 1988 will still be the basis on which the admission of the evidence in question will be decided and also the allied question as to whether that admission would render the trial unfair.

Similarly, in most cases, the well-established rules in our common law applicable to similar fact evidence could not easily be deviated from without resulting in trial-related prejudice that would potentially render the trial unfair. However, similar fact evidence may be an important mechanism by which the prosecution may seek to establish that a particular offence was committed as part of a pattern of racketeering activity of an enterprise.[13] So, for instance, if it is proved that a particular gang committed armed robberies or 'hits' on rivals in a certain 'signature' manner, the prosecution might seek to rely on the fact that other robberies or murders were committed with the same *modus operandi*. By so doing, the prosecution would seek to establish before court that they too were committed as part of the enterprise activities even if they did not involve the accused. The prosecution would bear the onus of demonstrating the relevance and probative value of such evidence against which the court must weigh any prejudice to the accused.

The need to prove previous convictions is clearly justifiable[14] to establish the existence of predicate offences in order to prove a pattern of racketeering activity.[15] However, even here, the court would have to tread carefully to ensure that previous convictions are not relied on to establish bad character or to create a negative impression in the mind of the court of the accused's alleged tendency to become involved in crime. Great care should be taken in cases where the accused is charged with both racketeering *and* with common law crimes of fraud and theft either as separate counts or as alternative charges.[16]

One case to refer to this issue, albeit obliquely, is the 2012 case of *S v De Vries and Others*.[17] In this case, De Vries and 11 others were arraigned on various charges relating to the hijacking of trucks transporting cigarettes. The appellant did not personally participate in any of the robberies. However, the State alleged that he had purchased the stolen cigarettes with the knowledge that they had been stolen and had received them for the purpose of resale. He was convicted on:

- two counts of theft – having purchased the cigarettes, knowing that they were stolen
- two counts of money laundering as envisaged in section 4 of the POCA – having stolen them for the purpose of resale

---

11 Law of Evidence Amendment Act 45 of 1988.
12 S 3(1)(*c*)(i) to (vii).
13 In other words, that the offences were 'planned, on-going, continuous or repeated'.
14 See the discussion in ch 19.3.2.
15 See the definitions of racketeering offences in s 2 read with s 1 of the POCA.
16 In *Singh and Others v S* 2016 (2) SACR 443 (SCA) the court took this into account in sentencing (para 26).
17 2012 (1) SACR 186 (SCA).

CHAPTER 61 EVIDENTIARY PROBLEMS WITH THE PREVENTION OF ORGANISED CRIME ACT, ... 541

- on one count of conducting or participating in a pattern of racketeering activity in contravention of section 2(1)(*e*) of the POCA – having associated with the enterprise of the gang of robbers and participated in the gang's affairs.

The appellant contended that section 2(2) of the POCA makes serious inroads into an accused's normal procedural rights by rendering admissible evidence that would otherwise be inadmissible in our law, thereby rendering his trial unfair. For that reason, the appellant contended that an accused cannot be charged in the same indictment with both an offence under section 2(1) (the racketeering 'umbrella' offence) as well as the underlying predicate offences.

However, the Court held that it was neither shown that such allegedly inadmissible evidence had been introduced to the prejudice of the appellant nor had it in any way compromised his defence or rendered his trial unfair. The Court said that to that extent the argument was purely academic and it was, therefore, unnecessary to consider it in any detail. In an *obiter* comment, the Court said:

> **Suffice it to say that the trained judicial mind should be able to limit the effect of otherwise inadmissible evidence to the charges in respect of which it is admissible – any section 2(1) charges – and to exclude it from consideration in respect of charges in which it is not. Indeed this is what occurs, daily by courts, for example, in hearing trials-within-trials.**[18]

What the Court appears to suggest is that the approach should be to admit evidence in terms of section 2(2) of the POCA even if *prima facie* inadmissible by applying the law of evidence. It should then carefully 'disabuse' the mind of any potential prejudicial inferences against the accused as is done in trials-within-trials. This begs the question: the very reason for the qualified admissibility criteria in section 2(2) is to permit the admission of otherwise inadmissible evidence against the accused. It seems pointless to admit the evidence, only then to attempt to rid the court's mind of prejudicial influences to pay lip-service to the fair trial requirement in section 2(2).

THIS CHAPTER IN ESSENCE

1   The Prevention of Organised Crime Act, 1998 (POCA) is the primary statutory tool for fighting organised crime in South Africa.
2   The POCA has replaced the common law *mens rea* concepts of intention (*dolus*) and negligence (*culpa*) with the concept of 'knowledge', which refers to:
   2.1   a person having knowledge of a particular fact
   2.2   a court being satisfied that a person believes in the reasonable possibility that a particular fact exists and he or she failed to obtain information to confirm the existence of that fact.
3   For purposes of the POCA an accused's *mens rea* is proved at the very low level of imputed knowledge based on the suspicions of the so-called reasonable person.
4   A court deciding on a matter of racketeering as provided for in the POCA may hear any evidence, including evidence of hearsay, similar facts or previous convictions, as long as such evidence does not result in an unfair trial. However, this position appears to be self-contradictory as there are few circumstances where ignoring the statutory prerequisites for the admission of hearsay evidence will not violate section 35(3) of the Constitution and consequently render a trial procedurally unfair.

---

18   *S v De Vries and Others* 2012 (1) SACR 186 (SCA) at para 52.

ANNEXURE A
Civil trial process

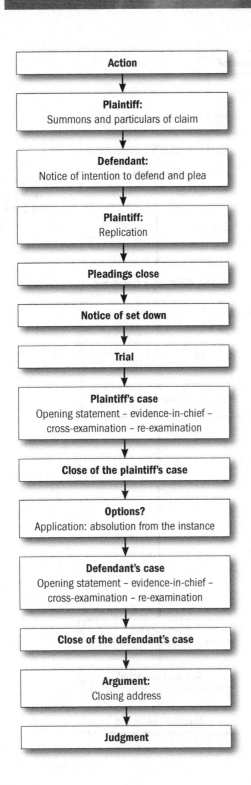
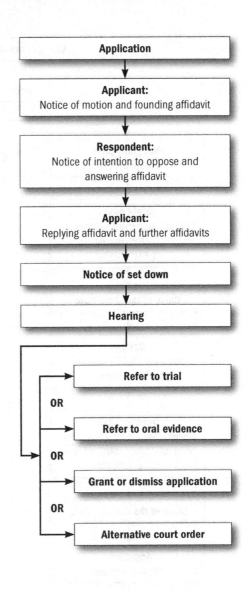

ANNEXURE B
Criminal trial process

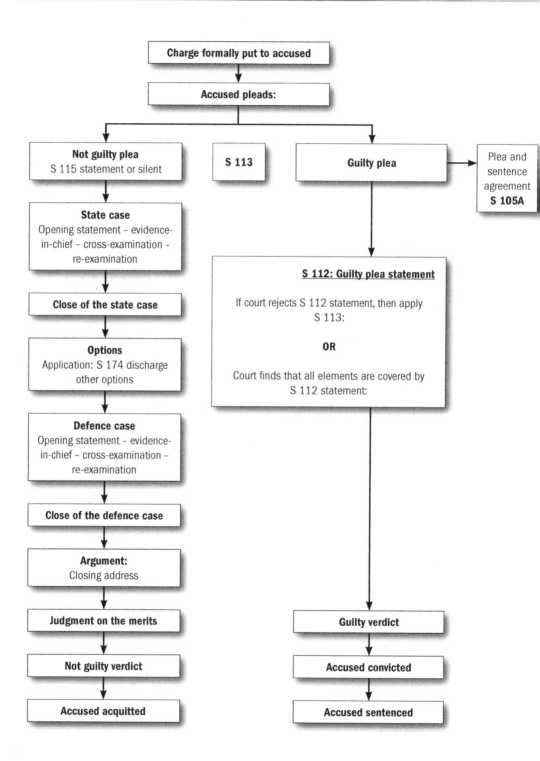

Bibliography

Books (including revision services)

Best, A *Evidence* 10 ed (2016) Wolters Kluwer.

Boyd, N *Canadian Law: An Introduction* 5 ed (2011) Nelson College Indigenous.

Burns, R *A Theory of the Trial* (1999) Princeton University Press.

Casey, E *Digital Evidence and Computer Crime: Forensic Science, Computers and the Internet* 2 ed (2004) Elsevier.

Choo, AL-T *Evidence* (2006) Oxford University Press.

Cohen, T, Rycroft, A and Whitcher, B *Trade Unions and the Law in South Africa* (2009) LexisNexis.

Colman, R *Cross-examination: A Practical Handbook* (1970) Juta.

Cowen, Z and Carter PB *Essays on the Law of Evidence* (1956) Clarendon Press.

Currie, I and De Waal, J *The Bill of Rights Handbook* 6 ed (2013) Juta.

De Bracton, H *Bracton on the Laws and Customs of England (translated with revisions and notes by SE Thorne)* (1968) Belknap Press.

Dressler, J and Michaels, AC *Understanding Criminal Procedure* 4 ed (2006) LexisNexis Matthew Bender.

Dugard, J *Human Rights and the South African Legal Order* (1978) Princeton University Press.

Du Toit, E, De Jager, FJ, Paizes, A, Skeen, AStQ and Van der Merwe, S *Commentary on the Criminal Procedure Act* (1987) Juta. [Revision Service].

Elliott, DW Elliott and Phipson *Manual of the Law of Evidence* 12 ed (1987) Sweet and Maxwell.

Friedman, LM and Hayden, GM *American Law: An Introduction* (2017) Oxford University Press.

Grogan, J Labour *Litigation and Dispute Resolution* (2010) Juta.

Harms, LTC *Civil Procedure in Magistrates' Courts* (1997) Butterworths. [Revision Service].

Himonga, C (ed), Nhlapo, T (ed), Maithufi, IP, Mnisi-Weeks, S, Mofokeng, L and Ndima, D *African Customary Law in South Africa: Post-Apartheid and Living Law Perspectives* (2014) Oxford University Press.

Holt, TJ, Bossler AM and Seigfried-Spellar, KC *Cybercrime and Digital Forensics: An Introduction* (2015) Routledge.

Huettel, SA, Song, AW and McCarthy, G *Functional Magnetic Resonance Imaging* 2 ed (2008) Sinauer Associates Inc.

Kemp, G, Walker, S, Palmer, R, Baqwa, D, Gevers, C, Leslie, B and Steynberg, A *Criminal Law in South Africa* (2012) Oxford University Press.

Kruger, A *Hiemstra's Criminal Procedure* (2008) LexisNexis. [Revision Service].

Lansdown, CWH, Hoal, WG and Lansdown, AV *South African Criminal Law and Procedure* 6 ed (1957) Juta.

Lempert, R and Salzburg, S *A Modern Approach to Evidence: Text, Problems, Transcripts and Cases* 2 ed (1982) West Academic Publishing.

Lulat, YG-M *United States Relations with South Africa: A Critical Overview from the Colonial Period to the Present* (2008) Peter Lang Inc., International Academic Publishers.

MacIntyre, A *After Virtue* (1984) University of Notre Dame Press.

Marnewick, CG *Litigation Skills for South African Lawyers* Rev ed (2003) LexisNexis Butterworths.

Mason, S (ed) *Electronic Evidence* 3rd ed (2012) LexisNexis.

Mason, S and Seng, D (eds) *Electronic Evidence* 4th ed (2017) University of London.

McEwan, J *Evidence and the Adversarial Process: The Modern Law* 2 ed (1998) Blackwell.

Meintjies-Van der Walt, L *DNA in the Courtroom: Principles and Practices* (2010) Juta.

Meintjies-Van der Walt, L *Expert Evidence in the Criminal Justice Procedure: A Comparative Perspective* (2001) Rozenberg.

Mofokeng, LL *Legal Pluralism in South Africa: Aspects of African customary, Muslim and Hindu Family Law* (2009) Van Schaik Publishers.

Morris, E *Technique in Litigation* 6 ed (revised and updated by J Mullins and C da Silva) (2010) Juta.

Müller, K *Preparing Children for Court: A Handbook for Practitioners* (2004) [Institute for Child Witness Research and Training].

Munday, R *Evidence* 4 ed (2007) Oxford University Press.

Murphy, P *A Practical Approach to Evidence* (1980) Oxford University Press.

Murphy, P *A Practical Approach to Evidence* 10 ed (2008) Oxford University Press.

Nicholas, HC 'Some aspects of opinion evidence' (1989) In C Visser (ed) *Essays in Honour of Ellison Kahn* Juta pp 225–237.

Paciocco, DM and Stuesser, L *The Law of Evidence* 7 ed (2015) Irwin Law.

Palmer, R and McQuoid-Mason, D *Basic Trial Advocacy Skills* (2000) LexisNexis Butterworths.

Peté, S, Hulme, D, Du Plessis, M, Palmer, R and Sibanda, O *Civil Procedure: A Practical Guide* 2 ed (2011) Oxford University Press.

Pretorius, JP *Cross-examination in South African Law* (1997) Butterworths.

Schmidt, CWH and Zeffertt, DT *Evidence* (revised by DP Van der Merwe) (1997) Butterworths.

Schwikkard, PJ and Van der Merwe, SE *Principles of Evidence* 3 ed (2009) Juta.

Schwikkard, PJ and Van der Merwe, SE *Principles of Evidence* 4 ed (2016) Juta.

Scoble, CN *The Law of Evidence in South Africa* 3 ed (1952) Butterworths.

Soga, JH *The AmaXosa: Life and Customs* (1932) Cambridge University Press.

Stephen, JF *Digest of the Law of Evidence* 12 ed (1914) Macmillan.

Steytler, N *Constitutional Criminal Procedure: A Commentary on the Constitution of the Republic of South Africa, 1996* (1998) Butterworths.

Swart, CWH and Rademeyer H *Bewysreg* 4 ed (2000) Butterworths.

Tapper, C *Cross and Tapper on Evidence* 8 ed (1995) Butterworths.

Tapper, C *Cross and Tapper on Evidence* 11 ed (2007) Butterworths.

Tapper, C *Cross and Tapper on Evidence* 12 ed (2010) Butterworths.

Terblanche, SS *Guide to Sentencing in South Africa* 2 ed (2007) LexisNexis.

Terblanche, SS and Van der Merwe, DP *The Law of Evidence: Cases and Statutes* 4 ed (2009) Juta.

Thayer, JB *Preliminary Treatise on Evidence at the Common Law* (1898) Little, Brown & Co.

Theophilopoulos, C, Rowan, A, Van Heerden, C and Boraine, A *Fundamental Principles of Civil Procedure* (2006) LexisNexis.

Theophilopoulos, C, Van Heerden, CM and Boraine, A *Fundamental Principles of Civil Procedure* 3 ed (2015) LexisNexis.

Twining, W *Theories of Evidence: Bentham and Wigmore* (1985) Weidenfeld and Nicolson.

Van der Merwe, D, Roos, A, Nel, W, Eiselen, S and Nel, S *Information and Communications Technology Law* (2016) LexisNexis.

Wigmore, JH *A Treatise on the Anglo-American System of Evidence in Trials at Common Law* 3 ed (1940) Little, Brown & Co.

Wigmore, JH *Wigmore on Evidence* 3 ed (1940) Little, Brown.

Zeffertt, DT and Paizes, AP *Essential Evidence* (2010) LexisNexis.

Zeffertt, DT and Paizes, AP *The South African Law of Evidence* (formerly Hoffmann and Zeffertt) 2 ed (2009) LexisNexis.

Zuckerman, AAS *The Principles of Criminal Evidence* (1992) Clarendon Press.

SALC and SALRC reports

South African Law Commission *Women and Sexual Offences Report* (1985).

South African Law Commission Project 71 Working Paper 28 *The Protection of the Child Witness* (1989).

South African Law Commission Project 84 Working Paper 52 *Applications of the Trapping System* (1993).

South African Law Commission Project 107 Discussion Paper 102 *Sexual Offences: Process and Procedure* (2002).

South African Law Reform Commission Project 126 Discussion Paper 113 *Review of the Law of Evidence: Hearsay and Relevance* (2008).

South African Law Reform Commission Project 126 Issue Paper 27 *Review of the Law of Evidence: Electronic Evidence in Criminal and Civil Proceedings: Admissibility and Related Issues* (2010).

Periodicals

Ashworth, A 'Corroboration and self-corroboration' (1978) *Justice of the Peace* 266–267.

Casey, E 'Error, uncertainty and loss in digital evidence' (2002) 1(2) *International Journal of Digital Evidence* Available at: https://utica.edu/academic/institutes/ecii/publications/articles/A0472DF7-ADC9-7FDEC80B5E5B306A85C4.pdf

Combrinck, H 'Monsters under the bed: Challenging existing views on the credibility of child witnesses in sexual offence cases' (1998) 8 *South African Journal of Criminal Justice* 326–330.

Dworkin, R 'The serpent beguiled me and I did eat: Entrapment and the creation of crime' (1985) 4 *Law and Philosophy* 19–39.

Farwell, L 'Brain fingerprinting: Corrections to Rosenfeld' (2011) 8(2) *Scientific Review of Mental Health Practice* 56–68.

Farwell, LA and Smith, SS 'Using brain MERMER testing to detect concealed knowledge despite efforts to conceal' (2001) 46(1) *Journal of Forensic Sciences* 135–143.

Fortt, C 'Child sexual abuse and the UK expert witness' (2001) *Solicitors Journal* 3. A version of this article is available at: http://www.expertsearch.co.uk/articles/fortt.htm

Hugo, JH 'A tale of two cases' (1999) 12 *South African Journal of Criminal Justice* 204–213.

James, GF 'Relevancy, Probability and the Law' (1941) 29(6) *California Law Review* 689.

Jonker, G and Swanzen, R 'Intermediary services for child witnesses testifying in South African criminal courts' (2007) 3(6) SUR – *Revista Internacional de Direitos Humanos [International Journal on Human Rights]* 95–119. Available at: http://socialsciences.

scielo.org/scielo.php?pid=S1806-64452007000100005&script=sci_arttext

Kerr, AJ 'Customary Family Law' *Family Law Service*, Issue 44, October.

Leroux, O 'Legal admissibility of electronic evidence' (2004) 18(2) *International Review of Law, Computers & Technology* (2004) 193–222.

Meintjies-Van der Walt, L 'Fingerprint evidence: Probing myth and reality' (2006) 19 *South African Journal of Criminal Justice* 152–172. Available at: http://www.academia.edu/931537/Fingerprint_evidence_probing_myth_or_reality_fingerprint_evidence

Mischke, C 'The monitoring and interception of electronic communications: Obtaining and using e-mail and other electronic evidence' (2001) 10 *Contemporary Labour Law* 91–98.

Müller, K 'The enigma of the child witness: A need for expert evidence' (2003) 4(2) *Child Abuse Research in South Africa* 2–9.

Müller, K and Van der Merwe, A 'Judicial management in child abuse cases: Empowering judicial officers to be "the boss of the court"' (2005) 18(1) *South African Journal of Criminal Justice* 41–55.

Nicholas, HC 'The credibility of witnesses' (1985) 102 *South African Law Journal* 32–44.

Nugent, RW 'Self-incrimination in perspective' (1999) 116 *South African Law Journal* 501–520.

Peiris, GL 'The rule against hearsay and the doctrine of *res gestae*: A comparative analysis of South African, English and Sri Lankan law' (1981) 14(1) *Comparative International Law Journal of Southern Africa* 1–33.

Pennington, K 'Torture and fear: Enemies of justice' (2008) 19 *Revista Internazionale di Diritto Comune* Available at: http://faculty.cua.edu/pennington/PenningtonTortureEssay.htm

Phillips, VM and Scheepers, CF 'Comparison between fingerprint and dental concordant characteristics' (1990) 8(1) *Journal of Odontostomatology* 17–19.

Roberts, AJ 'Everything new is old again: Brain fingerprinting and evidentiary analogy'

(2007) 9 *Yale Journal of Law and Technology* 234–270.

Schmidt, CWH '*S v Lwane* 1966 (2) SA 433 (A)' (1966) 29 *Tydskrif vir Hedendaagse Romeins-Hollandse Reg* 267–269.

Schwikkard, PJ 'Law of evidence' (2008) *Annual Survey of South African Law* Juta 855–90.

Shankarkumar, U 'The Human Leucocyte Antigen (HLA) System' (2004) 4(2) *International Journal of Human Genetics* 91–103.

Smith, JC 'The Admissibility of Statements by Computer' (1981) *Criminal Law Review* 387 at 390

Snyckers, F 'Law of evidence' (2003) *Annual Survey of South African Law* Juta 869–912.

Sorenson, T and Snow, B 'How children tell: The process of disclosure in child abuse' (2000) 1(2) *Child Abuse Research in South Africa* 41–48.

Theophilopoulos, C 'State privilege, protection of information and legal proceedings' (2012) 129(4) *South African Law Journal* 645–650.

Theophilopoulos, C 'The corporation and the privilege against self-incrimination' (2004) 16(1) *South African Mercantile Law Journal* 17–30.

Theophilopoulos, C 'The evidentiary value of adverse influences from the accused's right to silence' (2002) 15 *South African Journal of Criminal Justice* 321–336.

Theophilopoulos, C 'The historical antecedents of the right to silence and the evolution of the adversarial trial system' (2003) *Stellenbosch Law Review* 161–186.

Theophilopoulos, C 'The parameters of witness indemnity: A review of s 204 of the CPA' (2003) 120 *South African Law Journal* 373–387.

Theophilopoulos, C 'The privilege against self-incrimination and the distinction between testimonial and non-testimonial evidence' (2010) 127(1) *South African Law Journal* 107–140.

Underwood, RH 'Truth verifiers: From the hot iron to the lie detector' (1995-6) 84 *Kentucky Law Journal* 597–642.

Walker, L and Monahan, J 'Social frameworks: A new use of social science in law' (1987) 73 *Virginia Law Review* 559–598.

Zeffertt, D 'Law of evidence' (1997) *Annual Survey of South African Law* Juta 718–46.

Zeffertt, D 'Opinion evidence' (1976) 93 *South African Law Journal* 275–279.

Zieff, P 'The child victim as witness in sexual abuse cases: A comparative analysis of the law of evidence and procedure' (1991) 4 *South African Journal of Criminal Justice* 21–43.

Theses

I Moodley 'The Customary Law of Intestate Succession' (2012) PhD Thesis, University of South Africa.

Wells, J 'The admissibility of real evidence in the light of the Constitution of the Republic of South Africa, 1996'. Submitted in accordance with the requirements for the degree of Doctor of Laws at the University of South Africa. Supervisor: Professor SS Terblanche (November 2013).

Table of cases

A

A Company and Others v Commissioner South African Revenue Services 2014 (4) SA 549 (WCC)....283
AA Mutual Insurance Association Ltd v Biddulph and Another 1976 (1) SA 725 (A) 460
AA Onderlinge Assuransie-Assosiasie Bpk v De Beer 1982 (2) SA 603 (A) 59
AB and Another v Minister of Social Development 2016 (2) SA 27 (GP)..215
AB and Another v Minister of Social Development 2017 (3) SA 570 (CC) 211, 215
ABSA Bank Limited v Le Roux and Others 2014 (1) SA 475 (WCC)...130
Absa Bank Ltd v Blumberg and Wilkinson 1995 (4) SA 403 (W)...461
ABSA Bank Ltd v Hammerle Group 2015 (5) SA 215 (SCA) 294
Absa Bank Ltd v Le Roux and Others 2014 (1) SA 475 (WCC)...129
Absa Brokers (Pty) Ltd v Moshoana NO and Others [2005] 10 BLLR 939 (LAC) 529
ABSA Investment Management Services (Pty) Ltd v Crowhurst [2006] 2 BLLR 107 (LAC) 529, 530
ABSA Technology Finance Solutions Pty (Ltd) v Michael's Bid A House CC and Another 2013
    (3) SA 426 (SCA) 505
Africa Solar (Pty) Ltd v Divwatt (Pty) Ltd 2002 (4) SA 681 (SCA) 337
African Farms and Townships Ltd v Cape Town Municipality 1963 (2) SA 555 (A) 93
Albrecht v Newberry 1974 (4) SA 314 (E) 254
Alexkor Ltd and Another v Richtersveld Community and Others 2004 (5) SA 460 (CC)................211
Amod v S [2001] 4 All SA 13 (E) 533, 537
Annama v Chetty and Others 1946 AD 142 398
Anton Piller KG v Manufacturing Processes Ltd and Others [1976] 1 All ER 779 143
Aris Enterprises (Finance) (Pty) Ltd v Protea Assurance Co Ltd 1981 (3) SA 274 (A) 498
Armstrong v Tee and Others (1999) 20 ILJ 2568 (LC) 519
Arthur v Bezuidenhout and Mieny 1962 (2) SA 566 (A) 435
Association of Amusement and Novelty Machine Operators and Another v Minister of
    Justice and Another 1980 (2) SA 636 (A) 209
Attorney-General v Hitchcock (1847) 1 Exch 91..247
Attorney-General, Transvaal v Kader 1991 (4) SA 727 (A) 316
Avril Elizabeth Home for the Mentally Handicapped v CCMA and Others (2006) 27
    ILJ 1644 (LC)..516, 530
AZAPO and Others v President of the Republic of South Africa and Others 1996 (4)
    SA 671 (CC) 430

B

B and B Hardware Distributors (Pty) Ltd v Administrator, Cape and Another 1989 (1)
    SA 957 (A)...499
B and D Mines (Pty) Ltd v Sebotha NO and Another [1998] 6 BLLR 573 (LC) 519
Bamford and Others v Energiser (SA) Limited [2001] 12 BALR 1251 (P)..527
Barclays Western Bank Ltd v Creser 1982 (2) SA 104 (T) 104
Basson v Attorneys Notaries and Conveyancers' Fidelity Guarantee Fund
    Board of Control 1957 (3) SA 490 (C) 252
Beheersmaatschappij Helling I NV and Others v Magistrate Cape Town and Others 2007 (1)
    SACR 99 (C) 142, 143
Beukes v Mutual and Federal Insurance Co Ltd 1990 NR 105 (HC) 425

550 THE LAW OF EVIDENCE IN SOUTH AFRICA

Bhe & Others v Magistrate, Khayelitsha & Others (Commission for Gender Equality as
amicus curiae); Shibi v Sithole & Others; South African Human Rights Commission &
Another v President of the Republic of South Africa & Another 2005 (1) SA 580 (CC)...............23, 25
Blanchard, Krasner & French v Evans 2004 (4) SA 427 (W) 106
Blend and Another v Peri-Urban Areas Health Board 1952 (2) SA 287 (T) 93
Blue Ribbon Bakeries v Naicker and Others [2000] 12 BLLR 1411 (LC) 529
Bogoshi and Another v Director, Office for Serious Economic Offences and Others 1996 (1)
SA 785 (A)...............284
Bogoshi v Van Vuuren NO and Others; Bogoshi and Another v Director, Office for Serious
Economic Offences and Others 1996 (1) SA 785 (A)...............283, 284
Borcherds v Estate Naidoo 1955 (3) SA 78 (A) 398
Botha v Dreyer (now Moller) (4421/08) [2008] ZAGPHC 395 (19 November 2008)...............469
Bristow v Lycett 1971 (4) SA 223 (RA) 428
Buthelezi v Ndaba 2013 (5) SA 437 (SCA) 214, 435
Byers v Chinn and Another 1928 AD 322 140

C

Caji and African Personnel Services (Pty) Ltd (2005) 26 ILJ 150 (CCMA) 524
Cape Coast Exploration Ltd v Scholtz and Another 1933 AD 56...............250
Cape Town City Council v SAMWU and Others (2000) 21 ILJ 2409 (LC)...............524, 526
Carpede v Choene NO and Another 1986 (3) SA 445 (O) 105
Cash Wholesalers Ltd v Cash Meat Wholesalers 1933 (1) PH A24 (D) 90
Castle v Cross [1984] 1 WLR 1372, [1985] 1 All ER 87...............139, 140
Castle v Cross [1985] 1 All ER 87...............140, 149
Centre for Child Law and others v Media24 Ltd and others 2017 (2) SACR 416 (GP) 508
Chambers v Mississippi 410 US 284 (1973) 370
Char Technology (Pty) Ltd v Mnisi and Others [2000] 7 BLLR 778 (LC) 519
Chizuna v MTN (Pty) Ltd and Others [2008] 10 BLLR 940 (LC)...............516
City Panel Beaters v Bhana and Sons 1985 (2) SA 155 (D) 370
Claude Neon Lights SA (Ltd) v Daniel 1976 (4) SA 403 (A) 67
Cloete NO and Others v Birch R and Another 1993 (2) PH F17 (ECD) 416
Competition Commission v ArcelorMittal SA Ltd and Others 2013 (5) SA 538 (SCA)...............283
Conradie v Kleingeld 1950 (2) SA 594 (O) 93
Consolidated Diamond Mines of South West Africa Ltd v Administrator,
South West Africa 1958 (4) SA 572 (A)...............429
Consolidated Wire Industries (Pty) Ltd v CCMA and Others (1999) 20 ILJ 2602 (LC) 519
Conway v Rimmer and Another [1968] 1 All ER 874 (HL)...............296
Coopers (SA) (Pty) Ltd v Deutsche Gesellschaft Fur Schadlingsbekampfung MBH
1976 (3) SA 352 (A)...............212
County Fair Foods (Pty) Ltd v Theron NO and Others (2000) 21 ILJ 2649 (LC) 519
CUSA v Tao Ying Metal Industries and Others [2009] 1 BLLR 1 (CC) 519

D

Dairybelle (Pty) Ltd v FAWU and Others [2001] 6 BLLR 595 (LC) 379, 530
Daubert et ux., individually and as guardians ad litem for Daubert, et al. v. Merrell Dow
Pharmaceuticals, Inc.509 U.S. 579 (1993) 484
Daubert v Merrell Dow Pharmaceuticals, Inc. (1993) 509 U.S. 579 486

TABLE OF CASES | 551

Dauth v Brown and Weirs Cash & Carry [2002] 8 BALR 837 (CCMA) 525
Davis v Tip NO and Others 1996 (1) SA 1152 (W) 518
De Klerk v Absa Bank Ltd and Others 2003 (4) SA 315 (SCA)..500
De Klerk v Old Mutual Insurance Co. Ltd 1990 (3) SA 34 (E) 77
De Wet and Another v President Versekeringsmaatskappy Bpk 1978 (3) SA 495 (C) 57
Delew v Town Council of Springs 1945 TPD 128..165, 167
DHL Supply Chain (Pty) Ltd v De Beer NO and Others (2014) 35 ILJ 2379 (LAC) 478
DHL Supply Chain (Pty) Ltd v De Beer NO and Others (DA4/2013) [2014] ZALAC 15;
    [2014] 9 BLLR 860 (LAC); (2014) 35 ILJ 2379 (LAC) (13 May 2014) 476
Dimbaza Foundries Ltd v CCMA and Others (1999) 20 ILJ 1763 (LC) 519
Diniso v African Bank Limited 2017 JDR 0120 (ECG)..130
Director of Public Prosecution v Modise and Another 2012 (1) SACR 553 (GSJ)....................132
Director of Public Prosecutions v Kilbourne [1973] 1 All ER 440 58
Director of Public Prosecutions v S 2000 (2) SA 711 (T) 399, 512
Director of Public Prosecutions, KwaZulu-Natal v Mekka 2003 (4) SA 275 (SCA) 509, 510
Director of Public Prosecutions, Transvaal v Minister of Justice and Constitutional
    Development, and Others 2009 (4) SA 222 (CC) 84
Director of Public Prosecutions, Transvaal v Minister of Justice and Constitutional
    Development and Others 2009 (2) SACR 130 (CC) 314, 508, 509
Director of Public Prosecutions, Transvaal v Viljoen 2005 (1) SACR 505 (SCA)....................190
Doe d Church and Phillips v Perkins (1790) 3 Term Rep 749 753, 100 ER 838.....................363
DPP v Boardman [1975] AC 421 168
DPP v Boardman [1975] AC 421 (HL); [1974] 3 All ER 887 (HL)...............................199, 203
DPP v Heunis (196/2017) [2017] ZASCA 136 (29 September 2017) 443
DPP v Kilbourne [1973] 1 All ER 440..405
DPP v Kilbourne [1973] AC 729 ....54, 163, 164, 166
DPP v P [1991] 2 AC 447 (HL) 203
DPP, Transvaal v Viljoen 2005 (1) SACR 505 (SCA) 190
Dreyer and Another NNO v AXZS Industries (Pty) Ltd 2006 (5) SA 548 (SCA) 393
Du Toit v Grobler 1947 (3) SA 213 (SWA) 219
Duchen v Flax 1938 WLD 119...91
Duncan v Cammell Laird and Co Ltd [1942] 1 All ER 587 (HL) 295

E

Early Bird Farms (Pty) Ltd v Mlambo [1997] 5 BLLR 541 (LAC) 529
Els v Minister of Safety and Security 1998 (2) SACR 93 (N)..302
Estate de Wet v De Wet 1924 CPD 341...254, 266
Euroshipping Corporation of Monrovia v Minister of Agricultural Economics and Marketing
    and Others 1979 (1) SA 637 (C)..282
Ex parte Minister of Justice: In re R v Demingo and others 1951 (1) SA 36 (A) 311
Ex parte Minister of Justice: In re R v Jacobson and Levy 1931 AD 466 71
Ex parte Minister of Justice: In re R v Matemba 1941 AD 75...292, 465
Ex parte Minister of Justice: In re R v Pillay and Others 1945 AD 653 303
Ex Parte Minister of Native Affairs: In re Yako v Beyi 1948 (1) SA 388 (A) 22, 28
Ex parte Rosch [1998] 1 All SA 319 (W)..122, 136
Exactics-Pet (Pty) Ltd v Patelia NO and Others (2006) 27 ILJ 1126 (LC)...............................524

552 | THE LAW OF EVIDENCE IN SOUTH AFRICA

F

Fawu obo Kapesi and Others v Premier Foods Ltd t/a Blue Ribbon
Salt River [2010] 9 BLLR 903 (LC) 474, 475, 476, 521, 530
Fedics Group (Pty) Ltd and Another v Matus and Others, Fedics Group (Pty)
Ltd and Another v Murphy and Others 1998 (2) SA 617 (C)..172
Ferreira v Levin NO and Others; Vryenhoek and Others v Powell NO and Others 1996 (1)
SA 984 (CC)..287, 288
Firstrand Bank Limited v Venter [2012] JOL 29436 (SCA)..127, 137
Firstrand Bank Ltd v Venter (829/11) [2012] ZASCA 117...129
Fletcher and Another v S [2010] 2 All SA 205 (SCA) 405
FN Mzimela and United National Breweries (SA) (Pty) Ltd (2005) 14 CCMA 8.23.11 476
Foschini Group v Maidi and Others (2010) 31 ILJ 1787 (LAC) 521
Frye v United States (293 F 1013 [DC Cir 1923]) 486
Frye v United States, 293 F. 1013 (D.C. Cir. 1923) 484

G

Galante v Dickinson 1950 (2) SA 460 (A)..424
Gemalto South Africa (Pty) Ltd v Ceppwawu obo Louw and Others (2015) 36 ILJ 3002 (LAC) 477
General Accident Fire and Life Assurance Corporation Ltd v Goldberg 1912 TPD 494..........283, 285
Gentiruco AG v Firestone SA (Pty) Ltd 1972 (1) SA 589 (A) 208, 210
Giovagnoli v Di Meo 1960 (3) SA 393 (N)..282
Gleneagles Farm Dairy v Schoombee 1947 (4) SA 66 (E)...107, 254
Godla v S (A98/2009) [2011] ZAFSHC 46 413
Golden Fried Chicken (Proprietary) Limited v Yum Restaurants International (Proprietary) Limited
(1243/2004) [2005] ZAGPHC 311 (22 August 2005)
Gomes v Visser 1971 (1) SA 276 (T) 427
Goosen v Caroline's Frozen Yoghurt Parlour (Pty) Ltd and Another (1995) 16 ILJ 396 (IC) 525
Gouda Broedery Bpk v Transnet 2005 (5) SA 490 (SCA)..437
Government v National Bank of SA Ltd 1921 AD 121 501
Griffin v California, 380 US 609 (1965) 290
Gumede v S (800/2015) [2016] ZASCA 148; [2016] 4 ALL SA 692 (SCA); 2017(1)
SACR 253 (SCA) (30 September 2016)...175

H

HA Millard and Son (Pty) Ltd v Enzenhofer 1968 (1) SA 330 (T) 67
Harksen v Attorney-General, Cape and Others 1999 (1) SA 718 (C)..283
Harrington v State of Ohio 659 N.W. 2d 509 (IOWA 2003) 484, 485
Harris v DPP [1952] AC 694 (HC)..200, 205
Hassim (also known as Essack) v Incorporated Law Society, Natal 1979 (3) SA 298 (A)..............219
Hees HC v Nel JT 1994 (1) PH F11 (TPD) 383
Hees v Nel 1994 (1) PH F11 (T) 58
Helen Suzman Foundation v President of the Republic of South Africa and Others 2015 (2)
SA 1 (CC) 208
Herbst v R 1925 SWA 77 209
Heroldt v Wills 2013 (2) SA 530 (GSJ) 120
Herstigde Nasionale Party van Suid-Afrika v Sekretaris van Binnelandse Sake en Immigrasie
1979 (4) SA 274 (T) 102

TABLE OF CASES 553

Hikumwah v Nelumbu 2015 JDR 1202 (Nm)..27
Hlabathi v Nkosi 1970 BAC 51 (C)..34
Hlongwane and Others v Rector, St Francis College and Others 1989 (3) SA 318 (D) 90, 271, 272
Hlophe v Mahlalela and Another 1998 (1) SA 449 (T)..26
Hollingham v Head (1858) 140 ER 1135 163
Hollingham v Head (1858) 27 LJCP 241 163
Hollington v E Hewthorn & Co Ltd [1943] KB 587..159
Hollington v F Hewthorn & Co Ltd [1943] 2 All ER 35 (CA)..219
Hollington v F Hewthorne & Co Ltd [1943] 2 All ER 35 (CA) 208
Holtzhausen v Roodt 1997 (4) SA 766 (W)...............164, 208, 478, 167, 210, 213, 215, 257
Hoskisson v R 1906 TS 502 ....366, 369
Howard & Decker Witkoppen Agencies & Fourways Estates (Pty) Ltd v De Souza 1971 (3)
    SA 937 (T) 105
Howe v Malkin (1878) 40 LT 196 251

I

Independent Newspapers (Pty) Ltd v Minister for Intelligence Services In re
    Masetlha v President of the RSA and Another 2008 (5) SA 31 (CC) 297
Institute for Democracy in SA and Others v African National Congress and Others 2005 (5)
    SA 39 (C) 298
International Business Machines SA (Pty) Ltd v Commissioner for Customs and Excise 1985 (4)
    SA 852 (A) 209
Ismail v Nationwide Airlines Unreported (KN 23530)..522, 523

J

Jabaar v South African Railways and Harbours 1982 (4) SA 552 (C) 370
Jacobs and another v Transnet Ltd t/a Metrorail and Another 2015 (1) SA 139 (SCA) 210
Jafta v Ezemvelo KZN Wildlife (2009) 30 ILJ 131 (LC)...124, 137
Jafta v Ezemvelo KZN Wildlife [2008] ZALC 84 124
Janda v First National Bank (2006) 27 ILJ 2627 (LC)..516
Janit and Another v Motor Industry Fund Administrators (Pty) Ltd and Another 1995 (4) SA 293 (A)......172
Jeeva and Others v Receiver of Revenue, Port Elizabeth and Others 1995 (2) SA 433 (SE)................284
Johnston v Leal 1980 (3) SA 927 (A)..506
Jordaan v Bloemfontein Transitional Local Authority and Another 2004 (3) SA 371 (SCA) 424

K

K v The Regional Court Magistrate NO and Others 1996 (1) SACR 434 (E)................................83
Karbochem Sasolburg (A Division of Sentrachem Ltd) v Kriel and Others (1999) 20 ILJ 2889 (LC) 519
Katz and Another v Katz and Others [2004] 4 All SA 545 (C) 59
Kayser and Department of Correctional Services (1998) 7 CCMA 8.14.3 518
Ketler Investments CC t/a Ketler Presentations v Internet Service Providers'
    Association 2014 (2) SA 569 (GJ)...123
Kewana v Santam Insurance Co. Ltd 1993 (4) SA 771 (TkA)..37
Key v Attorney-General, Cape Provincial Division and Another 1996 (2) SACR 113 (CC)..................184
King's Transport v Viljoen 1954 (1) SA 133 (C)..61
Klaasen v Commission for Conciliation, Mediation and Arbitration and Others [2005] 10
    BLLR 964 (LC)..424

THE LAW OF EVIDENCE IN SOUTH AFRICA

KLD Residential CC v Empire Earth Investments 17 (Pty) Ltd 2017 (6) SA 55 (SCA) 294
Klep Valves (Pty) Ltd v Saunders Valve Co Ltd 1987 (2) SA 1 (A) 92
Kok v Osborne and Another 1993 (4) SA 788 (SE) 505
KPMG Chartered Accountants (SA) v Securefin Ltd and Another 2009 (4) SA 399 (SCA) 528
Kruger v Coetzee 1966 (2) SA 428 (A)...353
Kuruma, son of Kaniu v R [1955] AC 197 (PC) 171
Kutoone v Stofile 1971 BAC 142 (C)...34

L

LA Consortium & Vending CC t/a LA Enterprises v MTN Service Provider
     (Pty) Ltd 2011 (4) SA 577 (GSJ)....................123, 127, 128, 129, 130, 134, 135, 136, 137, 146
LA Consortium and Vending CC t/a LA Enterprises and Others v MTN Service Provider (Pty)
     Ltd and Others Case No A5014/08 (19 August 2009) (SCHC)..522
Lachman v S 2010 (2) SACR 52 (SCA..537
Land Securities plc v Westminster City Council [1993] 4 All ER 124 55
Langham and Another NNO v Milne NO and Others 1961 (1) SA 811 (N) 350
Latif v Obama 666 F.3d 746 (D.C. Cir. 2011) 140
Laubscher v National Foods Ltd 1986 (1) SA 553 (ZS)...205
Le Monde Luggage CC t/a Pakwells Petje v Dunn and Others [2007] 10 BLLR 909 (LAC) 521
Le Roux and Others v Viana NO and Others 2008 (2) SA 173 (SCA)..143
Le Roux v Direkteur-Generaal van Handel en Nywerheid 1997 (4) SA 174 (T)................................284
Leboho v CCMA and Others (2005) 26 ILJ 883 (LC) 519
Leeb and Another v Leeb and Another [1999] 2 All SA 588 (N) 219
Legal Aid Board v John NO and Another (1998) 19 ILJ 851 (LC) 519
Lenco Holdings Ltd and Others v Eckstein and Others 1996 (2) SA 693 (N) 48, 172, 491
Lenssen v R 1906 TS 154..251, 252
Levenstein and Others v Estate of the Late Sidney Lewis Frankel and Others 2018 ZACC 16 238
Levin v Saidman 1930 WLD 256 90
Liberty Group Limited v K & D Telemarketing CC 2015 JDR 1846 (GP) 130
Lithgow City Council v Jackson (2011) 244 CLR 352 162
Lloyd v Powell Duffryn Steam Coal Co Ltd [1914] AC 733 ....55, 162
Lorraine v Markel American Insurance Company 241 F.R.D. 534..152
Lotter v Arlow and Another 2002 (6) SA 60 (T)..525
Lourens en 'n Ander v Genis 1962 (1) SA 431 (T)..499
Louwrens v Oldwage 2006 (2) SA 161 (SCA)...214, 393
Lukhanji Municipality v Nonxuba NO and Others [2007] 2 BLLR 130 (LC) 529

M

M & V Tractor & Implement Agencies Bk v Venootskap DSU Cilliers en Seuns en
     Andere 2000 (2) SA 571 (N) 88
M v R 1989 (1) SA 416 (O) 469
Mabena v Letsoalo 1998 (2) SA 1068 (T)...25, 26
Mabona and Another v Minister of Law and Order and Others 1988 (2) SA 654 (SE)................377, 379
Mabuza v Mbatha 2003 (4) SA 218 (C) 25, 38
Macleod v Rens 1997 (3) SA 1039 (E) 414
Madubula v Mahlangu 1972/74 AC 449 (C)...34
Magmoed v Janse van Rensburg and Others 1993 (1) SA 777 (A) 287

TABLE OF CASES | 555

Mahlangu v CIM Deltak, Gallant v CIM Deltak (1986) 7 ILJ 346 (IC)...............................478
Mahomed v Attorney-General of Natal and Others 1996 (1) SACR 139 (N)....................269
Mahomed v Attorney-General of Natal and Others 1998 (1) SACR 73 (N) 287
Mahomed v Shaik 1978 (4) SA 523 (N)...211
Makate v Vodacom (Pty) Ltd 2014 (1) SA 191 (GSJ)...............................125, 143
Makate v Vodacom Ltd 2016 (4) SA 121 (CC) (26 April 2016) 500
Makhathini v Road Accident Fund 2002 (1) SA 511 (SCA)...................................272
Makin v Attorney-General New South Wales [1894] AC 57 (PC); [1891–1984]
    All ER 24 (PC)..199, 200, 202, 203
Maluleke (in her capacity as representative of the estate of the late Dumakude Patrick
    Mtshali) and Others v Minister of Home Affairs and Another (02/24921) [2008]
    ZAGPHC 129 (9 April 2008)...25
Maluleke and Others v The Minister of Home Affairs and Another (02/24921) [2008]
    ZAGPHC 129 (9 April 2008) 38
Man Truck and Bus (SA) (Pty) Ltd v Dusbus Leasing CC and Others 2004 (1) SA 454 (W)...........502
Mapota v Santam Versekeringsmaatskappy Bpk 1977 (4) SA 515 (A) 389
Mapp v Ohio (367 U.S. 643 (1961)...178
Maqutu v Sancizi 1936 NAC (C & O) 86...39
Marapula and Others v Consteen (Pty) Ltd [1999] 8 BLLR 829 (LC) 529
Maseti v S [2014] 1 All SA 420 (SCA)...127, 128, 137
Maseti v S 2014 (2) SACR 23 (SCA)...128
Masokanye v Additional Magistrate Stellenbosch and Others 1994 (1) SACR 21 (C) 288
Maswanganye v Baloyi N.O. and Another (62122/2014) [2015] ZAGPPHC 917
    (4 September 2015)...37
Matjhabeng Municipality v Mothupi NO and Others (2011) 32 ILJ 2154 (LC)....................516
Mayer v Williams 1981 (3) SA 348 (A) 398
Mbuli and Spartan Wiremakers CC (2004) 25 ILJ 1128 (BCA) 524
McDonald's Corporation v Joburgers Drive-Inn Restaurant (Pty) Ltd and Another 1997 (1) SA 1 (A).......268
Mdani v Allianz Insurance Ltd 1991 (1) SA 184 (A) 38
Mdumane v Mtshakule 1948 NAH (C20) 28...33
MEC for Education, KwaZulu-Natal and Others v Pillay 2008 (1) SA 474 (CC)...................26
Medscheme Holdings (Pty) Ltd and Another v Bhamjee 2005 (5) SA 339 (SCA) 417
Menday v Protea Assurance Co Ltd 1976 (1) SA 565 (EC) 212, 216
Metedad v National Employers' General Insurance Co Ltd 1992 (1) SA 494 (W)...................270, 271
Metiso v Padongelukfonds 2001 (3) SA 1142 (T)...37
Metropolitan Health Corporate (Pty) Ltd v Neil Harvey and Associates (Pty)
    Ltd and Another (10264/10) [2011] ZAWCHC 358 (19 August 2011)........................143
Mgobhozi v Naidoo NO and Others [2006] 3 BLLR 242 (LAC) 521
Mhlongo v S; Nkosi v S (CCT 148/14; CCT 149/14) [2015] ZACC 19; 2015(2)
    SACR 323 (CC); 2015(8) BCLR 887 (CC) (25 June 2015) 442
Mhlongo v S; Nkosi v S [2015] ZACC 19...446, 447, 448
Mhlongo v S; Nkosi v S 2015 (2) SACR 323 (CC)...38, 272
Minister of Safety and Security and Another v Gaqa 2002 (1) SACR 654 (C)....................292
Minister of Safety and Security and Another v Xaba 2004 (1) SACR 149 (D)....................292
Minister of Safety and Security and Others v Bennett and Others 2009 (2) SACR 17 (SCA).............282
Minister of Safety and Security and Others v Craig and Others NNO 2011 (1) SACR 469 (SCA).........377
MM v MN 2013 (4) SA 415 (CC)...26
MM v MN and Another 2013 (4) SA 415 (CC) 25

Mnyama v Gxalaba and Another 1990 (1) SA 650 (C) 40
Modiga v The State [2015] ZASCA 94 398
Mohamed v President of RSA and Others 2001 (2) SA 1145 (C) 282, 284
Mohammed v State (605/10) [2011] ZASCA 98 (31 May 2011) 335
Mohlala v Citibank and Others (2003) 24 ILJ 417 (LC) 518
Mokoena v Mokoena 1972/74 AC 382 (C) 34
Moonsamy v The Mailhouse (1999) 20 ILJ 464 (CCMA) 526
Morant v Roos and Another 1911 TPD 1092 460
Mosii v Motseoakhumo 1954 (3) SA 919 (A) 21, 29
Motaung v Dube 1930 NAC (N & T) 9 32
Motor Industry Fund Administrators (Pty) Ltd and Another v Janit and Another 1994 (3) SA 56 (W) 172
Mqobhozi v Naidoo NO and Others [2006] 3 BLLR 242 (LAC) 530
Msonti v Dingindawo 1927 AD 255 30
Msonti v Dingindawo 1927 AD 256 ......29, 30
Msonti v Dingindawo 1927 AD 531 22
MTN Service Provider (Pty) Ltd v LA Consortium & Vending CC t/a LA Enterprises and Others
    [2009] JOL 23394 (W) 127
Mtoto v S (A488/14) [2015] ZAWCHC 45 (22 April 2015) 466
Mugwedi v The State (694/13) [2014] ZASCA 23 (27 March 2014) 472
Mutual and Federal Insurance Co Ltd v CCMA and Others [1997] 12 BLLR 1610 (LC) 519
Myataza v Macasa 1952 NAC (S) 28 39

N

Naraindath v CCMA and Others (2000) 21 ILJ 1151 (LC) 519, 521
Narlis v South African Bank of Athens 1976 (2) SA 573 (A) 121, 128, 152
Natal Shoe Components CC v Ndawonde (1998) 19 ILJ 1527 (LC) 518, 519
National Board (Pretoria) (Pty) Ltd and Another v Estate Swanepoel 1975 (3) SA 16 (A) 505
National Justice Compania Naviera SA v Prudential Assurance Co Ltd ('The Ikarian Reefer')
    [1993] 2 Lloyd's Rep 68 214
National Media Ltd and Others v Bogoshi 1998 (4) SA 1196 (SCA) 517
Naude and Another v S [2011] 2 All SA 517 (SCA) 397
Ndhlovu and Others v S [2002] 3 All SA 760 (SCA) 446, 447
Ndlovu v Minister of Correctional Services and
    Another [2006] 4 All SA 165 (W) 122, 123, 127, 128, 130, 133, 136, 137, 147, 150
Nduli and another v Minister of Justice and others 1978 (1) SA 893 (A) 430
Nel v Law Society; Cape of Good Hope 2010 (6) SA 263 (ECG) 524
Nel v Le Roux NO and Others 1996 (3) SA 562 (CC) 317
Network Field Marketing (Pty) Ltd v Mngezana NO and Others (2011) 32
    ILJ 1705 (LC) 376, 377, 392, 529
New Forest Farming CC v Cachalia and Others (2003) 24 ILJ 1995 (LC) 518
Ngcobo v Ngcobo 1929 AD 233 21
Nkala v Nkosi 1975/77 AC 227 (NE) 34
Nkosi v Barlow NO en Andere 1984 (3) SA 148 (T) 292
Nombona v Mzileni and Another 1961 NAC 22 (S) 33
Northern Mounted Rifles v O'Callaghan 1909 TS 174 100
NUMSA and Volkswagen of SA (Pty) Ltd (2003) 12 Private 1.8.1 518
NUMSA obo Abrahams v Guestro Wheels [2004] 4 BALR 520 (CCMA) 524

TABLE OF CASES | 557

NUMSA obo Nqukwe and Others v Lowveld Implement and Farm
    Equipment (Life) [2003] 8 BALR 909 (CCMA) 524
Nxumalo v S [2010] 1 ALL SA 325 (SCA) 413

O

OK Bazaars (a division of Shoprite Checkers) v CCMA and Others (2000) 21 ILJ 1188 (LC) 527
Olivier v Minister of Safety and Security and Another 2008 (2) SACR 387 (W) 424
Omega, Louis Brandt et Frere SA and Another v African Textile Distributors 1982 (1) SA 951 (T) 204
Onassis v Vergottis [1968] 2 Lloyd's Rep 403 383
Oriental Products (Pty) Ltd v Pegma 178 Investments Trading CC and Others 2011 (2)
    SA 508 (SCA) 501
Orville Investments (Pty) Ltd v Sandfontein Motors 2000 (2) SA 886 (T) 499
Osman and Another v Attorney-General, Transvaal 1998 (4) SA 1224 (CC) 47, 290, 422, 423

P

Palmer v Minister of Safety and Security 2002 (1) SA 110 (W) 56, 251
Parbhoo and Others v Getz NO and Another 1997 (4) SA 1095 (CC) 288
Parker v Reed 1904 21 SC 496 428
People v. Johnson 62 Cal.App.4th 608 36
PFE International Inc (BVI) and Others v Industrial Development Corporation of
    South Africa Ltd 2013 (1) SA 1 (CC) 299
Phadu and Others v Department of Health: Free State [2004] 2 BALR 167 (PHWSBC) 524
Phalandira v Moloi 1978/80 AC 97 (C) 34
Phato v Attorney-General Eastern Cape and Another; Commissioner of SAPS v
    Attorney-General Eastern Cape and Others 1994 (2) SACR 734 (E) 285
Pillay and others v S 2004 (2) BCLR 158 (SCA) 186
Pillay v Krishna and Another 1946 AD 946 ....63, 65, 517
Pincus v Solomon (1) 1942 WLD 237 ....252, 258
Plascon-Evans Paints Ltd v Van Riebeeck Paints (Pty) Ltd 1984 (3) SA 623 (A) 91, 92
Portnet (a division of Transnet Ltd) v Finnemore and Others [1999] 2 BLLR 151 (LC) 530
Potgietersrus Platinum Ltd v CCMA and Others (1999) 20 ILJ 2679 (LC) 516
Pountas' Trustee v Lahanas 1924 WLD 67 90
Powell NO and Others v Van Der Merwe NO and Others 2005 (1) SACR 317 (SCA) 142
PPWAWU and Another v Commissioner CCMA (Port Elizabeth) and Another [1998] 5 BLLR 499 (LC) 519
Preen v Preen and Another 1935 NPD 138 398
President of RSA and Others v SA Rugby Football Union and Others 2000 (1) SA 1 (CC) 417
President of RSA and Others v Sarfu and Others 2000 (1) SA 1 (CC) 417
President of the Republic of SA and Others v SA Rugby Football Union and
    Others 2000 (1) SA 1 (CC) 315, 392
President Versekeringsmaatskappy Bpk v Moodley 1964 (4) SA 109 (T) 460
Pressma Services (Pty) Ltd v Schuttler and Another 1990 (2) SA 411 (C) 93
Prinsloo v Van der Linde and Another 1997 (3) SA 1012 (CC) 437
Prophet v National Director, Public Prosecutions 2007 (6) SA 169 (CC) 219
Protea Technology Ltd and Another v Wainer and Others 1997 (9) BCLR 1225 (W) 526
Purchase v Purchase 1960 (3) SA 383 (N) 93

R

R (on the application of O) v Coventry Justices [2004] All ER (D) 78 149

THE LAW OF EVIDENCE IN SOUTH AFRICA

R v A (No 2) [2001] UKHL 25; [2002] 1 AC 45 (HL)..241
R v A (No2) [2002] 1 AC 45 159
R v Abdoorham 1954 (3) SA 163 (N)..385
R v Abelson 1933 TPD 227 301
R v Adkins 1955 (4) SA 242 (GW) 428
R v Afrika 1949 (3) SA 627 (O)..454
R v Amod & Co (Pty) Ltd and Another 1947 (3) SA 32 (A).....................................103
R v Armstrong [1922] 2 KB 555...205
R v B (KG) [1993] 1 SCR 740 366
R v Baartman 1960 (3) SA 535 (A)...336
R v Ball [1911] AC 47 (HL) 200, 202, 204, 205
R v Baloi 1949 (1) SA 491 (T)..273
R v Barlin 1926 AD 459..289, 443, 445
R v Becker 1929 AD 167 451
R v Behrman 1957 (1) SA 433 (T) 112
R v Beland [1987] 2 SCR 398 478
R v Beukman 1950 (4) SA 261 (O) 366, 369
R v Bikitsha 1960 (4) SA 181 (E) 427
R v Blom 1939 AD 188...59, 413, 414
R v Blyth 1940 AD 355 ....407, 455, 457
R v Bond [1906] 2 KB 389 (CCR) 201, 202
R v Bunana 1958 (1) SA 573 (E) 428
R v Burgess 1927 TPD 14..260
R v Butterwasser [1948] 1 KB 4, [1947] 2 All ER 415 (CCA) 225
R v C 1955 (4) SA 40 (N)..237, 258
R v Camane and Others 1925 AD 570..285, 289, 292
R v Campbell [1999] 1 SCR 565..189
R v Cloutier (1979) 48 C.C.C. (2d) 159
R v Cloutier 1979 48 C.C.C. (2d) 1 163
R v Collins (1987) 1 SCR 265 ....183, 190
R v Cooper 1926 AD 54 350
R v Da Silva [1990] 1 All ER 29...362
R v Davies [1953] 1 QB 489, [1953] 1 All ER 341 228
R v Davis 1925 AD 30 200
R v Daye [1908] 2 KB 333...99
R v De Beer 1949 (3) SA 740 (A)...251
R v De Villiers 1944 AD 493 59
R v Dhlamini 1960 (1) SA 880 (N)...162, 205
R v Dhlumayo and Another 1948 (2) SA 677 (A)...417
R v Diedericks 1957 (3) SA 661 (E) 286
R v Dinehine 1910 CPD 371...273
R v Downey (1992) (13) Cr 4th 129 (SCC) 434
R v Downey 1992 (13) Cr 4th 129 (SCC) 71
R v Duetsimi 1950 (3) SA 674 (A)..452
R v Dumezweni 1961 (2) SA 751 (A)..29, 30
R v Dumezweni 1961 (2) SA 751 (AD) 30
R v Edwards (1991) 93 Cr App R 48...164
R v Fouche 1958 (3) SA 767 (T) 72

TABLE OF CASES 559

R v Gimingham 1946 EDL 156 224
R v Gordon (1995) 2 Cr App R 61 164
R v Grant (2009) SCC 32 .... 184, 188
R v Gumede 1949 (3) SA 749 (A) 384, 396
R v Hall [1998] B.C.J. No. 2515 151
R v Hanger 1928 AD 459 452
R v Harvey 1969 (2) SA 193 (RA) 429
R v Heilbron 1922 TPD 99 330
R v Hendrickz 1933 TPD 451 230
R v Innes Grant 1949 (1) SA 753 (A) 289
R v John 1929 WLD 50 253
R v Kaiser 1927 WLD 278 255
R v Katz 1946 AD 71 164
R v Katz and Another 1946 AD 71 162
R v Keller and Parker 1915 AD 98 205
R v Kelsey (1982) 74 Cr App R 213 363
R v Kitaitchik (2002), 166 CCC (3d) 14 (Ont. CA) 188
R v Kola 1949 (1) PH H100 (A) 410
R v Kola 1949 (1) PH H100 (AD) 400
R v Kritzinger 1953 (1) SA 438 (W) 320
R v Kukubula 1958 (3) SA 698 (SR) 252
R v Kumalo & Nkosi 1918 AD 500 167
R v Kumalo 1952 (3) SA 223 (T) 336
R v Kuyper 1915 TPD 308 286
R v Lalla 1945 EDL 156 253
R v Lipschitz 1921 AD 282 231
R v Lipsitch 1913 TPD 652 205
R v Lombard and Another 1957 (2) SA 42 (T) 103
R v Luttrell [2004] 2 Cr App R 31 (CA) 111
R v M 1959 (1) SA 434 (A) 261
R v Mack [1988] 2 SCR 903 537
R v Maduna 1946 EDL 334 428
R v Magoetie 1959 (2) SA 322 (A) 445
R v Makeip 1948 (1) SA 947 (A) 111, 466
R v Malindi 1966 (4) SA 123 (PC) 223
R v Manda 1951 (3) SA 158 (A) 399
R v Masapha 1958 (3) SA 480 (O) 427
R v Mashelele and Another 1944 AD 571 289
R v Matthews and Others 1960 (1) SA 752 (A) 54, 159, 167, 205
R v McCulloch [1992] B.C.J. 2282 151
R v Mendy (CA) (1976) 64 Cr App R 4 249
R v Michael and Another 1962 (3) SA 355 (SR) 446, 454
R v Minors; R v Harper [1989] 1 WLR 441 CA 140
R v Mlambo 1957 (4) SA 727 (A) 421
R v Mohan [1994] 2 S.C.R 9 165
R v Mokoena 1932 OPD 79 399

THE LAW OF EVIDENCE IN SOUTH AFRICA

R v Mondor 2014 ONCJ 135 150
R v Morela 1947 (3) SA 147 (A) 427
R v Mpanza 1915 AD 348 163
R v Mpanza 1915 AD 348 254
R v Mputing 1960 (1) SA 785 (T) 409
R v Nethercott [2002] 2 Cr App R 117 162
R v Nksatlala 1960 (3) SA 543 (A) 113, 212, 213
R v Noble (1997) 146 DLR (4th) 385 291
R v Ntshangela en Andere 1961 (4) SA 592 (A) 286
R v O'Linn 1960 (1) SA 545 (N) 363
R v Omar and Another 1948 (1) SA 76 (T) 534
R v Osborne [1905] 1 KB 551 259
R v Patel 1946 AD 903 289
R v Pelunsky 1914 AD 360 103
R v Persutam 1934 TPD 253 230
R v Qongwana 1959 (2) SA 227 (A) 287
R v Randall [2004] 1 WLR 56 (HL) 54
R v Regan (1887) 16 Cox CC 203 102
R v Roberts (1942) 28 Cr App R 102 257
R v Rorke 1915 AD 145 231
R v Rowton [1865] 169 ER 1497 168
R v Rowton 1865 Le and CA 520; 169 All ER 1497 222
R v Sacco 1958 (2) SA 349 (N) 377
R v Samhando 1943 AD 608 450
R v Schaube-Kuffler 1969 (2) SA 40 (RA) 55, 165
R v Scoble 1958 (3) SA 667 (N) 363
R v Seaboyer; R v Gayme (1991) 83 DLR (4th) 193; [1991] 2 SCR 577 241
R v Simon and Another 1925 TPD 297 200
R v Sims (1946) 31 Cr App R 158 163
R v Sims [1946] 1 KB 531 (CCA) 205
R v Smit 1952 (3) SA 447 (A) 113
R v Smith (1915) 11 Cr App Rep 229 202
R v Sole 2004 (2) SACR 599 (Les) 162
R v Solomons 1959 (2) SA 352 (A) 169, 225, 351
R v Sonyangwe 1908 22 EDC 394 314
R v Spiby [1990] 91 Cr App R 186 .... 149, 151
R v Steyn 1954 (1) SA 324 (A) 285, 299
R v Stillman 1997 42 CRR (2d) 189 (SCC); 1997 1 SCR 607 182
R v Straffen [1952] 2 QB 911 168
R v Straffen [1952] 2 QB 911 (CCA) 200, 202
R v Tager 1944 AD 426
R v Taylor 1961 (3) SA 616 (N) 252
R v Trupedo 1920 AD 58 .... 160, 164, 165, 166, 168, 169
R v Valachia & another 1945 826 (AD) 443
R v Valachia and Another 1945 AD 826 444
R v Valentine [1996] 2 Cr App R 213 237
R v Van Schalkwyk 1938 AD 543 302
R v Vilbro and Another 1957 (3) SA 223 (A) 208

TABLE OF CASES   561

R v W 1949 (3) SA 772 (A)...405
R v Wallwork [1958] 42 Cr App R 153 237
R v Weinberg 1939 AD 71..376, 421
R v Wellers 1918 TPD 234 370
R v Wilson [1991] 2 NZLR 707..165, 166
R v Yaeck (1991) 68 C.C.C. (3d) 545 162
R v Zahlan and Another 1951 PH H69 (AD) 1978 (3) SA 5 (O)................................534
R v Zungu 1953 (4) SA 660 (N) 103, 104
Rademeyer v Attorney-General and Another 1955 (1) SA 444 (T) 287
Rammoko v Director of Public Prosecutions 2003 (1) SACR 200 (SCA)....................217
Rank Film Distributors Ltd v Video Information Centre [1982] AC 380, 441–448 (HL) 288
Rasool v R 1932 NPD 112..261
Rio Tinto Zinc Corporation v Westinghouse Electric Corporation [1978] AC 547, 549, 563-66 (HL)....288
Road Accident Fund v Mothupi 2000 (4) SA 38 (SCA)..499
Robinson v State of South Australia (No 2) [1931] AC 704 (A)................................296
Room Hire Co (Pty) Ltd v Jeppe Street Mansions (Pty) Ltd 1949 (3) SA 1155 (T)..........92, 93
Ruto Flour Mills Ltd v Adelson (1) 1958 (4) SA 235 (T) 208

S
S v Abbott 1999 (1) SACR 489 (SCA) 450
S v Abrahams 2002 (1) SACR 116 (SCA) 217
S v Adendorff 2004 (2) SACR 185 (SCA)..34, 81
S v Agliotti 2011 (2) SACR 437 (GSJ) 66
S v Agnew and Another 1996 (2) SACR 535 (C) 458
S v AR Wholesalers (Pty) Ltd and Another 1975 (1) SA 551 (NC) 2
S v B 1976 (2) SA 54 (C) 405
S v B 1996 (2) SACR 543 (C) 327
S v B 2003 (1) SA 552 (SCA) 509
S v Bailey 2007 (2) SACR 1 (C)..333, 410
S v Bakane 2017 (1) SACR 576 (GP) and (1180/2016) [2017] ZASCA 182 (5 December 2017)....454
S v Baleka and Others (1) 1986 (4) SA 192 (T)..117
S v Banana 2000 (3) SA 885 (ZS)..259
S v Basson 2001 (2) SACR 537 (T) 336
S v Bergh 1976 (4) SA 857 (A)..168, 256, 257, 263, 361,
S v Bester 2004 (2) SACR 59 (C)...429
S v Bhulwana; S v Gwadiso 1996 (1) SA 388 (CC)..46, 436
S v Blom 1992 (1) SACR 649 (E) 466
S v Boesak 2000 (1) SACR 633 (SCA) 113, 337, 445
S v Boesak 2001 (1) SA 912 (CC)..46, 290, 291, 423, 424
S v Boesak 2001 (1) SACR 1 (CC) 337
S v Bontsi 1985 (4) SA 544 (BG) 492
S v Bosman and Another 1978 (3) SA 903 (O) 287
S v Brown (CC 54/2014) [2015] ZAWCHC 128 (17 August 2015)..........122, 125, 127, 135, 136
S v Brown [2015] ZAWCHC 128 128
S v Brown 2016 (1) SACR 206 (WCC) 120, 130, 146
S v Brown en 'n Ander 1996 (2) SACR 49 (NC) 95, 290, 423
S v Burger and Others 2010 (2) SACR 1 (SCA)..385, 421

S v Campos 2002 (1) SACR 233 (SCA)...........421
S v Carneson 1962 (3) SA 437 (T)...........287
S v Carolus 2008 (2) SACR 207 (SCA)...........472
S v Chabalala 2003 (1) SACR 134 (SCA)...........291, 378
S v Chesane 1975 (3) SA 172 (W)...........534
S v Coetzee and Others 1997 (1) SACR 379 (CC)...........46, 188
S v Coetzee and Others 1997 (3) SA 527 (CC)...........46, 436
S v Cornelissen; Cornelissen v Zeelie NO en Andere 1994 (2) SACR 41 (W)...........317
S v Cornick and Another 2007 (2) SACR 115 (SCA)...........237, 260, 378
S v Crossberg 2008 (2) SACR 317 (SCA)...........472
S v D 1991 (2) SACR 543 (A)...........203, 204
S v Daba 1996 (1) SACR 243 (E)...........400
S v Damalis 1984 (2) SA 105 (T)...........247
S v Daniels en 'n Ander 1983 (3) SA 275 (A)...........460
S v Davidson 1964 (1) SA 192 (T)...........321
S v De Lange 1972 (1) SA 139 (C)...........427
S v De Ruiter 2004 1 SACR 332 (W)...........2
S v De Villiers 1993 (1) SACR 574 (Nm)...........138
S v De Vries and Others 2012 (1) SACR 186 (SCA)...........540, 541
S v December 1995 (1) SACR 438 (A)...........444
S v Dladla 1980 (1) SA 526 (A)...........398
S v Dlamini 1978 (4) SA 917 (N)...........287
S v Dlamini, S v Dladla and Others; S v Joubert; S v Schietekat 1999 (4) SA 623 (CC)...........47
S v Dlamini; S v Dladla and Others; S v Joubert; S v Schietekat 1999 (2) SACR 51 (CC)...........293
S v Domingo 2005 (1) SACR 193 (C)...........85
S v Dube 2000 (2) SA 583 (N)...........527
S v Duna and Others 1984 (2) SA 591 (CkS)...........292
S v Dzukuda and Others; S v Thilo 2000 (2) SACR 443 (CC)...........183
S v Edley 1970 (2) SA 223 (N)...........523
S v Eiseb and Another 1991 (1) SACR 650 (Nm)...........443
S v Engelbrecht 2005 (2) SACR 41 (W)...........208
S v F 1999 (1) SACR 571 (C)...........83
S v Forbes and Another 1970 (2) SA 594 (C)...........171
S v Fuhri 1994 (2) SACR 829 (A)...........429
S v Gcaba 1965 (4) SA 325 (N)...........456
S v Gcam-gcam 2015 (2) SACR 501 (SCA)...........454
S v Gentle 2005 (1) SACR 420 (SCA)...........260, 405
S v Gouws 1968 (4) SA 354 (GW)...........351
S v Govender and Others 2006 (1) SACR 322 (E)...........366, 420
S v Green 1962 (3) SA 886 (A)...........201
S v Groenewald 2005 (2) SACR 597 (SCA)...........443, 444
S v Grove-Mitchell 1975 (3) SA 417 (A)...........443
S v Guess 1976 (4) SA 715 (A)...........379
S v Gumede and Others 1998 (5) BCLR 530 (D)...........188, 190, 191
S v Gxokwe and Others 1992 (2) SACR 355 (C)...........494
S v Haasbroek 1969 (2) SA 624 (A)...........209
S v Hammer and Others 1994 (2) SACR 496 (C)...........171
S v Hammond 2004 (2) SACR 303 (SCA)...........260, 261

TABLE OF CASES 563

S v Hanekom 2011 (1) SACR 430 (WCC)..399
S v Harper and Another 1981 (1) SA 88 (D) 99, 121, 138, 152
S v Hassim and Others 1973 (3) SA 443 (A) 86
S v Hayes en 'n Ander 1998 (1) SACR 625 (O) 537
S v Heilig 1999 (1) SACR 379 (W) 432
S v Helm 2015 (1) SACR 550 (WCC) 429
S v Hena And Another (2006) 2 SACR 33 (SE)..497
S v Hena and Another 2006 (2) SACR 33 (SE) 179
S v Hendrix and Others 1979 (3) SA 816 (D) 287
S v Heyman and Another 1966 (4) SA 598 (A) 287
S v Hlapezulu 1965 (4) SA 439 (A)..397
S v Hlongwa 2002 (2) SACR 37 (T)...87, 495
S v Hlongwane 1992 (2) SACR 484 (N) 290
S v Holshausen 1984 (4) SA 852 (A)...254
S v Huma and Another (2) 1995 (2) SACR 411 (W)................................292, 465
S v J 1998 (2) SA 984 (SCA)..418, 512
S v Jackson 1998 (1) SACR 470 (SCA)..................241, 396, 400, 401, 403, 512
S v Jama and Another 1998 (2) SACR 237 (N) 66
S v Janse van Rensburg & another 2009 (2) SACR 216 (C)..........................399
S v Janse van Rensburg and Another 2009 (2) SACR 216 (C)........................378
S v January 1994 (2) SACR 801 (A)..451
S v January 1995 (1) SACR 202 (O) 231
S v January: Prokureur-Generaal, Natal v Khumalo 1994 (2) SACR 801 (A) 450
S v Jochems 1991 (1) SACR 208 (A)................................379, 386, 388, 390, 392
S v Johannes 1980 (1) SA 531 (A) 398
S v Jones 2004 (1) SACR 420 (C) 216
S v Jordaan 1992 (2) SACR 498 (A)..451
S v Josephs 2001 (1) SACR 659 (C) 47
S v K and Another 1999 (2) SACR 388 (C) 492
S v Katoo 2005 (1) SACR 522 (SCA)..112, 310
S v Kearney 1964 (2) SA 495 (A)...283, 454
S v Kelly 1980 (3) SA 301 (A) 376
S v Khan 2010 (2) SACR 476 (KZP) 446
S v Khanyapa 1979 (1) SA 824 (A)..219
S v Khanye and Another 2017(2) SACR 630(CC)..272
S v Khumalo 1992 (2) SACR 411 (N)...451
S v Kimimbi 1963 (3) SA 250 (C)..216, 465
S v Kinney 171 Vt 239, 762 A 2d 833 (2000) 213
S v Kleynhans 2005 (2) SACR 582 (W) 208
S v Kotzè 2010 (1) SACR 100 (SCA) 534, 537
S v Kruger (612/13) [2013] ZASCA 198 (unreported, SCA case, 2 December 2013) 238
S v Langa and Others 1998 (1) SACR 21 (T)........................192, 289, 292, 445
S v Lavhengwa 1996 (2) SACR 453 (W) 290
S v Lawrence; S v Negal; S v Solberg 1997 (4) SA 1176 (CC)........................431
S v Le Grange and Others 2009 (1) SACR 125 (SCA)......................................336
S v Letsoko and Others 1964 (4) SA 768 (A) 162, 290
S v Limekayo 1969 (1) SA 540 (E) 466

S v Litako 2014 (2) SACR 431 (SCA) 446, 447
S v Litako and Others 2014 (2) SACR 431 (SCA) 38
S v Lotter 2008 (2) SACR 595 (C) 384
S v Lottering 1999 (12) BCLR 1478 (N) 182
S v Lubaxa 2001 (4) SA 1251 (SCA) 66
S v Lund 1987 (4) SA 548 (N) 427
S v Lungile and Another 1999 (2) SACR 597 (SCA) 312
S v Lwane 1966 (2) SA 433 (A) 286, 287
S v M 1963 (3) SA 183 (T) 410
S v M 1972 (4) SA 361 (T) 410
S v M 1999 (1) SACR 664 (C) 237
S v M 2002 (2) SACR 411 (SCA) 110, 240
S v M 2003 (1) SA 341 (SCA) 164, 203
S v M 2006 (1) SACR 135 (SCA) 376, 390, 421
S v M 2018 (1) SACR 357 (GP) 215
S v M M 2012 (2) SACR 18 (SCA) 269
S v Mabaso 1978 (3) SA 5 (O) 398
S v Mabaso 2016 (1) SACR 617 (SCA) 450
S v Mafaladiso en Andere 2003 (1) SACR 583 (SCA) 367, 369
S v Mafiri 2003 (2) SACR 121 (SCA) 389, 393
S v Magwaza 2016 (1) SACR 53 (SCA) 450
S v Mahlangu and another 2011 (2) SACR 164 (SCA) 399
S v Makhubo 1990 (2) SACR 320 (O) 290
S v Makwanyane and Another 1995 (3) SA 391 (CC) 28
S v Malebo en Andere 1979 (2) SA 636 (B) 444
S v Malinga and Others 1963 (1) SA 692 (A) 533
S v Manamela and Another (Director General of Justice Intervening) 2000 (3) SA 1 (CC) 47, 436, 539
S v Mankwanyane and Another 1995 (3) SA 391 (CC) 187
S v Maphumulo 1996 (2) SACR 84 (N) 292
S v Maqhina 2001 (1) SACR 241 (T) 114
S v Maradu 1994 (2) SACR 410 (W) 333
S v Maritz 1974 (1) SA 266 (NC) 289
S v Mashengoane 2014 (2) SACR 623 (GP) 455
S v Masuku 1969 (2) SA 375 (N) 397
S v Mathebula and Another 1997 (1) SACR 10 (W) 66, 288
S v Mathonsi 2012 (1) SACR 335 (KZP) 366, 369, 370
S v Matsabu 2009 (1) SACR 513 (SCA) 537
S v Mavundla and Another; S v Sibisi 1976 (2) SA 162 (N) 112
S v Mavuso 1987 (3) SA 499 (A) 219, 231
S v Mavuso 1987 3 SA 499 (A) 164
S v Mayo and Another 1990 (1) SACR 659 (E) 55, 169
S v Mbambo 1975 (2) SA 549 (A) 407
S v Mbata en andere 1977 (1) SA 379 (O) 321
S v Mbatha; S v Prinsloo 1996 (2) SA 464 (CC) 436
S v Mbothoma en 'n Ander 1978 (2) SA 530 (O) 461
S v Mbovana and others 1985 (1) SA 224 (C) 102

TABLE OF CASES | 565

S v Mcasa and Another 2005 (1) SACR 388 (SCA) 288, 412
S v Mdlongwa 2010 (2) SACR 419 (SCA)..................422
S v Melani 1996 (1) SACR 335 (E)..................188
S v Melani and Others 1996 (1) SACR 335 (E) 288
S v Mello and Another 1999 (2) SACR 255 (CC)..................436
S v Meyer 2017 JDR 1728 (GJ)..................120, 125, 126, 127, 128, 130, 136, 146, 153
S v Mfene and Another 1998 (9) BCLR 1157 (N)..................190, 191
S v MG 2010 (2) SACR 66 (ECG) 385
S v Mgcina 2007 (1) SACR 82 (T)..................190
S v Mgcwabe (2015) (2) SACR 517 (ECG) 313
S v Mgengwana 1964 (2) SA 149 (C)..................395
S v Mia and Another 2009 (1) SACR 330 (SCA)..................378
S v Mia and Another 2009 (1) SACR 330 (SCA); [2009] 1 All SA 447 (SCA)..................407
S v Miller and Others [2015] 4 All SA 503 (WCC) 141
S v Miller and Others 2016 (1) SACR 251 (WCC) 120, 123, 127, 133
S v Mjoli and Another 1981 (3) SA 1233 (A)..................2, 72, 407, 457
S v Mkhabela 1984 (1) SA 556 (A) 466
S v Mkhize (CC55/11 D) [2011] ZAKZDHC 62; 2012 (2) SACR 90 (KZD) (8 December 2011) 240
S v Mkohle 1990 (1) SACR 95 (A) 257
S v Mlimo 2008 (2) SACR 48 (SCA)..................208
S v Mocke 2008 (2) SACR 674 (SCA) 379
S v Mofokeng 1982 (4) SA 147 (T) 451
S v Mokahtsa 1993 (1) SACR 408 (C) 451
S v Mokgeledi 1968 (4) SA 335 (A) 2
S v Mokoena 1967 (1) SA 440 (A) 231
S v Mokoena; S v Phaswane 2008 (2) SACR 216 (T)..................83
S v Moletsane 1962 (2) SA 182 (E) 327
S v Molimi 2008 (3) SA 608 (CC)..................268, 495
S v Monyane and Others 2001 (1) SACR 115 (T) 292
S v Moolman 1996 (1) SACR 267 (A)..................168, 250, 256
S v Moroney 1978 (4) SA 389 (A) 72
S v Mosoinyane 1998 (1) SACR 583 (T)..................111
S v Mpetha and Others (2)1983 (1) SA 576 (C) 445
S v Mphala and Another 1998 (1) SACR 654 (W)..................186, 194
S v Mpofu 1993 (3) SA 864 (N) 253, 327
S v Mpumlo and Others 1986 (3) SA 485 (E)..................117
S v Mpumlo and others 1987 (2) SA 442 (SE) 100, 105
S v Msimango and Another 2010 (1) SACR 544 (GSJ)..................336
S v Mthembu 2008 (2) SACR 407 (SCA)..................179, 182, 191
S v Mthembu and Others 1988 (1) SA 145 (A) 231
S v Mthethwa 2004 (1) SACR 449 (E)..................192, 289
S v Mthethwa 2017 JDR 0551 (WCC)..................145
S v Mthetwa 1972 (3) SA 766 (A)..................70, 400, 409, 423
S v Mthimkulu 1975 (4) SA 759 (A)..................140, 427, 429
S v Mtsweni 1985 (1) SA 590 (A) 421
S v Muchindu 2000 (2) SACR 313 (W)..................492
S v Mulula [2014] ZASCA 103 400

S v Mushimba en Andere 1977 (2) SA 829 (A) 171
S v Naidoo and Another 1998 (1) SACR 479 (N).......182, 188
S v Nala 1965 (4) SA 360 (A) 465
S v Ncube and Another 1976 (1) SA 798 (RA) 287
S v Ncube; S v Mphateng en 'n Ander 1981 (3) SA 511 (T).......441
S v Ndawonde 2013 (2) SACR 192 (KZN).......397
S v Ndhlovu and Others 2001 (1) SACR 85 (W) 445
S v Ndhlovu and Others 2002 (2) SACR 325 (SCA).......268, 270, 271, 272
S v Ndika and Others 2002 (1) SACR 250 (SCA).......454
S v Ndiki and Others [2007] 2 All SA 185 (Ck).......137, 150
S v Ndiki and Others [2007] 2 ALL SA 185 (Ck) 122
S v Ndiki and Others 2008 (2) SACR 252 (Ck) 123, 124, 127, 128, 133, 134, 135, 136, 146, 147
S v Ndlovu 1987 (1) PH H37 (A) 57
S v Nduli and Others 1993 (2) SACR 501 (A).......444
S v Nduna 2011 (1) SACR 115 (SCA).......202
S v Nel 1990 (2) SACR 136 (C) 167
S v Nell 2009 (2) SACR 37 (CPD).......182
S v Ngcina 2007 (1) SACR 19 (SCA).......378
S v Ngcobo 1998 JDR 0747 (N).......186
S v Nglengethwa 1996 (1) SACR 737 (A) 492
S v Ngwani 1990 (1) SACR 449 (N).......269
S v Ngwenya and Others 1998 (2) SACR 503 (W) 192
S v Nieuwoudt 1990 (4) SA 217 (A).......118, 168
S v Nkata and Others 1990 (4) SA 250 (A).......283
S v Nkibane 1989 (2) SA 421 (NC) 337
S v Nkombani and Another 1963 (4) SA 877 (A) 290
S v Nkosi and Another 2011 (2) SACR 482 (SCA).......66
S v Nkwanyana 1978 (3) SA 404 (N) 449
S v Nombewu 1996 (2) SACR 396 (E).......188, 445
S v Nortjé 1996 (2) SACR 308 (C) 537
S v Ntlantsi [2007] 4 All SA 941 (C) 180
S v Nyabo [2009] 2 All SA 271 (SCA).......400
S v Nyathe 1988 (2) SA 211 (O) 466
S v O 2003 (2) SACR 147 (C) 212, 213, 217
S v Ohlenschlager 1992 (1) SACR 695 (T) 533, 534
S v Oosthuizen 1982 (3) SA 571 (T).......384, 420
S v Orrie and Another 2004 (1) SACR 162 (C) 292, 468
S v Orrie and Another 2005 (1) SACR 63 (C) 180, 192
S v Parrow 1973 (1) SA 603 (A) 289
S v Peake 1962 (4) SA 288 (C) 112, 301
S v Petane 1988 (3) SA 51 (C) 430
S v Peters 1992 (1) SACR 292 (E) 445
S v Pillay [2011] ZAWCHC 106.......397
S v Pillay and Others 2004 (2) SACR 419 (SCA).......179, 180, 182, 187
S v QN 2012 (1) SACR 380 (KZP).......510, 512
S v R 1965 (2) SA 463 (W).......259
S v Radebe and Another 1968 (4) SA 410 (A) 445
S v Raghubar (148/12) [2012] ZASCA 188 (30 November 2012) 314

TABLE OF CASES

S v Raghubar 2013 (1) SACR 398 (SCA) 509
S v Rall 1982 (1) SA 828 (A) 326
S v Ramabokela and Another 2011 (1) SACR 122 (GNP) 378
S v Ramaligela en 'n Ander 1983 (2) SA 424 (V) 286
S v Ramalope 1995 (1) SACR 616 (A) 346, 347
S v Ramavhale 1996 (1) SACR 639 (A) 252, 271
S v Ramgobin and Others 1986 (4) SA 117 (N) 117
S v Ramroop 1991 (1) SACR 555 (N) 398
S v Rathumbu 2012 (2) SACR 219 (SCA) 271
S v Rautenbach 2014 (1) SACR 1 (GSJ) 270
S v Reddy and Others 1996 (2) SACR 1 (A) 412, 414
S v Robertson en Andere 1981 (1) SA 460 (C) 445
S v Robiyana and Others 2009 (1) SACR 104 (Ck) 417
S v Ross 2013 (1) SACR 77 (WCC) 87
S v Rululu 2013 (1) SACR 117 (ECG) 87
S v S 1977 (3) SA 830 (A) 214
S v S 1990 (1) SACR 5 (A) 261
S v S 1995 (1) SACR 50 (ZS) 259, 510
S v Safatsa and Others 1988 (1) SA 868 (A) 281
S v Sampson and Another 1989 (3) SA 239 (A) 454
S v Sauls 1981 (3) SA 172 (A) 399
S v Sauls and Others 1981 (3) SA 172 (A) 398
S v SB 2014 (1) SACR 66 (SCA) 470
S v Schultz and Another 1989 (1) SA 465 (T) 445
S v Scott-Crossley 2008 (1) SACR 223 (SCA) 56, 168, 244, 256, 257, 390, 392
S v Sebejan and Others 1997 (1) SACR 626 (W) 192, 289
S v Sebejan and Others 1997 (8) BCLR 1806 (T) 192
S v Segone 1981 (1) SA 410 (T) 445
S v Seleke 1980 (3) SA 745 (A) 443
S v Seleke en 'n Ander 1980 (3) SA 745 (A) 72, 73, 444
S v Sesetse en 'n Ander 1981 (3) SA 353 (A) 444
S v Sesetse en Andere 1981 (3) SA 353 (A) 443
S v Shabalala 1966 (2) SA 297 (A) 412
S v Shabalala 1986 (4) SA 734 (A) 165, 168, 169
S v Shaik and Others 2007 (1) SA 240 (SCA) 270
S v Shaw [2011] ZAKZPHC 32: AR 342/10 (1 August 2011) 416
S v Sheehama 1991 (2) SA 860 (A) 450, 451, 458
S v Shuping and Others 1983 (2) SA 119 (B) 66
S v Sibisi 1976 (2) SA 162 (N) 112
S v Sihlani & Another 1966 (3) SA 148 (E) 29
S v Sihlani and Another 1966 (3) SA 148 (E) 29
S v Singh and Another 1975 (1) SA 330 (N) 117
S v Singo 2002 (4) SA 858 (CC) 47, 436
S v Sinkankanka and Another 1963 (2) SA 531 (A) 357
S v Sithole [2013] ZASCA 55 400
S v Snyman 1968 (2) SA 582 (A) 395, 534
S v Soci 1998 (2) SACR 275 (E) 180, 182, 188, 191
S v Soko and Another 1963 (2) SA 248 (T) 428

S v Sole 2004 (2) SACR 599 (Les) 203
S v Spies and Another 2000 (1) SACR 312 (SCA) 533
S v Staggie and Another 2003 (1) BCLR 43 (C) 239
S v Staggie and Another 2003 SACR 232 (C) 272
S v Stefaans 1999 (1) SACR 182 (C) 84
S v Steyn en Andere 1987 (1) SA 353 (W) 370
S v Strydom 1978 (4) SA 748 (E) 429
S v Swanepoel en 'n Ander 1980 (1) SA 144 (NC) 105
S v T 1963 (1) SA 484 (A) 236, 258
S v Tandwa 2008 (1) SACR 613 (SCA) 180, 186, 187
S v Tandwa and Others 2008 (1) SACR 613 (SCA) 182, 183, 187, 194, 283, 291, 424
S v Terblanche 2011 (1) SACR 77 (ECG) 397
S v Thebus and Another 2003 (2) SACR 319 (CC) 289
S v Theron 1968 (4) SA 61 (T) 290
S v Thurston en 'n Ander 1968 (3) SA 284 (A) 310
S v Trainor 2003 (1) SACR 35 (SCA) 57, 378
S v Tshabalala 1980 (3) SA 99 (A) 104
S v Tuge 1966 (4) SA 565 (A) 253
S v V 1961 (4) SA 201 (O) 259
S v V 1962 (3) SA 365 (E) 229, 230
S v V 1995 (1) SACR 173 (T) 321
S v Van der Sandt 1997 (2) SACR 116 (W) 87, 274
S v Van der Vyver 2008 (1) SA 556 (C) 467
S v Van der Westhuizen 2011 (2) SACR 26 (SCA) 328, 330, 444
S v Van Deventer and Another 2012 (2) SACR 263 (WCC) 193, 194
S v Van Dyk 1998 (2) SACR 363 (W) 398
S v Van Rensburg 1963 (2) SA 343 (N) 330
S v Van Schoor 1993 (1) SACR 202 (E) 288
S v Van Vuuren 1983 (2) SA 34 (SWA) 251
S v Vilakazi 2009 (1) SACR 552 (SCA) 511
S v Vumazonke 2000 (1) SACR 619 (C) 399
S v Waite 1978 (3) SA 896 (O) 287
S v Webber 1971 (3) SA 754 (A) 399
S v Williams 1991 (1) SACR 1 (C) 454
S v Wilmot 2002 (2) SACR 145 (SCA) 203, 231
S v Witbooi and others 2018 (1) SACR 670 (ECG) 449
S v Yanta 2000 (1) SACR 237 (Tk) 270, 336
S v Yende 1987 (3) SA 367 (A) 451
S v Yolelo 1981 (1) SA 1002 (A) 445
S v Zuma 1995 (2) SA 642 (CC) 436
S v Zuma 2006 (2) SACR 191 (W) 162, 199, 200
S v Zuma and Others 1995 (1) SACR 568 (CC) 183, 456
S v Zuma and Others 1995 (2) SA 642 (CC) 46, 434
S v Zwane and Others 1993 (1) SACR 748 (W) 247
S v Zwane and Others 1993 (3) SA 393 (W) 337
S v Zwayi 1997 (2) SACR 772 (Ck) 289

TABLE OF CASES 569

Saayman v Road Accident Fund 2011 (1) SA 106 (SCA) 351
SACCAWU obo Dolo v Somerset Wines International (Pty) Ltd [2009] 10 BALR 1069 (CCMA) 476
SAI Investments v Van der Schyff NO and Others 1999 (3) SA 340 (N) 505
Sajid v The Juma Masjid Trust (1999) 20 ILJ 1975 (CCMA) 520
SAMWU obo Abrahams and Others v City of Cape Town (2008) 17 LC 4.2.1 518
Santam Bpk v Biddulph 2004 (5) SA 586 (SCA) 376, 377
SAR v Hermanus Municipality 1931 CPD 184 91
Saridakis t/a Auto Nest v Lamont 1993 (2) SA 164 (C) 499
Sasol Mining (Pty) Ltd v Commissioner Nggeleni and Others [2011] 4 BLLR 404 (LC) 375
Sasol Mining (Pty) Ltd v Ngzeleni NO and Others (2011) 32 ILJ 723 (LC);
    (Unreported JR 1595/08) [2010] ZALC 141, 1 October 2010 529
SATAWU and Others v Protea Security Services
    (unreported case number JS754/2001: 24 November 2004) 476
Saturley v CIBC World Markets Inc. 2012 NSSC 226 ....150, 151
Savoi and Others v National Director of Public Prosecutions and Another 2014 (1) SACR 545 (CC) 539
Savoi and Others v National Director of Public Prosecutions and Another 2014 (5) SA 317 (CC) 539
Savoi and Others v NDPP and Another 2014 (1) SACR 545 (CC) 270
Scagell and Others v Attorney-General of the Western Cape and Others 1997 (2) SA 368 (CC) 76
Scagell and Others v Attorney-General, Western Cape and Others 1997 (2) SA 368 (CC)....46, 434, 437
Schneider NO and Others v AA and Another 2010 (5) SA 203 (WCC) 212, 213, 214, 215
Scholtz v Commissioner Maseko NO and Others (2000) 21 ILJ 1854 (LC) 519
Seccombe and Others v Attorney-General and Others 1919 TPD 270 99
Sedick and Another v Krisray (Pty) Ltd [2011] 8 BALR 879 (CCMA) 525
See Kroukam v SA Airlink (Pty) Ltd (2005) 26 ILJ 2153 (LAC) 516
Seetal v Pravitha NO and Another 1983 (3) SA 827 (D) 292, 469
Senior and Another v CIR 1960 (1) SA 709 (A) 254
Seyisi v S (117/12) [2012] ZASCA 144 (28 September 2012) 464
Shabalala and Others v Attorney-General of Transvaal and Another 1995 (2) SACR 761 (CC) 469, 472
Shabalala and Others v Attorney-General Transvaal and Another 1995 (2)
    SACR 761 (CC) 218, 300, 302, 303
Shabalala and Others v Attorney-General, Transvaal and Another 1995 (2) SACR 761 (CC) 47
Shell SA (Edms) Bpk en Andere v Voorsitter, Dorperaad van die Oranje-Vrystaat en Andere
    1992 (1) SA 906 (O) 172, 491
Shilubana and Others v Nwamitwa 2007 (5) SA 620 (CC) 27
Shilubana and Others v Nwamitwa 2009 (2) SA 66 (CC) 19
Shilubana and Others v Nwamitwa and Others 2009 (2) SA 66 (CC) 22, 25
Shoba v Officer Commanding, Temporary Police Camp, Wagendrift Dam 1995 (4) SA 1 (A) 143
Shoprite Checkers (Pty) Ltd v Ramdaw NO and Others (2000) 21 ILJ 1232 (LC) 519
Sigasa v Kemklean Hygiene Systems [1997] 4 BLLR 494 (CCMA) 522
Sigcau v Sigcau 1944 AD 67 ....22, 25
Sihlali v South African Broadcasting Corporation Ltd (2010) 31 ILJ 1477 (LC) 125
Sikhula Sonke obo Pedro v CCMA and Others (2007) 28 ILJ 1322 (LC) 519
Sila & Another v Masuku 1937 NAC (N&T) 121 37
Singh and Others v S 2016 (2) SACR 443 (SCA) 537, 540
Singh v Govender Brothers Construction 1986 (3) SA 613 (N) 104
Skilya Property Investments (Pty) Ltd v Lloyds of London Underwriting 2002 (3) SA 765 (T) 273

Slaughter v State 108 P 3d 1052, 2005 OK CR 6	483
Smit v His Majesty King Goodwill Zwelithini Kabhekuzulu 2009 JDR 1361 (KZP)	30, 37
Smith v The Queen (2001) 206 CLR 650	162
Smuts v Backup Storage Facilities and Others [2003] 2 BALR 219 (CCMA)	525
Sosibo and Others v Ceramic Tile Market (2001) 22 ILJ 811 (CCMA)	476
South African Airways Soc v BDFM Publishers (Pty) Ltd and Others 2016 (2) SA 561 (GJ)	281
South African Airways Society v BDFM Publishers Pty Ltd and others 2016 (2) SA 561 (GJ)	284

South African Rugby Football Union and Others v President of the
RSA and Others 1998 (4) SA 296 (T) 284

South Cape Corporation (Pty) Ltd v Engineering Management
Services (Pty) Ltd 1977 (3) SA 534 (A) 63, 64, 65

Southern Life Association Ltd v Beyleveld NO 1989 (1) SA 496 (A)	499
Southern Sun Hotel Interests (Pty) Ltd v CCMA and Others (2010) 31 ILJ 452 (LC)	529
Southern Sun Hotels (Pty) Ltd v SACCAWU and Another (2000) 21 ILJ 1315 (LAC)	521
Spencer v R 1946 NPD 696	230

Spring Forest Trading CC v Wilberry (Pty) Ltd t/a Ecowash and Another 2015 (2)
SA 118 (SCA) 125, 126

Standard Bank of SA Ltd v Cohen (1) 1993 (3) SA 846 (SE)	77
Standard Bank of SA Ltd v Minister of Bantu Education 1966 (1) SA 229 (N)	321
Standard Bank of SA Ltd v Mosime NO and Another [2008] 10 BLLR 1010 (LC)	530
Standard Bank of SA Ltd v Neugarten and Others 1987 (3) SA 695 (W)	92
Standard Bank of SA Ltd v Stama (Pty) Ltd 1975 (1) SA 730 (A)	499
Standard Merchant Bank Ltd v Rowe and Others 1982 (4) SA 671 (W)	102
Steen and Wetherleys (Pty) Ltd (2005) 15 CCMA 7.1.6	476

Stellenbosch Farmers' Winery Group Ltd and Another v Martell et
Cie and Others 2003 (1) SA 11 (SCA) 375, 382, 383, 385, 529

Stellenbosch Farmers' Winery Ltd v Vlachos t/a The Liquor Den 2001 (3) SA 597 (SCA)	500
Steyn v Gagiono en 'n Ander 1982 (3) SA 562 (NC)	107
Stirland v Director of Public Prosecutions [1944] AC 315	223
Stocks & Stocks Properties (Pty) Ltd v City of Cape Town 2003 (5) SA 140 (C)	106
Sublime Technologies (Pty) Ltd v Jonker and Another [2009] JOL 24639 (SCA)	129
Sublime Technologies (Pty) Ltd v Jonker and Another 2010 (2) SA 522 (SCA)	129
Sugreen v Standard Bank of SA (2002) 23 ILJ 1319 (CCMA)	526
Suliman v Hansa 1971 (4) SA 69 (D)	303
Swanepoel v Minister van Veiligheid en Sekuriteit 1999 (2) SACR 284 (T)	303

Swissborough Diamond Mines (Pty) Ltd and Others v Government of RSA and
Others 1999 (2) SA 279 (T) 270, 296, 298

T

Tactical Reaction Services CC v Beverley Estate II Homeowners' Association
(2007/16441) [2010] ZAGPJHC 102 (5 November 2010) 499

Telewizja Polska USA Inc. v Echostar Satellite Corp 2004 WL 2367740	152
Teper v R [1952] 2 All ER 447 (PC)	252

Thatcher v Minister of Justice and Constitutional Development and Others 2005 (1)
SACR 238 (C) 288

The Citizen v McBride 2010 (4) SA 148 (SCA)	427

TABLE OF CASES | 571

The President of the Republic of South Africa and Others v M & G
  Media Ltd 2011 (2) SA 1 (SCA) 298
Thint (Pty) Ltd v National Director of Public Prosecutions and Others;
  Zuma v National Director of Public Prosecutions and Others 2008 (2) SACR 421 (CC)................284
Thint (Pty) Ltd v NDPP and Others; Zuma v NDPP and Others 2009 (1) SA 1 (CC)......................142
Thomas v David 1836 (7) C&P 350 249
Thompson v R [1918] AC 221 (HL) 200
Thompson v R [1918] AC 221 (HL); [1918] All ER 521 (HL)..202
Titty's Bar and Bottle Store (Pty) Ltd v ABC Garage (Pty) Ltd and Others 1974 (4) SA 362 (T)............91
Transnet Ltd v Newlyn Investments (Pty) Ltd 2011 (5) SA 543 (SCA) 102, 357
Transvaal Industrial Foods Ltd v BMM Process (Pty) Ltd 1973 (1) SA 627 (A) 350
Tregea and Another v Godart and Another 1939 AD 16...75, 433
Trend Finance (Pty) Ltd and another v Commissioner for SARS and Another [2005] 4
  All SA 657 (C)...129
Triplex Safety Glass Co Ltd v Lancegaye Safety Glass (1934) Ltd [1939] 2 KB 395, 408–9
  (Eng CA 1938)...288
Trust Bank of Africa Ltd v Senekal 1977 2 SA 587(W) 71
Trust Bank van Afrika Bpk v Eksteen 1964 (3) SA 402 (A) 498
Trustees for the Time Being of the Delsheray Trust and Others v ABSA Bank Limited [2014]
  JOL 32417 (WCC) 120
Trustees for the time being of the Delsheray Trust and Others v ABSA Bank Limited [2014]
  4 All SA 748 (WCC)...139, 140, 141
Truworths Ltd v CCMA and Others [2008] JOL 22565 (LC) 476
Twine v Rubber Rollers (Pty) Ltd [1999] 3 BLLR 285 (LC) 529

U

U-Haul Intern Inc. v Lumbermens Mut. Cas.Co 576 F.3d 1040 (9th Cir. 2009) 151
Union Government v Vianini Ferro-Concrete Pipes Pty (Ltd) 1941 AD 43 77
United States v Chemical Foundation Inc. 272 U.S. 1, 14-15 (1926)..140
United States v Lard 734 F 2d 1290 (8th Cir)(1984) 537
United States v Lizarraga-Tirado (9th Cir. 2015) F 3d. 2015 WL 3772772................................152
United States v Posado 57 F 3rd 428 (5th Cir) (1995) 476
United States v Rollins 2004 WL 26780...152
United States v Scheffer 523 US 303 (1998) 478
United States v Semrau (2012) 2nd Circuit Court of Appeals of the United States.
  No. 11-5396, 6 486
United States v Semrau 693 F.3d 510 (6th Cir. 2012) 486
Uramin (Incorporated in British Columbia) t/a Areva Resources Southern Africa v Perie 2017
  (1) SA 236 (GJ) 85, 143

V

Vaatz v Law Society of Namibia 1991 (3) SA 563 (Nm) 90
Van Aswegen and Another v Drotskie and Another 1964 (2) SA 391 (O) 93
van Breda and Others v Jacobs and Others, 1921 AD 330...11, 22
Van der Berg v Coopers & Lybrand Trust (Pty) Ltd and Others 2001 (2) SA 242 (SCA)..................162
Van der Harst v Viljoen 1977 (1) SA 795 (C) 469

572 THE LAW OF EVIDENCE IN SOUTH AFRICA

Van der Heever v Die Meester en Andere 1997 (3) SA 93 (T)..........282
Van der Linde v Calitz 1967 (2) SA 239 (A) 5, 6, 7, 9, 296
Van der Merwe and Others v Additional Magistrate, Cape Town and Others 2010 (1)
    SACR 470 (C)..........142
Van Niekerk v Pretoria City Council 1997 (3) SA 839 (T)..........284
Van Willing and Another v S (109/2014) [2015] ZASCA 52 (27 March 2015) 252
Venevene v Hlandlini 1972/74 AC 109 (S) (Elliotdale)..........37
Volkwyn v Truworths Ltd [2002] 4 BALR 455 (CCMA) 525

W

Waddell Eyles NO and Welsh NO 1939 TPD 198..........286
Waste Products Utilisation (Pty) Ltd v Wilkes and Another 2003 (2) SA 515 (W) 172
Weintraub v Oxford Brick Works (Pty) Ltd 1948 (1) SA 1090 (T) 320, 321
Welz and Another v Hall and Others 1996 (4) SA 1073 (C)..........103, 272
Whittaker v Roos and Another 1911 TPD 1092 460
Wilson v Corestaff Services. L.P. 2010 NY Slip Op 20176 [28 Misc 3d 425] 486
Winsor v Dove 1951 (4) SA 42 (N) 93
Woji v Santam Insurance Co Ltd 1981 (1) SA 1020 (A)..........512
Woolworths (Pty) Ltd v CCMA and Others (2011) 32 ILJ 2455 (LAC) 517

Y

YM v LB (465/09) [2010] ZASCA 106 (17 September 2010)..........469
YM v LB 2010 (6) SA 338 (SCA) 114

Table of legislation

A

Admiralty Jurisdiction Regulation Act 105 of 1983

Section 6(3) 270
Section 6(4) 270
Appellate Jurisdiction Act of 1876 4
Arms and Ammunition Act 75 of
1969 (repealed) 436
Section 40(1) 436
Australian Evidence Act, 1995
Section 29(2) 39

B

Basic Conditions of Employment Act 75
of 1997 515
Bill of Rights 7, 9, 20, 24, 27, 44, 45, 46,
64, 172, 175, 176, 180, 295, 410, 441, 536
Section 35(5) 170
Black Administration Act 38 of 1927 31
Section 12 .... 31, 33
Section 12(4) 32
Section 20 .... 31, 33
Section 20(2) 32
Budapest Convention of Cybercrime 143

C

Canada Evidence Act, 1985 150
Section 30 150
Section 31 150
Canadian Charter of Rights and Freedoms,
Part I of the Constitution Act 1982 .... 176, 188
Section 24(2) 188
Cape Evidence Ordinance 4, 5
Chiefs and Headmen's Civil Courts Rules 32
Rule 5 32
Rule 6 32
Rule 7 32
Rule 11 32
Child Justice Act 75 of 2008 76
Section 7(1) 76, 434
Children's Act 38 of 2005 215
Section 36 .... 72, 438, 470
Section 37 .... 113, 470
Civil Evidence Act 1995 (England) 148

Civil Evidence Act of 1968 219
Sections 11-13 219
Civil Proceedings Evidence Act 25
of 1965 .... 5, 6, 7, 108, 121, 131,
132, 138, 219, 273, 275, 522
Part IV 360
Section 2 .... 54, 163, 168
Section 4 .... 113, 210
Section 5 430
Section 7 369
Section 8 309
Section 9 310
Section 10 294
Section 10(1) 312
Section 10(2) 312
Section 10A 312
Section 12 .... 294, 312
Section 14 .... 286, 288
Section 15 459
Section 16 398
Section 17 86
Section 18(1) 105
Section 19(1) 100, 105
Section 20 105
Section 22(1) 86, 275
Section 25 86
Section 26 .... 275, 428
Sections 27-32 106
Sections 27-38 148
Section 28 275
Section 31 293
Section 33 .... 99, 117
Sections 33-38 (Part VI) 8, 87, 101,
131, 132, 138, 275, 522
Section 34 .... 121, 127, 131, 132, 275, 528
Section 34(1) 106
Section 34(1)(a)(i) 131
Section 34(1)(a)(ii) 131
Section 34(2) 106, 262
Section 35(2) 360
Section 36 105
Section 37 106
Section 39 .... 81, 314
Section 40 .... 81, 314

574 | THE LAW OF EVIDENCE IN SOUTH AFRICA

Section 41...81
Section 42.................6, 81, 286, 288, 295,
                                    309, 365, 524
Civil Union Act 17 of 2006................................294
    Section 13..312
Colonial Laws Validity Act, 1865 (Britain)
    (repealed) 19
Combating of Rape Act 8 of 2000................258
    Section 6...258
    Section 7...258
Companies Act, 1973................................287
    Section 417(2)(b)...................................287
Companies Act 71 of 2008
    Section 50(4)...276
    Section 51(1)(c)......................................276
Computer Evidence Act 57 of 1983 ....8, 122, 123
Constitution Act, 1982
    Section 35(1), being Schedule B to the
        Canada Act, 1982, c. 11 (U.K.)...........39
Constitution of the Republic of South Africa, Act 200
    of 1993 (Interim Constitution).........28, 44, 175
    Section 25..46
Constitution of the Republic of
    South Africa, 1996 ....3, 6, 7, 9, 20, 31, 44,
                55, 66, 138, 296, 317, 450, 491
    Chapter 1, section 2.................................44
    Chapter 2...44
    Section 2..7, 536
    Sections 7–39 ....44, 172, 181
    Section 8(1) 44
    Section 8(2) 45
    Section 10...................................287, 292
    Section 10..465
    Section 12..181
    Section 12(1)(e).....................................292
    Section 12(2)..292
    Section 14..287
    Section 14..292
    Section 14(a)..465
    Section 14(d)..293
    Section 16..285
    Section 16(1)..297
    Section 16(1) of Schedule 6.......................31
    Section 28...114
    Section 28(2).....................................83, 469
    Section 32.......................................48, 284

Section 32(1)...298
Section 33(1)..49
Section 34..49, 297
Section 35.................45, 181, 282, 292, 441,
                                    450, 518
Section 35(1)......................................183, 185
Section 35(1)(a)................95, 180, 286, 422
Section 35(1)(b)..............................45, 286
Section 35(1)(c)............180, 286, 292, 465
Sections 35(1)–(3)....................................168
Section 35(3)............226, 241, 286, 539, 540
Section 35(3)(c).......................................297
Section 35(3)(e)..95
Section 35(3)(f).......................................180
Section 35(3)(f) and (g)..............................45
Section 35(3)(g).......................................180
Section 35(3)(h)...........45, 64, 95, 180, 290,
                                    422, 436, 465, 539
Section 35(3)(i)..............13, 45, 81, 95, 241,
                                    266, 268, 272, 336
Section 35(3)(j)..............180, 286, 287, 290,
                                    292, 311, 422, 465
Section 35(5)..........49, 168, 175, 178, 180,
                        190, 238, 291, 410, 437, 441, 536
Section 36............44, 48, 83, 181, 290, 539
Section 36(1)..44
Section 39(1)(b)..430
Section 39(1)(c)..................................176, 430
Section 39(2)......................................7, 9, 172
Section 44(2)...297
Section 166(e)...31
Section 146(2)..297
Section 198..297
Section 200(2)..297
Section 205(3)..297
Section 209(1)..297
Section 211..33
Constitutional Court Rules
    Rule 31...431
Consumer Protection Act 68 of 2008
    Section 50(1)..505
    Section 51(1)(g)......................................505
Council of Europe's Convention on
    Cybercrime 143
    23.XI.2001 143

Criminal Code	258
Section 275	258
Criminal Justice Act 2003 (England)	148
Section 118(2)	273
Criminal Law and Criminal Procedure Law	
Amendment Act 39 of 1989	239
Criminal Law (Forensic Procedures) Amendment	
Act 6 of 2010	464, 465
Criminal Law (Forensic Procedures) Amendment	
Act 37 of 2013	471
Criminal Law (Sexual Offences and Related	
Matters) Amendment Act 32 of 2007	
(Sexual Offences Act, 2007)	236, 401, 511
Section 58	237, 258, 511
Section 59	237, 258, 511
Section 60	242, 396, 400, 512
Section 20 of the draft Sexual	
Offences Bill	512
Criminal Procedure Act of 1865	
Section 6	248
Criminal Procedure Act 56 of 1955	442
Criminal Procedure Act 51 of 1977	2, 3, 5, 6,
7, 121, 131, 132, 138, 141, 142, 181, 224,	
262, 273, 320, 327, 336, 346, 350, 398,	
442, 445, 464, 491, 508, 522, 534	
Chapter 2	141
Chapters 21, 22, 23 and 24	3
Chapter 24 (sections 208–253)	138
Part III Schedule 2	316
Section 1	455
Section 3	39
Section 33	138
Section 36A	464
Section 36A	471
Section 36A(1)(*b*)	471
Section 36A(1) (cB)	472
Section 37	291, 464, 468, 469
Section 37(3)	291
Section 37(1)(*a*)	291
Section 37(1)(*c*)	291
Section 37(2)(*a*)	468
Section 41	192
Section 60(11)(*a*)	301
Section 60(11B)(*b*)	88
Section 60(11B)(*c*)	274, 293
Section 60(14)	48, 301, 302
Section 72(4)	48
Section 73(1), (2)	294

Section 77	490
Section 78(1A)	65
Section 78(1B)	65
Section 79	490
Section 79(7)	293
Section 87(1)	102
Section 107	64
Section 112	94
Section 112(1)	445
Section 113	445
Section 115	94, 321, 407, 442, 445, 457
Section 115(2)(*b*)	442
Section 115(3)	443
Section 145(4)	491
Section 150	320
Section 150(1)	323
Section 151	320, 328
Section 151(1)(*b*)(i)	95, 327
Section 151(1)(*b*)(ii)	58, 95
Section 153	508
Section 158	327
Section 158	508
Section 158(2)(*a*)	85
Section 158(3)	85
Section 159	327
Section 161	81
Section 162	81, 509
Section 162(1)	314
Section 163	81, 82, 314, 509
Section 164(1)	509
Section 166(1)	336, 346
Section 166(2)	336
Section 166(3)(*a*)	337
Section 169	114
Section 170A	82, 84, 508
Section 170A(2)(*b*)	83
Section 170A(3)(*b*)	83
Section 170A(3)(*c*)	83
Section 171(1)(*a*)	85
Section 174	66, 320
Section 175	350
Section 175(2)	350
Section 189	316
Section 189(1)	317
Section 190	365
Section 190(2)	369
Section 192	293, 309
Section 193	317

Section 194	310
Section 195(1)(*a–i*)	313
Section 196(1)	312
Section 196(1)(*a*)	311
Section 196(1)(*b*)	312
Section 196(2)	313
Section 197	225, 226, 228, 249
Section 197(*a*)	169, 229
Section 197(*a*)–(*d*)	229
Section 197(*b*)	230
Section 197(*c*)	169, 228, 230
Section 197(*d*)	230
Section 198	312
Section 198(1)	294, 312
Section 198(2)	294
Section 199	294
Section 200	286
Section 201	283
Section 202	295
Section 203	286, 288
Section 204	286, 287, 311, 370, 397
Section 204(1)(*a*)(iii)	287
Section 204(1)(*a*)(iv)	287
Section 205	286, 302, 316
Section 206	6, 309
Section 208	398
Section 209	404, 406, 407, 456
Section 210	54, 138, 166, 168, 246
Section 211	225, 249
Section 212	87, 88, 274, 464, 465
Section 212(1)	274
Section 212(2)	274
Section 212(3)	274
Section 212(4)	113, 274, 275
Section 212(4)(*a*)	87, 464
Section 212(5)	274
Section 212(6)	113
Section 212(7)	274
Section 212(8)	274, 469
Section 212A	87, 274
Section 213	262, 274
Section 214	274
Section 215	274, 528
Section 216	39
Section 217	442, 449, 452
Section 217(1)	453, 458
Section 217(1)(*a*)	455
Section 217(1)(*b*)(ii)	46, 436, 456

Section 218	442, 445, 450
Section 218(1)	450
Section 218(2)	450
Section 219	442, 447
Section 219A	286, 445, 447, 450, 458
Section 219A(1)	451
Section 220	72, 442, 443
Section 221	99, 122, 131, 138, 148, 274, 276, 522
Section 221(5)	138
Section 222	8, 87, 106, 127, 131, 138, 148, 262, 360, 522
Section 223	39
Section 224	430
Section 225	464
Section 225(1)	291
Section 225(2)	291
Section 227, as amended by the Sexual Offences Act, 2007	511
Section 227(2)	239
Section 227(2)–227(7)	337
Section 227(2)(*a*)	512
Section 227(4)	512
Section 227(5)	240
Section 227(6)	241, 512
Section 228	105, 113, 210
Section 229	428
Section 231(*a*)	106
Section 231(*b*)	106
Section 232	117, 430
Section 233	430
Section 233(1)	105
Section 234(1)	105
Section 235	275
Section 236	106, 131, 132, 138, 148, 275
Section 236(4)	293
Section 236A	132
Section 237	434, 438
Section 241	226
Section 246	106, 138
Section 247	138
Section 252	6, 224
Section 252(A)	524, 534, 536
Section 252A(1–7)	534
Section 252A(1)	534
Section 252A(2)	534
Section 252A(2)(*a*)	534
Section 252A(3)	534, 537

Section 252A(3)(*a*)	535, 536	Sections 12–15		275

Section 252A(3)(*a*) 535, 536
Section 252A(3)(*b*) 535, 536
Section 252A(6) 437, 495, 537
Section 271 ....226, 231
Section 276(1)(*i*) 193
Section 309A(1) 33
Section 337 ....112, 276
Section 337(*b*) 112
Criminal Procedure Amendment Act 56
   of 1979 445
Criminal Procedure Second Amendment
   Act 85 of 1996
   Section 1 534
Criminal Procedure Code Act 31 of 1917 442
Criminal Procedure and Evidence
   Act 31 of 1917 5
Cybercrimes and Cybersecurity Bill B-2015
   version
   Chapter 8 139
Cybercrimes and Cybersecurity Bill
   B6-2017 ....124, 138, 142, 143,145
   Chapter 5 142
   Section 24 144
   Section 61 146

D

Diplomatic Immunities and Privileges Act 37
   of 2001
   Section 3 315
Dissolution of Marriages on Presumption
   of Death Act 23 of 1979
   Section 1 438
Drugs and Drug Trafficking Act 140 of
   1992 ....436, 538
   Section 21(1)(*a*)(i) 46

E

Electronic Communications and
   Transactions Act 25 of 2002 ....3, 8, 9,
      116, 121, 123, 124, 129, 136, 138, 146
   Chapter Three 9
   Chapter XII 141
   Section 1 ....100, 126
   Section 2(*f*) 123
   Section 4 ....124, 138
   Section 11 124
   Section 12 124

Sections 12–15 275
Section 13 126
Section 13(1) 126
Section 13(2) 126
Section 13(3)(*a*) 126
Section 13(3)(*b*) 126
Section 13(4) 126
Section 14 125
section 14(2) 125
Section 15 ....127, 128, 146, 522
Section 15(1) 127
Section 15(1)(*a*) 127
Section 15(1)(*b*) 127, 128
Section 15(2) 136
Section 15(3) 136, 137
Section 15(4) 128, 131, 132, 147, 148
Section 17 126
Section 29(3) 293
Section 37 126
Section 82 141
Section 83 141
Section 92 123
Employee Polygraph Protection Act of 1994 476
Employment Equity Act 55 of 1998 516
   Section 6(1) 516
   Section 10 515
   Section 11 516
   Section 20(5) 516
English Criminal Procedure Act, 1865 288
   Section 4 365
   Section 5 366
Evidence Act of 1962 (repealed)
   Section 5 106
Evidence Act, 1995 (Australia)
   Section 72 39
Evidence Amendment Act
   Section 3 168
Evidence Proclamations of the Zuid-Afrikaanse
   Republiek (ZAR) and the Orange
   River Colony 4, 5

F

Federal Rules of
   Evidence (USA) 151, 153, 166, 484
   Rule 401 ....163, 166
   Rule 403 166
   Rule 702 484

578 | THE LAW OF EVIDENCE IN SOUTH AFRICA

Fifth Amendment (USA) ... 290
Finance and Financial Adjustments Acts
    Consolidation Act 11 of 1977
    Section 3 ... 535
Financial Intelligence Centre Act 38 of
    2001 (FICA) ... 538
    Section 38(3) ... 304
Forest Act 122 of 1984
    Section 84 ... 437

G

Gambling Act 51 of 1965 ... 437
    Section 6(3) ... 46, 437
General Law Amendment Act 62 of 1955
    Section 36 ... 48
    Section 37 ... 48

H

High Court Rules ... 67, 346
    Rule 6(15) ... 90
    Rule 6(5)(g) ... 92
    Rule 6(6) ... 93
    Rule 22(2) ... 459
    Rule 22(3) ... 460
    Rule 29 ... 346
    Rule 35 ... 102
    Rule 35(9) ... 105
    Rule 36(1) and (2) ... 217
    Rule 36(2) ... 217
    Rule 36(3) ... 218
    Rule 36(4) ... 218
    Rule 36(8) ... 218
    Rule 36(9)(a) ... 217
    Rule 36(9)(b) ... 217
    Rule 38 ... 315
    Rule 38(3) ... 86
    Rule 38(5)
    Rule 39(10) ... 350
    Rule 39(10) ... 350
    Rule 39(11) ... 67
    Rule 39(11) ... 67
    Rule 39(13) ... 67
    Rule 39(16)(d) ... 114
    Rule 39(5) ... 320, 326
    Rule 39(5) ... 67
    Rule 39(5) ... 67
    Rule 39(5) ... 67

Rule 39(7) ... 320, 326
Rule 39(8) ... 336, 346
Rule 39(9) ... 67
Rule 63 ... 100, 101
Rule 63(1)–(5) read with Rule 27(3) ... 106

I

Income Tax Act 58 of 1962 ... 193
Inquests Act 58 of 1959
    Section 2 ... 438
Insolvency Act 24 of 1936
    Section 69 ... 143
Interception and Monitoring Prohibition
    Act 127 of 1992 ... 527
International Co-operation in Criminal
    Matters Act 75 of 1996 ... 142
Internal Security Act 74 of 1982
    Section 66 ... 296
    Section 66(1) ... 296
    Section 66(2) ... 296
Interpretation Act 33 of 1957 ... 8
Intimidation Act 72 of 1982 ... 316
    Section 1 and 1A ... 316

J

Judicature Acts of 1873 and 1875 ... 4
Justice Laws Rationalisation Act 18
    of 1996 ... 20
Justices of the Peace and Commissioners
    of Oaths Act 16 of 1963 ... 87, 88, 455

L

Labour Relations Act 66 of 1995
    Section 6 ... 526
    Section 24 ... 515
    Section 68 ... 375, 515
    Section 138 ... 515,518, 520, 521, 525
    Section 187 ... 515
    Section 191(5)(a) ... 515
    Section 191(5)(b) ... 515
    Section 192 ... 515
    Section 200A ... 528
Law of Evidence Amendment Act 45
    of 1988 ... 3, 8, 24, 38, 121, 131, 132,
    138, 139, 147, 447, 540
    Section 1 ... 430
    Section 1(1) ... 20, 21, 211, 430, 431
    Section 1(2) ... 21, 211

TABLE OF LEGISLATION 579

Section 1(3)................................23
Section 3.................101, 127, 130, 131, 148,
238, 266, 273, 277, 448, 540
Section 3(1)................132, 251, 252,
253, 276, 540
Section 3(1)(a)...................132, 269
Section 3(1)(b)...................132, 268, 269
Section 3(1)(c)...........40, 130, 132, 137,
268, 269, 272, 273, 446
Section 3(1)(c)(i) to (vii)...........540
Section 3(2)....................448
Section 3(3).........................265, 270
Section 3(4).........................265, 267
Section 9...........................39

M

Magistrates' Courts Act 32 of 1944
Section 29A.........................32
Section 29A.........................33
Section 29A(1)–(2)..................33
Section 34..........................31
Section 51.........................315
Section 52...........................86
Section 53...........................86
Magistrates' Courts Amendment Act 67 of 1998
Section 1..........................31
Magistrates' Courts Rules...........67, 144, 346
Rule 23 102
Rule 24(1) and (2)(a) and (b) 217
Rule 24(2)(a) 217
Rule 24(3)(a) 218
Rule 24(4) 218
Rule 24(8) 218
Rule 24(9)(a)......................217
Rule 24(9)(b) 217
Rule 26...........................315
Rule 29(14).......................350
Rule 29(3).........................320, 321
Rule 29(7)..........................67, 326
Rule 29(8)...........................67
Rule 29(9)...........................67
Rule 29(10).........................67
Rule 30(1)(d) 114
Model Law on Electronic Commerce (the
UN 1996 Model Law)...........122, 123, 124,
126, 148, 150

N

Natal Code of Zulu Law GG No 10966, Proc
R.151 of 1987
Section 1............................35
Natal Colony Law 17 of 1859...........5
National Credit Act 34 of 2005
Section 93.........................505
Section 90(2)(h) and (i).............505
National Prosecuting Authority Act 32 of 1998
Section 28.........................284
Section 29.........................284
National Veld and Forest Fire Act 101 of 1998
Section 34.........................437

O

Ordinance 72 of 1830 4

P

Powers, Privileges and Immunities of
Parliament and Provincial Legislatures
Act 4 of 2004 315
Section 9.........................315
Prevention and Combating of Corruption and
Corrupt Activities Act 12 of 2004.......538
Section 25 528
Prevention of Organised Crime Act 121
of 1998...........................227, 538
Chapter 5.........................139
Chapter 6.........................139
Definitions and Interpretations.......538
Section 1(2)........................538
Section 1(3)........................538, 539
Section 2...........................538, 539
Section 2(1)........................227
Section 2(1)(e).....................541
Section 2(2)........................270, 538, 539
Section 4...........................538
Section 5...........................538
Section 6...........................538
Section 9...........................538
Proceeds of Crime Act 76 of 1996.......538
Proclamation 11 of 1902 4
Promotion of Access to Information Act 2
of 2000 (PAIA).....................295, 298
Chapter 4.........................299
Section 3..........................298

580 THE LAW OF EVIDENCE IN SOUTH AFRICA

Section 5 299
Section 11 299
Section 39 302
Section 39(1) 302
Section 46 .... 299, 302
Section 46(b) 303
Protection of Constitutional Democracy
Against Terrorist and Related Activities
Act 33 of 2004 538
Protection of Information Bill 6 of 2010 295
Protection of Information Act 84 of 1982 295

R

Recognition of Customary Marriages Act 120
of 1998 26
Section 3(6) 40
Reform of Customary Law of Succession and
Regulation of Related Matters Act 11
of 2009 41
Section 1 35
Section 1(a) 41
Section 4(2) 35
Regulation of Interception of Communications
and Provisions of Communication-related
Information Act 70 of 2002 (RICA) 524, 526
Chapter 3 141
Section 6 525
Restitution of Land Rights Act 22 of 1994
Section 30(2)(a) 270
Revenue Laws Amendment Act 60 of 2008
Section 103 107
Rules for the Conduct of Proceedings in the
Labour Court
Rule 6 530

S

Safety Matters Rationalisation Act 90 of 1996
Section 1 296
Small Claims Courts Act 61 of 1984 270
Section 26 270
South African Citizenship Act 88 of 1995
Section 2 24

South African Police Service Act 68
of 1995 .... 465, 471
Chapter 5B 468
Section 15A 465
Section 15B 465
Special Courts for Blacks Abolition Act 34
of 1986 .... 28, 31
Stamp Duties Act 77 of 1968
Section 12 107
Superior Courts Act 10 of 2013
Section 36 315
Section 39 86
Section 40 86
Section 47 315

T

Traditional Authorities Act 25 of 2000 (Namibia)
Section 7 27
Traditional Courts Bill
Section 7(4)(b) 32
Traditional Leadership and Governance
Framework Act 41 of 2003 27
Section 18(1)(a) 27
Section 20(1) 27
Tax Administration Act 28 of 2011
Section 67(1) 304
Section 68(1)(b) 304
Section 68(4) 304

U

Uniform Electronic Evidence Act, 1999 150
Uniform Rules of Court
Rule 35 .... 125, 143

V

Value Added Tax Act 89 of 1991 193
Section 58(a) 193
Section 58(c) 193
section 58(d) 193

Glossary

a quo (Latin): from which; for example the court *a quo* – the court from which the decision came

accused: a person (private or legal) charged with a crime (*see* defendant)

actus reus (Latin): the action or conduct which is a constituent element of the crime

ad (Latin): towards (used in the current sense of 'about' or 'with regard to'

adjectival law: *see* procedural law

administration of justice: refers to various persons who and bodies which administer justice such as the police, courts, legal profession, correctional services and the National Prosecuting Authority (NPA)

admissibility: permitting information to be considered by the court – once information is *admitted (*allowed into court), it becomes evidence before the court

admissions: statements made orally or in writing in civil and criminal matters where certain facts or issues are admitted and therefore, generally, evidence need not be led to prove them (*see* formal and informal admissions)

adversarial procedure: in a trial the opposing parties are responsible for finding and presenting evidence

adversarial system: a court system characterised by a passive judge and where the litigants, or lawyers on their behalf, lead and cross-examine witnesses. The judge is effectively a referee of the dispute but has the power to intervene in prescribed circumstances, a power that is sparingly exercised (*see* inquisitorial system)

affidavit: a written statement that is sworn to or affirmed by the person making it before a commissioner of oaths; it is written evidence; it is the primary means of placing evidence before a court in application proceedings

affirmation: this is where witnesses in criminal and civil matters affirm that they will speak the truth and has the same legal effect as taking an oath (*see* oath)

aliunde (Latin): from elsewhere

animus confitendi (Latin): the intention to make a confession

antagonistic *animus*: a witness who does not actually want to tell the truth 'at the instance of the party calling him'

appeal: a procedure whereby a decision of a lower court is considered by a higher court to establish whether the decision of the lower court was correct

appellant: a party appealing against a judgment or order

Appellate Division: previously the highest court of appeal in South Africa; it has now been renamed the Supreme Court of Appeal

applicant: a party applying to court for an order

application: court proceedings brought by a notice of motion supported by affidavits; oral applications may also be made by counsel from the bar at court

audi alteram partem (Latin): hear the other side; it is a principle of our law that courts will not generally grant an order without hearing the version of the party against whom the order is sought

authenticity (of document): one of the requirements for admitting a document into court is that the authorship of the document must be proved

autrefois acquit (French): a plea that an accused can raise if he or she has previously been acquitted of a crime and is subsequently charged again with the same offence

autrefois convict (French): a plea that an accused can raise if he or she has been previously convicted of a crime and is subsequently charged again with the same offence

bail: security, usually a sum of money, that is paid in exchange for the release of an arrested person. If bail cannot be paid or is refused by the court, the arrested person is detained until his or her next court appearance. Bail is used as a guarantee of that person's appearance for his or her trial and will be refunded once the person appears at the next court date

bar: this could refer to one of two things, related in their origins. The bar is the part of the

582 THE LAW OF EVIDENCE IN SOUTH AFRICA

courtroom from where legal representatives present and argue their cases. It is also the term used for the professional voluntary society (Society of Advocates) to which most practising advocates belong, hence 'member of the Bar', and the English term for advocate, namely barrister

Bill of Rights: the fundamental rights contained in sections 7 to 39 of the Constitution

bona fide (Latin): in good faith

burden of proof: *see* onus of proof

capacity (to litigate): the general rule is that every natural person has legal capacity to litigate. Certain persons lack full legal capacity, for instance the mentally disabled and children, and require someone with full legal capacity to represent them or assist them in litigation

cautionary rule: a rule of evidentiary practice that has been developed over time to ensure that courts follow a cautionary approach when evaluating certain categories of evidence, usually where experience has shown those categories of evidence to be particularly unreliable

character evidence: evidence about a variety of character traits or characteristics of a specific person such as honesty, deceitfulness, integrity, moral values or violent tendencies. These character traits are also referred to as a person's disposition. For certain purposes in law, character may also include a person's general reputation

child: any person under 18 years of age

circumstantial evidence (indirect evidence): evidence where there are no direct assertions about a fact in dispute but instead evidence is presented about other facts or situations from which conclusions can be drawn. Note that different rules apply to the drawing of inferences from circumstantial evidence in civil and criminal cases

civil law system: *see* inquisitorial system

civil procedure: the framework of laws, rules, practices and procedures that govern the administration of justice in civil cases, including both civil trial and application proceedings

closing address: also called closing argument or the argument stage; this is the address by the parties to the court after all witnesses have been called, arguing how the witnesses' evidence should be interpreted and what conclusions should be drawn by the court

cognitive (functions): brain processes whereby a person becomes aware of, perceives or comprehends things

collateral evidence: evidence which, on the face of it, is not directly linked to an issue the court has to decide. Usually, collateral evidence does not add value to the resolution of the issues in dispute. Note, however, that what may appear to be collateral evidence may nevertheless be relevant to issues such as the credibility of witnesses

commissioner of oaths: a person legally empowered to witness and certify the validity of documents and to commission affidavits in terms of the Justices of the Peace and Commissioners of Oaths Act 16 of 1963

common cause: an issue or set of facts is common cause when both parties agree that it is not in dispute

common law: all the law of the land that is not codified; initially inherited from Holland and England, and developed by repeated usage and custom

common purpose: where two or more people associate together to commit a crime, each of them will be liable for any criminal conduct of the others falling within the scope of their common purpose; they will be regarded as co-perpetrators

compellable witness: a witness is compellable if he or she can lawfully be obliged to give evidence

competent witness: a witness is competent, in other words, qualified and able, to give evidence if he or she is permitted to do so in terms of the law

complainant: a person who reports a complaint about the commission of an alleged crime to the police

conclusive proof: evidence which has become proof and can usually no longer be contradicted

GLOSSARY | 583

condonation: where a court, on application, excuses non-compliance with the rules of court

confession: a series of admissions to all the elements of a crime that collectively amount to an unequivocal admission of guilt to that crime

Continental system: see inquisitorial system

contradictions (in evidence): where an item of evidence submitted conflicts in a material respect with other admitted evidence (*see* discrepancies)

corroboration: the evaluation process whereby an item of evidence is supported or confirmed by another item of evidence from a different source, usually increasing the weight of the first item of evidence

corruption: the crime of corruption is now defined in section 3 of the Prevention and Combating of Corruption and Corrupt Activities Act 12 of 2004

credibility: the believability of a witness; in other words, an assessment of whether the witness is telling the truth or lying

credit: when used correctly, should only be used as an abbreviation for creditworthiness, but is also sometimes used as a shorthand reference for credibility, for example cross-examination as to credit

creditworthiness: also shortened to credit; an assessment of the overall acceptability of a witness's evidence, including the witness's consistency, reliability, demeanour and credibility, when deciding what weight to give the witness's evidence

criminal procedure: the framework of laws, rules, practices and procedures that govern the administration of justice in criminal cases, from investigation and arrest through to the conclusion of appeal procedures

cross-examination: the questioning of an opposing witness in civil and criminal matters, or any witnesses called by the court

culpa (Latin): negligence

culpable homicide: the unlawful, negligent causing of the death of a human being

de novo (Latin): to start anew or afresh, i.e. from the beginning

defendant: the party who defends a civil action (criminal defendants are called the accused in South African law)

delict: a civil wrong giving rise to a civil claim for compensation

demeanour (of a witness): the witness's behaviour, manner of testifying, his or her personality, and the general impression that he or she creates in the witness box

deponent: a person who gives testimony under oath or affirmation in the form of an affidavit

direct evidence: evidence given by witnesses who have made direct assertions and usually have direct knowledge with regard to a fact in dispute

discrepancies (in evidence): items of evidence that appear to contradict one another but which, on closer examination, are not material contradictions but are explicable as differences that arise in the course of normal human experience. For example, one witness may estimate a certain distance to be 50 m while another witness may estimate the same distance to be 80 m

disposition (of a person): see character evidence

dispute of fact: a dispute between parties to litigation regarding a material fact or set of facts. Where a party decides to initiate court proceedings against another party and foresees that a real dispute of fact will arise between the parties, it is necessary for that party to proceed by way of action as opposed to application (*see also* the Plascon-Evans rule)

DNA testing: deoxyribonucleic acid testing is the comparison of the genetic coding of a tissue sample taken from a suspect with a DNA sample obtained elsewhere to link the suspect to a crime or activity, or to identify a person or their relationship to another person

documentary evidence: an item of evidence is considered a document if the content of that item is relied on in court, irrespective of the material out of which the item is made. For example, a piece of wood containing writing is considered a document if the court has reference to the writing on the wood and a photograph is a document if evidence is lead

584 | THE LAW OF EVIDENCE IN SOUTH AFRICA

about the people or objects depicted in the photograph

dolus (Latin): intention

dominus litis (Latin): master of the case/ litigation; the party presenting the case chooses which witnesses to call, the sequence of the witnesses and what questions to ask of each of the witnesses

duty to begin: the obligation on one of the parties to begin in a civil or criminal trial

entrapment: a criminal procedural process used by applying section 252A of Criminal Procedure Act, 1977 to trap suspects by giving them an opportunity to commit a crime (*see* trap)

estoppel: a rule that prevents a party from denying the truth of a representation made to another party if the latter, believing the representation to be true, acted on the strength of it to his or her detriment or prejudice

evaluation of evidence: admitted evidence is evaluated by the court after the closing argument stage to determine what weight to attach to that evidence (*see* weight of evidence)

evidence on commission: evidence obtained in civil or criminal proceedings by a magistrate in another jurisdiction. This evidence is transcribed and then sent back to the trial court and becomes part of the trial record

evidence*:* any information that has been formally admitted by a court or tribunal in civil or criminal proceedings, or at administrative or quasi-judicial proceedings

evidentiary burden: the duty (or burden) that rests on a party to litigation to lead sufficient evidence to force the other side to respond

evidentiary material: a category of information received during trial proceedings which is not formally admitted by the court, but on which the court can nevertheless rely in coming to its decision

examination-in-chief: the leading of a witness by a party to support the elements of the party's case

exclusionary rules: a collective term for all rules of evidence which may be relied on to exclude

evidence from being admitted into court, the primary exclusionary rule being that evidence cannot be admitted if it is irrelevant

exculpatory statement: an oral or written statement in which a person attempts to remove blame from him- or herself. For example, in a criminal matter an accused may state: 'I was at their house when he was stabbed but I had nothing to do with the stabbing.' This contains an informal admission: 'I was at their house when he was stabbed ...' combined with an exculpatory statement: '... but I had nothing to do with the stabbing.'

expert evidence: opinion evidence given by an expert who is legally permitted to do so due to his or her knowledge, education and/or experience in the field of expertise concerned

external inconsistency: arises when one witness contradicts another witness on the same side

factum probandum (pl *facta probanda*) (Latin): a fact that is in issue

factum probans (pl *facta probantia*) (Latin): a fact relevant to the fact in issue

forensic: for the purpose of taking criminal or civil action, for example forensic investigation is an investigation to build a case for criminal or civil action; forensic medicine is applying medical information for the purpose of criminal and civil legal action

formal admissions: in criminal cases formal admissions are made in terms of section 220 of the Criminal Procedure Act, 1977 and may be made either by the accused or the State

formal truth: the court's finding of what *probably* happened (*see* material truth)

Government Gazette: the official government publication in which legal information relating to various functions of the government as well as other information of an official and legal nature is published. For example, Bills of Parliament that are to become law are published in the *Government Gazette*, as are regulations passed by ministers in terms of various laws

hearsay evidence: evidence, whether oral or in writing, the probative value of which depends on the credibility of any person other than the person giving such evidence

HLA (human leukocyte antigen) tissue typing system: a blood test that measures substances called antigens on the surface of body cells and tissues

Hollington rule: evidence of the conviction of an accused in a criminal case is not admissible to prove any evidence relating to the same incident in a subsequent civil case

hostile witness: a witness called by a party to support its case but who then actively attempts to undermine the case of the person who called him or her. Once a witness has been declared hostile, that witness may be cross-examined by the party who called him or her

illegally obtained evidence: evidence obtained in violation of relevant legislation

illegally: conduct that violates legislation

improperly obtained evidence: evidence obtained contrary to good practice and ethics but not *unlawfully* obtained

improperly: not in accordance with accepted standards

in camera (Latin): the exclusion of the public or non-essential persons from court; can also mean in chambers in some jurisdictions

in casu (Latin): in this case or matter; in this instance

inferences: logical conclusions drawn from evidence or argument

informal admissions: in criminal matters, informal admissions are items of evidence detrimental to the accused in the sense that they help the State prove its case against the accused; they may be made intentionally or unintentionally, and inside the courtroom during the trial, or outside the courtroom prior to the commencement of the trial (*see* exculpatory statement)

information: information of any kind becomes evidence when admitted by a court

inherent jurisdiction: a discretionary power of the High Courts, the Supreme Court of Appeal and the Constitutional Court that enables these courts to prevent procedural injustices from occurring by either overriding the rules of court or providing some procedural remedy where none exists

inherent probabilities: the action being assessed is *inherently probable* if it accords with the general probabilities of the case and with the way one expects things to happen in the ordinary course of life based on common human experiences

inquisitorial system: also known as the civil law system or the Continental system; in this system, trials are presided over by a judge without a jury and there are no evidentiary rules preventing the admission of evidence that may prejudice a jury. Trials are inquisitorial not adversarial in nature and there is thus no cross-examination by either party of the other side's witnesses. All questioning of witnesses is done by the presiding judge, the lawyers merely leading the witnesses (*see* adversarial system)

inspection in loco: where a court (the magistrate or judge with assessors if applicable) and the litigants with their representatives inspect a particular location which is relevant to the matter being heard or are taken to inspect an object which cannot practically be brought to court

inter alia (Latin): among others or among other things

interests of justice: this is a general test applied in criminal proceedings to determine what, in a set of given circumstances, is in the best interests of society as a whole when the procedure in question is considered

intermediary: a person appointed in terms of section 170A(1) of the Criminal Procedure Act, 1977 to assist child witnesses in criminal proceedings

internal inconsistency: self-contradiction; arises when there is a contradiction between versions given by the same witness

interrogatories: a list of questions sent to a court in another jurisdiction to be put to a witness there. The answers to the questions are then recorded and sent back to the trial court where the questions and answers become part of the trial record

intoxication: a state in which a person's normal capacity to act or reason is inhibited by alcohol or drugs

ipse dixit (Latin): he himself said it; an unsupported statement that relies solely on the authority of the individual who makes it

ipsissima verba (Latin): the very words, for example a quotation

irrebuttable presumptions: an irrebuttable presumption of law is simply an ordinary rule of substantive law formulated to look like the law of evidence (*see* presumptions of fact)

Judges Rules: a set of rules formulated at a judges' conference in 1931 in Cape Town, setting out procedural safeguards for suspects, and arrested and accused persons in criminal matters. These rules were subsequently adopted as administrative directions by the police authorities

judicial notice: a legal rule that allows a fact to be accepted without proof if it is so notorious or well known that it cannot reasonably be doubted

jural: based in law. A jural act is an action taken by a legal official in a legal context

jurisdiction: the power or competence of a particular court to hear and determine an issue between parties brought before it

juristic person: an artificial person, usually a corporate entity, which has a legal persona or legal personality for purposes of the law

law of evidence: also called 'rules' of evidence; governs what requirements have to be met and what steps have to be followed to render information admissible in court as evidence or evidentiary material, and how admitted evidence must be evaluated to come to a decision

leave of the court: with permission of the court

legislation: collective noun for statutes passed by an elected body, such as the National Assembly; also called codified law

lie-detector: *see* polygraph

local area networks (LANs): a computer network that links devices within a building or group of adjacent buildings, especially one with a radius of less than 1 km

locus standi (Latin): the full expression is *locus standi in iudicio*, meaning legal standing to litigate. To possess *locus standi*, a person must have both legal capacity as well as a direct and substantial interest in the right which is the subject matter of litigation

major (person): this term should no longer be used as the Age of Majority Act 57 of 1972 has been repealed. A *child* is a person who is below 18 years of age and an *adult* is a person 18 years or older

marital privilege: this privilege exists between spouses who may refuse to disclose any communication from the other spouse made during the course of their marriage

material truth: what *actually* happened as opposed to what the court *decided* had happened (*see* formal truth)

mendacity: the tendency to be untruthful (to lie)

mens rea (Latin): the mental state of the accused in criminal matters

mero motu (Latin): of its own accord, for example the court decided, *mero motu*, to recall the witness

minor (person): this term should no longer be used as the Age of Majority Act 57 of 1972 has been repealed. A *child* is a person who is below 18 years of age and an *adult* is a person 18 years or older

mutatis mutandis (Latin): with the necessary changes having been made for the change in context

negligence (*culpa* in Latin): a failure to exercise the standard of behaviour that would be expected from a reasonable person in the circumstances of the case; also called the reasonable person test

nexus: a close connection

notice of motion: a court document that contains the order a party wishes the court to grant

oath: once taken in civil and criminal proceedings, it converts oral evidence into testimony, for example section 162 of the Criminal Procedure Act, 1977 where the prescribed oath reads as follows: 'I swear to tell the truth, and nothing but the truth, so help me God.' (*see* affidavit)

objection (in court): a party to litigation may, in court, object to evidence led by his or her

GLOSSARY | 587

opponent on various grounds. The usual basis of an objection in court is that the evidence an opponent is attempting to lead is inadmissible on some legal basis

offence: a crime created in terms of a statute

onus of proof: the burden placed on a party by law and which that party must overcome to succeed in a case; also called burden of proof

opening statement: before leading evidence in both civil and criminal trials the plaintiff (or prosecutor) and defendant (or accused) may make an opening statement outlining their case

opinion evidence: the general rule is that the opinion of a witness is not relevant as it is the court's function to draw inferences from the evidence led. Note, however, that it is not always easy to decide what is admissible or inadmissible opinion evidence as witnesses will often testify as to the impressions that they form based on certain incidents, and the evidence of their state of mind is generally admissible if relevant (*see* expert evidence)

oral evidence: evidence given by mouth, in other words orally – derived from the Latin word '*ora*' meaning mouth. Note that in a strict legal sense, *verbal* evidence is not the equivalent of oral evidence as the word 'verbal' is derived from the Latin word '*verbis*' meaning a word. Therefore, a verbal statement may be oral or in writing as both these statements are constituted by words

oral testimony: *see* oral evidence

originality (of document): one of the requirements for admitting a document into court is the general rule that only the original of the document concerned is admissible

parol evidence rule: any terms that are not embodied in the contract (often called extraneous terms or terms extrinsic to the contract) are irrelevant when interpreting the contract

party: a person (natural or legal) involved in litigation

per se (Latin): as such; by itself

perjury: making a false statement under oath or affirmation. This is a common law crime and has a statutory counterpart – see section

319(3) of the Criminal Procedure Act 56 of 1955

Plascon-Evans rule: a final order may only be granted by a court if the allegations in the applicant's affidavits which have been admitted by the respondent, considered together with the allegations made by the respondent, justify such an order

pointing out: an overt act whereby the accused indicates physically the presence or location of some thing or place visible to the inquisitor (pointings out are now considered informal admissions by conduct in our law)

police docket privilege: in criminal cases the general privilege over the contents of the docket is limited to part B (letters and memoranda) and part C (investigation diary). In terms of *Shabalala*'s case, the accused generally has access, for the purposes of trial preparation, to part A of the police docket which contains statements of state witnesses and forensic reports. For the purposes of a fair trial, however, the accused may apply to the court for access to parts B and C as well in specific circumstances. In civil cases, the plaintiff normally has access to the entire police docket

polygraph: also called a lie-detector. A device that measures and records momentary physiological changes in respiration, blood pressure, heart rate, pulse and skin current (associated with the sweating of the palms) which takes place in response to questions put to the examinee. From these responses, conclusions are drawn about the truthfulness of the examinee

potential weight: a preliminary assessment of the weight an item of information has to determine whether it has the potential to assist a court to draw inferences about an issue that the court has to decide (*see* relevance)

precedent: a reference to previous court judgments. Precedents may, in some cases, be binding on a court hearing the matter; in others they may be persuasive but not binding; or they may be of no assistance depending on the circumstances

precognition: the process of preparing a witness to give evidence at trial

presumption: a rule of evidence that entitles a court to assume that a fact, set of circumstances or state of affairs exists until the contrary is proved

presumptions of fact: these are not really presumptions at all, but really statements of substantive law (*see* irrebuttable presumptions)

previous consistent statement: a statement, oral or written, made by a witness on a previous occasion out of court and that is substantially the same as the witness's testimony in court. These statements are usually inadmissible as they violate the rule against self-corroboration

previous inconsistent statement: a statement, oral or written, made by a witness on a previous occasion out of court and that is inconsistent with the witness's testimony in court

prima facie (Latin): on the face of it; also an initial, non-evaluative assessment

prima facie case: a case where, on the face of it, there appears to be sufficient evidence to find in favour of the plaintiff (in civil cases) or to convict the accused (in criminal cases)

prima facie evidence: evidence that on the face of it appears compelling and requires a response from the opposing party (often used as a synonym for *prima facie* proof)

prima facie proof: this is where there is sufficient evidence to establish a *prima facie* case. This *prima facie* case can still be challenged by contradicting evidence (see *prima facie* evidence)

primary onus of proof: the burden of proof that is fixed on a particular party at the outset of a trial and that remains fixed throughout the trial

principle of party control: parties to litigation choose which witnesses they wish to call, which ones to omit and what evidence they wish to present

private privilege: legal professional privilege (attorney–client privilege) may be claimed for any confidential communication or document made by a client to his or her legal representative (acting in his or her professional capacity) for the purpose of pending litigation; the privilege against self-incrimination means no one may be compelled to give evidence incriminating him- or herself either before or during a trial; an accused has a pre-trial and trial right to remain silent; other private privileges include the marital privilege, parent–child privilege and statements made without prejudice

privilege: in certain circumstances an individual or the state may lawfully refuse to disclose relevant evidence at trial even if the privileged evidence is the only evidence available to a court. The two broad categories of privilege are state privilege and private privilege, with the latter including legal professional privilege and witnesses' privilege

Privy Council: the highest court of appeal for all colonies of Great Britain

probative force or probative value: in the context of admissibility, the potential the information has to help prove an issue to establish relevance; in the context of weight, the potential certain items of evidence have to help the court assess weight, in other words the potential the admitted evidence has to tilt the probabilities in favour of one party to the litigation during the process of evaluating the evidence

probative material: properly admitted evidence or evidentiary material

probative value: *see* probative force

procedural law: the procedures to enforce legal claims in civil or criminal law; its two main branches are the law of civil procedure and the law of criminal procedure

proof: refers to whether a party has proved his or her case beyond a reasonable doubt in a criminal case or on a balance of probabilities in a civil case (*see* onus of proof)

propensity evidence: evidence to show that the accused is the kind of person who may have committed the crime in question

racketeering: a criminal offence that is performed through an 'enterprise' (a crime syndicate). It originated with the criminal practice of demanding 'protection payments' from legitimate businesses by criminal organisations such as the Mafia, hence the reference to this type of behaviour as a 'racket' (see section 2 of the Prevention of Organised Crime Act 121 of 1998

real evidence: objects and related things which, if relevant, will be admissible evidence, for example a knife, photograph, voice recording, letter or even the facial features of a person. Only the object itself is identified and the contents of the object, if any, are not relied on. For example, a stolen photograph submitted as evidence of a theft is an item of real evidence because the content of the photograph is not being relied on

rebuttable presumption: an assumption made by a court that may be accepted as true unless contested by persuasive evidence

re-examination: follows cross-examination and is the questioning of the party's own witness to clarify or place into context the evidence of the witness after he or she has been cross-examined

refreshing memory: a witness is entitled to refresh his or her memory before testifying in court, while in the witness box during the process of giving evidence or during an adjournment of proceedings for the purpose of refreshing memory

relevance: the primary test for the admissibility of evidence. Information is relevant if it has the potential to assist the court to draw inferences about an issue that will ultimately help to prove or disprove the case

reliability (of a witness's evidence): depends on various factors, including the credibility and creditworthiness of the witness and the inherent probabilities. The assessment of the reliability of a witness will determine how much weight a court will give to that witness's testimony

res gestae (Latin): things that matter; facts that are so closely connected in time, place and circumstance with some transaction which is at issue that they can be said to form part of that transaction. In other words, facts that are irrelevant may be admitted if bound up with relevant facts or facts in issue

residuary sections: various sections that confirm that if the South African law of evidence is silent on an issue, then recourse must be had to English law as it was at 30 May 1961, for example section 252 of the Criminal Procedure Act, 1977 which reads, 'The law as to the admissibility of evidence, which was in force in respect of criminal proceedings on the thirtieth day of May 1961, shall apply in any case not expressly provided for by this Act or any other law'

Roman-Dutch law: a legal system based on Roman law as applied in the Netherlands in the seventeenth and eighteenth centuries and transported to the Cape of Good Hope in 1652. The South African common law developed as a 'mixed' system through the intermingling of Roman-Dutch and English law principles

SALRC: South African Law Reform Commission (previously called the SALC, the South African Law Commission)

self-corroboration: where a witness provides earlier evidence that supports his or her present evidence. The rule against self-corroboration is a general rule that a witness cannot repeat something he or she wrote or said on a previous occasion to corroborate evidence later given in court by him or her (*see* previous consistent statement)

sentence: the punishment for an offender handed down by a magistrate or judge after an accused person has been convicted. Sentences include imprisonment, correctional supervision, fines and so on

similar fact evidence: evidence of illegal or immoral conduct by a person in circumstances that are logically connected or substantially similar to the same person's conduct in a circumstance that is the subject of the charge or dispute

sine qua non (Latin): without which not; a description of a prerequisite or condition that is indispensable; known as the 'but for' rule

state privilege: the state may, subject to certain prerequisites, refuse to disclose relevant evidence to a court when it would be prejudicial to the public interest

subject (person): in this context, a person who is being subjected to a procedure, for example being subjected to brain-scanning procedures

trap: a person who is used as bait to entrap another into committing a crime

trial-within-a-trial: a hearing held *within* a trial, in other words the trial proceedings are interrupted and suspended until the trial-within-a trial has been completed. The purpose of the trial-within-a trial hearing is to determine the *admissibility* of information alleged to be inadmissible, such as statements containing alleged confessions or informal admissions, disputed pointings out and alleged unconstitutionally obtained information

truth verifiers: methods and systems used to try to determine the truth

unconstitutionally obtained evidence: evidence obtained in violation of a right in the Constitution's Bill of Rights (see Bill of Rights)

unfairly obtained evidence: evidence obtained in a procedurally unfair manner

unfairly: not based on or behaving according to principles of equality and justice

unlawfully obtained evidence: evidence obtained contrary to the law (common law or legislation)

unsworn evidence: evidence not given under oath or affirmation, for example where the witness is too young to understand the meaning of an oath or affirmation

vicarious liability: employers or principals are jointly liable for damages caused by the wrongful and negligent conduct of their employees or agents, their 'representatives', acting in the *course and scope* of their employment or within their authority as agent. The test for the vicarious liability of state employees is whether they were *acting within the scope of their authority as servants of the state*

viva voce (Latin): with living voice; usually used in the context of *viva voce* evidence, meaning direct oral evidence given by witnesses in court

voice-stress analyser: a device for testing voice patterns to draw an inference about possible mendacity. These devices, usually attached to telephones, are generally considered unreliable

void: having no legal force or effect; not legally binding or enforceable, for example a void contract

voir dire (French): a term used for a trial-within-a-trial in some jurisdictions. In the United States of America, it is also a preliminary examination of prospective jurors or witnesses under oath to determine their competence or suitability

weight of evidence: a determination made by the court after evaluating evidence in order to decide whether the case has been proved or not

Index

Please note: Page numbers in *italics* refer to images, tables and figures.

A

accused
- and admissibility of previous convictions 225–227
- and cross-examination by prosecution 225, 229
- and lifting the shield 228–231
- and previous conviction of receiving stolen property 227–228, 230
- privileges of 228, 229
- and right to silence 288–289
- as witness 311

action proceedings 88, 94

adjectival law 15

adjudicator 14

adjudicatory function 14

admissibility
- concept of 52, 53
- determination of 55–56
- and exclusionary rules 164
- and probative value 164–165
- relationship with relevance 159, 160, *161*
- rules relating to 54
- vs weight *53*

admissions *449*
- by accomplices 447–448
- and common purpose 446
- vs confessions 452, *458–459*
- in criminal proceedings 442–449
- description of 441
- legal test for 458

advanced electronic signature 126, *153*

adversarial model/system (of fact-finding)
- vs inquisitorial model/system 11–13, *12–13, 15*
- and presumption of innocence 64
- role of evidence in 15

adversarial procedure 14

adversarial trial
- basic jurisprudential principles of 13–14
- basic rules for system of 14–15

affidavit
- in civil application proceedings 88
- description of 86
- form and content of civil 88

- inadmissible evidence in 90–91
- permissibility of 81
- purposes of 87–88
- types of 87
- *see also* oath

African customary law 19
- and colonial governments 19

analogue evidence, forms of 116–118

ancient documents 100, *101*, 106, *107*

animus confitendi 451

antagonistic *animus* 370

application proceedings 91–93

arbitration hearings
- documentary evidence in 518
- duty to begin in 520
- oral evidence in 518
- real evidence in 518

arbitrations
- admissibility of evidence in 520–521
- evaluation of evidence in 529–530
- as hearings *de novo* 520
- hearsay evidence in 521–523
- opinion evidence in 523–524

assessors 14, 31, 491

audi alteram partem 81, 96

audio tapes 116, 117–119

authenticity (of documentary evidence) 99, 101
- proof of 105–107
- waiver of proof of 106, *107*

autrefois acquit 503

autrefois convict 503

B

best evidence rule 154
- and electronic evidence 128
- vs secondary evidence 102–103

Bill of Rights 7
- and customary law 20
- and relevance to law of evidence 44, 45
- and unconstitutionally obtained evidence 180, 181

blanket docket privilege 47, 299

blood tests
- in civil cases 469–470
- in criminal cases 468–469

592 THE LAW OF EVIDENCE IN SOUTH AFRICA

and paternity 469, 470
Boardman formulation 203–204
body-print 464, 465
brain fingerprinting 480, 481
    and the *Harrington* case 483, 484, 485

C
Cape Evidence Ordinance 4, 5
cardinal rules of logic 413, *414*
cautionary rule *402*
    abolition of 241–242
    applications of 396–398
    aspects to 394
    and children 512
    and children's testimony 399–400
    and complainants in sexual offences
        cases 241–242, *242*, 400–401
    compliance with 395–396
    and corroboration 404
    definition of 395
    and deliberate false evidence 396–398
    and identification testimony 400
    purpose of 395, 406
    and single witness's testimony 398–399
    status of 395
character
    of accused 224–231
    of complainant in criminal cases 231
    meaning of 222, 223
    of plaintiff and defendant in civil
        cases 231–232
    of witnesses 225, 232–233
character evidence
    on accused 224–231
    and admissibility in common law 223–224
    and admissibility in criminal cases 224–231
    in civil cases 231–232
    on complainant 231
    description of 222, 223
    and prejudice 223
    principles defining *233*
    probative value of 223
    and residuary rule 224–225
    and sexual history 238
    types of 222, 223
Chiefs and Headmen's Civil Courts Rules 32
child witnesses, accommodating of 508, 509

children
    and cautionary rule 512
    and delay in reporting 511
    evaluating testimony of 510–511
    and the oath 509–510
    and previous consistent statements 511
    as witnesses 314
cinematographic (celluloid) films 116–117
circumstantial evidence 59, *414*
    in civil proceedings 414
    in criminal proceedings 412–414
civil
    decision 14
    law system, *see* inquisitorial system
    procedure 15
    trail process 543
    trials, impact of Constitution on 48
closed-circuit television 85
closing addresses/arguments 319
    examples of 353–355
    important issues with regard to 351, 352
    legal basis for 350–351
    organising of 352–353
    purpose of 351
    sequence of 350
    and written heads of argument 351, 352
co-accused, as witness 311
collateral evidence
    and bias 249
    description of 246
    and previous convictions 248–249
    and questions as to credit 247–249
Commissioners' Courts 27, 28, 31
common law of evidence, and residuary
    sections 5, 6, 7
common law, rules of evidence 3
common purpose 446
competence and compellability
    procedural aspects of 315–317
    of witnesses 309–315, 317
completeness, *res gestae* principle of 168
computer(-generated) evidence 122
    admissibility of 152
    in arbitrations 522
    and hearsay rule 148, 275
    and recovery of 144
    see also data message; electronic evidence

conclusive proof 72
condonation and variation and rescission of
    awards, applications for 515
confession *457*
    admissibility of 452–457
    vs admission 452, *458–459*
    confirmation of 456–457
    definition of 441, 451
    falsely induced 455
    intention to make 451–452
    legal test for 458
    to lesser/related offences 456
    and reverse onus clauses 46
    and the State's burden of proof 456
confrontation, right of 14
contempt of court 316
continental system, *see* inquisitorial system
contradiction 391–391
convictions, admissibility of previous 225–227
corroborating evidence, characteristics
    of 405–406
corroboration
    and cautionary rule 404, 406
    of confessions 406–407
    description of 405
    process of 405
    and weight of evidence 58
credibility (of witness) 58
    assessment of 376
    and evaluation of truthfulness (veracity)
        of 382–384
    and probabilities of the case 376–377
creditworthiness, meaning 382
crime control vs due process model/rights/
    values 175, 182, 186
crime detection privileges 302–303
criminal
    judgment 14
    trial process 544
cross-examination
    of accused 225
    to attack credibility of witnesses 232–233
    description of 335
    examples of 337–345
    of expert witness 213
    legal basis for 336
    and lifting the shield 229, 230, 231
    objectives of 232

and oral evidence 81, 95, 96
purpose of 335
rules on 336–337
through intermediary 83, 84, 85
of witnesses 232–233
cryptography 293
culpa 456, 538, 539
cultural affiliation 23–24
customary law/rule
    application of 24
    and the Constitution 21
    description 18, 19, 23
    evidence of content of 23, 27
    evidence of existence of 21–22, 27
    and gender prejudices 40
    and hearsay evidence 38, 39
    inquisitorial nature of 35, 36
    living version of 23, 25–31
    and presumptions about seduction and
        marriage 40–41
    and proof of cultural affiliation 23–24
    and relationship by blood or affinity 40, 41
    relevance of rituals in 37–38
    and traditional leaders 27
    see also living customary law
customary tribunals (and disputes) 5

D
data, definition of 100, *153*
data message
    admissibility of 127, 128, 136, 146, 153
    authenticity of 125, 126
    and cryptography 293
    definition of 100, 124, 146, *153*
    and Electronic Communications and
        Transactions Act *154*
    evidential weight of 127, 136–137, 153
    hearsay in 128–136, 146, 147, 149, 153, 276
    legal recognition of 124
    as original 125
    and paper-based document 123, 147
    and presumption of reliability 139
    as real and/or documentary
        evidence 133–136, 147, 149
    in writing 124–125
Daubert Rule 484, 486
demeanour
    fallibility of 417

594 THE LAW OF EVIDENCE IN SOUTH AFRICA

meaning of 416
trial court's observations of 417–418
of witnesses 58
digital evidence 144, 145
    see also data message; electronic evidence
digital forensics 144
direct evidence 59
    example of 412
    and identification 408
    and probability 389
    and state of mind 253
    weight of 59
disposition 222, 223
dispute of fact 375–376
disputes, and customary tribunals 5, 6
DNA coding/fingerprinting 114
DNA evidence
    chain of custody of 474
    pre-trial disclosure of 472–473
    procedure for admitting 471–472
DNA testing
    forensic evidentiary value of 470
    probative value of 471
    process of 470–471, *471*
dock identification 261, 262, 410
docket privilege 47
    and crime detection privileges 302
    scope and procedural application of 301
doctrine of precedent 14
document
    admissibility of 101, *104*
    and authenticity 99, 101, 105–107, *107*
    categories of 100–101, *101*
    and computer printout 122, 134, 522
    definition of 99, 138
    inspection and discovery of 102
    and originality 99, 101, 102, *104*
    production of original 102–103
    and relevance 99, 101
    steps when adducing 108
    see also documentary evidence
documentary evidence 8
    admissibility of secondary 103–105, *104*
    see also documents
dolus 456, 538, 539
dominus litis 14, 328
double jeopardy 503

due process model/rights/values 175,
    182, 186
duty to begin 14, 67, 520

E
elders, and euphemistic language 34
electroencephalography (EEG) 480, 481, 484
electronic
    communication, definition of *153*
    document 100, 127, 150
    media 85
electronic evidence
    admissibility of 8, 9, 127
    and best evidence rule 128
    and Cybercrimes and Cybersecurity
        Bill 138–139, 146
    evolution of 121
    foreign law in respect of 148–153
    and forensic science 144–145
    and functional equivalence 123
    and hearsay 128–136, 275
    and legislation 137–139
    and legislative reform 120, 121, 122, 123,
        145–148
    and Model Law on Electronic
        Commerce 122–123, 124
    and presumption of liability 139–141
    recovery of 144
    SALRC review of 145–148
    search and seizure of 141–144
    and technological developments 120, 123
    and technology neutrality in legislation 123
    weight of 136–137
    see also data message; digital evidence
electronic signature 126, *153, 154*
English law
    reception of 5, 6
    residuary sections of 4, 6, 7
entrapment 490
    authorisation of 534
    and the Constitution 536
    and the Criminal Procedure Act 533–536
    description of 533
    in labour matters 524, 526
    procedure for challenging 537
    safeguards to ensure integrity
        of 534, 535, 536

INDEX 595

estoppel 76, *502*
   definition of 498
   elements of 498–499
   by judgment 502–503
   legal rules applicable to 501–502
evaluation (of evidence) *380*
   establishing factual basis of case 374
   example of principles of 379–381
   meaning of 374
   and piecemeal reasoning 377–378
   principles of 376–381
evidence
   by way of affidavit 86
   characteristics of corroborating 405–406
   on commission 85–86
   common law rules of 3
   of cultural affiliation 23–24
   of customary law/rule content of 23
   of existence of customary law/rule 21–22
   definition of 2, 3
   deliberate false 396–398
   free system of 13
   illegally obtained 48
   of incompetence 310, 311
   principles for evaluation of 57
   regarding sexual history 238–241
   role in adversarial system 15
   rules of 15
   rules regulating admissibility of 52
   sources of 8, 8
   statutes on the law of 7–8
   testing in trial 62
   types of 116
   weighing of 57–59
Evidence Proclamations 4, 6
evidence-in-chief
   basic rule of 326
   description of 325
   duty of prosecutor in 330
   examples of 330–333
   and expert witnesses 328
   legal basis for 325–326
   procedure for 327–328
   sequence of questioning in 328, 329
evidentiary burden 46
   in civil cases 67
   in criminal cases 66
   definition of 65

   features of 65–66
evidentiary
   fact 3
   legislation, residuary sections of English
      law in 4, 6
   material 2, 3, 406, 407
   rebuttal 14
examination-in-chief, *see* evidence-in-chief
expert evidence 210
   in civil litigation 217–218
   in criminal litigation 218
   failure to follow 214–215
   and hearsay 216
   vs opinion evidence 210, *220*
   probative value of 212–214
   procedure for leading of 217–218
   see also expert opinion; expert witness
expert opinion
   admissibility of 210
   probative value of 212–214
   reasons for 212–214
   see also expert evidence; expert witness
expert witness
   duties of 214–215
   requirement to qualify as 211–212
   for sentencing purposes 216–217
   written reports by 213
external inconsistency 391
extra-curial admission 446–447
extrinsic evidence rule 504

F
fact, dispute of 375–376
facta probanda 94
   and admissibility 55
   and evidence of proof 61
   relationship with *facta probantia 159*
   and relevance 159, 163
facta probantia
   and admissibility 55
   and evidence of proof 61
   relationship with *facta probanda 159*
   and relevance 159, 163
facts
   of general notoriety 427
   based on general knowledge 427
   of local notoriety 428
failure to testify 422–425

596 | THE LAW OF EVIDENCE IN SOUTH AFRICA

fair trial
    and admissions 182–185, 447
    and entrapment 536
    and intermediaries 84–85
    and legal professional privilege 282
    and oral evidence 95
    and pointings out 450
    and police docket privilege 300, 301
    principles of 182
    right to 48
    and right to silence 290, 293
    and self-incrimination 285, 287, 288
    and unconstitutionally obtained
        evidence 183, 184
Farwell, Lawrence 481, 483, 484, 485
fingerprint 112–113
    analyses 465–466, *466*
footprint 464, 466–467
foreign documents 100, *101*, 106, *107*
forensic brain scan analysis (FBSA)
    480, 481–482, *482*
    in criminal cases 483–484
    future application of 485–486
    and *Harrington* case 483, 484, 485
    testing methodology of 482–483
forensic
    debate 14
    science 144–145, 480
formal admission 2
    in civil matters 459–461
    in criminal proceeding 442–444
    intention to make 460
    withdrawal of 460–461
formal truth, vs material truth 62, *62*
functional equivalence, principle of 147
functional magnetic resonance
    imaging (fMRI) 480, 481
    used in court cases 485–486
    future application of 486
fundamental rights
    and the Constitution 45, 46
    and legal professional privilege 282,
        284–285

G

gang-related offences 538
gender, prejudices 40
genetic coding 114

group
    affiliation to 23–25
    in customary law 18

H

handwriting 113
Harrington case 483, 484, 485
hearing or speech impaired persons, as
    witnesses 314
hearsay
    and affidavits 90
    and data messages 128–136
    rule, exceptions to 132, 138, 147
hearsay evidence
    admissible 268–273, *269*
    assessing nature of 270–271
    in civil proceedings 270
    common law definition of 265, 266
    constitutionality of admission of 268
    corroboration of 39, 40
    in criminal trials 270
    and cross-examination 265–266
    determining relevance of 271
    and exceptions to exclusionary rule 147
    and interests of justice test 270–273, 277
    and prejudice to opponents 272–273
    probative value of 271, 272
    requirements for admissibility of 39
    and SALRC discussion papers 8, 9
    and SALRC recommendations 276–277
    statutes allowing for 273–276
    statutory definition of 265, 266–268
    and vicarious admissions 38, 39
HLA tissue typing 469
hlompho 34
Hollington rule 218–220
hostile witnesses 368–371
hostility, declaration of 370–371

I

identification
    legal rules applicable to 409–410
    parades 410, 378, 400
    testimony and cautionary rule 400
    types of 408–410
illegally obtained evidence 48
immediate real evidence 111
in camera proceedings 239, 298, 508

incompetence, evidence of 310, 311
indirect evidence 412, 414
    see also circumstantial evidence
inferences 56, 59
    of an accused's guilt 414
    and circumstantial evidence 412, 413
    and opinion evidence in arbitrations 523
    and piecemeal reasoning 377
    from polygraph testing 475
    and similar fact evidence 199, 203
    vs speculation 57
    and witness's opinion 207, 208, 210
informal admissions 444–449
    admissibility of 445–446
    definition of 444–445
information
    evidentiary material 2
    relevance of 3
    types of 2
informers, and state privilege 295, 300, 301,
    302, 303
inherent
    improbability 389, 390
    jurisdiction 91
    probabilities 376, 388, 391
inhlonipho 34
initiation 38
inquisitorial model/system 11
    vs adversarial model/system 11–13, 12–13
    of fact-finding 35–36, 53
    in labour matters 519
inspection in loco 114
interests of justice
    and hearsay evidence 268, 270–273, 277
    and oral evidence 85
    and state privilege 298
intermediary
    appointment of 84–85
    for child witnesses 82–84
internal
    disciplinary hearings 530
    inconsistency 391
interpreters 96
irrebuttable presumptions 76, 434
irrelevant opinion evidence 208

J

judges rules 45

judgment 319
judicial notice *431*
    categories of 427–428
    of common law 430
    by the Constitutional Court 431
    description of 426
    and examples of notorious facts 428–429
    of foreign law 430
    of indigenous law 341–432
    legal rules applicable to 432
just excuse 316, 317

L

labour arbitration procedure 518–519
Labour Court 515, 525, 530
labour disputes/matters
    admissibility of improperly obtained evidence
        in 525–527
    admissions and confessions in 527
    and bargaining councils 515
    and the CCMA 515
    entrapment in 524
    evidentiary burden in 517, 518
    and internal disciplinary hearings 530
    and jurisdiction of the Labour Court 515
    interception of communication in 524–525
    legal privilege in 528
    monitoring and searches in 527
    onus of proof in 515–516
    parol evidence rule in 527–528
    proof without evidence in 528–529
    and right to silence 517–518
    similar fact evidence in 528
    standard of proof in 516–517
leading questions (rule against) 326, 327
legal professional privilege 281–285
legal relevance vs logical relevance 166–167
lie-detector, see polygraphs
lifting the shield 228–231
litigation privilege vs legal professional
    privilege 285
living customary law
    in apartheid era 27, 28, 31
    and assessors' opinions 31
    and codified customary law 26, 27
    description of 25, 26
    methods to identify 25
    and presiding officer's knowledge 27–30

598 THE LAW OF EVIDENCE IN SOUTH AFRICA

logic, cardinal rules of 413, *414*
logical relevance vs legal relevance 166–167
logically relevant evidence 55

M

magnetic resonance imaging (MRI) 481
Makin formulation 199–201, *201*
marital privilege 294, 312
material truth, vs formal truth 62, *62*
memory
    adjourning to refresh 362
    and oral testimony 360
    and preparation of witnesses 361
    refreshing of a witness's 360–363
    and unreliability of evidence 360
mendacity (of witness) 384–385, 386
    description of 419
    legal rules applicable to 420–421
    means of assessing 419–420
mental incapacity 65
MERMER test 481, 483, 484, 485
Model Law on Electronic Commerce (1996)
    122–123, 124
money laundering 538
motion proceedings 94, 95

N

narrative evidence/testimony
    benefits of 34, 35
    definition of 33
    disadvantage of 34
    and euphemistic language 34
    recognition of 39
    see also oral evidence; *viva voce* evidence
narrative, rule against 244
    see also self-corroboration
Native Appeals Courts 31
neurological evidence 480
neurotechnology 480
notice of motion 88–90
notorious facts 426, 427, 428

O

oath 81
    evidence under 3
    see also affirmation
objection
    description of 357

    examples of 358–359
    legal aspects of 357–358
    practical aspects of 358
official documents 100, *104*, 105
onus of proof 63, 64, 190–191
opening statement/address
    content of 320
    description of 319
    examples of 322–324
    practical aspects of 321
    procedure for 320–321
    and rules of court 320
opinion
    of court and *Hollington* rule 218–220
    of expert 210–218
    of lay person 209–210
    meanings of 207
    rule 208–209
opinion evidence 208
    admissibility of 209–218
    vs expert evidence *220*
oral argument (principle of orality) 14
oral evidence
    in civil matters 94
    in criminal trails 94
    definition of 80, 81
    general rule of 81
    narrative methods of 34
    principles of *97*
    summary of *96*
organised crime, and POCA 538
originality (of documentary evidence) 99, 101,
    102, *104*

P

P300 test 481, 483, 484, 485
palmprint 454, 466
parent–child privilege 293, 294
parol evidence rule 77, *506*
    description of 504
    exceptions to 505–506
    requirements for 504–505
party control, principle of 368
paternity 72, 113, 114, 438, 469, 470
perjury 81, 96
photographic identification 410
photographs 116–117
plaintiff, law of the 23

Plascon-Evans rule 91–92
pointings out
    admissibility of 450
    definition of 441, 449
    legal test for 458
    and *Samhando* exception 450–451
police docket privilege 47, 299–301
polygraph
    admissibility of 475–476
    arguments against admissibility of 476–478
    definition of 474
    scientific reliability/validity of 474–475, 476
    in the USA 476
polygraph tests 474–475, *475*
    admissibility of 477, 478
    inferences from 475
potential
    evidence 3
    prejudice 171, 172
    weight 56
precedent *13*
    and determination of admissibility 56, 169
    doctrine of 14
    and test of relevance 171
precognition 96
prejudice
    and admissibility of polygraph tests 477
    and admission of hearsay 272, 273
    and character evidence 223
    and hearsay 272–273
    to opponents 272, 277
    vs probative value 56, 161, 164, 271, 477
    and similar fact evidence 203
    statement made without 294
    and withdrawal of admission 460, 461
    see also procedural prejudice
presumptions 2, *435*
    description of 433
    examples of 438
    of fact 71
    of innocence 46, 47, 64, 436, 437
    and reverse onus 436–437, *437*
    types of 433
Prevention of Organised Crime Act 121 of 1998
    (POCA)
    new concept of knowledge in 538–539
    and new types of criminal offences 538

and racketeering offences 539–541
previous consistent statement
    admissibility of 257–263
    and children 511
    and common law 236–237
    description of 256
    and prior identification 261–262
    and refreshing of memory 263
    as part of *res gestae* 262
    rule against 235–238, 256–257
    in sexual offence cases 236–237, 258–261
    and statements made on arrest 263
    and statutory time limit 237, 238
previous convictions
    admissibility of 225–227
    and lifting the shield 228–231
    and prejudice 226
    and receiving stolen property 227–228
previous inconsistent statement 256
    evidentiary consequences of 366–367
    and impeaching credibility of own
        witness 369–370
    proving cross-examination on basis of 365
    procedure to deal with 365–366
prima facie
    case 70
    evidence 71, 72
    proof 71
primary evidence 102, 103
prior identification 261–262
private documents 100, *101*
private privilege
    categories of 281–294
    vs state privilege 295
privilege *305*
    of accused 228, 229
    definition of 280–281
    and exclusionary rules of evidence 281
    and juristic persons 288
privileged communications 90
Privy Council 6, 296
probative
    force 3, 204, 257
    material 2
    value 3, 164, 165
procedural law, and substantive law 74–75
procedural prejudice 164, 165

600 | THE LAW OF EVIDENCE IN SOUTH AFRICA

and exclusion of evidence 171–172
meaning of 167–168
proof
  burden of 63–65, 75
  in civil cases 63, 65
  in criminal cases 63, 64–65
  onus of 63, 64, 190–191
  primary burden of 14
  and substantive law 64, 65
propensity evidence 225
public documents
  definition of 100
  and hearsay 276
  vs private documents *101*
  as secondary evidence *104*, 105
public policy
  and unconstitutionally obtained
    evidence 182, 183, 185
  and privilege 281, 293, 294, 295, 296,
    297, 303
public privilege 301, *305*
  see also state privilege

Q
questions as to credit 237–249

R
racketeering 227, 538, 539–541
rape, psychological effects of 237
real evidence
  admissibility requirement for 111
  and blood tests 113–114
  description of 110
  examples of 110
  and fingerprints 112–113
  and handwriting 113
  inspections *in loco* 114
  and paternity 113, 114
  physical appearance as 111–112
  and tape recording 112
rebuttable presumptions
  effect on burden of proof 434
  examples of 438
  of fact 435
  of law 434–435
recalcitrant witnesses 315–316
red blood cell tests 469

re-examination 81
  examples of 347–348
  legal basis for 346
  procedure for 347
  purposes of 346
relevance
  and admissibility exclusionary rules 164
  common law requirements of 99, 101
  compared to admissibility 160
  concept of 158, 159–160, 162
  determining of 54
  of documentary evidence 99
  and exclusionary rule 246
  foundational characteristic of 166
  functional elements of 169–170
  functional/general test of 160–161, *161*
  practical test of 170–171
  principles of 160
  and probative value 164–165
  relationship with admissibility 159
  rule of 54
  and SALRC discussion papers 8
  threshold test of 163
relevant opinion evidence 208
reliability (of witness) 385–387
reported real evidence 111
reputation 222, 223
res gestae
  definition of 250–251, *255*
  doctrine of 251
  evidence 171
  principle of completeness 168
  statements forming part of 251–255, *255*
res judicata 502
residuary rule, effect of 6, 7
reverse onus
  clauses 46–47
  statutory presumption 436–437, *437*
right to silence 285, 286, 288–293, *304*
  and burden of proof 436
  common law 289–290
  constitutional 290–293
  and trial-within-a-trial 493
rights
  of arrested, accused and detained persons 45
  constitutionally entrenched 45, 46
ritual
  and adoption of children 37

in African customary marriages 37, 38
definition of 36
and initiation 38
objectives of 37

S

Samhando exception 450–451
secondary evidence
admissibility of 103–105, *104*
definition of 102
vs primary evidence 103
self-contradiction 391
self-corroboration (rule against) 58, 235
basis of 244
purpose of 244–245
scope of 245
self-incrimination
constitutional right against 287
witness's privilege against 285–288, *304*
self-serving statements, rule against 244
see also self-corroboration
sexual offence cases
cautionary rule applicable to complainants
in 241–242
complainant in *242*
and evidence regarding sexual
history 238–241
and previous consistent statement 258–261
and statutory time limit 237, 238
silence
common law right to 289–290
constitutional right to 290–293, *304*
similar fact evidence
admissibility of 199
and *Boardman* formulation 203–204
example of non-admittance of 205
examples of admittance of 204–205
and identity of accused 202–203
and jury system 198
and *Makin* formulation 199–201, *201*
meaning of 197
and mere coincidence 201–202
purpose of 197–198, characteristics of 198
reasons for inadmissibility of 198–199
and supporting evidence 204
South African Law Reform Commission (SALRC) 7
discussion papers 8–9
Issue Paper 9

project 8–9
South African procedural system 13
spouse as co-accused 313
stare decisis 14
state privilege 47, *305*
and access to information 298–299
common law approach to definition of 296,
297
common law development of 295–295
constitutional approach to definition
of 296–298
and national security policy 297
and police informers 295, 300, 301, 302,
303
and provisions of PAIA 298–299
vs private privilege 295
unique theory of 303
statement made without prejudice 294
Statute of Westminster 19
statutory
perjury 81
presumptions 436–437, *437*
tribunals 13
strict liability 456
substantive law, and procedural law 74–75
sufficient proof 72–73

T

terminology, correct use of 3
tissue typing tests 113, 114
tracker dog evidence 164–165, 168, 169
traditional courts
rules of evidence and procedure 32
viva voce evidence in 32–36
and appeal in Magistrates' Court 32, 33
traditional leaders
and customary law 27
rules of evidence in courts of 31–33
trial-within-a-trial 57, 193, 314, 317
appeal against ruling in 495–496
burden of proof in 495
description of 490, 491
principles of 491–492
procedure 492–494
ruling 494
views on reform of 496–497
and voluntariness 358, 446

602 THE LAW OF EVIDENCE IN SOUTH AFRICA

U

Ubuntu, interpretation of term 28
ultimate issue doctrine 208
unconstitutionally obtained evidence 48, *195*
    and admissions 182-189
    and Bill of Rights 180, 181
    and due process model/rights/values 175,
        182, 186
    and fair trial principles 182, 183, 184
    implications of excluding 179-180
    and *locus standi* 191-192
    and onus of proof 190-191
    and public policy 182, 183, 185, 194
    rationales for exclusion of 176-179
    section 35(5) test for excluding 181-189
unfairly obtained evidence, and privilege 283
Union of South Africa, map of 5, *5*
unlawfully obtained evidence 175
    see also unconstitutionally obtained evidence
unsolicited statement 230
unsworn evidence 82

V

value concept, of *hlompho/inhlonipho* 34
vicarious
    admission 446-447
    liability 438, 456
video tapes 116, 117-119
visual identification 408, 409
viva voce evidence 81
    in traditional courts 32-36
    see also narrative evidence; oral evidence
voice identification 408, 410
voice-stress analyser 478

W

weight (of evidence) 3
    vs admissibility *53*

concept of 52, 53
Westminster, Statute of 19
witness
    accused as 311
    and character evidence 223
    character of 229, 232-233
    child as 314
    co-accused as 311
    compellability of 309
    competence of 309
    and contempt of court 316
    to counter unfavourable evidence 368
    credibility of 224, 232, 376-377, 382-384
    cross-examination of 232-233
    evaluation of truthfulness (veracity)
        of 382-384
    and evidence-in-chief 326-329
    foreign language speakers as 314
    function of 14
    hearing or speech impaired persons as 314
    legal rules applicable to 309-310
    mendacity of 384-385, 386
    and mental disability and
        intoxication 310-311
    objections by 315
    and preparation for trial 361-362
    privilege against self-incrimination 285-288
    refreshing of memory of 360-363
    reliability of 309, 385-387
    sequence of 328, 329
    spouse of accused as 312-313
    spouses as co-accused 313
    support of 330
    and unsolicited statement 230

Z

Zuid-Afrikaanse Republiek (ZAR) 4, 5